AF560575

THE Āᶜ ĪN-I AKBARĪ

THE
Āᶜīn-i Akbarī

(The Complete English Translation)

Abū 'L-Faẓl ᶜAllāmī

Translated into English by
COL. H.S. JARRETT

Corrected and further annotated by
SIR JADU NATH SARKAR

IN THREE VOLUMES
VOLUME TWO

MANOHAR
2024

First published 1869-94
Reprinted 2022, 2023, 2024

ISBN 978-93-91928-20-9 (Vol. 2)
ISBN 978-93-91928-36-0 (Set)

Published by
Ajay Kumar Jain *for*
Manohar Publishers & Distributors
4753/23 Ansari Road, Daryaganj
New Delhi 110 002

Printed at
Replika Press Pvt. Ltd.

THE
ĀᶜĪn-i Akbarī

Abū 'l-Fazl ʿAllāmī

Vol. I

Translated into English by
H. BLOCHMANN

Edited by
LIEUT.-COLONEL D.C. PHILLOTT

Vol. II & III

Translated into English by
COLONEL H. S. JARRETT

Corrected and further annotated by
SIR JADU NATH SARKAR

THE ASIATIC SOCIETY
1 PARK STREET ■ KOLKATA-700 016

THE
Āʿīn-i Akbarī

THE
Āʿīn-i Akbarī

(A Gazetteer and Administrative Manual of Akbar's Empire and Past History of India)

by

Abū 'l-Faẓl ʿAllāmī

Vol. II

Translated into English by
COLONEL H. S. JARRETT

SECOND EDITION

Corrected and further annotated by
SIR JADU NATH SARKAR

C.I.E., HONY. D. LITT.

Honorary Member, Royal Asiatic Society of Great Britain and Ireland; Corresponding Member, Royal Historical Society, Honorary Fellow, Royal Asiatic Society of Bengal, and of Bombay Branch, Royal Asiatic Society of G. Britain.

Work No. 271
Issue No. 1558

THE ASIATIC SOCIETY
1 PARK STREET KOLKATA-700 016

EDITOR'S INTRODUCTION

After the lamented death of H. Blochmann on 13th July, 1878, at the early age of 40 years only, a search among his papers showed that he had not translated any portion of the *Ain-i-Akbari* beyond the first volume which the Asiatic Society of Bengal was then publishing. In fact, his careful editing of the vast text of the *Ain* had been such a laborious task, and his English version of the first volume of it was such a monument of scholarship and tireless research in annotation, that he could not have had the time to begin the translation of the second volume. The Society entrusted his unfinished work to Lt.-Col. H. S. Jarrett, who finished printing the translation of the second volume in 1891. Thus, Jarrett had at his disposal only such works of reference and learned treatises on India as were in print in 1884-1889. The authorities cited by him in his notes, as I have pointed out in the Introduction to my revised edition of the 3rd volume of his translation, have proved to be obsolete and often useless in the light of our knowledge today.

Since 1890, a complete revolution in these branches of orientology and the history of Hindu and Muslim India has been effected by the publication of Hastings's *Encyclopædia of Religion and Ethics*, the *Encyclopædia of Islam*, the *Grundriss* of Buhler, Elliot and Dowson's *History of India as told by its own Historians*, the *Cambridge History of India*, and many learned monographs on particular sovereigns and dynasties by Indian writers which touch the high-water mark of modern critical scholarship and exhaustive research.

All these authorities were unknown to Jarrett. His sole resource for the Hindu dynastic lists was Prinsep's *Useful Tables* (published in 1832) which is often based on this very *Ain-i-Akbari* and improved by reference to the mythical *Purānas* (as summarised in Wilson's translation of the *Vishnu Purāna*.) As for the Muslim rulers, he had to depend on the primitive *History of India* by Elphinstone (1841) or its source Firishta. Our reconstruction of Indo-Muslim history from inscriptions, coins and original Persian manuscripts was naturally missed by a writer of the years 1885-1889.

Therefore a mere reprint of Jarrett's translation and notes today would not do justice to the present state of Oriental scholarship and would naturally disappoint the modern reader. Thus the first task of an editor of Jarrett's translation is to correct and modernise his notes and elucidations by sweeping away his heaps of dead leaves, and giving more accurate information from the latest authorities. My second aim has been to lighten the burden of his notes, many of which are not only obsolete in information, but prolix to the point of superfluity. It is, I think, a mistake of the translator's duty to try to make a modern reader get all his ideas of Hindu philosophy, science, mythology, hagiography, and the topography and history of Muslim and Hindu India from the notes to an English translation of the *Ain-i-Akbari*. The modern reader will find very much fuller and far more accurate information on these subjects in the voluminous encyclopædias, gazetteers and standard monographs published in the present century, which are available in the libraries of learned societies.

I have also economised space and saved the reader from frequent unnecessary interruptions, by the omission of Jarrett's notes on the emendations of the printed Persian text made by him (except in a few cases of vital importance.) The numberless variant readings which encumbered the pages of his second volume have been mostly cleared away by the acceptance of the true forms in the body of the book and rejecting all those that are palpably wrong or unhelpful in solving our doubt. It is well-known to the learned world that the editing of many of the volumes in the Persian and Arabic section of the Bibliotheca Indica series, was not done with the care and accuracy which characterise the oriental texts published in London or Paris, Leyden or Beyrut. Therefore all obvious misprints and wrong readings in the text of the *Ain* have been silently correctd in this revised edition of the translation, and many hundreds of notes of the first edition deleted.

The third volume of the *Ain-i-Akbari* is an encyclopædia of the religion, philosophy and sciences of the Hindus, preceded by the chronology and cosmography of the Muslims, as required by literary convention, for comparison with the Hindu ideas on the same subjects. The second volume was designed to serve as a Gazetteer of the Mughal Empire under Akbar. Its value lies in its minute topographical descriptions and statistics about numberless small places and its survey of the Empire's finances, trade and industry, castes and tribes.

Jarrett's translation of Volume II is weakest in this essential respect. For the more than six thousand place-names in this volume he could consult only Hunter's *Imperial Gazetteer of India* (in the rather crude early edition of 1887) ; but that work is quite unhelpful for the purpose of identifying the minute places mentioned in the *Ain*, and its volume of maps is on too small a scale to give the information we need. The highly useful and detailed provincial Gazetteers—such as Atkinson's *N. W. P. Gazetteer* and Campbell's *Bombay Gazetteer*, were completed after the Eighteen-eighties, too late for Jarrett's use. Nor did he consult the quarter-inch-to the mile maps of India published by the Surveyor-General and entitled the *Indian Atlas*. These two authorities,—the provincial Gazetteers and the Survey maps—are indispensably necessary for correctly tracing the place-names in the *Ain-i-Akbari*.

I have consulted these two primary works of reference and corrected Jarrett's (or Abul Fazl's) names and notes, with infinite labour, the nature of which can be understood only by comparing the list of *mahals* in a district (*sarkār*) in Jarrett's edition with the corresponding page in mine. Nine-tenths of the place-names in this book have been identified and entered in the corrected spelling in the course of my revision. This improvement of Abul Fazl's work will be completed and the nature of the gain to our knowledge of Mughal Indian topography will become evident to the modern reader, after the publication of a supplementary volume, on which Prof. Nirod Bhusan Roy is now working and which will contain a very much enlarged geographical index giving the location and exact references to mapsheets and Gazetteer-pages for each place mentioned here and discussing the probable location or necessary emendation of the small proportion of places not satisfactorily traced by me. Very many of the mistakes in Jarrett (or rather in the printed Persian text followed by him) were due to the wrong placing or omission of dots (*nuqta*) and the well-known confusion of certain letters of the Arabic alphabet by our copyists. These I have silently corrected.

The chapter on the subah of Kashmir, which was the most confused and wrongly spelt in this volume,—has been revised throughout by Professor Nirod Bhusan Roy, on the basis of Stein's *Memoir* and *Chronicle of the Kings* and the official *Gazetteer* (by Bates). But the necessary changes are so many that the new information has been lumped together at the end, instead of being distributed in countless footnotes on the respective pages, and the useless notes and extracts of the first edition have been omitted.

I am deeply obliged to Prof. N. B. Roy for the care and persistence with which he has assisted me in this work of revision and performed the exacting task of reading the proofs (up to p. 192) of such a difficult book. A special word of thanks is due to the Sri Gouranga Press, which has patiently and efficiently done the rather exasperating work of printing this volume from a copy of the first edition, whose rotten paper crumbled at the touch, and on which my ink corrections had made the text even less readable than before. The sight of this press copy had scared away two first-rate printing establishments in Calcutta to whom it was previously offered, and the acceptance of the work of printing it was really a favour shown to the Society and to learning, by the Sri Gouranga Press. For my appreciation of the manner in which, on the whole, Jarrett completed a stupendous task, I refer the reader to my Introduction to the Translation of the Third Volume of the *Ain*, 2nd edition.

The absence of uniformity in the transliteration of oriental words in the Roman alphabet, is explained by the facts, (1) that Jarrett himself did not follow one uniform system throughout the first edition printed by him, (2) that the rotten paper of the single copy of this first edition which was given to me for preparing my press-copy, made it impossible for me to erase wrong marks and insert the latest-current signs in most places, and (3) that the typing of the entire book and the insertion of diacritical marks uniformly according to the system at present followed by the Society, could not be carried out for financial reasons. In short, this edition had to be printed in the rough practical form that I have given to it, or not at all. But two little hints may be given here: in the unchanged portions of Jarrett's work the inverted comma stands for the letter *āliph* (in names like—*ud-din*), while in my portion it stands for the letter *'ain*; and the mark over the long *A* (capital) could not be inserted owing to some technical difficulty in linotype composition.

Calcutta,
30th December, 1949.

JADUNATH SARKAR.

EXTRACTS FROM JARRETT'S PREFACE

Whatever the verdict of those competent from linguistic knowledge and acquaintance with the abrupt, close and enigmatic style of the original to judge of the merits of my translation, no pains at least have been spared to render it a faithful counterpart consistently with a clearness of statement which the text does not everywhere show. The peculiar tone and spirit of Abul Fazl are difficult to catch and to sustain in a foreign tongue. His style, in my opinion, is not deserving of imitation even in his own. His merits as a writer have, in general, been greatly exaggerated. Omitting the contemporary and interesting memoirs of Al Badāoni, whose scathing comments on the deeds and motives of king and minister have an independent value of their own, the accident that Abul Fazl's works form the most complete and authoritative history of the events of Akbar's reign, has given them a great and peculiar importance as state records. This they eminently deserve, but as exemplars of style, in comparison with the immutable types of excellence fixed for ever by Greece and Rome, they have no place. His unique position in Akbar's court and service enhanced the reputation of all that he wrote, and his great industry in a position which secured wealth and invited indolence, fully merited the admiration of his countrymen. Regarded as a statistician, no details from the revenues of a province to the cost of a pine-apple, from the organisation of an army and the grades and duties of the nobility to the shape of a candlestick and the price of a curry-comb, are beyond his microscopic and patient investigation : as an annalist, the movements and conduct of his sovereign are surrounded with the impeccability that fences and deifies Oriental despotism, and chronicled with none of the skill and power, and more than the flattery of Velleius Paterculus : as a finished diplomatist, his letters to recalcitrant generals and rebellious viceroys are Eastern models of astute persuasion, veiling threats with compliments, and insinuating rewards and promises without committing his master to their fulfilment. But these epistles which form one of his monuments to fame, consist of interminable sentences involved in frequent parentheses difficult to unravel, and paralleled in the West only by the decadence of taste, soaring in prose, as Gibbon justly remarks, to the vicious affectation of poetry, and in poetry sinking below the flatness and insipidity of prose, which characterizes Byzantine eloquence in the tenth century. A similar affectation, and probably its prototype, is to be found in the most approved Arab masters of florid composition of the same epoch, held by Ibn Khallikan's crude and undisciplined criticism to be the perfection of art, and which still remains in Hindustan the ideal of every aspiring scribe.

His annals have none of the pregnant meaning and point that in a few masterly strokes, exalt or brand a name to all time, and flash the actors of his drama across the living page in scenes that dwell for ever in the memory. The history of nearly forty-six years of his master's reign contains not a line that lives in household words among his own countrymen, not a beautiful image that the mind delights to recall, not a description that rises to great power or pathos, nor the unconscious simplicity redeeming its wearisome length which lends such a charm to Herodotus, and which in the very exordium of Thucydides, in Lucian's happy phrase, breathes the fragrance of Attic thyme. His narrative affects a quaint and stiff phraseology which renders it often obscure, and continues in an even monotone, never rising or falling save in reference to the Emperor whose lightest mention compels the adoring prostration of his pen, and round whom the world of his characters and events revolves as its central sun. Whatever its merit as a faithful representation, in a restricted sense, of a reign in which he was a capable and distinguished actor, it lacks the interesting details and portraiture of the life and manners of the nation which are commonly thought to be below the dignity of history but which brighten the pages of Eastern historians less celebrated than himself, and are necessary to the light and shade of a perfect picture.

His statistical and geographical survey of the empire which this volume comprises is a laborious though somewhat lifeless compilation, of the first importance indeed as a record of a past and almost forgotten administration to guide and instruct the historian of the future or the statesman of to-day, but uninformed by deductive comment and illustration which might relieve the long array of bald detail. His historical summaries of dynasties and events in the various Subahs under their ancient autonomous rule, are incoherent abridgements, often so obscurely phrased as not to be understood without a previous knowledge of the events to which they relate and his meaning is rather to be conjectured than elicited from the grammatical analysis of his sentences. The sources from which he drew his information are never acknowledged. This of itself would have been of no moment and their indication might perhaps have disturbed the unity of his design had he otherwise so incorporated the labours of others with his own as to stamp the whole with the impress of originality, but he not seldom extracts passages word for word from other authors undeterred by the fear or heedless of the charge, of plagiarism.

Such, in my opinion, is the reverse of the medal which represents Abul Fazl as unrivalled as a writer and beyond the reach of imitation. The fashion of exaggerating the importance and merits of a subject or an author by those who make them their special study, especially when that study lies outside the common track of letters, inevitably brings its own retribution and ends by casting general discredit on what in its place and of its kind has its due share of honour or utility. The merit and the only merit of the *Ain-i-Akbari* is in what it tells and not in the manner of its telling which has little to recommend it. It will deservedly go down to posterity as a unique compilation of the systems of administration and control throughout the various departments of Government in a great empire, faithfully and minutely recorded in their smallest detail, with such an array of facts illustrative of its extent, resources, condition, population, industry and wealth as the abundant material supplied from official sources could furnish. This in itself is praise and fortune of no common order and it needs not the fictitious ascription of unparalleled powers of historiography in its support. The value of the *Ain* in this regard has been universally acknowledged by European scholars and it may not be out of place to quote here the opinion* of the learned Reinaud on this work in his 1st vol. of the *Geographie d' Abulfeda,* as it accurately represents its nature and worth and the style and quality of its literary composition. He writes :—

"Muslim India offers us, at the commencement of the 17th century, a work of compilation, which is of great interest for geography ; it is a Persian treatise composed by Abul Fazl, the minister of the Mughal Emperor Akbar, and entitled the *Ain-i-Akbari* or the Institutes of Akbar. . . . . The empire founded in India by Babur, had attained, under the reign of Akbar, a great extension, and stretched from Afghanistan up to the head of the Gulf of Bengal, from the Himalaya up to the Deccan. Due to the excellent government established by Akbar, the provinces, long ravaged by intestine wars, had acquired a new shape. On the other hand, the liberal views of the Emperor and of his ministers, had nothing in common with the narrow and exclusive spirit which characterises Islam, and they had caused to be translated into Persian the best works of Sanskrit literature. Abul Fazl, putting himself at the head of a body of scholars, undertook a geographical, physical and historical description of the empire, accompanied by statistical tables. Each of the sixteen *subahs* or Governments of which the Mughal empire was then composed, is there described with minute exactitude ; the geographical and relative situation of the cities and boroughs (market towns, *qasba*) is there indicated ; the enumeration of the natural and industrial products is carefully traced there ; as also the names of the princes, both Hindu and Musalman, to whom the *subah* had been subject before its inclusion in the empire. We next find an exhibition of the military condition of the empire and an enumeration of those who formed the household of the sovereign, &c. The work ends in a summary, made in general from indigenous sources, of the Brahmanic religion, of the diverse systems of Hindu philosophy, &c.

The author, by the pursuit of a misplaced erudition has accomplished the style of the ancient Persian authors ; it is often difficult to understand it. In 1783, Francis Gladwin, encouraged by the Governor-General Hastings, published an abridged English version of the work. (He then condemns Gladwin's defects,—inaccuracy, confusion, and 'horrible alteration' of indigenous, particularly Sanskrit, words in transcribing them in the Arabic Alphabet, and calls for a new edition as a very useful service to students.)

In the table of the names of places confusion exists in the original text. Evidently, the person who in that early age was charged with the drawing up of the table had little knowledge of geography."

H. S. JARRETT.

Calcutta,
1891

---

* Translated from French into English by J. Sarkar for the second edition.

CONTENTS

BOOK THIRD

IMPERIAL ADMINISTRATION

Since somewhat of the recent imperial institutions regulating the Army and the Household have been set down, I shall now record the excellent ordinances of that sagacious intellect that energizes the world.

'A IN I

THE DIVINE ERA

The connection of monetary transactions without fixity of date would slip from the grasp, and through forgetfulness and falsehood raise a tumult of strife; for this reason every community devises a remedy and fixes an epoch. Since thought fosters well-being and is an aid to facility (*of action*),to displace obsolete chronology and establish a new usage is a necessity of government. For this reason, the prince regent on the throne of felicity in the 29th year of the *Ilāhi* Divine Era,[1] for the purpose of refreshing that pleasure-ground of dominion and revenue, directed its irrigation and rendered blooming and lush the palace-garden of the State.

Compassing events within a determinate time, the Persian calls *māhroz* (date); the Arab has converted this into *mu'arrakh* (*chronicled*), and thence "*tārikh* (*date*) is a household word. Some derive the Arabic from *irākh,* a wild bull.[2] This conjugation of the measure of *tafa'il* means, to polish. As ignorance of the time of an event grew less, it

---

[1] *Akbarnāmah* (Beveridge's trans), iii. 644; this era was introduced at the beginning of the 29th regnal year, 8 Rabi A. 992=10th March 1584.

[2] *Encyclopaedia of Islam,* Supplement, p. 230 : "The root of the word *tārikh* (meaning era, date) is *w-r-kh,* common to the Semitic languages, which we find for example in the Hebrew *yerah,* month. . . . The survival of a tradition in al-Biruni is interesting; according to this, the word is an arabisation of the Persian *māhruz:* here again there is the vague consciousness that the word has something to do with fixing the beginning of the month. al-Khwarizmi in his *Mafātih al-'Ulum* expressly states that this tradition is to be rejected." Abul Fazl's etymology is sometimes as bad as his geography. [J. S.]

became distinguished by this name. Some assert that it is transposed from '*tākhir* which is referring a late period to an antecedent age. Others understand it to be a limit of time wherein an event determines. They say "such a one is the *tārikh* of his tribe," that is, from whom dates the nobility of his line. It is commonly understood to be a definite day to which subsequent time is referred and which constitutes an epoch. On this account they choose a day distinguished by some remarkable event,[3] such as the birth of a sect, a royal accession, a flood or an earthquake. By considerable labour and the aid of fortune, by constant divine worship and the observance of times, by illumination of the understanding and felicity of destiny, by the gathering together of far-seeing intelligences and by varied knowledge especially in the exact sciences and the Almighty favour, observatories were built: wonderful upper and lower rooms with diversity of window and stair arose on elevated sites little affected by dust.

By this means and with the aid of instruments such as the armillary sphere and others double-limbed and bi-tubular,[4] and the quadrant of altitude,[5] the astrolabe, the globe and others, the face of astronomy was illumined and the computation of the heavens, the position of the stars, the extent of their orbits in length and breadth, their distance from each other and from the earth, the comparative magnitude of the heavenly bodies and the like were ascertained. So great a work without the daily increasing auspiciousness of a just monarch and his abundant solicitude, is not to be accomplished. The gathering together of learned men of liberal minds is not achievable simply by means of ample

---

[3] This passage is so strikingly similar to the opening of the 3rd chapter of Al Biruni's *Athār ul Bāqiya* that it can scarcely be accidental. There is nothing to hinder the supposition that Abul Fazl was acquainted with that writer's works and not a little indebted to him. [H. S. J.]

[4] I cannot determine accurately what these may be. It is possible that the first may be the *skaphium* of Aristarchus which was a gnomon, the shadow of which was received on a concave hemispherical surface, having the extremity of its style at the centre, so that angles might be measured directly by arcs instead of the tangents. The second may refer to the invention of Archimedes to ascertain the apparent diameter of the sun by an apparatus of double cylinders. There was another, too, of Aristarchus to find the distance of the sun by measuring the angle of elongation of the moon when dichotomized. The *kitab ul Fihrist* mentions only the astrolabe and the armillary sphere, p. 284. Sedillot (*Prologomenes des Tables Astron. d'Olong Beg*) speaks of a "gnomon ā trou" used by Nasiruddin Tusi.

[5] So I venture to interpret the term. Dozy (Supplem. *Dict. Arab.*) quotes Berbrugger on this word "*Ruba'a-el-moudjib,* le quart de cercle horodictique, instrument d'une grande simplicite dont on fait usage pour connaitre l'heure par la hauteur du soleil." *Moudjib* should be "*mujayyab*',

wealth, and the philosophic treatises of the past and the institutions of the ancients cannot be secured without the most strenuous endeavours of the sovereign. With all this, thirty years are needed to observe a single revolution of the seven planets.[6] The longer the period and the greater the care bestowed upon a task, the more perfect its completion.

In this time-worn world of affliction Divine Providence has vouchsafed its aid to many who have attained considerable renown in these constructions, such as Archimedes, Aristarchus and Hipparchus in Egypt, from whose time to the present, the 40th year of the divine era, 1769 years have elapsed;[7] such as Plotemy in Alexandria who flourished some 1410 years ago; as the Caliph Māmun in Baghdad, 790 years past, and Sind[8] bin 'Ali and Khālid[9] bin 'Abdul Malik al Marwazi 764 years since at Damascus. Hākim and Ibn[10] Aa'lam also laid the foundations of an observatory at Baghdad which remained unfinished, 712 years, and Battāni[11] at Raqqa 654 years previous to this time. Three

---

[6] The ancients gave the name of *planets* to the five planets visible to the naked eye, and the sun and moon. The names of the five—Mercury, Venus, Mars, Jupiter, and Saturn first occur in the cosmical scheme of Philolaus. (Lewis. *Astron. of the Ancients*) The thirty years must refer to that planet of the seven occupying the longest period in its revolution, namely, Saturn which was the most remote then known. It takes 29 years and 5½ months (very nearly) to return to the same place among the fixed stars, whether the centre of motion be the Sun or the Earth.

[7] It is needless to say that all these figures are very inexact. Archimedes flourished 287-212 B.C., Aristarchus somewhwere about 280-264 B.C. and Hipparchus is placed by Suidas at from B.C. 160 to 145, and yet they are all bracketed together. The date of Plotemy, illustrious as he is as a mathematician, astronomer and geographer, is uncertain. He observed at Alexandria, A.D. 139 and was alive in A.D. 161. Mamun succeeded to the Caliphate on the 24th September 813. He caused all Greek works that he could procure to be translated, and in particular the *Almagest* of Plotemy. *Almagest* is a compound of the Greek with a prefix of the Arabic article. (*Encycl. Metropolitana.* Art. Astron.)

[8] *Abu Tayyib Sind-b-'Ali* was a Jew converted to Islam in the Caliphate of Māmun and was appointed his astronomer and superintendent of observatories.

[9] *Khalid-b-'Abdul Malik,* A.H. 217 (832) a native of Merv. He is included among three astronomers who first among the Arabs, instituted observations from the Shammāsiyah observatory at Baghdad

[10] *Ibn ul 'Ā'a'lam* A.H. 375 (A.D. 985), stood in great credit with Adhad ud daulah, but finding himself in less estimation with his son Shamsud Daulah, he left the court but returned to Baghdad a year before his death. His astronomical tables were celebrated not only in his own time but by later astronomers.

[11] *Muhammad b. Jābir al Battani* (Albatenius), a native of Harrān and inhabitant of Raqqa. His observations were begun in A.H. 264 (A.D. 877-8) and he continued them till A.H. 306. *Ency. Islam,* i. 680, "one of the greatest of Arab astronomers," (where details about his writings and achievement); he died in 317 A.H. He was surnamed the Ptolemy of the Arabs. He corrected the determination of Ptolemy respecting the motion of the stars in longitude, ascertaining it to be one degree in 70 instead of 100 years; modern observations make it one degree in 72 years. He also determined very exactly the eccentricity of the ecliptic and corrected the

hundred and sixty-two solar years have passed since Khwājah[12] Nasir of Tus built another at Murāgha near Tabriz and 155 is the age of that of Mirzā Ulugh Beg[13] in Samarqand.

Rasad signifies 'watching' in the Arabic tongue and the watchers, therefore, are a body who, in a specially-adapted edifice, observe the movements of the stars and study their aspects. The results of their investigations and their discoveries regarding these sublime mysteries are tabulated and reduced to writing. This is called an astronomical table (*zij*). This word is an Arabicized form of the Persian, *zik* which means the threads that guide the embroiderers in weaving brocaded stuffs. In the same way an astronomical table is a guide to the astronomer in recognising the conditions of the heavens, and the linear extensions and columns, in length and breadth, resemble these threads. It is said to be the Arabic rendering of *zih* from the frequent necessity of its use, which the intelligent will understand. Some maintain it to be Persian, signi-

---

length of the year, making it consist of 365 days, 5 hours, 46 minutes, 24 seconds, which is about 2 minutes short of but 4 minutes nearer the truth than had been given by Ptolemy. He also discovered the motion of the apogee.

[12] *Nasiru'ddin* is the surname of Abu Ja'far Md. b. Muhammad-b-Hasan or Ibn Muhammad at Tusi, often simply called Khwājah Nasiru'ddin (A.H. 597-672). Hulāku the Tartar chief placed him at the head of the philosophers and astronomers whom his clemency had spared in the sack of Moslem towns, and gave him the administration of all the colleges in his acquired dominions. The town of Marāgha in Azarbayjān was assigned to him and he was ordered to prepare the astronomical tables which were termed Imperial (Elkhān). [*Enc. Islam*, iv. 980, under al-Tusi.]

[13] Ulugh Beg, (name Muhammad Turghāi) born 1393, died 1449 A.D., was the son of Shah Rukh and grandson of Tamerlane. In 810 he possessed the government of some provinces of Khorasān and Mazanderān and in 812, that of Turkistān and Transoxania. He, however, quickly abandoned politics and devoted himself passionately to his favourite studies. He desired that his tables should be scrupulously exact and procured the best instruments then available. These at this period, were of extraordinary size. The obliquity of the ecliptic was observed in A.D. 995 with a quadrant of 15 cubits' radius (21 feet 8 inches). The sextant of Abu Muhammed al Khojandi used in 992 had a radius of 40 cubits (57 feet 9 inches). The quadrant used by Ulugh Beg to determine the elevation of the pole at Samarqand, was as high as the summit of St. Sophia at Constantinople (about 180 feet). The astronomical tables were first published in A.H. 841 (A.D. 1437). The ancient astronomy had produced only one catalogue of the fixed stars, that of Hipparchus. Ulugh Beg, after an interval of sixteen centuries, produced the second. His observatory at Samarqand (begun in 1428 under the architect Ali Qushji), in its day was regarded as one of the wonders of the world. He corrected Ptolemy's computations and compiled the *Zij-i-Jadid Sultāni*. These tables became celebrated in Europe—trans. by Hyde in 1665, by Sedillot (prolegomena only) in 1847, and by Knobel in 1917." With him the period of astronomical works in the East finishes." [*Ency. Islam*, iv. 994-996.]

For the compilation of Astronomical Tables by Muslims (*zij*), see *Enc. Islam*, i. 498.

fying a mason's rule, and as he, through its instrumentality determines the evenness of a building, so an astronomer aims at accuracy by means of this astronomical table.

Many men have left such compilations to chronicle their fame. Among these are the Canons of.

1. MĀJUR THE TURK.

There are two of this family whom Sedillot terms the Benou Amajour. Hammer-Purgstall makes them the same person but adds another name Abul Qāsim 'Abdullah. According to him, they were brothers, and the former was the author of the Canon called al Bedia or "the Wonderful ;" the latter of works on other astronomical tables with disputed titles. He appears to quote from the Fihrist and from Casiri who borrows from Ibn Jounis, but the Fihrist distinctly states that Abu'l Hasan was the son not the brother of Ali b. Amajur. Ibn Jounis speaks of Abul Qāsim also, and as a native of Herat. The Benou Amajur were astronomers of repute and made their observations between the years 885-933, leading the way to important discoveries. (Sed p. xxxv *et seq*).

2. HIPPARCHUS.
3. PTOLEMY.
4. PYTHAGORAS.
5. ZOROASTER.
6. THEON OF ALEXANDRIA.
7. SāMĀT THE GREEK.

Another reading is Sābāt but I cannot recognize nor trace the name satisfactorily. The epithet *Yunāni* inclines me to believe the name to be that of a Greek astronomer in Islamic times.

8. THĀBIT-b-QURRAH b Hārun was a native of Harrān, of the Sabean sect, and rose to eminence in medicine, mathematics and philosophy, born A. H. 221 (A.D. 836), died in A. H. 288 (A.D. 901). He was much favoured by the Caliph al Muatadhid who kept him at Court as an astrologer. He wrote on the Spherics of Theodosius, and retranslated Euclid already turned into Arabic by Hunain-b-Ishāq al Ibādi. He was also author of a work in Syriac on the Sabean doctrines and the customs and ceremonies of their adherents. Ibn Khall. D'Herb. Sediilot. p. xxv. *et seq.* For a list of his works, see the Fihrist, p. 272.

9. HUSĀM b. SINAN (var. Shabān.)

I believe the first name to be an error. The Fihrist mentions a son of Sinan with the patronymic Abul Hasan who is no doubt here meant. He was grandson of Thābit-b-Qurrah, and named also Thābit according to D'Herb. as well as Abul Hasan after his grandfather. (Sedillot). Equally proficient in astronomy with his grandfather, he was also a celebrated physician and practised in Baghdad. He wrote a history of his own time from about A.H. 290 to his death in 360. Abul Faraj speaks of it as an excellent work. See also Ibn Khall. De Slane. Vol. II. p. 289 and note 7. His father Sinān the son of Thābit-b-Quarrah, died at Baghdad A.H. 331. They were both Harranians, the last representatives of ancient Greek learning through whom Greek sciences were communicated to the illiterate Arabs.

Sinān made a collection of meteorological observations called the Kitāb ul anwā, compiled from ancient sources, incorporated by Albiruni in his Chronology, and thereby preserved to us the most complete Parapegma of the ancient Greek world. See Albiruni, *Chronol*, Sachau's Transl. p. 427. n.

10. THĀBIT-b-MUSA.

I can find no such name. The Fihrist gives Thābit-b-Ahusa, head of the Sabean sect in Harrān.

11. MUHAMMAD-b-JABIR AL BATTĀNI. See p. 3, note 11.

12. AHMAD-b-'ABDULLAH JABĀ.

Jaba is a copyist's error for Habsh. He was one of Al Māmun's astronomers, and distinguished by the title of Al Hāsib or the Reckoner. He was employed by Māmun at Sinjar to observe the obliquity of the Ecliptic and to test the measurements of geometrical degrees. He compiled a set of tables by the Caliph's order. Ham. Purg. B. III, p. 260. Abul Faraj (ed. 1663, p. 247) says that he was the author of three Canons ; the first modelled on the Sindhind, the second termed Mumtahan or Proven (after his return from his observations) and the third the Lesser Canon, known as the 'Shāh'.

13. ABU RAYHĀN.

Abu Rayhān-Muhammad-b-Ahmad Albiruni, born 362. A. H. (A. D. 973), d. 440. (Ar. D. 1048). For further particulars I refer the reader to Sachau's preface to the *Indica* and the *Chronology* of this famous savant.

14. KHĀLID-b-'ABDUL MALIK. See p. 3, note 9.

15. YAHYA-b-MANSUR.

More correctly Yahya-b-Abi Mansur, was one of Al Māmun's most famous astronomers. Abul Faraj (p. 248), says that he was appointed by that Caliph to the Shammāsiyah observatory at Baghdad and to that of Mount Qāsiun at Damascus. The Fihrist gives a list of his works (p. 275) and (p. 143) his genealogy and descendants who appear to have shared and augmented their father's fame. He died about 833, (A. H. 218) in Māmun's expedition to Tarsus and was buried at Aleppo. *Enc. Islam*, iv. 1150.

16. HĀMID MARWARUDI.

This is doubtless, Abu Hāmid, Ahmad-b-Muhammad as Sāghāni. Sāghān is a town near Marw. Ibn Khallikān's derivation of Marwarrud will explain the difference in the titular adjectives of place. I transcribe De Slane, V. I, p. 50. "*Marwarrudi* means *native of Marwarrud*, a well known city in Khorāsān, built on a river, in Persian *ar-rud*, and situated 40 parasangs from Marw as Shāhjān ; these are the *two Marws* so frequently mentioned by poets: the word Shāhjān is added to the name of the larger one from which also is derived the relative adjective *Marwazi ;* the word rud is joined to that of the other city in order to distinguish between them. *Marwarud* has for relative adjective Marwarrudi and *Marwazi*, also, according to as Samāni." Shāhjān is, of course, Sāghān. Abu Hāmid was one of the first geometricians and astronomers of his time (d. 379, A. H. 898), and a maker of astrolabes at Baghdad and was employed to certify the correctness of the royal astronomical reports. Ham Purg. B. V. 313.

17. MUGHITHI. Perhaps, Mughni tabulae astronomicae sufficientes, mentioned by Hāji Khalifa, p. 568, Art. Zich.

18. SHARQI. (Var. Sharfi.) probably Abul Qāsim as Saraqi of whom Casiri writes. 'Abulcassam Alsaraki Aractensis (of Raqqa), Atrologiæ judiciariæ et astronomiæ doctrina, uti etiam Tabularum et Spheræ peritia haud ignobilis, inter familiares atque intimos Saifeldaulati Ali-ben-Abdalla-ben Hamdan, per ea tempora Regis, habitus est, quibuscumque Sermones Academicos frequens conferebat (Saifeldaulatus Syriæ Rex, anno Egiræ 356 obiit. (Sedillot, p. xlviii.)

19. ABUL WAFĀ-NURHĀNI. An error for Buzjāni. Buzjān is a small town in the Nisābur district in the direction of Herāt. He was born A. H. 328 (939) d. 388 (998). In his 20th year he settled in Irāq. A list of his works will be found in the Fihrist, p. 283. Ham. Purg. B. V. 306. His Canon was termed "as Shāmil." His most important work was the Almagest, which contains the formulas of tangents and secants employed by Arab geometricians in the same manner as in trigonometrical calculations of the present day. In the time of Al Battāni, sines were substituted for chords. By the introduction of tangents he simplified and shortened the expression of circular ratios. His anticipation of the discoveries of Tycho Brahe, may be seen in Sed. p. ix. *Enc. Isl,* i. 133, s.v. *Abu-l-Wafa.*

20. THE JAMI'. (Plura continens) }
21. THE BALIGH. (Summum attingens) } Kyahushyar.
22. THE 'ADHADI. }

Kushyār-b-Kenān al Hanbali, wrote three Canons, according to Hāji Khalifa. Two were the *Jāmi'* and the *Sāli'* (Bāligh is however confirmed by D'Herbelot, art. *Zig*). These works were on stellar computations, on almanacs, the motions of the heavenly bodies and their number, supported by geometrical proofs. His compendium (mujmal) summarises their contents (p. 564.) The *Jāmi'* is again mentioned lower down as a work in 85 chapters applied by the author to rectify or elucidate the Persian era. He added to it a supplement in illustration of each chapter of the *Jāmi'*. The third Canon is called simply *Zij Kushyār* translated into Persian by Md-b-'Umar-b-Abi Tālib at Tabrizi. This was probably dedicated to Adhad ud Daulah Alp Arslan, lord of Khorāsān, who had condescended to accept this title from his creature the feeble Qāim bi amri llāh at Baghdad. Hence, I conjecture, the name Adhadi.

23. SULAYMĀN-b-MUHAMMAD. Untraceable. This name does not occur in one of the MSS. of the Ain.

24. ABU HĀMID ANSĀRI.

The only descendant of the Ansārs that I can find among the astronomers is Ibn us Shatir. d. 777 A. H. (1375) ; the name was Alāuddin, patronymic not given. See Haj. Khal. pp. 557, 566. It is possible that the celebrated Abu Hāmid al Ghazzāli may be meant

25. SAFĀIH. Evidently the name of a Canon and not of its author.

26. ABUL FARAH SHIRĀZI.

27. MAJMUa'. Apparently the name of a Canon mentioned by Hāji Khalifa, auctore Ibn Shari', collecta de astrologia judiciaria.

28. MUKHTĀR auct. Shaikh Abu Mansur Sulaiman b. al Husain-b-Bardowaih, Another work of the same name (Dilectus e libris

electionis dierum, astrologicæ) was composed by the physician Abu Nasr Yahya b. Jarir at Takriti for Sadid ud Daulah Abul Ghanāim Karim.

29. ABUL HASAN TUSI. This name occurs in the Fihrist (p. 71) as that of a scholar learned in tribal history and poetry. A son of the same name is mentioned as a distinguished doctor, but there is no notice of his astronomical knowledge.

30. AHMAD-b-ISHĀQ SARAKHSI.

The name of Ishāq does not occur in the genealogy of any Sarakhsi that I can discover. The text probably refers to Ahmad-b-Md. b. at Tayyib, the well known preceptor of the Caliph al Muatadhid by whom he was put to death in A. H. 286 (899) for revealing his pupil's confidences. D'Herb. states that he wrote on the *Eisagaege* of Porphirius, and Albiruni (Chronology) mentions him as an astrologer and cites a prophecy of his where he speaks of the conjunction of Saturn and Mars in the sign of Cancer.

31. GHARĀRI. Probably Al Fazāri. Abu Ishāq Ibrahim-b-Habib the earliest maker of astrolabes among the Arabs, who was the author of a canon and several astronomical works. Fihrist, p. 273, date not given.

32. AL HĀRUNI.

It is difficult in such bald mention of names, where so many are alike, to be sure of the correctness of allusion. This is, probably, Hārun-b-al Munajjim, an astrologer, native of Baghdad and an accomplished scholar. His great grandfather was astrologer to the Caliph al-Mansur and his son Yahya served al Fadhl-b-Sahl in the same capacity, died A. H. 288 (901). Ibn Khall. IV, p. 605.

33. ADWĀR I KIRĀIN (Cycles of conjunctions) the name of a Canon whose author I cannot discover.

34. YAKUB-b-TĀUS.

I may safely hazard the emendation Tariq for Tāus. This astronomer is mentioned by Albiruni. Ham. Purg. gives his date A. H. 218 (833) and a list of his works apparently copied from the Fihrist, p. 278.

35. KHWĀRAZMI.

Muhammad-b-Musa, by command of al Māmun, compiled an abridgement of the Sindhind (*Siddhānta*) ; better known as a mathematician than as astronomer—see Sedillot, I. xvi. He was the author of a Canon according to the Fihrist, p. 274. *Enc. Isl.* ii. 912.

36. YUSUFI. The secretary of Al Māmun, Abut Tayyib-b-'Abdillah is the only name I discover in this relative form. The Fihrist, (p. 123) mentions no astronomical works of his. Perhaps, Yusuf-b-Ali Thatta (1043) or Ibn Yusuf al Massisi may be meant: the text is too vague to determine accurately.

37. WĀFI—the work of Ulugh Beg "fi *Mawāfi* ul āamāl un Najumiya" (de transtitibus operationum astronomicarum) is the only title approaching that of the text that I discover.

38. JAUZHARAYN—Jauzhar the Arabic form of Gauzhar, is the head and tail of Draco. The two points in the Ecliptic which mark its intersection by the orbit of a planet in ascent and descent, are called its Nodes or two Jauzhars—(Istilābāt ul Funon.) There is a Canon called *Fi Maqawǎm al Juzhar* de motu vero capitis et caudœ draconis, by Shaikh Ibn ul Qādir al Barallusi—see Haj-Khall, p. 561,

39. Sama'ānī. D'Herbelot mentions under this surname Abu Saad Abdul Karim Muhammad, the author of a work on Mathematics entitled *Adāb fi istimāl il Hisāb*. A. H. 506—62. The Fihrist p. 244, records another Samaān as a commentator on the Canon of Ptolemy, and a third Ibn Samaān, the slave of Abu Mashar, and author of an astronomical work.

40. Ibn Sahra.

The variants of this name suggest its doubtful orthography. Ibn Abi Sahari is mentioned by Ham. Purg. as an astrologer of Baghdad whose predictions were fortunate. He lived in the latter half of the century, 132—232, (749—846) the most brilliant period in the annals of Arab literature.

41. Abul Fadhl Māshallah, incorrectly Māshada in the text. —Born in Al Mansur's reign, he lived to that of Al Māmun. His name "What God wills" is simply a rendering of the Hebrew Mischa. The Fihrist calls him Ibn Athra and notes his voluminous writings, copied by Ham, Purg. B. III. 257.

42. 'Aāsimi—untraceable.

43. Kabir of Abu Ma'shar—a native of Balkh, a contemporary and envious rival of Al Kindi.—At first a traditionist, he did not begin the study of astronomy till after the age of 47. He died at Wāsit exceeding the age of 100, A. H. 272, (885)—An astronomer and astrologer of great renown. In the latter capacity, he paid the penalty of success in a prediction by receiving a flogging at the command of Al Musta'in ; upon which his epigram is recorded. "I hit and got hit." Thirty-three of his works are named in the Fihrist, p. 277. He was known in Europe as Albumaser and his works translated into Latin, see Sachau's Albiruni (Chronol.) p. 375,—also Haj. Khal. art. zij.

44. Sind-b-'Ali. See note p. 3.

45. Ibn Aālam. See note p. 3.

46. Shahryārān.

This Canon occurs in Albiruni (*Chronol.*) with the addition of the word Shāh.—Sachau confesses his ignorance of it. Haj. Khal. gives a Canon called Shahryar which is well-known—translated into Arabic by At Tamimi from the Persian. Fihrist, 244. v. also Sachau's preface to Albiruni's *India*, p. xxx.

47. Arkand.—In Albiruni called "the days of Arkand." The more correct form according to Reinaud, *Memoire sur l Inde*, p. 322, would be the Sanskrit *Ahargana*—See Sachau's note p. 375 of Albiruni's *Chronol.* from which I quote.

Albiruni made a new edition of the Days of Arkand, putting into clearer words and more idiomatic Arabic, the then existing translation which followed too closely the Sanskrit original.

48. Ibn Sufi.

Al Shaikh Md. b. Abil Fath as Sufi al Misri wrote an epitome of the Canon of Ulugh Beg with additional tables and notes. It was with reference to this epitome that the work of Al Barallusi, *Bihjat ul Fakr fi Hall is Shams Wāl Qamr* was written, of which the Jauzhar, one of its three parts, is alluded to in 38.

49. Sehalān Kāshi.

Sehelān, Sehilān or Ibn Sehilān according to D'Herbelot was the name of the Minister of Sultān ud Daulah of the Buyide famlly, whose enmity with his brother Mushrafud Doulah was due to the policy or personal feeling of that statesman. A canon might have been published under his patronage and name.

50. AHWĀZI. D'Herbelot alludes to several authors under this name ; one a commentator on Euclid. The Fihrist names Md-b-Ishāq al Ahwazi, without date. He appears to have written on agriculture and architecture.

51. THE 'URUS OF ABU JAFAR BUSHANJI.

Bushanj, according to Yaqut (*Mujam il Buldān*) is a small town about 40 miles from Herat, which has given birth to some eminent scholars, but I can find no astronomer among them.

52. ABUL FATH—Shaikh Abul Fath as Sufi who amended the tables termed Samarqandi. Haji Khal, 566, III.

53. A'KKAH RĀHIBI—untraceable.

54. MASAUDI.—The *Canon Masudicus* is extant in 4 good copies in European libraries, and waits for the combination of two scholars, an astronomer and an Arabic philologist, for the purpose of an addition and translation, v. Sachau, pref. to Alberuni's *India,* p. xvi. *Enc. Islam,* iii. 403.

55. MUATABAR OF SANJARI. The surname of Abul Fath Abdur Rahman, called the treasurer ; he was a slave of Greek origin, in the service of A'li al Khāzin al Marwazi and much in his favour. On the completion of his Canon, the Sultan Sanjar sent him a thousand dinars which he returned. Haj. Khal. III. 564.

56. WAJIZ-I-MUATABAR is doubtless, as its name imports, an epitome of the foregoing.

57. AHMAD ABDUL JALIL SANJARI, author of two treatises on stellar influences. D'Herbelot mentions him as an astrologer of note, but adds no particulars.

58. MUHAMMAD HASIB TABARI.
Untraceable.

59. 'ADANI.
60. TAYLASĀNI.
61. ASĀBAI.
62. KIRMĀNI.

These are names of tables which I do not find mentioned. By the term Taylasān is meant a paradigm showing astronomical calculations, in the shape of half an oblong quadrangular field divided by a diagonal. It is named after the form of the Scarf (Taylasān) worn by learned men in the East. A model will be found in Albiruni's Chronology. (Sachau), p. 133.

63. SULTAN 'ALI KHWĀRAZMI. Ali, Shah-b-Md-b-il Qāsim commonly known as 'Alāuddin Al Khwārazmi, the author of a Canon called *Shāhi*—the royal ; also of a Persian epitome from the Elkhāni Tables, called the *Umdat ul Elkhāniya.* Haj. Khal. p. 565, III.

64. FĀKHIR 'ALI NASABI.
The variants indicate a corrupt reading—untraceable.

65. THE 'ALAI OF SHIRWĀNI. Fariduddin Abul Hasan Ali-b-il Karim as Shirwani, known as Al Fahhād, eminent among the later astronomers, the author of several canons besides the one mentioned —See Haj. Khal. p. 567, in two places.

There are two other Canons called *'Alai,* H. K. 556-7.

66. RĀHIRI—var. Zahidi—untraceable.

67. MUSTAWFI—mentioned by Haj. Khal. without author's name.

68. MUNTAKHAB (Selectus) OF YAZDI.

69. ABU RAZĀ YAZDI.

Yazd is a town between Naysabur and Shirāz. I find no record of either the canon or the astronomer.

70. KAYDURAH.

71. IKLILI.

Al Iklil is the 17th Lunar Station—three stars in the head of Scorpio. I infer from the absence of any mention of such astronomers that these canons are named after stars. I can learn nothing of Kaydurah.

72. NĀSIRI—perhaps called after Nāsirud-Daulah-b-Hamdān, temp. Mutii billah, A.H. 334. (946 A D.)

73. MULAKHKHAS. (Summarium).

74. DASTUR. *Dastur ul Aml fi Tashih il Jadwal*—a Persian commentary by Mahmud-b-Mahd.-b-Kādhizāda (known as Meriem Chelebi, in H. K. and D'Herb.) of the Canon of Ulugh Beg. See H. K. p. 560, III, and Sedillot, clv. I.

75. MURAKKAB. (Compositus).

76. MIKLAMAH. (Calamarium).

77. 'ASĀ. (Baculas)

78. SHATSALAH. Var. Sashtalah.

79. HASIL. (Commodum).

80. KHATĀI. A name of N. China: its people possessed an Astronomical Calendar in common with the Aighur Tribe, v. D'Herb. Art. *Igur.*

81. DAYLAMI.

This is a bare list of tables of whose authors there is no certain record. Two of them, Khatāi and Daylam point to the countries where they were in vogue. Kublai Khan the brother of Hulāku after his conquest of China, introduced into the Celestial Empire the astronomical learning of Baghdad, and Cocheon-king in 1280, received the tables of Ibn Yunas from the hands of the Persian Jamāluddin. For the extent of Chinese science at this time, see Sedillot. ci. I.

82. MUFRAD. (Simplex) OF MD.-b-AYYUB.

This Canon is in H. K. without the author's name.

83. KĀMIL (Integer) OF ABU RASHID.

There is a commentary of the *Shamil* of al Buzjani by Hasan-b-Ali al qumnāti, entitled the *Kāmil,* mentioned in H. K. p. 565. III.

84. ELKHĀNI.

There are the tables of Nasiruddin Tusi.

85. JAMSHIDI. Ghiyāthuddin Jamshid together with the astronomer known as Kadhizadah, assisted Ulugh Beg in the preparation of his Canon. The former died during the beginning of the work, the latter before its completion. H. K. 559. D'Herbelot (Art. *zig. Ulug. Beg.*) reverses this order and asserts that Jamshid finished it. I suspect that he has copied and mistaken the sense of H. K.

86. GURGANI. Another name for the Canon of Ulugh Beg. See Sed. p. cxix.

Whatever they set down, year by year from an astronomical table, as to the particular motions and individual positions *of the heavenly bodies,* they call an Almanac. It embodies, in fact, the diurnal progression of a planet from its first entrance into Aries to a determinate point in the ecliptic, in succession, and is in Hindi called *patrah.* The Indian sage considers astronomy to be inspired by divine intelligences. A mortal endowed with purity of nature, disposed to meditation, with accordant harmony of conduct, transported in soul beyond the restraints of sense and matter, may attain to such an elevation that earthly and divine forms, whether as universals or particularized, in the sublime or nethermost regions, future or past, are conceived in his mind. From kindliness of disposition and in the interests of science they impart their knowledge to enquirers of auspicious character, who commit their lessons to writing, and this writing they term *Siddhānt.* Nine such books are still extant; the *Brahm-Siddhānt,* the *Suraj-Siddhānt,* the *Som-Siddhānt,* the *Brahaspat-Siddhānt,* inspired by Brahma, the sun, moon, and Jupiter respectively. Their origin is referred to immemorial time and they are held in great veneration, especially the first two. The Garg-Siddhānt,[14] the Nārad-Siddhānt, the Parāsar-Siddhānt, the Pulast-Siddhānt, the Bashista-Siddhānt,—these five they ascribe to an earthly source. The unenlightened may loosen the tongue of reproval and imagine that these mysteries acquired by observation of *Stellar* movements, have been kept secret and revealed only in such a way as to ensure the gratitude of *reverential* hearts, but the keen-sighted and just observer will, nevertheless, not refuse his assent, the more especially as men of innate excellence and outward respectability of character have for myriads of years transmitted a uniform tradition.

[14] These last are named after five celebrated Rishis or Munis. The antiquity of Indian astronomy is a matter of dispute among the learned. The curious inquirer may refer to the 8th Vol. of the Asiatic Researches where Mr. Bentley reduces its age, maintained by Monsieur Bailly to date back to the commencement of the Kali Yug, 3102 B.C.—to within a few hundred years, and fixes the date of the Súraj-Siddhānt—the most ancient astronomical treatise of the Hindus and professed to have been inspired by divine revelation 2,164,899 years ago,—to 1038 of our era. Mr. Bentley is in turn learnedly answered by a writer in the *Edinburgh Review* for July 1807. Sir W. Jones' essay on the Chronology of the Hindus may be read in conjunction with the preceding papers, v. Alb. India, Chap. XIV, where the names of the Sidhánts and their sources are differently given.

Among all nations the Nychthemeron[15] is the measure of time and this in two aspects, *firstly,* Natural, as in Turān and the West, from noon to noon, or as in China and Chinese Tartary[16] from midnight to midnight; but the reckoning from sunset to sunset more universally prevails. According to the Hindu sages, in Jagmot[17]—the eastern extremity of the globe, they reckon it from sunrise to sunrise; in Rumak—the extreme west, from sunset to sunset; in Ceylon, the extreme south, from midnight to midnight and the same computation obtains in Delhi : in Siddhapur, the extreme north, from noon to noon. *Secondly,* the Equated also called Artificial, which consists of a complete revolution of the celestial sphere measured by the sun's course in the ecliptic. For facility of calculation, they take the whole period of the sun's revolution and divide equally the days thereof and consider the fractional remainder as the mean of each day, but as the duration of the revolutions is found to vary, a difference *between the natural and artificial day* arises. The tables of Al-Battāni assume it as 59 minutes, 8 seconds, 8 thirds, 46 fourths, 56 fifths and 14 sixths. Those of Elkhāni make the minutes and seconds the same, but have 19 thirds, 44 fourths, 10 fifths and 37 sixths. The recent Gurgāni tables agree with the Khwājah[18] up to the thirds, but give 37 fourths, and 43 fifths. Ptolemy in the Almagest accords in minutes and seconds, but sets down 17 thirds, 13 fourths, 12 fifths and 31 sixths. In the same way ancient tables record discrepancies, which doubtless arise from varying knowledge and difference of instruments. The cycle of the year and the seasons depend upon the sun. From the time of his quitting one determinate point till his return to it, they reckon as one year. The period that he remains in one sign is a solar month. The

---

[15] This term for the twenty-four hours of light and darkness was used by the later Greeks and occurs in 2 Cor. xi. 25. Its precision of meaning commends its use which Sachau has adopted.

[16] Uighūr is the name of a Chaghtai tribe eponymously applied to this country, see D'Herb. Art. Igur and the observations thereon Vol. IV, p. 300.

[17] Cf. Albirúni's *India,* Edit. Sachau, p. 133, Chap. XXVI. This word should be "Jamkót." Albirúni quotes from the *Siddhānta.* The 4 cardinal points mentioned are given as the names of 4 large towns—the globe is described a spheroid, half land, half water : the mountain Míru occupies the centre, through which the Equator (*Nalkash*) passes. The Northern half of the mountain is the abode of angelic spirits, the southern that of Daityas and Nāgs and is therefore called Daitantar. When the sun is in the medidian of Meru, it is midday at Jamkót, midnight at Rumak and evening at Siddpúr. The latter name is spelt by Abirúni with a double *d.* See a map of this peculiar geographical system prefixed, to Gladwin's translation of the *Aín* and in Blochmann's text edition, following the preface.

[18] Naṣíru'ddín Ṭúsi, author of the Elkhāni tables.

interval of the moon's departure from a given position to its return thereto with the sun in conjunction or opposition or the like, is a lunar month. And since twelve lunations are nearly[19] equal to one *annual* revolution of the sun, they are called a lunar year. Thus both the year and the month are solar and lunar : and each of these two is Natural when the planetary revolutions are regarded and not the computation of days, and Equated when the computation is in days and not in the time of revolution. The Hindu sage divides the year, like the month, into four parts, allotting a particular purpose to each. Having now given a short account of the night, the day, the year and the month which form the basis of chronological notation, we herein set down somewhat of the ancient eras to complete our exposition.

A note on Islamic astronomy (compiled from the *Encyclopaedia of Islam,* i. 497-501.) For the Muslims, as for the Greeks, astronomy only aims at studying the apparent movements of the stars and giving a geometrical representation of them; it comprises therefore what we call spherical astronomy and the "theory of the instruments". . . . The sum total of the practical knowledge necessary for determining by calculation or instruments the hours of day and night, having especially in view the fixing of the times of the five canonical prayers in the mosques, is called *'ilm al mawaqit* or science of the fixed times. In the beginning of Islam the Arabs already possessed some knowledge of practical astronomy. . . . But it was only in the 2nd century of the Hijra (=8th century A.D.) that the scientific study of astronomy was entered on, under the influence of two Indian books : the *Brahma-sphuta-Siddhānta* of Brahmagupta (628) which was brought to the Court at Baghdad in 771 and was used as a model in Arabic by Ibrahim b. Habib al Fazari and Yaqub b. Tariq; and the treatise of Aryabhatta composed in 500, from which Abul-Hasan al Ahwazi derived his tables of the planetary movements. . . .

To these selections from Indian books there was soon added the Arabic translation of the Pahlavi tables entitled *Zik-i-shatroayar* ("royal astronomical tables") compiled in

---

[19] A synodical month, the interval between two conjunctions of the sun and moon, is 29 d. 12 h. 44 m. It was founded on the most obvious determination of the moon's course and and furnished the original month of the Greeks, which was taken in round numbers at 30 days. By combining the course of the sun with that of the moon, the tropical year was assumed at a rough computation to consist of 12 unations or 360 days. See *Astron. of the Ancients* by Lewis, p. 16.

the last period of the Sassanian empire; but about the 11th century A.D. they ceased to be used.

The Greek influence was the last in order of time, but first in order of importance. It introduced into Muslim astronomy the geometrical representation of the celestial movement. The first (and unsatisfactory) Arabic translation of the *Almagest* dates from about 800 A.D.; it was followed by two other versions much superior (in 828 and *c.* 850.) Translations of other Greek works on astronomy, esp. Tables were made later in large numbers.

(The author of the above account, Signior C. A. Nallino, has treated the subject much more fully in Hastings's *Encyclopaedia of Religion and Ethics,* xii. 94-101, under "Sun Moon and Stars".

—[*J. Sarkar.*]

ERA OF THE HINDUS

The creation of Brahmā is taken as its commencement and each of his days is an epoch. They assert that when 70 *kalps* are completed, each consisting of 4 Yugs[20] and the total of these being 4,320,000 years, a Manu appears. He is the offspring of the volition of Brahma and his co-operator in the creation. In each of his days fourteen *successive* Manus arise. At this time which is the beginning of the 51st year of the age of Brahma, there have been six Manus, and of the seventh, 27 *kalps* have elapsed, and three Yugs of the 28th, and of the fourth Yug, 4,700 years. In the beginning of the present Yug, Rājā Judhishthira conquered the universe and being at the completion of an epoch, constituted his own reign an era and since that time to the present which is the fortieth of the Divine era, 4,696 years have elapsed. It continued in observance 3,044 years. After him Bikramājit[21] reckoned from his own accession to

[20] *Viz.,* the Satya or Krita, Tretā, Dwāpar and Kali; the first comprises 1,728,000 years; the second, 1,296,000, the third, 864,000, the fourth, 432,000—being a total of 4,320,000. For Hindu Cosmogony and Cosmology, Hastings's *Encyclo. of Religion,* iv. 155-161 (H. Jacobi) and Hindu Calendar, *ibid.,* v. 870 (Hopkins.) The best and most detailed practical table is Swami-Kannu Pillai's *Indian Ephemeris,* 7vols. (1922), which supersedes all earlier and smaller works, but it covers only 700—1999 A.D. [J. Sarkar.]

The first is Svayambhuva (as sprung from Svayam-bhu, the self-existent,) the author of the famous Code: the next five are Svarochesha, Uttama, Tāmasa, Raivata, Chakshusha; the seventh is called Vaivasvata, or the Sun-born and is the Manu of the present period,—conjectured to be Noah, as the first is thought to be Adam.—Prinsep's *Useful Tables.*

[21] This era to which the luni-solar system is exclusively adapted is called Sanvat, Vulg. Sambat. It began when 3044 years of the *Kali Yug* had elapsed, *i.e.,* 57 years before Christ, so that if any year, say 4925 of the *Kali*

the throne and thus in some measure gave relief to mankind. He reigned 135 years. In this year 1652 years have since then gone by. They relate that a youth named Sālbāhan,[22] was victorious through some supernatural agency and took the Rājā prisoner on the field of battle. Since the captive was not deserving of death, he treated him with consideration and asked him if he had any request to make. He replied that though all his desire was centred in retirement from the world and in the worship of the one Supreme Creator, he still retained the wish that his era might not be obliterated from the records of the age. It is said that the boon was granted, and although he introduced his own era, he did not interfere with the observance of the other. Since this era, 1517 years have expired, and they believe that it will continue in use for 18,000 years more, after which Raja Ḅijiyābhinandan will institute a new era from his own reign which will last 10,000 years. Then Nāgā Arjun will come to the throne and promulgate another era which will continue for 400,000 years, after which Kalki,[23] whom they regard as an *avatar,* will establish a fresh era to last 821 years. These six are considered the principal eras and are called Saka, for there were many epochs and each termed "Sanpat."[24] After the invasion of Sālbāhan, the era of Bikramājit was changed from "Sāka" to "Sanpat." After *the expiration of these six,* the Sat[25] Yug will re-commence and a new epoch be instituted.

The Hindu astronomers regard the months and years as of four kinds—1st, "Saurmās," which is the sun's continuance in one sign of the Zodiac, and such a year consists

---

Yug be proposed and the last expired year of Vikramaditya be required, subtract 3044 therefrom and the result, 1881, is the year sought. To convert Samvat into Christian years, subtract, 57; unless they are less than 58 in which case deduct the amount from 58 and the result will be the date B.C. This era is in general use throughout Hindustan properly so called.—*Useful Tables,* Part II, p. 26.

[22] Sālivāhan, a mythological prince of Deccan who opposed Vikramāditya raja of Ujjain. His capital was Pratishthāna on the Godaveri. The Sáka era, dates from his birth and commences on the 1st Bysákh, 3179. K. Y. which fell on Monday, 14th March, 78 A.D. Julian style.—*Ibid.* p. 22.

[23] Vishnu, in his future capacity of destroyer of the wicked and liberator of the world. This is to constitute the tenth and last *avatār* and is to take place at the end of the four *yugs.* He is to re-appear as a Brahman, in the town of Sambhal, in the family of Vishnu Sarmá.

[24] Properly 'Sanwat.' *Sākā* signifies an era or epoch and is generally applied to that of Sálivâhan.

[25] The text is here in error. The full stop after *āst* nullifies the sense. It should be omitted together with the alif of *āst.* The sentence is then complete and the meaning obvious and consistent. *Sat* is the ordinary Persian transliteration of the Sanskrit *satya.*

of 365 days, 15 *gharis*,[26] 30 *pals*, and 22½ *bipals*; 2nd, "Chāndramās," which is computed from the first day of the moon's increase to the night of the new moon. This year is of 354 days, 22 *gharis*[27] and one '*pal*.' The beginning of the year is reckoned from the entry of the sun into Aries. This month consists of 30 lunar days (*tithi*). Each twelve degrees of the moon's course, reckoning from its departure from conjunction[28] with the sun is a *tithi*: and from the slowness or speed of the moon's progress there is a difference in the number of *gharis* from a maximum of 65 to a minimum of 54. The first, *tithi* is called Pariwā; the second Duj; the third Tij; the fourth Chauth; the fifth Panchamin; the sixth Chhath; the seventh Saptamin; the eighth Ashtamin; the ninth Naumin; the tenth Dasmin; the eleventh Ekādasi; the twelfth Duādasi; the thirteenth Tirudasi; the fourteenth Chaudas; the fifteenth Puranmāsi; and from the 16th to the 29th, they use the same names up to the 14th. The 30th is called Amāwas. From Pariwā the 1st to the 15th they call Shukla-pachch, and the other half Kishna-pachch. Some begin the month from the 1st of Kishna-pachch. In their ephemerides generally the year is solar and the month lunar.

And since the lunar year is less than the solar by ten days, 53 *gharis* 29 *pals* and 22½ *bipals*, on the calculation of a mean rate of motion *of the sun and moon*, the difference, after 2 years, 8 months, 15 days and 3 *gharis*, would amount to one month, and according to the reckoning in the ephemeris would occur in not more than 3 years or in less than 2 years and one month. According to the first calculation, there is this difference in every twelve months and in such a year they reckon one month twice: according to the latter system, in every solar month when there are two conjunctions,[29] and this must necessarily occur between

[26] A *ghari* is 24 minutes, a *pal* 24 seconds, a *bipal*, a second. This would give 6 hours, 12 minutes and 22½ seconds, whereas according to our calculation, it should be 5 hours, 48 m. 47½ s. very nearly.

[27] This minus the *pal* is our calculation exactly.

[28] The year commences at the true instant of conjunction with the sun and moon, that is on the new moon which immediately precedes the beginning of the solar year, falling, somewhere within the 30 or 31 days of the solar month Chaitra. The day of conjunction (*amāvasyā*) is the last day of the expired month; the first of the new month being the day after conjunction. The *tithis* are computed according to *apparent* time, yet registered in *civil* time. For the comprehension of this perplexing notation I refer the reader to the *Useful Tables*, Part II, p. 24.

[29] When two new moons fall within one solar month, the name of the corresponding lunar month is repeated, the year being then intercalary or

Chait and Kuār (*āsvin*) and does not go beyond these seven months. They term this *intercalary* month Ādhik (*added*), vulgarly called Laund.

The third kind of month is Sāwan Mās. They fix its commencement at any day they please : it is completed in thirty days. The year is 360 days.

The fourth, Nachhattar, is reckoned from the time the moon quits any mansion to her return thereto. This month consists of 27 days and the year of 324.

The number of the seasons is, with them, six[30] and each they call *Ritu*. The period that the sun remains in Pisces and Aries, they term *Basant* : this is the temperate season : when in Taurus and Gemini, *Girekham,* the hot season; in Cancer and Leo, *Barkha,* the rainy season; in Virgo and Libra, *Sard,* the close of the rainy season and the beginning of winter; in Scorpio and Sagittarius, *Hemant,* winter; in Capricornus and Aquarius, *Shishra,* the season between winter and spring.

They divide the year likewise into three parts : to each they give the name of *Kāl,* beginning from Phāgun. They call the four hot months *Dhupkāl;* the four rainy months *Barkhakāl* and the four cold months *Sitkāl.* Throughout the cultivable area of Hindustan, there are but three seasons. Pisces, Aries, Taurus and Gemini are the summer; Cancer, Leo, Virgo, Libra, the rains; Scorpio, Sagittarius, Capricornus and Aquarius, the winter. The solar year they divide into two parts. The first beginning with Aries to the extreme of Virgo they term *Uttargol,* which is the sun's progress to the north of the Equator, and from the beginning of Libra to the extreme of Pisces, *Dakkhangol,* the sun's course to the south of the Equator. Also from the first of Capricorn to the end of Gemini, they call *Uttarāyan,* the sun's northern declination (the summer solstice) : and from the 1st of Cancer to the end of Sagittarius *Dachchhanāyan*, or the sun's southern declination (the winter solstice). Many events, occurring in the first of these divisions, especially death, are deemed fortunate.

The Nycthemeron they divide into 60 equal parts and to each they give the name of *ghatis,* more commonly *ghari.* Each *ghari* is subdivided into the same number of parts,

---

containing 13 months. The two months of the same name are distinguished by the terms *adhika* (added) and *nija* (proper or ordinary). *U. T.* p. 23.

[30] Of two sidereal months each, the succession of which is always the same : but the vicissitudes of climate in them will depend upon the position of the equinoctial colure.—*U. T.* II, 18.

each of which they call *pal*. In the same way they apportion the *pal*, and each part they term *nāri* and also *bipal*. Each *nāri* is equal to six respirations of a man of an equable temperament, undisturbed by running, the emotions of anger and the like.

A man in good health respires 360 times in the space of one *ghari*, and 21,600 times in a Nycthemeron. Some affirm that the breath which is respired, they term *Swās* and that which is inspired *Parswās*, and both together they called a *parān*. Six *parāns* make a *pal*, and 60 *pals* a *ghari*. An astronomical hour which is the 24th part of a Nycthemeron is equal to 2½ *gharis*. Each night and each day is again divided into 4 parts, each of which is called a *pahr*, but these are not all equal.

The Khatāi era.

They reckon from the creation of the world, which in their belief took place 8,884 *Wans* and 60 years previous to the present date. Each *Wan* is 10,000 years. They believe that the duration of the world will be 300,000 *Wans*—according to some 360,000. They employ the natural solar year and the natural lunar month. They begin the year from the sun's mid passage through Aquarius. Muhiuddin[31] Maghrebi places it at the 16th degree, others between the 16th and 18th. They divide the Nycthemeron into 12 *Chāghs*. Each of which is subdivided into 8 *Kehs*, and to evey one of these they give a different name.

They divide the Nycthemeron also into *Feneks*. For this computation of time they have three cycles, *viz.*, *Shāng Wan*, *Jung Wan*, and *Khā Wan*, each comprising 60 years and each year of the cycle is defined by a double[32]

---

[31] He was a distinguished philosopher and mathematician in the service of the Sultan of Aleppo. Surnamed al Mughrebi from his having been educated in Spain and Africa, associated in A. H. 658 with Nasir-u'ddin Tusi in the superintendence of the observatory at Murāgha, and shared in the composition of the Elkhāni tables. D'Herbelot. See D'Herb. (Vol. IV. p. 42.) on this nomenclature and his tables of the cycles. For Chinese era, Hastings' *Ency.*, iii. 82.

[32] The word *badu* may also grammatically but in point of fact less accurately apply to the cycle. The following explanation taken from the *Useful Tables* (Part II. p. 14-15 under 'Chinese era'), will elucidate the text. They have two series of words, one of ten and the other of twelve words; a combination of the first words in both orders is the name of the 1st year; the next in each series are taken for the 2nd year, and so to the 10th; in the 11th, the series of 10 being exhausted, they begin again with the first combining it with the eleventh of the second series; in the 12th year, the second word of the first series is combined with the twelfth of the second;

notation. The revolution of the cycle is marked by a series of ten and a series of twelve *symbols*. The first is employed for the notation of the year and the day; the second is similarly applied and is likewise horary. By the combination of these two series, they form the cycle of 60 and work out detailed calculations.

The Turkish Era.

Called also the Uighuri. It is similar to the foregoing, except that this cycle is based on the series of 12. They reckon their years and days after the same manner, but it is said that some astronomical tables also employ the series of 10. The commencement of their era is unknown. Abu Raihān (Albiruni) says[33] that the Turks add nine to the incomplete Syromacedonian years and divide it by 12 : and in whatever animal the remainder terminates, counting from the Sign of the Mouse, the year is named therefrom. But weighed in the balance of experiment, this is found wanting by one year. The intention, undoubtedly, is to carry the remainder down the animal signs of the series,

---

for the 13th year, the third word of the first list with the first of the second list is taken, that list also being now exhausted. Thus designating the series of 10 by Roman letters, and that of 12 by italics, the cycle of 60 will stand thus.

1 a a	21 a i	41 a e
2 b b	22 b k	42 b f
3 c c	23 c l	43 c g
4 d d	24 d m	44 d h
5 e e	25 e a	45 e i
6 f f	26 f b	46 f k
7 g g	27 g c	47 g l
8 h h	28 h d	48 h m
9 i i	29 i e	49 i a
10 k k	30 k f	50 k b
11 a l	31 a g	51 a c
12 b m	32 b h	52 b d
13 c a	33 c i	53 c e
14 d b	34 d k	54 d f
15 e c	35 e l	55 e g
16 f d	36 f m	56 f h
17 g e	37 g a	57 g i
18 h f	38 h b	58 h k
19 i g	39 i c	59 i l
20 k h	40 k d	60 k m

The first cycle, according to the Jesuits, began in February 2397 B.C.; we are now, therefore, in the 72nd cycle, the 28th of which will begin in 1890. To find the Chinese time, multiply the elapsed cycle by 60, and add the odd years: then if the time be before Christ, subtract the sum from 2398; but after Christ, subtract 2397 from it; the remainder will be the year required.

[33] This reference I have not been able to trace in Albiruni's *Athār ul Baqiya*, or his India. [Jarrett] The Turkish era has fallen into disuse, but the names of the Cyclic years as borrowed in Indo-China, Champa and Japan, are given in Hastings, *Encycl.*, iii. 110-115. [J. S.]

and beginning from the Mouse, to adopt the name of the animal in which it terminates. Although the commencement of the era is unknown, yet we gather sufficient information regarding the year of the cycle and its name. And if 7 years be added to the imperfect years of the Maliki era, dividing by 12, whatever remains is the year of the animal reckoning from the Mouse. This will prove correct according[34] to the following series.

Names of the twelve years of the Cycle.

1. *Sijqān,* the Mouse. 2. *Ud,* the Ox. 3. *Pārs,* the Leopard. 4. *Tawishqān,* the Hare. 5. *Loiy,* the Dragon, 6. *Y'ilān,* the Serpent. 7. *Yunt,* the Horse. 8. *Qu,* the Sheep. 9. *Bij,* the Ape. 10. *Takhāku,* the Cock. 11. *Yit,* the Dog. 12. *Tankuz,* the Hog. They add the word *el* to each of these words, which signifies year.

The Astrological Era.

The astrologers reckon from the Creation and assert that all the planets were then in Aries. The year is solar. According to their calculation, from that time to the present 184,696 years have elapsed.

The Era of Adam.

Its beginning dates from his birth. The years are solar, the months lunar. According to the Elkhāni tables, 5,353 solar years have elapsed to the present date. But some of those possessing a book of divine revelation make it 6,346 solar years; others 6,938 solar: others again, 6,920, solar, but according to what has been reported from learned Christians, it is 6,793.

The Jewish Era.

Begins with the creation of Adam. Their years are natural, solar: their months, artificial, lunar. They reckon their months and days like the Arabians according to an intermediate system. The years is of two kinds, *viz.*, Simple, which is not intercalary, and Composite, in which

[34] These 12 signs of the Zodiac exactly correspond with the animals in the series of the Japanese Cycle given in the *Useful Tables*, but the vernacular names are different. The calculations based on them are vaguely stated: in Albiruni's *Chronology*, some information may be obtained from the Rules for the reduction of Eras.

an intercalation is effected. Like the Hindus they intercalate a month every three years.[35]

The Era of the Deluge.

This era is computed from this event; the year is natural, solar, the month natural, lunar. The year begins from the entry of the Sun into Aries. Abu Ma'shar of Balkh based his calculations regarding the mean places of the stars on this era from which to the present year 4,696 years have elapsed.

The Era of Bukht Nassar (Nebuchadnezzar).

This monarch instituted an era from the beginning of his own reign. The year is solar, artificial, of 365 days without a fraction. The month, likewise, is of 30 days and five days are added at the end of the year. Ptolemy in his Almagest computed the planetary motions on this era. Since its commencement 2,341 years have elapsed.

The Era of Philipus (Arrhidæus).[36]

Called also Filbus or Filqus. It is also known as the Era of Alexander of Macedon. It dates from his death. The years and months are artificial, solar. Theon of Alexandria has based his calculations of the mean places of the stars in his Canon on this Era, and Ptolemy has recorded some of his observations regarding it, in the Almagest. Of this period, 1,917 years have elapsed.

The Coptic Era.[37]

This is of ancient date. Al Battāni states that its years are solar, artificial, consisting of 365 days without a fraction. The Sultāni tables say that its years and months

---

[35] Or 7 months in 19 lunar years. Cf. Albiruni's *Chronology*, p. 13. For the Jewish era, Hastings's *Encyclo.* iii. 117-123, after which Prinsep's *Useful Tab*, ii. 8 is unnecessary. For the era of Nebuchadnezzar, *Encyclo. of Islam*, under *Bukht-Nasar* (i. 784) and under *Tarikh* (Suppl. 231.) The Arabs have confounded Nabonassar with Nebuchadnezzar (though 143 years separate the two.) Ptolemy makes this era begin in 742 B.C. For calculating dates in this system, see Prinsep's *Useful Tab.* ii. 9. [J. S.]

[36] He was half brother of Alexander the Great, the son of Philip and a female dancer, Philinna of Larissa. Prinsep's *U. T.* ii. 10. *Enc. Islam,* Supp. 231, this era began on 12 Nov. 324 B.C.

[37] This is the era of Diocletian or the Martyrs; was much used by the Christian writers till the introduction of the Christian era in the 6th century, and is still employed by the Abyssinians and Copts. It dates from 29th August, 284. Prinsep, ii. 7. *Ency. Isl.* iv. 1211.

resemble the Syro-Macedonian. It has the same intercalations, but the Coptic intercalary days precede those of the Syro-Macedonian by six months.

The Syro-Macedonian Era.

The years and months are artificial, solar, and they reckon the year at 365¼ days exactly. In some astronomical observations, the fraction in excess is less than ¼. According to Ptolemy, it is 14 m. 48 s. The Elkhāni observations make the minutes the same, but 32 seconds and 30 thirds. According to the calculations of the Cathayans the minutes are the same, and 36 seconds, 57 thirds; to the recent Gurgāni observations, the minutes agree, with 33 seconds; the Maghrebi has 12 m.: the Battāni, 13 m. 36 s. Muhiyuddin Maghrebi says that some of the Syro-Macedonian calculations make the fraction more than a quarter, others less than a quarter, and thus a quarter has been taken as the medium. Others assert that the Syro-Macedonians have by observation determined the fraction to be a full ¼. Consequently it is a natural solar year, although Mulla 'Ali Kushji makes it a solar year even on the first mentioned basis. This era dates from the death of Alexander the second, [corr. IV] *Bicornutus,* but was not employed till 12 years after his death. Others assert that he established it in the 7th year of his reign when he set out from Macedonia, his kingdom, bent on foreign conquest. Muhiyuddin Mughrebi on the other hand, states that it began with the reign of Seleucus (*Nicator*) who founded Antioch. This era was in use both with the Jews and Syrians. They relate that when Alexander the son of Philip marched from Greece to the conquest of Persia, he passed through Jerusalem. Summoning the learned Jews of Syria he directed them to discontinue the Mosaical era and to employ his own. They thus answered him. "Our forefathers never observed any era above a thousand years and this year our Era will complete the thousand; from next year, therefore, thy command shall be obeyed." And they acted accordingly. And this took place in Alexander's 27th year. Some maintain that this Grecian era is of Hebrew origin. Kushyar in his Jāmi' says that there is no difference between the Syro-Macedonian and the Syrian era, except in the names of the months. The Syrian year begins on the 1st day of Tishrin ul Awwal. This happened formerly when the sun was in the 4th degree of Libra, and now falls on the 11th.[38] With the Syro-Macedonians, that date is the 1st of Qanuni i Sāni, when the sun is near the 20th degree of Capricorn. Battāni mentions this era[39] as beginning with Philip, father of Alexander Bicornutus, but that he called it after his son to exalt his fame; and he has based on it the calculation of the mean places of the planets in his Canon. Of this era 1905 years have elapsed.

The Augustan Era.

He was the first of the Roman Emperors. The birth of Jesus Christ happened in his reign. The era begins with his accession. The year is the same as the Syro-Macedonian, and the months are Coptic; the last month in the common years has 35 days and in leap years 36. Of this era 1623 years have elapsed.[40]

The Christian Era.

Begins with the birth of Jesus Christ. The year consists, like the Syro-Macedonian, of 365 d. 5 h. At the end of 4 years, they add a day to the end of the second month. The beginning of their Nycthemeron is reckoned from midnight. Like the Arabians, they name the days of the week, beginning with Sunday. The commencement of their year, some take to be the entry of the sun in Capricorn : others, from the 8th degree of the same.

The Era of Antoninus of Rome.

It begins with his accession [138 A.D.]. The years are Syro-Macedonian, the months Coptic. Ptolemy deter-

[38] Another reading is 15th. Gladwin has 16th. Better known as the Seleucid era, began on 1 Oct. 312 B.C. (acc. to Ginzel.) *Ency. Islam,* Supp 231; also iv. 1211.

[39] There is a discrepancy among chronologers as to the commencement of this era. Some determine it to the 1st October 312 B.C. (W. Smith, *Cl. Dic.* art Seleuc); the *U. T.* (ii. 11) places it, 311 y. 4 m. B.C. The Syrian Greeks began their years in September, other Syrians in October : the Jews, about the autumnal equinox. It is used in the book of Maccabees and appears to have begun in Nisan. Supposing it to begin on 1st September 312 B.C.; to reduce it to our era, subtract 311 y. 4 m.

[40] The Spanish era of the Caesars is reckoned from 1st January, 38 B.C., being the year following the conquest of Spain by Augustus. It was much used in Africa, Spain, and the south of France. By a Synod held in 1180, its use was abolished in all the churches dependent on Barcelona. Pedro IV of Arragon abolished it in 1350. John of Castile in 1382. It continued to be used in Portugal till 1455.—*U. T.,* ii. 11. But *Enc. Islam,* Supp. 231, differs ; "its epoch 14 Feb. 27 B.C.".

mined the position of the fixed stars in his *Almagest* on this era of which 1,457 years have elapsed.

The Era of Diocletian[41] *of Rome.*

He was a Christian emperor. The era begins with his accession. The years are Syro-Macedonian, the months Coptic; 1,010 years have since elapsed.

The Era of the Hijra.

In pre-Islamic times, the Arabs had various eras, such as the building of the Ka'bah, and the sovereignty of Omar[42] b. Rabii'a to whom was due the rise of idolatry in Hijāz, and this continued in use till the year of the Elephant,[43] which they, in turn, observed as a fresh epoch. Every Arab tribe constituted any important event in their history, an era. In the time of the prophet this thread *of custom* had no coherence, but from the date of the Hijra, they gave each year a special name. Thus that year was called the "year of Permission," that is, the permission to go from Mecca to Medina. The second year was named the "year of Command," *i.e.,* to fight the unbelievers.[44]

---

[41] The name in the text is Diocletian. Abul Fazl evidently meant Constantine, but probably following the text of Albiruni, (*Chronol*) he copied the heading of the Era of Diocletian, without noticing in the body of the passage, the change of name to Constantine, as the 1st Christian Emperor. The number 1010 is an error. Gladwin has 1410. If Abul Fazl counts from the era of Diocletian A.D. 284, the intermediate years would be about 1310; if from A.D. 324, the date of Constantine's sole mastership of the empire 1270, if from his proclamation as Emperor by the legions in 306, the number would be 1290. His father Constantius was proclaimed Caesar by Diocletian in A.D. 292.

[42] An error (taken from Albiruni) for 'Amr-b-Lohayy, born about 167 A.D., was king of Hijaz; for his genealogy see *Ency. Isl.* i. 336, and Caus. de Perc. *Essai Sur l'hist. Arab.* Tabl. II, VIII. The great tribe of Khuzaa'h trace their descent from him. Whilst at Balkā in Syria, he had seen its inhabitants practising idolatry; their idols, they averred, protected and favoured them, granting rain at their prayers. At his request they presented him with the idol, Hobal, which he set up in Mecca and introduced its worship.

[43] 570 A.D. the year in which Mahomed was born, and the name of which commemorates the defeat of Abraha, the Ethiopian king of Yaman. *Qurān*, Sura 105.

[44] The 3rd year was called, the year of the trial.

4th	,,	,,	,,	year of Congratulation on the occasion of marriage.
5th	,,	,,	,,	year of the earthquake.
6th	,,	,,	,,	year of inquiring.
7th	,,	,,	,,	year of victory.
8th	,,	,,	,,	year of equality.
9th	,,	,,	,,	year of exception.
10th	,,	,,	,,	year of farewell.

Chronol. Albiruni, Sachau, p. 35.

At the accession of the second Caliph (Omar), Abu Musa Asha'ri,[45] governor of Yaman made the following representation: "Your despatches have arrived dated the month of Shabān. I cannot discover what date is understood by Shabān." The Caliph summoned the learned. Some of the Jews advised the use of their era. The sage Hurmuzān[46] said; "the Persians have a computation which they call Māhroz" and this he explained. But as there were intercalations in both, their skill in calculation was slight, he did not accept either but adopted the era of the Hijrah. The month according to their system is reckoned from the sight of one new moon, after the sun has completely set, till the next is visible. It is never more than 30 nor less than 29 days. It sometimes occurs that four successive months are of 30 days, and three of 29. Chronologers putting aside calculations based on the moon's appearance, reckon lunar months in two ways, *viz.*, Natural, which is the interval of the moon's departure from a determinate position, with the sun in conjunction or opposition or the like to its return thereto; 2ndly, Artificial; since the motions of the moon are inconstant and their methodisation as well as an exact discrimination of its phases difficult, its mean rate of motion is taken and thus the task is facilitated. In the recent (*Gurgāni*) tables, this is 29 days, 12 hours and 44 minutes.[47] The rule is this, that when the fraction is in excess of half, it is reckoned as one day. Thus when the excess is over a half, they take the month of Muharram as 30 days, and the second month 29, and so on alternately to the last. In common years, therefore, Dhil Hijjah is 29 days. The mean lunar year consists of 354 d. 8 h. 48 m.[48] which is less than a solar artificial year by

[45] Abu Musa Al Asha'ri was one of the Companions, a native of Kufah. He joined the prophet at Mecca and was a convert before the Flight to Medina. He was also one of the fugitives to Abyssinia and including his journey from Yaman to Mecca, shared in the unusual distinction of three flights. *Ency. Islam*, I. 481.

[46] Hurmuzan was a learned Persian, taken prisoner by Abu Musa and sent to the Caliph Omar by whom his life was spared, though the grace was obtained with some difficulty. He subsequently became a convert. *Ency. Islam*, ii. 338. Nawawi, *Tahzib-ul-Asmā*.

[47] This is a lunation or synodical month, the interval between two conjunctions of the Sun and Moon. The periodical month, as distinguished from this, is the time taken in transit by the moon from any point of the Zodiac back to the same point: it consists of 27 d. 7 h. 43 m. Hence a lunar month is sometimes taken in round numbers at 28 d. and this is the length of a lunar month according to the law of England. Lewis. *Astr. of the Anc*, p. 20.

[48] And 36 seconds. *Ibid.*

10 d. 21 h. 12 m. Mirza Ulugh Beg has based his new Canon on this era of which 1002 years have elapsed to the present time.

The Era of Yazdajird.

He was the son of Shahryār Aparwez[49] b. Hurmuz b. Noshirwān. It began with the accession of Jamshid. After him every succeeding monarch renewed his designation by his own accession and Yazdajird also re-instituted it from his assumption of sovereignty.[50] The years are like the Syro-Macedonian; but the fraction in excess was reserved till at the end of 120 years, it amounted to a whole month, and that year was reckoned at 13 months. The first intercalation was after *Farwardin,* and it was called by the name of that month. Then *Urdibihisht* was twice counted and so on. When the era was renewed under the name of Yazdajird, and his authority terminated in disaster, the continuity of intercalation was neglected. The years and months are artificial, solar. 963 years have since elapsed.[51]

Note on the Hijera era. "The question on what day the 1st Muharram of the year 1 A.H. fell is not yet decided." (Discussion of different theories; *Encyclopædia of Islam,* Suppl. 231).

"Authorities are not agreed on the exact date of the Hidjra. According to the most usual account, it took place on the 8th Rabi' I (20th Sept. 622 A.D.). But this would not be the date of the departure from Mecca but of the arrival in Medina. According to other versions, it was the 2nd or the 12th Rabi' I . . . . The 8th was preferred as it was a Monday. According to a tradition, the Prophet is said to have answered when asked why he observed Monday especially, 'on this day I was born, on this day I received my prophetic mission, and on this day I migrated'. The fixing of the Hidjra as the beginning of the Muhammadan era dates from the Caliph 'Omar. The traditions which try

---

[49] In Albiruni, Shahryār-b-Parwez. Parwez or Aparwez signifies Victorious. Era of Yazdajird, *Ency. Islam,* Supp. 232, also Prinsep's *Useful* T. ii. 12. *Ency. Islam,* iv. 178, gives Yazdigird III. (r. 632-651 A.D.) after Ardashir III. (r. 628-630), with "several ephemeral rulers" between them. J. S.

[50] A.D. 632.

[51] "In Persia, sinec the age of Zoroaster, the revolution of the sun has been known and celebrated as an annual festival, but after the fall of the Magian empire, the intercalation had been neglected: the fractions of minutes and hours were multiplied into days, and the date of the spring was removed from the sign of Aries to that of Pisces." Gibbon. *Decl. and Fall.* Vol. X. p. 367, Ed. 1797.

to trace it to the Prophet himself are devoid of all probability." (*Ency. Islam,* ii. 302).

In *Ency. Islam,* iv. 1210 (under *Zamān*), there is a full discussion of the calendar adopted by the Muslims.

"Although the era of Islam begins with the 15th (16th) of July, 622 A.D., the lunar year, peculiar to the Muslims, was not established till the year A.H. 10. When Muhammad in that year (A.D. 631) made his last pilgrimage to Mecca, ... he arranged . . . that the year should consist of 12 lunar months of 29, (28, 30) days each, and that intercalation (*nasi'*) was to be forbidden (*Quran,* ix. 36 ff.) . . . The Meccans had had a more or less perfect solar year (before this, as) the names of the months in part indicate clearly certain definite seasons of the year—a situation, in the case of a changeable lunar year, evidently out of the question. . . . The Arabs adopted the week of the Jews and Christians." (K. Vollers in Hastings's *Encyclopædia of Religion,* iii. 126-127).—*J. Sarkar.*

The Maliki Era.

It is also called Jalāli. The Persian Era was used at that period. Through the interruption of continuity in intercalation, the commencements of the years fell into confusion. At the instance of Sultān Jalāluddin[52] Malik Shāh Saljuki, Omar Khayyam and several other learned men instituted this era. The beginning of the year was determined from the sun's entry into Aries. The years and months were *at first* Natural, but now the month is the ordinary Artificial. Each month consists of 30 days and at the end of *Isfandārmuz,* they add 5 or 6 days. Of this era, 516 years have elapsed.

The Khāni Era

dates from the reign of Ghāzān[53] Khān and is founded on the Elkhāni tables. The years and months are Natural,

[52] A brilliant sketch of his life may be read in Gibbon, Ch. 57, and *Enc. Isl.* iii. 211. For his era *Ency. Islam,* i. 1006 (under *Djalāli*), also iv. 672 (under *Tarikh*) and iii. 888 (under *Nawruz.*) The era begins on 15 March 1079 A.D.

[53] Ghazan Khan, Mahmud, eldest son of Arghun, the 8th from Mangu Khan son of Jenghiz, of the Moghul Tartar or Ilkhanian Dynasty of Persia. He ascended the throne in A. H. 694 (A.D. 1294) and was succeeded by Ghiasu'ddin Au-gaptu Khuda bandah Muhammad, A. H. 703 (A. D. 1303). *U. T. P.* II, p. 146. The Ilkhani era, in *Ency. Isl.* Supp. 232. Ghāzān Kh. in *ibid.* ii. 149.

solar. Before its adoption the State records bore date from the Hijrah and the lunar year was current. By this means the road was opened to grievous oppression, because 31 lunar years are equal to only 30 solar years and great loss occurred to the agriculturists, as the revenue was taken on the lunar years and the harvest depended on the solar. Abolishing this practice Ghāzān Khān promoted the cause of justice by the introduction of this era. The names of the month are the Turkish with the addition of the word *khāni.* Of this, 293 years have elapsed.

The Ilāhi Era.

His Majesty had long desired to introduce a new computation of years and months throughout the fair regions of Hindustan in order that perplexity might give place to easiness. He was likewise averse to the era of the Hijra (*Flight*) which was of ominous signification, but because of the number of short-sighted, ignorant men who believe the currency of the era to be inseparable from religion, His Imperial Majesty in his graciousness, dearly regarding the attachment of the hearts *of his subjects* did not carry out his design of *suppressing it.* Although it is evident to right-minded people of the world, what relevancy exists between the market-coin of commercial dealing and the night gleaming jewel of faith, and what participation between this chain of objective connection and the twofold cord of spiritual truth, yet the world is full of the dust of indiscrimination, and the discerning are heedful of the fable of the fox[54] that took to flight when camels were being impressed. In 992 of the Novilunar year, the lamp of knowledge received another light from the flame of his sublime intelligence and its full blaze shone upon mankind. The fortunately gifted, lovers of truth raised their heads from the pillow of disappointment and the crooked-charactered, drowsy-willed lay in the corner of disuse. Meanwhile the imperial design was accomplished. Amir Fathullah Shirāzi,[55] the representative

[54] *Gulistan* I. Story XVI. 'What connection, Madcap', they said to him 'has a camel with thee and what resemblance hast thou to it?' 'Peace!' he answered 'for if the envious should, to serve their own ends, say"—"This is a camel," who would care about my release so as to inquire into my condition?"

The Ilāhi era was introduced by Akbar at the beginning of the 29th year of his reign, 8th Rabi-ul Awwal 992 A.H. = 10th March 1584 (*Akbarnamak,* tr. iii. 644.) Prinsep, *Useful Tables,* ii. 37.

[55] See *Ain Akb. trans.,* Vol. I, p. 33, *n.*

of ancient sages, the paragon of the house of wisdom, set himself to the fulfilment of this object, and taking as his base the recent Gurgāni Canon, began the era with the accession of his Imperial Majesty. The splendour of visible sublimity which had its manifestation in the lord of the universe commended itself to this chosen one, especially as it also concentrated the leadership of the world of spirituality, and for its cognition by vassals of auspicious mind, the characteristics of the divine essence were ascribed to it, and the glad tidings of its perpetual adoption proclaimed. The years and months are natural, solar, without intercalation and the Persian names of the months and days have been left unaltered. The days of the month are reckoned from 29 to 32, and the two days of the last are called *Roz o Shab* (Day and Night). The names of the months of each era are tabulated for facility of reference. [Tr.'s *note.* The Uighur and Coptic months are spelt differently by Albiruni from Abul Fazl. The spelling of the Jewish month names also is incorrect in the printed text of the *Ain.*]

1. Hindu months.	2. Khatāi months.	3. The Uighur Era.	4. The Era of the astrologers.	5. The Era of Adam.	6. The Era of the Jews.	7. The Era of the Deluge.	8. The Era of Nabonasar.	9. The Era of Philipus Arrhidaeus.	10. The Era of the Copts.
Chait	Chanweh	Arām Ay.	,,	,,	Tishri	,,	Thoth	Thoth	Thoth
Baisākh	Zhezheweh	Ikandi Ay.	,,	,,	Marheshwān	,,	Bāpeh	Bāpeh	Pāopi
Jeth	Sāmweh	Ochanj Ay.	,,	,,	Kislew	,,	Hātor	Hator	Athyr
Asārh	Harweh	Dardanj Ay.	,,	,,	Tebeth	,,	Kahak	Kehak	Khawāk
Sānwan	Uweh	Beshanj Ay.	,,	,,	Shebāt	,,	Tubah	Tubah	Tybi
Bhādon	Luweh	Altinj Ay.	,,	,,	Adhār	,,	Amsher	Amsher	Makhir
Kunwar	Cheweh	Yetinj Ay.	,,	,,	Nisān	,,	9	Barmahāt	Phamanoth
Kātik	Bāweh	Saksanj Ay.	,,	,,	Iyār	,,	9	Barmulah	Pharmuthi
Aghan	Kheweh	Tuksanj Ay.	,,	,,	Siwān	,,	9	Bashans	Pachon
Pus	Shabweh	Onnanj Ay.	,,	,,	Tammuz	,,	9	Bonah	Payni
Māgh	Shayayweh	Onbaranj Ay.	,,	,,	Áb	,,	9	Abib	Epiphi
Phāgun	Sirweh	Haksabāt Ay.	,,	,,	Elul	,,	9	Misri	Mesori

11. Syro-Macedonian Era.	12. The Augustan Era.	13. The Christian Era.	14. The Era of Antoninus.	15. The Era of Diocletian.	16. Era of the Hijrah.	17. Era of Yazdijird.	18. The Maliki Era.	19. The Khāni Era.	20. The Divine Era.
Tashrinul Awwal	Identical with those of Nabonasar.	January	Identical with those of Nabonasar.		Muharram	Farwadin Māh. Old Style	Farwardin Māh i Jalāli &c.	Arām Ay. Khani	Farwardin Māh i Ilāhi &c.
'ashrinu'l Ākhir		February			Safar	Ardibihisht Māh. O. S.		&c.	like 18,
ānun'l Awwal		March			Rabia' I.	Khurdād Māh. O.S.	&c.	&c. like 3 with the word "Khāni" after "Ay"	substituting "Ilāhi" for "Jalāli."
ānunu'l Ākhir		April			Rabia' II.	Tir Māh. O. S.	&c.		
hebāt		May			Jumāda I.	Amurdād Māh. O.S.	like 17, with the word "Jalāli" after "Mah."	In the 4th month the word "Tortanj" occurs, where in Col. 3, it is "Dardanj."	
zār		June			Jumāda II.	Sharewar Māh. O.S.			
isān		July			Rajab	Mihr Māh. O. S.			
yyār		August			Sha'bān	Abān Māh. O. S.			
uzurān		September			Ramadhān	Āzar Māh. O. S.			
amuz		October			Shawwāl	Day Māh. O. S.			
b		November			Dhi Ka'da	Bahman Māh. O.S.			
ylul		December			Dhi Hijjah	Isfandārmaz Māh. O. S.			

The events of the world recorded in chronological sequence, are accounted the science of history, and he who is proficient in them, is a historian. Many writings in this branch of knowledge regarding India, Khatā, the Franks, Jews and other peoples are extinct. Of the Muhammadan sect, the first who in Hijaz occupied himself with this subject was Muhammad-b-Ishāq, then follow Wahab-b-Murabbih, Wāqidi, Asma'i, Tabari, Abu A'bdullah Muslim-b-Qutaybah, Aa'tham of Kufa, Muhammad Muqanna, Hakim A'li Miskawaih, Fakhruddin Muhammad-b-Ali, Dāud Sulaiman Binākiti, Abul Faraj, 'Imadu-ddin-b-Kathir, Muqaddasi, Abu Hanifah Dinawari, Muhammad-b-Abdullah Masa'udi, Ibn Khallākān, Yāfa'i, Abu Nasr Utbi; amongst the Persians, Firdausi Tusi, Abul Hasan Baihaqi, Abul Husain author of the *Tārikh-i-Khusrawi*, Khwājah Abul Fazl Baihaqi, A'bbās-b-Musa'b, Ahmad-b-Sayyār, Abu Ishāq Bazz'az, Muhammad Balkhi, Abul Qāsim Ka'bi, Abu'l Hasan Fārsi, Sadruddin Muhammad author of the *Tājul-Maāsir,* (*Corona monumentorum*), Abu Abdullah Juzjāni (author of the *Tabaqāt-i-Nāsiri*), Kabiruddin Irāqi, Abul Qāsim Kāshi, author of *Zubdah* (*Lactis flos*), Khwājah Abul Fazl, author of the *Makhzan ul Balāghat* (*Promtuarium eloquentiœ*) and *Fadhāil-ul-Muluk* (*Virtutes principum prœstantes*) A'lauddin Juwaini, brother of the Khwājah Shamsuddin, author of a Diwān, (he wrote the *Tārikh Jahānkushā, Historia orbis terrarum victrix*), Hamdullah Mustaufi Qazwini, Qādhi Nidhām Baydhāwi, Khwājah Rashidi Tabib, Hāfiz Abru, and other trustworthy writers.

For a long time past, likewise, it has been the practice to record current events by a chronogram and to make the computation of years appear from a single word, a hemistich and the like, and this too they term a date; as for instance, for the accession of his Majesty, they have devised the words *Nasrat-i-Akbar* (*victoria insignis*) and *Kām Bakhsh* (*Optatis respondens*), but the ancients practised it little: thus the following was written on Avicenna,—

The Demonstration of Truth, Abu A'li Sina,
Entered in Shaja' (373) from non-existence into being.
In Shasā (391) he acquired complete knowledge.
In Takaz (427) he bade the world farewell.

BIOGRAPHICAL NOTES

"The whole of this series of authors is taken bodily and in the same order by Abul Fazl from the *Raudhat-us-Safā* without acknowledgement." (*H. S. Jarett.*)

For convenience of printing and also of study, Jarrett's notes on the ancient authors, a bare list of whose names is given by Abul Fazl, have been here collected in one place, instead of being dispersed as separate footnotes. For more modern and detailed information consult the *Encyclopædia of Islam* under each name." (*J. Sarkar.*)

Md.-b-Ishāq,—author of the well-known work *Al Maghāzi wa's Siyar* (expeditiones bellicæ et biographiæ); he was a native of Medina and as a traditionist held a high rank, and regarded by Al-Bukhāri and As-Shāfa'i as the first authority on the Muslim conquests. He died at Baghdad A.H. 151 (A.D. 768). It is from his work that Ibn Hishām extracted the materials for his life of the Prophet.

Wahab-b-Murabbih,—was a native of Yaman and one of the "Abnā", *i.e.,* a descendant of one of the persian soldiers settled there. He died at Sana'ā in Yaman A.H. 110, in Muharram (April-May A.D. 728)—(others say in 114 or 116) at the age of 90. He was a great transmitter of narrations and legends. A great part of the information given by Moslem historians regarding the pre-Islamic history of Persia, Greece, Yaman, Egypt, etc., comes from him. He was an audacious liar, as Moslem critics of a later period discovered. Ibn Khall. De. Sl. IV. p. 672-3.

Wāqidi,—Abu A'bdullah, Muhammad-b-Omar. Wāqid, al Wāqidi, a native of Mecca, author of the well-known *"Conquests"* of the Moslems, born A.H. 130 (Sept. A.D. 745), died on the eve of Monday 11 Zul Hijjah, A.H. 206 (27th April A.D. 823).

Asma'i,—Abu Sa'id A'bdu'l Malik-b-Kuraib al Asma'i, the celebrated philologer, a complete master of Arabic. He was a native of Basra, but removed to Baghdad in the reign of Hārun-ar-Rashid. It is said he knew by heart 16,000 pieces of verse; born A.H. 122 (A.D. 740) and died in Safar A.H. 213 (March-April A.D. 728). *Ency. Isl.* i. 490.

Tabari,—Abu Jafar M-b-Jarir at-Tabari, author of the Great Commentary of the *Qurān* and of the celebrated history. He is regarded as an exact traditionist, born A.H.

224 (A.D. 838-9) at Amol in Tabaristān and died at Baghdad A.H. 319 (A.D. 923). *Ency. Isl.* iv. 578.

Abu Abdullah Muslim,—(213-270 A.H.) A native of Dinawar, some say of Marw, author of the *Kitāb-ul-Ma'ārif* and *Adāb-ul-Kātib* (=the Writer's Guide): the first a work of general knowledge, from which Eichhorn extracted his genealogies of the Arabs published in his *Monumenta historiæ Arabum*: it contains a number of short biographical notices of the early Moslems.

Aa'tham Kufi,—Muhammad-b-A'li, known as Aa'sim Kufi; his work the *Futuḥ Aa'thim* (H.K.) is a short account of events from the death of the prophet to the death of Husain at Karbalā. It was translated into Persian by Aḥmad-b-Muṣtaufi.

Md. Muqanna',—Freytag gives his name from the Scholia as Muhammad-b-Ohmaizah. He is said to have been called Muqanna' from the veil he wore to protect the beauty of his person. He squandered his wealth in lavish gifts and in the time of the Omayyads was still living, of much account with his people, but in poverty. Not to be confounded with Abu 'Amr (afterwards Abu Md.) *Ibn al Muqaffa'* (*Ency. Islam* ii. 404), who was known as the Katib or Secretary and was the author of some celebrated epistles, and also translated *Kalila and Damna* into Arabic.

Abu Ali Ahmad-b-Miskawaih,—a Persian of good birth and distinguished attainments. He was treasurer tc Malik Adhd-ud-daulah-b-Buwaih, who placed the utmost trust in him. He was the author of several works. Abul Faraj relates (*Hist. Dynast.* p. 328) that Avicenna consulted him on a certian abstruse point; and finding him slow of intelligence and incapable of solving his difficulty, left him. His death is placed about A.H. 420.

Daud Sulaiman Binakiti,—author of the *Raudhat-ul-Albāb* (*Viridarium cordatorum*) a compendium of Persian history. He lived tempore Jinghiz Khan and wrote on the history of Khātāi kings at the request or command of Sultan Abu Said Bahādur.

Abul Faraj,—(1) 897-967 A.D., author of the great *Kitāb al Aghani.* (2) Barhebraeus, 1226-1286, author of a famous Universal History (See *Ency. Isl.* under the above two names).

Hafidh I'maduddin,—Ismail-b-A'bdu'llah ad Dimashqi died in A.H. 774 (A.D. 1372). The name of his history is

'Al Bidāyah wa'l Nihāyah (*Initium et finis*) and is continued to his own time.

Muqaddasi,—There are several of this name. Shamsuddin Abdullah was the author of a geography entitled Ahsanu'l taqasim fi Ma'rifati'l aqalim, a description of the seven climates, died A.H. 341 (A.D. 1049, *Ency. Isl.* iii. 708); a second Husāmuddin Md. b. A'bul Wāhid author of a work on judicial decisions; died A.H. 642 (A.D. 1245); a third, probably the one alluded to, Shahābuddin Abu Mahmud as Shāfa'i author of the work *Muthirul Gharam ila' Ziāratil Quds wāl Shām* (*Liber cupidinem excitans Hierosolyma et Damascum visendi*). He died in 765 (A.D. 1363). H. K.

Abu Hanifa Ahmad-b-Dāud ad Dinawari, author of a work *Islah ul Mantiq* (*Emendatio sermonis*). He died 290 (A.D. 902) H. K.

Masāudi,—author of the *Muruj-ud-Dahāb.* (*Prata Auria*) which he composed in the reign of the Caliph Mutia' Billah and many other works. It begins with the creation of the world, and is continued through the Caliphs to his own time. He died in Cairo in 346 A.H. (A.D. 957). *Ency. Isl.* iii. 403.

Ibn Khallakan,—the famous biographer: his work the Wafayātul Aa'yān containing the lives of illustrious men is well-known. It was composed in Egypt under Sultān Baybars of the Mameluke dynasty. He has given a few particulars of his life at the close of this work which was finished in A.H. 672 (A.D. 1273-4). He was born in 608 (A.D. 1211) and died in 681 (A.D. 1282, *Ency. Isl.*, ii. 396).

Abdullah-b-Asa'd al Yafa'i al Yamani, died 768 A.H. (A.D. 1266). He wrote the *Mirat ul Janān wa I'brat ul Yakdhān* (speculum cordis et exemplum vigilantis), a historical work beginning with the Flight and continued to his own time. Another is the *Raudhatul Riahin* (*Viridarium hyacinthorum*) containing lives of Moslem saints. *Ency. Isl.*, iv. 1134.

Utbi,—author of the *Tārikh Yamini* which contains the history of the Ghaznivide Sultan Yamin ud Daulah Mahmud-b-Subuktigin of whom he was a contemporary: it is brought down to the year 427 (A.D. 1036-7).

Baihaqi,—(1) Abu Hasan' Ali-b-Zayd al Baihaqi author of the *Wishāhi Dumyatil Qasr*: a supplement to the *Dumyat ul Qasr* of al Bakharzi the poet, who died A.H. 467

(A.D. 1075), and author of work called *Tārikhi Baihaq. Ency. Isl.*, i. 592.

Baihaqi,—(2) Abul Fazl Md. b. Husain, author of a history of the Ghaznavids in more than 30 vols., of which only five volumes covering the reign of Masa'ud b. Mahmud has been preserved. *Ency. Islam,* i. 592-593.

Abul Husain,—Muhammad-b-Sulaiman Al Asha'ri; the *Tārikh Khusrawi,* is a history of the Persian kings.

Abbas b. Musa'b,—author of the *Tārikh Khorāsān.*

Ahmad-b-Sayyār-b-Ayyub,—the Hāfidh; Abul Ḥasan al Marwazi, a traditionist of great repute and accuracy. Died A.H. 268, A.D. 881. *Abul Mahasin* V. II. p. 45.

Abu Ishaq-Muhammad-b-al Bazzāz was the author of a history of Herat.

Muhammad-b-Akil al Balkhi-d—A.H. 316 (A.D. 928). (Abul Mahasin II. p. 235) author of a history of Balkh. H. K.

Abu'l Qāsim Ali-b-Mahmud, author of a history of Balkh.

Abu'l Hasan,—Abdul Ghāfir-b-Ismail *Al Fārsi,* author of the *Siyāq fi daili tārikh Nishabur* (*Cursus orationis appendix ad historiam Nishaburae*). He died A.H. 527 (A.D. 1132). H. K.

Juzjāni,—The *Tabaqāt-i Nāsiri* is on the military expeditions of Nāsiruddin Mahmud Shāh-b-Iltamish of Delhi. The name of the author is Abu Omar, Othman-b-Muhammad al Minhāj, Sirāj al Juzjāni. Translated by Raverty in Biblio. Indica series.

Kabiruddin Irāqi,—son of Tajuddin Irāqi, who wrote of the conquests of Sultan Alāuddin Khilji. He was a skilled rhetorician, and writer; see a slight sketch of him in the *Tārikh Firoz Shāhi,* of Ziāuddin Barni, p. 361.

Abul Qāsim Jamāluddin Muhammad,—d. 836 (A.D. 1432), author of the *Zubdatut Tawārikh,* in Persian.

Abul Fadhl Ubaidullah—(H.K. : in *Raudhat us Safa,* 'Abdullah) -b-Abi Nasr Ahmad-b-Ali-b-al Mikāl; both the works mentioned are historical.

Alauddin Ata Malik al Juwaini,—the author of the *Jahān Kushā'* a Persian history, *Ency. Isl.,* i. 1067-1070, under *Djuwaini.*

Hamdullah Qazvini,—author of the *Tārikh Guzida* (*Prœstantissima ex historia*) which ranks among the best general histories of the East, written for the Wazir Ghiāthuddin Muhammad. It was first composed in 50,000 verses, and then turned into prose about A.H. 730 (A.D. 1329-30). *Ency. Isl.*, ii. 844.

Qadhi Nasiruddin Abdullah-b-Omar al *Baidhāwi-d*—A.H. 684 (A.D. 1285), author of the *Nidhamut Tawārikh* (*Ordo historiarum*), a compendium of Persian history with an account of Moslem dynasties from the house of Umayyah to that of Khwārazm and the Mongols (1275 A.D.). *Ency. Isl.*, i. 590.

Khj. Rashidi,—Khwājah Rashiduddin Fadhlullah, Tabib, "one of the greatest historians of Persia (put to death in 718, A.D. 1318), author of the *Jamiut Tawārikh* (*Historia universalis*). He began it just before the death of Ghāzān Khan A.H. 704 (1304 A.D.). His successor Khudabandah Muhammad ordered him to complete it and preface it with his name and to add to the history of the Jingiz dynasty, a more general account, *Ency. Isl.*, iii. 1124.

Hāfidh Abru,—Shihābuddin Abdullah b. Lutfullah b. Abdur Rashid al Khwāfi (and not *al-Haravi*), author of the *Zubdatut Tawārikh* composed for Baisonghor Mirzā, an account of the principal events and strange or extraordinary occurrences recorded in the history of the world, carried down to A.H. 829 (1425 A.D.). He died in 834 (A.D. 1430). *Ency. Isl.*, ii. 213.

Avicenna,—The full name of this philosopher is Abu Ali Husain-b-Abdullah-b-Sina, as Shaikh, ar-Rāis. He is therefore known in the East as *Ibn Sina* and *Pur-i-Sina,* from his father's name. *Ency. Isl.*, ii. 419-420 (under *Ibn Sina*). He was born in Bukhārā A.H. 370 (A.D. 980) and died in 428 (A.D. 1036) at the age of 58.

A'IN I.

The Provincial Viceroy, Sipah Sālār, literally, *Commander of the Forces.*[56]

He is the vicegerent of His Majesty. The troops and people of the provinces are under his orders and their welfare depends upon his just administration. He must seek the

[56] The Sipah-Sālār's duties are described also in a *farmān* of Akbar included in *Mirāt-i-Ahmadi* (Gaekwad's Or. Series), i. 163-170. See *Mughal Administration* by Jadunath Sarkar, 3rd ed., ch. iv. §2 for further details and references to additional sources. The distintcion between the provincial

will of God in all that he undertakes and be constant in praise and supplication. He must never lay aside the consideration of the people's prosperity nor suffer his zeal to sleep. He must not be prompt to vain converse or asperity of manner. Vigilance and the due distinction of ranks must be his care, especially towards subordinates near his person and officials at a distance. What is the duty of dependents must not be committed to his sons, and what these can perform he should not execute himself. In all transactions he should confide in one wiser than himself and if he can find none such, he should confer with a few chosen individuals and weigh carefully their deliberations.

It haps at times, the hoary sage
May fail at need in counsel right,
And unskilled hands of tender age
A chance shaft wing within the white.
[S'adi, *Gulistān,* Ch. 3.]

He should not admit many men to his secret councils, for the prudent, zealous, warm, disinterested adviser is rare, lest one of them should provoke dissension, and opportunities for timely action escape. He should regard his office of command as that of a guardian, and exercise caution, and making a knowledge of the disposition of men a rule of government, live as it behoves his office. Levity and anger he should keep under the restraint of reason. He should reclaim the rebellious by a just insight into the conduct of affairs and by good counsel, failing which, he should be swift to punish by reprimands, threats, imprisonment, stripes or amputation of limb, but he must use the utmost deliberation before severing the bond of the principle of life. He should not pollute his tongue with abuse which is the manner of noisy vagabonds of the market place. He should refrain from the use of oaths in speech for this is imputing falsehood to himself by implication and distrust in the person he addresses. In judicial investigations, he should not be

---

viceroy (*sipah sālār*) and the revenue-head (*diwān*) is as old as the first government set up by the Arabs after the conquest of Egypt: "In the early centuries of Arab rule (in Egypt) two political functions are sharply distinguished, the governorship and the treasury. The governor, *Amir,* had control over the military and police only. . . . Alongside of him was the head of the treasury the '*Amil.* . . . These two officials had to keep a strict watch on one another." (C. H. Becker in *Ency. Islam,* ii. 13.) These provincial viceroys were afterways called *nāzims* and *subah-dārs*. Akbar divided his empire into 12 provinces and appointed a uniform set of officials to each, first in his 24th regnal year (1579). See *Akbarnāmah,* tr. ii. 413. [*J. Sarkar.*]

satisfied with witnesses and oaths, but pursue them by manifold inquiries, by the study of physiognomy and the exercise of foresight, nor, laying the burden of it on others, live absolved from solicitude.

Beware lest justice to that judge belong,
Whose own ill-deed hath wrought the suppliant's wrong.

Let him not inflict the distress of expectation upon supplicants for justice. He should shut his eyes against faults and accept excuses, and adopt such a course of conduct as will not disparage his good breeding and dignity. He should not intefere with any man's creed. A wise man, in worldly affairs that are transient, seeks not his own loss, why then should he knowingly abandon the spiritual life that is eternal, for if it be true, disturbance is criminal and if otherwise it is the malady of ignorance and is deserving of kind treatment. Each division of the kingdom, he should entrust to zealous upright men and provide for the safety of the roads by the establishment of trusty guards and from time to time receive reports of them. He should select for purposes of secret intelligence honest, provident, truthful and unavaricious men, and if such needful individuals are not to be obtained, in every affair he should associate several who are unknown to each other and inspecting their several reports thus ascertain the truth. His expenditure should be less than his income, and from his treasury he should supply the needy, especially those who loose not their tongues in solicitation. He should never be negligent of the supplies and accoutrements of the troops. He should not refrain from the practice of horsemanship, and should use the bow and the matchlock and command this exercise to his men. In attaching individuals to his own person and in the increase of confidence, he should employ a cautious circumspection. Many are the evil dispositioned and licentious of nature who profess sincerity and sell themselves at a high price. He should turn his attention to the increase of agriculture and the flourishing condition of the land and earn the gratitude of the people by the faithful discharge of his obligations and account the befriending of the agriculturists as an excellent service to the Almighty. He should retain impartial collectors of revenue and from time to time obtain information regarding their actions. Let him store for himself a goodly reward in the making of reservoirs, wells, watercourses, gardens, serais and other pious foundations, and set about the repairing of what has fallen into ruin. He should not be given to retirement nor be unsettled in mind which is the manner of recluses, nor make a practice of associating with the common people nor be ever surrounded by a crowd which is the fashion of blind worshippers of outward appearances.

Court not the world nor to it wholly die;
Walk wisely : neither phœnix be nor fly.

Let him hold in honour the chosen servants of God, and entreat the assistance of spiritually-minded anchorites and of mendicants of tangled hair and naked of foot. The imploring of blessings from the sun and the solar lamp, he should not consider as its deification or a worshipping of fire.[57] Let him accustom himself to night vigils and partake of sleep and food in moderation. He should pass the dawn and the evening in meditation and pray at noon and at midnight. When he is at leisure from worldly affairs and introspection of conscience, he should study works of philosophy and act according to their precepts. If this does not satisfy his mind, he should peruse the spiritual admonitions of the Masnawi [of Jalāl-ud-din Rumi] and regardless of the letter imbibe its spirit. He should entertain his mind with the instructive stories of Kalila and Damna, and thus gaining a knowledge of the vicissitudes of life, regard the experience of the ancients as his own. Let him apply himself to the cultivation of true knowledge and put aside childish tales. Let him associate with a discreet and trusty friend and give him permission to look carefully into his daily conduct in order that he may privately represent whatever, in the balance of his discretion, appears blameworthy and if at any time his penetration should be at fault he should not be thereat displeased for men have ever been backward in uttering a displeasing truth especially in a season of anger when reason slumbers and the spirit is aflame. Courtiers, for the most part, seek pretexts of evasion and lend a false colouring to error, and if perchance one of them should be really concerned, he will hold his peace for fear, for he is indeed difficult to find who would prefer another's benefit to his own injury. Let him not be roused to anger by the representations of detractors, but rest in the path of circumspection, for men of evil nature, dissemblers in speech, palm off their tales with the semblance of truth and representing themselves as disinterested, labour to in-

[57] See Vol. I, pp. 200-202.

jure others. He should not consider himself as fixed of residence but hold himself ever ready for a summons to the presence. Let him not be malevolent, but prefer courtesy and gentleness. He should not subvert ancient families but let an illustrious ancestry redeem unworthy successors. Let him see that the younger among his followers when they meet, use the greeting *Allah u ākbar,*[58] 'God is greatest', and the elder reply *Jalla-jalāluhu,* 'His majesty is eminent'. Let him not take as food a sheep or a goat of under one year and he should abstain from flesh for a month after the anniversary of his birthday. He shall not eat of anything that he has himself killed. He should restrict himself in sensual gratification and approach not a pregnant woman: The food which is bestowed in memory of the deceased, he should prepare each year on his birthday and regale the needy.

With heavenly treasures store thy grave—provide
While yet in life—none may when he hath died.
[*Gulistan.*]

When the sun advances from one sign of the zodiac to another, let him offer up a thanksgiving and discharge cannon and musketry to arouse the slumberers in forgetfulness. At the first beams of the world-illumining sun and at midnight which is the turning point of its re-ascension, let him sound the kettle-drum and enforce vigilance.

A'IN II.

The Faujdār.

In the same way that His Majesty, for the prosperity of the empire, has appointed a Commander of the forces for

[58] *Allahu akbar.*—This formula, as the briefest expression of the absolute superiority of the One God (Allah) over the idols of the pagan Arabs, is used in Muslim life in different circumstances, in which the idea of Allah, His greatness and goodness is suggested. . . . The call to the daily prayer (*azan*) is opened with a four-fold *takbir* (=the cry *Allahu ākbar.*) The Prophet is said to have uttered very frequently the *takbir* during the Hajj. (*Ency. Islam,* iv. 627 under *takbir.*)

Akbar's order for its general use as a form of salutation among the public in the place of the customary *salām 'alaikum* (sanctified by its frequent occurrence in the *Qurān,* xvi. 34, xxxix. 73 &c.), led the ignorant populace to believe that he wished to be acknowledged as God. "This caused great commotion." (Badayuni, tr. ii. 308.) For Abul Fazl's vexation at this misrepresentation, *Akbarnāmah,* tr. iii. 397. V. Smith's *Akbar,* p. 177 ("ambiguous phrase"), 218 and *n.* [*J. Sarkar.*]

each province, so by his rectitude of judgment and wise statesmanship he apportions several pargannahs to the care of one of his trusty, just and disinterested servants,[59] appreciative of what is equitable, and faithful to his engagements; and him they style by the above name. As a subordinate and assistant he holds the first place. Should a cultivator or a collector of the crown lands or an assignee of government estates prove rebellious, he should induce him to submit by fair words, and if this fail, he shall take the written evidence of the principal officers and proceed to chastise him. He should pitch his camp in the neighbourhood of the body of rebels and at every opportunity inflict loss upon their persons and property but not risk at once a general engagement. If the affair can be concluded with the infantry he should not employ cavalry. He should not be rash in attacking a fort, but encamp beyond bowshot and the reach of its guns and musketry, and obstruct the roads of communication. He should be vigilant against night attacks and devise a place of retreat, and be constant in patrolling. When he has captured the rebel camp, he must observe equity in the division of the spoil and reserve a fifth for the royal exchequer. If a balance of revenue be due from the village, this should be first taken into account. He should constantly inspect the horses and accoutrements of the troops. If a trooper be without a horse, his comrades should be assessed to provide for him and if a horse be killed in action, it should be made good at the expense of the State. He must duly furnish a roll of the troops present and absent, to the royal court and ever bear in mind the duty of carrying out its sacred ordinances.

A'IN III.

The Mir A'dl and the Qāzi.

Although the supreme authority and the redress of grievances rests with sovereign monarchs, yet the capacity of a single person is inadequate to the superintendence of

[59] For the duties of the *faujdar* (modern district magistrate *cum* superintendent of police and commandant of local forces but *not* collector), see Sarkar's *Mughal Administration*, 3rd. ed., IV. § 4.

the entire administration. It is therefore necessary that he should appoint one of his discreet and unbiassed servants as his judiciary delegate. This person must not be content with witnesses and oaths, but hold diligent investigation of the first importance, for the inquirer is uninformed and the two litigants are cognisant of the facts. Without full inquiry, and just insight, it is difficult to acquire requisite certitude. From the excessive depravity of human nature and its covetousness, no dependence can be placed on a witness or his oath. By impartiality and knowledge of character, he should distinguish the oppressed from the oppressor and boldly and equitably take action on his conclusions. He must begin with a thorough interrogation and learn the circumstances of the case; and should keep in view what is fitting in each particular and take the question in detail, and in this manner set down separately the evidence of each witness. When he has accomplished his task with intelligence, deliberation and perspicacity, he should, for a time, turn to other business and keep his counsel from others. He should then take up the case and reinvestigate and inquire into it anew, and with discrimination and singleness of view search it to its core. If capacity and vigour are not to be found united, he should appoint two persons, one to investigate whom they call a Qāzi;[60] the other the Mir A'dl to carry out his finding.

A'IN IV.

The Kotwāl.[61]

The appropriate person for this office should be vigorous, experienced, active, deliberate, patient, astute and humane. Through his watchfulness and night patrolling the citizens should enjoy the repose of security, and the evil-disposed lie in the slough of non-existence. He should keep a register of houses, and frequented roads, and engage the citizens in a pledge of reciprocal assistance, and

---

[60] *Qazi* in Sarkar's *Mughal Administration,* Ch. II, § 7.

[61] *Kotwal* in *ibid.*, Ch. IV, § 5, *Mirat-i-Ahmadi,* i. 168. In the later Mughal Empire the inspection of markets was often entrusted to the *muhtasib* (from Aurangzib's reign).

bind them to a common participation of weal and woe. He should form a quarter by the union of a certain number of habitations, and name one of his intelligent subordinates for its superintendence and receive a daily report under his seal of those who enter or leave it, and of whatever events therein occur. And he should appoint as a spy one among the obscure residents with whom the other should have no acquaintance, and keeping their reports in writing, employ a heedful scrutiny. He should establish a separate *serāi* and cause unknown arrivals to alight therein, and by the aid of divers detectives take account of them. He should minutely observe the income and expenditure of the various classes of men and by a refined address, make his vigilance reflect honour on his administration. Of every guild of artificers, he should name one as guildmaster, and another as broker, by whose intelligence the business of purchase and sale should be conducted. From these also he should require frequent reports. He should see to the open thoroughfare of the streets and erect barriers at the entrances and secure freedom from defilement. When night is a little advanced, he should prohibit people from entering or leaving the city. He should set the idle to some handicraft. He should remove former grievances and forbid any one from forcibly entering the house of another. He shall discover thieves and the goods they have stolen or be responsible for the loss. He should so direct that no one shall demand a tax or cess (*bāj wa tamghā*) save on arms, elephants, horses, cattle, camels, sheep, goats and merchandise. In every Subah a slight impost shall be levied at an appointed place. Old coins should be given in to be melted down or consigned to the treasury as bullion. He should suffer no alteration of value in the gold and silver coin of the realm, and its diminution by wear in circulation, he shall recover to the amount of the deficiency. He should use his discretion in the reduction of prices and not allow purchases to be made outside the city. The rich shall not take beyond what is necessary for their consumption. Hs shall examine the weights and make the *ser* not more nor less than thirty *dāms*. In the *gaz* hereinafter to be mentioned, he should permit neither decrease or increase, and restrain the people from the making, the dispensing, the buying or selling of wine, but refrain from invading the privacy of domestic life. Of the property of a deceased or missing person who may have no heir, he shall take an inventory and keep it in his care. He should reserve separate ferries and wells for men and women.

He should appoint persons of respectable character to supply the public watercourses, and prohibit women from riding on horseback. He should direct that no ox or buffalo or horse, or camel be slaughtered, and forbid the restriction of personal liberty and the selling of slaves. He should not suffer a woman to be burnt against her inclination, nor a criminal deserving of death, to be impaled, nor any one to be circumcised under the age of twelve. Above this limit of age, the permission may be accorded. Religious enthusiasts, calenders, and dishonest tradesmen he should expel or deter from their course of conduct, but he should be careful in this matter not to molest a God-fearing recluse, or persecute barefooted wandering anchorites. He should allot separate quarters to butchers, hunters of animals, washers of the dead, and sweepers, and restrain men from associating with such stony-hearted gloomy-dispositioned creatures. He shall amputate the hand of any who is the pot-companion of an executioner, and the finger of such as converse with his family. He should locate the cemetery outside of, and to the west of the city. He should prohibit his adherents from wearing sombre garments in mourning and induce them to wear red. From the first till the nineteenth of the month of Farwardin, during the whole month of Abān, the days of the sun's passage from one sign of the zodiac to another, *viz.*, the first of every solar month, the sixteenth of the same, the Ilāhi festivals, the days of the eclipse of the sun and moon, and on the first day of the week, he shall prohibit men from slaughtering animals, but hold it lawful as a necessity for feeding animals used in hunting and for the sick. He shall remove the place of execution to without the city and see that the Ilāhi festivals are observed. He shall have lamps lit on the night of the Nauroz (New Year's day) and on the night of the 19th of Farwardin. On the eve of a festival, as well as on the festival itself he shall cause a kettle-drum to be sounded at each watch. In the Persian and Hindu almanacs, he shall cause the Ilāhi era to be adopted and the beginning of the month according to the Hindu nomenclature he shall place in *Shukla-pachch*.

A'IN V.

The 'Aml-guzār or Collector of the Revenue.

Should be a friend of the agriculturist. Zeal and truthfulness should be his rule of conduct. He should consider himself the representative of the lord paramount and establish himself where every one may have easy access to him without the intervention of a mediator. He should deal with the contumacious and the dishonest by admonition and if this avail not, proceed to chastisement, nor should he be in apprehension of the land falling waste. He should not cease from punishing highway robbers, murderers and evildoers, nor from heavily mulcting them, and so administer that the cry of complaint shall be stilled. He should assist the needy husbandman with advances of money and recover them gradually. And when through the exertions of the village headman the full rental is received, he should allow him half a *biswah*[62] on each *bigha,* or otherwise reward him according to the measure of his services. He should ascertain the extent of the soil in cultivation and weigh each several portion in the scales of personal observation and be acquainted with its quality. The agricultural value of land varies in different districts and certain soils are adapted to certain crops. He should deal differently, therefore, with each agriculturist and take his case into consideration. He should take into account with discrimination the engagements of former collectors and remedy the produce of ignorance or dishonesty. He should strive to bring waste lands into cultivation and take heed that what is in cultivation fall not waste. He should stimulate the increase of valuable produce and remit somewhat of the assessment with a view to its augmentation. And if the husbandman cultivate less and urge a plausible excuse, let him not accept it. Should there be no waste land in a village and a husbandman be capable of adding to his cultivation, he should allow him land in some other village.

He should be just and provident in his measurements. Let him increase the facilities of the husbandman year by year, and under the pledge of his engagements, take nothing beyond the actual area under tillage. Should some

---

[62] The 20th part of a *bigha.*

prefer to engage by measurement and others by appraisement of crops, let him forward the contracts with all despatch to the royal presence. Let him not make it a practice of taking only in cash payments but also in kind. This latter is effected in several ways. First, *kankut*: *kan* in the Hindi language signifies grain, and *kut*, estimate. The whole land is taken either by actual mensuration or by pacing it, and the standing crops estimated in the balance of inspection. The experienced in these matters say that this comes little short of the mark. If any doubt arise, the crops should be cut and estimated in three lots, the good, the middling and the inferior, and the hesitation removed. Often, too, the land taken by appraisement, gives a sufficiently accurate return. Secondly, *bātāi*, also called *bhāoli*, the crops are reaped and stacked and divided by agreement in the presence of the parties. But in this case several intelligent inspectors are required, otherwise the evil-minded and false are given to deception. Thirdly, *khet batāi*, when they divide the fields after they are sown. Fourthly, *lāng batāi*; after cutting the grain, they form it in heaps and divide it among themselves, and each takes his share home to clean it and turn it to profit. If it be not prejudicial to the husbandman, he may take the value of the corn-bearing land in cash at the market rate. If on this land they sow the best kinds of produce,[63] in the first year he should remit a fourth of the usual assessment. If at the time of collection, the better produce is found to be larger in quantity than the previous year, but less land cultivated, and the revenue be the same, let him not be provoked or removed to contention. He should always seek to satisfy the owner of the crops.. He should not entrust the appraisement to the headman of the village lest it give rise to remissness and incompetence and undue authority be conferred on highhanded oppressors, but he should deal with each husbandman, present his demand, and separately and civilly receive his dues.

He must take security from land surveyors, assessors and other officers of revenue. He should supply the officials engaged in the land measurements, for each day on which

---

[63] *Jins-i-Kāmil* such as sugar, *pān*, indigo, opium or cotton in contradistinction to *jins-i-ādna*, inferior crops, such as maize.

they are employed, with 16 *dāms* and 31 *sers,* and as a monthly ration, on the following scale :

	Flour. ser	Oil. ser	Grain. ser	Vegetables &c. dām
Superintendent of survey ...	5	½	7	4
Writer	4	½	4	4
Land surveyor and four thanadars, each ...	8	1	5	5

He shall affix a mark to the land surveyed and shall take a bond from the headman that there shall be no concealment regarding the land, and the various crops shall be duly reported. In the process of measurement if any inferior portion of land be observed, he shall at once estimate its quantity, and from day to day take a note of its quality and this voucher he shall deliver to the husbandman. But if this discovery be made after the collection of the revenue, he shall gather information from the neighbours and from unofficial documents and strike an average. In the same way as the *kārkun* (registrar of collections) sets down the transactions of the assessments, the *muqaddam*[64] (chief village revenue officer) and the *patwāri* (land-steward) shall keep their respective accounts. The Collector shall compare these documents and keep them under his seal and give a copy thereof to the clerk. When the assessment of the village is completed, he shall enter it in the abstract of the village accounts, and after verifying it anew, cause its authentication by the *kārkun* and *patwāri,* and this document he shall forward weekly to the royal presence and never delay it beyond fifteen days. After the despatch of the draft estimates to the imperial court, should any disaster to the crops occur, on ascertaining the exact particulars on the spot, he shall calculate the extent of the loss and recording it in writing, transmit it without delay in order that it may be approved or a commissioner despatched. He should collect the revenue in an amicable manner and extend not the hand of demand out of season. He should begin the collection of the spring harvest from the *Holi,* which is a Hindu festival occurring when the sun is about to pass from Aquarius and is entering or has reached midway in Pisces and the Autumn harvest from the *Dasharah,* which is a festival falling when the sun is in the middle or

---

[64] For *muqaddam,* Wilson, 351.

last days of Virgo or the first ten of Libra. Let him see that the treasurer does not demand any special[65] kind of coin, but take what is of standard weight and proof and receive the equivalent of the deficiency at the value of current coin and record the difference in the voucher. He should stipulate that the husbandman bring his rents himself at definite periods so that the malpractices of low intermediaries may be avoided. When there is a full harvest, he should collect the appropriate revenue and accept no adjournment of payments on future crops.

Whosoever does not cultivate land liable to taxation but encloses it for pasturage, the Collector shall take for each buffalo six *dāms,* and for an ox, three *dāms* yearly, but for a calf or a buffalo which has not yet calved, he shall make no demand. He shall assign four oxen, two cows and one buffalo to each plough and shall lay no impost on these. Whatever is paid into the treasury, he shall himself examine and count and compare it with the day-ledger of the *kārkun.* This he shall verify by signature of the treasurer and placing it in bags under seal, shall deposit it in a strong room and fasten the door thereof with several locks of different construction. He shall keep the key of one himself and leave the others with the treasurer. At the end of the month, he shall take from the writer (*bitikchi*) the account of the daily receipts and expenditure and forward it to the presence. When two lakhs of *dāms* are collected, he shall remit them by the hands of trusty agents. He shall carefully instruct the *pātwari* of each village to enter in detail in the memorandum which he gives to the husbandman, the amount he receives from the same; any balances he shall enter under each name in a book and forward it attested by the signatures of the headmen; and these, at the next harvest, he shall recover without distress. He shall carefully inspect the *suyurghal*[66] tenures, sending copies of them to the registry office to be compared. He should ascertain the correctness of the *chaknāmah,*[67] and resume the share of a deceased grantee or one who is an

---

[65] *Zar-i-khās* in the text should be translated as His present Majesty's coin. Jarrett took it to mean 'any special kind of coin', but this interpretation is wrong. It is not necesary to read *Khālis* for *Khās* (from a variant) as suggested by Jarrett (="fine gold"). *J. S.*

[66] An assignment of land revenue for charitable purposes: also a grant of land without stipulation of any condition or service. Wilson, 495.

[67] This is a grant of alienated lands specifying the boundary limits thereof. *Chak,* according to Elliot, is a patch of rent-free land detached from a village. Wilson, 97.

absentee or actually in service of the state. He should take care that land cultivated by the farmer himself and not by the tenant, as well as resumed lands, should not be suffered to fall waste; the property of the absentee or of him that dies without an heir he should duly keep under ward and report the circumstances. He should see that no capitation-tax be imposed nor interfere with the remission of dues granted by former governments.

He shall not make the occasions of journeying, feasting or mourning an opportunity for exactions, and refrain from accepting presents. Whenever a *muqaddam* or *patwāri* shall bring money or, advancing to the dais, shall present a *dām* in obeisance, he shall not accept it. In the same way he shall renounce *balkati,* which is the practice of taking a small fee from each village when the harvest is ready for reaping. He shall also waive all perquisites on handicrafts, market-booths, police, travelling passports, garden produce, temporary sheds, enclosure, fishing rights, port-dues, butter, oil of sesame, blanketing, leather, wool, and the like malpractices of the avaricious who fear not God. He shall provide for the periodic appointment of one among those best acquainted with the district, to reside at the royal court and furnish it with the minutest particulars. Every month he shall submit a statement of the condition of the people, of the *jāgirdārs,* the neighbouring residents, the submission of the rebellious, the market prices, the current rents of tenements, the state of the destitute poor, of artificers and all other contingencies. Should there be no *kotwāl,* the Collector must take the duties of that office upon himself.

A'IN VI.

The Bitikchi[68]

Must be conscientious, a good writer, and a skilful accountant. He is indispensable to the collector. It is his duty to take from the *kanungo*[69] the average decennial state

[68] A word of Turkish origin, signifying a writer or scribe. *Enc. Isl.* i. 734.

[69] An officer in each district acquainted with its customs and land-tenures and whose appointment is usually hereditary. He receives report from the *patwāris* of new cases of alluvion and diluvion, sales, leases, gifts of land &c. which entail a change in the register of mutations. He is a revenue officer and subordinate to the tahsildār. Carnegy, *Kachh. Technical.* Wilson, 260.

of the village revenues in money and kind, and having made himself acquainted with the customs and regulations of the district, satisfy the Collector in this regard, and lend his utmost assistance and attention. He shall record all engagements made with the agriculturists, define the village boundaries, and estimate the amount of arable and waste land. He shall note the names of the *munsif*,[70] the superintendent (*zābit*), the land-surveyor and *thānadār*, also that of the cultivator and headman, and record below, the kind of produce cultivated. He should also set down the village, the pergunnah and the harvest, and subtracting the deficiency take the value of the assets, or after the manner of the people of the country, inscribe the name, the kind of produce, and the deficiency below the date of cultivation.

When the survey of the village is complete, he shall determine the assessment of each cultivator and specify the revenue of the whole village. The Collector shall take the revenue on this basis, and forward a copy of the survey, called in Hindi *khasra* to the royal court. When drawing out the rolls, if the former documents are not available, he should take down in writing from the *patwāri* the cultivation of each husbandman by name and thus effect his purpose, and transmit the roll together with the balances and collections punctually, and he shall enter the name of the *tahsildar* below each village, in the day-ledger. He shall record the name of each husbandman who brings his rent and grant him a receipt signed by the treasurer. Copies of the rolls of the *patwāri* and *muqaddam* by means of which they have made the collections, together with the *sarkhat*, that is the memorandum given to the husbandman, he shall receive from the *patwāri*, and inspecting them, shall carefully scrutinize them. If any falsification appears, he shall fine them and report to the Collector daily and the collection and balances of each village and facilitate the performance of his duty. Whenever any cultivator desires a reference to his account, he shall settle it without delay and at the close of each harvest he shall record the collections and balances of each village and compare them with the *patwāri's*, and enter each day in the ledger the receipts and disbursements under each name and heading, and authenticate it

---

[70] *Munsif*—An officer employed to superintend the measurement of the lands of a village in concert with the villagers. [Wilson, 356]. For the position of the *munsif* in Sher Shah's revenue system, see 'Abbās Sarwāni, near the end. [*J. S.*]

by the signature of the Collector and treasurer. At the end of the month, he shall enclose it in a bag under the seal of the Collector and forward it to the presence. He shall also despatch daily the price-current of mohurs and rupees and other articles under the seals of the principal men, and at the end of each harvest, he shall take the receipts and disbursements of the treasurer, and forward it authenticated by his signature. The abstract and settlement of the assessment, at the close of each year, he shall transmit under the signature of the Collector. He shall enter the effects and cattle plundered in any village, in the day-ledger, and report the circumstances. At the year's end, when the time of the revenue-collections has closed, he shall record the balances due from the village and deliver the record to the Collector and forward a copy to the royal court. When removed from office, he shall make over to the Collector for the time being his account under the heads of balances, advances &c., and after satisfying him in this regard, take the detail thereof and repair to the Court.

ĀIN VII.

The Treasurer (*Khazānadār*)

Called in the language of the day *Fotadār*.[71] The treasury should be located near the residence of the governor and the situation should be such where it is not liable to injury. He should receive from the cultivator any kind of mohurs, rupees or copper that he may bring,- and not demand any particular coin. He shall require no rebate on the august coinage of the realm but take merely the equivalent of the deficiency in coin-weight. Coinage of former reigns he shall accept as bullion. He shall keep the treasure in a strong room with the knowledge of the *shiqdār*[72] and the registrar, and count it every evening and

---

[71] The term *fota* is applied in Arabic, to cloths used as waist wrappers brought from Sind, and the word itself is supposed to be derived from that country and not to be of Arabic origin. The office was no doubt originally named from this distinguishing portion of apparel; whence the common name *Poddār* applied to a banker, cash-keeper, or an officer in public establishments for weighing money or bullion. See Wilson's *Gloss.*, 160 and 422.

[72] *Shiqdār*, an officer appointed to collect the revenue from a certain division of land under the Moghul government; it was sometimes applied to the chief financial officer of a province or to the viceroy in his financial capacity.—Wilson's *Glossary*, 480. For this officer in Sher Shah's system, see 'Abbās Sarwāni, near the end.

cause a memorandum thereof to be signed by the Collector and compare the day-ledger with the registrar's account and authenticate it by his signature. On the door of the treasury as sealed by the Collector, he should place a lock of his own, and open it only with the cognisance of the Collector and registrar. He shall not receive any monies from the cultivator save with the knowledge of the Collector and registrar, and he shall grant a receipt for the same. He shall cause the *patwāri's* signature to be affixed to the ledger known in Hindustan as *bahi*, so that discrepancy may be avoided. He shall consent to no disbursements without the voucher of the *diwān*,[73] and shall enter into no usurious transactions. If any expenditure should be necessary that admits of no delay, he may act under the authority of the registrar and *shiqdār* and represent the case to government. The aforementioned duties, from those of the commander of the troops up to this point, are primarily under the direct cognisance of the sovereign authority and as no one individual can perform them, a deputy is appointed for each function and thus the necessary links in administration are strengthened.

Currency of the means of Subsistence.

Since the benefit and vigour of human action are referrible to bodily sustenance, so in proportion to its purity is the spirit strengthened; the body, were it otherwise, would grow corpulent and the spirit weak : the thoughts too under such a regimen, incline to refinement and actions to virtue. The seekers of felicity, sober in conduct, are before all things particularly careful in the matter of food and do not pollute their hands with every meat. To the simple in heart who fear God, labour is difficult and their means of living straitened. They have not that luminous insight which penetrating to the essence of things, dwells in repose, but through fear of the displeasure of God, are sunk in exhaustion of soul from the pangs of hunger. As for instance in the case of the man who possessed a few cows, his legitimate property, and subsisted on their milk. By the accident of fortune, it chanced that they were

[73] *Diwān*. This term was especially applied to the head financial minister whether of the state or of a province, being charged in the latter with the collection of the revenue, its remittance to the imperial treasury and invested with extensive judicial powers in all civil and financial causes. Wilson's *Glossary*, 144-145. For a full description, see Sarkar's *Mughal Administration*, Ch. 3, § 1-5.

carried off, and he passed some days fasting. An active fellow after diligent pursuit brought them back, but he would not accept them and replied, "I know not whence those dumb animals have had food during these past few days." In a short space this simple soul died. Many tales are told of such dull-witted creatures who have thus passed away. There are also avaricious worldlings who do not recognize the difference between other people's property and their own, and gratify themselves at the expense of their spiritual and temporal good. The ignorant and distraught in mind, making their own necessities an occasion of spoliation and seizure, prepare for themselves eternal punishment.

Simple, innocent-minded folk consider that there are no unappropriated waste lands and were they obtainable, it would be difficult to furnish the implements of cultivation, and if these could be had, the means of providing food which would enable them to labour, are not manifest. They can discover no mine to excavate, and if one were pointed out to them which had no owner, it would be extremely onerous to obtain a living therefrom. They are averse too, from the profession of arms, lest dear life be the exchange for base lucre. They withdraw themselves also from commerce for this reason that many ask a high price for their goods, conceal their deficiencies and praise them for qualities which are not in them, while they close their eyes to the evident excellencies of what they purchase and disparage it for faults it does not possess, preferring their own benefit to another's loss. And they disapprove also of those who are content to hold lawful the sequestration of the goods of rival sectaries, and they affirm that if the fautor of such pretension be discerning and wise, it will seem an occasion for additional anxiety rather than a sanction to retain the property of another; for how can the illicit seizure of what is another's be commendable on the score of a difference of faith? On the contrary, it is a suggestion of the evil one, a phantasy of the dreams of the avaricious and unfit for the ears of the good. At the present time His Majesty has placed a lamp upon the highway before all men, that they may distinguish the road from the pitfalls, and sink not into the slough of perdition, nor pass their dear lives in unprofitableness.

Since there is infinite diversity in the natures of men and distractions, internal and external, daily increase, and heavy-footed greed travels post haste, and light-headed rage breaks its rein, where friendship in this demon-haunted waste of dishonour is rare, and justice lost to view, there is, in sooth, no remedy for such a world of confusion but in autocracy, and this panacea in administration is attainable only in the majesty of just monarchs. If a house or a quarter cannot be administered without the sanctions of hope and fear of a sagacious ruler, how can the tumult of this world-nest of hornets be silenced save by the authority of a vicegerent of Almighty power? How, in such a case can the property, lives, honour, and religion of the people be protected, notwithstanding that some recluses have imagined that this can be supernaturally accomplished, but a well-ordered administration has never been effected without the aid of sovereign monarchs. That fiery wilderness of talismanic power, too, is haunted by spells and sorcerers, and storms of confusion from this sea of undiscernment have arisen and arise, and many souls, through simplicity and shortsightedness, in the turbulent billows of inexperience have been and are still ever engulfed, while those who by the light of wisdom and through the grace of acceptance have bridled their desires and garnered provisions for the long journey to come, have, in the cross-roads of distraction, become the reproach of high and low, for their folly, irreligion and unbelief. In that assembly of ignorance should a philosopher of experience enter, he must needs take up the fashion of fools and so escape from the contumely of the base.

It is evident that in all cultivated areas, the possessors of property are numerous, and they hold their lands by ancestral descent, but through malevolence and despite, their titles become obscured by the dust of uncertainty and the hand of firmness is no longer stretched above them. If the cultivator hold in awe the power of the Adorner of the universe and the Elixir of the living, and the merchant turn back from evil designing and reflect in his heart on the favour of the lord of the world, the depository of divine grace, his possessions would assuredly be approved of wisdom. Thus the virtue of property lies in the pledge of intention, and a just ruler, like a saltbed, makes clean the unclean, and the evil good. But without honest coadjustors, abundant accessories of state and a full treasury even he could effect nothing and the condition of subserviency and obedience would lack the bloom of discipline. Now the man of robust frame should, in the first place, choose the profession of arms and reflect on the assistance which he is capable of rendering, so as to regard his life as devoted to the task of preserving human society from dissolution. The means of sustenance are likewise as abundant to the labourer as forage for his cattle. But if a man is unequal to this, he should endeavour, in some way, to enter into the number of state servants. Thus the currency of the means of subsistence rests on a twofold basis, *viz.*, the justice of sovereign monarchs and regard to the welfare of well-disposed dependents. The base materialist understands not the language of reason and never transcends the limits of bodily sense. This unfertile soil needs the water of the sword, not the limpid spring of demonstration. In the presence of the majesty of the prince, the proud and perverse of disposition sink into obscurity while the prosperity of the good who seek after justice is ever continuous.

Of a truth, whatever be the recompense of the guardianship over the four[74] priceless elements of the constitution, it is both meet and expedient and according to the Almighty will. To the watchmen over the house, the lord thereof appoints the guerdon, and to the watchmen of the universe, its shepherds. If the whole of a man's possessions were spent for the protection of his honour, it would be but fitting if in gratitude he further pledged his whole credit, how much the more when it is a question of the guardianship of the four great elements of State polity? But just monarchs exact not more than is necessary to effect their purpose and stain not their hands with avarice; and hence it is that this principle varies, as has been stated, according to diversities of age and country. From this suggestive digression, it will be evident that whatever circumspect rulers exact from their subjects after due deliberation and to subserve the interests of justice and grant to their submissive dependents, has a perfect propriety and is universally in vogue. It is also clear that the maintenance of the soldier should be ampler and more choice. Next follow the cultivators and then other artisans.

---

[74] In Vol. I. Abul Fazl's preface, they are named as (1) the warriors, (2) the artificers and merchants, (3) the learned, and (4) the husbandmen and labourers,—who are respectively likened to the four elements, fire, air, water and earth. [J. S.]

Ancient Greek[75] treatises affirm that professions are circumscribed to three classes, the Noble, the Base, and the Intermediate. The former refers to the mind and is, also, of not more than three kinds: the first concerns the pure intellect, as sagacity and capability of administration; the second, acquired knowledge, as composition or eloquence. the third personal courage, as military duty. The Base also is of three kinds: the first is opposed to the common weal of mankind, such as the hoarding of grain; the second is the contrary of any one virtue, as buffoonery; the third is such as the disposition is naturally averse from, as the trade of a barber, a tanner or a sweeper. The Intermediate comprises various callings and trades; some that are of necessity, such as agriculture; others which could be dispensed with, as dyeing; others again simple, as carpentry and ironmongery; and some compound, as the manufacturing of scales or knives.

From this exposition the distinguished character of the military profession is evident. In short, the noblest source of maintenance is to be found in a profession which is associated with just dealing, self-restraint and bravery and apart from evil doing and sensuality. The good regard three things as necessary in a profession—avoidance of tyranny, refraining from what is dishonourable, abstinence from all that is mean; by what is dishonourable, is meant buffoonery and the like low pursuits; by what is mean, is understood an inclination to base callings.

When an appropriate means of maintenance is secured, it is a requisite condition of economy to husband a portion of one's means, provided that the household is not thereby straitened. The mendicant should not be turned away disappointed nor subjected to the reproof of covetousness and greed. The proper control of an estate is conditional on the expenditure being less than the income; it is permitted to indulge a little in commercial speculation and engage in remunerative undertakings, reserving a part in coin and valuables, a part in goods and wares, and somewhat invested in the speculations of others, and yet a por-

---

[75] The reference is, no doubt, to Aristotle's *Politics* z. (△) the true sense of which has been lost by filtration through some Arabic version or paraphrase. [H. S. J.]

The reader will find most of these ideas in a rather different form in Aristotle's *Politics*, Walford's translation in Bohn's Classical Library (1898), Bk. IV. Ch. IV (pp. 130 *sqq.*) Bk. III. Ch. V (p. 91) [J. S.]

tion in lands and immoveable estates, and a share may be entrusted to borrowers of credit, and expenditure regulated with circumspection, justice and modesty. Let such a one be frank in his commercial dealings and give no place in his heart to self-reproach. He should keep in view of his purpose, the will of God, not the hope of gratitude, the increase of reputation or the expectation of reward. He should also give freely to the needy whose destitution is unexposed. There is also a twofold manner of munificence which if exercised in just measure, is meritorious. Firstly, what is given in pure generosity or largesse such as a present and the like. This should be done quickly and secretly and without setting store on its amplitude or abundance, nor yet so as to cripple one's resources or exhaust them.

Secondly what is called for by occasional exigencies, either in procuring comforts or removing grievances, such as what is given to oppressors or to the profligate in order that person, property and honour may escape their injury. But in this he should use moderation. In procuring the conveniences of life, however, it is better that the bounty should be liberal.

People of the world in the matter of living are to be resolved into three classes. One class are fallen into such heedlessness that spiritual needs do not enter their comprehension, much less are practically considered. Another through their luminous fortune are so immersed in the consideration of essential truths that they give no thought to their means of sustenance. But those who seek the felicity to come, the circumspect in conduct, neglect not a just appreciation of life but make external conditions the instrument of interior well being in the hope of admission among those absorbed in divine love, and so attaining to the third degree of felicity, whence after traversing the arid waste of deliverance, they may repose in the second.[76]

The dues of sovereignty have thus been set forth. The circulation of the means of sustenance, thus, is seen to rest on the justice of prudent monarchs and the integrity of conscientious dependents. And because the conditions of

---

[76] That is, according to the theology of the mystics, the third stage in the progressive spiritual life is the attraction of the soul to God *Allah;* the second is immersion in the Divine love *fi-Allah;* the supreme stage is the unitive *Ma' Allah* reserved for his chosen saints.

the royal state and prerogative vary in different countries, and soils are diverse in character, some producing abundantly with little labour, and others the reverse, and as inequalities exist also, through the remoteness or vicinity of water and cultivated tracts, the administration of each state must take these circumstances into consideration and fix its demands accordingly. Throughout the whole extent of Hindustan where at all times so many enlightened monarchs have reigned, one-sixth of the produce was exacted; in the Turkish empire, Irān and Turān a fifth, a sixth, and a tenth respectively. In ancient times a capitation tax was imposed called, *khirāj*. Kubād disapproved of this practice, and resolved that the revenue should be fixed upon arable land accurately surveyed. But his death occurred before he could accomplish his design. Noshirwān (his son) carried it to completion and made the *jarib* of ten square reeds.[77] This was sixty royal yards square. One fourth of this was taken as a *qafiz*[78] and valued at three dirhams,[79] and the third part was fixed as the contribution due to the state. *Qafiz* is a measure, called also *sāa'* weighing eight *ratl*,[80] and, some say, more. The dirham is equal in weight to one *misqāl*. When the Caliphate fell to Omar, at the suggestion of the learned, he adopted the plan of Noshirwān but through the vicissitudes of temporal conditions, he introduced some alterations which may be gathered from ancient volumes. In Turān and Irān from ages past, they have exacted a tenth, but the exactions have increased to more than a half which does not appear exorbitant to a despotic government. In Egypt they take for a

Faddān of the best soil,	3	*Ibrahimis*
,, ,, ,, middling,	2	,,
,, ,, ,, worst,	1	,,

[77] In the original, the word *qabzah* is written erroneously for *qasbah* which is corrected in the subsequent page with the following note. "According to the glossaries, 6 barleycorns make an *asba'*, (finger breadth) : 4 *asba'*, a *qabzah* : 8 *qabzah*, a *zarāa'* (cubit) : 10 cubits, a *qasbah* : 10 *qasbah*, an *ashl* : a *jarib* is 1 square *ashl*, *i.e.*, 10 square *qasbah* or 100 square cubits. According to the *qudāmah*, 4 *asba'* is equal to a *qabzah*, and 10 *qabzah* a cubit, and 60 cubits an *ashl*. According to this, a *jarib* would be 60 square cubits."

[78] *Qafiz.*—A space of ground containing from about 124 to 144 cubits square. It is also a dry measure. *Enc. Isl.* ii. 622.

[79] *Dirham* in *Ency. of Islam*, i. 978; and *Ain-i-Akbari*, Vol. I. Ain II.

[80] *Ratl* is variously rated at 12 to 16 oz. At Bombay it is said to be equal to 36 Surat rupees. In the Red Sea littoral the Rottolo, as it is corruptly called, varies from 10 to 24 oz. avoirdupois. Wilson's *Gloss.*, 441.

The *faddān*[80a] is a measure of land of 100 square reeds, each of which is equal to one *bāa'*. An *Ibrahimi* is current for 40 *kabirs* and 14 *kabirs* is equal to a rupee of Akbar Shāh. In some parts of the Turkish empire, they exact from the husbandman 30 *Ākchehs* for every yoke of oxen. The *Ākcheh* is a silver coin equal to 81 *Ibrahimis*. And from crown lands the demand is 42 *Ākcheh*, and from each soldier 21, besides which the governor of the Subah takes 15 more. In some parts for each plough 20, and from each soldier 7 *Ākcheh*, while the Governor takes six. In others, the *Sanjaqbegi*[81] receives 27 and the *Subashi* (kotwāl) twelve. Other systems are also given which obtain in that empire.

Note on Islamic land-tax.

The very obscure and complicated subject of the land system of early Islam can be best studied in the *Encylopædia of Islam* by piecing together information scattered under the following words :—*Kharadj* (ii. 902), *Muqasama* (Suppl. 154), *'Ushr* (iv. 1050-1052), *Dār-al-Sulh* (i. 919), and *Fai'* (ii. 38). Abu Yusuf Ibn Yaqub's *Kitāb-ul-Khirāj* (Fr. tr. by. E. Fagan) is not very helpful. The application of the system to India in Aurangzib's reign is discussed in detail in Jadunath Sarkar's *Mughal Administration*, 3rd ed., ch. XI.

The term *sulhiy*, for the meaning of which Abul Fazl refers us to "ancient documents," will be understood from the following passages of the *Ency. Islam* (i. 919, under *Dār ul Sulh*) : "With the Christian population of Najran Muhammad himself entered on treaty relationships, guaranteeing their safety and laying on them a certain tribute. See on the whole story, Baladhuri, *Futuh-al-Buldān*. The constitutional situation on the matter is thus

---

[80a] *Faddān*, a certain measure of land, subdivided into 24 *qirāt*—loosely reckoned as the quantity which a yoke of oxen will plough in one day and commonly defined as consisting of 333¼ *qasabehs*, the latter being 24 *qabdah*, and the *qabḍah* being the measure of a man's fist with the thumb erect, or about 6¼ inches. Lane's *Arab. Lex. Ency. Islam*, ii. 36.

[81] *Sanjaq* is a word in Turkish, signifying a flag or standard : it also means a minor province of which several form one Eyālat or Government. It is in this latter sense that the word should probably be taken, signifying the provincial governor. An *Akcheh* is ⅓ of a *pāra* and consequently the 1/120 of a piastre or the 1/36 of a penny; it is frequently mentioned under the name of *asper*, a corruption of the Greek equivalent for the proper Turkish word. [*Ency. Islam*, iv. 148. *Aqcha*, in *ibid.*, i. 229].

formally laid down by Mawardi : All territories . . . under Muslim control . . . fall into three divisions : (*i*) those taken by force of arms; (*ii*) those taken without fighting after the flight of their previous owners; (*iii*) those taken by treaty (*Sulh*). . . In the last (class) if the title to the soil remains with the original owners, . . . the terms of the treaty are that the owners retain their lands and pay a *Kharāj* from their produce; that this *kharāj* is regarded as a *jizya* which falls away when they embrace Islam; that their lands are absolutely their own to sell or pledge; and that their country is neither *Dār-ul-Islām* nor *Dār-ul-Harb* but *Dār-ul-Sulh*. When these lands pass to a Muslim, *Kharāj* can no longer be collected . . . Mawardi includes among the *Bilād al Islām* this *Dār-ul-Sulh*." Also, *ibid.*, ii. 38 under *Fai'* :—"Verses lix. 6, 3 and 10 of the *Qurān* were revealed when Muhammad had resolved not to divide the fields and orchards left by the Ban u'l Nādir, who had been driven out of the country, as booty of war among those who had taken part in the siege, but to give them to the Muhājirs exclusively. He justified this action by arguing that these were really obtained not by fighting, but in a peaceful fashion, by surrender."

"At a later period 'Umar I thought that this principle should be applied to the newly conquered territories also. He ordered that only movable property captured should be divided among the Arab conquerors, but not the land. . . . As a rule only the native population was to till the ground and pay . . . tribute to the Muslim treasury. This payment (*kharāj*) was to be bound up with the possession of land for all time . . . The only exception was those districts, whose inhabitants had voluntarily surrendered on the approach of the Arab army on condition that they were allowed to retain possession of their lands. In such districts (the so called *Dār-al-Sulh*) the land did not belong to the *fāi*." [*J. Sarkar.*]

The Muhammadans account conquered lands of 3 kinds : *U'shri, Khirāji* and *Sulhiy*. The first two are subdivided into five kinds and the last into two. *U'shri,* 1st kind; the district of Tehāmah which comprises Mecca, Tāif, Yemen, O'mān, Bahrayn.[82] 2nd kind; land of which

[82] The text has a word following "Bahrayn" which may possibly be read as a proper name. Either Rabah or Rayah, but Abu'l Fazl quotes evidently from the Fatāwa of Qāzi Khan (A.H. 592, Hāj. Khal.) where the definition

the owner has voluntarily embraced that faith. 3rd, Lands which have been conquered and apportioned. 4th, Land on which an adherent of that faith has built a mosque or planted a vine or laid out a garden or fertilized it with rain water; otherwise other conditions apply. 4th, Waste land which has been brought into cultivation by permission of the owner. *Khirāji* 1st kind; Persia proper and Kirmān. 2nd, Land which a tributary subject has laid out as grounds round about his house. 3rd, Land which a Muslim has reclaimed and irrigates from a source constructed from the public revenues. 4th, Land which has been acquired by convention. 5th, Land cultivated by means of water that pays revenue. *Sulhiy,* Lands of the Bani Najrān and Bani Taghlib;[83] the details of these may be learnt from ancient documents. Likewise, in some treatises, land is regarded under three heads. 1st, Land cultivated by Muslims which they deem *U'shr.*[84] 2nd, Land of which the proprietors have accepted that faith. According to some, this is *U'shri,* and others say that it is *U'shri* or *Khirāji,* according to the determination of the Imām. 3rd, Land acquired by conquest, which some make *U'shri* and others *khirāji,* and others again affirm that its classification rests with the Imām. 4th, Land which those outside the faith retain on convention. This they call *khirāji.* Tribute paid by *khirāji* lands is of two kinds. 1. *Muqāsamah* (divided), is the 5th or 6th produce of the soil. 2. *Wazifah*[85] which is settled according to the capability and convenience of the tributaries. Some call the whole produce of the revenue *khirāj,* and as the share of the producing body is in excess of their expenditure, the *Zakāt*[86] is taken from the amount under certain stipulations and this they call a tithe, but on

---

of the limits of *U'shri* are laid down exactly as in the text with the omission of Rabah. The Fatāwa i A'lamgiri follows Qāzi Khān. From the variants of this doubtful reading given in the notes, it is clear that there is some corruption and perhaps the variant of M.S. *Dal* is correct.

[83] The text has Tha'lab, a misprint. The details of the submission of these two tribes may be gathered from Caussin De Perc. *Essai sur l'histoire des Arabes. Ency. Islam,* iii. 825 (under *Nadjirān*), *Sup.* 254 (under *Uqail*), Sup. 223 (under *Taghlib*).

[84] This word signifies a tenth and is the tithe assessed on lands under Muslim rule. *U'shri* are therefore those lands subject to the tithe.

[85] *Wazifah* signifies a stipend or any thing stipulated or agreed upon; hence, revenue collected at a stipulated or fixed rate for a certain quantity of land. Wilson's *Gloss.,* 557.

[86] *Zakat,* the poor rate, the portion therefrom given as the due of God by the possessor that he may *purify* it thereby, the root of the word, *zakā,* denoting purity. The proportion varies, but is generally a fortieth or 2½ p.c. provided that the property is of a certain amount and has been in possession eleven months. See *Ency. Isl.* iv. 1202-1204.

each of these points there is much difference of opinion. The Caliph Omar, during his time, taxed those who were not of his faith at the rate of 48 dirhams for persons of condition, 24 for those of the middle class, and 12 for the lowest class. This was called the *Jaziyah* (capitation tax).

In every kingdom government taxes the property of the subject over and above the land revenue and this they call *Tamghah.*[87] In Irān and Turān they collect the land tax from some, from others the *Jihāt* and from others again the *Sāir Jihāt,* while other cesses under the name of *Wajuhāt* and *Farua'āt* are exacted. In short, what is imposed on cultivated lands by way of quit-rent is termed *Māl.* Imports on manufactures of respectable kinds are called *Jihāt,* and the remainder *Sair*[88] *Jihāt.* Extra collections over and above the land tax if taken by revenue officers are *Wajuhāt;* otherwise they are termed *Furua'āt.*

In every country such demands are troublesome and vexatious to the people. His Majesty in his wise statesmanship and benevolence of rule carefully examined the subject and abolished all arbitrary taxation, disapproving that these oppressions should become established by custom. He first defined the *gaz,* the *tanāb,* and the *bighah* and laid down their bases of measurement: after which he classed the lands according to their relative values in production and fixed the revenue accordingly.

---

[87] The Turkish word *tamghā* means a royal seal or stamp: sometimes written *altamgha* from the Turkish *āl.* red. The word also signifies a royal grant under the seal of some of the former native princes and recognised by the British Government as conferring a title to rent-free land in perpetuity, hereditary and transferable. Although, perhaps, originally bearing a red or purple stamp, the colour of the imperial seal or signature became in Indian practice indifferent. Wilson's *Gloss.*, 19. *Ency. Isl.* ii. 171.

[88] In its original purport, the word signifies moving, walking, or the remainder: from the latter it came to denote the *remaining* or all other sources of revenue in addition to the land tax from a variety of imposts, as customs, transit dues, houses, fees, market tax &c., in which sense it is current throughout India: the several imposts under this name were abolished by the British Government, except customs, duties on spirituous liquors and other minor items. The privilege of imposing local taxes under the name of *Sāir,* was also taken away from private individuals, but it still applies to various items of the income from landed property not comprised in the produce of cultivation, as rent from fisheries, timber, fruit-trees, bees'-wax &c.; it also designates certain admitted manorial rights or prescriptive fees and cesses levied from residents in a village, or from cultivators by the proprietors, which have long been established and are upon the record: the former of these additions are usually taken into account, the latter not, in fixing the assessment. It is also a tax on personal property. In Marathi it also signifies the place where the customs are levied. Wilson's *Gloss.*, 454.

A'IN VIII.

The Ilāhi Gaz

Is a measure of length and a standard gauge. High and low refer to it, and it is the desire of the righteous and the unrighteous. Throughout Hindustan there were three such measures current, *viz.*, long, middling and short. Each was divided into 24 equal parts and each part called *Tassuj.*[88a] A *Tassuj* of the 1st kind was equal to 8 ordinary barley-corns placed together breadthways, and of the other two respectively, to 7 and 6 barley-corns. The long *gaz* was used for the measurement of cultivated lands, roads, distances, forts, reservoirs and mud walls. The middling was employed to measure buildings of stone and wood, bamboo-built houses, places of worship, wells and gardens, and the short *gaz* for cloth, arms, beds, seats of state, sedan chairs, palanquins, chairs, carts and the like.

In some other countries, although they reckon the *gaz* as consisting of 24 *Tassuj*, they make

1 Tassuj	equal to	2 Habbah (grain).
1 Habbah	,,	2 Barley-corns.
1 Barley-corn	,,	6 Mustard seeds.
1 Mustard seed	,,	12 Fals.
1 Fals	,,	6 Fatila.
1 Fatila	,,	6 Naqir.
1 Naqir	,,	8 Qitmir.
1 Qitmir	,,	12 Zarrah.
1 Zarrah	,,	8 Habā.
1 Habā	,,	2 Wahmah.

Some make 4 Tassuj equal to 1 Dāng.
6 Dāng ,, 1 Gaz.

Others reckon the *gaz* as 24 fingers, each finger equal to the breadth of 6 barley-corns, and each barley-corn equal in thickness to 6 hairs from the mane of a cob. In some ancient books they make the *gaz* equal to two spans and twice round the joint (*girih*) of the thumb, and they divided it into 16 *girih* and each *girih* was subdivided into 4 parts

[88a] *Tassuj* is an arabicized word from the Pers. *tasu*, a weight of 4 barley-corns, the 24th part of a weight measure or day. *Ency. Islam*, iv. 692 (under *Tasudj*).

which they called 4 *pahr,* so that a *pahr* was the sixty-fourth part of a *gaz.*

In other ancient records the *gaz* is reckoned of seven kinds. 1st, The *Gaz i Sauda* (*Gaz* of traffic) consisting of 24 digits and two-thirds of a digit. Harun ur Rashid of the House of 'Abbās took this measure from the hand of an Abyssinian slave who was one of his attendants: the Nilometer[88b] of Egypt is on this measure, and houses and cloths are also measured by it. 2nd, *Zirāa' i qasbah,* (Reed-yard) called also *A'āmah,* and *Daur,* of 24 digits: this was introduced by Ibn Abi Laila.[89] 3rd, The *Yusufiyah,* used by the provincial governors of Baghdad for the measurement of houses: it consisted of 25 digits. 4th, The short *Hāshimiyah,* of 28 digits and a third. Bilāl[90] the son of Abi Bardah introduced it: according to some it was Abu Musa Ash'ari his grandfather. 5th, The long *Hāshimiyah* of 29 digits and two-thirds which Mansur the A'bbaside favoured. It is also called the *Maliq* and *Ziyādiyah.* Ziyād[91] was the so-called son of Abu Sufiyān who used it to measure the lands in Arabian I'rāq. 6th, The *Omariyah* of 31 digits. During his Caliphate, Omar carefully considered the long, short and middling *gaz.* He took the three kinds together and to one-third of the aggregate he added the height of the closed fist and the thumb erect. He closed both ends of the measure with tin and sent it to Hudaifah[92] and Othmān[93]-b-Hunaif which they used for the measurement of the villages in Arabian Irāq. 7th, The *Māmuniyah* of 70 digits less a third. Mamun brought it into use, and it was employed for measuring rivers, plains and road distances.

[88b] The cubit of the Nilometer is supposed to be the same as that of the Jews, which is exactly two feet English: if so the 24 digits will be precisely inches. A finger's breadth may be safely taken as three quarters of an inch. *Useful Tables,* pp. 87, 88. For *Zirā'* see *Ency. Isl.* i. 959 (under *Dhirā'*).

[89] *Muhammad-b-Abdur Rahmān,* surnamed Ibn Abi Layla, was a distinguished jurisconsult and one of the *Tābiis.* He was Qadhi of Kufa where he was born A.H. 74, and died in A.H. 148. D'Herb.

[90] *Bilāl.*—The grandson of Abu Musa al Ashari, Qādhi of Basrah, of which his grandfather had been Governor. See a brief notice of him in Ibn Khall. Vol. II, p. 2.

[91] *Ziyād,* the governor of Irāq. (*Enc. Isl.* iv. 1232).

[92] *Hudaifah,* one of the most eminent of the Companions of Muhammad. Omar appointed him to the government of Madāin, where he died after the assassination of Othmān and 40 days after the accession of 'Ali. Ibn Hajar. *Biog. Dict.*

[93] *Othmān.*—He was governor of Basrah under the Caliph 'Ali. Ibn Khall, p. 391, Vol. IV.

Some in former times reckoned the cloth-measure (*gaz*) to be seven times the fist, and the fist was equal to four fingers closed; according to others, one finger less. The survey *gaz,* according to some, was the same seven fists: others made it seven fists together with one finger (thumb?) erect added to the seventh fist. Others again added another finger to that fist; while some made it seven fists with one finger adjoined to each fist.

Sultan Sikander Lodi in Hindustān introduced another *gaz* of the breadth of 41 *Iskandaris* and a half. This was a copper coin mixed with silver. Humayun added a half and it was thus completed to 42. Its length was 32 digits. But some authors anterior to his time make mention of a similar measure. Sher Khān and Salim Khān [Sur], under whom Hindustān was released from the custom of dividing the grain and its apportionment, in measuring land used this *gaz.* Till the thirty first-year of the Divine Era, although the *Akbar Shāhi gaz* of 46 fingers was used as a cloth-measure, the *Iskandari gaz* was used for cultivated lands and buildings. His Majesty in his wisdom, seeing that the variety of measures was a source of inconvenience to his subjects, and regarding it as subservient only to the dishonest, abolished them all and brought a medium *gaz* of 41 digits into general use. He named it the *Ilāhi gaz* and it is employed by the public for all purposes.

A'IN IX.

The Tanāb.[94]

His Majesty fixed for the *jarib* the former reckoning in yards and chose the measurement of sixty square, but adopted the *Ilāhi gaz.* The *Tanāb* (tent rope) was in Hindustān a measure of hempen rope twisted which became

[94] The *Tanāb, Jarib* and *Bigha* seem to have been indiscriminately used as nearly interchangeable terms. The *Jarib* in its original use, according to Wilson (*Glossary*), was a measure of capacity equal to 60 *qafiz* or 384 *madd,* about 768 pounds. It then became applied to a land measure, or as much land as could be sown with a *jarib* of seed-corn, and then appears to have been loosely used for a *bigha.* In course of time it occurs as a measure of land of various extent, and as the chain or rope for measuring. In the N. W. P. the measurements were made by a chain, and the *jarib* is=to 5

shorter or longer according to the dryness or moisture of the atmosphere. It would be left in the dew and thus fraudfully moistened. Oftentimes it would be employed in the early morning when it had got damp and had shrunk, and by the end of the day it had become dry and had lengthened. In the former case, the husbandmen suffered loss, in the latter the royal revenues were diminished. In the 19th year of the Divine era, the *jarib* was made of bamboos joined by iron rings. Thus it is subject to no variation, and the relief to the public was felt everywhere while the hand of dishonest greed was shortened.

A'IN X.

The Bigha

Is a name applied to the *jarib*. It is a quantity of land 60 *gaz* long by 60 broad. Should there be any diminution in length or breadth or excess in either, it is brought into square measure and made to consist of 3600 square *gaz*.[95] They divide the *bigha* into 20 parts, each of which is called *biswah,* and this is divided into 20 parts each of which is termed *biswānsah*. In measuring they reduce no further. No revenue is required from 9 *biswānsah,* but ten they account as one *biswah.* Some, however, subdivide the biswänsah into 20 parts, each of which they called *taswān-*

---

chains of 11 yards each, or to 60 *gaz* or 20 gathas or knots. A square of one *jarib* is a *bigha*. Before the new system of survey, it was usual to measure lands paying revenue with a *jarib* of 18 knots only, two being coiled round the measurer, but free lands were measured with the entire rope of 20 knots. In Sindh a *jarib* is a measure of a 150 square feet. In Telegu, it is applied to garden land or its produce. The standard *bigha* of the revenue surveyors of the N. W. P. is=to 3,025 sq. yds. or ⅝ of an acre. In Bengal the *bigha* contained only 1,600 sq. yds. or a little less than ⅓ of an acre. In Benares at the time of the settlement, it was determined at 3,136 sq. yds. In other perganahs it was equal to 2,025 to 3,600 or 3,925 sq. yds. A *kachha bigha* is in some places a third, in others only a fourth of a full *bigha*. Akbar's *bigha* of 3,600 Ilahi *gaz* was considered=to 3,025 sq. yds. of the *bigha* of Hindustān. In Cuttack the *bigha* is now considered to be an English acre. The Maratha *bigha* is called 20 *pānds* or 400 sq. *kālhis* or rods of (each) 5 cubits and 5 hand-breadths. The Guzerät *bigha* contains only 284$\frac{4}{9}$ sq. yds. Mr. Elliot specifies six variations found in the Upper Provinces. See Wilson's *Gloss*. under *Bigha* and *Jarib*. *Ency. Islam,* iii. 530-539 (under *al-Mizān*) and i. 1018 (under *Djarib*). Elliot *Memoirs,* ii. 189 (*jarib*).

[95] The text has an error of 60 for 600. 3600 sq. *gaz*=2,600 sq. yards=0·538 or somewhat more than half an acre. *U. T.,* p. 88.

sah, which they again divide into 20 parts, calling each *tapwānsah*. This again they partition into 20 portions, and name them severally *answānsah*. A *bigha* as measured by the *tanāb* of hemp, was two *biswah* and 12 *biswānsah* smaller in extent than the *bigha* measured by the *tanāb* of bamboo. This makes a difference of 10 *bigha* in a hundred. Although the *tanāb* of hemp was of 60 *gaz*, yet in the twisting it shrank to 56. The *Ilāhi gaz* was longer than the *Iskandari* by one *biswah*, 16 *biswānsah*, 13 *taswānsah*, 8 *tapwānsah*, and 4 *answānsah*. The difference between the two reduced the *bigha* by 14 *biswah*, 20 *biswānsah*, 13 *taswānsah*, 8 *tapwānsah*, *and* 4 *answānsah*. In one hundred *bighas* the variation in the two measures amounted to 22 bighas, 3 *biswah* and 7 *biswānsah*.

A'IN XI.

Land and its classification, and the proportionate dues of Sovereignty.

When His Majesty had determined the *gaz*, the *tanāb*, and the *bigha*, in his profound sagacity he classified the lands and fixed a different revenue to be paid by each.

Polaj is land which is annually cultivated for each crop in succession and is never allowed to lie fallow.

Parauti is land left out of cultivation for a time that it may recover its strength.

Chachar is land that has lain fallow for three or four years.

Banjar is land uncultivated for five years and more.

Of the two first kinds of land, there are three classes, good, middling and bad. They add together the produce of each sort, and a third of this represents the medium produce, one-third part of which is exacted as the royal dues. The revenue levied by Sher Khān, which at the present day is represented in all provinces as the lowest rate of assessment, generally obtained, and for the convenience of the cultivators and the soldiery, the value was taken in ready money.

Produce of Polaj Land.[96] *Spring Harvest, called in Hindi Asādhi.*

	Produce of a *bigha* of the best sort of *Polaj.*		Produce of a *bigha* of the middling sort.		Produce of a *bigha* of the worst sort.		Aggregate produce of three *bighas* of different sorts.		One third of the preceding, being the medium produce of a *bigha* of *polaj.*		One third of the medium produce, being the proportion fixed for the **revenue.**	
	Md.	**Sr.**	**Md.**	**Sr.**	**Md.**	**Sr.**	**Md.**	**Sr.**	**Md.**	**Sr.**	**Md.**	**Sr.**
Wheat	18		12		8	35	38	35	12	38¼	4	12¾
Nukhud—(Vetches) ...	13		10	20	7	20	31	0	10	13½	3	18
Adas—Pulse (Cicer lins) in Hindi. *Masur* ...	8	10	6	20	4	25	19	15	6	18½	2	6
Barley	18	0	12	20	8	15	38	35	12	38¼	4	12¾
Linseed	6	20	5	10	3	30	15	20	5	7	1	29
Safflower—(carthamus tinctorius)	8	30	6	30	5	10	20	30	6	36½	2	12
Arzan—Millet (Penicum miliaceum (in Hindi ***China***)	10	20	8	20	5	5	24	5	8	1⅓	2	27⅛
Mustard	10	20	8	20	5	5	24	5	8	1⅔	2	27⅛
Peas	13	0	10	20	8	25	32	5	10	23	3	28
Fenugreek (*Methi*) ...	14	0	11	0	9	35	34	35	11	25	3	35
Kur rice	24	0	18	0	14	10	56	10	18	30	6	10

The revenue from musk melons, *ajwāin* (*Ligusticum ajowan*), onions and other greens not counted as produce, was ordered to be paid in ready money at the rates hereinafter mentioned.

---

[96] I have copied the *form* of the 4 following tables from Gladwin. Abul Fazl makes the calculation for the 4th and 5th columns for wheat only. For vetches and pulse he omits the 4th column and omits the 4th and 5th of all the remainder. The fractions below a quarter of a seer are discarded in calculating the proportion fixed for revenue : the thirds are not always mathematically exact, and fractions are sometimes raised to a unit or altogether omitted.

Polaj Land.

The Autumn Harvest, called in Hindi SĀWANI.

	Produce of a *bigha* of the best sort of *Polaj.*		Produce of a *bigha* of the middling sort.		Produce of a *bigha* of the worst sort.		Aggregate produce of three *bighas* of different sorts.		One third of the preceding, being the medium produce of a *bigha* of *polaj.*		One third of the medium produce, being the proportion fixed for the revenue.	
	Md.	Sr.	Md.	Sr.	Md.	Sr.	Md.	Sr.	Md.	Sr.	Md.	Sr.
Molasses[97]	13	0	10	20	7	20	31	0	10	13½	3	18
Cotton	10	0	7	20	5	0	22	20	7	20	2	20
Shāli Mushkin—Dark coloured, small in grain and white, fragrant, that ripens quickly and pleasant to taste ...	24	0	18	0	14	10	56	10	18	80	6	10
Common rice, not of the above quality ...	17	0	12	20	9	15	38	85	12	38½	4	13
Māash—in Hindi *Mung* (Phaseolus mungo) ...	10	20	7	20	5	10	28	10	7	80	2	23½
Mush Siah—H. *Uridh* (a kind of vetch) ...	10	20	7	20	5	10	28	10	7	80	2	28½
Moth (lentils), coarser than the white *mung* and better than the dark ...	6	20	5	10	3	30	15	20	5	6½	1	29
Jowār (Andropogon Sorghum. Roxb.) ...	13	0	10	20	7	20	31	0	10	13½	8	18
Shamākh—H. *Sanwān* (Panicum frumentaceum. Roxb.)	10	20	8	20	5	5	24	5	8	1½	2	27½
Kodron[98] (like Sanwān) but its outer husk darkish red	17	0	12	20	9	15	38	85	12	88½	4	12½
Sesame	8	0	6	0	4	0	18	0	6	0	2	0
Kanguni (Panicum italicum)	6	20	5	10	8	80	15	20	5	7	1	29
Turiya, like mustard seed, but inclined to red ...	6	20	5	10	8	80	15	20	5	7	1	29
Arzan (Panicum miliaceum) generally a spring crop	16	0	18	20	10	25	40	5	18	1½	4	18½
Lahdarah grows in ear, the grain like *Kanguni*	10	20	7	20	5	10	28	10	7	80	2	23½
Mandwah (Cynosurus corocanus) the ear like Sānwan, the seed like mustard seed, but some red, some white ...	11	20	9	0	6	20	27	0	9	0	8	0

[97] The 4th and 5th columns have been omitted by Abul Fazl.

[98] A variant gives *Kodon* and *Koderam* probably the same as *Kodo*—a small grain (Paspalum frumentaceum). Wilson's *Glossary,* 292.

The Autumn Harvest, called in Hindi SĀWANI.—*Contd.*

	Produce of a *bigha* of the best sort of *Polaj.*		Produce of a *bigha* of the middling sort.		Produce of a *bigha* of the worst sort.		Aggregate produce of three *bighas* of different sorts		One third of the preceding, being the medium produce of a *bigha* of *polaj.*		One third of the medium produce, being the proportion fixed for the **revenue.**	
	Md.	Sr.	Md.	Sr.	Md.	Sr.	Md.	Sr.	Md.	Sr.	Md.	Sr.
Lobiya (Dolichos sinensis), resembles a bean, somewhat small	10	20	7	20	5	10	28	10	7	30	2	20½
Kudiri, like *Sānwan* but coarser	6	20	5	10	3	30	15	20	5	7	1	29
Kult, (Dolichos uniflorus) like a lentil somewhat darker, its juice good for camels : it softens stone and renders it easy to cut	10	20	7	20	5	10	23	10	17	30	2	20½
Barti, like *Sanwān* but whiter (a species of Panicum)	6	20	5	10	3	30	15	20	5	7	1	29

As a consideration for watching the crops a quarter of a seer (per maund) is allowed in some places and in others more, as will be shown.

The revenue from indigo, poppy, *pān,* turmeric, water chestnut[99] (trapa bispinosa), hemp, *kachālu* (arum colocasia) pumpkin, *hinna* (Lawsonia inermis) cucumbers, *bādrang* (a species of cucumber), the egg-plant (solanum melongena), radishes, carrots, *karelā* (momordica charantia) *kakura* (Momordica Muricata), *tendas,*[100] and musk-melons,

[99] This is the *Singārah* or Singharah. In the month of November, the nut ripens and such of the fruit as remains ungathered, falls off and sinks to the bottom of the pond. When the water dries up in May or June, these nuts or bulbs are found to have thrown out a number of shoots. They are then carefully collected and placed in a small hole in the deepest portion of the tank and covered with water. In the rains when the ponds begin to fill, the bulbs are taken up, each shoot is broken off, enveloped in a ball of clay to sink it and thrown into the water at different distances. They at once take root and grow rapidly until in a short time the surface of the water is covered with leaves. The fruit forms in October. The produce of a standard *bigha* is about 2½ *mans* which at the selling price of 10 *sers* for the rupee, represent a total value of Rs. 10. It is much more extensively consumed by the Hindus than the Mahomedans. Carnegie's *Kachhari Technicalities.*

[100] Also called *tendu* : resinous fruit of the tree Diospyros glutinosa,

not counted as produce, was ordered to be paid in ready money at the rates hereafter mentioned.

Parauti land when cultivated, pays the same revenue as *polaj*.

His Majesty in his wisdom thus regulated the revenues in the abovementioned favourable manner. He reduced the duty on manufactures from ten to five per cent. and two per cent. was divided between the *patwari* and the *qānungo*. The former is a writer employed on the part of the cultivator. He keeps an account of receipts and disbursements, and no village is without one. The latter is the refuge of the husbandman. There is one in every district. At the present time the share of the *qānungo* (one per cent.) is remitted and the three classes of them are paid by the State according to their rank. The salary of the first is fifty rupees: of the second, thirty; of the third, twenty; and they have an assignment for personal support equivalent thereto. It was the rule that the commissaries of the *shiqdar*, *karkun*,[101] and *Amin* should receive daily 58 *dāms* as a perquisite, provided that in spring they did not measure less than 200, nor in autumn less than 250 *bighas*. His Majesty whose heart is capacious as the ocean, abolished this custom and allowed only one *dām* for each *bigha*.

Many imposts, equal in amount to the income of Hindustān were remitted by His Majesty as a thank-offering to the Almighty. Among these were the following:

The capitation tax, *jizya*.
The port duties, *mir-bahari*.
Tax[102] per head on gathering at places of worship, *kar*.
A tax on each head of oxen, *gāo-shumāri*.
A tax on each tree, *sar-i-darakhti*.
Presents, *peshkash*.
Distraints, *qurq*.
A tax on the various classes of artificers, *peshawar*.
Dārogha's fees, *dāroghānah*.
Tahsildār's fees, *tahsildāri*.
Treasurer's fees, *fotahdāri*.

---

[101] *Kārkun*, the registrar of the collections under a *Zamindar*. The *Amin* was an officer employed either in the revenue department to take charge of an estate and collect the revenues on account of government, or to investigate and report their amount: or in the judicial department, as a judge and arbitrator in civil causes. Wilson's *Gloss.*, 261.

[102] The word is *kar* in the text, and is probably from the Sansk. कर an impost, fee or cess. These imposts are called *wajuhāt* in the text, and *ābwābs* in the later Mughal days. For a full account of the *ābwābs*, see Sarkar's *Mughal Adm.*, 3rd ed., ch. v. § 8 and 9.

Complimentary offerings on receiving a lease and the like, *salāmi*.

Lodging charges, *wajih kirāya*.
Money bags, *kharitah*
Testing and exchanging money, *sarrāfi*.
Market duties, *hāsil-i-bāzār*.

Sale of cattle (*nakhās*); also on hemp, blankets, oil, raw hides, weighing (*Kayyāli*), scaling; likewise butcher's dues, tanning, playing at dice,[103] passports for goods, turbans,[104] hearth-money [*dudi, har ke ātish āfruzad chize bar dehad, i.e.*, fee for illumination?] fees on the purchase and sale of a house, on salt made from nitrous earth, *balkati* on permission to reap the harvest, felt, manufacture of lime, spirituous liquors, brokerage, catching fish, the product of the tree Āl (*Morinda citrifolia*);[105] in fine all those imposts which the natives of Hindustān include under the term *Sair Jihāt*,[106] were remitted.

ĀIN XII.

Chachar land.

When either from excessive rain or through an inundation, the land falls out of cultivation, the husbandmen are, at first, in considerable distress. In the first year, therefore, but two fifths of the produce is taken: in the second three-fifths; in the third,[107] four-fifths and in the fifth, the ordinary revenue. According to differences of situation, the revenue is paid either in money or in kind. In the third year the charges of 5 per cent. and one *dām* for each bigha[108] are added.

---

103 Two words follow which are marked in the text as doubtful, there is doubtless an omission.

104 The word is *pag*, contraction of *pagri*, a turban. It was a kind of poll tax levied on every turban.

105 From which a dye is extracted.

106 See p. 63.

107 There is probably an error in the text as the fourth year is omitted. Gladwin has "the third *and fourth* years fourth-fifths each."

108 I take the *wa* between *dah wa nim* to be an error, as by retaining it the percentage would rise to 15 or at least to 10½. Five per cent. was levied on manufactures; it may therefore have been an extra charge on land though I do not see its reason or its justice. Gladwin translates as I have done.

ĀIN XIII.

Banjar land.

When through excessive inundations production has seriously diminished, the revenue is collected in the following proportions :

Spring Harvest.

Proportion of revenue from one Bigha of Banjar land for five years.

		1st year		2nd year		3rd year		4th year		5th year
		Md.	Sr.	Md.	Sr.	Md.	Sr.	Md.	Sr.	
Wheat	I.	0	20	1	0	2	0	8	0	as *polaj*
Mustard	R.	0	5	0	25	0	35	1	10	,,
Vetches *Nukhud*	I.	0	10	0	30	1	10	2	10	,,
Do.	R.	0	5	0	80	1	10	2	10	,,
Barley	I.	0	20	1	0	2	0	8	0	,,
Do.	R.	0	5	0	85	1	20	2	20	,,
Pulse (*Cicer lens*) *Adas* ...	I.	0	10	0	30	1	10	1	80	,,
Do.	R.	0	5	0	80	1	10	1	80	,,
Millet (*Panicum miliaecum*) *Arzan* ...	I.	0	10	0	25	0	35	1	0	,,
Do.	R.	0	5	0	25	0	85	1	0	,,
Linseed	I.	0	10	0	20	0	30	1	10	,,
Do.	R.	0	5	0	5	0	80	1	10	,,

Note. I stands for inundated land, and R for that which has suffered from rain.

Autumn Harvest.

Proportion of revenue from one Bigha of Banjar land for five years.

		1st year		2nd year		3rd year		4th year		5th year
		Md.	Sr.	Md.	Sr.	Md.	Sr.	Md.	Sr.	
Māsh	I.	0	20	1	0	1	20	2	10	as *polaj*
Do.	R.	0	5	0	20	1	0	1	20	,,
Jowār	I.	0	20	1	0	2	0	8	0	,,
Do.	R.	0	5	0	20	1	0	2	0	,,
Moth	R.	0	5	0	20	0	30	1	10	,,
Lahdarah	R.	0	5	0	20	1	10	2	0	,,
Kodron	I.	0	20	1	0	2	0	3	0	,,
Do.	R.	0	5	0	20	1	20	2	20	,,
Mandwah	I.	0	20	1	0	2	0	3	0	,,
Do.	R.	0	5	0	80	1	10	2	10	,,
Kudiri	I.	0	10	0	25	0	85	1	10	,,
Do.	R.	0	5	0	25	0	85	1	10	,,
Kanguni, (Pers. *kāl*) ...	I.	0	10	0	25	0	35	1	10	,,
Do.	R.	0	5	0	25	0	35	1	10	,,
Turiya	I.	0	20	1	0	1	10	1	20	,,
Do.	R.	0	5	0	25	0	35	1	10	,,
Sanwān (Pers. *Shamākh*) ...	I.	0	10	0	25	0	35	1	10	,,
Do.	R.	0	5	0	25	0	85	1	10	,,
Arzan	I.	0	10	0	80	1	0	1	10	,,
Do.	R.	0	5	0	30	1	0	1	10	,,
Sesame	R.	0	5	0	20	0	80	1	10	,,

In the 4th year the charges of 5 per cent and one *dām* for each *bigha* were collected and this is still in force.

In *Banjar* land for the 1st year, one or two *sers* are taken from each *bigha;* in the 2nd year, 5 *sers;* in the 3rd year, a sixth of the produce; in the 4th year, a fourth share together with one *dām* : in other years a third suffices. This varies somewhat during inundations. In all cases the husbandman may pay in money or kind as is most convenient. *Banjar* land at the foot of the hills and land subject to inundations in the districts of Sanbhal and Bahrāich, do not remain as *banjar,* for so much new soil is brought down with the overflow that it is richer and more productive than *polaj*. His Majesty, however, in his large munificence places it in the same class. It is in the option of the cultivator to pay in ready money or by *kankut or bhaoli.*

ĀIN XIV.

The Nineteen Years' Rates.[109]

Intelligent people have from time to time set themselves to record the prices current of the Empire, and after careful inquiry the valuation of grain was accepted on this basis.

The revenue rates for *a bigha of polaj* land were fixed as has been stated. From the 6th year of the Divine Era which runs with the Novilunar year 968 (A. D., 1560-1) and concluding with the 24th year of this reign, the statistics were collected and have been tabulated for reference after the most diligent investigation. The figures are entered under the heading of each year.

---

[109] Nineteen years correspond with a cycle of the moon during which period the seasons are supposed to undergo a complete revolution. Gladwin, p. 292, Vol. I.

Spring Harvest of the Subah of Agra. Nineteen years' rates.

	6th and 7th years.	8th year.	9th year.	10th year.	11th year.	12th year.	13th year.	14th year.	15th year.	16th year.	17th year	18th year.	19th year	20th year.	21st year.	22nd year.	23rd year.	24th year.
Wheat ...	90 *dams* D.	80 to 90 D	90 D.	50 to 60 D.	56 to 60 D.	56 to 60 D.	56 to 60 D.	52 to 60 D.	38 to 48 D.	36 to 52 D.	36 to 74 D	43 to 54 D.	32 to 50 D.	40 to 58 D.	42½ to 80 D.	64 to 94 D.	40 to 58 D.	52 to 116 D.
Cabul Vetches	...	...	...	...	...	...	...	...	38-57	38-57	38-57	38-57	38-57	38-57	38-57	38-57	26-52	50-85
Indian do ...	80	76-80	80	44-56	44-56	44-56	44-56	32-40	20-38	20-30	20-48	19-28	19-20	21-38	19-44½	26½-40	22-37	40-86
Barley ...	80	60-76	60	38-50	38-50	40-52	40-54	36-40	21-28	21-34	21-54	28-30	20-40	26-40	28-52½	36-54	23-36	40-90
Pot-herbs ...	80	80	80	80	80	80	80	80	52-60	50-70	50-60	40-54	40-60	44-62	44-60	44-60	46-60	46-60
Poppy ...	160	160	160.	140	140	140	140	140	130	100-130	100-130	100-130	100-130	100-130	100-130	100-130	100-130	100-130
Safflower	20 *sers*	20 sers.	20 sers	80 D.	80	80	80	70-76	60-70	60-70	52-70	50-70	40-78	54-78	54-78	54-78	54-73	54-73
Linseed	...	...	80 D.	60-80	60-80	60-80	60-80	50-56	24-30	18-30	18-28	23-26	24-28	24-26	16-34½	16-34½	18-26	24-42
Mustard	80 D	80	80	60-80	60-80	60-80	60-80	50-56	22-30	20-30	24-32	22-30	22-26	19½-30	19-32	20½-32	18½-26	30-48
Adas (Pulse)	60	60-68	50	32-50	32-50	32-50	32-50	26-32	15-24½	15-28	15-30	15-22	15-28	17-25	16-40½	16-20½	16-24	25-50
Arzan (Millet)	44	44	20	30	30	30	80	26-28	14-20	15-22	15-24	14-18	14-17	16-19	11½-25	12½-24	12-24	16-34
Peas ...	...	68	...	...	...	...	44	15-26	15-42	15-42	15-42	19-24	17-28	17-30	17-30	17-30	18-28	32½-56
Persian Musk-melons ...	...	...	...	...	...	...	...	120	86-120	86-120	86-120	86-120	86-120	86-120	82-120	82-120	82-120	82-120
Indian do ...	10	10	...	...	8	8	8	16	16	15-16	15-16	8-16	15-16	15-16	10-16	12-16	12-16	12-16
Kur rice ...	60	60	60	50-60	54-60	60	54-70	40-54	36-48	36-44	36-54	32-50	32-42	32-54	34-56	34-48	34-48	50-70
Ajwain Ligusticum ajowan ...	80	80	80	80	80	80	80	70	70	70-90	70-71	60-90	70	50-80	70-90	70-90	70-74	72-74

Note. In these tables D stands for *dām* and J for *Jetal* the 25th part of a *dām* which is the 40th part of a rupee.

Spring Harvest of the Subah of Agra, continued. Nineteen years' rates.

	6th & 7th years	8th year.	9th year.	10th year.	11th year.	12th year.	13th year.	14th year.	15th year.	16th year.	17th year.	18th year.	19th year.	20th year.	21st year.	22nd year.	23rd year.	24th year.
									D.	D.	D.	D.	D.	D.	D.	D.	D.	D.
Onions ..	...	...	...	...	...	...	...	...	17 to 73	54-70	70-73	70-72	72-80	-80	70-80	70-80	70-80	70-80
Fenugreek ..	...	...	...	...	...	...	...	...	70	70	50-70	40-70	70	0-80	60-70	28-80	32-80	40-80
Carrots ..	*1 man*	*1 man*	*1 man*	...	...	...	...	...	20-80	20-30	20-28	20-40	20-40	16-26	16-26	18-25	18-25	22-40
Lettuce ..	...	...	...	...	...	...	...	...	24-25	24-25	24-25	24-25	24 5	25	25	25	16	16

Autumn Harvest of the Subah of Agra.

	6th & 7th years	8th year.	9th year.	10th year.	11th year.	12th year.	13th year.	14th year.	15th year.	16th year.	17th year.	18th year.	19th year.	20th year.	21st year.	22nd year.	23rd year.	24th year.
	D.	D.	D.	D.	D.	D.	D.	D.	D.	D.	D.	D.	D.	D.	D.	D.	D.	D.
Sugar-cane (*paunda*) ..	...	...	...	180-200	180-200	180-200	180·200	180-200	150-200	150-200	180-200	170-200	160-200	180-200	180-200	180-200	180-200	180-200
Common sugar-cane ..	180	180	180	140-160	140-160	140-160	140-160	184-154	112-174	100-150	90-134	96-134	96-134	94-189	104-170	100-140	76-100	88-126
Shali Mushkin Dark coloured rice ..	...	...	...	70-80	70-80	70-80	70-80	64-70	52-64	29-74	40-64	52-70	42-70	47-87	47-80	47-80	56-80	60-80
Common rice	70	70	70	60	52-60	52-60	56-65	44-52	86-45	36-52	86-45	36-42	34-50	29-50	25-58	40-74	38½-66	46-48
Munji rice ..	...	...	...	...	...	...	...	...	48	48-65	48-65	48-65	48-65	48-65	48-65	48-65	48-65	48-65
Cotton ..	120	120	130	110	110	110	110	70-92	90	85-90	70-90	62-90	70-90	59-94	76-101½	60-90	44 58	44-60
Potsherbs ..	80	80	80	80	80	80	80	80	70	70	60-70	50-70	50-70	60-80	30-80	60-80	56-70	56-76
Seasame seed	60	60	80	70	70	70	70	60-64	50	50	40-50	28-50	25½-50	21-38	21-32½	19-36½	24-37	10½-42
Moth lentils	48	48	54	36-44	40-50	40-48	80-36	20-28	19-86	19-26	14-22	18-23½	16-21	10½-25	19-26	13-21	18-25	16½-32
Māsh ..	48	48	54	36-44	44	44-50	40-44	32-86	28-32	25½-82	26-32 D. and 18 J	25-36	22-40	25½-45	22-40	22-89½	27-47½	26½-50

Autumn Harvest of the Subah of Agra, continued. Nineteen years' rates.

	6th and 7th years.	8th year.	9th year.	10th year.	11th year.	12th year.	13th year.	14th year.	15th year.	16th year.	17th year.	18th year.	19th year.	20th year.	21st year.	22nd year.	23rd year.	24th year.
	D.	D.	D.	D.	D.	D.	D.	D.	D.	D.	D.	D.	D.	D.	D.	D.	D.	D.
Mung ..	48	48	48	44	44	44	44	32-40	32-40	32-40	32-40	26-40	22-34	27½-48	22-65½	22-50	27-44	32-50
Jowar ..	50	50	60	40-48	40-48	40-48	40-48	30-40	26-30	24-38	24-30	24-34	22-34	20-34½	22½-46½	26-47	34-48	34-53
Lahdarah ..	48	48	48-50	36-44	36-50	36-44	20-24	20-36	20-24	20-36	18-24	18-24	17-31½	17-31½	18-38	18-38	20-30	24-40
Lobiya ..	...	...	...	...	...	...	...	...	20-32	15-42	20-32	14-32	19-32	19-37	16-36½	20-36½	19-27	22-37
Kodaram ..	44	44	50	44	40-44	40-48	30-36	20-23	20-32	21-22½	19-24	16-32	18½-35	18½-35	21-41	21-42½	21-39½	24-50
Kori ..	40	40	50	24	24	24	24	16-20	10-23	8-23½	8-26	10-26	7-23½	5-28½	5-28½	7-23½	7-20	7-28
Shamākh ..	36	36	50	26-30	26-30	30-36	26-34	18-20	10-12	10-20	10-12	7-12	8-16	6½-15½	6½-14	7-17	7-13	9-14
Gāl (a sort of millet) ..	44	44	50	36-40	36-40	40	40	22-28	13-14	13-28	13-14	18-14	8-14	9-17	9-23	8½-28	8½-18½	12-18
Arzan ..	44	44	50	30-40	32-40	} 36-40	36-40	34-36	15-24	15-36	15-24	15-36	13-24	13-24	13-24	12-28	12-28	12-26
Mandwah ..	48	48	50	36-40	32-40													
Indigo ..	140	140	160	140	140	130	126-130	126-136	124-132	116-140	116-136	130-160	136-140	136-140	137-140	130-140	136-140	136-140
Hemp ..	80	80	80	80	80	80	80	70-78	70-76	70-78	70-76	60	60-76	70-76	74-78	68-80	60-84	60-84
Turiya ..	80	80	...	...	...	...	...	...	32-40	30-40	32-40	24-40	23½-32	29-40	17½	17½-40	23-40	23-40
Turmeric ..	...	...	...	...	...	...	...	...	100	100	100	100	100	100	100	100	100	100
Kachālu (arum-colocasia) ..	...	...	...	...	...	...	...	...	70	70	60-70	54-70	54-70	60-70	60-70	60-70	60	60
Kult ..	...	...	...	...	...	...	...	...	28	26	26	22	22	28	24	24	20	26
Hinna ..	...	...	...	...	...	...	...	...	58	58	58	58	58	60-70	24	53-72	58	53
Watermelons	...	...	...	...	...	...	...	...	10	10	10-12	9-11	9½-15	10-13	10-13	10-13	10-13	10-14
Pān ..	...	...	...	...	...	...	...	...	180	...	...	...	...	...	...	...	...	...
Singhārah ..	...	...	...	...	...	...	...	...	100	...	...	...	...	...	...	...	...	...

Spring Harvest of the Subah of Allahabad. Nineteen years' Rates.

	6th and 7th years.	8th year.	9th year.	10th year.	11th year.	12th year.	13th year.	14th year.	15th year.	16th year.
	D.	D.	D.	D.	D.	D.	D.	D.	D.	D.
Wheat ..	90	90	90	60-64	80-100	80-100	70	62	48-70	42-100
Cabul Vetches	...	...	...	...	...	...	...	...	38-50	50
Indian do. ..	80	80	80	56-64	76-90	76-90	76-90	76-90	24-70	13-40
Barley ..	70	80	80	80-120	80	80	80	70-76	50-106	50-100
Pot-herbs ..	80	80	80	80-120	80	80	70-76	60-70	44	28-70
Poppy ..	160	160	160	140	140	140	140	130	100-130	100-130
Safflower ..	½ *man*	½ *man*	½ *man*	70-80	80	80	80	76	60-70	60-70
Linseed ..	80	80	80	70-80	80	80	80	64	30-80	26-64
Mustard ..	80	80	80	70-80	80	80	80	20-50	30-80	26-44
Adas ..	60	60	50	40-54	54-60	54-60	54-60	42	17-60	18-40
Arzan ..	44	44	20	30	40	30-40	26-36	19-36	17-36	17-36
Peas ..	...	...	...	...	...	...	...	15-60	18-43	17-40
Persian Musk-melons ..	...	...	...	...	...	...	...	120	120-160	120-160
Indian do. ..	10	10	10	10	10	10	10	10-12	12-16	12-16
Kur rice ..	60	60	60	60	54-80	60	60-70	40-60	44-46	40-48
Ajwāin ..	80	80	80	80	80	80	80	80	70-100	70-100
Onions ..	...	...	...	...	...	...	...	...	70-100	70-100
Fenugreek ..	...	...	...	...	...	...	...	...	36-70	36-70
Carrots ..	1 *man*	do.	do.	do.	do.	do.	do.	do.	24-30	24-30
Lettuce ..	...	...	...	...	...	...	...	...	24	24

	17th year.	18th year.	19th year.	20th year.	21st year.	22nd year.	23rd year.	24th year.
	D.	D.	D.	D.	D.	D.	D.	D.
Wheat ..	42-100	48-70	40-70	42½-64½	48½-86	62½-86	40-62	40-75
Cabul Vetches	50	50	50	33-50	33-50	33-75	26-75	40-63½
Indian do. ..	32-45	20-45	20-45	30-74½	43½-57½	38-50	22½-44	24-43
Barley ..	50-100	40-100	40-100	40-100	44-60	46-60	43-60	37-60
Pot-herbs ..	32-50	30-50	21-50	22-50	22½-47	45-83	38-56	24-56
Poppy ..	100-130	100-130	100-130	100-130	100-130	100-130	100-130	100-130
Safflower ..	60-70	52-70	50-70	43-70	56-70	56-70	56-70	56-70
Linseed ..	30-64	18-64	20-64	22-31	23-28	20-28	18-22	18-24
Mustard ..	26-44	22-44	24-44	25-43	26½-46½	28-36	22-30	22-44
Adas ..	24-40	15-40	15-40	18-43	24-36	21-35½	25-28	17-38½
Arzan ..	14-36	16-36	16-23	14-23	16-23	14-23	14-23	14-30½
Peas ..	14-40	15-40	17-34	17-44	17-44	17-44	17-28	18-41½
Persian Musk-melons ..	120-160	80-160	66-160	43-160	86-120	86-120	86-120	86-120
Indian do. ..	12-16	8-16	9-16	12-40	12-16	12-16	12-16	12-16
Kur rice ..	40-48	36-46	38-46	22-42	36-42	32-42	40-42	42-50
Ajwāin ..	70-100	60-100	52-100	52-70	52-73	70-73	52-73	52-78
Onions ..	70-100	70-100	70-100	70-76	62-76	72-76	72-76	70-95½
Fenugreek ..	36-70	36-70	36-70	50-73	52-72	52-72	28-80	40-80
Carrots ..	24-30	23-40	20-40	20-32	20-26	20-25	14-25	16-24
Lettuce ..	24	24	25	25	25	25	16	25

Autumn Harvest of the Subah of Allahabad. Nineteen years' rates.

	6th and 7th years.	8th year.	9th year.	10th year.	11th year.	12th year.	13th year.	14th year.	15th year.	16th year.	17th year.	18th year.	19th year.	20th year,	21st year.	22nd year.	23rd year.	24th year.
	D.	D.	D.	D.	D.	D.	D.	D.	D.	D.	D.	D.	D.	D.	D.	D.	D.	D.
Sugar-cane (*paunda*) ..	...	...	...	...	200	200	200	200	200	200	200	200	170-200	160-200	180-200	180-200	180-200	180-200
Common sugar-cane	180	180	180	180	180	180	180	170-180	174-180	100-144	86½-102	100-120	100-130	86½-134	86½-165½	86-70	86-70	70-126
Dark coloured rice (*Shāli Mushkin*) ..	...	...	...	80	80	80-90	80	80	56-100	56-76½	56-76	56-76	50-76	54½-77	49-77	49-77	56-76	56-76
Common rice	70	70	70	60	80-90	80-90	70	48	86-80	36-50	36-57½	84-57½	37-57½	37-58	42-59	40-50	86-44	80-61
Munji rice ..	...	...	...	...	...	...	...	...	48	48	48	48	48	60	44½	65	65	65
Cotton ..	120	120	130	110	120	120	120	96	90-120	90-120	70-120	70-120	70-120	70-120	70-123	80½-102½	70-102½	50-70
Pot herbs ..	70	80	80	80	80	80	80	80	70	70-100	60-100	50-100	50-100	60-94	60-94	60-94	60-86	60-99½
Sesame seed	60	60	80	70	80	80	80	64	50-100	39-50	89-40	28-40	28-40	26½-38	22-32	24-32	24-52	24-46
Moth (lentils)	48	48	54	44	54-70	50	50	36	22-60	29-46	22-46	20-46	18-46	13-30	22-28	16½-20	16-27	16½-28
Māsh ..	48	48	54	44	54-70	50	48	36	28-70	28-42	28-42	24-42	25-42	27-44	21-44	21-40	24-45	24-45
Mung ..	48	48	48	44	44	44	44	44	82-72	32-46	32-46	80-46	38-46	82½-48	28½-56	34-56	80-50	26-56
Jowār ..	50	50	60	48	60	48	48	40	26	26	26	26-27	22-26	29-46½	22½-54	30-54	82-40	24-44
Lahdarah ..	48	48	48	44	50-56	50-56	50-56	40-56	20	20	20	20-22	16-40	20-48	20-48	20-48	24-40	28-61
Lobiya ..	...	...	...	...	...	...	...	...	56	42	82-42	32-42	82-42	21-43	34-44½	28-58	20-36½	20-44
Kodaram ..	44	44	44	44	44-64	54-64	54-64	36	21-60	21-83	20-44	20-22	16-86½	20½-88	76-48	81-48	22-80	21-89½
Kori ..	40	40	50	24	30	30	30	20	10	10	10	10	7-22	7-14	7-14	7-14	10	7-14
Shamākh ..	36	36	50	30	36	54	36-54	30	30	20	10-40	10-22	10-22	7-22	8-22	7-14	10½-18	10-17
Gāl ..	44	44	50	40	50-56	50-56	50-56	28	13-44	13-24	18-24	10-24	8-24	10½-21½	15-23	15-23	14½-24	12-22½

Autumn Harvest of the Subah of Allahabad (continued). Nineteen years' rates.

	6th and 7th years.	8th year.	9th year.	10th year.	11th year.	12th year.	13th year.	14th year.	15th year.	16th year.	17th year.	18th year.	19th year.	20th year.	21st year.	22nd year.	23rd year.	24th year.
	D.	D.	D.	D.	D.	D.	D.	D.	D.	D.	D.	D.	D.	D.	D.	D.	D.	D.
Arzan ...	44	44	50	40	40	40	40	36	20-36	20-36	20-36	20-36	18-36	20-38	14-28	14-28	14-28	14-30
Mandwah ...	46	48	50	40	40	52-56	52-56	34	22-56	22-29½	22-29½	17-29½	13-29	19-39½	25-32	25-32	22-28	18-28
Indigo ...	140	140	160	140	140	140	140	136	150-160	130-160	120-180	130-160	130-180	130-140	132-140	132-140	132-140	132-160
Hemp ...	80	80	80	80	80	80	80	77	70-120	70-80	70-80	76-80	76-80	60-88	60-90½	80	80	80
Turiya ...	80	80	80	...	...	...	...	...	32-80	32-44	32-44	24-44	24-44	32-40	26-40	26½-40	26½-40	26½-40½
Turmeric ...	...	...	...	...	...	...	...	...	100	100	100	100	100	100	100	100	100	100
Kāchālu ...	...	...	...	...	...	...	...	...	70	70	60	60	60	60	60	60	60	60
Kult ...	...	...	...	...	...	...	...	...	20	36	36	36	36	24	24	24	18	29½
Hinna ...	...	...	...	...	...	...	...	...	58	58	58	58	58	60-80	60-80	60-80	60-80	60-80
Watermelons	...	...	...	...	...	...	...	...	10-12	10-12	10-12	10-12	19½-12	10-14	10-14	10-14	10-14	10-14
Pān ...	...	...	...	...	...	...	...	...	180	180	180	180	180	160	200	200	240	240
Singhāra ...	...	...	...	...	...	...	...	...	100	100	100	100	100	100	100	100	100	100
Arhar (Cytisus Cajan) ...	...	...	...	...	...	...	...	...	...	...	...	...	...	20	20	20	20	20

Spring Harvest of the Subah of Oudh. Nineteen years' rates.

	6th and 7th years.	8th year.	9th year,	10th year.	11th year,	12th year.	18th year.	14th year.	15th yeor.	16th year.	17th year.	18th year.	19th year.	20th year.	21st year.	22nd year.	23rd year.	24th year.
	D.	D.	D.	D.	D.	D.	D.	D.	D.	D.	D.	D.	D.	D.	D.	D.	D.	D.
Wheat	90	90	90	52-60	52-80	52-80	52-70	46-65	48	42-50	50-52	33-46	33-43	46-50½	46-70	54-74½	32-44	38-46
Cabul vetches ...	...	...	...	...	...	...	...	...	50	50	50	50	50	50	50	50	50	50
Indian do. ...	80	80	80	40-56	48-76	48-76	48-74	34-58	24-33	26-33	26-33	20-27	20-28	30-41	42-57	30-57½	19-44	21-40
Barley	80	70	60	42-50	42-60	52	48-50	36-44	28-32	30-32	32-61	20-27	20-28	29½-45	43-62	34-56½	2[illegible]-30	24-40
Pot-herbs	80	80	80	80	80	80	80	62-72	56-60	50-6[illegible]	5[illegible]-6[illegible]	40-62	40-60	40-52	40-52	40-52	44-60	24-60
Poppy	160	160	160	140	140	140	140	130	130	130	100-130	100-130	100-130	100-130	100-130	100-130	100-130	100-130
Safflower	½ *man*	½ *man*	½ *man*	80	80	80	80	60-70	70	60-70	6[illegible]-70	52-70	52-70	54-60	54-60	54-70	54-70	54-70
Linseed	80	80	80	68-80	68-80	68-80	68-80	50-68	30-31	26-31	26-31	30-31	18-31	20-27	21-31	17½-28	17-20	17-24
Mustard	80	80	80	68-80	68-80	68-80	68-80	54-60	30-33	28-33	26-33	22-33	22-33	25-39	19-31	25-31	20-28	21-22
Adas	60	60	50	40	40-54	40-54	50-54	32-40	18-27	19-2[illegible]	20	14-19	14-18	17-24	20-24	19-28	19-22	18½-25
Arzan	44	44	20	80	30-40	30-40	30-40	26	15-17	17-20	17-20	14-18	14-16	16-18	14-17	16-17	14-16	14-17
Peas	...	...	...	...	...	...	...	...	...	28	28	16-28	15-31½	15	16-28	16-22	16-24	16-31
Persian Muskmelons	...	...	...	...	...	...	...	120	120	120	120	160-180	66-120	86-120	86-120	86-120	86-120	86-120
Indian do. ...	10	10	10	10	8-10	8-10	8-10	8-10	16	8-16	16	13-16	8-16	15-16	12-16	12-16	12-16	12-16
Kur rice	66	66	66	50-60	50-60	50-60	60-72	52-60	44-46	36-46	36-46	36-46	23-46	22-42	32-42	35-42	35-42	36-53
Ajwāin	80	80	80	80	80	80	80	70	70	70	70-71	60-70	70	5[illegible]-70	52-73	70-73	52-73	52-73
Onions	...	...	...	...	...	...	...	...	70-73	70	70-73	70-73	70	70-74	70-74	70-74	70-74	70-74
Fenugreek ...	...	...	...	...	...	...	...	...	70	70	70	70	70	52-80	52-80	50-80	52-80	50-80
Carrots	1 *man*	do.	do.	...	...	...	...	...	80	24	24	50-90	24	20-25	20-28	20-28	14-28	17-28
	...	...	...	...	...	...	...	...	... 24	24	24	24	25	25	25	25	16	25

Autumn Harvest of the Subah of Oudh. Nineteen years' rates.

	6th and 7th years.	8th year.	9th year.	10th year.	11th year.	12th year.	13th year.	14th year.	15th year.	16th year.	17th year.	18th year.	19th year.	20th year.	21st year.	22nd year.	23rd year.	24th year.
	D.	D.	D.	D.	D.	D.	D.	D.	D.	D.	D.	D.	D.	D.	D.	D.	D.	D.
Sugar-cane (*paunda*)	...	...	...	200	200	200	200	200	200	200	200	200	200	200	200	200	200	200
Common Sugar-cane	180	180	180	160	160-180	160-180	160-180	160-180	144	124-144	100-110	100-110	100-110	90-106	70-100	70-100	64-80	64-107
Dark coloured rice (*Shaālī Mushkin*)	...	...	...	80	80	80	80	60	56	56-68	56	56-70	50-70	54-70	49½-68	44-76	40-76	36-60
Common rice ...	70	70	70	60	60-80	60-80	60-80	48-52	36	36-48	36-38	36-38	28-36	24-38	22-46	36-40	21-36	22-36
Munji rice ...	...	...	...	...	...	...	...	...	...	48	48	48	48	48	60	44½	65	65
Cotton	120	120	130	110	110-130	110-120	110-120	88	90	90	70-90	70-74	72-130	72-130	65-79	64-70	50-60	46-90
Pot-herbs	80	80	80	80	80	80	80	70	70	60-70	50-76	60-70	64-94	64-94	64-94	64-94	60-70	60-64
Sesame seed ...	60	60	80	70	70-80	70-80	70-80	64	50	50	40-50	28-50	24-50	28-32	29-90½	21½-33	21½-30	19-26
Moth	48	48	54	44	44	44	44	44	22	22-36	22	20-22	20-22	13-21½	18-25	16-25	12-20	16-20
Māsh	48	48	54	44	44-54	44-50	50-54	36	28	28-36	28	27-28	26-28	23-35	28-42½	28-34	19-36	16-28
Mung	48	48	48	44	44	44	44	44	32-40	32-40	32-40	32-40	32-40	32-48	28½-44	30-52	36-46	25-30
Jowār	50	50	60	48	48-60	46-60	48-60	40	26	26-40	26	26-27	24-26	23-40	23-48	25½-48	30-40	24-46
Lahdarah ...	48	48	48-50	44	16-44	44-50	44-50	20-70	20-40	20	20-40	18-48	18-48	20-40	18-48½	30-40	18-30	18-30
Lobiya	...	...	16-44	44	44-54	...	...	...	24	15-50	32	32	30	36½	35	20	20	20
Kodaran	44	44	44-50	44	44-54	44-54	50-54	36	21-23	21-36	20-21	20-21	16-24	22-30	28-41	22-34	18-28	15-28
Kori	40	40	50	24	24-30	24-30	30	20	10	10	8-10	10	10	9-10	9-12½	9-12½	9-12½	10½-18½
Shamākh ...	36	36	50	30	30-36	30	36	20	10	10-20	10	9-10	9-10	9-12½	8½-18	10-16	8-12	11-16½
Gāl	44	44	50	40	40-50	40-50	44-50	26	13	13-28	13	10-13	10-13	11-15	12-23	12-23	14-14½	12-14
Arzan	44	44	50	40	40	40	40	34-36	20	20	20	20	18-28	20-28	14-28	14-28	14-22	14-25
Mandwah ...	48	48	50	40	40	40-52	50-52	34	22-23	22-23	22-23	16-22	18-20½	18-31½	22-31	18-28	14-28	14-28
Indigo	140	140	160	140	140	140	140	136	132	130-136	130-136	136	130-136	140	140	140	140	140
Hemp	80	80	80	80	80	80	80	70-78	70	70-78	70	70	70	70-80	80	80	60-80	60-80
Turiya	80	80	80	...	...	...	...	...	32	32	32	24-32	24-32	20-32	18-32	20-32	20-32	14½-24

Autumn Harvest of the Subah of Oudh (continued). Nineteen years' rates.

	6th and 7th years.	8th year.	9th year.	10th year.	11th year.	12th year.	13th year.	14th year.	15th year.	16th year.	17th year.	18th year.	19th year.	20th year.	21st year.	22nd year.	23rd year.	24th year.
	D.	D.	D.	D.	D.	D.	D.	D.	D.	D.	D.	D.	D.	D.	D.	D.	D.	D.
Turmeric ...	...	...	...	...	...	...	...	...	100	100	100	100	100	100	100	100	100	100
Kachālu ...	...	...	...	...	...	...	...	...	60	70	60	60	60	60	60	60	60	60
Kult ...	...	...	...	...	...	...	...	...	20	36	36	36	36	24	24	24	18	29½
Hinna ...	...	...	...	...	...	...	...	...	58	58	58	58	58	58-70	58-70	60-70	60-70	60-70
Water melons	...	...	...	...	...	...	...	...	10	16-18	10	10	10	10-12	10-12	10-12	10-12	10-12
Pān ...	...	...	...	...	...	...	...	...	180	180	180	180	180	300	200	200	240	240
Singhārah ...	...	...	...	...	...	...	...	...	100	100	100	100	100	100	100	100	100	100
Arhar ...	...	...	...	...	...	...	...	...	...	...	...	...	...	20	20	20	20	20

Spring Harvest of the Subah of Delhi. Nineteen years' rates.

	6th and 7th years.	8th year.	9th year.	10th year.	11th year.	12th year.	13th year.	14th year.	15th year.	16th year.	17th year.	18th year.	19th year.	20th year.	21st year.	22nd year.	23rd year.	24th year.
	D.	D.	D.	D.	D.	D.	D.	D.	D.	D.	D.	D.	D.	D.	D.	D.	D.	D.
Wheat ...	90	84-90	90	44-60	48-56	56	56	50-56	44-57	36-48	37-64	40-48	24-40	31½-50	45-83	36½-82	20-56	65-102
Cabul vetches	...	...	...	...	...	...	...	...	54½	54	54	54	33-58	54	54-57	54½-57	50-57	57-60½
Indian do. ...	70	70-86	80	44-56	40-44	40-50	40-50	30-44	20-30	21-30	21-30	21-40	19-30	19-50	19-24	21-30½	24-38	19-37
Barley ...	80	60-70	60	32-50	32-40	40	40	36	16-37	16-39	20-44	12-37	12-30	12-30	20-34	19-37	26-42	40-72½
Pot-herbs ...	80	80	80	80	80	80	80	70	40-70	40-70	40-60	40-54	40-60	40-60	40-60	40-69	40-60	40-60
Poppy ...	108	108	108	108	140	140	140	130-140	100-130	100-130	100-130	100-130	100-130	100-130	100-130	100-130	100-130	100-130
Safflower ...	½ *man*	½ *man*	½ *man*	80	80	80	80	76-80	60-70	60-70	60-70	50-70	50-70	50-70	54-70	54-70	54-70	54-70
Linseed ...	...	...	80	60-80	60	...	60-70	50	20-30	20-30	20-30	19-30	19-30	19-30	28-70	14½-28	8-19	26-30
Mustard ...	80	80	80	60-70	60	60-70	60-70	48-60	22-30	19-30	27-28	19-26	19-27	19-27	14½-24	19½-30	19½-24	28-48

Spring Harvest of the Subah of Delhi (continued). Nineteen years' rate.

	6th and 7th years.	8th year.	9th year.	10th year.	11th year.	12th year.	13th year	14th year.	15th year.	16th year.	17th year.	18th year.	19th year.	20th year.	21st year.	22nd year.	23rd year.	24t year.
	D.	D.	D.	D.	D.	D.	D.	D.	D.	D.	D.	D.	D.	D.	D.	D.	D.	D.
Adas	60	60-70	50	34-40	34-36	86-40	36-40	26-28	19-24	19-24½	19-28	15-18	15-18	15-18	14-30	16-25	16-25	30-40
Arzan	44	44	20	30	80	80	30	24-28	15-20	15-20	15-20	12-30	12-17	12-17	12½-18	12-18	12-20	16-30
Peas	...	66-70	...	...	...	...	...	...	15-26	15-24	15-30	15-44	15-24	15-24	15-25	17-32	17-24	20-56
Persian Muck Melons	...	...	...	...	...	...	...	120	80-120	80-120	80-120	80-120	80-120	66-130	80-120	80-120	80-120	80-120
Indian ditto ...	10	10	...	...	8-10	8-10	8-10	11-15	11-16	11-16	10½-16	11-16	11-16	10-16	12-16	12-16	12-16	12-16
Kur rice ...	60	60	60	40-60	40-60	60	54	40-54	36-64	34-45	34-48	28-52	24-54	24-54	30-56	30-56	30-56	30-70
Ajwāin	80	80	...	70-80	70-80	70-80	70-80	70	70	70	70	70	70	70	70-73	70-73	70-73	70-73
Onions	...	...	...	...	...	...	...	70-78	70-78	70-73	70-73	70-73	70-73	70-73	70-74	70-74	70-74	70-74
Fenugreek	...	...	...	...	—	...	...	70	70	70	70	70	70	30-70	22-70	30-40	42-60	42-60
Carrots	...	...	...	...	...	...	...	19-24	19-26	19-26	19-24	19-25	22-25	16-25	16-25	16-25	28-40	28-40
Lettuce	...	...	...	...	...	...	...	24-25	24-25	24-25	24-25	25	25	25	25	25	16-18	24-25

Autumn Harvest of the Subah of Delhi. Nineteen years' rate.

	6th and 7th years.	8th year.	9th year.	10th year.	11th year.	12th year.	13th year.	14th year.	15th year.	16th year.	17th year.	18th year.	19th year.	20th year.	21st year.	22nd year.	23rd year.	24th year.
	D.	D.	D.	D.	D.	D.	D.	D.	D.	D.	D.	D.	D.	D.	D.	D.	D.	D.
Sugar-cane (*paunda*)	...	...	...	200	180-200	180-200	do.	do.	do.	do.	do.	do.	do.	do.	do.	do.	do.	do.
Common sugar-cane	180	180	180	106-140	106-140	106-140	106-140	106-140	112-164	104-130	90-134	96-134	90-134	90-106	90-123½	94-104	60-100	80-102
Dark coloured rice *Shāli mushkin* ...	...	...	...	70-80	70-80	70-80	70-72	64	47-57	48-57	47-57	48-57	44-57	64-77	47½-70	47½-77	54-78	42-90
Common rice ...	70	70	70	70	52-60	52-60	52-60	56	44-48	32-45	31-45	30-49	28-50	18-50	32-57	20-58	36-64	34-66
Munji rice ...	...	...	...	...	...	...	...	...	47-65	48-65	43-65	48-65	40-65	50-65	44½-65	43-65	43-65	38-65

Autumn Harvest of the Subah of Delhi—(continued). *Nineteen years' rates.*

	6th & 7th years.	8th year.	9th year.	10th year.	11th year.	12th year.	13th year.	14th year.	15th year.	16th year.	17th year.	18th year.	19th year.	20th year.	21st year.	22nd year.	23rd year.	24th year.
	D.	D.	D.	D.	D.	D.	D.	D.	D.	D.	D.	D.	D.	D.	D.	D.	D.	D.
Cotton	120	120	130	110	110	110	110	90	90	75-90	70-90	60-90	70-90	76-112	88-150	56-120	44-68	45-70
Pot-herbs	80	80	80	80	80	80	80	80	70	70	44-70	54-70	54-70	54-70	54-70	57-60	57-60	57-60
Sesame seed	60	60	80	80	80	80	80	80	60-64	50	32-50	35-80	35-50	21-50	21-43	19½-45	19½-36½	20-36
Moth	48	48	54	36-44	40	40	32	20-22	18-22	18-22	19-21	16-22	19½-22	10-19½	10-18	16-21	19-36	19-36
Māsh	48	48	54	36-44	36-44	44	40	32	26-30	25½-35	26-35	22-32	19-31	22-36	19-29½	16-22	25-44	28-54
Mung	48	48	48	44	44	44	44	44	28-32	28-32	28-32	28-32	22-45	24-40	22-40½	23-36	30-44	30-55
Jowār	50	50	60	40-48	40-48	40-48	40-44	32-34	26	22-26	22-26	22-26	18-26	20-42	19-42	19-42	25-32	26-53
Lahdarah	48	48	50	40-44	36-44	36-44	36-44	28-30	20	20	20	18-20	16-21	19-27	17-22	19-28	18-31	18-44
Lobiya	...	...	...	...	...	...	...	...	20-32	20-32	20-32	20-32	14-23	19-33	20-33	20-33	20-33	20-33
Kodaram	44	44	50	44	40-44	40-44	40	30	20-21	21	21	16-20	14-24	17½-35	17½-36	19½-43	20-39	29-30
Kori	40	40	50	24	24	24	24	16	10	9½	10	10	6-10	4-10	5-10½	5-14	5-12½	10½-15
Shamukh	36	36	50	30	26-30	30-36	26	16-20	10-15	9½-15	9½-15	9½-15	6½-15	6½-11½	5½-12	12-28	7-13	10½-15
Gāl	44	44	50	32-40	32-40	36-40	36-40	34-36	20	20	16-20	16-20	13-20	12-22	8½-21	12½-22	16-25	14½-25
Arzan	44	44	50	32-40	32-40	36-40	36-40	34-36	20	20	16-20	16-20	13-20	12-22	8½-21	10½-22	14-25	14½-25
Mandwah	48	48	50	36-40	36-40	40	40	30-34	22	22	22	16-22	14-22	14½-25	13-22	17½-33	24-35	23-44
Indigo	140	140	160	140	140	140	140	136	120-136	126-132	200-136	124-136	126-136	126-136	134-136	136-150	136-150	130-150
Hemp	80	80	80	80	80	80	80	78	70	67-70	67-70	66-70	66-70	66-70	50-66	66-70	60-80	60-80
Turiya	80	80	80	...	60-80	...	...	...	32	32	32	28-32	32	19½-40	17½-40	30½-38	18½-40	18½-38
Turmeric	...	...	...	...	...	...	...	...	100-120	100	100	100	100	100	100	100	100	100
Kachālu	...	...	...	...	...	...	...	...	70	70	60-70	54-70	54-70	57-60	57-60	57-60	52-60	54-60
Kult	...	...	...	...	...	...	...	...	28	26	26	22	22	28	24	24	20	26
Hinna	...	...	...	...	...	...	...	...	58	58	58	58	58	60-70	60-70	60-70	60-70	60-70
Water-melons	...	...	...	...	...	...	...	...	10	10	10-12	10-12	9½-15	10-12	10-12½	15	10-12½	10-12½

Spring Harvest of the Subah of Lahore—(continued). Nineteen years' rates.

	6th & 7th years.	8th year.	9th year.	10th year.	11th year.	12th year.	13th year.	14th year.	15th year.	16th year.	17th year.	18th year.	19th year.	20th year.	21st year.	22nd yeor.	23rd year.	24th year.
	D.	D.	D.	D.	D.	D.	D.	D.	D.	D.	D.	D.	D.	D.	D.	D.	D.	D.
Wheat	90	80	90	50	56	56	60	60	44-52	48-52	40	24	30	40-43	28-38	44-55	38-64	55-68
Cabul Vetches / Indian ditto ...	... / 80	... / 70	... / 80	... / 48	... / 48	... / 48	... / 50	... / 50	43½-53*	D. J- 57½-3½	D. J. d●.	D. J. 57-16	D. J. 57½-3½	57	D. J. 57½-3½	D. J. 57-3½	57½-63	do.
Barley	70	70	60	40	40	40	40	40	26-30	32-33	25	16	20	24½-28	16-21	28-34	28-34	40-53
Potherbs	80	80	80	80	80	80	80	80	26-34	32-36	24	12	21	22-27	18-24	26-40	30-51	40-51
Poppy	160	160	160	...	...	...	...	130	60-70	50-60	60	50	50	54	54	54	54-74	54-74
Safflower	½ man	do.	do	80	80	80	80	80	120	100	100	100	104	104	104	104	104	104
Linseed	...	...	50	60	60	60	50	50	76	70	60	60	70	64	64	64	64	64
Mustard	80	80	80	60	60	60	60	60	28-30	28-30	25	19	24	20-23	14-23	15-30	16-30	25-40
Adas	60	60	50	36	36	36	40	40	28-30	25	19	30	22-23	16-23	18-28	18-28	20-26	30-42
Arzan	44	44	20	30	30	30	30	24	27-28	24-27	20	12	16	12½-19	13-16½	19-26	26-42	29-42
Peas	...	...	...	...	...	...	...	...	19-22	20-22	16	13	20	16-18	7½-10½	7½-14	12-20	18-24
Persian Muskmelons	...	...	...	...	...	...	...	...	15	15	19-28	28-36	15	19-23	19	19-28	19-30	28-36
Indian ditto ...	10	10	...	...	8	8	12-24	12-24	50-100	120	120	120	120	80	66	86	86	86
Kur rice	60	60	60	54	54	60	54	40-44	13	13	13	15	15	11-12	12	12	12	12
Ajwāin	80	80	80	80	80	80	70	70	40-44	24	24	27	27	26-27	26-27	34-40	36-50	36-50
Onions	...	...	...	...	...	...	...	...	70	70	70	70	70	70-74	70-76	70-76	73-74	73-74
Fenugreek	...	...	...	...	...	...	...	...	73	73	73	73	73	70-74	70-74	70-74	70-74	70-74
Carrots	½ man	½ man	½ man	...	...	...	...	...	70	70	70	70	70	42-54	20-74	20-32	30-64	40-64
Lettuce	...	...	...	...	...	...	...	...	24	24	24	24	20-21	20-21	20-21	20-21	18-26	21-32
									25	25	25	25	21	21	18½	18½	16-20	25-50

* D stands for *Dām* and J for *Jetal*. In these six columns, the J applies only to the Cabul Vetches and not to the following figures.

Autumn Harvest of the Subah of Lahore. Nineteen years' rates.

	6th & 7th years.	8th year.	9th year.	10th year.	11th year.	12th year.	18th year.	14th year.	15th year.	16th year.	17th year.	18th year.	19th year.	20th year.	21st year.	22nd year.	23rd year.	24th year.
	D.	D.	D.	D.	D.	D.	D.	D.	D.	D.	D.	D.	D.	D.	D.	D.	D.	D.
Sugarcane (*paunda*) ...	...	...	200	200	200	200	200	200	200	200	200	200	200	200	200	200	200	200
Common sugarcane ...	180	180	180	160	160	160	160	150	100-120	100-120	100-120	100-120	117½-120	40-107½	94-131	94-130	70-130	105-130
Dark coloured rice (*Shāli Mushkin*) ...	...	...	...	80	80	80	80	60	60	46	46	42	40	50-60	40½-62	44-60	43-60	60-75
Common rice ...	80	70	70	60	60	60	60	44	45-50	36-40	36-40	32-36	26-32	32½-42½	22-32½	24-38	30-48	45-56
Munji do. ...	...	...	...	...	...	...	...	...	65	65	65	65	65	50	50	43-50	30-56	50-52
Cotton	120	120	130	110	110	110	110	99	120	96-104	70	64	80	90-95½	90-120	80-160	44-70	55-68
Pot-herbs	80	80	80	80	80	80	80	80	76	70	60-70	50-60	50-60	60-70	60-70	60-70	60-70	60-70
Sesame seed	60	60	80	70	70	70	80	64	50-58	48	40	36	36	25-40	22-28	18-26	20-34	32-40
Moth	48	48	54	44	44	44	46	30	36	28-30	30-38	24-25	20-21	20-21	18½-23	12-17	10½-17	14-28
Māsh	48	48	54	44	44	44	46	36	30-28	36-50	24-25	24-25	34	20-26	18-32	22-60	39-50	39-50
Mung	48	48	48	44	44	44	44	30	28-30	26-28	20-28	24-26	21	23	15-20	18½-23	16-24	26-34
Jowār	50	50	60	48	48	48	44	32	30-32	32	32-36	25-27	25	38½	24½-30	23-30	18-40	40-60
Lahdarah	48	48	50	44	44	44	44	30	30-32	26-28	20-28	24-26	21	23	15-23	15½-23	16-24	26-34
Lobiya	...	...	...	...	...	...	...	...	30	30	30	30	30	23	14-23	12½-27	20-30	24-28
Kodaram	44	44	50	44	44	44	44	30	30-32	32	30-32	30	26	24-30	18½-28	18½-28	18½-28	26-44
Kori	40	40	50	24	24	24	24	16	16	10	10	10	5	10	5-12	6½-10	8-12	5-14½
Shamākh	36	36	50	30	30	30	30	16	16	10	10	10	7	7-10½	7-10	8-10	9-12	12-18
Gāl	44	44	50	40	40	40	40	20	18-20	17	16-17	12-14	13-14½	7½-15½	8½-11½	10-14	10-14½	12½-20
Arzan	44	44	50	40	40	40	40	36	18-20	20-24	20-24	16-20	14-18	16-21½	6½-15	8-15	10-20	15-20
Mandwah	48	48	50	40	40	40	40	30	28-30	26-28	26-28	26-28	22-26	21	25	18-25	20-26	26-36½
Indigo	140	140	160	140	140	140	140	136	136	136	136	120	120	130-134	130-134	134	134	134
Hemp	80	80	80	80	80	80	80	78	78	78	78	70	70	72	...	60-80	60-80	60-80
Turiya	80	80	80	...	...	...	...	...	32	32	32	32	34	34	34	34	29-34	23-34
Turmeric	...	...	...	...	...	...	...	...	120	120	120	104	104	104	104	104	104	104
Kachālu	...	...	...	...	...	...	...	...	76	70	70	60	60	68-70	70	68-70	68-70	28-70
Kult	...	...	...	...	...	...	...	...	28	26	26	22	22	24-28	24	24	48	26-32
Hinna	...	...	...	...	...	...	...	...	58	58	58	68-71	67-70	67-70	67-70	67-70	67-70	67-70
Water melons ...	...	...	...	...	...	...	...	...	10	10	10	10	10	11	11	11	11	11
Pān	...	...	...	...	...	...	...	...	...	...	...	...	...	...	...	223-5 D. J. to 263	...	...

Spring Harvest of the Subah of the Multān. Ninteen years' rates.

	6th and 7th years.	8th year.	9th year.	10th year.	11th year.	12th year.	13th year.	14th year.	15th year.	16th year.	17th year.	18th year.	19th year.	20th year.	21st year.	22nd year.	23rd year.	24th year.
	D.	D.	D.	D.	D.	D.	D.	D.	D.	D.	D.	D.	D.	D.	D.	D.	D.	D.
Wheat	...	...	...	...	...	...	...	...	52	52	36	24	30	36-60	21½-40	...	40-52	46-64
Kabul Vetches	...	...	...	...	...	...	...	...	57-16 D. J.	ditto	ditto	ditto	ditto	ditto	ditto	ditto	ditto	ditto
Indian ditto	...	...	...	...	...	...	...	...	30	32	23-25	16	20	21½-40	13½-40	20½-40	20-48	26-48
Barley	...	...	...	...	...	...	...	...	34	36	22	12	21	20½-40	16-40	20½-40	20-48	26-48
Potherbs	...	...	...	...	...	...	...	...	70	60	56-60	50	50	53-60	44-50	34-40	52-60	52-60
Poppy	...	...	...	...	...	...	...	...	130	130	100	100	100	60-104	60-104	60-104	60-104	60-104
Safflower	...	...	...	...	...	...	...	...	76	70	60	60	70	60-64	40-64	64-70	64-70	60-70
Linseed	...	...	...	...	...	...	...	...	30	30	20	19	24	24	23	23	16-30	28-30
Mustard	...	...	...	...	...	...	...	...	30	30	25	19	30	18-60	15½-40	14½-28	20-36	36
A'das	...	...	...	...	...	...	...	...	28	28	19	12	16	6-20½	12½-40	18½-40	10-42	27-42
Arzan	...	...	...	...	...	...	...	...	22	22	16	13	20	16-37	18½-40	10-16	13-20	17-24
Peas	...	...	...	...	...	...	...	...	15	15	19-20	26-30	15½	19	19	18½	9-22	26-30
Persian Muskmelons ...	...	...	...	...	...	...	...	...	120	120	120	82	66	60-80	86	86	86	86
Indian ditto ...	...	...	...	...	...	...	...	...	13	13	13	11	11	12-19	12-40	11-12	11-16	12
Kur rice	...	...	...	...	...	...	...	...	44	44	44	44	27	26	28-36	40	40	40
Ajwāin	...	...	...	...	...	...	...	...	73	70	70	70	70	64-70	44-70	52-74	56-74	44-60
Onions	...	...	...	...	...	...	...	...	70	70	70	70	70	60-74	40-74	52-74	56-74	44-60
Fenugreek	...	...	...	...	...	...	...	...	72	70	70	70	70	60	35-40	14½-52	40-70	40-70½
Carrots	...	...	...	...	...	...	...	...	24	24	24	24	20-21	20-21	20-21	20	16	24-26
Lettuce	...	...	...	...	...	...	...	...	25	25	25	25	21	20	18½	18½	20	25

Autumn Harvest of the Subah of Multān. Nineteen years' rates.

	6th & 7th years.	8th year.	9th year.	10th year.	11th year.	12th year.	13th year.	14th year.	15th year.	16th year.	17th year.	18th year.	19th year.	20th year.	21st year.	22nd year.	23rd year.	24th year.
	D.	D.	D.	D.	D.	D.	D.	D.	D.	D.	D.	D.	D.	D.	D.	D.	D.	D.
Sugarcane (*paunda*) ...	...	...	...	...	...	...	...	...	200	200	200	200	200	200	200	200	200	200
Common sugarcane ...	...	...	...	...	...	...	...	...	150	120	100-120	100-120	100-120	100-120	100	100-110	70-100	100
Dark coloured rice ...	...	...	...	...	...	...	...	...	60	46	46	40	40	*60	45-62	45-62	54-62	65-72
Common rice	...	...	...	...	...	...	...	...	50	40	40	32	32	48½-48	28-40	28-40	32½-40	38-48
Munji do.	...	...	...	...	...	...	...	...	65	65	65	65	65	50	50	50	56	52
Cotton	...	...	...	...	...	...	...	...	120	104	70	64	80	70-96	40-95½	70-76	44-90	56-90
Potherbs	...	...	...	...	...	...	...	...	76	70	60-70	60	50	40-76	40-70	70	60-70	60-70
Sesame seed	...	...	...	...	...	...	...	...	58	48	40	36	36	40-48	19½-40	24-26	20-26	26-40
Moth	...	...	...	...	...	...	...	...	31	25	25	21	20	23-40	13-40	13-40	14-18	24-26
Māsh	...	...	...	...	...	...	...	...	36	30	30	25	24-25	34-48	18-40	20-32	20-26	26-40
Mung	...	...	...	...	...	...	...	...	32	32	32	32	27	34-48	34-40	26-36	32-23	32-50
Jowār	...	...	...	...	...	...	...	...	39	32	32	27	25	39-48	15½-40	24-26	25-32	32-48
Lahdarah	...	...	...	...	...	...	...	...	30	28	28	26	21	23-48	23-40	13	16	26-30
Lobiya	...	...	...	...	—	...	...	...	32	32	32	32	25	23-36	22-40	26-27½	22-26	26-38
Kodaram	...	...	...	...	...	...	...	...	32	32	32	32	32	23-36	22-40	26-27½	22-26	26-38
Kori	...	...	...	...	...	...	...	...	32	32	32	32	26	24-30	18½-30	18⅓-30	16	26—
Shamākh	...	...	...	...	...	...	...	...	18	10	16	10	5	10-16	9-10	9-10	10-12	5-12½

* Gladwin has 46½ but the text has no variant.

Autumn Harvest of the Subah of Multān—(continued). Nineteen years' rates.

	6th & 7th years.	8th year.	9th year.	10th year.	11th year.	12th year.	13th year.	14th year.	15th year.	16th year.	17th year.	18th year.	19th year.	20th year.	21st year.	22ad year.	23rd year.	24th year.
	D.	D.	D.	D.	D.	D.	D.	D.	D.	D.	D.	D.	D.	D.	D.	D.	D.	D.
Gāl	...	...	...	...	...	...	...	...	16	10	10	10	7	10-12½	9-10	9-10	8-10½	12-12½
Arzan	...	...	...	...	...	...	...	...	20	24	24	24	14	20½-48	20½-40	10-21	10-20	15-20
Mandwah	...	...	...	...	...	...	...	...	30	28	28	24	21	25	25	25	18-25	26-30
Indigo	...	...	...	...	...	...	...	...	136	136	136	120	120	130-134	134	134	134	134
Hemp	...	...	...	...	...	...	...	...	78	78	78	70	70	48-72	48-72	48-72	60-70	70-82
Turiya	...	...	...	...	...	...	...	...	32	32	32	32	32	34	34	34	24-34	23-34
Turmeric	...	...	...	...	...	...	...	...	120	120	120	104	104	104	104	104	104	104
Kāchālu	...	...	...	...	...	...	...	...	76	70	70	60	60	68-70	68-70	68-70	70	70
Kult	...	...	...	...	...	...	...	...	28	26	26	22	22	28	24	24	24	24-30
Hinna	...	...	...	...	...	...	...	...	58	58	58	58	58	48-70	40-70	70	70	70
Water melons ...	...	...	...	...	...	...	...	...	10	10	10	10	10	11	11	11	11	11
Pān	...	...	...	...	...	...	...	...	180	6¼ Rp.	do.	do.	do.	300	200	200	200	200
Singhārah	...	...	...	...	...	...	...	...	100	100	100	100	100	100	100	100	100	100
Arhar	...	...	...	...	...	...	...	...	...	...	...	...	...	20	20	20	20	20

Spring Harvest of the Subah of Mālwah. Nineteen years' rates.

	6th & 7th years.	8th year.	9th year.	10th year.	11th year.	12th year.	13th year.	14th year.	15th year.	16th year.	17th year.	18th year.	19th year.	20th year.	21st year.	22nd year.	23rd year.	24th year.
	D.	D.	D.	D.	D.	D.	D,	D.										
Wheat	50	50	50	50	50	50	50	50	Muzaffairs[1] 2 to 50	do.	do.	do.	do.	1$\frac{3}{4}$M to 43$\frac{1}{2}$	do.	do.	do.	do.
Cabul Vetches ...	...	...	...	...	...	...	...	...	1$\frac{3}{4}$M to 48$\frac{1}{2}$	do.	do.	do.	do.	do.	do.	do.	do.	do.
Indian do. ...	50	50 (Indian do. and Barley)	50	50	50	50	50	50	2M to 50D	do.	do.	do.	do.	1$\frac{3}{4}$M to 43$\frac{1}{2}$	do.	do.	do.	do.
Barley	70	...	...	...	...	...	...	...										
Pot-herbs ...	75	75	75	75	75	75	75	75										
Poppy	50	50	50	50	50	50	50	50		3	Muzaffaris to 75 dams.							
Safflower ...	...	...	...	...	...	...	...	...										
Linseed ...	50	50	50	50	50	50	50	50										
Mustard ...	...	...	...	...	...	...	...	...										
Adas and *Arzan*	50	50	50	50	50	50	50	50										
Peas ...	...	...	...	...	...	...	...	...		2	Muzaffaris to 50.							
Persian muskmelons	...	...	...	...	...	...	...	...										
Indian do. ...	10	10	10	10	50	50	50	50										
Kur rice ...	60	60	60	54	54	60	54-70	56										
Ajwāin ...	80	80	30	80	80	80	80	80		3	Muzaffaris to 75.							
Onions, Fenugreek										2	Muzaffaris to 50.							
Carrots, lettuce ...	...	...	...	...	...	...	...	...										

[1] See Vol. I, p. 23. There were three Sovereigns of Gujarāt of the name of Muzaffar: the 1st reigned A.H. 799 (A.D. 1396): the 2nd in A.H. 917 (A.D. 1511): the 3rd in 969 (A.D. 1561). The last named abdicated in favour of Akbar in 980 (A.D. 1572), but in 991, he collected a force, defeated Akbar's general and re-ascended the throne. His second reign was brief and the kingdom became a province of the Empire. Mālwah was united to Gujarāt under Bahādur a king of the latter dynasty A.H. 937, (A.D. 1530). I take these details from Mr. Oliver's note on the the coins of the Muhammadan kings of Gujarāt. In the list of coins there are two of copper of Muzaffar Shāh II, of 169 and 160 grains respectively, and three of silver of Muhammad Shāh III, of 73 and 175 grains. The latter, No. XXXI, of the Catalogue, is remarkable as having been struck during the second brief accession of this monarch to power. See also History of Gujarāt, Bayley, Index, Muzaffar.

Autumn Harvest of the Subah of Mālwah. Nineteen years' rates.

	6th & 7th years.	8th year.	9th year.	10th year.	11th year.	12th year.	13th year.	14th year.	15th year.	16th year.	17th year.	18th year.	19th year.	20th year.	21st year.	22nd year.	23rd year.	24th year.
	D.	D.	D.	D.	D.	D.	D.	D.	M. D.	D.	D.	D.	D.	M. D.	D.	D.	D.	D.
Sugarcane (*paunda*) ...	...	...	...	...	150	150	150	150	6-150	do.	do.	do.	do.	7 to 75	do.	do.	do.	do.
Common Sugarcane ...	150	do.	do.	do.	do.	do.	do.	do.	6-150	do.	do.	do.	do.	M. 7 to 75	do.	do.	do.	do.
Dark coloured rice ...	...	...	...	62½	do.	do.	do.	do.	2½-62½	do.	do.	do.	do.	M. 3 to 75	do.	do.	do.	do.
Common rice ...	50	do.	do.	do.	do.	do.	do.	do.	2-50	do.	do.	do.	do.	M. 1 to 48½	do.	do.	do.	do.
Munji ,, ...	...	...	...	...	...	...	...	...	2-50	do.	do.	do.	do.	do.	do.	M. 1-43½	do.	do.
Cotton	50	do.	do.	do.	do.	do.	do.	do.	2-50	do.	do.	do.	do.	M. 2½-62½	do.	do.	do.	do.
Pot-herbs	75	do.	do.	do.	do.	do.	do.	do.	3-75	do.	do.	do.	do.	do.	do.	do.	do.	do.
Sesame seed																		
Moth																		
Māash																		
Peas																		
Jowār																		
Lahdarah																		
Lobiya	50	do.	do.	do.	do.	do.	do.	do.	do.	do.	do.	do.	do.	M. D. 1-48½	do.	do.	do.	do.
Kodaram																		
Kori																		
Shamākh																		
Gāl																		
Arzan																		
Mandwāh																		
Indigo	150	do.	do.	do.	do.	do.	do.	do.	M. D. 6-150	do.	do.	do.						
Hemp	50	do.	do.	do.	do.	do.	do.	do.	2-50	do.	do.	do.						
Turiya	50	do.	do.	do.	do.	do.	do.	do.	2-50	do.	do.	do.						

AIN 15.

The Ten Years' Settlement.

From the beginning of this immortal reign, persons of intelligence and void of rapacity, together with zealous men of experience, have been annually engaged in noting the current prices and reporting them to His Majesty, and taking the gross produce and estimating its value, they determined the rates of collection, but this mode was attended with considerable inconvenience. When Khwajah Abdul Majid Āsaf Khan was raised to the dignity of Prime Minister, the total revenue was taken at an estimation, and the assignments were increased as the caprice of the moment suggested. And because at that time the extent of the empire was small, and there was a constant increase of dignities among the servants of the State, the variations were contingent on the extent of corruption and self-interest. When this great office devolved on Muzaffar Khān and Rajah Todar Mull, in the 15th year of the reign, a re-distribution of the imperial assessment was made through the *qanungos*, and estimating the produce of the lands, they made a fresh settlement. Ten *qanungos* were appointed who collected the accounts from the provincial *qanungos* and lodged them in the imperial exchequer. Although this settlement was somewhat less than the preceding one, nevertheless there had been formerly a wide discrepancy between the estimate and the receipts.

When through the prudent management of the Sovereign the empire was enlarged in extent, it became difficult to ascertain each year the prices current and much inconvenience was caused by the delay. On the one hand the husbandman complained of extensive exactions, and on the other the holder of assigned lands was aggrieved on account of the revenue balances. His Majesty devised a remedy for these evils and in the discernment of his world-adorning mind fixed a settlement for ten years : the people were thus made contented and their gratitude was abundantly manifested. From the beginning of the 15th year of the Divine era to the 24th, an aggregate of the rates of collection was formed and a tenth of the total was fixed as the annual assessment ; but from the 20th to the 24th year the collections were accurately determined and the five former ones accepted on the authority of persons of probity.

The best crops were taken into account in each year and the year of the most abundant harvest accepted, as the table shows.

(A Note on *Dastur-ul-'aml* : *Sarkar*, &c.)

For a full description and discussion of the official manuals called *Dastur-ul-'aml,* see J. Sarkar's *Mughal Administration* 3rd. ed., ch. XIV. § 2.

Sir Henry Elliot writes, in his *Supplemental Glossary,* revised ed. by J. Beames, entitled *Memoirs of the History* &c. of *N.W.P.* (1869), :—"*Dastur-ul-aml,* a body of instructions, and tables for the use of revenue officers under the Native Government. . . . No two copies can ever be found which correspond with each other, and in most respects they widely differ. Those which profess to be copied from the *Dastur-ul-'aml* of Akbar, are found to contain on close examination sundry interpolations of subsequent periods.

"Besides the *Dastur-ul-'aml,* another book, called the *'Aml Dastur,* was kept by the Qanungoes, in which were recorded all orders which were issued in supersession of *Dastur-ul-'aml.*" (ii. 156-157.)

"A *Sarkār* is a subdivision of a *subah.* Each *subah* is divided into a certain number of *sarkārs,* and each *sarkār* into *parganahs* or *mahals* (which are used as equivalent expressions), and the parganahs again are aggregated into *Dasturs* or districts. . . .

"*Dastur* besides signifying a rule, is also a minister, a munshi. *Parganah* means tax-paying land; the *Burhan-i-Qati'* gives the meaning *Zamine ke āz ān māl wa kharāj bagirand.* . . .

"The words used before Akbar's time to represent tracts of country larger than a *parganah* were *shiqq, Khita, 'arsa diyār, vilāyat,* and *iqta',* but the latter (term) was generally applied when the land was assigned for the support of the nobility or their contingents." (See *Ikta'* in *Encyclopaedia of Islam,* ii. 461, for a fuller treatment. J.S.)

"I have endeavoured to restore the *sarkars, dasturs,* and *parganahs* (in the N. W. Provinces of Allahabad and Agra) as they stood in the time of the Emperor Akbar. The copies of the *Ain-i-Akbari* vary so much, and such ignorance is frequently exhibited by the transcribers, that to verify the names of *parganahs* has been a work of great labour. . . . .

"But it is in separating the *sarkārs* into *dasturs* that the ignorance of the copyists has been chiefly exhibited, for all the *parganahs* are frequently mixed together, as if there were no meaning at all attached to *dastur.*" (ii. 201-203.)

The word *dastur* in the sense of a subdivision of land for revenue purposes, went out of use in the official histories of the Mughal empire after Akbar's time. It may have lingered on in the N.W. Provinces up to the Mutiny, but only in the village records, as it does not occur in any history or revenue-manual of the Central Government of the later Mughals known to me. (*Jadunath Sarkar.*)

The *Subah* of *Allahabad* comprises nine *sarkārs* (districts) and possesses fifteen separate revenue codes. (*dastur-ul-'aml.*)

1. The *Sarkār* of *Allahabad* includes fifteen mahals and has three revenue codes.

The suburban district of Allahabad comprises three mahals, *viz.*, the suburbs of *Allahabad, Kantit,* and a tract on the extreme limits of the *subah* of Agra, and possesses one revenue code.

Jalālābād [*i.e.*, Arail] has three mahals and a revenue code.

Bhadoi, seven mahals, *viz., Bhadoi, Sikandarpur, Sorāon, Singror, Mah, Kewāi, Hādiābās* [=Jhusi]—and a revenue code.

2. The *Sarkār* of *Benāres* has eight mahals and a revenue code. The detail is as follows—the suburban district of *Benares,* the township of *Benares, Pandrah, Kaswār, Harhwā, Byālisi.*

3. The *Sarkār* of *Jaunpur* has 41 mahals and two codes.

The suburban district of *Jaunpur,* 39 mahals, one code, *viz.* :—

Aldimao, 'Angli, Bhileri, Bhadāon, Talhani, Jaunpur, Suburban Jaunpur, Chandipur Badhar, Chāndah, Chiriyā Kot, Chakesar, Kharid, Khāspur Tāndah, Khānpur, Deogaon, Rāri, Sanjholi, Sinkandarpur, Sagdi, Sarharpur, Shādi-ābād, Zafarābād, Karyāt Mittu, Karyāt Dostpur, Karyāt-Mendia, Karyāt Swetah, Gheswah, Ghosi, Kodiya, Gopālpur, Karākat, Mandiāho, Muhammad-ābād, Majhorā, Mau, Nizāmābād, Naigun, Nathupur.

4. The *Sarkār of Chanādah* [=Chunār], 14 mahals and one revenue code, *viz.*, the suburban district of *Chanadah, Aherwārah, Bholi, Badhol, Tāndah, Dhos, Rāghupur*[110]—the villages on the western bank of the river, *Majhwārah, Mahāech, Mahwāri, Mahoi, Silpur, Naran.*

5. The *Sarkār* of *Ghāzipur,* 18 mahals, one code, *viz.*, the suburban district of *Ghāzipur, Baliā, Pachotar, Balhābās, Bhariābād, Barāich, Chausā Dehma, Sayyidpur Namdi, Zahurābād, Karyāt Pali, Kopā Chhit, Gadhā, Karandah, Lakhnesar, Madan Benāras, Muhammadābād, Parhābāri.*

6. The *Sarkār* of *Karrah,* 12 mahals, one code, *viz.*, the township of *Karrah,* its suburban district, *Aichhi, Atharban, Ayāsā, Rāri, Karāri, Kotla, Kaunra* commonly called *Karson, Fatehpur Hanswah, Hatgāon, Hanswah.*

7. The *Sarkār* of *Korah,* 8 mahals, 3 codes, *viz.*, thus detailed. The suburban district of *Korah* has one code and 2 mahals, *viz.*, itself and *Ghātampur; Kotiā,* 3 mahals, *Kotiā, Goner, Keranpur Kinār,*[111] and one code ; *Jajmau,* 3 mahals, *viz.*, *Jājmau, Muhsinpur, Majhāon,* and one code.

8. The *Sarkār* of *Kālinjar,* 10 mahals, one code, *viz.*, *Kālinjar* with its suburbs, *Ugāsi, Ajigarh, Sihonda, Simoni, Shādipur, Rasan, Khandeh, Mahobā, Maudhā.*

9. The *Sarkār* of *Mānikpur,* 14 mahals, 2 codes. The suburbs of *Mānikpur* have 10 mahals and one code, *viz.*, *Mānikpur* together with its suburban district, *Arwal Bhalol, Salon, Jalālpur Balkhar, Karyāt Karārah, Karyāt Paegāh, Khatot, Nāsirābād.*

Rāe Bareli, etc., 4 mahals, one code, *viz.*, *Rāe Bareli, Talhandi, Jāes, Dalmau.*

---

[110] A note to the text gives *Rālhupūr* as the present name of this mahal—the other names have nearly all variants in the MSS., no doubt due as much to dialectic variations in pronunciation as to errors of copyists. Tieffenthaler adds to the above, the fortress of *Tschinarghar* (Chanār) built of stone, on an eminence on the western bank of the Ganges.

[111] Thus in all MSS. but Elliot has *Kiratpur Kananda,*

Spring Harvest of the Subah of Allahabad—Ten Years' rates.

	Suburban district of Allahabad. 3 Mahals.	Jalālābās, &c. 5 Mahals.	Bhaḍoi, &c. 7 Mahals.	Sarkār of Benāres 8 Mahals.	Suburban district of Jaunpur. 39 Mahals.	Parganah of Mongrah, &c. 2 Mahals.	Sarkār of Chanāḍah 14 Mahals.	Ghāzipur, &c. 18 Mahals.	Parganah of Karrah 12 Mahals.	Parganah of Korah. 2 Mahals.	Parganah of Kotia. 3 Mahals.	Jājmau, &c. 3 Mahals.	Sarkār of Kālinjar. 10 Mahals.	Sarkār of Mānikpur. 10 Mahals.	Rāe Bareli. 4 Mahals.
	D. J.	D. J.	D. J.	D. J.	D. J.	D. J.	D. J.	D. J.	D. J.	D. J.	D. J-	D. J.	D. J.	D. J.	D. J.
Wheat	60-9	58-4	64-21	64-1	64-1	58-4	64-21	64-21	60-3	69-18	60-3	60-23	63-15	58-4	62-15
Cabul Vetches	...	......	...	71-14	71-14	...	71-14	71-14	...	55-23	...	...	55-23	...	71-14
Indian do.	38-0	39-3	...	41-9	41-9	39-3	41-9	41-9	38-0	34-17	38-0	37-0	34-17	39-3	39-3
Barley ... ... }	40-6	40-12	...	48.2	67-2	40-12	47-2	47-2	...	40-6	40-6	40-6	40-6	42-12	45-21
Green barley not in ear }				67-3			68-2	68-2							67-2
Adas	24-15	23-12	...	38-0	38-0	23-12	38-0	38-0	24-15	24-15	24-15	25-16	24-15	23-14	35-8
Safflower	83-15	83-21	...	70-3	70-3	83-21	70-3	83-3	83-21	70-17	83-21	69-22	72-17	83-21	82-3
Poppy	150-13	150-13	...	115-20	115-20	156-13	115-20	115-20	156-13	127-15	153-13	128-0	55-23	156-18	115-8
Potherbs	27-2	28-5	...	80-13	80-13	67-5	82-13	80-13	67-2	55-23	67.20	21½-0	30-15	68-5	76-1
Linseed	31-8	27-4	...	40-6	40-6	32-15	40-6	40-6	31-8	32-15	31-20	30-5	32-15	32-15	35-8
Mustard	35-8	28-4	...	40-6	40-6	27-24	40-6	40-6	35-8	32.15	35-8	31-21½	20-3	38-21	38-21
Arzan	20-3	15-19	...	6-21	26-21	16-19	26-21	26-21	20.3	20-3	20-3	20-3	20-2	16-19	24-15
Peas (*Mashang*)	24-15	29-2	...	40-6	40-6	29-2	40-6	40-6	24-15	22-6	24-0	20-2	26-21	29-2	38-0
Carrots	25-18	26-21	...	26-21	26-21	16-21	26-21	26-21	25-18	32-21	25-18	31-21	70-18	26-21	26-21
Onions	83-21	79-2	...	80-13	80-13	79-10	80-13	80-13	83.21	82-18	83-21	82-18	...	84-10	80-93
Fenugreek	74-23	87-4	...	54-29	54-24	54-24	54-24	54-24	74-23	...	74-23	82-18	109-14	58-4	54-20
Persian muskmelons	144-6	150-13	...	134-4	134-11	150-1	134-4	134-4	144-6	109-14	144-6	119-16	115-16	150-1	134-4
Indian ditto	19-0	7-22	...	14-14	14-14	17-20	14-14	14-14	19-0	15-16	19-0	14-13	...	17-7	14-13
Cumin seed	...	61-12	...	83-15	89-15	61-12	89-15	89-15	...	82-18	...	...	82-18	61-12	89-15
Coriander seed	...	...	...	105-2	105-2	...	105-2	105-2	...	...	...	...	...	...	105-2
Kur rice	52-14	56-24	...	56-24	46-24	46-24	46-24	46-24	52-14	50-20	52-14	46-24	50-20	46-24	46-24
Ajwān	83-21	79-10	...	89-15	89-15	89-15	89-15	89-15	83-4	86-15	83-21	83-21	86-2	83-10	97-7

* In these tables, *D* **stands for** ***dām*** and *J* for *jetal,* the 25th part of a *dām* which is the 40th part of a rupee.

Autumn Harvest of the Subah of Allahabad.

	Sub-District of Allahabad.	Jalālābās.	Bhadoi.	Sarkār of Benāres.	Sub-District of Jaunpur.	Parganah of Mongrah.	Sarkār of Chanādah.	Ghāzipur.	Parganah of Karrah	Parganah of Korarah.	Parganah of Kotia.	Jājmau.	Sarkār of Kālinjar.	Sarkār of Mānikpur.	Rāe Bareli.
	D. J.	D. J.	D. J.	D. J.	D. J.	D. J.	D. J.	D. J.	D. J.	D. J.	D. J.	D. J.	D. J.	D. J.	D. J.
Sugarcane (*paundah*)	240-9	...	230-20	208-15	223-15	234-20	223-15	223-15	240-3	223-15	240-9	231-15	223-15	232-20	223-15
Common Sugarcane	...	...	126-9	123-0	123 0	126-9	123-9	123-0	109-17	143-3	103-17	143-3	143-17	126-6	123-0
Dark coloured rice	71-14	...	71-14	71-14	71-14	71-14	71-14	71-14	81-14	67-2	81-14	73-20	67-2	71-14	71-14
Common rice	44-18	...	42-12	49-5	49-5	43-12	49-5	49-5	44-18	46-24	44-28	43-24	46-24	42-12	46-24
Āl (morinda citrifolia, from which a red dye is extracted) ...	...	...	...	...	...	...	...	...	...	205-18	[illegible]	205-18	...	...	...
Cotton	89-15	...	91-18	96-4	96-4	91-17	96-4	96-4	89-15	91-18	89-0	93-3	91-18	91-18	93-23
Moth	25-18	...	26-21	33-14	33-14	26-21	33-14	33-14	25-18	24-15	25-18	22-23	14-11	26-21	31-8
Arzan	23-12	...	18-24	26-21	26-21	17-22	32-21	26-21	23-12	24-15	23-16	26-21	24-15	17-20	24-18
Indigo	163-6	...	162-3	162-3	162-3	162-3	162-3	162-3	163-5	163-6	163-6	163-6	163-6	162-6	162-6
Hinna	76-0	...	89-15	89-15	89.15	89-15	89-15	89-15	76-0	79-20	86-0	86-1	69-20	83-15	89-15
Hemp	84-24	...	84-24	84-24	84-24	84-24	84-24	84-24	84-24	89-24	84-24	84-24	89-15	84-4	84-24
Potherbs	80-0	...	87-5	83-15	83-15	87-5	89-15	89-15	82-17	84-23	82-18	87-7	84-20	87-5	87-0
Pān	210-0	...	244-21	268-20	268-20	244-21	268-14	268-14	210-3	267-20	210-4	268-20	267-20	267-20	267-20
Singhārah	120-18	...	115-2	115-20	115-20	115-20	115-20	115-20	120-18	120-20	115-20	115-20	115-20	115.20	115-20
Jawāri, (Jawār)	34-17	...	35-20	40-6	40-6	35-20	40-6	40-6	34-4	33-7	34-17	32-15	37-7	35-8	38-0
Kuri (a kind of wild grain) ...	...	...	...	13-15	13-15	...	13-15	15-15	...	13-15	...	...	18-15	...	13-15
Persian muskmelons	...	...	...	105-2	105-2	...	205-2	105-2	...	...	...	...	...	...	105-2
Sesame seed	40-0	...	43-15	44-18	44-15	44-18	44-18	42-12	42-12	42-12	41-9	101-9	43-15	43-15	43-15
Mung	42-12	...	48-2	49-5	49-5	48-5	49-5	49-5	42-12	42-6	42-12	41-9	40-6	48-2	48-2
Turmeric	...	...	...	115-20	115-20	...	115-20	115-20	...	...	...	...	...	...	...

The Subah of *Oudh* comprises five *sarkārs* and possesses twelve codes.

1. The *Sarkār* of *Oudh*, 21 mahals, 3 codes. The suburban district has 19 mahals and one code. Two parganahs are comprised in Khairābād. They are as follows:

Oudh with its suburban district; *Anbodha, Anhonah, Pachhamrāth, Bilehri, Basodhi, Thānah Bhadāon, Bakthā, Daryābād, Rudauli, Selak, Sultānpur, Sātanpur, Supahah, Sarwāpāli, Satrakah, Gawārchah, Manglasi Naipur.*

Ibrahimābad and Kishni are each a parganah with one code.

2. The *Sarkār* of *Bharāitch* has 11 mahals, one code. The suburban district of *Bharāitch,* &c. 8 mahals, one code. *Bharāitch* with its suburbs 6 mahals, *Bahrah, Husampur, Wankdun, Rajhāt, Sanjhauli, Fakhrpur,* Fort *Nawāgarh.*

Firuzābād, &c., two parganahs, one code, *viz., Firuzābad, Sultānpur.*

Kharosna, one mahal, one code.

3. The *Sarkār* of *Khairābad,* 2 mahals, 3 codes. *Khairābād,* &c., 12 parganahs, one code, *viz.,* suburbs of *Khairābād,Basārā, Baswah, Basrah, Chhitāpur, Khairigarh, Sadrpur, Kheri, Kharkhela,* and *Laharpur,* two mahals; *Machharhattah,* and Hargarāon, two mahals. *Pāli,* &c. has 8 mahals, one code, *viz., Pāli, Barurānjnah, Bāwan, Sāndi, Sirah, Gopamau, Khankatmau, Nimkhā; Bharwārah,* &c. two mahals, included in *Oudh, viz. Bharwārah* and *Pilā,*— and one code.

4. The *Sarkār* of *Gorakhpur,* 24 parganahs, one code. The suburban district of Gorakhpur with the town, 2 mahals, *Atraulā, Anholā; Bināekpur* &c. 4 mahals, *Bāhmnipārah, Bhāwāpārā, Tilpur, Chilupara, Dharyapara, Dhewapārā* and *Kotlah* [*Kuhānā*] 2 mahals, *Rihli; Ramgarh* and *Gauri* 2 mahals, *Rasulpur* and *Ghaus* 2 mahals; *Kathlā, Khilāpārā* [=*Rihlāpara*] *Maholi, Mundwah, Mandlah; Maghar* and *Ratanpur,* 2 mahals; *Maharanthoi.*

5. The *Sarkār* of *Lucknow* has 55 mahals, 2 codes. The suburban district of Lucknow, &c., 47 parganahs, one code. *Abethi, Isauli, Asiyun, Asohā, Unchah Gāon, Balkar Bijlour?* [*Bijnor*], *Bāri, Bharimau Pangwan, Betholi, Panhan, Parsandhān, Pātan, Bārāshākor, Jhaloter, Dewi, Deorakh, Dadrah, Ranbirpur, Rāmkot, Sandilah, Saipur, Sarosi, Sahāli, Sidhor, Sidhupur, Sandi, Saron, Fatehpur,*

Fort of *Ambhati, Kursi, Kakori, Khanjrah, Ghātampur, Karanda, Konbhi Lucknow* with its suburbs, ***Lashkar Malihābād, Mohān, Morāon, Madiāon, Mahonah, Manawi, Makrāed, Hadha, Inhār.***

Onām &c., 8 parganahs, one code, *viz.*, ***Onām, Bilgrāon, Bangarmau, Hardoi, Sātanpur, Fatehpur Chaurāsi, Kachhāndu, Malāwah.***

Spring Harvest of the Subah of Oudh.

	Parganah of the suburban district of Oudh, &c.	Ibrahimabād, &c.	Kishni, &c.	Bharāitch, &c.	Firuzabād, &c.	Kharānsah, &c.	
	D. J.	D. J.	D. J.	D' J.	D. J.	D. J.	
Wheat	54-20	62-15	58-4	54-20	55-23	55-20	*Note.*—The difference in the two classes of mustard seed is in the size and colour of the grain.
Indian Vetches ...	34-17	39-3	39-3	33-14	32-11	33-14	
Mustard seed (*Khardal*)	...	40-6	...	...	...	...	
Barley ...	39-3	45-21	42-12	38-0	35-20	38-0	
Adas	23-12	35-20	23-12	22-9	21-6	22-10	
Safflower	71-14	72-0	83 21	71-14	69-8	71-14	
Poppy	127-15	115-20	156-13	127-12	127-11	127-11	
Potherbs	69-9	76-1	68-5	56-12	54-20	56-12	
Linseed	29-0	35-20	32-15	27-24	26-21	27-24	
Mustard seed (*Sarshaf*)	30-5	38-0	27-24	29-2	29-2	29-2	
Arzan	20-3	24-15	16-19	15-3	7-22	23-4	
Peas	29-2	38-0	29-2	25-8	24-15	25-15	
Carrots	30-5	36-21	36-21	28-7	29-2	29-2	
Onions ...	78-0	80-18	79-10	78-7	78-7	78-7	
Fenugreek	55-22	54-20	58-4	58-4	78-20	...	
Persian Muskmelons ...	115-20	230-4	150-1	110-20	115-20	115-30	
Indian do. ...	4-13	14-23	17-22	15-16	15-16	15-16	
Cumin seed	79-15	61-12	...	...	...	...	
Coriander seed ...	...	150-2	...	...	...	...	
Kur rice	...	46-24	46-24	45-21	44-18	45-21	
Ajwāin	...	97-5	79-10	83-21	83-21	82-21	

Autumn Harvest of the Subah of Oudh.

	Parganah of the subur-ban district of Oudh, &c.	Ibrahimā bād, &c.	Kishni, &c.	Bharāitch, &c.	Firuzābād, &c.	Kharonsa, &c.	Suburban district of Khairābād.	Pāli, &c.	Bharwārah, &c.	Suburban district of Gorakhpur.	Lucknow, &c.	Onām, &c.
	D. J.	D. J.	D. J.	D. J.	D. J.	D. J.	D. J.	D. J.	D. J.	D. J.	D. J.	D. J.
Sugarcane (*paundah*) ...	240-9	223-15	230-8	240-9	203-15	240-9	220-15	231-15	240-9.	240-9	231-15	231-35
Common sugarcane ...	190-15	123-0	126-0	123-0	134-4	123-0	134-4	131-23	190-15	123-0	127-15	131-3
Dark coloured rice ...	67-2	71-14	71-14	62-5	65-4	62-15	66-24	73-20	67-2	62-15	74-20	73-20
Common rice	43-16	46-24	42-12	40-6	41-9	40-6	41-9	46-24	43-17	40-6	44-18	46-24
Māsh	33-15	34-17	40-6	31-8	32-15	31-8	32-15	34-17	33-15	31-8	34-2½	34-17
Cotton	83-21	93-23	91-18	89-15	89-11	89-15	89-15	93-23	83-21	89-15	93-18	93-28
Moth	35-18	41-20	26-21	24-15	23-12	24-15	23-12	22-23	25-18	24-15	24-15	22-23
Gāl	16-19	21-6	15-16	15-16	15-16	15-16	...	...	...	...	...	...
Turiya	31-8	38-0	35-20	31-8	33-14	31-6	...	...	...	...	...	...
Arzan	25-18	24-15	17-22	22-9	24-15	22-9	...	...	...	...	...	...
Indigo	123-15	162-3	162-3	163-6	163-6	162-6	...	...	...	...	...	...
Hinna	70-15	79-15	79-15	69-8	71-14	69-20	...	...	...	...	...	...
Hemp	89-15	84-24	84-24	85-21	89-15	89-15	...	...	...	...	...	...
Potherbs	89-2	84-5	87-5	82-18	82-16	83-21	...	...	...	...	...	...
Kachrah (*Cucumis melo*)	12-20	4-3	13-15	12-8	14-4	12-8	...	...	...	...	...	...
Pān	230-14	260-3	244-21	223-15	223-15	223-15	...	...	...	...	...	...
Singhārah	115-8	115-8	115-8	115-8	115-8	115-8	...	...	...	...	...	...
Lobiya	...	38-0	...	...	...	...	...	...	...	...	...	...
Jowāri, (millet)	35.20	38-0	35-8	38-0	33-14	38	33-14	32-15	35-2	38-0	85	32-15
Carrots	...	81-15	...	...	...	...	...	...	...	...	...	...
Kuri (a kind of wild grain)	...	13-15	...	15-5	...	...	...	...	...	...	...	...
Persian* watermelon ...	105-2	...	...	...	...	...	...	...	...	...	...	...
Arhar	...	...	...	22-9	...	22-9	23-12	25-4	...	...	...	...
Lahdarah	24-15	25-18	24-15	23-12	24-15	23-12	24-15	25-18	24-18	23-12	25-4	25-18
Kodaram	28-20	31-8	29-2	26-22	26-18	26-15	25-18	31-8	28-8	26-21	28-24	41-8
Mandwah	25-18	31-8	26-21	25-18	24-15	25-18	24-15	29-2	35-18	55-18	32-21	23-2
Sesame seed	41-9	31-8	43-15	44-18	45-1	44-18	45-21	41-9	41-1	44-18	40-20	41-9
Shamākh	18-15	19-0	12-8	12-8	12-8	12-8	12-8	13-10	13-11	12-8	12-8	13-10
Mung	43-15	48-2	48-3	41-2	43-15	41-9	43-15	41-9	43-15	41-10	43-15	41-9

* So the text, but it is probably a misprint of tarbuja for kharbuja.

1. The *Sarkār of Agra*—the royal residence. **44** parganahs, 4 codes. The suburban district of Agra, &c., 6 mahals, one code, *viz.*, *Agra* and its suburbs, *Chanwār, Jalesar,* the city of *Agra, Dholpur, Mahāwan, Beānah* &c., 33 mahals, one code; the suburbs of *Beānah,* 2 mahals, *Oudehi, Od, Ol, Bhasāwar Todahbhim, Bināwar, Chausath, Khānwā, Rajhohar, Fatehpur* known as *Sikri, Seonkar Seonkri, Mathura, Maholi, Mangotlah, Bhaskar, Wazirpur, Helak, Hindon, Rāpari, Bāri, Bajwārah. Etāwah* &c. 3 mahals, one code, *viz.*, *Etāwah, Rāpri,*[112] *Hatkānt. Mandāwar* &c. 2 mahals, one code, *viz.*, *Mandāwar, Kakhonmar.*

2. *Sarkār* of *Alwar.* 43 paragraphs, 3 codes. The parganahs of *Alwar* &c. 33 mahals, one code, *viz.*, the suburbs of *Alwar, Dharā, Dadekar, Bahādurpur, Panāin, Khelohar, Jalālpur, Bihrozpur, Rāth, Bālhattah, Bahrkol, Hājipur, Budahthal, Anthulah Hābru, Parāt, Balhār, Barodah Fathkhan, Barodahmeo, Basānah, Hasanpur, Badohar, Hasanpur Gori, Deoli Sājāri, Sakhan, Kiyārah, Ghat Seon, Kohrana, Monkonā, Mandāwarah, Naugāon Nāhargarh, Harsori* and *Harpur,* 2 mahals, *Harsānā. Bachherah,* &c. 5 mahals, one code, *viz.*, *Bachherah, Khohariranā, Bhiwān, Ismailpur, Amran, Mubārakpur,* &c., 5 mahals, one code, *viz.*, *Mubārakpur, Harsoni, Mandāwar, Khirtahali, Mojpur.*

3, 4. *Sarkārs* of *Tijārah* and *Erāj*, 4 codes. The *Sarkār* of *Eraj*, 16 mahals, *viz.*, *Eraj, Parhār, Bhānder, Bijpur, Pāndur, Chhatrah, Riyābānah, Shāhzādahpur, Khatolah* &c., *Kajhodah, Kedār, Kunj, Khekas, Kānti, Khāerah, Maholi.* The *Sarkār* of *Tijārah,* 18 mahals, 1 code, *viz.*, *Tijārah, Indor, Ujaina, Umarā Umari, Por, Begwān, Basohrā, Chamrāwat, Khānpur, Sākras, Santhadāri, Firuzpur, Fatehpur Mongarta, Kotlah, Karherā, Naginān. Thānah* of *Kahwār,* one code. *Besru,* one code.

5. *Sarkār* of *Kanauj,* 5 codes. The suburban district of *Kanauj,* &c. 11 mahals, one code. The suburbs of *Kanauj Bārā, Bithur, Bilhur, Bilgrāon, Deohā, Sikandarpur, Seoli, Seonrakh, Malkusah, Nānamau. Saketh* &c. 6 mahals, one code. *Sāketh, Karāoli, Barnah, Sahār, Patiāli, Sahāur. Bhagaon,* &c. 10 mahals, one code. *Bhogāon, Sonj, Sakrāon, Sakatpur, Saror, Chhabarmau,*

[112] A note to the text suggests this name to be an error, as not in Elliot nor in the account of the province of Agra. Neither is it in Tieffenthaler.

Shamshābād, Pati 'Alipur, Kanpal, Bhojpur. Sinkandarpur, one code. *Phapund,* one code.

6. *Sarkār* of *Sahār. Sahār,* &c. 6 madals, one code, *viz., Sahār, Pahāri, Bhadoli, Kāmah, Koh Majahid, Hodal. Nonhera,* one code.

7, 8, 9. *Sarkār* of *Gwalior,* &c., one code. *Sarkār* of *Gwalior,* 13 mahals, one code. *Sarkār* of *Narorpanj,* 5 mahals, one code. *Sarkār* of *Beanwan,* 28 mahals, one code.

10. *Sarkār* of *Kalpi,* 16 parganahs, one code. *Ulai, Bilāspur, Badhneth Derāpur, Deokali, Rāth, Rāipur, Suganpur, Shāhpur, suburbs of Kālpi, Kenār, Khandot, Khandela, city of Kālpi, Muhammadābād, Hamirpur.*

11. *Sarkār of Kol,* 4 codes. *Thānah Farida,* &c. 10 mahals, one code, *viz., Thānah Farida, Pahāsu, Danbhāi, Malikpur, Shikārpur, Nuh, Chandos, Khurjah, Ahār, Tapal.* Suburban district of *Kol,* &c., 4 mahals, one code, *viz., Kol, Jalāli, Sikandar rāo, Gangeri. Mārharah,* &c., 5 mahals, one code, viz., *Mārharah, Bairām, Soron, Pachlānah* and *Sidhpur,* 2 mahals. *Akbarābād,* 2 mahals, one code, *viz., Akbarābād, Atrauli.*

12. *Sarkār* of *Nārnol,* 4 codes. Suburban district of *Nārnol,* &c., 8 mahals, *viz.,* suburbs of *Nārnol* and city, *Bārh, Kot Potli, Bābāi, Khandela, Sankhāna, Kānori,* villages at the foot of the hill. *Barodah rana,* &c. 2 mahals, *viz., Barodah ranā Lāpoti. Chāl Kalānah,* &c. 2 mahals, *Chālkalānah, Khodānā. Kanodah,* &c. 3 mahals, *Kanodah, Narharah, Jhojeon.*

See Table next page.

Spring Harvest of the royal residence of Agra.

	Suburban district of Agra.	Etāwah.	Suburban district of Bayānah.	Mandāwar.	Alwar.	Bachherah.	Mubārakpur.	Eraj.	Tijārah.	Thānah of Kahwār.	Besru.	Sahār.	Pahāri.	Nonhera.	Kanauj.
	D. J.	D. J.	D. J.	D. J.	D. J.	D. J.	D. J.	D. J.	D. J.	D. J.	D. J.	D. J.	D. J.	D. J.	D. J.
Wheat	67-2	0-9	67.2	67-2	67-2	64-21	63-10	63-17	64-21	67-2	67-2	67-2	64-21	68-2	60-21
Cabul Vetches	67-9	...	...	...	...	...	...	55-23	...	...	...	...	...	...	...
Indian do.	44-18	35-20	42-12	40-6	40-6	36-23	35-20	34-17	36-23	40-6	36-23	36-23	36-23	40-6	37-15
Barley	49-5	40-6	44-17	44-18	44-18	42-12	41-9	46-0	42-12	44-17	42-12	42-12	42-12	44-17	40-0
Adas	29-2	25-17	29-17	26-21	26-21	26-21	26-21	26-21	26-21	26-21	26-21	26-21	26-21	26-21	25-17
Safflower	127-11	120-1	127-11	123-[illegible]	123-0	127-0	127-0	127-0	127-0	120-0	127-11	127-11	127-11	123-0	69-22
Poppy	127-11	120-20	127-11	123-0	127-0	127-11	127-11	127-11	127-11	123-0	127 11	127-11	123-0	123-0	128-0
Potherbs	67-2	58-4	61-12	60-9	60-9	59-7	60-9	55-23	59-8	60-9	59-8	59-8	59-8	60-9	61-12
Mustard seed	31-14	31-8	31-14	33-14	33-14	31-8	31-8	32-11	31-8	33-14	31-8	31-8	31-8	33-14	31-21
Arzan	24-15	23-3	20-3	21-6	21-6	22-9	23-3	23-9	21-6	22-9	22-9	22-9	22-9	21-6	20-6
Peas	31-8	29-2	33-14	32-11	32-11	31-20	29-2	29-2	31-8	32-11	31-8	31-8	31-8	32-15	39-2
Carrots	29-2	29-2	33-14	29-2	29-2	25.18	26-21	26-21	25-18	29-2	25-18	25-18	25-8	29-2	31-21
Onions	84-24	80-12	80-11	80-18	82-17	81-16	81-16	82-17	81-16	80-2	31-16	81-16	81-16	82-17	82-17
Fenugreek	44-18	50-8	84-24	55-8	55-29	84-24	81-16	...	83-24	55-23	...	...	84-24	55-23	82-18
Persian muskmelons ...	111-20	87-17	111-20	111-20	111-20	100-16	100-16	100-16	100-14	100-16	...	100-16	100-16	111-20	119-16
Indian ditto ...	15-11	14-13	15-16	15-16	15-16	14-14	15-16	15-16	14-14	15-16	15-16	15-16	14-14	15-16	14-13
Cumin seed	84-24	83-21	82-24	84-24	84-24	81-18	84-24	82-17	...	84-24	...	...	81-16	84-24	...
Kur rice	55-23	59-5	87-8	51-11	51-11	53-17	51-11	50-8	50-18	51-11	53-17	53-17	56-17	51-11	46-24
Ajwāin	84-24	83-21	84-24	84-24	84-24	81-17	84-24	86-2	81-16	84-24	81-16	81-16	81-16	84-24	83-21

Autumn Harvest of the Subah of Agra.

	Suburban district of Agra.	Etāwah.	Suburban district of Bayānah.	Mandāwar.	Alwar.	Bachherah.	Mubārakpur.	Eraj.	Tijārah.	Thānah of Kahwār.	Besru.	Sāhar.	Pahāri.	Nonhera.	Kanauj.
	D. J.	D. J.	D. J.	D. J.	D. J.	D. J.	D. J-	D. J.	D. J.	D. J.	D. J.	D. J.	D. J.	D' J.	D. J.
Sugarcane (*paundah*) ...	239-6	239-8	223-15	200-18	205-0	223-15	223-15	223-15	223-15	217-0	218-18	217-0	220-15	217-0	...
Common sugarcane ...	147-11	134-4	148-17	134-4	134-4	125-6	120-11	173-3	185-6	134-4	138-16	138-6	125-6	134-4	131-23
Dark coloured rice	84-20	60-9	82-17	81-14	81-14	78-7	76-0	67-2	78-1	71-14	76-0	76-1	78-7	71-14	73-20
Common rice	6-9	44-17	58-4	63-18	63-17	63-18	63-17	48-4	63-18	63-17	58-4	58-0	63-18	63-17	26-24
Āl	...	...	...	...	...	...	...	250-17	...	...	...	...	...	...	...
Māsh	40-6	34-17	38-0	35-20	35-9	35-20	35-20	35-19	35-20	35-20	36-23	36-23	35-20	35-20	34-17
Cotton	7-5	89-15	89-11	89-11	89-11	89-11	89-15	91-17	89-11	89-11	95-1	95-0	89-11	89-11	93-23
Moth	29-2	24-15	...	22-9	22-9	22-9	22-9	24-15	22-9	22-9	24-15	24-15	22-9	22-9	22-23
Gāl	20-3	14-13	17-22	16-19	16-10	16 19	16-19	15-15	16-19	16-19	15-16	15-16	16-19	16-19	15-19
Turiya	40-12	34-17	40-6	39-3	39-3	38-0	35-20	38-0	38-0	39-3	42-12	42-13	38-0	39-3	34-17
Arzan	29-2	22-9	...	22-9	22-9	23-12	24-15	24-15	23-12	22-9	23-12	23-12	23-13	22-9	26-21
Indigo	156-13	159-22	158-19	161-0	161-0	161-0	156-18	163-0	161-0	161-0	163-6	163-0	161-0	161-0	163-1
Hinna	70-7	78-7	67-2	77-7	78-7	78-7	78-7	69-8	78-0	78-7	78-7	78-7	78-7	78-7	76-1
Hemp	93-23	89-11	89-11	89-11	13(?)11	88-20	89-11	89-11	88-8	89-11	88-8	88-8	88-8	89-11	84-24
Potherbs	84-24	80-12½	81-14	81-14	81-14	82-17	81-14	84-23	82-17	81-14	78 7	88-7	72-17	71-14	78-7
Kachrah	13-15	12-8	15-5	13-11	11-15	13-15	13-11	12-7	13-11	13-11	13-11	13-11	13-11	13-11	11-5
Pān	223-20	223-15	223-15	223-15	223-15	223-15	223-0	267-0	223-15	223-15	223-15	223-15	223-15	223-15	268-20
Singhārah	115-20	...	115-20	115-20	115-20	115-20	115-20	115-20	115-20	115-20	115-20	115-20	115-20	115-15	115-20
Lobiya	31-8	30-15	38-0	37-24	27-24	32-5	31-8	33-14	30-5	27-24	33-14	33-14	30-5	27-24	...
Jowāri	44-18	35-6	40-6	35-20	35-20	35-20	38-7	35-20	35-20	36-23	36-23	35-20	35-20	32-15	32-15
Kuri	...	...	...	...	...	...	...	...	...	...	...	...	...	...	...
Lahdarah	...	...	...	...	...	...	...	...	...	...	...	...	...	...	...
Kodaram	...	...	...	...	...	...	...	...	...	...	...	...	...	...	...
Mandwah	...	...	...	...	...	...	...	...	...	...	...	...	...	...	...
Sesame seed	...	...	...	...	...	...	...	...	...	...	...	...	...	...	...
Shamākh	...	...	...	...	...	...	...	...	...	...	...	...	...	...	...
Mung	...	...	...	...	...	...	...	...	...	...	...	...	...	...	...

Supplement to the Spring Harvest of the Subah of Agra.

	Saketh.	Bhagāon.	Sikandarpur.	Phapund.	Gwalior, &c.	Kālpi.	Kol.	Thānah Farida.	Akbarābād.	Mārharah.	Nārnol.	Barodahrana.	Chāl Kalānah.
	D. J.	D. J.	D. J.	D. J.	D. J.	D. J.	D. J.	D. J.	D. J.	D. J.	D. J.	D. J.	D. J.
Wheat ...	64-21	58-4	60-9	63-18	69-8	63-18	63-9	58-4	63-18	60-9	62-15	63-18	61-12
Cabul Vetches ...	...	...	...	55-23	...	55-23	...	...	...	...	...	...	...
Indian do. ...	39-3	33-14	38-0	34-18	42-12	34-17	35-20	34-17	35-20	38-0	36-22½	35-20	35-20
Barley ...	40-12	38-	40-6	40-6	40-6	40-6	40-6	38-0	40-12	40-6	41-9½	41-9	41-9
Adas ...	26-21	24-15	24-15	24-15	20-2	24-15	26-21	22-9	24-15	24-15	24-15	23-15	24-15
Safflower ...	73-20	73-20	74-23	72-17	69-8	72-17	71-14	83-21	81-14	74-23	72-17	71-14	71-14
Poppy ...	127-15	127-15	127-15	127-15	127-15	127-15	123-0	124-9	123-0	128-12	119-17	127-15	123-0
Potherbs ...	60-9	57-4	57-4	55-23	60-9	50-23	58-4	64-21	63-2	58-4	65-4	60-9	60-9
Mustard seed ...	32-15	30-5	30-15	30-15	33-14	32-15	29-2	30-5	29-2	30-15	37-½	31-8	31-8
Arzan ...	21-6	20-3	21-6	20-3	16-12	20.3	20-9	19-0	22-9	21-6	20-9	22-9	20-3
Peas ...	31-20	24-15	29-2	20-9	31-8	22-9	26-21	29-2	29-2	29-2	27-23	29-21	26-21
Carrots ...	31-20	39-20	31-20	26-21	26-24	26-21	24-15	24-15	26-21	31-8	26-1	24-20	24-15
Onions ...	87-5	80-18	87-5	82-18	84-24	82-18	89-15	81-15	81-16	47-15	84-12	81-16	77-7
Fenugreek ...	89-15	...	89-11	...	...	...	...	49-5	...	89-15	...	81-16	...
Persian Musk Melons ...	...	101-19	...	109-14	115-20	109-14	100-16	145-9	111-8	...	102-21	100-16	...
Indian ditto ...	19-16	15-16	14-14	15-16	15-16	15-16	17-22	15-16	14-14	15-16	15-16	15-16	1 (?) 16
Cumin seed ...	84-24	82-18	87-5	82-18	84-14	80-18	...	86-2	84-24	87-5	84-2	84-24	...
Kur rice ...	51-15	...	51-15	50-8	59-8	50-20	49-5	59-23	53-17	51-15	46-2	51-11	60-9
Ajwāin ...	84-24	80-18	87-5	82-2	86-2	86-2	84-24	86-2	84-24	87-23	84-12	84-24	84-24

Supplement to the Autumn Harvest of the Subah of Agra.

	Saketh.	Bhugāon.	Sikandarpur.	Phapund.	Gwalior, &c.	Kālpi.	Kol.
	D. J.	D. J.	D. J.	D. J.	D. J.	D. J.	D. J.
Sugarcane (*paunda*) ...	...	223-5	...	223-15	239-6	...	223-18
Common Sugar-cane ...	138-16	146-3	147-16	143-3	147-15	143-0	134-4
Dark coloured rice	70-14	59-7	71-14	67-2	70-12	67-2	64-21
Common rice ...	0-5	44-18	49-5	46-24	55-20	46-24	46-24
Āl ...	4...	...	...	205-18	...	205-18	...
Māsh ...	35-20	34-18	34-18	35-19	40-6	35-19	33-14
Cotton ...	93-23	84-24	93-23	91-17	87-5	91-18	89-15
Moth ...	25-18	22-18	24-15	24-5	26-21	24-15	22-9
Gāl ...	16-19	15-16	16-19	15-16	20-9	15-16	15-16
Turiya ...	38-0	34-17	35-20	38-0	40-8	38-0	38-0
Arzan ...	24-15	21-6	23-12	40-6	27-24	24-15	24-15
Indigo ...	160-3	158-19	160-0	160-6	160-3	162-1	163-1
Hinna ...	...	77.4	...	69-8	69-8	69-8	77-4
Hemp ...	82-11	86-2	87-5	89-11	84-20	89-11	84-24
Potherbs ...	78-7	78-7	78-7	74-23	76-1	74-21	76-0
Kachrah ...	13-11	12-8	13-11	12-7	12-7	12-7	12.7
Pān ...	...	267-20	...	268-8	223-15	268-8	223-13
Singhārah ...	...	102-22	...	111-20	111-20	111-20	111-20
Lobiya ...	30-5	27-24	131-8	33-17	31-8	33-14	36-21
Jowāri ...	39-8	35-20	39-3	38-7	34-18	38-7	35-19
Kuri ...	...	...	...	...	15-16	...	...
Lahdarah ...	26-21	24-5	26-21	26-21	31-8	26-21	24-15
Kodaram ...	30-5	27-24	30-5	27-24	31-8	27-24	29-2
Mandwah ...	30-5	26-21	29-2	26-2	31-8	25-21	27-24
Shamākh ...	25-18	12-8	24-11	11-5	14-0	11-5	12-8
Peas ...	49-6	42-24	49-5	40-6	49-5	40-6	40-6
Turmeric ...	89-11	...	111-20	...	...	...	...

	Thānah Farida.	Akbarābād.	Mārharah.	Nārnol.	Barodahrana.	Chāl Kalānah
	D. J.	D. J.	D. J.	D. J.	D. J.	D. J.
Sugarcane (*paunda*) ...	219-2	223-15	...	216-22	223-15	205-18
Common Sugar-cane ...	134-4	134-4	138-16	134-4	127-11	125-6
Dark coloured rice	67-2	64-21	74-2	77-6½	76-1	73-20
Common rice ...	46-20	46-24	49-5	60-90	63-18	53-17
Āl ...	...	...	...	...	...	...
Māsh ...	23-14	33-14	34-17	38-0	35-20	33-14
Cotton ...	93-23	89-15	93-23	89-11	89-11	89-11
Moth ...	23-12	22-9	24-15	29-3	22-3	23-12
Gāl ...	14-14	15-16	16-19	16-19	15-19	15-16
Turiya ...	33-14	38-0	35-20	42-12	35-9	46-½
Arzan ...	21-6	24-11	23-12	23-12	24-11	22-9½
Indigo ...	160-24	161-0	165-15	156-0	161-0	161-0
Hinna ...	76-17	77-4	...	76-½	78-7	77-4
Hemp ...	77-5	84-24	87-5	89-15	89-11	84-24
Potherbs ...	88-8	76-0	77-7	71-13	71-14	11-14
Kachrah ...	12-8	12-8	13-11	13-1½	13-11	12-8
Pān ...	223 15	223-15	...	223-15	223-15	223-15
Singhārah ...	111-20	108-11	...	115-20	111-20	111-20
Lobiya ...	36-21	33-14	31-8	35-19	31-8	26-21
Jowāri ...	35-14	35-19	39-3	35-19	35-20	38-14
Kuri ...	11-14½	(?) 11	...	...	12-8	...
Lahdarah ...	24-15	24-15	26-21	27.23	26-23	26-23
Kodaram ...	32-5	29-2	30-5	29-1	33-14	29-2
Mandwah ...	27-14	27-24	29-2	20-8	25-18	27-24
Shamākh ...	11-8	12-8	24-15	12-7	13-15	15-19
Peas ...	33-0	40-6	49-5	35-19	35-20	35-20
Turmeric ...	...	...	111-20	...	...	...

Subah of *Ājmere,* 7 Sarkārs, 9 codes.

1. *Sarkār* of *Ājmere,* 2 codes. Suburban district of *Ājmere,* &c. 24 Parganahs, 1 code. City and suburbs of *Ājmere,* 2 mahals, *Arāine, Parbat, Bahnāi,*[113] *Bharānah, Bawāl, Bāhal, Bāndhan Sandheri, Bharonda, Tusina,*[114] *Jobnair,*[115] *Deogāon, Roshanpur, Sānbhar, Sarwār, Sathelā, Sulaimānābād, Kekri, Kherwah, Māhrot, Masaudābad, Narāina, Harsor, Anber,* &c., 4 Parganahs, 1 code, *viz., Anber, Bhakoi, Jhāg, Muzābād.*

2. *Sarkār* of *Jodhpur,* 21 Parganahs, 1 code. Suburbs and city of *Jodhpur, Asop, Endrāoti, Bhodhi, Palpārah, Belārā, Pāli,* &c., 3 mahals, *Bāhilah, Podhh, Bhadrājaun, Jetāran, Dotārā, Sujhat, Sātalmer, Sewāna, Kherwa, Kheonsar, Kundoj, Mahewah.*

3. *Sarkār* of *Chitor,* 28 Parganahs, 1 code. Suburbs and city of *Chitor,* 2 mahals, *Islāmpur* commonly *Rāmpur, Udaipur,* &c., 3 mahals, *Aparmāl,*[116] *Artod, Islāmpur commonly Mohan, Bodhnur, Phuliā, Banhera, Pur, Bihin Surur, Bāgor, Begun, Pati Hājipur, Jeran, Sānwarkhāti, Sāndri, Samel* with the cultivated land, *Kosiānah, Māndalgarh, Māndal, Madāriya Nimach* &c., 3 mahals.

4. *Sarkār* of *Ranthambor,* 4 codes, *Ranthambor* &c., 36 Parganahs, 1 code. Subarban district of *Ranthambor, Alhanpur, Etāda, Aton, Islāmpur, Iwān Bosamer, Barodah, Bhadlāon, Baklānt, Palātiāh, Bhosor, Belonah, Bālakhatri, Bhoripahāri, Bārān, Talād, Jetpur, Jhāin, Khaljipur, Dhari, Sanhusāri, Kotā, Khandār, Khatoli, Kadaud, Lakhri, Londah, Lahaud, Māngror, Momedānah* &c., 16 mahals. *Chātsu* &c., 16 Parganahs, 1 code. *viz., Chātsu, Barwārah, Uniyārā, Pātan, Banhatā, Sarsup, Boli, Bejri, Kharni, Nawāhi, Jhalāwah, Khankharah, Sui Supar, Malārnah, Karor, Bondi, Delhwārah,* &c., 7 Parganahs, 1 code, *viz., Delhwārah, Rewāndhnah, Nagar, Antrorah, Delānah, Amkhorah, Loharwārah, Todā,* &c., 3 Parganahs, 1 code, viz., *Todā, Tonk, Tori.*

5. *Sarkār* of *Nāgor,* 30 Parganahs, 1 code. Suburban district of *Nāgor, Amar Sarnain, Indānah, Bhadānah,*

---

[113] *Bahacoi,* Tieff.
[114] *Bossina, Ibid.*
[115] *Zounbora, Ibid.*
[116] *Aparpāl, Ibid.*

Baldubalām,[117] *Batodhā, Baroda, Bārah gāin, Chāel, Charodah, Jākhrah, Khārijkhatu, Dendwānah, Donpur, Rewāsā, Ron, Rasulpur, Rahot, Sādelah, Fathpur Jhanjmun, Kāsli, Khāelah Kojurah, Kolewah, Kumhāri, Keran, Lādon, Merath, Manohar nagar, Nokhā.*

6 & 7. *Sarkārs* of *Sarohi* and *Bikāner*. The codes of these two *Sarkārs are* not laid down.

Spring Harvest of the Subah of Ājmere.

	Suburban district of Ājmere, &c.	Parganah of Amber, &c.	Parganah of Jodhpur, &c.	Parganah of Chitor, &c.	Parganah of Rantambhor &c.	Parganah of Chātsu, &c.	Parganah of Delhwārah, &c.	Parganah of Todah, &c.	Parganah of Nāgor, &c.
	D. J.	D. J.	D. J.	D. J.	D. J.	D. J.	D. J.	D. J.	D. J.
Wheat	49-5	31-8	100-16	55-23	55-23	53-18	67-2	46-24	100-16
Indian Vetches ...	33-14	20-3	55-23	31-8	31-8	38-0	42-12	27-24	55-23
Barley	33-14	20-3	67-2	33-14	33-14	38-0	49-5	32-11	67-2
Adas	22-3	13-11	...	22-9	22-9	24-15	20-3	...	...
Safflower	62-15	38-9	67-2	55-23	55-22	58-9	59-4	36-29	67-2
Poppy	85-15	60-9	115-20	89-24	84-24	115-20	116-8	77-4	115-20
Potherbs	55-23	35-20	62-15	55-23	55-23	46-8	55-22	36-24	62-15
Linseed	31-8	20-3	31-8	26-21	26-21	26-21	29-2	...	31-8
Mustard seed ...	44-18	26-21	55-23	26-21	24-15	...	27-24	18-11	55-23
Arzan	20-9	13-11	55-23	13-11	13-11	17-22	17-22	14-15	55-23
Peas	26-9	20-3	...	22-2	20-9	...	...	...	...
Carrots	26-21	15-16	...	22-9	22-21	...	27-24	18-11	...
Onions	67-2	44-18	67-2	59-21	59-21	80-13	89-13	53-17	68-2
Fenugreek ...	...	...	55-0	...	67.	...	...	55-23	...
Persian Musk-Melons	100-16	67-2	...	83-11	89-11	...	89-11	89-8	...
Indian ditto	11-5	6-18	...	13-11	13-11	13-11	13-11	13-11	8-24
Cumin	70-7	53-17	77-8	67-2	67-2	80-13	80-13	53-17	...
Kur rice	51-11	33-0	...	52-14	52-24	40.6	33-14	...	...
Ajwāin	70-7	53-17	78-7	67-2	67.	80-13	80-13	53-17	88-7

[117] In the text *Bakdu*, but the above is the name in the account of this Subah which occurs later on.

Autumn Harvest of the Subah of Ājmere.

	Suburban district of Ājmere, &c.	Parganah of Amber, &c.	Parganah of Jodhpur, &c.	Parganah of Chitor, &c.	Parganah of Rantambhor &c.	Parganah of Chātsu, &c.	Parganah of Delhwārah, &c.	Parganah of Todah, &c.	Parganah of Nāgor, &c.
	D. J.	D. J.	D. J.	D. J.	D. J.	D. J.	D. J.	D. J.	D. J.
Sugarcane (*paundah*) ...	...	...	...	239-6	239-6	...	...	...	...
Common sugarcane	115½-20	86-1	115-8	115-8	115-8	134-4	115-20	81-16	115-20
Dark coloured rice	55-23	35-20	55-23	67-2	68-2	72-20	67-22	44-18	...
Common rice ...	44-20	23-2	44-2	53-17	50-17	67-2	46-24	31-8	44-18
Māsh ...	33-14	29-2	31-7	33-14	33-14	39-3	27-24	18-15	31-8
Cotton ...	60-15	40-6	67-2	76-1	76-1	78-8	72-17	54-0	67-0
Moth ...	24-15	15-16	36-3	26-1	26-1	22-9	40-6	26-21	20-3
Gāl ...	13-15	8-24	38-21	13-15	13-15	15-16	16-16	10-16	38-8
Turiya ...	38-1	24-16	...	33-14	33-14	15-5	...	...	...
Arzan ...	17-22	12-7	55-21	17-22	17-22	17-22	22-9	17-24	55-6
Indigo ...	134-4	85-11	134-4	111-20	134-4	134-4	134-4	89-11	134-4
Hinna ...	67-2	44-18	67-2	55-23	55-23	67-2	62-15	40-21	67-2
Hemp ...	82-19	53-8	87-7	78-8	78-7	89-15	76-13	76-13	53-17
Potherbs ...	55-22	35-20	62-15	55-23	55-23	62-15	76-13	26-9	62-15
Kachran ...	13-2	8-24	13-11	11-5	15-5	13-11	13-11	8-24	13-11
Singhārah ...	115-20	116-20	115-20	115-20	115-20	115-20	115-20	118-20	115-20
Lobiya ...	31-20	20-9	22-9	31-8	31-8	32-11	22-9	13-14	22-9
Jowāri ...	24-15	11-16	31-8	29-2	29-12	32-22	42-2	30-0	31-8
Lahdarah ...	20-3	12-8	17-20	22-9	22-9	25-18	31-8	19-0	17-22
Kodarama ...	22-3	11-5	...	22-9	22-9	33-14	33-14	27-24	...
Mandwah ...	22-2	14-4	...	22-3	22-9	26-21	26-21	17-22	...
Sesame seed ...	33-14	20-3	33-4	33-14	33-14	24-16	34-17	22-24	33-14
Shamākh ...	15-5	6-18	...	11-5	11-5	11-5	11-5	6-0	...
Mung ...	24-11	15-16	26-21	40-6	40-6	36-22	42-12	27-10	26-21
Kurī ...	21-5	6-18	...	8-24	8-24	...	11-5	6-3	...
Kalt ...	...	...	...	...	33-14	...	...	22-9	...

The rates of the *Sarkārs* of Bikāner and Sarohi are not given.

The *Subah* of Delhi, 8 *Sarkārs*, 28 codes.

1. The *Sarkār* of Delhi, 48 Parganahs, 7 codes. The old suburban district, the new ditto *Pālam, Jhārsah, Masaudābād, Tilpat, Luni, Shakarpur, Bāghpat, Kāsnah, Dāsnah, Sulaimānābād, Kharkhudah, Sonipat, Talbegampur, Talālpur.*

Pānipat, &c., 2 Parganahs, 1 code, *viz., Pānipat, Karnāl, Safedun, Kutānah, Chhaproli, Tāndah Bhagwān, Gonor, Jhanjhānah, Kāndhlah, Gangerkhera.*

Baran, &c., 8 Parganahs, 1 code. *Baran, Siyānah, Jewar, Dankor, Ādh, Pothh, Senthhah, Sikandarābād,*

Merath, &c., 7 Parganahs· 1 code. *Merath, Hāpur, Barnāwah, Jalālābād, Sarwārah, Garh Muktesar, Hatnāwar.*[118]

Jhajhar, &c., 4 Parganahs, 1 code. *Jhajhar, Dādri-Tāha· Māndothi, Beri Dobaldhan.*

Rohtak, 1 Parganah, 1 code.

Palol· 1 Parganah, 1 code.

2. *Sarkār* of *Badāon*, 16 Parganahs, 1 code. *Ajāon, Aonla, Badāon* and suburbs, *Bareli· Barsar, Pond, Telhi, Sahsāwn, Sonāsi Mandehah· Saniyā, Kānt, Kot Sālbahan, Golah.*

3. *Sarkār* of *Hisār Firozah*· 18 mahals, 4 codes. Suburbs of *Hisār Firozah*, &c., 7 parganahs, 1 code. Suburbs and city of *Hānsi, Barwalah, Barwā· Toshām* and *Agrohah*, 2 mahals, *Fatehābād*. *Gohānah*, &c., 4 parganahs, 1 code. *Gohānah, Ahroni, Bhattu* and 16 villages. *Sirsā*, 1 parganah· 1 code. *Muhim*, &c., 6 parganahs, 1 code. *Muhim· Rohtak, Jind, Khāndah, Tahānah, Athkerah.*

4. *Sarkār* of *Rewāri*, 11 mahals, 4 codes. *Rewāri*, &c., 8 parganahs· 1 code. *Rewāri, Bāwal, Kot Kāsim Ali, Pātaudi, Bhoharah, Ghelot, Ratāi Jatāi, Nimrānah*. *Tāoru*, 1 parganah, 1 code. *Sunnah*, 1 parganah, 1 code. *Kohānah*, 1 parganah, 1 code.

5. *Sarkār* of *Sahāranpur*, 36 mahals, 4 codes. *Deoband*, &c.· 26 mahals, 1 code. *Deoband, Sahāranpur, Bhatkhanjāwar, Manglor· Nānoth Rāmpur, Sarot, Purchhapār, Jorāsi, Sikri Bhukarhari, Sarsāwah, Charthāwal· Rurki, Baghra, Thānah Bhewan, Muzuffarābād, Raepurtātār, Ambeth· Nakor* and *Toghlaqpur*, 2 mahals, *Bhogpur· Bhattah, Thānah Bhim, Sanbalhera, Khodi* and *Gangwah*, 2 mahals· *Lakhnauti Kerunah*, &c., 2 parganahs· 1 code. *Kerānah· Bedoli.*

Sardhanah, &c., 7 parganahs, 1 code. *Surdhanah, Bhonah, Suranpalri, Badhānah, Joli, Khatoli* and *Baghra*, 2 mahals. *Indri*. 1 mahal, 1 code.

6. *Sarkār* of *Sirhind*· 2 mahals, 4 codes. Suburbs of *Sirhind*, &c.· 13 parganahs. Suburbs of *Sirhind· Rupar,*

---

[118] *Hastinapur*, Elliot & Tieff.

Pāel, Benor, Jahat, Dhotah, Dorālah, Deorānah, Kuhrām, Masenkan, villages of *Rāe Samu, Ambālah* and *Kaithal. Thānesar,* &c., 8 parganahs. *Thānesar, Sadhurah, Shāhābād, Khizrābād, Mustafa-ābād, Bhodar, Sultanpur, Pundri. Thārah,* &c., 2 parganahs. *Thārah, Ludhiānah, Samānah,* &c., 9 parganahs. *Samānah, Sunnām, Mansurpur, Mālner, Hāpuri, Pundri, Fatehpur* and *Bhatindah, Machhipur.*

8. *Sarkār* of *Sambal,* (*Sambhal*) 47 mahals, 3 codes. City of *Sambal,* &c., 23 parganahs. City of *Sambal,* suburbs of *Sambal, Sarsi, Naroli, Manjholah, Jadwār, Gonor, Neodhanah, Deorah, Dabhārsi, Dhakah, Rajabpur, Amrohah, Ujhāri, Kachh, Āazampur, Islimpur Dargu, Islāmpur Bharu, Afghānpur, Chopālah, Kundarki, Bachharaon, Gundor. Chāndpur,* &c., 16 parganahs. *Chāndpur, Sherkot, Bijnaur, Mandāwar, Keratpur, Jalālābād, Sahanspur, Nihtor, Naginah, Akbarābād, Islimābad, Seohāra* and *Jhala,* 2 mahals. *Lakhnor,* &c., 11 parganahs. *Lakhnor, Shāhi, Kābar* and *Kānkhari* 2 mahals. *Hatamnah, Rājpur, Dodelah, Leswah, Sarsāwah, Basārā, Parohi* [=*Barohi*].

Sarkār of *Kumāon.* (The names of its parganahs are not entered in the MSS.)

Spring Harvest of the Súbah of Delhi.

	Old suburban district.	Pānipat, &c.	Merath, &c.	Baran, &c.	Jhajhar, &c.	Palol.	Rohtak.	Sarkār of Badāon.	Suburban district of of Hisār.	Gohānah, &c.	Sirsā.	Muhim.	Rewārī.	Tāoru.
	D. J.	D. J.	D. J.	D. J.	D. J.	D. J.	D. J.	D. J.	D. J.	D. J.	D. J.	D. J.	D. J	D. J.
Wheat	63-0	58-4	58-4	58-4	61-12	64-21	58-4	50-8	62-15	57-4	58-4	58-4	68-10	64-16
Cabul Vetches	...	...	...	...	...	...	...	...	67-2	...	...	...	...	...
Indian ditto	36-3	36-23	40-6	32-11	33-14	33-14	29-16	30-5	29-2	29-16	30-5	7-19	35-20	31-20
Barley	42-12	40-6	38-0	38-0	41-9	42-12	34-17	45-20	40-6	42-12	42-12½	42-12½	24-11	22-12
Adas	24-15	24-15	25-11	22-9	24-15	26-1	24-11	15-23	24-15	22-9	24-16	24-11	24-11	26-21
Safflower	71-14	71-14	84-24	83-21	71-14	72-14	68-20	70-11	67-2	67-0	67-2	60-20	71-14	71-14
Poppy	123-0	125-3	145-9	120-45	123-11	127-11	119-16	128 0	119-16	119-16	119-16	127-16	127-11	127-11
Potherbs	67-2	55-23	64-21	64-21	60-9	59-7	48-0	57-1	60-2	55-23	51-12	57-0	60-9	50-7
Linseed	31-20	31-7	29-20	33-14	33-14	32-11	36 21	24-0	25-13	25-17	24-15	23-21	29-2	34-17
Mustard seed	29-2	29-2	31-20	35-5	31-20	31-20	30-20	26-7	31-20	29-2	29-2	30-5	31-20	31-20
Arzan	22-9	20-3	19-0	19-0	20-3	22-2	20-3	17-9	20-3	17-20	20-3	20-3	22-9	22-9
Peas	29-2	26-21	24-16	29-2	26-21	31-20	26-21	...	29-9	29-9	29-9	26-21	29-2	29-2
Carrots	21-23	24-15	23-12	24-11	24-11	53-17	29-2	26-21	23-5	39-2	29-2	29-2	26-21	25-18
Onions	81-16	78-7	81-16	81-16	77-7	81-16	80-0	80-8	85-0	85-0	85-0	81-16	81-16	81-16
Fenugreek	...	62-15	49-5	49-5	...	...	...	...	35-0	38-0	...	...	81-16	81-16
Persian Musk Melons ...	111-20	100-16	45-9	145-9	100-16	100-16	96-4	13-12	98-10	96-4	98-2	96-4	100-16	100-16
Indian ditto ...	11-16	15-16	117-16	17-22	15-16	15-16	13-11	11-16	15-16	13-11	13-11	13-14	11-16	14-14
Kur rice	53-17	53-17	53-17	55-23	60-9	50-17	46-24	38-0	46-24	45-21	46-24	46-24	21-11	53-17
Ajwāin	84-24	89-12	84-24	86-2	84-24	81-16	85-0	85-0	85-0	85-0	84-24	85-0	...	81-16

Autumn Harvest of the Súbah of Delhi.

	Old suburban district.	Panipat, &c.	Merath, &c.	Baran, &c.	Jhajhar, &c.	Palol.	Rohtak.	Sarkār of Badāon.	Suburban district of Hisar.	Gohānah, &c.	Sirsā.	Muhim.	Rewāri.	Tāoru.
	D. J.	D. J.	D. J.	D. J.	D. J.	D. J.	D. J.	D. J.	D. J.	D. J.	D. J.	D. J.	D. J.	D. J.
Sugarcane (*paundah*) ...	210-5	204-17	216-22	219-3	250-18	218-5	217-0	216-9	214-20	214-20	214-20	217-0	220-11	223-11
Common sugarcane ...	127-11	123-0	123-0	134-4	125-6	138-11	127-19	125-6	125-6	128-2	127-24	127-4	137-11	125-6
Dark coloured rice ...	78-7	67-0	43-18	67-2	73-8	76-1	62-11	64-21	62-15	63-18	64-21	76-1	76-1	77-7
	55-7	44-18	48-2	46-20	53-17	58-14	49-5	38-15	51-14	...	45-21	48-20	63-18	63-18
Māsh	35-20	33-14	34-17	33-14	33-14	31-23	38-0	31-20	38-0	35-20	38-0	38-0	35-20	35-20
Cotton	89-11	91-17	89-11	93-23	89-11	95-1	89-21	96-4	89-11	89-11	89-11	89-12	89-11	89-11
Moth	23-12	26-21	22-9	23-12	23-13	24-11	23-12	23-3	24-11	23-12	23-12	23-12	22-0	22-9
Gāl	16-15	15-9	16-19	14-14	15-16	11-16	16-12	15-3	16-19	15-16	15-16	16-12	16-12	16-12
Arzān	20-3	20-3	29-9	21-6	22-9	23-12	23-12	19-4	23-12	23-12	23-12	23-12	24-15	23-12
Indigo	121-0	121-0	121-0	121-0	121-0	121-0	120-12½	121-14	125-12	125-12½	125-12½	156-0	156-3	161-0
Hinna	77-4	76-1	71-14	72-17	78-3	78-7	76-0	42-14	76-0	76-0	76-0	76-0	76-0	77-7
Hemp	84-24	89-18	83-21	87-5	84-24	81-0	80-18	89-11	80-18	80-18	87-5	86-18	89-11	88-8
Potherbs	70-17	71-14	78-7	78-7	71-14	71-7	73-20	73-20	71-14	71-14	71-14	73-20	71-14	72-17
Kachrah	11-0	11-0	12-7	12-20	13-11	13-11	12-20	13-11	13-11	13-11	12-11	13-11	13-11	13-11
Pān	223-15	200-15	220-11	220-11	220-11	220-11	220-11	220-11	220-11	220-11	220-11	220-11	220-11	220-11
Singhārah	111-15	111-20	111-20	111-20	111-20	111-20	111-20	111-20	111-20	111-20	111-20	111-20	111-20	111-20
Lobiya	31-0	...	26-21	26-21	26-21	33-14	31-20	27-10	35-20	34-17	38-0	38-0	35-20	30-5
Jowāri	33-14	33-14	33-14	33-14	33-14	26-20	35-20	34-17	38-0	38-0	98-0	35-0	35-20	35-20
Kuri	11-5	11-5	12-20	11-5	13-11	11-5	...	11-5	11-5	...	11-20	...	12-8	12-8
European radish ...	500?0	500?0	12-20	12-20	13-11	13-11	12-20	13-20	13-11	13-11	13-11	13-11	...	13-11
Lahdarah	26-21	26-21	22-9	24-11	26-21	26-21	29-2	22-9	28-0	27-24	26-21	29-2	...	21-21
Kodaram	32-11	33-4	29-2	32-5	29-2	33-14	29-2	27-24	29-2	29-2	33-14	23-8	...	34-17
Mandwah	29-2	31-20	23-2	27-14	27-24	27-10	28-0	25-17	26-21	26-21	25-17	28-0	25-17	29-9
Sesame seed	42-12	40-0	44-18	44-18	52-12	49-5	46-24	39-3	44-18	45-21	41-24	46-24	...	44-18
Shamākh	11-5	11-5	12-8	11-5	11-19	12.20	11-19	11-19	11-5	11-4	11-5	11-5	13-11	13-11
Mung	38-0	42-0	43-11	38-6	35-26	40-6	36-23	26-22	[illegible]	[illegible]	[illegible]	[illegible]	[illegible]	[illegible]

Supplement to the Spring Harvest of the Súbah of Delhi.

	Suhnah.	Kohānah.	Deoband, &c.	Sardhanah, &c.	Kerānah, &c.	Indri.	Suburban district of Sirhind.	Thānesar, &c.	Thārah, &c.	Samānah, &c.	Suburban district of Sambhal.	Chāndpur, &c.	Lakhnor, &c.
	D. J.	D. J.	D. J.	D. J.	D. J.	D. J.	D. J.	D. J.	D. J.	D. J.	D. J.	D. J.	D. J.
Wheat	34-21	67-2	55-23	58-4	58 0	51-11	51-11	59-5	51-11	51-11	55-21	54-20	50-8
Cabul Vetches ...	...	...	...	...	...	...	...	...	...	...	59-22½	...	...
Indian do. ...	35 0	33-14	33-14	34-17	35-8	32-23	35-0	31-22	33-3	33-14	33-14	35-20	35-20
Barley	42-12	44-18	35-8	38-0	40-6	36-23	35-0	31-22	39 3	33-14	33-14	35-20	35-20
Adas	24-15	24-15	25-11	29-9	23-15	26-1	24-11	11-23	22-9	15-23	24-15	24-15	24-18
Safflower	76-17	71-14	84-24	84-24	71-14	76 0	176-0	76-0	76-0	76-0	71-14	69-20	70-11
Poppy	...	123-0	150 7	145-9	125-3	126-9	126 9	126-9	126-9	126-9	127-11	127-1	120-0
Potherbs	...	60-9	64-21	64 21	55-21	58-7	59-7	59-7	58-5	57-5	57-½	57-1	58-1
Linseed	32 11	30-14	27-24	29-9	31-8	25-18	26-21	25 18	25-18	26-21	24-11	24-15	24-16
Mustard seed ...	...	33-14	29-2	31-20	29-2	21-21	26-21	25 17	26-0	26-21	29 2	27-24	26-7
Arzān	...	21-6	20-9	19 0	20-9	17 22	17-22	17 22	17 22	17-22	17-22	17-9	17-9
Peas	31-20	31-20	32-11	30-5	26-21	20-9	22 9	22-3	22-20	25-0	30-5½	30 0	...
Carrots	...	29-2	26-21	23-12	24-16	26-21	26 21	22-7	26-1	26 1	26-1	26-1	26-1
Onions	...	...	82-19	84 24	81-16	87-7	82-18	82 18	82-18	83-21	...	82-18	82-18
Fenugreek	...	55-23	...	49 0	60-17	51-11	...	40 6	51-11	41-2	67-10	62-11	...
Persian Musk Melons	...	111-20	145-0	145-9	100-16	115-20	112-23	113-12	111 20	111-20	114-1	111-20	113-12
Indian ditto ...	11-16	11-16	19-0	17 22	11-16	14-9	14-14	14-14	14-14	15-16	15-16	11-20	11-16
Kur rice	...	51-11	60 9	53-17	53-17	41-9	41-9	49-17	41-9	42-12	42-12	...	38-0
Ajwāin	...	84-24	84-24	84-24	89-15	84-24	85-0	84-24	84-24	85-0	84-24	42-12 (?)	24-24 (?)

Supplement to the Autumn Harvest of the Subah of Delhi.

	Suhnah.	Kolānah.	Deoband, &c	Sardhanah, &c.	Kerānah, &c.	Indri.	Suburban district of Sirhind.	Thānesar, &c.	Thārah, &c.	Sāmanah, &c.	Suburban district of Sambal.	Chāndpur, &c.	Lakhnor, &c.
	D. J.	D. J.	D. J.	D. J.	D. J.	D. J.	D. J.	D. J.	D. J.	D. J.	D. J.	D. J.	D. J.
Sugarcane (*paundah*)	218-0	...	216-20	216-20	214-1	240-12	240-12	240-12	240-12	230-12	220-6	220-0	216-0
Common Sugarcane	134-16	134-16	123-0	123-0	123-0	118-13	121-22	120-19	118-13	118-12	129-17	130-20	120-29
Common rice ...	58-4	33-17	42-12	48-9	44-48	42-12	42-12	42-18	44-14	49-15	42-12	41-9	42-12
Māsh	36-23	35-20	32-11	34-17	33-14	32-15	33-14	33-0	32-12	31-8	34-12	35.19	31-20
Cotton	95-1	89-11	89-11	89-11	91-17	107-8	107-8	150-2	58-20	105-2	102-21½	97-10	46-14
Moth	24-15	26-9	20-9	22-0	26-21	21-6½	22-9	22-9	21-1	21-6	22-9	22-9	22-3
Gāl	15-16	16-19	15-16	16-19	16-9	13-11	14-14	14-14	13-11	14-14	15-16	15-16	15-3
Arzan	23-12	22-9	20-9	22-9	23-3	23-3	23-3	23-3	23-3	21-3	21-6	22-9	19-14
Indigo	168-0	161-0	157-13	161-0	161-0	161-0	161-0	161-0	161-0	161-0	163-6	156-13	161-14
Hinna	78-20	88-7	77-4	71-14	86-1	70-11	69-20	70-11	70-11	70-11	73-20½	72-17	72-17
Hemp		89-11	82-18	83-21	82-18	82-12	82-12	82-12	82-12	82-12	89-11	89-11	89-11
Potherbs	77-7	71-14	71-14	78-7	70-14	71-14	71-14	70-11	71-14	71-14	78-6	78-7	73-20
Kachrah	13-11	13-11	12-8	12-8	12-8	11-5	11-19	11-5	11-19	11-19	11-5	11-14½	12-20
Pān	223-11	223-15	245-24	223-15	223-15	223-15	223-15	223-15	223-15	223-15	223-15	223-15	...
Singhārah	...	...	...	111-20	111-20	111-20	111-20	111-20	111-20	111-20	111-20	111-20	...
Lobiya	33-14	27-24	30-5	25-21	...	...	...	...	...	...	26-23	26-21	27-10
Jowār	36-23	35-20	26-21	35-14	33-14	33-14	33-14	34-17	33-14	33-14	36-22	38-18	36-23
Kuri	13-11	13-11	11-5	12-8	10-3	12-23	13-20	12-22	12-22	12-8	...	...	...
European radish ...	13-11	13-11	12-8	12-8	12-20	11-5	11-19	11-5	11-19	11-19	11-5	11-14½	12-20
Lahdarah	26-21	26-21	22-9	22-9	26-21	24-15	25-4	24-15	24-25	24-15	24-15	24-15	22-9
Kodaram	33-14	35-20	38-24	29-9	33-14	26-7	25-18	26-21	26-7	24-15	27-23	26-20	26-7
Mandwah	27-10	27-24	24-15	29-9	30-20	24-15	25-18	24-15	24-15	24-15	26-6½	27-24	25-18
Sesame seed ...	49-5	44-18	34-17	44-18	40-6	40-6	41-3	41-9	40-6	40-6	44-18	48-2	39-3
Shamākh	12-8	13-11	11-5	12-20	11-5	11-5	11-5	11-5	11-5	11-5	11-18	11-5	11-19
Mung	40-6	38-0	38-0	34-15	40-6	40-6	40-6	40-6	40-6	38-0	40-6	40-6	36-22
Turmeric	...	...	27-24	...	...	...	...	...	...	111-20	...	...	...

The *Subah* of *Lāhore* contains 8 populated areas[119] (*Tieff. pagi et oppida*).

1. The area of *Lāhore*, &c. has 20 mahals, 1 code. Area of *Lāhore*, &c. 4 mahals; metropolitan area, *Bāri Doāb; Barhiāsat;*[120] lands of *Panj Bari Shāhpur*: lands of *Kālapand, Rachnāu Doāb.*

Panjāb, 16 mahals: Tappah[121] *Bheluwāl* of the *Bari Doāb, Tappah Bharli, Tappah Phulwāri, Punjgarāmi, Sandhwāl, Sāhu Mali, Sidhpur, Mankatwālah, Ghāzipur, Chandanwarak, Amrāki Bhatah, Parsaror, Rachnau, Sidhpur Panchnagar, Garbandwāl.*

2. *Sarkār* of *Jālandhar*, 30 hahals. 1 code. *Jālandhar, Sultānpur, Shaikhpur, Melsi, Lohi Dheri, Nakodar, Talon, Muhammadpur, Miani Nuriya, Kharkharaon, Rahimabad, Jalalabad, Hādiābād, Bajwārah, Harhānah*, and *Akbarabad*, 2 mahals, *Balot, Bhonkā, Hājipur, Pati Dhināt, Dardak Sāhimalot, Andwarah, Dadiāl, Kard Jālar? Sarkar* (?). *Deswahah, Chaurāsi, Naunankal, Nobi.*

3. *Sarkār* of *Batālah*, &c. 14 mahals, 1 code. *Battālah, Kanuwāhan, Kalānor, Jamāri, Hanwād* and *Baba*, 2 mahals, *Thandot, Dābhāwālah, Khokhowāl, Paniyal, Bhalot, Katwahā* and *Bethān*, 2 mahals, Salimābād separate from Battālah.

4. *Pati Haibatpur*, &c., 6 mahals, 1 code. *Haibatpur, Hoshiār Karnālah, Firozpur, Qasur, Muhammadot, Deosah.?*

5. *Sarkār* of *Parsaror*, &c., 7 mahals, 1 code. *Parsaror, Maukri, Mahror, Pati Zafarwāl, Pati Bārmak, Haminagar.*

6. *Sarkār* of *Rohtās*, &c., 9 mahals. 1 code. *Rohtās, Kari, Kariāli, Bahni, Andarhal, Losdah, Sardahi, Malotrai Kedāri, Nandanpur.*

7. *Sarkār* of *Siālkot*, &c., 11 mahals, 1 code. *Siālkot, Mānkot, Wan, Sodrah, Narot, Renhā, Jimah Chatah, Marāt, Mankoknor Sialkot?*

---

[119] The term *sawād* is usually applied to the towns and villages of Arabian Irāq [*i.e.*, the *sown* or cultivated area, as distinct from the desert], as those in Khurasān are called *rustāk*, and in Arabia Felix *makhālif*.

[120] This name does not occur in the account of Lahore later on. The variants are *Barhiāt, Barhāt, Barsāhāt, Barsahasāt*. It is scarcely necessary to note that the words *Bāri* and *Rachna* in connection with Doāb are formed by the crasis of *Beās* and *Rāvi*, in the former case, and *Rāvi* and *Chenāb* in the latter.

[121] *Tappah* denotes a small tract or division of country smaller than a parganah, but comprising one or more villages. In some parts of the North-West, it denotes a tract in which there is one principal town or a large village with lands and villages acknowledging the supremacy of one amongst them and forming a sort of corporate body, although not otherwise identical. Wilson's *Gloss.*

8. *Sarkār* of *Hazārah*, &c., 16 mahals, 1 code. *Hazārah, Chandanwat* of the *Chenāu Doāb, Bherah, Khokharwāl, Khushāb, Kal Bhelak,*[122] *Khār Darwāzah, Tāral, Shor, Shamshābād,* separate from *Bherah, Shorpur* separate from *Chandanwat, Shakarpur* separate from *Shor.*

Spring Harvest of the Subah of Lahore.

	Lahore, &c.	Battālah, &c.	Parsaror, &c.	Pati Haibatpur, &c.	Jālandhar, &c.	Rohtās, &c.	Siālkot, &c.	Hazārah, &c.
	D. J.	D. J.	D. J.	D. J.	D. J.	D. J.	D. J.	D. J.
Wheat	50-18	49-5	53-17	58-17	53-17	44-18	38-17	55-23
Cabul Vetches ...	64-21	...	...	...		60-10	70-15	...
Indian do. ...	85-20	33-14	85-20	83-14	...	31-8	85-20	34-17
Barley	46-0	35-20	88-0	38-0	...	31-8	38-0	38-0
Adas	26-21	24-15	24-15	24-15	...	22-9	28-21	26-2
Safflower	79-10	79-10	78-10	79-2	...	67-2	78-7	79-10
Poppy	129-17	129-17	129-17	129-17	...	115-20	129-18	129-17
Potherbs	71 14	67-2	67-2	67-2		55-20	67-0	67-2
Linseed	31-8	27-24	27-24	31-8	...	22-9	29-22	81-8
Mustard seed ...	81-8	29-2	31-8	31-8	...	26-21	81-8	35-21
Arzan	21-6	19-0	19-0	21-6	...	15-16	20-3	20-8
Peas	24-15	26-21	27-4	26-21	...	26-21	81-8	27-24
Carrots	24-15	25-18	24-15	24-15	...	19-0	24-15	24-15
Onions	88-21	83-21	86-18	83-21	...	71-13	88-21	84-24
Fenugreek	50-8	46-24	61-12	40-6	...	60-10	67-2	36-28
Persian Water Melons	115-20	115-20	115-20	115-20	...	89-15	111-20	111-20
Indian ditto ...	15-16	15-16	15-16	15-16	...	11-13	15-16	15-16
Cummin	57-5	84-24	84-5	87-5	...	81-4	84-24	87-5
Ajwāin	87-5	84-24	84-0	87-0	...	71-4	84-34	87-5

Autumn Harvest of the Subah of Lahore.

	Lahore, &c.	Battālah, &c.	Parsaror, &c.	Pati Haibatpur, &c.	Jālandhar, &c.	Rohtās, &c.	Siālkot, &c.	Hazārah, &c.
	D. J.	D. J.	D. J.	D. J.	D. J.	D. J.	D. J.	D. J.
Sugarcane (*paundah*)	240-12	240-12	240-12	240-12	240-12	183-12½	...	240-12
Common Sugarcane ...	145-9	136-10	145-0	134-4	123-0	123-0		170-15
Dark coloured rice ...	64-21	60-9	60-15	60-15	58-4	50-8	67-0	66-0
Common rice ...	49-5	40-6	40-6	46-24	46-12½	33-14	41-9	49-5
Kalt	32-11	31-8	31-8	30-5	32-15	26-21	81-8	29-2
Māsh	35-20	33-4	35-20	38-14	38-14	31-8	85-20	36-28
Cotton	80-15	85-0	87-5	88-5	89-15	76-5	77-5	91-18

[122] In the account of Lahor, *Bhalak.*

Autumn Harvest of the Subah of Lahore.—continued.

	Lahore. &c.	Battālah, &c.	Parsaror, &c.	Pati Haibat-pur, &c.	Jālandhar, &c.	Rohtās, &c.	Siālkot, &c.	Hazārah, &c.
	D. J.	D. J.	D. J.	D. J.	D. J.	D. J.	D. J.	D. J.
Moth	20-9	22-9	23-23	22-9	22-9	20-3	23-12½	23-12½
Gāl	17-22	15-16	17-20	17-20	15-16	13-12	16-15	19-0
Turiya	...	33-14	35-20	26-21	...	31-8	38-0	...
Arzan	20-9	17-0	17-22	22-9	15-22	14-14	17-22	29-2
Indigo	156-23	156-13	156-13	156-13	156-13	134-4	134-18	158-19
Hinna	70-0	70-0	74-23	76-0	74-23	67-6	74-23	77-24
Hemp	93-23	93-23	93-23	93-23	89-15	80-12	93-23	93-23
Potherbs	80-12½	80-17	80-17	80-12½	80-17	60-9	70-17	80-12½
Kachrah	12-8	12-8	12-8	12-8	12-8	10-6	12-8	13-11
Pān	123-15	123-15	...	123-15	...	...	...	123-15
Singhārah	115-20	115-20	...	115-20	...	...	...	115-20
Jowāri	40-6	35-20	38-0	38-0	35-20	31-8	38-0	38-0
Lahdarah	31-8	29-2	30-5	29-2	26-21	24-15	23-2	31-8
Kodaram	33-14	35-20	34-17	31-8	33-14	31-8	35-20	35-20
Mandwah	33-14	31-8	31-8	32-15	26-21	26-21	21-20	32-15
Sesame	46-24	42-12	42-12½	44-18	40-6	33-14	48-12½	46-24
Shamākh	13-15	12-20	12-8	12-8	12-9	10-2	12-8	13-15
Mung	40-12½	...	...	...	40-6	26-21	44-18	44-18
Kori	13-15	12-8	12-8	12-8	15-5	10-2	12-8	12-8
Turmeric	133-0	133-0	138-0	134-4	133-0	115-20	134-4	133-20

Subah of Mālwah.

1. *Sarkār* of *Ujjain*, 10 mahals. City of *Ujjain* with suburban district, *Dipālpur, Ratlām, Nawlāi, Badhnāwar, Kanel, Anhal, Khāchrod, Sānwer, Pānbihār.*

2. *Sarkār* of *Hindiah*, 22 mahals.
3. ,, ,, *Kotri*, 9 do.
4. ,, ,, *Sārangpur*, 23 do.
5. ,, ,, *Bijagarh*, 32 do.
6. ,, ,, *Gāgron*, 11 do.

7. *Sarkārs* of *Raisin* and *Chanderi*, 1 code. *Sarkār* of *Raisin, Asāpori*, &c.· 6 mahals. *Bhilsah, Bhori· Bhojpur, Bālābhat, Thānah Mir Khān, Jājoi, Jhatānawi, Jalodah, Khiljipur, Dhāmoni, Dekhwārah, Deorod, Dhāniah·* *Raisin* with suburban district, *Sewāni· Sarsiah, Shāhpur, Khimlāsah, Khera, Kesorah, Khāmgarh, Kargarh, Korai· Laharpur, Māhsamand.* *Sarkār* of *Mando*, 12 mahals. City of *Mando, Amjharah, Mahesar, Dikthān, Dharmagāon, Sānkor, Panmān, Dhār, Barodah, Hāsilpur, Sanasi, Kotrah, Manāwarah Nalchah* and *Nawali*, 2 mahals.

Subah of Multān.

Sarkār of *Dipālpur.* Dipālpur, &c., 14 mahals; one *Dastur; Dipālpur, Lakhi bālā Bhoj, Lakhi Kalnārki, Lakhi Yusfāni,*[123] *Lakhi. Khokharāin, Kabulah, Lakhi Rahimābād, Lakhi Chahni, Lakhi Qiyāmpur, Lakhi Jangli, Lakhi Aālampur, Jalālābād, Tappah Sadkarah,* 2 mahals. *Tappah Sadkarah, Shahzādah Baloj, Karal, Khānpur, Rasulpur, Shahzādah Hajrau, Mundi.*

Spring Harvest of the Subah of Multān.[124] — *Spring Harvest of the Subah of Mālwah.*

	Multān, &c. 26 mahals.	Dipālpur, &c. 14 mahals.	Sadkarah, &c. 11 mahals.	Ujjain, &c.			Raisen, &c.	Māndo, &c.
	D. J.	D. J.	D. J.	M.[123]	D.	J.	D. J.	D. J.
Wheat	58-17	44-18	51-11		...		29-20	...
Cabul Vetches ...	...	...	...		...		40-12	...
Barley	49-5	30-5	30-20		...		46-24	...
Adas	44-5	24-15	47-14		...		30-5	...
Safflower	73-20	78-20	70-8	3¼	2	13	69-20	...
Poppy	115-20	128-15	129-0	4¼	5	20	127-15	...
Pot-herbs	67-2	70-15	67-2	8¼	2	13	60-9	...
Linseed	...	29.2	31-8		...		31-8	...
Mustard seed ...	44-18	29-2	31-2	3½	2	13	...	...
Arzan	29-2	20-17	20-8		...		16-12	...
Peas	...	23-12	25-17		...		31-8	...
Carrots	...	22-9	36-1		...		27-24	...
Onions	71-14	74-7	72-18		...		...	...
Fenugreek ...	69-20	89-8	44-18		...		...	...
Persian musk melons	...	116-0	115-20	8¼	1	3	115-20	...
Indian do. ...	22-9	15-16	15-16		...		15-0	...
Cumin	73-20	74-8	77-11		...		46-2	...
Kur rice	...	...	...		...		85-0	...
Ajwāin	...	...	...		...		86-2	...

[123] *M.* stands for *Muzaffari*, see Vol. I, p. 23.

[124] In this and the table of the Spring harvest of Lahore I consider *mang* a misprint for *mashang* which occurs in this order in all the previous tables. *Mung,* the *Phaseolus mungo,* is recorded only in the Autumn harvest.

Autumn Harvest of the Subah of Multān. *Autumn Harvest of the Subah of Mālwah.*

	Multān& c. 22 mahals.	Dipālpur &c. 14 mahals.	Sadkarah &c. 11 mahals.	Ujjain, &c.			Raisen, &c.	Mando, &c.		
	D. J.	D. J.	D. J.	M.	D.	J.	D. J.	M.	D.	J.
Sugarcane (*paundah*) ...	...	240-12	240-11	7½	1	21	239-6		...	
Common Sugarcane	134-4	126-9	143-3	4¼	5	8	48-15	6	1	0
Dark coloured rice	...	60-3	64-21		...		70-18		...	
Common rice ...	49-5	49-15	49-5		...		55-3		...	
Kalt	...	27-24	31-3		...		46-6		...	
Māsh	40-0	32-11	35-20		...		...		...	
Cotton	93-23	87-5	89-11	2¾	1	2	87-5	2¾	3	1
Moth	38-0	22-9	23-12		...		26-21		...	
Gāl	26-21	17-22	19-0		...		8-3		...	
Arzan	31-20	23-12	22-9		...		...		...	
Indigo	145-9	150-19	159-22	2¾	1	2	4-24		...	
Hinna	76-0	76-0	76-0		...		...	2½	1	1
Hemp	85-0	91-17	93-23		...		...		...	
Pot-herbs	73-20	77-4	82-18		...		...		...	
Pān	...	123-0	...		...		...		...	
Singhārah ...	...	111-0	...	4¼	5	20	115-20	6¼	4	7
Lobiya	38-0	38-0	33-14		...		...		...	
Jowāri	42-12	35-20	38-0		...		44-18		...	
Kuri	...	13-11	12-8		...		15-16		...	
Lahdarah ...	44-18	29-2	31-2		...		...		...	
Kodaram ...	...	33-14	33-14		...		...		...	
Mandwah ...	...	30-19	31-8		...		31-8		...	
Sesame	41-9	43-15	44-18		...		40-12		...	
Shamākh ...	12-8	12-8	13-11		...		...		...	
Mung	...	...	...		...		40-5		...	

Note.—I cannot understand nor explain the notation in Muzaffaris and am not sure if I have interpreted it correctly.

EDITOR'S NOTE

On the correction of place-names and dynastic lists in Jarrett's translation, vol. II.

In tracing the Hindu personal names and the numerous less important place-names, the variant readings given in the printed Persian text of the *'Ain-i-Akbari* are of no help to us, unless we know the correct names from other sources, such as (in the case of topography) large-scale maps and the records in the modern revenue and judge's courts of those areas. Similarly, Tieffenthaler's *Geography of Hindustan* (Fr. trans. by Bernoulli, 1786) is of no real use to us; he merely translated from Persian mss of the *'Ain,* and where his names differ from those in our printed text of the *'Ain,* he can be correct only in the rare instances of his having had a more correct and legible ms. of the book before him and his having transcribed these names in Roman letters without a mistake. Most of the mistakes in the proper names are due to the ignorance or carelessness of the Muslim clerks of Abul Fazl and the later copyists of his book. Students of Persian mss know that the usual sources of mistake in mss are the confusion, in writing, of the letters *R, D,* and *W,* (and sometimes also *HU* for *DU*) and the wrong placing (or omission) of dots (*nuqta*) by which *B, T, N, Y, P* and *H* are confounded together.

The only dependable means of correcting the place-names in the *'Ain-i-Akbari* is to use the Survey of India maps (quarter-inch or even one inch to the mile sheets), and this I have done. But absolute certainly on this point can be gained only by carefully verifying these names from the old revenue and civil court records of each particular sub-division included in the *'Ain.* I wish that local inquirers would do this work and send the result to the Royal Asiatic Society of Bengal (Calcutta) for incorporation in a future edition of this translation.

Unlike his brother Faizi who was a Sanskrit scholar, Abul Fazl did not know that difficult language. So, the author of Akbar's *Imperial Gazetteer* had to engage a number of Brahman pandits and Kayasth scribes, and they read out and summarised in Urdu the legendary Hindu history from the Sanskrit epics and Purānas and quasi-historical works like the *Rajatarangini* and the guide-books to famous Hindu shrines (*i.e., māhātmyas* and *khandas.*) These summaries were put down in Persian by Abul Fazl's clerks. Pickings from these Persian notes went to the making of ancient Hindu history as given by Abul Fazl in the final shape of the *'Ain-i-Akbari.*

When Col. Jarrett made his translation of the second volume of the *'Ain-i-Akbari* in the Eighteen-eighties, his only sources for ancient Hindu history were Wilson's *Vishnu Purāna* and Prinsep's *Useful Tables*, and for early Muslim history, Firishtah, *Riyāz-us-Salātin* and similar uncritical early works. During the sixty years and more that have passed since then, the study of Indian history has made such a great advance that it would be an injustice to the modern reader—and also to Jarrett's memory,—to reprint his notes from obsolete authors. I have therefore felt it necessary to sweep away his heaps of dead leaves (as I have called them in my introduction to the revised edition of the third volume of the *'Ain*), and to give extracts only from modern authorities, such as the Dacca University *History of Bengal* (vol. I. Hindu period, vol. II. Muslim Rule), R. D. Banerji's *History of Orissa* in 2 volumes (1930-1931, replacing the ante-diluvian Hunter's *Orissa* of 1872, which Jarrett cited,), the *Cambridge History of India,* Elliot and Dowson, &c.

In fact, Abul Fazl's Hindu history is of no real value, as it was entirely drawn from traditions and myths, long before the age of critical historiography based upon inscriptions, coins and records. Hence, I have not wasted paper by trying to refute every error in this portion of the *'Ain,* but I have given exact references to modern sources, where the reader will find the necessary correct information on the subject.

The pandits employed by Abul Fazl have made a hotch-potch of the old history of Hindustan by mixing together legendary and historical kings, inserting real royal names of one dynasty or province into the dynastic list of another, and thus inextricably mingling truth and fancy together, *e.g.,* Anangahbima was a real king of Orissa (three of the dynasty bearing that name) shortly before the Muslim invasion, but Abul Fazl makes him the son of the pre-historic Bhagadatta, the comrade of Duryodhan of the *Mahābhārat* and a king of Bengal! So also, Bhoja, who reigned elsewhere than in Bengal and was a Kshatriya, is made in the *'Ain* a Kāyastha and the founder of the second line of Bengal kings.

As for Raja *Naujah,* Abul Fazl is confused, making him the last king of the Sena dynasty in one place, and the father of Lakshman Sena in another. I cannot conceive how *Nārāyan* can be misspelt in Persian writing as *Naujah.* I suggest the emendation *Budh-sen* (a real king at the end of the Senas) for *Naujah* in the list, and *Raja of Nudia* for *Raja-i-Naujah* at the first mention.

Correct list of the Pala kings of Bengal—

Gopāla I., accession ...	... *c.* 750 A.D.
Dharma-pāla ...	... 770
Deva-pāla	... 810
Vigraha-pāla I or Sura-pāla I	... 850
Nārāyana-pāla ...	... 854
Rājya-pāla	... 908
Gopāla II.	... 940
Vigraha-pāla II ...	... 960
Mahi-pāla I	... 988
Naya-pāla	... 1038
Vigraha-pāla III ...	... 1055
Mahi-pāla II ...	... 1070
Sura-pāla II	... 1075
Rāma-pāla	... 1077
Kumāra-pāla ...	... 1120
Gopāla III	... 1125
Madana-pāla ...	... 1140
Govinda-pāla ...	... 1155

(D.U. *Bengal,* i. 176-177.)

Correct list of the Sena kings of Bengal—

Vira-sena (progenitor, not Raja)

Sāmanta-sena

Hemanta-sena, 1st Raja, in Rārh acc. *c.* 1080.

Vijaya-sena, conquered all Bengal except Gaur, (r. 1125-58)

Vallāla-sena, *r.c.* 1158-1179

Lakshman-sena, *r.c.* 1179-1206. His sons Vishwa-rupa-sena and Keshav-sena ruled in East Bengal till *c.* 1230. Surya-sena and Purushottama-sena were probably the sons of Vishwa-rupa, and were in power till *c.* 1245. Among the chiefs with names ending in Sena, in Eastern India in the 13th century, are Buddha-sena (of Pithi) and his son Jaya-sena, and Madhu-sena (date prob. 1289); but they were mere local barons or zamindārs and not ruling sovereigns. (D.U. *Bengal,* i. 205-228.)

Correct list of the Pre-Mughal Muslim rulers of Bengal leaving out the viceroys and rebel sultans from Qutbuddin Aibak to Md. Tughluq Shah, 1202-1339.)—

Ala-ud-din Ali (Mubārak) accession 1339 A.D.

Early Ilyās Shāhi dynasty

Shams-ud-din Ilyās (Bhangāra),	... r.	1348-'57
Sikandar Shah ...	... r.	1357-c. '91
Ghiyās-ud-din Ā'zam Shāh	... c.	1391-1409
Ghiyās-ud-din Ā'zam Shāh	... c.	1391-1409
Saifuddin Hamza Sh.	...	1409-10
Shihābuddin Bāyezid Sh. (title Shams-ud-dīn) ...	...	1411-13
'Alauddin Firuz Sh. ...	...	1414

Hindu dynasty

Ganesh (*var.* Kans) ...	...	1414-1418
Jalāluddin, s. of Ganesh	...	1418-31
Shams-ud-din Ahmad	...	1431-42

Later Ilyās Shāhi dynasty.

Nāsir-ud-din Mahmud I	...	1442-59
Rukn-ud-din Bārbak Sh.	...	1459-74
Shams-ud-din Yūsuf Sh.	...	1471-81
Jalāl-ud-din Fath Sh. ...	...	1481-87

Abyssinian dynasty.

Bārbak Shah	... 6 months,	1487
Saif-ud-din Firuz Sh.	...	1487-90
Nāsir-ud-din Mahmud II	...	1490-91
Shams-ud-din Muzaffar	...	1491-93

(Arab) Husain Shāhi dynasty.

A'la-ud-din Husain Shāh,	...	1493-1510
Nāsir-ud-din A. M. Nasrat Sh.	...	1519-32
A'la-ud-din Firuz ...	...	1532-33
Ghiyās-ud-din Mahmud,	...	1533-38

Sur dynasty.

Sher Shāh	... ...	1539-45
Islām Shāh	... ...	1545-53
Shams-ud-din Md. Sh.	...	1553-55
Ghiyās-ud-din Bahādur (Khizr Kh.)		1556-60
Ghiyās-ud-din II	... ...	1561-63
His son ...	... 7 months,	1563
Ghiyās-ud-din III	... one year	1564

Karrāni dynasty (Afghan).

Tāj Kh. Karrāni	... ... r.	1564-65
Sulaiman Karrāni	... ...	1565-72
Bāyezid Karrāni	... ...	1572
Dāud Karrāni	... ...	1573-76

(See D.U. *Bengal,* vol. II)

Note on the sarkars of Bengal in Akbar's time.

In view of the frequent changes in the administrative geography of Bengal under British rule and the radical change resulting from the partition of Bengal in August 1947, it is impossible to indicate briefly the extent of any of the *sarkārs* of the *'Ain* in terms of the districts of the two parts of Bengal as they are today. Among the striking points of difference are that under Mughal rule (*a*) southern and western Midnapur belonged to Orissa and not to Bengal, (*b*) the district of Purnia and the eastern portion of Bhagalpur were attached to Bengal and not to Bihar, and (*c*) Sikhar-bhum (old name of Pachet), Dhaval-bhum, and Singbhum formed parts of the *Sarkār* of Mandaran belonging to Bengal.

The following table of approximate equivalents between Akbar's *sarkārs* and the Bengal districts in the last stage of British rule may be of some help to the modern reader.

Sarkars		*Districts*
Udambar	...	Rajmahal subdivision, N.W. Murshidabad, and N. Birbhum.
Jannatābād	...	Malda (mainly)
Fathābād	...	Faridpur, South Bakarganj and the islands at the mouth of the Ganges.
Mahmudābād	...	North Nadia, North Jessore, and West Faridpur.
Khilāfatābād	...	South Jessore and West Bakarganj.

Sarkars		*Districts*
Baklā ...	...	North and East Bakarganj and S.-W. Dacca.
Tājpur	...	East Purnia and West Dinajpur.
Ghorāghāt	...	S. Rangpur, S.-E. Dinajpur, and N. Bogra.
Pinjāra	...	Dinajpur and parts of Rangpur and Rajshahi.
Bārbakābād	...	mainly Rajshahi, S.W. Bogra and S.E. Malda.
Bāzuhā	...	partly Rajshahi, Bogra, Pabna and Dacca.
Sonārgāon	...	West Tippera and Noakhali.
Sharifatābād	...	mostly Burdwan.
Sulaimanābād	...	North Hugli, and adjacent parts of Nadia and E. Burdwan.
Sātgāon	...	24 Parganas, W. Nadia (?) and Howrah.
Mandāran	...	Bankura, Vishnupur, S.E. Burdwan and W. Hugli.

Bāzuhā—This word is the Persian plural of *bāzu* meaning 'an arm', *i.e.*, the direction of a locality with reference to a central point such as the capital town. In early times the provinces of a kingdom were indicated as its different directions (*e.g.*, *Tarf*, *subah* from *sub*, whence the titles of provincial governors *Tarf-dār*, *subah-dār*, &c.) As will be noticed in the lists of the *'Ain*, in Orissa locality-names are compounded with the word *dik* meaning direction of the compass, and in Bengal and elsewhere with the word *dast*, meaning the right arm or the left arm, of the speaker. In Akbar's time the portion of Bengal known as *Bāzuhā* had not yet been consolidated into a compact area, but lay sprawling over many neighbouring districts and having no clear-marked boundaries. *Rāst* and *chap* mean the right and left hands respectively.

J. Sarkar.

ACCOUNT OF THE TWELVE SUBAHS.

In the fortieth year of the Divine Era [1594] His Majesty's dominions consisted of one hundred and five *Sarkārs* (divisions of a Subah) subdivided into two thousand seven hundred and thirty-seven townships (*qasba*). When the ten years' settlement of the revenue was made (which amounted to an annual rental of three *Arbs,* sixty-two *krors,* ninety-seven *lakhs,* fifty-five thousand two hundred and forty-six *dāms* [Rs. 9,07,43,881] and twelve *lakhs* of betel leaves), His Majesty apportioned the Empire into twelve divisions, to each of which he gave the name of *Subah* and distinguished them by the appellation of the tract of country or its capital city. These were Allahabad, Agra, Oudh, Ajmer, Ahmadābād, Behār, Bengal, Delhi, Kābul, Lāhor, Multān, Mālwah : and when Berār, Khandesh and Ahmadnagar were conquered, their number was fixed at fifteen. A brief description of each is here set down, and an account of their rulers together with the periods in which they flourished, duly recorded.

BENGAL SUBAH.

Since the conceptions of sovereign rule embrace the universe, I propose to begin with Bengal which is at one extremity of Hindustān and to proceed to Zabulistān[1] and I hope that Turān and Irān and other countries may be added to the count. The country lying to the east will be first described, followed by the north, the south, and the west.

This *Subah* is situated in the second clime.[2] Its length

---

[1] Kābul and the adjacent territory as far as Ghazna and even beyond come under this appellation which is derived by Yākut, *Majmu'a-ul-Buldān*) from Zābul, grandfather of Rustam.

[2] *Iqlim,* literally a slope or inclination, was used in the mathematical geography of the Greeks with reference to the inclination of various parts of the earth's surface to the plane of the equator. Before the globular figure of the earth was known, it was supposed that there was a general slope of its surface from S. to N. and this was called *klima.* But as the science of mathematical geography advanced, the word was applied to belts of the earth's surface, divided by lines parallel to the equator, those lines being determined by the different lengths, at different places, of the shadow cast by a gnomon of the same altitude, at noon of the same day. This division into climates was applied only to the N. hemisphere as the geographers had no practical knowledge of the earth S. of the equator. There were 19 climates as given by Ptolemy (*Geogr.* i, 23). The term was afterwards applied to the average temperature of each of these regions and hence our modern use of the word, (Smith's *Dict. of Antiq,* 2nd ed., art. Climates; also *Ency. of Islam,* ii. 460).

from Chittagong to *Garhi*[3] is four hundred *kos*. Its breadth from the northern range of mountains to the southern frontier of the *Sarkār* of *Mandāran*, is two hundred *kos*, and when the country of Orissa was added to this *Subah*, the additional length was forty-three *kos* and the breadth twenty-three. It is bounded on the east by the sea, on the north and south by mountains and on the west by the *Subah* of Behār. The tract of country on the east called *Bhāti*,[4] is reckoned a part of this province. It is ruled by Isa Afghān and the *Khutbah* is read and the coin struck in the name of his present Majesty. In this country the mango trees grow to the height of a man or not so high and produce abundant fruit. Adjoining it, is an extensive tract of country inhabited by the Tipperah tribes. The name of the ruler is *Bijay Mānik*. Whosoever obtains the chieftainship, bears the title of *Mānik* after his name, and the nobles that of *Nārāin*. He has a force of two hundred thousand footmen and a thousand elephants. Horses are scarce. To the north is a country called *Kuch*. Its chief commands a thousand horse and a hundred thousand foot. *Kāmrup*, commonly called also *Kāonrup* and *Kāmtā*, is subject to him. The inhabitants are as a race good looking and addicted to the practice of magic. Strange stories are told regarding them. It is said that they build houses, of which the pillars, walls and roofs are made of men. Some of these they compel by the power of sorcery, and criminals deserving of death are also thus made use of. Whoever voluntarily surrenders

---

The Arabs adopted this system but restricted the number to seven. They considered three-fourths of the globe to be submerged and one-fourth above water. Of this latter $\frac{1}{30}$ was habitable and the remainder waste or desert. The habitable portion was 33 150,000 square miles in extent, each mile being 4000 cubits, each cubit 24 digits. It was situated between the Equator and the N. pole and was divided into 7 climates.

[3] This is Teliagarhi, a pass in the Santhāl Parganahs, Bihar, lying between the Rājmahāl hills on the S. and the Ganges on the N. Formerly of strategic importance as commanding the military approaches to Bengal proper. The ruins of a large fort still exist, through which the E. I. Railway passes. It seems never to have been completed and was constructed in the last century by the Teli *zamindār* who was forcibly converted by the Muhammadans. Hence the name of the fort and the *parganah* in which it is situated. *Imp. Gazetteer*.

The *kos* is for convenience generally taken at two English miles. The basis of all linear systems is the same, *viz.*, the cubit or human forearm. Proceeding upwards four *hāths* or cubits = a *danda* or staff: and 2000 *dandas* a *kos*, which by this calculation should be 4000 yards English or nearly 2¼ miles. *Useful Tables*, p. 87. Also Elliot's *Memoir of Races, N. W. P.* II, 194.

[4] The name given by the Muhammadan historians to the coast-strip of the Sundarbans from Hijili to the Meghna Lat. 20° 30′ to 22° 30′ N., long. 88° to 91° 14′ E. The name means "low lands overflowed by the tide" and is still applied to the Sundarban tracts of Khulna and Bākarganj Districts. *I. G.* For Isa Kh., D.U. *Bengal*, ii. 194-212.

himself for this purpose, escapes retribution for a year. Various conveniences are reserved for him. In due time, men armed with swords cut them down, and from their movements or immobility or other aspects, they have cognizance of scarcity or plenty or duration of years [of the reign] or the longevity of the ruler or defeat of enemies. They also cut open a pregnant woman who has gone her full term of months and taking out the child, divine somewhat as to the future. There grows a wonderful tree whose branches when cut, exude a sweet liquid which quenches the drought of those athirst. They have also a mango tree[5] that has no trunk; it trails like a climbing vine, over a tree and produces fruit. There is likewise a flower[6] which after it has been gathered for two months, does not wither nor lose its colour or smell. Of this they make necklaces.

Bordering on this country are the dominions of the Rājah of Ashām (Assam) whose great pomp and state are subjects of general report. When he dies, his principal attendants of both sexes voluntarily bury themselves alive in his grave. Neighbouring this is Lower Tibet and to its left is *Khata.*[7] This is also called *Mahāchin* which the vulgar pronounce *Māchin.* From *Khān Bāligh*[8] its capital, to the ocean, a forty days' journey, they have cut a canal both sides of which are embanked with stone and mortar. Alexander of Greece advanced to that country by this route.[9] Another road is also mentioned which can be traversed in four days and four nights.

---

[5] The *Willoughbeia edulis.* It is known to natives of Bengal, Assam and the Chittagong Hill tracts, as the Loti Ā'm (*Loti,* for Sanskrit *latā,* a creeper) but botanically is far removed from the true mango. The fruit is said to be pleasant to taste. The leaf of the dried specimen is very similar to the ordinary mango leaf: the fruit is about 2½ inches long and 2¼ broad (Dr. King.)

[6] The *Tulsi,* (Ocymum Sanctum).

[7] China for nearly 1000 years, writes Yule (*Marco Polo,* 2nd ed. Introd., p. 11) has been known to Asia under the name of Khitai, Khata or *Cathay* and is still called Khitai by the Russians. [*Ency. Islam,* ii. 737 under *Kara Khitai.*]

[8] De Guignes (*Hist. des Huns.* gives this name to Pekin, called also Tatou the *grand court* or Khān Bāligh, *the court of the Khān.* Several towns have received this name which as it signifies the royal residence is transferable to any that the monarch may honour with his presence. It is the *Cambalu* of Western geographers and historians and placed by them in Northern China or Grand Tartary, while the Orientals locate it in China Proper. (*Ency. Islam,* ii. 898).

[9] In B.C. 329 Alexander crossed the Oxus in pursuit of Bessus and after putting him to death, he passed the Jaxartes (Sir Daria) and defeated several cythian tribes north of that river. This was the northernmost point that he reached. A. Fazl is merely relating the Muslim legend of Alexander, for which see *Ency. Islam,* ii. 533 under *al-Iskandar.* [J. S.]

To the south-east of Bengal is a considerable tract called *Arakan* which possesses the port of *Chittagong*. Elephants abound, but horses are scarce and of small size.[10] Camels are high priced : cows and buffaloes there are none, but there is an animal which has somewhat of the characteristics of both, piebald and particoloured, whose milk the people drink. Their religion is said to be different to that of the Hindus and Muhammadans. Sisters may marry their own twin brothers, and they refrain only from marriages between a son and his mother. The ascetics, who are their repositories of learning, they style *Wali* whose teaching they implicitly follow. It is the custom when the chief holds a court, for the wives of the military to be present, the men themselves not attending to make their obeisance. The complexion of the people is dark and the men have little or no beard.

Near to this tribe is *Pegu* which is also called *Chin*. In some ancient accounts it is set down as the capital city of *Chin*. There is a large military force of elephants and infantry, and white elephants are to be found. On one side of it is *Arakan*. There are mines of rubies, diamonds, gold, silver, copper, naphtha and sulphur, and over these mines there is continual contention between this country and the *Maghs* as well as the tribes of Tipperah.

The original name of Bengal was *Bang*. Its former rulers raised mounds measuring ten yards in height and twenty in breadth throughout the province which were called *Āl*.[1] From this suffix, the name Bengal took its rise and currency. The summer heats are temperate and the cold season very short. The rains begin when the sun is midway in Taurus, (May) and continue for somewhat more than six months, the plains being under water and the mounds alone visible. For a long time past, at the end of the rains, the air had been felt to be pestilential and seriously affected

---

[10] The domestic animals of the Arakan Hill Tracts according to the *Imp. Gaz.* are the *gayal*, buffalo, ox, goat, pig, dog. "The Gayal (*Bos Frontalis*) has interbred with the common Indian cattle; these hybrids are brought down by the Bhutiahs to the annual fair in the Darrung District : though they thrive in Shillong they soon die if kept in the plains. The Gayal is plentiful along the spurs of the Bhutān hills, amongst the Dufflas, Lushais, and along the hilly tract well into Chittagong." *Sport in British Burmah* by Lieut-Col. Pollock. An alternative reading gives, "horses are scarce, and asses and camels are high-priced," which Gladwin has adopted.

[1] Sansk. *āli* a mound of earth or ridge for crossing ditches, dividing fields and the like.

animal life, but under the auspices of his present Majesty, this calamity has ceased.

Its rivers are countless and the first of them in this province is the *Ganges*: its source cannot be traced. The Hindu sages say that it flows down from the hair of *Mahadeva's* head. Rising in the mountains towards the north, it passes through the province of Delhi, and imperial Agra, and Allahabad and Behār into the province of Bengal, and near *Qāzihattah* in the *Sarkar* of *Bārbakābād,* it divides into two streams. One of these, flowing east-wards, falls into the sea at the port of Chittagong. At the parting of the waters, it takes the name of *Padmāwati* and pursues a southern course. It is divided into three streams; one, the *Sarsuti* [Saraswati]; the second the *Jamna* (Jamuna) and the third the Ganges, called *collectively* in the Hindi language *Tribeni,*[2] and held in high veneration. The third stream after spreading into a thousand channels, joins the sea at *Sātgāon* [Hugli]. The *Sarsuti* and the Jamna unite with it. In praise of this stream the Hindu sages have written volumes. From its source to its mouth it is considered sacred, but some spots have a peculiar sanctity. Its water is carried as an offering of price to far distant places. Believing it to be a wave of the primeval river, they hold its worship to be an adoration of the supreme being, but this is no part of the ancient tradition. Its sweetness, lightness and wholesomeness attest its essential virtues. Added to this, it may be kept in a vessel for years without undergoing change.

Another river is the Brahmaputra. It flows from *Khatā*[3] (China) to *Kuch* and thence through the *Sarkār* of Bāzuhā and fertilising the country, falls into the sea.

And again there is the sea which is here a gulf of the great ocean, extending on one side as far as Basrah and on the other to the Egyptian Qulzum[4] and thence it washes

---

[2] Sansk. *tribeni* three braids of hair. Wilford says (*Asiatic Research,* Vol. XIV, p. 396) that the waters of these three rivers do not mix. The waters of the Jumna are blue, those of the Sarasvati white and the Ganges is of a muddy yellowish colour.

[3] Its rise is supposed to be from the S. E. base of the sacred Kailás hill, on the opposite side of the water-parting in which the Sutlej and the Indus also take their rise. Its course, con-fluents and history may be read in the *I. G.*

[4] This is the ancient Klysma, the site of the modern Suez, in the neighbourhood of which the Tel Qulzum still retains the name which has been given to the Red Sea. *Ency. Islam,* ii, 1114.

both Persia and Ethiopia where are Dahlak and Suākin, and is called (the Gulf of) Omān and the Persian Sea.

The principal cultivation is rice of which there are numerous kinds. If a single grain of each kind were collected, they would fill a large vase. It is sown and reaped three times a year on the same piece of land with little injury to the crop. As fast as the water rises, the stalks grow, so that the ear is never immersed, inasmuch as those experienced in such matters have taken the measure of a single night's growth at sixty cubits.[5] The people are submissive and pay their rents duly. The demands of each year are paid by instalments in eight months, they themselves bringing mohars and rupees to the appointed place for the receipt of revenue, as the division of grain between the government and the husbandman is not here customary. The harvests are always abundant, measurement is not insisted upon, and the revenue demands are determined by estimate of the crop. His Majesty in his goodness has confirmed this custom. Their staple food is rice and fish; wheat, barley and the like not being esteemed wholesome. Men and women for the most part go naked wearing only a cloth (*lungi*) about the loins. The chief public transactions fall to the lot of the women. Their houses are made of bamboos, some of which are so constructed that the cost of a single one will be five thousand rupees or more and they last a long time. Travelling is by boat, especially in the rains, and they make them of different kinds for purposes of war, carriage or swift sailing. For attacking a fort they are so constructed that when run ashore, their prow overtops the fort and facilitates its capture. For land travel they employ the *Sukhāsan*. This is a crescent-shaped litter covered with camlet or scarlet cloth and the like, the two sides of which have fastenings of various metals, and a pole supporting it is attached by means of iron hooks. It is conveniently adapted for sitting in, lying at full length or sleeping during travel. As a protection against sun and rain they provide a commodious covering which is removable at pleasure. Some enjoy the luxury of riding on elephants but they rarely take to horseback. The mats made here often resemble woven silk.

[5] Gladwin has *six* for *sixty*. The long stemmed rice, according to the *I.G.* is extensively cultivated in the swamps. The seed is sown when the marshes are dry or nearly so, and when the rains set in the plant shoots up with the rise of the water and can be grown in water to a depth of from 18 to 20 feet, but even this is not in one night.

Tria[6] inde genera eunuchorum veniunt, quo Sandalos, Bādāmos et Kāfuros nuncupant. Priores, partibus genitalibus radicaliter exsectis, Atlises etiam nominant. Bādāmis pars solum penis relinquitur. Kāfuros adhuc teneræ ætatis, testes vel compressi conficiuntur vel exsecantur: tamen notatum est, castrationem, quæ pervicaciam cæteris omnibus animalibus tollit, hominibus solis excitare.

Salt is in great demand and is brought from long distances. Diamonds, emeralds, pearls, cornelians and agates are imported. Flowers and fruit are in plenty. The betel-nut is of a kind that stains of a red colour the lips of those who chew it.

Jannatābād is an ancient city: for a time, it was the capital of Bengal and was widely known as Lakhnauti and for a while as Gaur. His Majesty the late Emperor Humāyun distinguished it by this title of Jannatābād. It has a fine fort and to the eastward of it is a lake called *Chhatiāpatiā* in which are many islands. Were the dam that confines it to break, the city would be under water. About a *kos* to the north of the fort, is a large building and a reservoir, monuments of great antiquity. From time immemorial, its water has been considered to be of a poisonous character. The place was called *Piyāsbāri* (abode of thirst), and criminals condemned to death, were there confined who in a short time perished from the effects of this brackish water. At present in the blessed reign of His Majesty, this practice has been discontinued.

Mahmudābād.—The marshes around the fort have added to its impregnability. The ruler of this district, at the time of its conquest by Sher Khān, let some of his elephants loose in its forests from which time they have abounded. Long pepper grows in this tract.

The *Sarkār* of *Khalifatābād* is well wooded and holds wild elephants. The *Sarkār* of *Baklā* extends along the sea shore. The fort is surrounded by woods. On the first day of the new moon the sea steadily rises until the fourteenth, and from the fifteenth till the end of the month as gradually falls. In the 29th year of the Divine Era, a terrible inundation occurred at three o'clock in the afternoon, which swept

[6] I have imitated the example of Gladwin in veiling the following passage under the mask of a learned language and with a slight alteration have borrowed his words. (Jarrett.)

over the whole *Sarkār*. The Rājah held an entertainment at the time. He at once embarked on board a boat, while his son Parmānand Rāe with some others climbed to the top of a temple and a merchant took refuge in a high loft. For four hours and a half the sea raged amid thunder and a hurricane of wind. Houses and boats were engulfed but no damage occurred to the temple or the loft. Nearly two hundred thousand living creatures perished in this flood.

In the *Sarkār* of *Ghoraghāt*, silk is produced and a kind of sackcloth [jute]. Numbers of eunuchs are here and hill ponies in plenty are procurable. There are many kinds of indigenous fruits, especially one called *Latkan*.[7] It is the size of a walnut with the taste of a pomegranate and contains three seeds.

The *Sarkār* of *Bārbakābād* produces a fine cloth called *Gangājal* (*Ganges water*), and a great abundance of oranges.

In the *Sarkār* of *Bāzuhā* are extensive forests which furnish long and thick timbers of which masts are made. There are also iron mines.

The *Sarkār* of *Sonārgāon*[8] produces a species of muslin very fine and in great quantity. In the township of *Egāra Sindur* is a large reservoir which gives a peculiar whiteness to the cloths that are washed in it.

In the *Sarkār* of Sylhet there are nine[9] ranges of hills. It furnishes many eunuchs.

There is a fruit called *Suntarah*[10] in colour like an orange

---

[7] Dr. King of the Royal Botanical Gardens, Calcutta, considers this to be a species of *Elœcarpus*. The fruits of all the species are a good deal alike, varying in size from an olive to a walnut, having an external flushy pulp more or less palatable (in some species of fair flavour) and containing a stone. The later is usually found to be divided into 3 cells, one of which contains a mature seed, the seeds in the other two being abortive. The taste of the pulp of the *E. serratus* and *E. lancœofolius* (both natives of Rangpúr) is a good deal like that of the pomegranate.

[8] This was the ancient Maḥammadan capital of Eastern Bengal but is now an insignificant village called Painám in the Dacca District. *I.G.*

[9] In the south of the district, says the *Gazetteer*, eight low ranges of hills run out into the plain, being spurs of the Tipperah mountains. The highest is about 1000 feet above sea level. There is also a small detached group, the Ita hills, in the centre of the district.

[10] Commonly *Sangtarah*. The name is supposed to be a corruption of Cintra, but its mention by Baber in his Memoirs seems subversive of this derivation, for though the fruit is said to have been an eastern importation into Portugal, it is improbable that the foreign name could have been current in India at so early a date. Humayun praises it highly saying that no one cares for any other fruit who has this. He states that it is found only at Sonárgáon in Bengal and in the greatest perfection only at one place. A note to the *Memoirs* (p. 329) says that the description of the fruit by Baber suits more the *Citrus decumana* than any other, and its Bengali name *Batavi nimbu*, the Batavia lime, denotes its being an exotic.

but large and very sweet. The China root[2] is produced in plenty. In ancient times it had not been discovered until some scientific travellers from European Turkey introduced it to universal notice. Aloes-wood is abundant in these mountains. At the end of the rains they fell the trees to the ground, and after a certain time they give them various names according to their greenness or maturity.

The *Bhangrāj*[3] is a bird of a black colour, with red eyes and a long tail. Two of the feathers extend to a length of a *gaz*. They are snared and tamed. It catches the note of any animal that it hears, and eats flesh. The *Sherganj* is of the same kind but its beak and legs are red; in imitating sounds, it matches the other and pursues sparrows and the like and eats them.

Chātgāon (Chittagong) is a large city situated by the sea and belted by woods. It is considered an excellent port and is the resort of Christian and other merchants.

In the *Sarkār* of *Sharifābād* is a beautiful species of cattle, white in colour, and of a fine build : like camels they are laden kneeling down and carry fifteen *man* weight. It is noted for the Barbary goat and for fighting cocks.

In the *Sarkār* of *Sātgāon*,[4] there are two ports at a distance of half a *kos* from each other; the one is Sātgāon, the other Hugli : the latter the chief; both are in the possession of the Europeans. Fine pomegranates grow here.

---

[2] The root of a species of smilax of a pale reddish colour with no smell and very little taste. The *smilax glabra* or *lanceœfolia*, not distinguishable, according to Roxburg, by the eye from the drug known as *China root*. It is a native of Sylhet and the adjacent Garrow country.

[3] Bhringa-rāj, *Edolius paradiseus* or large racket-tailed Drongo. Plumage uniformly black with a steel-blue gloss. Length to end of ordinary tail 14 inches; wing 6¾; tail to middle 6½; outer tail feather 12 to 13 inches more; the shaft having the terminal end for about 3½ inches barbed externally, but towards the tip only on the inner side, and turning inwards so that the under-side becomes uppermost. It will eat raw meat, lizards, and almost any kind of food offered to it. It imitates all sorts of sounds, as of dogs, cats, poultry. The Bhring-ráj, (king of the bees) is found in the dense forests of India from the Himalays to the Eastern Ghats as far S. as N.L.15°. Jerdon. *Sherganj* Cissa Sinensis, Brisson. Cissa Venatoria, Blyth—the green jay. It is found in the South Eastern Himalays and in the hill ranges of Assam, Sylhet, Arakan and Tenasserim. These birds wander about from tree to tree and pick grasshoppers, mantides and other insects, are frequently tamed and caged and are amusing and imitative. They sing lustily a loud screeching strain and are highly carnivorous. The shrike-like habit, in confinement, of placing a bit of food between the bars of their cage is in no species more exemplified than in this—Jerdon. II, 312.

[4] The traditional mercantile capital of Bengal from the Puranic age to the time of the foundation of the town of Hugli by the Portuguese. Its decay commenced in the latter part of the 16th century owing to the silting up ofthe channel of the Saraswati. In 1632, Hugli being made a royal port, all the public offices were withdrawn from Sátgáon which soon sunk into ruin. *Stat. Acct. of Bengal* ,III, 307—310.

In the *Sarkār* of *Mandāran* is a place called Harpah in which there is a diamond mine producing chiefly very small stones.

Orissa.

This was formerly a separate State. The climate is extremely healthy. His Majesty apportioned it into five *Sarkārs, viz., Jalesar, Bhadrak, Katak* (Cuttack), *Kaling Dandpāt* and *Raja Mahandrah.* These five are now included in the province of Bengal. It contains one hundred and twenty-nine masonry forts. Its ruler is entitled Gajpati.[1] The rainy season extends over eight months; there are three cold months and one month only that is hot. The staple cultivation is rice and the food of the inhabitants consists of rice, fish, the egg-plant and vegetables. When the rice is cooked, they steep it in cold water and eat it on the second day. The men are effeminate, anointing their bodies with sandal oil and wearing golden ornaments. The women cover only the lower part of the body and many make themselves coverings of the leaves of trees.[2]. The walls of their huts are of reeds and their temples are of stone and of great height. Elephants abound. The inhabitants of Bengal do not understand the language of this country. A woman may have more. than one husband. They write on palm leaves[3] with an iron pen, holding it with the clenched fist, and pen and ink are rarely employed. The litters called *Sukhāsan* are much in use: cloths are manufactured and the province furnishes eunuchs: fruits and flowers are in great plenty, especially the *gul-i-nasrin*[4] which is very delicate and sweet-scented: its outer petals are white, the inner yellow. The *keorah*[5] grows in great abundance and there are various kinds of betel-leaf. Money transactions are in *kauris* which is a small white shell generally divided down the middle; it is found on the sea shore. Four *kauris* make a *ganda,* five *gandas,* a *budi,* four *budis,* a *pan,* sixteen or according to

---

[1] Lord or rider of the elephant. The suit of cards used by Akbar (Vol. I. p. 316) under the name of Gajpati, symbolised the power and reputation of Orissa in the possession of these animals.

[2] For the leaf-wearing tribes of Orissa, the *Juangs* or *Patwas,* see Hunter's *Orissa,* ii. 116. Banerji, *Orissa,* i. 19 et.

[3] The Brahmanical archives of the temple of Jagannāth consist of bundles of palm leaves, neatly cut and written over with a sharp iron pen without ink. *I. G.*

[4] In Hindi, *Seoti* the *Rosa glandulifera.* Roxb.

[5] *Pandanus odoratissimus,* Roxb.

some twenty *pan*, a *khāwan* [*kāhan*] and ten *khāwan*, a rupee.

Katak (CUTTACK.) The city has a stone fort situated at the bifurcation of the two rivers, the *Mahānadi*, held in high veneration by the Hindus, and the *Katjuri*.[6] It is the residence of the governor and contains some fine buildings. For five or six *kos* round the fort during the rains, the country is under water. Rajah Mukund Deo[7] built a palace here nine stories in height; the first story was taken up for the elephants and the stables : the second was occupied by the artillery and the guards and quarters for attendants : the third by the patrol and gatekeepers : the fourth by the workshops : the fifth, by the kitchen : the sixth contained the public reception rooms : the seventh, the private apartments; the eighth, the women's apartments, and the ninth, the sleeping chamber of the governor. To the south is a very ancient temple. Overlooking this, in the city of Purushottama (Puri) on the sea shore stands the shrine of Jagannāth. Near to it are the images of Krishna and of his brother and sister,[8] made of sandal-wood. It is said that over four thousand years ago Rājah Indradaman (Indradyumna) ruler of the Nilgiri hill sent a learned Brāhman to select a suitable spot for the building of a city. He wandered much in search of his object and found a fitting site which he preferred to all other places. On a sudden he beheld a crow plunge into the water and after bathing itself, pay its devotions to the sea. He was astonished at this action and as he understood the language of animals, he inquired of the crow the reason of its proceeding. He received this answer. "I was once of the number of the *deotas* and through the curse of an ascetic was transformed into this shape. A spiritual guide of high illumination affirms that the Supreme Creator has a special regard for this spot and whosoever dwells here and applies his soul to the worship of God, quickly attains his desire. For some years past I have supplicated for my deliverance in this

[6] One of the deltaic tributaries of the Mahānadi dividing into two branches, one of which retains its own name while the other takes that of Koyākhai and supplies the Puri district.

[7] Telinga Mukund Deo (Harichandan); in this reign the sovereignty of Orissa was overthrown by the King of Bengal. Banerji, *Orissa*, i. 342—348, palace-building not supported by history.

[8] *Purush-ottama* means "the best of men" *i.e.*, Vishnu or Krishna. His brother and sister are Balabhadra and Subhadrā. The images are rude logs coarsely fashioned in the shape of a human bust, and are actually in the sanctuary itself. For a description of the temple and other local shrines, Banerji, *Orissa*, ii. 369—418.

manner and the time is now at hand when my prayer will be answered. Since thou art essentially meritorious, watch in expectation and comprehend the wonders of this land." The Brāhman in a short time witnessed with his own eyes the things he had heard. He apprised the Rājah of these occurrences, who built a large city and appointed a special place of worship. The Rājah, one night, after having administered justice, was reposing on the couch of divine praise when it was thus revealed to him, "On a certain day, watch in expectation upon the sea shore. A piece of wood of fifty-two fingers in length and a cubit and a half in breadth will approach : this is the special image of the deity : take it and placing it in thy house, guard it for seven days and whatever shape it then assumes, place it in the temple and enshrine it." After waking, the thing happened in the same wise, and by a divine inspiration, he named it Jagannāth and decked it with gold and jewels. It became a place of devotion to high and low and many miracles are reported[9] regarding it. Kālā Paḥār the General of Sulaymān Karrāni, on his conquest of the country, flung the image into the fire and burnt it and afterwards cast it into the sea. But it is now restored and these popular fables are related of it.

The three images are washed six times every day and freshly clothed. Fifty or sixty priests wearing the Brahmanical thread, stand to do them service and each time large dishes of food are brought out and offered to the images, so that twenty thousand people partake of the leavings [*prasād.*] They construct a car of sixteen wheels which in Hindi, they call *Rath,* upon which the images are mounted, and they believe that whosoever draws it, is absolved from sin and is visited by no temporal distress. Near Jagannāth is a temple dedicated to the Sun. [at Konārak]* Its cost was defrayed by twelve years revenue of the province. Even those whose judgment is critical and who are difficult to please stand astonished at its sight. The height of the wall is 150 cubits high and 19 thick. It has three portals. The eastern has carved upon it the figures of two finely designed elephants, each of them carrying a man upon his trunk. The western bears sculptures of two horsemen with trappings

[9] The legend will be found related at length in Hunter's *Orissa,* Vol. I, p. 89.
Kālāpāhār's desecration of the Jagannath temple and images, Banerji's *Orissa,* i. 345.

* Konārak temple, description in Banerji's *Orissa,* ii. 380—392; its art, ii. 410—415.

and ornaments and an attendant. The northern has two tigers, each of which is rampant upon an elephant that it has overpowered. In front[10] is an octagonal column of black stone, 50 yards high. When nine flights of steps are passed, a spacious court appears with a large arch of stone upon which are carved the sun and other planets. Around them are a variety of worshippers of every class, each after its manner with bowed heads, standing, sitting, prostrate, laughing, weeping, lost in amaze or in wrapt attention and following these are divers musicians and strange animals which never existed but in imagination. It is said that somewhat over 730 years ago, Rāja Narsing Deo completed this stupendous fabric and left this mighty memorial to posterity. Twenty-eight temples stand in its vicinity; six before the entrance and twenty-two without the enclosure, each of which has its separate legend. Some affirm that Kabir Mua'hhid (monotheist) reposes here and many authentic traditions are related regarding his sayings and doings to this day. He was revered by both Hindu and Muhammadan for his catholicity of doctrine and the illumination of his mind, and when he died, the Brāhmans wished to burn his body and the Muhammadans to bury it.

The Subah of Bengal consists of 24 *Sarkārs* and 787 *Mahals*. The revenue is 59 crores, 84 lakhs, 59,319 *dāms* (Rs. 14,961,482-15-7) in money. [Of this Orissa has 5 sarkārs, 99 mahals and 1,25,732,638 dāms.] The zamindars are mostly *Kayaths*. The troops number 23,330 cavalry, 801,150 infantry, 1,170 elephants, 4,260 guns, and 4,400 boats.

N.B.—The *Parganahs* will now be entered in alphabetical order in long double columns to each page accompanied by a few descriptive notices.

In the list of mahals, the editor has given the correct name first, with the letter R* or A* added, to mean that the place has been found in Rennell's Maps or in the Atlas of the Survey of India (quarter-inch scale). The name of the place as misspelt in the Persian text or wrongly transcribed by Jarrett has been given within brackets after the word *mistake*.—J. Sarkar.

---

[10] This now stands in front of the Lion-gate of Jagannāth. *Orissa*, I. 290. The Konārak temple was built by Narasimha I. of the Eastern Ganga dynasty (r. 1238—1264.) Banerji, *Orissa*, I. 267—269. For Kabir, *Ency. Islam*, ii. 592 (T. W. Arnold) and Hastings, *Ency. Religion and Ethics*, vii. 632—634. (R. Burn).

Sarkār of Udambar commonly known as Tāndā.[1]

Containing 52 *Mahals*. Rev. 24,079,399⅓ *Dāms*.

	Dāms.		*Dāms.*
Āg mahal ...	133,017	Dāud Shāhi ...	242,802
Achlā, Darsanpārah, Ashrafnihāl ..	404,287½	Dugāchhi ...	225,745
Ibrahimpur ...	360,357	Rāmpur ...	115,532
Ajiyāl-ghāti ...	231,957	Rubaspur ...	138,122
Amgāchhi ...	369,357½	Sarup Singh ...	1,368,877
Barhgangal ...	666,200	Sultānpur Ajiyāl	456,394
Bhatāl ...	415,470	Sulaimān Shāhi	198,742
Bahādurpur ...	314,870	Sulaimānābād ...	197,760
Bāhrāri ...	24,655	Salimpur ...	187,097
Phulbāri ...	193,025	Sambalā ...	174,550
Bahādur Shāhi ...	138,102	Shershāhi ...	178,230
Tāndā with Suburban district ...	4,326,102	Shams Khāni ...	361,952
Tājpur ...	291,997	Sherpur ...	163,097
Taalluq Barbhākar	11,725	Firozpur ...	347,787½
Tanauli ...	196,380	Kunwar-partāb	1,607,200
Chunaghāti ...	589,967	Kānakjok [Kānkjol] ...	1,589,332
Chāndpur ...	190,027	Kāthgarh ...	1,265,632
Nasibi ...	160,205	Gankarah ...	894,027
Chungnadiyā ...	145,305	Kāshipur ...	36,240
Hājipur ...	106,255	Kachlā ...	36,240
Husainābād ...	266,545	Kāfurdiya ...	1,440
Khānpur ...	31,410	Mudesar ...	1,503,352
Dhāwah ...	250,597	Mangalpur ...	226,770
Deviyāpur ...	559,557	Receipts from scattered estates*	45,837
		Nawanagar ...	825,985
		Nasibpur ...	377,750

[1] For *Udambar* the reading *Udner* was accepted in the 1st ed. *Tanda* became the capital of Bengal after the decadence of Gaur: now a petty village in Maldah District; it was to the S. W. of Gaur beyond the Bāgirathi. Old Tānda has been utterly swept away by the changes in the course of the Pāglā. Sulaimān Shāh Karrāni, the last but one of the Afghan kings of Bengal, moved the seat of government to Tāndā in 1564, A.D. eleven years before the final depopulation of Gaur. It was a favourite residence of the Mughal governors of Bengal until the middle of the following century. In 1660 the rebel Shāh Shujāa' was defeated in its vicinity.

* The term *Mazkurain* was applied in old revenue accounts to small and scattered estates not included in the accounts of the district in which they are situated, and of which the assessments were paid direct to the Government officers: subsequently it denoted a revenue payer, paying through the intervention of another, except in Cuttack where it implied the reverse, or the heads of villages paying the revenue immediately to the Collector. Wilson's *Gloss*.

Sarkār of Jannatābād or Lakhnauti.
66 *Mahals.* Rev. 18,846,967 *Dāms.*
Castes *Kāyaths* and *Brahmans.* Cavalry 500.
Infantry, 17,000.

	Dāms.
Jannatābād, commonly known as Gaur. It has been a brick fort	7,869,202
Adjacent villages of Ākrā forming 14 *Parganahs* as follows : ...	1,573,296
Ajor ...	138,925
Bāzkhokrā ...	192,508
Baler ...	127,060
Ākra suburban district ...	211,260
Dhanpur ...	140,340
Deviya ...	112,208
Serhwar[1] ...	71,000
Shāhbālā ...	98,400
Shāhlalsari ...	8,000
Khektar ...	50,200
Madnāwāti ...	151,890
Modihāt ...	6,980
Nāhat ...	242,710
Hashtganjpur ...	28,515
Adjacent villages of Darsarak 16 *mahals* as follows : ...	2,009,344
Achārikhānah where they sell undried ginger	7,800
Bhatiya ...	826,432
Belbāri ...	91,560
Bāzāri Kadim (Old Bāzār) ...	3,720
Darsarak ...	62,835
Rāngāmāti ...	3,200
Sāir duties from Gangapat and neighbourhood of Hindui† ...	170,800
Sherpur and Gangalpur 2 *mahals*	2,000
Shāhbāzpur within the city ...	400
Ghiyāspur ...	41,920
Kamalā ...	16,377
Kāthachhāpā ...	12,000
Modi Mahal ...	13,000
Mewa Mahal ...	360
Duties from the New Market ...	11,760
Adjacent villages of Dihikot 7 *mahals* ...	869,000
Barāripinjar ...	698,900
Pākor ...	37,720
Dihikot ...	31,624
Dahlgāon ...	130,320
Shāhzādahpur ...	84,360
Māligāon ...	141,460
Modipur ...	61,880
Adjacent villages of Ramrauti 7 *mahals* ...	749.795
Badhtahli ...	207,500
Rāmauti ...	194,767
Selghariya ...	103,000
Sangkalkarā ...	93,320

[1] T. Sirapour, G. Seerpoor.
† Probably a mistake for *Mandavi* or grain-mart, emporium.

		Dāms.
Sultānpur	...	29,210
Sangdwār	...	14,447
Māhinagar	...	107,550
Adjacent villages of Sarsābād rev. of 10 *mahals*		13,192,377
Akbarpur	...	9,736
Pārdiyār	...	85,280
Khizrpur	...	396,100
Sarsābād	...	553,080
Kotwāli	...	788,427
Garhand	...	334,880
Garhi	...	200,000
Makrāin	...	106,480
Manikpur and Hatanda, 2 *mahals*		630,770

Adjacent villages of Māldah, 11 *mahls*.

Bārbakpur, Bāzār i Yusuf, Suburban district of Māldah, Dherpur, Sujāpur, Sarbādahlpur, Sankodiya, Shālesari, Shāhmandawi, Fathpur, Mui'zzu'ddinpur.

Sarkār of Fathābād.

31 *mahals*. Rev. 7,969,568 *dāms*.

Zamindārs of three classes (i.e. castes).

Cavalry, 990. Infantry, 50,700.

		Dāms.
Isrāchāraj	...	34,024
Bholiyābil	...	384,452
Belor	...	124,872
Bhāgalpur	...	2,115
Bādhādiyā	...	1,442
Telhati	...	377,290
Charnlakhi	...	35,645
Charhāi	...	30,200
Suburban district and town of Fathābād	...	902,662
Salt duties	...	277,758
Hazratpur	...	11,640
Market dues	...	11,467
Rasulpur	...	103,767
Sondip	...	1,182,450
Sarhārkal	...	787,430
Sarisāni	...	173,227
Sardiyā	...	53,882
Sadhwā	...	37,127
Sawāil, commonly called Jalālpur		1,857,230
Shahbāzpur	...	732,172
Kharagpur	...	118,135
Kasodiyā	...	102,405
Kosā	...	68,350
Makorgāon	...	3,157
Masnadpur	...	55,312
Mirānpur	...	22,172
Receipts from scattered estates		133,365
Naklesar	...	49,422
Nia'matpur	...	20,960
Hazārahati	...	21,597
Yusufpur	...	258,025

Sarkār of Mahmudābād.

88 *mahals.* Rev. 11,602,256.

Caste *Kāyath.* Cavalry, 200. Infantry, 10,100.

	Dāms.		*Dāms.*
Adniyā ...	76,113	Husain Ajiyāl ...	345,135
Anupampur ...	43,365	Haweli [suburb]	91,575
Ajiyālpur ...	37,307	Khālispur ...	56,805
Indarkalli ...	11,250	Khizrākhāni ...	1,092
Āmdah ...	192	Khurrampur ...	265
Bāzu-rāst ...	652,507	Dakāsi[3] ...	51,740
Bāzu-chap ...	271,240	Durlabhpur ...	13,775
Barādi ...	604,122	Dhuli ...	13,665
Bisi ...	25,247	Deora ...	107
Barin Jumlah ...	102,210	Dahlat Jalālpur	1,200
Betbariya ...	96,117	Dostihnā ...	1,052
Bāthnān ...	85,447	Dhomarhāt ...	42,505
Bātkān ...	41,317	Sadkichāl Kotiyā	
Belwāri ...	80,195	or Kota ...	8,205
Bandwāl ...	26,155	Sārotiyā ...	6,530
Pātika māra ...	22,710	Sarsariyā ...	72,147
Bābhankarlā ...	14,895	Sankardiyā ...	10,212
Parānpur ...	12,572	Salimpur ...	23,637
Barmahpur ...	6,717	Soltāra Ajiyāl,	
Patkābāri ...	3,567	commonly Koma	789,220
Pipalbariyā ...	2,045	Suruppur ...	7,482
Bāghotiyā ...	217	Sālibariyā ...	6,760
Belkasi ...	123,387	Sātor ...	290,727
Tāragonā ...	675,790	Shāhajiyāl ...	644,787
Tiyāghāti ...	96	Sherpurbari ...	9,402
Tārāajiyāl ...	391,365	Sherpur Utasholi	2,797
Chhāduiyā or		Azmatpur ...	14,422
Chhāddiya ...	9,125	Ghaznipur ...	12,367
Jiyārukhi ...	11,505	Farhatpur ...	301,790
Jagannāthpur ...	762	Fathpur Nosika	102,525
Chadibāriyā[1] ...	44,007	Qutabpur ...	23,352
Jediya ...	44,700	Qazipur ...	2,652
Chitanbāzu[2] ...	952,950	Kandaliyā ...	20,417

[1] T. and *var.* Jedibariya.
[2] G. Chytun, *var.* Jastan and Chain.
[3] T. and *var.* Dakāri.

Sarkār of Mahmudābād—Contd.

	Dāms.
Khelphāti ...	19,940
Kandi Nawi ...	8,477
Kolbariyā ...	6,517
Kaudasā[4] ...	6,435
Kāliyānpur ...	26,235
Kali Mahal ...	26,717
Lāniyāṇ ...	313,286
Launkohāl ...	15,425
Mihmān Shāhi ...	575,727
Makhiyā ...	14,505
Mahmud Shāhi	226,552
Mirpur ...	2,370
Maheswarpur ...	42,852
Madhodiya ...	695
Maruf-diya ...	2,302
Naldi ...	804,440
Nasrat Shāhi ...	272,450
Nagarchāl Kotiyā	61,235
Nagar Bānkā ...	3,382
Nāshipur called also Ujain ...	91,080
Hemtapur ...	477,360
Haldā ...	122,566
Hawāl Ghāti ...	66,217
Hatapān (?Hatiān)	3,665
Hosipur ...	17,425

Sarkār of Khalifatābād.

35 *mahals*. Rev. 5,402,140 *dāms*.

Castes, various. Cavalry, 100. Infantry, 15,150.

	Dāms.
Bhāl, with township	475,102
Bhālkā ...	230,515
Polah ...	135,932
Potkā ...	104,205
Bāgh Mārā ...	81,807
Bhāngā ...	25,300
Bhades ...	11,225
Bhaliyānah ...	9,527
Phulnagar ...	66,660
Taālluq of Kāsināth	297,720
Tālā ...	174,676
Taālluq of Srirang	26,427
,, Mahes Māndal	23,727
,, Dāmodar Bhattachāraj	13,860
,, Sripat Kavirāj	8,675
Jesar, commonly, Rasulpur ...	1,723,850
Charaulā ...	99,550
Chhalerā[1] ...	60,920
Suburban dist. of Khalifatābād ...	31,442
Khālispur ...	32,770
Dāniyā ...	522,885
Rāngdiya ...	129,910
Sahaspur ...	260,340
Sulaimānābād ...	168,504
Sāhas ...	91,500
Sobhnāth ...	51,662
Sālesarbāhi[2] ...	11,484
Imādpur ...	97,102
Khokrāl ...	105,520
Kanges, Taalluq Parmanand ...	166,360
Mundāgācha ...	126,360
Malikpur ...	61,327
Madhariyā ...	45,007
Mangorghāt ...	16,842
Mahresā ...	11,170

[4] G. T. and *var.* Gāuda.
[1] G. and *var.* Chabrah.
[2] T, and G. and *var.* Sālesari,

Sarkār of Baklā.

Containing 4 *mahals*. Rev. 7,150,605.

Castes, various. Elephants, 320. Infantry, 15,000.

	Dāms.		*Dāms.*
Ismailpur, commonly Bakla ...	4,348,960	Shāhzādahpur ...	977,245
Srirāmpur ...	252,000	Adilpur [Idilpur] ...	1,553,440

Sarkār of Purniyah.

9 *mahals*. Rev. 6,408,775 *dāms*.

Infantry, 5,000.

	Dāms.		*Dāms.*
Asonja ...	734,225	Sripur ...	390,200
Jairāmpur ...	467,785	*Sāir* duties from elephants ...	85,000
Suburban dist. of Purniyah ...	2,686,995	Kathiyāri ...	590,100
Dalmālpur ...	671,530	Kadwān ...	280,592
Sultānpur ...	502,206		

Sarkār of Tājpur.

29 *mahals*. Rev. 6,483,857 *dāms*.

Castes, various. Cavalry, 100. Infantry, 50,000.

	Dāms.		*Dāms.*
Pangat (*mist.* Bankat) ...	3,307,885	Mālduār (*mist.* Tāldwār) ...	208,540
Badokhar ...	238,855	Chhāpartāl ...	243,255
Phāli ...	60,860	Suburban dist. and town of Tājpur	886,254
Bandol ...	190,830	Dilāwarpur ...	944,055
Bobarā ...	23,192	Daihat ...	124,196
Bhonharā ...	118,295	Sesahrā ...	376,760
Badgāon ...	9,330	Shujāpur ...	244,507
Bāsigāon ...	104,492	Shāhpur ...	126,235
Bangāon ...	115,990	Kuwārpur ...	406,000
Bahādurpur ...	96,012	Kasārgāon ...	258,742
Bahānagar ...	91,630	Gopālnagar ...	233,160
Badalkā ...	71,564		

Sarkār of Tājpur—Contd.

	Dāms.		Dāms.
Goghra ...	147,392	Nilun ...	147,510
Mahur (*mist.* Mahon) ...	194,475	Yusuf ...	146,240
Nilnagar (Nilpur)	267,612	Zakāt (tax) ...	78,487

Sarkār of Chorāghāt.

84 *mahals.* Rev. 8,083,072½ *dāms.*

Castes, various. Cavalry, 900. Elephants, 50.

Infantry, 32,800.

	Dāms.		Dāms.
Adhwā ...	91,292	Banwārkājar ...	4,452
Andhar ...	75,010	Belghāti ...	3,245
Andalgāon ...	154,337	Bāzār Chhatāghāt	387
Anwarbān ...	31,022	Palāsbāri[1] ...	
Ālgāon ...	171,695	Panch Mālka ...	5,340
Ambathurā, Abthurā	25,326	Tulsighāt ...	164,340
Āhmadābād ...	18,517	Taalluq Husain	35,410
Anbalāgāchhi ...	9,200	,, Bālnāth	27,962
Anwar Malik ...	8,020	,, Siwān	15,490
Āl Hāt ...	7,508	,, Kasāi	15,267
Ilāhdādpur ...	2,190	Tāchahal ...	8,290
Bāzu Zafar Shāhi, 2 mahals ...	735,835	Taalluq Ahmad Khān ...	238,475
Bāzu Faulād Shāhi	711,412	Hāmilā ...	6,580
Bāgdwār ...	102,440	Khairābādi ...	5,602
Phulbāri ...	6,580	Khāsbāri ...	2,735
Bārbakpur ...	84,952	Rungpur [Ruknpur]	10,950
Bāmanpur ...	349,070	Sultānpur ...	108,377
Town of Nasratābād ...	336,445	Sikhshahar[2] ...	93,071
		Sāthipur ...	49,570
Barsalā ...	233,680	Sirhata ...	344,097
Bari Sābakbālā	146,767	Sabdi ...	206,224
,, Ghorāghāt	165,827	Sitpur ...	128,775
Bāyazidpur ...	144,227	Siriyā Kāndi ...	24,622
Pātāldeh ...	41,365	Sāghāt ...	16,412
Bālkā ...	30,335	Sherpur Koibāri (S. Kafurā) ...	15,675
Bholi ...	12,040	Fathpur ...	353,355
Bājpatāri ...	7,900		

[1] In text figures wanting, G. has 7,000. *Var.* 5,340
[2] *Var.* Sabtakah, Beshekh, Silah. T. Sankha.

Sarkār of Ghorāghāt—Contd.

	Dāms.
Khetāri ...	1,344,280
Gayapur ...	107,205
Kābulpur ...	98,465
Ganj Sākhmālā	98,465
Khadkhadi ...	81,565
Gokul ...	56,865
Kothi Bāri 2 *mahals*	48,807
Khalsi ...	264,322
Kandibāri ...	125,797
Kuli Bāzār, commonly Jorpuri	115,680
Gobindpur Akhand	40,675
Kanhtāl[3] ...	40,367
Kanak Sakhar ...	28,065
Ghātnagar ...	27,922
Kawā Gāchhi ...	24,600
Kālibāri ...	24,847

	Dāms.
Korā, receipts from Zakāt ...	18,000
Kokaran ...	13,120
Kābul ...	11,690
Garhiya ...	10,980
Gokanpārā ...	9,850
Magatpur ...	124,005
Muhabbatpur ...	46,512
Musjid Husain Shāhi	28,945
,, Andarkhāni	3,447
Malāir ...	24,800
Nandahra ...	61,050
Naupāra ...	19,202
Nahajaun Bātor	49,010
Wakar Hazir ...	30,646
Wachhi ...	16,832
Wahrib ...	4,230

*Sarkār of Pinjarah.**

21 *mahals.* Rev. 5,803,275 *dāms*

Castes, various. Cavalry, 50. Infantry, 7,000.

	Dāms.
Ambel ...	1,058,725
Ambāri A* ...	36,525
Amgochah ...	101,882
Bārbakpur (Bārangpur) ...	635,390
Bijānagar A* ...	719,107
Bāyazidpur A*	255,445
Baharnagar ...	119,720
Bāri Gher ...	84,277
Bādughar (? Balurhat) ...	55,205
Tegasi (Takāsi) A*	374,490
Chaloon (Hālon) A*	82,142

	Dāms.
Suburban district of Pinjarah ...	93,967
Digha ...	146,837
Deopārā (Deorā) A*	107,727
Sadharbāri (?Jharbari) ...	273,045
Sankatā (Suktigacha) ...	251,410
Sultānpur A* ...	203,292
Sāsber A* ...	165,180
Sulaimānābād ...	42,532
Khattā (?Khetlāl)	777,255
Kedābāri† ...	213,382

---

[3] *Var.* Gātrāl, G. Gautnāll.

* *Pinjarah,* evidently a copyist's error. No such name in any map. Tieffenthaler reads *Bijara.*

† Cannot be *Godāgāri.* May be *Kāmdevpur.*

Sarkār of Bārbakābād.

38 *mahals.* Rev. 17,451,532 *dāms.*
Castes, various. Cavalry, 50. Infantry, 7,000.

	Dāms.
Amrul ...	560,382
City of abovementioned (Bārbakābād) ...	315,340
Basuoul (Bāsdol) A*	190,885
Polārhār ...	136,712
Pustu (Bastol) A*	652,367
Barbariyā ...	64,335
Bangāon ...	319,000
Pāltāpur A* ...	179,840
Chhandiya Bāzu	755,522
Chaurā A* ...	159,832
Jeasindh (Jahāsand) and Chaugāon, 2 *mahals* ...	407,007
Chāndlāi (Jandlāi) A* ...	289,340
Janāsu (? Jhankur) A* ...	85,787
Suburb. district of Sukh Shahar	1,629,175
Dhāmin (Dhārman) A* ...	350,895
Dāudpur A* ...	8,902
Sankārdal, commonly Nizāmpur	389,975
Shikārpur A* ...	327,342
Sherpur and Bahāmpur, 2 *mahals* A*	391,625
Tāhirpur A* ...	505,825
Qāzihatti A* ...	620,477
Kardoho A* ...	1,390,572
Guzrhāt ...	1,296,240
Khās ...	881,080
Ganj known as Jagdal A* ...	694,655
Gobindpur ...	410,535
Kāligāe Kotha ...	341,057
Khurael (Kharāl) A* ...	210,132
Kodānagar ...	129,550
Kāligaon (Kaligāe) A* ...	196,932
Laskarpur ...	255,090
Mājilpur (Māljipur) ...	925,680
Mosida (Masdhā) A* ...	689,712
Man Samāli ...	594,792
Mahmudpur ...	124,532
Wazirpur ...	169,190

Sarkār of Bāzuhā.

32 *mahals.* Rev. 39,516,871 *dāms.*
Castes, various. Cavalry, 1,700. Elephants, 10.
Infantry, 5,300.

Ālap Shāhi ...	760,667
Badmār, Nasrat Shāhi, Mehraunah, Kāhārwana, Sirali, 5 *mahals*	1,178,140
Bhoriya Bāzu ...	2,820,740
Bhawāl Bāzu ...	1,935,160
Partāb-Bāzu ...	1,881,265
Bakhariyā Bāzu	1,715,170
Husain Shāhi ...	182,750

Sarkār of Bāzuhā—Contd.

	Dāms.
Dashkāhaniyā Bāzu ...	1,945,602
Dhakā Bāzu ...	1,901,202
Salim Partāb Bāzu, Chānd Partāb Bāzu, Sultān Bāzu	4,625,475
Sonāghāti Bāzu	1,910,440
Sonā Bāzu ...	1,705,290
Silbaras ...	1,484,320
Dues on produce and piscary of rivers, tanks, &c. ...	261,280
Shāh Ajiyāl Bāzu	405,120
Zafar Ajiyal Bāzu	250,047
Katārmal Bāzu	2,804,390
Khatā Bāzu ...	137,720
Mihmān Shāhi, known as Sherp-pur Murcha ...	2,207,715
Mumin Singh, Nasrat Shāhi, Husain Singh, Nasrat Ajiyāl 4 *mahals*	1,867,640
Mubārak Ajiyāl	468,780
Hariyāl Bāzu ...	344,440
Yusuf Shāhi ...	1,670,900

Sarkār of Sonārgāon.

52 *mahals*. Rev. 10,331,333 *dāms*.

Castes, various. Cavalry, 1,500. Elephants, 200.

Infantry, 46,000.

	Dāms.
Uttar Shāhpur	388,442
Āl Jihāt ...	53,090
Uttar Usmānpur	24,880
Bikrampur ...	3,335,052
Bhulwā-jowār ...	1,331,480
Baldākhāl ...	694,090
Bawāliyā ...	237,320
Barchandi ...	120,100
Bāth Karā ...	4,080
Palās-ghāti, &c.	43,265
Baradiyā ...	19,000
Phulari ...	19,000
Pānhatta ...	7,367
Torā ...	104,910
Tājpur ...	60,000
Tarki ...	18,270
Jogidiyā ...	512,080
Environs of Port	82,632
Chhokhandi, from shop dues ...	17,827
Chand Bāzār ...	30,322
Chāndpur ...	120,000
Suburban district of Sonārgāon with city ...	459,532
Khizrpur ...	40,308
Dohār ...	458,524
Dānderā ...	421,380
Dakhin Shāhpur	239,910
Dilāwarpur : receipts from *zakāt*	127,207
Dakhin Usmānpur	8,840
Rāepur ...	4,535
Sekhargāon ...	340,365
Sakri ...	184,780
Salimpur ...	91,090

Sarkār of Sonārgāon—Contd.

	Dāms.		Dāms.
Sālisari with produce and piscary of rivers, tanks, &c., *raiyati** and the like ...	40,724	Kothri (Kothari)	35,160
Sakhwā from *raiyati*	280,000	Gāthi Nadhi (G. Danai) ...	20,000
,, ,, *sāir* dues	28,000	Mehrkol ...	1,039,470
Sakhādia ...	28,000	Muazzampur ...	236,830
Sejoāl† ...	13,000	Mehār ...	60,800
Shamspur ...	22,000	Manoharpur ...	53,301
Kerāpur ...	293,402	Mahijāl ...	25,000
Gardi ...	89,590	Narāenpur, from *sāir* dues, *zakāt* and *raiyati* ...	940,760
Kārtikpur ...	80,000	Nāwākot ...	16,080
Khāndi ...	40,140	Hamtā Bāzu ...	281,280
		Hāt Ghāti ...	10,285

Sarkār of Sylhet.

8 *mahals*. Rev. 6,681,308 *dāms*.

Castes, various. Cavalry, 1,100. Elephants, 190. Infantry, 42,920.

	Dāms.		Dāms.
Partābgarh, called also Panjkhand	370,000	Suburban district of Sylhet ...	2,290,717
Baniā Chang ...	1,672,080	Sarkhandal ...	390,472
Bajwa Biyāju ...	804,080	Laur ...	246,202
Jesa (Jaintiya?)	272,200	Harnagār, *raiyati* and *sāir* ...	1,010,857

Sarkār of Chittagong.

7 *mahals*. Rev. 11,424,310 *dāms*.

Castes, various. Cavalry, 100. Infantry, 1,500.

	Dāms.		Dāms.
Tālāgāon [?Mālgaon] ...	506,000	Sulaimānpur, commonly Shaikhpur	1,572,400
Chātgāon (Chittagong) ...	6,649,410	*Sāir* dues from salt-pits ...	737,520
Deogaon ...	775,540	Sahwā ...	5,079,340
		Nawāpārā ...	703,300

* Applied in Bengal to lands of which the revenue is paid in money in opposition to *khamār* lands of which revenue was paid in kind: also to a settlement direct with the cultivators.—Wilson's *Gloss*.

† G. and *var.* Sabarchāl.

Sarkār of Sharīfābād.

26 *mahals*. Rev. 2,488,750 *dāms*.

Castes, various. Cavalry, 200. Infantry, 5,000.

	Dāms.		*Dāms.*
Burdwān ...	1,876,142	Suburban district of Sherpur Atāi	816,068
Bahror ...	1,736,795	Azmatpur ...	1,660,045
Barbaksail ...	540,395	Fath Singh ...	2,096,460
Bharkondah, and Akbharshāhi, commonly Sāndal, 2 *mahals*	1,276,195	Husain Ajiyāl ...	393,345
Bāghā ...	509,340	Kargāon ...	348,260
Bhātsilā ...	307,340	Kiratpur ...	225,775
Bāzār Ibrāhimpur	15,740	Khand [Ghosh]	196,380
Janki ...	937,705	Khanga ...	174,360
Khot Makand ...	2,315	Kodrā ...	63,125
Dhaniyān ...	1,508,850	Mahland ...	1,831,890
Sulaimān Shāhi	721,335	Manohar Shāhi	1,709,920
Soniyā ...	90,370	Muzaffar Shāhi	1,552,175
		Nasak ...	782,517
		Natrān ...	203,560

Sarkār of Sulaimānābād.

31 *mahals*. Rev. 17,629,964 *dāms*.

Castes, various. Cavalry, 100. Infantry, 5,000.

	Dāms.		*Dāms.*
Indarāin ...	592,120	Husainpur ...	355,090
Ismāilpur ...	184,540	Dhārsah ...	95,250
Anliyā ...	124,577	Rāenah ...	68,257
Ulā ...	89;277	Suburban district of Sulaimānābād ...	2,051,090
Basandhari ...	2,266,280	Sātsikā† ...	757,111
Bhursat ...	1,968,990	Sahspur ...	314,842
Panduah ...	1,823,292	Sanghauli ...	72,747
Pāchnor ...	601,495	Sultānpur ...	44,575
Bāli Bhangā 2 *mahals** ...	417,185	Umarpur ...	223,320
Chhotipur ...	554,956	Aālampur ...	38,280
Chumhā ...	455,901	Qabāzpur ...	747,200
Jaipur ...	44,250		

* There is a Bāli Danga in Nadiya.

† G. and *var.* Satsanga. Note—Now in the district of Bardwān.

Sarkār of Sulaimānābād—*contd.*

	Dāms.		*Dāms.*
Gobinda (Kosada ?)	357,942	Molghar ...	792,107
Receipts from independent *taluqdārs* ...	213,067	Nagin ...	910,990
Muhammadpur	48,515	Nāirā ...	872,945
		Nasang ...	500,765
		Nabiya [? Nipā]	77,017

Sarkār of Sātgāon.

53 *mahals.* Rev. 16,724,724 *dāms.*

Castes, various. Cavalry, 50. Infantry, 6,000.

	Dāms.		*Dāms.*
Banwa, Kotwāli, Farāsatghar, (?) 3 *mahals* ...	1,540,770	Sādghāti ...	468,058
Ukrā ...	726,360	Sakotā ...	204,072
Anwarpur ...	236,950	Srirājpur ...	125,792
Arsa Tāwāli† Sātgāon 2 *mahals*	234,890	*Sāir* dues from Bandarbān and Mandawi, 2 *mahals* ...	1,200,000
Akbārpur ...	115,590	Sākhāt, Kātsāl, 2 *mahals* ...	45,757
Bodhan ...	956,457	Fāthpur ...	80,702
Panwān and Salimpur ...	952,505	Calcutta, Bakoya†† Bārbakpur, 3 *mahals* ...	936,215
Purah ...	652,470	Khārar ...	365,275
Barmhattar and Mānikhatti ...	383,803	Kandāliyā ...	242,160
Belgāon ...	233,602	Kalaruā ...	197,522
Bālindā ...	125,250	Magrā ...	801,302
Bāgwān and Bangābāri ...	100,000	Matiyāri ...	307,845
Baliyā ...	94,725	Medni Mal ...	186,242
Phalkā ...	38,245	Muzaffarpur ...	108,332
Baridhati ...	25,027	Mundāgāchhā ...	98,565
Tortariyā ...	36,604	Nāhihatti ...	49,935
Haveli Shahr ...	502,330	Nadiya and Sāntipur, 2 *mahals*	1,508,820
Husainpur ...	324,322	Helki ...	90,042
Hājipur, Bārbakpur, 2 *mahals*	142,592	Hāthi Kandhā ...	55,702
Dhuliyāpur ...	78,815	Hatiyāgarh ...	781,360
Ranihāt ...	1,358,510		

† Can it be *A'rsa haveli-e-Sātgān* ? [J. Sarkar].

†† G. and *var.* Makuma *Calcutta* is unlikely. I prefer the variant in text *Kalna* [J. S.]

Sarkār of Mandāran.

16 *mahals*. Rev. 9,403,400 *dāms*.

Castes, various. Cavalry, 150. Infantry, 7,000.

	Dāms.		*Dāms.*
Panihatti ...	122,655	Shergarh, commonly Sikharbhum ...	915,237
Bagri (Bālgarhi) R* ...	937,077	Shāhpur ...	634,160
Birbhum ...	541,245	Ket ...	46,447
Dhawālbhum (*mis.* Bawal) ...	495,220	Mandalghāt ...	906,775
Chitwā A* ...	806,542	Nāgor¶ ...	4,025,620
Champānagari ...	412,250	Minakbāg (T. Mansapāt) ...	279,322
Suburban district of Mandāran ...	1,727,077	Hesla (*mist.* Hesoli) A* ...	263,207
Sin[g]bhum ...	615,805		
Samar Sānhas (Sarhat) ...	274,461		

Orissa.

Sarkār of Jalesar.

28 *mahals*. Rev. 5,052,738 *dāms*.

Castes, various. Elephants, 2. Cavalry, 3,470.

Infantry, 43,810.

	Dāms.		*Dāms.*
Bānsanda, commonly Haftchor has five strong forts. Castes, *Khandait*, *Brāhman*, and *Bhej*. Cavalry, 100. Infantry, 5,800.	4,211,430	Parbadā. Cav. 400, Inf. 1,600; has a strong fort, partly on a hill, partly fenced by forest.	640,000
Bibli (Pipli) Cavalry, 10, Infantry, 40 ...	2,001,430	Bhogrāi, has a fortress of great strength; Caste *Khandait*, Cav. 100, Inf. 2,200, archers and matchlockmen.	497,140
Bāli Shāhi Cav. 200. Inf. 2,000	963,430	Bagri, *Rajput*, Cav. 100, Inf. 200	39,428
Bālkoshi, has three forts: 1, Sokrah. 2, Bānhas Tāli; 3, Daddhpur. Cav. 20, Inf. 300.	756,220	Bāzār	125,720
		Bābbanbhum, *Brāhman*, Cav. 20, Inf. 400 ...	114,208

¶ For *Nāgor* T. reads *Magor*. We know of a Nagar of Birbhum. For *Mandalghāt*, Rennell gives *Mangalgulla*, a little south of the Ajay river, and Atlas *Mangalkot*. *Hesla* is eight miles west by south of Purulia town, but one ms. reads *Mahisdal*.

Sarkār of Jalesar—*contd.*

	Dāms.
Taliya with town of Jalesar, has a brick fort. Caste, *Khandait*, Cav. 300, Inf. 6,250.	12,007,110
Tamluk Cav. 50, Inf. 1,000, has a strong fort, *Khandait*	2,571,430
Tarkua: a fort in the jungle, Cav. 30, Inf. 170	720,570
Dāwar Shorbhum, comly Bārah, Cav. 100, Inf. 100.	1,342,360
Ramuna, has five forts, 1 adjacent to city; 2, Ramchandpur; 3 Rabgā; 4, Dut; 5, Saldah, Cav. 700, Inf. 3,500, hold the five.	5,062,306
Rayn, on the border of Orissa, has three forts, Cav. 150, Inf. 1,500.	218,806
Rāepur, a large city, with a strong fortress, Cav. 200, Inf. 1,000.	986,970
Sabang, strong fort in the jungle, Cav. 100, Inf. 2,000.	1,257,140
Kesiari	108,570

	Dāms.
Kāsijorā, Cav. 200, Inf. 2,500, matchlock and bowmen.	893,160
Kharagpur, a strong fort in the wooded hills, 500 footmen and machlock-men.	528,570
Kedārkhand, three strong forts, Cav. 50, Inf. 500	468,570
Karāi, Infantry 100 ...	285,720
Gagnāpur, *Rajput*, Cav. 50, Inf. 400 ..	85,720
Karohi*	68,570
Māljhata, Cav. 500, Inf. 5,000	9,312,610
Mednipur, a large city with two forts, one ancient and the other modern. Caste *Khandait*, Cav. 60, Inf. 500.	1,019,930
Mahākānghāt commonly Qutbpur, a fortress of great strength, Cav. 30, Inf. 1,000.	240,000
Narāinpur, commonly Kandhār, with a strong fort on a hill, Cav. 100, Inf. 4,000.	2,280,860

Sarkār of Bhadrak.

7 *mahals.* Rev. 18,687,170 *dāms.*

Castes, various. Cavalry, 750. Infantry, 3,730.

	Dāms.
Barwa, two strong fortresses, Bānak and Raskoi, castes, *Khandait*, and *Kāyath*, Cav. 50, Inf. 400.	3,240,000
Jankajri	57,140
Suburban district of Bhadrak, has a fort called Dhāmnagar, with a resident governor, *Khandait*, Cav. 200, Inf. 3,500.	9,542,760

	Dāms.
Sahansu, 2 strong forts, *Khandait*, Cav. 300, Inf. 1,700.	3,514,280
Kāaimān, a strong fort of the greatest strength, *Khandait*, Cav. 100, Inf. 400.	1,515,840
Kadsu	730,430
Independent Talukdārs; three forts, Pachchhim Dik, Khandait, and Majori, Cav. 100, Inf. 300; the three forts, held by *Khandaits*.	85,720

* G. and *var.* Kerauli.

Sarkār of Katak (Cuttack.)

21 *mahals*. Rev. 91,432,730 *dāms*.

Castes, various. Cavalry, 900. Infantry, 108,160.

	Dāms.		*Dāms.*
Al, Inf. 2,100 ...	6,429,130	Jash commonly Jājpur, a strong fort, *Brāhman*, Cav. 200, Inf. 1,800.	2,073,780
Āsakah, Inf. 15,000 ...	3,160,380	Dakhin Dik, 4 forts, Cav. 180, Inf. 13,060.	22,065,770
Athgarh, with a strong fort, *Brāhman*, Cav. 200, Inf. 7,000.	1,184,980	Sirān	207,830
Purab Dik, four forts, Cav. 200, Inf. 6,000 ...	22,881,580	Shergarh, *Brāhman*, Cav. 20, Inf. 200.	1,408,580
Pachchhim Dik, Cav. 100, Inf. 50,000 ...	662,490	Kotdesh with three forts, the original fort, Kasibagh, Caste, *Khandait*, Cav. 5,008, Inf. 300.	4,720,980
Bahār	5,129,820	Katak Banāres, suburban district with city, has a stone fort of great strength, and a masonry palace within, *Brāhman* and *Khandait*, Cav. 200, Inf. 1,000.	605,600
Basāi Diwarmār, Inf. 1,000	2,746,650	Khatrah, with strong fortress, *Khandaits*, Cav. 100, Inf. 400.	1,120,230
Barang, 9 forts, among the hills and jungles, Caste, *ahir*, Cav. 20, Inf. 300.	2,132,940	Mānakpatan, a large port, where salt dues are collected.	600,000
Bhijnagar with strong fort, *Telingha*, Cav. 50, Inf. 22,000.	860,390		
Banju, *Rajput*, Cav. 100, Inf. 20,000 ...	866,206		
Parsotam	691,530		
Chaubiskot, 4 forts of great strength, Cav. 500, Inf. 20,000.	2,398,970		

Sarkār of Kaling Dandpāt.

27 *mahals*. Rev. 5,560,000 *dāms*.

Cavalry, 500. Infantry, 30,000.

Sarkār of Rāj Mahendrih.

16 *mahals*. *Rev.* 5,00,000 *dāms*.

Cavalry, 1,000. Infantry, 5,000.

A general view of the country having now been cursorily given, I proceed to record the succession of its rulers and the duration of their reigns. Twenty-four princes of the *Khatri* caste, kept aflame the torch of sovereignty from father to son in succession during 2418 years.

	Years.		Years.
Rājā Bhagdat, *Khatri* reigned ...	218	Sadhrak reigned ...	91
Anangbhim ,, ...	175	Jaydhrak ,, ...	102
Ranghim ,, ...	108	Udai Singh ,, ...	85
Gajbhim ,, ...	82	Bisu Singh ,, ...	88
Deodat ,, ...	95	Birmāth ,, ...	88
Jag Singh ,, ...	106	Rukhdeva ,, ...	81
Barmah Singh ,, ...	97	Rākhbind (Rukhnand) ,, ...	79
Mohandat ,, ...	102	Jagjiwan ,, ...	107
Benod Singh ,, ...	97	Kāludand ,, ...	85
Silar Sen ,, ...	96	Kāmdeva ,, ...	90
Sattarjit ,, ...	101	Bijai Karn ,, ...	71
Bhupat ,, ...	90	Sat Singh ,, ...	89

Nine princes of the *Kāyeth* caste ruled in succesion 520 years after which the sovereignty passed to another *Kāyeth* house.

	Years.		Years.
Rājā Bhoj Gauriya reigned ...	75	Rājā Jaint reigned ...	60
Lālsen ,, ...	70	Pirthu Rajā ,, ...	52
Rājā Madhu ,, ...	67	Rājā Grrar ,, ...	45
Samantbhoj ,, ...	48	,, Lachhman ,, ...	50
		,, Nandbhoj ,, ...	53

Eleven princes reigned in succession 714 years, after which another *Kāyeth* family bore rule.

	Years.		Years.
Rājā Udsur, (Adisur) reigned ...	75	Rājā Rukdeva ,, ...	62
,, Jāmanibhān ,, ...	73	,, Giridhar reigned ...	80
,, Unrud ,, ...	78	,, Pirthidhar ,, ...	68
,, Partāb Rudr ,, ...	65	,, Shishtdhar ,, ...	58
,, Bhawdāt ,, ...	69	,, Prabhākar ,, ...	63
		,, Jaidhar ,, ...	23

Ten princes reigned 698 years, after which the sway of another *Kāyeth* family was established.

	Years.		*Years.*
Rājā Bhopāl reigned ...	55	Rājā Bigan (Bijan) pāl, reigned ...	75
,, Dhripāl ,, ...	95	,, Jaipāl ,, ...	98
,, Devapāl ,, ...	83	Rājpāl ,, ...	98
,, Bhupati-pāl ,, ...	70	Bhogpāl, his brother ,, ...	5
,, Dhanpati-pāl ,, ...	45	Jagpāl, his son ,, ...	74

Seven princes governed in succession during 160 years.

	Years.		*Years.*
Sukh Sen reigned ...	3	Madhu Sen reigned ...	10
Balāl Sen, who built the fort of Gaur ,, ...	50	Kesu Sen ,, ...	15
Lakhan (Lachhman) Sen ,, ...	7	Sada (Sura) Sen ,, ...	18
		Rājā Nāujah (?Buddha-sen) ,, ...	3

Sixty-one princes thus reigned for the space of 4,544 years when Bengal became subject tc the Kings of Delhi.

From the time of Sultān Qutb u' ddin Aibak to Sultān Muhammad Tughlaq Shāh 17 governors ruled during a period of 156 years.

These were followed by—

A.H.	A.D.		*Years.*	*Months*
741	1340	Malik Fakhr'uddin Silāhdār, reigned	2	some
743	1342	Sultān Alāu'ddin	1	,,
744	1343	Shamsu'ddin Bhangarah Ilyās ...	16	,,
760	1358	Sikandar (Shāh) his son ...	9	,,
769	1367	Sultān Ghiyāsu'ddin his son ...	7	,,
775	1373	Sultān 'us Salātin, his son ...	10	0
785	1383	Shamsu'ddin, his son ...	3	some
787	1385	Kānsi native of Bengal ...	7	0
794	1392	Sultān Jalālu'ddin ...	17	0
812	1409	Sultān Ahmad, his son ...	16	0
		Nāsir his slave, a week or according to others, half a day.		

A.H.	A.D.		Years.	Months.
830	1426-7	Nāsir Shah, descendant of Shamsu'ddin Bhangarah ...	32	0
862	1457	Bārbak Shāh	17	0
879	1474	Yusuf Shāh	7	0
887	1482	Sikandar Shāh	half a day	
887	1482	Fath Shāh	7	5
896	1490	Bārbak Shāh ...	two and a half days.	
897	1491	Firoz Shāh	3	0
899	1494	Mahmud Shah, his son ...	1	0
900	1495	Muzaffar Habshi	3	5
903	1498	Alāu'ddin	27 (?)	some
927	1521	Nasrat Shāh, his son ...	11 (?)	
940	1534	*Mahmud Shāh, son of Alāu'd defeated by*		
944	1537	Sher Khān.		
945	1538	Humayun (held his court at Gaur).		
946	1539	Sher Khan, a second time.		
952	1545	Muhammad Khān.		
962	1555	Bahādur Shāh, his son.		
968	1560	Jalālu'ddin, his brother.		
Not in U. T.		Ghiyāsu'ddin.		
		Tāj Khān.		
971	1563-4	Sulaimān (Karāni), his brother.		
981	1573	Bāyazid, his son.		
981	1573	Dāud, his brother (*defeated by Akbar's forces*).		

Fifty princes ruled during about 357 years and one hundred and eleven kept alive the torch of sovereignty throughout the period, approximately, of 4,813 years and passed into the sleep of dissolution.

The first Rājā, (Bhagadatta) came to Delhi by reason of his friendship for Rājā Durjodhan, and fell manfully fighting in the war of the Mahābhārat, 4,096 years previous to the present time. When the cup of life of Rājā Naujah [*correct into* Rājāh of Nodia] overflowed, the sovereignty fell to Lakhmaniya, son of Rāe Lakhman. Nadiyā was at that time the capital of Bengal and the seat of various learning. Nowadays its prosperity has somewhat abated but the traces of its erudition are still evident. The astrologers predicted the overthrow of his kingdom and the establishment of another faith and they discovered in Muhammad Bakhtiyār Khilji the individual by whom these two events would be accomplished. Although the Rājā regarding these as idle tales refused to credit them, many of his subjects sought refuge in distant provinces. At the time when Qutbu'ddin Aibak held India for Shahābu'ddin, the Khilji took possession of Bihār by force of arms, and when he marched upon Bengal, the Rājā, escaped in a boat. Muhammad Bakhtiyar, entered Bengal and having amassed enormous plunder, he destroyed the city of Nadiyā and transferred the capital to Lakhnauti. From that time Bengal has been subject to the kings of Delhi.

During the reign of Sultān Tughlaq, Qadar Khān was viceroy in Bengal. Malik Fakhru'ddin his sword-bearer through greed of power, disloyally determined upon the death of his master and plotting in secret, slew him and with pretentious allegations fraudfully possessed himself of the government and refused allegiance to the sovereigns of Delhi. Malik Ali Mubārak, who had been one of the principal adherents of Qadar Khān, assumed the title of Alāu'ddin and rose against Fakhru'ddin, and taking him alive in action, put him to death. Hāji Iliyās 'Alāi, one of the nobles of Bengal, entering into a confederacy with some others, slew him and took the title of Shamsu'ddin. He is also called *Bhangrah*. Sultān Firoz set out from Delhi to chastise him and a severe struggle ensued, but as the rainy season was approaching, he concluded a hasty treaty and returned. When Shamsu'ddin died, the chiefs of the army raised his eldest son to the throne under the title of Sikandar Shāh. Sultān Firoz again marched into Bengal but retreated after arranging terms of peace. On Sikandar's death his son was elected to succeed him and was proclaimed under the title of Ghiyāsu'ddin. Khwājah Hāfiz of Shirāz sent him an ode in which occurs the following verse :

And now shall India's parroquets on sugar revel all,
In this sweet Persian lyric that is borne to far Bengal.

A native of Bengal named Kānsi fraudfully dispossessed Shamsu'ddin who was his [Ghiyās-ud-din's] grandson. When he died, his son embraced Islām and took the name of Sultān Jalālu'ddin. It was the custom in that country for seven thousand footmen called *Pāyiks* to patrol round the palace. One evening a eunuch conspiring with these guards slew Fath Shāh and assumed the title of Bārbak Shāh.

Firoz Shāh was also slain by these guards and his son Mahmud was raised to the sovereignty. An Abyssinian slave Muzaffar with the assistance of the same guards put him to death and mounted the throne. Alāu'ddin, an attendant of Muzaffar, in turn, in conspiracy with these guards despatched his master and established himself in power. Thus through the caprice of fortune, these low footsoldiers for a considerable time played an important part in the state. Alāu'ddin placed the administration of justice on a better footing and disbanded the *Pāyiks*. Nasrat Shah is said to have followed the example of his father in his justice and liberality and treated his brothers with consideration. When Sultān Ibrahim (Lodi) met his death in the engagement with Sultan Bābar, [1526] his brother and the chiefs of the army took refuge with this monarch and lived in security. Humayun appointed Jahāngir Quli Beg to the governorship of the province. When Sher Khān a second time rose to power, he beguiled Jahāngir under pretext of an amicable settlement and put him to death. During the reign of Salim Khān (at Delhi) Muhammad Khān his kinsman, united loyalty to his lord with justice to his subjects. When he fell in action against Mamrez Khān, his son Khizr Khān succeeded him and assumed the title of Bahādur Shāh. Mamrez Khān entered the field against him but perished in battle. Tāj Khān [Karrāni] one of the nobles of Salim Khān, slew Jalālu'ddin and assumed the government. His younger brother Sulaimān, although of a tyrannous disposition, reigned for some time, after which his sons Bāyazid and Dāud through misconduct dishonoured the royal privileges of the mint and the pulpit. Thus concludes my abstract.

Praise be to God, that this prosperous country receives an additional splendour through the justice of imperial majesty.

THE SUBAH OF BIHĀR.

It is situated in the second climate. Its length from *Gadhi* to *Rhotās* is 120 *kos;* its breadth from *Tirhut* to the northern mountains, 110 *kos*. On its eastern boundary is Bengal; to the west lie *Allahabad* and *Oudh*. On the north and south it is bounded by hills of considerable elevation. Its chief rivers are the *Ganges* and the *Son*. Whatever of wood or leather and the like falls into the Son, becomes petrified. The head springs of these three rivers, the *Son*, the *Narbada* and the *Johila*, bubble up from a single reed-bed* in the neighbourhood of *Gadha* [Mandla]. The Son

* The three great rivers, Narmadā, Son and Mahānadi, rise in a sacred pond at the Amar-Kantak, a village in the Rewā State, only three miles from

is pleasant to the taste, wholesome and cool; flowing in a northerly direction, it joins the Ganges near *Maner.* The *Gandak* flows from the north and unites with the Ganges near *Hājipur.* Such as drink of it suffer from a swelling in the throat, (goitre) which gradually increases, especially in young children, to the size of a cocoanut.

The *Sāligrām*† is a small black stone which the Hindus account among divine objects and pay it great veneration. If round and small and unctuous, they hold it in the highest regard and according to the variety of its form, different names and properties are ascribed to it. The generality have a single perforation, others more and some are without any. They contain gold ore. Some say that a worm is bred within which eats its way through; others maintain that it works its way in from the outside. The Hindus have written a considerable work on the qualities of this stone. According to the Brahmanical creed, every idol that is broken loses its claim to veneration, but with these, it is not so. They are found in the Son for a distance of 40 *kos* between its northernmost extremity and the south of the hills.

The *Karamnāsa* flowing from the south unites with the Ganges near *Chausā.* Its waters are regarded with aversion.[1] The *Punpun* flows also from the south and joins

---

the eastern border of the Garh Mandlā district of the C.P., where the Maikāl range begins. The *Johillā,* a very small river, is really a feeder of the *Son* and, after flowing north and west from its source for a little more than a hundred miles as a thin stream, loses itself in the *Son,* in the north-west corner of the Rewā State, 13 miles east of Bandhu-garh. It should not, therefore, be counted as separate from the *Son,* which does not really rise from the same tank at Amar-Kantak but some distance to the east of it. The third great river with its source at the same place is the *Mahānadi,* which Abul Fazl has entirely left out. The *Mahānadi* flowing eastward across half the breadth of the Indian peninsula, falls into the Bay of Bengal in Orissa, more than 1800 miles from the mouth of its twin-sister the Narmadā, in the Arabian sea, though both rivers started from the same cradle.

The sacred tank at Amar-Kantak is 8 yards long and 6 yards wide, and surrounded by a brick-wall. It is situated 90 miles due east of Mandla city. (Tieffenthaler quoting an English engineer's report). "The Narmada in issuing from its source is only one yard in breadth. The *Son* is visible only for a distance of half a mile from the tank, and then it descends in a water-fall 25 yards high, and after a course of five miles, it loses itself in the sand, but newly acquiring greater volume it (finally) becomes a large river." (Tieffenthaler, i, 416-417.) The *Son* used to fall into the Ganges near Maner, when Rennell made his survey (*Bengal Atlas,* 1772), but the junction is now about ten miles higher up, at Koilwar (Rl. Stn.) *Jadunath Sarkar.*

† A species of black quartzose found in the Gandhak containing the impression of one or more ammonites conceived by the Hindus to represent Vishnu. This river is also known as the Sālgirām.

[1] Its name signifies 'the ruin of religious merit.' No person of any caste will drink its waters. The reason of its impurity is said to be that a Brahman having been murdered by a Raja of the Solar line, a saint purified him of his sins by collecting water from all the streams of the world and washing him

the Ganges near Patna. The smaller rivers of this Subah cannot be recorded. The summer months are intensely hot, while the winter is temperate. Warm garments are not worn for more than two months. The rains continue during six months and throughout the year the country is green and fertile. No severe winds blow nor clouds of dust prevail. Agriculture flourishes in a high degree, especially the cultivation of rice which, for its quality and quantity is rarely to be equalled. *Kisāri*[2] is the name of a pulse, resembling peas, eaten by the poor, but is unwholesome. Sugarcane is abundant and of excellent quality. Betel-leaf, especially the kind called *Maghi,* is delicate and beautiful in colour, thin in texture, fragrant and pleasant to the taste. Fruits and flowers are in great plenty. At *Maner,* a flower grows named *Muchakand,*[3] somewhat like the flower of the *Dhātura,* very fragrant and found nowhere else. Milk is rich in quality and cheap. The custom of dividing the crops is not here prevalent. The husbandman pays his rents in person and on the first occasion presents himself in his best attire. The houses for the most part are roofed with tiles. Good elephants are procurable in plenty and boats likewise. Horses and camels are scarce. Parrots abound and a fine species of goat of the Barbary breed which they castrate: from their extreme fatness they are unable to walk and are carried on litters. The fighting cocks are famous. Game is abundant. Gilded glass is manufactured here.

In the *Sarkār* of *Bihār,* near the village of *Rājgir* is a quarry of stone resembling marble, of which ornaments are made. Good paper is here manufactured. *Gayā* the place of Hindu pilgrimage, is in this province: it is also called *Brahma Gayā* being dedicated to *Brahma.* Precious stones from foreign ports are brought here and a constant traffic carried on.

In the *Sarkār* of *Hājipur* the fruits *Kaṭhal*[4] and *Barhal* grow in abundance. The former attain such a size that a man can with difficulty carry one.

---

in their waters which were collected in the spiring from which the Karamnāsā now issues. *I. G.*

[2] Lathyrus sativus.

[3] Dr. King of the Royal Botanical Gardens, Calcutta, suggests that this may be the *Jasminum pubescens.* The flower resembles a miniature Dhatura flower and is very fragrant.

[4] Known as the Jack fruit (Artocarpus integrifolia Roxb.). The *Barhal* according to the dictionary is a small round fruit, also an Artocarpus, doubtfully distinguished as "*lacucha.*"

In the *Sarkār* of *Champāran* the seed of vetch *Māsh*[5] is cast on unploughed soil where it grows without labour or tilling. Long pepper grows wild in its forests.

Tirhut has from immemorial time, been a seat of Hindu learning. Its climate is excellent. Milk curds keep for a year without alteration. If those who sell milk adulterate it with water, some mysterious accident befalls them. The buffaloes are so savage that they will attack a tiger. There are many lakes and in one of them the water never decreases, and its depth is unfathomable. Groves of orange trees extend to a distance of thirty *kos*, delighting the eye. In the rainy season gazelle and deer and tiger frequent together the cultivated spots and are hunted by the inhabitants. Many of these with broken limbs are 'loosened in an enclosure, and they take them at their leisure.

Rohtās is a stronghold on the summit of a lofty mountain, difficult of access. It has a circumference of 14 *kos* and the land is cultivated. It contains many springs, and wherever the soil is excavated to the depth of three or four yards, water is visible. In the rainy season many lakes are formed, and more than two hundred waterfalls gladden the eye and ear. The climate is remarkably healthy.

This *Subah* contains seven *Sarkārs* subdivided into 199 *Parganahs*. The gross revenue is 22 *krors*, 19 lakhs, 19,404½ *dāms*. (Rs. 55,47,985-1-3). Of these *Parganahs*, 138, pay revenue in cash from crops charged at special rates.[6] The extent of measured land is 24 *lakhs*, 44,120 *bighas*, yielding a revenue of 17 *krors*, 26 *lakhs*, 81,774 *dāms* (Rs. 43,17,044) in cash. The remaining 61 *Parganahs* are rated at 4 *krors*, 22 *lakhs*, 37,630½ *dāms*. (Rs. 12,30,940-12-5), out of which 22 *lakhs*, 72,174 *dāms* are *Suyurghāl* (Rs. 56,803-8-10). The province furnishes 11,415 Cavalry, 449,350 Infantry and 100 boats.

Sarkār of Bihār.

Containing 46 *Mahals*, 952,598 *Bighas*. Revenue, 80,196,390 *dāms* in cash from special crops, and from land

---

[5] Phaseolus radiatus.

[6] The term *Zabti* though originally applied to lands sequestrated by the State, was used of rent free lands subjected to assessment in Bengal, to lands which had been resumed from Jagir grants by Jafar Khān : in the north-west, to money rents on the more valuable crops, such as sugar, tobacco, and cotton where rent in kind was the rule. Abul Fazl employs it loosely elsewhere for the revenue collection or assessment of a village.

paying the general *bigha rate*. *Suyurghāl,* 2,270,147 *dāms*. Castes various. Cavalry 2,115. Infantry 67,350.

	Bighas and Biswas	Revenue Dām	Cav.	Inf.	Suyurghal Dām	Castes
Arwal	57,089-5	426,780	...	1000	...	
Aukhri [?Khokri] ..	49-401-10	3,747,940	...	...	...	
Ikhal	40,404-4	335,260	...	200	...	Afghān & Brāhman
Amritu	24,387-19	1,821,333	...	...	16035	Do.
Anbalu	...	847,920	...	250	...	Brāhman
Anchha	10,290-57	6,700,000	20	300	...	Afghān
Antri	1,998-9	147,980	20	200	...	Kayath
Behār with suburban district, has a fort of stone and brick	70,683-9	5,534,151	10	400	653,200	
Bahlāwar	48,310-3	3,651,640	...	500	9000	Brāhman
Basok	35,318-18	2,706,539	...	300	1,708,130	Shaikhzādah
Palach	30,030-18	2,270,538	...	500	59,185	Brāhman,
Baliā	26,000-18	2,056,502	20	400	85,747	Rājput
Patna, has two forts, one of brick and the other of mud	21,846-8	1,922,430	...	...	131,807	
Phulwāri	20,225-19	1,585,420	20	700	118,120	Rājput
Pahra	12,285 6	941,160	20	400	18,560	Brāhman
Bhimpur	10,862-15	824,584	...	...	24,424	
Pandārak	...	727,640	300	2000	...	
Tilādah	39,053-12	2,920,366	20	300	232,080	Shaikhzāda
Jarar	12,930-10	979,363	50	500	880	Do.
Chargāon	...	904,440	20	300	...	Brāhman
Jai Champa ..	...	620,000	20	600	...	
Dādar	...	262,500	...	...	...	
Dhakner	...	215,680	...	...	...	
Ruh	...	250,100	20	1500	...	Brāhman
Rāmpur	...	363.820	...	...	...	
Rājgir	3,756-12	288,228	...	...	17,225	
Sanot	36 780-7	2,824,180	20	500	...	
Samāi	32,514-3	2,537,080	10	200	62,380	Kāyath
Sahrah	...	2,079,000	...	500	...	Rājput,
Sāndah	24,562-2	1,889,956	...	500	...	Afghān
Seor, has a strong fort on a hill ..	14,145-8	1,250,591	200	5000	...	Brāhman
Ghiāspur	84,205-7	5,657,290	...	...	227,454	
Gidhaur, has a strong fort on a hill in the jungle	...	1,452,500	250	10,000	...	Rājput
Kātibahra	...	737,540	...	...	...	
Kābar	7,400-9	560,875	30	700	...	Kāyath
Guh	...	374,880	100	1000	...	Rājput
Ghātisār	...	360,820	...	...	...	
Karanpur	...	363,820	...	...	...	
Gaya	951-4	74,270	...	...	14,235	
Muner	89,039-15	7,049,179	...	...	325,380	
Masodhā	68,191-10	4,631,080	...	...	...	
Māldah	28,128-9	2,151,575	100	3000	49,805	Brāhman
Manroā	7,706-9	585,500	20	500	...	Do.
Maher	23,937-19	1,779,540	...	200	47,700	Do.
Narhat	30,555-7	2,380,309	5	200	...	Kāyath

Sarkār of Monghyr.

Containing 31 *Mahals.* Revenue 109,625,981½ *dāms.* Castes various, 2,150 Cavalry, 50,000 Infantry.

	Revenue D.
Abhipur	2,000,000
Osla	89,760
Bhāgalpur	4,696,110
Baliā	3,287,320
Paharkiah	3,000,000
Pathrārah	140,920
Basai	132,000
Tanur	88,420
Chai	9,280,000
Chandoi	360,000
Dharmpur	4,000,000
Dānd Sakhwārah ...	136,000
Rohni	95,360
Sarohi	1,773,000
Sukhdehra	690,240
Saghauli	360,000
Angu	147,800
Anbalu	50,000
Surajgarh	299,445
Sakhrasāni	160,000
Satyāri	58,730
Kahalgāon	2,800,000
Kharhi	689,044
Kozrah	260,602
Khatki	160,000
Lakhanpur	633,280
Masjidpur	1,259,750
Monghyr and suburban district	808,907½
Masdi	29,725
Hindui	108,000
Hazār taki	9,182

Sarkār of Champāran.

Containing 3 *Mahals,* 85,711 *Bighas,* 5 *Biswas.* Revenue 5,513,420 *Dāms,* Horsemen, 700. Infantry 30,000.

	B.	& B.	Dāms
Samrun ...	7,200	,, 2	500,095
Mehsi ...	56,095	,, 7	3,518,435
Majhora	22,415	,, 16	1,404,890

Sarkār of Hājipur.

Containing 11 *Mahals,* 10 Villages, 436,952 *Bighas,* 15 *Biswas.* Revenue 27,331,030 *dāms.*

...	B.	& B.	Revenue
Akbarpur ...	3,366	,, 17	195,040
Boswāwi ...	10,851	,, 14	624,791
Basārā ...	106,370	,, 7	6,380,000
Bālāgachah ...	14,638	,, 2	913,660
Teghra ...	58,306	,, 13	3,518,354
Hājipur with suburban district	62,653	,, 17	3,833,460
Rati ...	30,438	,, 13	1,824,980
Saresā ...	102,461	,, 8	6,704,300
Imādpur ...	12,987	,, 7	795,870
Garhsarah ...	,,	,,	876,200
Naipur ...	27,877	,, 9	1,663,980

Sarkār of Sāran.

Containing 17 *Mahals.* Measured land 229, 052 *Bighas,* 15 *Biswas.* Revenue 60,172,004½ *dāms.* Castes various. Cavalry 1,000. Infantry 50,000.

	B.	& B.	Dāms
Indar ...	7,218	,, 4	534,990
Barāri ...	7,117	,, 10	533,820
Narhan ...	8,611	,, 8	654,508
Pachlakh ...	9,266	,, 15	437,997
Chanend ...	8,413	,, 13	633,270
Chaubāra ...	,,		400,000
Juwainah ...	6,963	,, 8	309,285
Degsi ...	5,825		277,630
Sipāh ...	3,662		290,592
Pāl ...	66,320	,, 5	4,893,378
Bārā ...	15,059	,, 3	383,797½
Godah (Gawā ?) ...	28,049	,, 3	2,012,950
Kaliyānpur ...	17,437		774,696
Kashmir · ...	16,915		1,314,539
Māngjhi ...	8,752	,, 19	611,813
Mandhal ...	9,405	,, 7	698,140
Maker ...	10,936	,, 14	811,095

Sarkār of Tirhut.

Containing 74 *Mahals*, Measured land 266,464 *Bighas* 2 *Biswas*. Revenue 19,179,777½ *dāms*. Castes various Cavalry 700. Infantry 80,000.

	B.	& B.R	Dāms
Āhaspur	4,880	,,	302,550
Utarkhand	2,068	,,	128,412
Ahlwār	1,001	,, 1	62,212
Aubhi	,,		60,000
Aughārā	836	,, 15	53,980
Athāis	559	,, 17	34,356
Basri &c., 4 Mahals	,,	,,	1,125,000
Bahrwārah	16,176	,,	942,000
Bānpur	40,347	,,	894,792
Barel	6,185	,,	789,858
Pepra	1,823	,, 18	112,591
Padri	9,048	,,	554,258
Basotra	8,864	,,	546,627
Panchhi [?Bachhi)]	5,816	,,	361,920
Bahnor	5,033	,,	289,773½
Bachhnor	4,956	,,	275,185
Pachham Bhagu	4,095	,,	271,826
Bagda	3,716	,,	267,862½
Purab Bhagu	3,022	,, 17	222,280
Pandrājah	3,135	,, 4	195,837½
Bādi Bhosādi	2,823	,,	175,585
Bhālā	2,840	,,	145,437
Bhadwār	2,087	,,	130,471½
Parhārpur	1,968	,,	121,067½
Bahādurpur	1,936	,, 16	119,305
Barai	1,455	,, 12	90,369½
Parhār Rāghu	1,303	,, 17	81,605
Bhaurā	1,170	,, 9	69,608
Palwāah	1,060	,, 9	65,628
Borā	875	,, 15	55,757
Bauwā	,,	,,	40,539
Parhārpur, Jabdi	604	,, 14	37,736
Bagi	505	,, 5	31,550
Bochhāwār	188	,, 10	12,875
Barsāni	200	,, 18	12,695
Tarāni	7,171	,,	443,242
Tilokchāwand	2,411	,, 7	149,896
Tājpur	1,351	,, 14	85,434
Tāndah	1,038	,, 4	63,768
Tarson	980	,, 4	61,180
Tirhut with suburban district	21,398	,,	1,307,706
Jākhar	17,140	,,	1,068,020
Jarāyal	8,297	,,	515,732
Chakmani	5,173	,,	321,326
Jakhal [-pur]	3,092	,,	196,020
Jabdi	,,	,,	45,025
Dahror	3,165	,,	202,818
Darbhāngā	2,038	,,	159,052
Rāmjaund	7,409	,,	470,005½
Sareshtā	15,474	,,	941,010
Salimpur	458	,, 14	29,094
Salimābād	44	,, 15	4,184
Sanjoli Tadrā	2,450	,,	150,843½
Alāpur	8,796	,,	442,466
Fakhrābād	1,170	,, 6	72,355
Khānauli	4,644	,,	408,804
Ghar Chāwand	5,510	,,	349,480½
Kodākhand	3,888	,,	243,677
Korādi	,,	,,	90,000
Khandā	330	,, 6	21,443
Ladwāri	2,609	,,	142,495
Mahlā	15,295	,,	946,048
Morwah	8,289	,,	515,485
Mandah, (Mahend?)	1,077	,, 12	66,693
Margā [?Naranga]	632	,, 18	39,022
Malahmi	151	,, 1	9,728
Nauram	,,	,,	288,140
Nautan	3,381	,, 7	209,153
Hāthi	2,563	,, 18	159,790½
Harni	796	,, 17	50,342
Hābi [?Hali)	3,665	,, 8	230,700

Sarkār of Rohtās.

Containing 18 *Mahals*, 47,334 *Bighas*, 15 *Biswas*. Revenue, 40,819,493 *Dāms*. Castes various. Cavalry 4,550. Infantry 162,000.

	B.	& B.R	Dāms
Ārah	53,512	,, 16	4,028,100
Bhojpur	66,078	,, 17	4,903,310
Piru	,,	,,	3,407,840
Panwār	22,733	,, 3	1,677,000
Baragāon	10,540	,, 17	842,400
Chakund (Jaund)	45,251	,, 3	4,440,360
Jaidar	26,538	,, 16	1,634,110
Danwār	29,154	,, 4	2,076,520
Dinār	,,	,,	350,000
Rohtās with suburban dist.	34,330	,, 10	2,258,620
Ratanpur, has a strong fort	,,	,,	783,425
Siris (Sarsi)	44,710	,, 3	2,769,446
Sahsaram	31,220	,, 18	2,370,790
Fathpur bhaiya	50,474	,, 15	3,736,000
Kotrā	29,167	,, 15	1,829,300
Kot, has a strong fort	,,	,,	847,920
Mangror (Munora?)	,,	,,	924,000
Naunor	29,621	,,	2,000,000

The Subah of Illāhābād. (*Allahabad.*)

It is situated in the second climate. Its length from *Sinjhauli* in the *Jaunpur* district to the southern hills is 160 *kos*; its breadth from *Chausa* ferry to *Ghātampur* 122 *kos*. On the East is *Behār*. To the North, *Oudh*. *Bāndhu** lies to the South and *Agra* to the West.

Its principal rivers are the *Ganges* and the *Jamna*, and there are other small streams such as the *Rind, Ken, Saru* (Sarju), *Barna*, &c.

Its climate is healthy. It produces a variety of fruits, flowers and garden herbs, and it has always an abundant supply of melons and grapes. Agriculture is in a flourishing state. *Jowāri* and *Lahdarah*, however, do not grow and *Moth* is scarce. Cloths, such as *Jholi*, and *Mihrkal* and the like are beautifully woven, especially at *Benāres*, *Jalālābād* and *Mau*. At *Jaunpur*, *Zafarwāl* and other places woollen carpets are manufactured. A variety of game is also to be found.

Illahabād anciently called *Prayāg* was distinguished by His Imperial Majesty by the former name. A stone fort was completed and many handsome edifices erected. The Hindus regard it as the King of shrines. Near it, the *Ganges*, the *Jamna* and the *Saraswati* meet, though the latter is not visible. Near the village of *Kantat* considerable captures of elephants are made. What is most strange is that when Jupiter enters the constellation Leo, a small hill appears from out of the Ganges and remains there during the space of one month upon which the people offer divine worship.

Bārānasi, universally known as Benares, is a large city situated between the two rivers, the *Barna* and the *Āsi*.† In ancient books, it is styled *Kāsi*. It is built in the shape of a bow of which the Ganges forms the string. In former days there was here an idol temple, round which procession was made after the manner of the *kaabah* and similar ceremonials of the pilgrims conducted. From time immemorial, it has been the chief seat of learning in Hindustān.

---

* *Bandhu* is Rewa State, and *not* Banda as Jarrett noted in the 1st edition.

† The Asi is a mere brook and the city is situated on the left bank of the Ganges, between the *Barnā Nadi* on the N. E. and the *Asi Nala* on the S. W. The former rises to the N. of Allahabad and has a course of 100 miles. From the joint names of the two which bound the city, N. and S. the Brāhmans derive Varanasi, the Sanskrit form of Benares. Cunningham, *Ancient Geog. of India*, p. 437.

Crowds of people flock to it from the most distant parts for the purpose of instruction to which they apply themselves with the most devoted assiduity. Some particulars of its history shall be related in what follows.

In A.H. 410 Sultān Mahmud of Ghazni marched hither, and some disruption of the old faith was effected. In A.H. 416, he again invaded the country. He first invested Gwalior but raised the siege under a treaty of peace. He then resolved to take the fort of *Kālinjar.* The governor sent him 300 elephants with his respectful submission and proffered some eulogistic verses. Mahmud was so much pleased that he bestowed on him the governorship of the fort together with the charge of fourteen other places.

Jaunpur is a large city. Sultān Firoz (Tughlaq) king of Delhi laid its foundations and named it after his cousin Fakhruddin Jaunah. Its longitude is 190° 6″; its latitude 16° 15″.

Chanādah (Chanār) is a stone fort on the summit of a hill, scarce equalled for its loftiness and strength. The Ganges flows at its foot.

In its vicinity, there is a tribe of men who go naked, living in the wilds, and subsist by their bows and arrows and the game they kill. Elephants are also found in the forests.

Kālinjar is a stone fortress situated upon a heaven-reaching* hill. No one can trace its origin. It contains many idol temples and an idol is there, called *Kāl Bhairob,* 18 cubits high of which marvellous tales are related. Springs rise within the fort and there are many tanks. Adjoining it is a dense forest in which wild elephants, and kestrels and hawks and other animals are trapped. Ebony is here found and many kinds of fruits grow spontaneously. There is also an iron mine. In the neighbourhood, within eight *kos,* the peasants find small diamonds.

It is said that Rājā Kirat Singh the governor of the fort possessed six precious treasures, a learned Brāhman of saintly life, a youth of great beauty and amiable disposi-

* Its elevation is 1230 feet above sea level. Ferishta ascribes the fort to Kedār Rājā, a contemporary of Muhammad, but local legend connects it with Chandra Varma, ancestor of the great Chandel family of Rajputs, who removed hither after their defeat by Prithi Rāj, the Chauhān ruler of Delhi. *I. G.*

tion, a parrot that answered any questions put to it and some say, remembered everything that it heard, a musician named Bakshu unequalled in the knowledge and practice of his art, and two handmaidens lovely to behold and skilled in song. Sultān Bāhadur Gujrāti having formed a friendship with the Rājā asked him for one of these. The Rājah generously and with a provident wisdom sent him Bakshu. Next Sher Khān of the House of Sur requested the gift of the two wonderful songstresses, and when his messenger returned without them, he invested the fort. Works were erected and the besieged were reduced to great straits. In despair, the Rājā, after the manner of the Hindus who hold their honour dear, burnt his women, for in the slumbering of his reason, he had set his affections upon the things of this fleeting life, and so giving his body to ashes, according to the desire of his enemies, he became soiled with the dust of dissolution. As to Sher Khān, who had conceived this wicked design, he fell at the powder magazine when the fire opened on the fort and the harvest of his life was consumed.*

The *Subah* contains ten *Sarkārs,* and 177 *Parganahs.* Revenue 21 *krors,* 14 *lakhs* and 17,819 *dāms* (Rs. 53,10,695-7-9)), and 12 *lakhs* of betel leaves. Of these *Parganahs* 131 pay revenue from crops charged at special rates. Measured land 39, 68,018 *bighas,* 3 *biswas,* yielding a revenue of 20 *krors,* 29 *lakhs,* 71,224 *dāms* (Rs. 50,74,280-9). The remaining 46 *Parganahs* pay the general *bigah* rate. They are rated at 94 *lakhs,* 56,595 *dāms* (Rs. 2,36,424-14). Of this, 1 *kror,* 11 *lakhs,* 65,417 *dāms* (Rs. 279,135-6-6) are *Suyurghāl.* The province furnishes 11,375 Cavalry, 237,870 Infantry and 323 elephants.

Note.—In the names of the *parganahs* under the following *Sarkārs,* I have altered the spelling where the variants allow, in accordance with Elliot's list, as his personal acquaintance with their true pronunciation is probably more correct than those of my previous lists which were adapted as far as possible to reconcile the readings of Gladwin and Tieffenthaler. The discrepancies are slight and will not interfere with their recognition.

* This took place in 1545. During the siege a live shell rebounded from the walls into the battery where Sher Shāh stood and set fire to the gunpowder. He was brought out severely burnt and died next day, having previously ordered an assault which was at once made with success. K. R. Qanungo's *Sher Shah,* 339.

Subah of Illāhābād. *Sarkārs.*	*Subah of Agra.* *Sarkārs.*	*Subah of Oudh.* *Sarkārs.*	*Subah of Delhi.* *Sarkārs.*
Illāhābas.	Agra.	Garakhpur.	Delhi.
Karrah.	Kanauj.		Rewāri.
Korarah (Kora).	Kālpi.		Sahāranpur.
Kālinjar.	Kol.		Hisār Firozah.
Jaunpur.	Tijārah.		Sambhal.
Ghāzipur.	Irij.		Badāon.
Benares.	Sahār.		
Chanār.			

Sarkār of Illāhābās (Allahabad).

Containing 11 *Mahals,* 573,311 *Bighas,* 14 *Biswas.* Of these 9 *Mahals* yield 20,833,374½ *Dāms,* in money. *Suyurghāl,* 747,001½ *Dāms.* Castes various. Cavalry 580. Infantry 7,100.

	Bighas and Biswas	Revenue D.	Suyurghāl D.	Cavalry	Infantry	Castes
Illāhābās, with suburban district: has a stone fort ..	284,057	9,267,359	253,261	...	1,000	Brāhman
Bhadoi, with a brick fort on the bank of the Ganges ..	73,252-2	3,660,918	37,534	200	5,000	Rājput, a few Bhars[1]
Jalālābād,[2] 5 Mahals	...	737,220	...	10	400	Brāhman
Sorāon	63,932-4	3,247,127	161,527	40	1,000	Rājput, Chandel, Brāhman
Singraur, has a brick fort on the bank of the Ganges	38,536-6	1,885,066	74,883	...	...	Brāhman, Kāyath, Rahmatullāhi
Sikandarpur ..	34,756-8	1,867,704	92,138	25	500	Brāhman
Kantit, has a stone fort on the Ganges	...	856,555	...	50	2,000	Khandāl ?[3]
Kusi. (Elliot Kewāi)	14,385-3	721,115	19,005	15	400	Rājput, Brāhman
Khairagarh, has a stone fort on a hill	...	400,000	...	200	5,000	Rājput, Birāsi (Bhar ?)
Mah, has a stone fort on the hill Alwand[4] ..	21,982	1,139,980	22,495½	20	400	Rājput, Gaharwāl
Hādiābās,[4] (now called Jhusi. Elliot) ..	42,422-5	2,018,014	79,078	20	400	Rājput, Brāhman

[1] The Bhars were a powerful tribe during the period of Buddhist ascendancy. In Southern and Eastern Oudh there are many relics of their wealth and power in the shape of tanks, wells, embankments and deserted sites of brick built forts and towns. Beames, *Memoir,*. i. p. 33. *Oudh Gazetteer,* i. p. xxxvi.

[2] Three names follow without diacritical points, intelligible in the MSS. Tieff. gives "Sobehe, Anelā, Bando, Barbar.

[3] A note to the text suggests, *Gaharwāl,* one of the 36 royal tribes of Rājputs.

[4] A note states that in the maps there is no hill. *Alwand* is the name of a well-known mountain in Hamadān, 80 leagues from Ispahan, often employed in Persian imagery as a synonym for loftiness.

Sarkār of Ghāzipur, (East.)

Containing 19 *Mahals*, 288,770 *Bighas*, 7 *Biswas*. Revenue 13,431,308 *Dāms*, in money. *Suyurghāl*, 131,825 *Dāms*. Castes various. Cavalry 310. Infantry 16,650.

	Bighas and Biswas	Revenue D.	Suyurghāl D.	Cavalry	Infantry	Castes
Baliā	28,344-15	1,250,000	...	200	2000	Rājput
Pachotar	13,679-9	6,982,040	2,250	50	2000	Do.
Bilhābās*	12,306	652,360	...	10	200	Do.
Bāhriābad	6,983-10	355,340	1,720	...	200	Do.
Bhalāech, (E. Barāich)	2.255-19	112,461	...	...	...	
Chausā, (E. Chaunsā) ..	15,602-11	791,653	...	10	500	Brāhman
Dihbā, (E. Dihmah) ..	2,808-15	128,815	2,077	...	50	Rājput
Sayyidpur Namdi ..	25,721-3	1,250,280	18,172	20	1000	Brāhman
Zahurābād	13,802-12	657,808	29,528	500	20	Do.
Ghāzipur with suburban district	12,325-9	570,350	39,680	10	20	Kayath, Rājput
Kariyāt Pali	1,394-5	75,467	...	...	...	
Kopāchhit	19,266-11	942,190	893	20	2000	Rājput
Gandhā, (E. Garhā) ..	10,049-10	500,000	...	...	200	Do.
Karendā	6,260-15	293,551	...	...	300	Do.
Lakhner, (E. Lakhnesar)	2,883-3	126,636	834	...	...	
Madan Benāres ..	66,548-7	2,760 000	1,356	50	5000	Brāhman
Muhammadābād, and Parhārbāri	48,774-16	2,2607707	4,777	2000	100	Do.

Sarkār of Benāres (East.)

Containing 8 *Mahals*, 36,869 *Bighas*, 12 *Biswas*. Revenue 8,869,315 *Dāms* in money. *Suyurghāl* 3,38,184. Castes various. Cavalry 830. Infantry 8,400.

	Bighas and Biswas	Revenue D.	Suyurghāl D.	Cavalry	Infantry	Castes
Afrād	10,655-6	853,226	20,080	...	400	Brāhman, Rājput
Benāres, with suburban district	31,657-1	1,734,721	22,190	50	1000	Brāhman
Byālisi	60,961-3	547,634	...	20	300	Do.
Pandarhā, (var. and E. Pandrah)	4,610-15	844,221	15,836	10	400	Do.
Kaswār	41,184-14	2-2[illegible],160	80,120	50	2000	Do.
Katehar, has a brick fort	30,495-14	1,874,230	48,070	500	4000	Raghuvansi
Harhuā	13,098-3	713,426	8,145	...	300	Brāhman

* G. and T. Baliabass.

Sarkār of Jaunpur (North).

Containing 41 *Mahals,* 870,265 *Bighas,* 4 *Biswas.*
Revenue 56,394,107 *dāms* in money.
Suyurghāl, 4,717,654. Castes various.
Cavalry 915. Infantry 36,000.

	Bighas and Biswas	Revenue D.	Suyurghāl D.	Cavalry	Infantry	Castes
Aldimau	46,888-12	3,099,990	88,976	50	3,000	Rājput
Angli	42,992-14	2,713,551	464,516	50	2,000	Sayyid, Rājput, and Rahmatullāhi Bachgoti
Bihtari	17,703	844,357	12,520	10	100	Ansari*
Bhadāon	4,300	229,315	...	10	100	Saddiki
Tilhani	10,983-8	654,363	27,457	10	100	Rājput
Jaunpur with suburbs, has a fort, the lower part stone, and the upper constructed of brick	65,739-4	4,247,043	807,821	120	2,500	Rājput Kosak, Brāhman, Kurmi
Chāndipur Badhar, (E. Birhar)	22,826-7	1,467,205	157,641	20	400	Rahmatullāhi, Brāhman
Chāndah	17,590	989,286	...	20	300	Bachgoti
Chiriyākot	14,153	807,848	13,689	20	200	Rājput
Jakesar (E. Chakesar)	5,415-10	286,586	...	10	100	Saddiki
Kharid, has a brick fort on the banks of the Sarah	30,914-13	1,445,743	3,140	50	5,000	Rājput Kausik
Khāspur Tāndah ..	17,365	986,953	40,189	10	300	Kāyath
Khānpur	6-628-10	3, 06,020	5,387	...	150	Rājput
Deogāon	44,524-18	2,583,205	196,238	25	1,000	Do. Gautami†
Rāri	24,360	1,326,299	84,502	10	300	Rājput
Sanjhauli	46,815-3	2,938,209	334,932	50	100	Sayyid, Rājput, Braman
Sikandarpur, has a brick fort ..	32,574-10	1,706,417	5,325	10	3,000	Brāhman
Sagdi, (E. Sagri) ..	19,792	1,274,721	102,224	10	200	Rājput
Surharpur	18,851	1,164,095	7,094	10	20	Do.

* These according to the I.G. (Bahraich) were the descendants of the early Mussalman settlers and invaders. For their descent and history, see Beames *Memoir,* I, 7. For Bachgoti, see Elliot (*Races of the N. W. P.*) who says that all Chauhans are Bachgotis, being of the *gotra* of Bach, but Sherring proves this to be an error, instancing the *gotras* of Vatsa and Kāsyap. *Hindu Tribes,* I, p. 164.

† A clan of Rājputs of the Chandarbans, once a powerful clan in the Lower Doab. See Elliot, p. 118, I, and Sherring, I, 202.

Sarkār of Jaunpur (North).—(*Contd.*)

	Bighas and Biswas	Revenue D.	Suyurghāl D.	Cavalry	Infantry	Castes
Shādiābād	30,848-8	1,700.742	10.020	20	400	Rājput
Zafarābād	2,822-9	156,926	13,806½	...	50	Do.
Qariyāt Mittu ..	8,991-11	551,410	...	10	300	Do.
" Dostpur ..	8,857	481 524	42,227	...	100	Do.
" Mendhah ..	7,416	394,870	21,260	...	100	Do.
" Seothah ..	2,988-10	206,733	14,224	...	100	Do.
Kolah	24,231	1,363,332	14,971	10	300	Do.
Ghiswah	30,775	1,241,291	42,366	10	200	Do.
Ghosi .. .	18,913	1,037,934	69,650	10	200	Do.
Gadwārah	2,191	513,942	2,682	50	5,000	Rājput Bachgoti
Kāudiyah, (E. Kauria)	5,764-12	341,890	...	...	200	Rājput
Gopālpur	3 266-8	18,043	4,948	...	100	Do.
Karākat	48,332-14	23,002,748	77,339	20	500	Do.
Mandiāhu, has a brick fort (E. Mariahu)	88,899-5	5,259,465	273,788	50	2,000	Rājput Kausik
Muhammadābād ..	56,350-14	3,229,063	220,442	30	1,000	Rājput, Brāhman
Mungra	9,626-5	529,730	...	...	200	Rājput
Majhāura	6,417-6	420,164	14,427	...	200	Rahmatullāhi
Mau	2,645-3	209,067	...	...	50	Shaikh zādah
Nizamābād	6,074-13	602,592	478,026	200	4,000	Rājput Gautami, Brāhman, Rahmatullāhi
Negun	10,145	758,796	145,350	...	200	Brāhman
Nathupur	4,948-14	278,472	21,239	10	200	Saddiki

Sarkār of Mānikpur.
Containing 14 *Mahals*, 666,222 *Bighas*, 5 *Biswas*.
Revenue 33,916,527 *Dāms* in money.
Suyurghāl, 8,446,173. Castes various.
Cavalry 2,040. Infantry 2,900.

	Bighas and Biswas	Revenue D.	Suyurghāl D.	Cavalry	Infantry	Castes
Arwal, has a brick fort	62.131-10	2,957,077	37 220	114	7.000	Rājput
Bhalol	32,343-3	1,832,283	175,753	20	500	Rājput Kāyath, Baoriya*
Tilhandi	11,721-6	383,251	54,821	10	300	Do.
Jalalpur Balkhar, has a brick fort	76,517-8	3,913,017	140,325	400	5,000	Brāhman Bachgoti,

* *Var.* Gauriya, Puriya : perhaps Baoria a tribe of professional thieves widely spread, and in a loose way, a distinct caste. *I. G.* under, Rajputana and Sherring, II. 82.

Sarkār of Mānikpur.—(Contd.)

	Bighas and Biswas	Revenue D.	Suyur-ghāl D.	Cavalry	Infantry	Castes
Jāes, has a brick fort, (I. G. Jais)	25,625	1,424,737	277,863	250	7,000	Various
Dalmau, has a brick fort on the Ganges ..	67,508-9	3,626,067	344,130	50	200	Turkomān
Rae Bareli, has a brick fort on the Sai ..	65,751-17	3,650,984	180,080	40	2,000	Rājput, Khand, Baoria
Salon, has a brick fort	56,102	2,717,391	394,774	180	8,900	Rājput Khandwāl,† Bisen.
Qaryāt Karārah ..	51,505-19	2,461,077	115,774	20	700	Rājput, Bisen
„ Pāegāh ..	22,130	1,117,926	6,794	20	400	Do. do.
Kathot, has a brick fort	9,456-8	514,909	3,187	100	2,000	Bachgoti
Mānikpur with suburbs, has a brick fort on the Ganges	129,830-1	6,737,729	542,312	500	6,000	Bisen
Nasirābād	55,599-4	2,582,079	108,148	40	1,000	Rājput, Kāyath, Gaoria, Bais

Sarkār of Chanādah (Chanār), South.
Containing 13 *Mahals*, 106,270 *Bighas*, 8 *Biswas*.
Revenue 5,810,654 *Dāms* in money.
Suyurghāl, 109,065. Cavalry 500.
Infantry 18,000.

	Bighas and Biswas	Revenue D.	Suyur-ghāl D.	Cavalry	Infantry	Castes
Ahirwārah	1,858-8	109,073	...	...	...	
Bholi, (E. Bhuili) ..	18,975-10	1,112,656	33,605	...	...	
Badhaul, (E. Barhaul) ..	6,412-11	361,364	605	...	...	
Tāndah	...	488,010	...	...	...	
Chanādah, with suburban district, has a stone fort . ..	12,939-14	833,908	8,467	500	18,000	Saddiki, Faruki, Ansāri
Dhus	4,274-10	235,644	14,548	...	...	
Rāghupur, now pronounced Rāhupur E.)	7,267-12	451,962	17,869	...	...	
Villages, this side of the river	18,098	845,371	14,492	...	...	
Majhwārah	9,312-3	549,817	14,597	...	...	
Mahāich	7,950-2	390,609	2,069	...	...	
Mahwāri	4,878-3	227,067	...	...	...	
Mahoi, (E. Mawai) ..	4,301-2	206,283	3,353	...	...	

† Sherring gives the name of *Khondchwāl* to a trading caste in Bhurtpur. iii. 52.

Sarkār of Bhathkhora, (South.)

Containing 39 *Mahals*. Revenue 7,262,780 *Dāms* in money.

Cavalry 4,304. Elephants 200. Infantry 57,000.

Sarkār of Kālinjar, (South.)

Containing 11 *Mahals*. Measured land, 508,273 *Bighas*, 12 *Biswas*. Revenue 23,839,470 *Dāms*, in money.

Suyurghāl 614,580 *Dāms*. Castes various.

Cavalry 1,210. Elephants 112. Infantry 18,100.

	Bighas and Biswas	Revenue D.	Suyurghāl D.	Cavalry	Infantry	Elephants	Castes
Uguāsi, has a brick fort, (E. Ugāsi)	53,963-6	2,502,898	60,776	400	5,000	10	Sayyid, Gadhwāl, Parihār
Ajaigarh, has a stone fort on a hill ..							
Sendha, (E. Sihondā) has a stone fort on	...	200,000	...	20	2,000	10	Gond
the Ken	138,467-12	6,262,833½	129,412	20	3.000	25	Gond, Chandel, &c.
Simauni, has a brick fort	48,866-3	2,247,346	15,300	300	3,000	...	Khandwāl
Shādipur, has a stone fort	62,755-15	2,798,329½	96,312	40	700	...	Rājput, &c.
Rasan	11,988-10	512,026	...	50	100	20	Bhar, Bais
Kālinjar with suburban district	22,494	970,259	130,490	20	500	7	
Kharelah, has a brick fort	25,940-1	1,275,325	...	50	1,500	...	Rāput, Bais
Mahobā, has a stone fort, and each side of the village is flanked by two high hills	81,567-13	4,042.014 &120,000 *pān*leaves	860,528	100	3,000	40	Bagri* Rahmatu'l-lāhi, Parihār
Māudhā, has a stone fort	62,530-7	2,998,062	154,062	30	400	..	

* The Bāgri are a tribe inhabiting the Bāgar country, a tract between the S.-W. border of Hariana and the Ghāra. Bāgar is also the name of a tract in the Mālwah, but in the N.-W. P. applied to the Bāgri Jats of Hissār and Bhattiāna. Elliot, *Memoir* (Beale), I, 9-10.

*Sarkār of Kurrah,** (*West.*)

Containing 9 *Mahals,* 341,170 *Bighas,* 10 *Biswas.*

Revenue 17,397,567 *Dāms. Suyurghāl* 469,350 *Dāms.*

Castes various. Cavalry 500. Elephants 10.
Infantry 15,000.

	Bighas and Biswas	Revenue D.	Suyur-ghāl D.	Cavalry	Infantry	Elephants	Castes
Jājmāo, has a fort on the Ganges ..	62,195-10	3,106,346	139,936	200	4,000	7	Afghān Lodi, Rājput, Bais.
Kurrah, with suburban district, has a brick fort on the Rind river	124,748-12	6,771,891	257,373	50	300	...	Brāhman
Ghātampur	73,876-3	3,667,564	48,654	100	2,000	10	Rājput Dikhit (Dikshit) Kāyath
Majhāwan	26,980-8	1,323,339	2,574	20	1,000	...	Brāhman
Kutiā	12,178-11	584,274	20,815	30	1,000	...	Rājput Gautami
Guner	10,041-16	513.457	...	20	1,000	...	Do.
Kiranpur Kinār, (Elliot Kiratpur Kanānda) ..	17,935	830,070	...	30	1,000	...	Do.
Muhsanpur	13,181	600,586	...	50	2,000	2	Rājput Chandel

* Kurrah is a decayed town in Fatehpur district; formerly the capital of this Sarkār under the Mughals : it still retains traces of its former importance. A few words follow this name which are either omitted or illegible in the other MSS. Literally they run thus : "And there is a village called Numi which produces flowers and colour."

Karah is now a ruined town on the right bank of the Ganges, 40 miles N.-W. of Allahābād. It was the scene of the famous meeting between Muizu'ddin and his father in 1286 which forms the subject of Mir Khusru's well-known Persian epic, the *Kirānu's Saadain.* Two *sarkārs* of the Allahabad province bearing names liable to be confounded with each other in careless Persian writing, are *Korā* and *Kārā.* They were later distinguished as Korā-Jahānābād (situated in the Fathpur dist. of the U. P.) and Kārā-Mānikpur, (Kārā being in the Allahabad dist., and Mānikpur on the north bank of the Ganges opposite to Kārā and therefore in the Oudh province). The two places are 70 miles apart east to west. The best device for avoiding confusion is to spell *Korā* as *Kurrāh,* which form of the word we find in the Marathi and some Persian records. [J. Sarkar.]

Sarkār of Karah, (West.)

Containing 12 *Mahals*, 447,556 *Bighas*, 19 *Biswas*.... Revenue 22,682,048 *Dāms*. *Suyurghāl*, 1,498,862 *Dāms*. Castes various. Cavalry 390. Infantry 8,700.

	Bighas and Biswas	D. Revenue	Suyurghāl D.	Cavalry	Infantry	Elephants	Castes
Eichhi, (Elliot Enchhi)	35,825-11	1,624,034½	34,974	10	500	...	Do.
Atharban	18,517-14	894,036½	4,770	10	200	...	Do.
Āyāsā	15,783-11	845.766	...	10	500	...	Rājput
Havelī, (suburban district) of Kara ..	9,638-17	5,192,170	442,080	100	1,000	...	Kāyath, Rājput, Brāhman, Khari
Rāri	56,727-18	2,707,034	26,350	10	4.000	...	Rājput Brāhman
Baldah* of Kara, has a fort on the Ganges, lower part stone, upper, brick	70,001-12	236,868	...	...	...	...	Various
Karāri, has a brick foot on the Jumna ..	39,686-19	141,953	...	...	...	...	
Kotlā	18,043-1	909,234	122,191	10	300	...	Brāhman Rājput
Kunrā, commonly Koson, (Elliot, Karson), has a brick fort ..	11,782-9	693,487½	...	100	2,000	...	Various
Fatehpur Hanswah, (Elliot Haswā) ..	55,915-8	2,892,705	370,420	50	1,000	...	Rājput, Brāhman
Hatgāon	55,322-12	2,723,508½	24,329	40	1,000	...	Do.
Hanswah	42,521-3	2,123,661½	15,506	30	1,000	...	Afghān, Rājput

Its rulers.

Sultānu's Sharq	reigned;	16 years.
Mubārak Shāh	,,	1 year and a fraction.
Sultān Ibrahim	,,	40 years ,,
Sultān Mahmud	,,	21 years and a few months.
Mahmud [=Muhammad] Shah	,,	5 months.
Husain	,,	19 years.

* Mr. Beames in a note to Elliot's Gloss., p. 83, II, distinguishes between *Haveli* and *Baldah*, the former alluding to the district close to the Capital and the latter to that at a distance.

Malik Sarwar Khwāja Jahān	A.H. 796/1394 A.D.
Malik Qaranful, Mubārak Sh.	802/1399
Shams-ud-din Ibrāhim Sh.	804/1402
Mahmud Sh.	840/1436
Muhammad Sh.	862/1458
Husain Sh.	862-884/1458-79

—(*Cambridge Hist. India, iii*).

These six princes held sway for 97 years and a few months.*

This province was formerly administered by the sovereigns of Delhi. When the imperial authority devolved on Sultān Muhammad-b-Firuz Shāh, he bestowed the title of Sultān us Sharq upon Malik Sarwar a eunuch who had received from his predecessor the dignity of *Khān-i-Jahān,* and sent him to this province. He gave lustre to his reign by his judgment, clemency, justice and valour and thus garnered a provision for his life's last journey. When the cup of his days was full, the son whom he had adopted, named Mubārak Qaranful, by the assistance of the chief men of the State, raised himself to power and had the *khutbah* read and the coin struck in his own name. When the news of this event reached Mallu (*Khān*), he collected troops and marched from Delhi to oppose him and encamped in readiness for battle on the bank of the Ganges, but nothing decisive having been effected, both armies returned home.

When this prince died, his younger brother Ibrahim was raised to the throne. By his knowledge of men and capacity for affairs he administered the kingdom with justice and made the chastisement of the unruly a source of prosperity to his government. Wisdom was eagerly sought and the prospects of the intelligent in every profession was advanced. Qāzi Shahābu'ddin, a sage of Hindustan flourished about this time. He was born at Delhi and in that city acquired a comprehensive knowledge of the inductive sciences and traditional lore, and at the time of the arrival of Timur, he set out for Jaunpur in the company of his master Maulānā Khwājagi who was the successor of Nasiru'ddin Chirāgh of Delhi and there continued his progress and became the envy of his time. Shāh Madār, however, who is esteemed one of the saints of Hindustān and the chief of his contemporary series of divines, through the disagreement that ever exists between philosophers who regard the material world, and masters of the spiritual life, entertained no esteem for the Qāzi.

When the days of Ibrahim came to a close, his eldest son Bikhan Khān, under the name of Sultan Mahmud, assumed the sovereignty. As his deeds were not approved, the sentence of deposition was issued against him and his

* Six *Jaunpur* rulers,—97 years.

brother Husain raised to power. He made rectitude his rule of conduct and his chief object the conciliation of all hearts. Fortune favoured his desires and the world praised him but intoxicated by the maddening fumes of worldly success, he became arrogant. He was involved in war with Sultān Bahlol and was defeated. Sultān Bahlol left his son Bārbak at Jaunpur and entrusted him with the government. [1478.] On the death of Sultān Bahlol the throne of Delhi devolved on Sultān Sikandar. Sultān Husain with the connivance of Bārbak collected troops, made several attempts against Delhi, but with him the *Sharqi* dynasty closed.*

The Subah of Oudh.

It is situated in the second climate. Its length from the Sarkār of *Gorakhpur* to *Kanauj* is 135 *kos*. Its breadth from the northern mountains to *Sidhpur* on the frontier of the *Subah* of Allahabad is 115 *kos*. To the east is *Bihar;* to the north, the mountains; to the south, *Manikpur,* and to the west *Kanauj*. Its climate is good. Summer and winter are nearly temperate. Its principal streams are the *Saru* (*Sarju*), the *Ghaghar* (*Gogra*) the *Sai* and the *Godi* (*Gumti*). In the first mentioned, divers aquatic animals and forms of strange appearance show themselves. Agriculture is in a flourishing state, especially rice of the kinds called *Sukhdās, Madhkar,* and *Jhanwān,* which for whiteness, delicacy, fragrance and wholesomeness are scarcely to be matched. They sow their rice three months earlier than in other parts of Hindustān. When the drought begins, the Sai and the Gogra rise high in flood and before the beginning of the rains, the land is inundated, and as the waters rise, the stalks of rice shoot up and proportionately lengthen : the crop, however, is destroyed if the floods are in full force before the rice is in ear. Flowers, fruits and game are abundant. Wild buffaloes are numerous. When the

* Jaunpur continued to be governed by the Lodi synasty till the defeat and death of Ibrahim grandson of Bahlol and last of the line, at Panipat by Bābar in 1526. A local kingdom was for a short time established under Bahadur Khān governor of Jaunpur who asserted his independence. It was recovered by Humayun, passed again into the hands of Sher Khān and his son of Salim. Humayun on his reconquest of Hindustān died before he could master his eastern possessions. Jaunpur continued under the Afghāns until Akbar in the 4th year of his reign, took possession of it through Ali Quli Khān and incorporated it with his dominions. In 1575 the Viceregal Court was removed to Allahabad and Jaunpur was governed thenceforth by a Nizam.

plains are inundated the animals take to the high ground where the people find sport in hunting them. Some of the animals remain all day in the water and only at night approach the dry ground and breathe in freedom. *Awadh* (*Ajodhyā*) is one of the largest cities of India. In is situated in longitude 118°, 6′, and latitude 27°, 22′. It ancient times its populous site covered an extent of 148 *kos* in length and 36 in breadth, and it is esteemed one of the holiest places of antiquity. Around the environs of the city, they sift the earth and gold is obtained. It was the residence of Rāmachandra* who in the *Treta* age combined in his own person both the spiritual supremacy and the kingly office.

At the distance of one *kos* from the city, the *Gogra,* after its junction with the Sai, [*Saraju*] flows below the fort. Near the city stand two considerable tombs of six and seven yards in length respectively. The vulgar believe them to be the resting-places of Seth and the prophet Job, and extraordinary tales are related of them. Some say that at *Ratanpur* is the tomb of Kabir,† the assertor of the unity of God. The portals of spiritual discernment were partly opened to him and he discarded the effete doctrines of his own time. Numerous verses in the Hindi language are still extant of him containing important theological truths. *Bahraich* is a large town on the banks of the river Sarju. Its environs are delightful with numerous gardens. *Sālār Masud*[1] and Rajab Sālār are both buried here. The common people of the Muhammadan faith greatly reverence this spot and pilgrims visit it from distant parts, forming themselves in bands and bearing gilded banners. The first mentioned was connected by blood with Mahmud Ghaznavi, and sold his life bravely in battle and left an imperishable name. The second was the

---

* The 7th *avatār,* who in this capital of the solar dynasty founded on the chariot wheel of Brahma, consummated the glories of sixty generations of solar princes and as the incarnate Rāmā, is the hero of the famous epic that bears his name.

† His doctrines were preached between A.D. 1380 and 1420 and attempted the union of Hindu and Muhammadan in the worship of one God whether invoked as Ali or Rāmā. On his decease both these sects claimed the body and while they contested it, Kabir suddenly stood in their midst and commanding them to look under the shoud, vanished. A heap of beautiful flowers was there discovered, which, divided among the rival worshippers, were buried or burnt according to their respective rites. Pilgrims from upper India to this day beg a spoonful of rice water from the Kabir Monastery at Puri in Orissa.

[1] Under the orders of Mahmud of Ghazni, he penetrated the country in A.D. 1033, but was eventually defeated at Bahraich and fell fighting, *sanguine purpuratum,* as Tieffenthaler writes, crowned with the double glories of the hero and the martyr.

father of Sultān Firoz king of Delhi and won renown by the recitude of his life.

In the vicinity of the town, there is a village called *Dogon* which for a long time possessed a mint for copper coinage.

From the northern mountains quantities of goods are carried on the backs of men, of stout ponies and of goats, such as gold, copper, lead, musk, tails[2] of the *kutās* cow, honey, *chuk* (an acid composed of orange juice and lemon boiled together), pomegranate seeds, ginger, long pepper, *majith*[3] root, borax, zedoary, wax, woollen stuffs, wooden ware, hawks, falcons, black falcons, merlins, and other articles. In exchange they carry back white and coloured cloths, amber, salt, assafœtida, ornaments, glass and earthen ware.

Nimkhār is a fort of considerable note and a shrine of great resort. The river Godi (Gumti) flows near it, and around are numerous temples. There is a tank called *Brahmāwartkund* in which the water boils and with such a swirl, that a man cannot sink therein,[4] and it ejects whatever is thrown into it. In the neighbourhood is also a deep hollow, the springhead of a stream, one yard in breadth and four digits deep that flows into the Gumti. The Brāhmans tell strange tales of it and pay it worship. Its sand shapes itself into the form of *Mahādeo* which quickly disappears again and of whatever is thrown in, as rice and the like, no trace remains.

There is likewise a place called *Charāmiti,* whence, during the *Holi* festival, flames spontaneously issue forth with astonishing effect.

---

[2] It would seem from a passage of Ferishta mentioning an inroad of Tibetans into Kashmir in the reign of Ibrahim, son of Nāzuk Shāh (p. 359, II) that the yāk is meant. The Kashmiris retaliated by pursuing the marauders, and exacting as compensation 500 horses, 1000 pieces of *pattu,* 200 sheep and 50 kutās cows. Later on, it is mentioned by Abul Fazl among the fauna of India and described as little differing from the common cow except in the tail which is a distinguishing peculiarity, and the origin of its name, *kutās.*

[3] Rubia Munjista, Roxb. a native of Nepal and other mountainous countries N.-E. of Bengal. Its root yields a red dye.

[4] Tieffenthaler asserts that it derives its name from Brahma who is supposed to have sacrificed here, but according to the *I. G.* there is a legend that in one of these tanks, Rāmā washed away his sin of having slain a Brāhman in the person of Ravana, who had carried off his wife Sita.

Lucknow is a large city on the banks of the Gumti, delightful in its surroundings. *Shaikh Mina* whom the people consider a saint, lies buried here.

*Surajkand** is a place of worship frequented by various classes of people from the most distant places.

Kheri is a town on the banks of the river *Sai* upon which the people go in boats to spear fish.

Bilgrām is a small town the air of which is healthy and its inhabitants are generally distinguished for their quick wit and their love of singing. There is a well here which adds to the intelligence and comeliness of whomsoever drinks of it for forty days.

This *Subah* is divided into five *Sarkārs* and thirty-eight *parganas*. The measured lands are 1 *kror,* 1 *lakh,* 71,180 *bighas*. Its revenue, 20*krors,* 17 *lakhs,* 58,172 *dāms,* (Rs. 5,043,954-4), of which 85 *lakhs,* 21,658 *dāms* (Rs. 213,041-7). are *Suyurghāl*. The provincial force consists of 7.640 Cavalry, 168,250, Infantry and 59 Elephants.

Sarkār of Oudh.

Containing 21 *Mahals,* 2,796,206 *Bighas,* 19 *Biswahs,* Revenue, 40,956,347 *Dāms* in money. *Suyurghāl,* 1,680,248 *Dāms*. Castes various. Cavalry 1,340, Elephants 23, Infantry 31,700.

	Bighas Biswas	Revenue D.	Suyur-ghāl D.	Infantry	Cavalry	Elephants	Castes
Oudh, with suburban district, 2 mahals ..	38,649-17	2,008,366	158,741	5	500	...	Brāhman Kumbi
Ambodha, has a brick fort	282,037	1,298,724	7,318	30	700	...	Bais
Ibrahimābād	19,338-8	445,417	103,806	...	...	...	Ansāri

* Identified with Asokpur, between Ajodhya and Gonda [Elliot, ii, 549].

Sarkār of Oudh—(contd.).

	Bighas Biswas	Revenue D.	Suyurghāl D.	Infantry	Cavalry	Elephants	Castes
Anhonah, has a brick fort	74,090	1,268,470	...	100	2,000	...	Chauhān, newly converted to Islām
Panchhamrāth ..	289,085	4,247,104	38,885	20	500	...	Rājput, Bāchhāl, Ghelot
	15,859	815,831	...	50	2,000	...	Bachgoti
Bilehri, has a brick fort	31,188	505,473	1,500	20	500	...	Do.
Basodhi	8,703-2	427,509	36,172	...	1,000	...	Do.
Thānah Bhadāon Bakthā	44,401	385,008	3,960	...	500	...	Do.
Daryābād, has a brick fort	487,014	5,369,521	226,871	100	2,000	...	Rājput Chauhān, Raikwār*
Rudauli, has a brick fort	351,533	3,248,680	269,083	50	2,000	...	Rājput, Chauhān, Bais
Silak, do. ..	571,071	4,723,209	200,945	100	2,000	...	Rājput, Raikwār
Sultānpur do. ..	75,903	3,832,530	98,967	200	7,000	8	Bachgoti
Sātanpur do. ..	80,154	1,600,741	109,788	300	4,000	...	Bais, newly converted to Islām, Bachgoti, Joshi
Subeha†	104,780	1,609,293	87,200	30	1,000	...	Rājput
Sarwapāli	58,170	1,210,335	47,107	...	1,000	...	Bachgoti
Satrikah (Satrikh) ..	37,041	1,126,295	92,695	20	1,000	...	Ansāri
Gawārchak	79,158	3,773,417	3,782	50	1,070	...	Raikwār
Kishni, has a brick fort	25,674	1,339,286	123,847	...	1,500	3	Rājput
Mangalsi	116,401	1,360,753	86,504	20	1,000	...	Sombānsi
Naipur	5,997	308,788	2,940	...	500	...	Various

* The origin of this tribe *Raikwār* is given in the I. G. (Bahraich) and their settlements in Sherring I, 219.

† Subeha is a well-known *parganah* in Bāra Bankī District. In the *I. G.* its area is recorded as 88 square miles, or 56,467 acres of which 30,783 are cultivated. Govt. land revenue £6611. In Akbar's time according to the above figures Rs. 40,232-7, and the average taking the bigha ⅝ of an acre, 65,487½ acres nearly.

Sarkār of Gorakhpur.

Containing 24 *Mahals,* 244,283 *Bighas,* 13 *Biswas.* Revenue 11, 926,790. *Dams* in money. *Suyurghal* 51,235 *Dams.* Castes various. Cavalry 1,010. Infantry 22,000.

	Bighas Biswas	Revenue D.	Suyurghāl D.	Cavalry	Infantry	Elephants	Castes
Utraulā, has a brick fort	32,052	1,397,367	6,935	50	1,500	...	Afghān-i-Miyānah
Unhaulā	4,114-17	201,120	2 170	...	400	...	Bisen
Bināikpur, has a brick fort	13,857-7	600,000	...	400	3,000	...	Rājput Surajbansi
Bānbhanpārah (E. Bamhni, p.)	6,688	414,194	...	...	2,000	...	Rājput
Bhawāpārah	3,105-15	155,900	...		200	...	Bisen
Telpur, has a brick fort	9,005-17	400,000	...	100	2,000	...	Rājput Surajbansi
Chilupārh, do. ..	6,536-14	289,302	...	...	2,000	...	Rājput
Daryāpārh (E. Dhuria, (p.)	31,357-19	1,517,078	5,067	60	400	...	Bisen
Dewāpārah and Kotlah* 2 mahals	16,194-17	717,840	...	20	2,000	...	Do.
Rihli, (or Rudauli) ..	33,183-19	1,618,074	20,873	...	1,000	...	Rājput Bisen
Rasulpur and Ghosi, 2 mahals (E. Ghaus) ..	4,200	622,030	...	...	500	...	Sombansi
Rāmgarh and Gauri, 2 mahals	10,762	485 943	...	...	...	...	Do., troops entered under Bināikpur
Gorakhpur with suburban district, has a brick fort on the Rapti, 2 mahals ..	12,656-8	567,385	3,919	40	200	...	Surajbansi
Katihlā, has a brick fort	900-12	40,000	...	300	2,000	...	Bansi
Rahlāpārh, Do. (E. Rihlā, p.)	16,012	425,845	...	20	300	...	Bisen
Mahauli. Do. ..	2,523	618,256	...	...	2,000	...	Bisen
Mandwah	1,909-19	452,321	...	20	500	...	Sombansi
Mandlah	1,252-6	51,100	...	...	...	...	
Maghar and Ratanpur, 2 mahals, has a brick fort	26,062	1,352,585	16,771	...	2,000	...	Bisen, Bais

* Elliot, Dhewāpāra Kuhānā.

Sarkār of Bahraich.

Containing 11 *Mahals,* 1,823,435 *Bighas,* 8 *Biswas.* Revenue 24,120,525 *Dāms* in money. *Suyurghal,* 466,482 *Dāms.* Castes various. Cavalry 1,170. Infantry 14,000.

	Bighas Biswas	Revenue D.	Suyurghāl D.	Cavalry	Infantry	Elephants	Castes
Bahraich with suburban district has a fort on the river Sarju ..	697,231	9,139,141	402,111	600	4,500	...	Rājput
Bahralı	926	37,135	...	...	500	...	Kahnah (Kher ?)
Husāmpur, has a brick fort	157,415	4,707,035	1,601	70	900	...	Raikwār, Bisen
Dāngdun	84,436	440,562	...	...	2,000	...	Janwār*
Rajhat	4,064-11	166,780	...	...	1,000	...	Ditto
Sujhauli	124,810	877,007	...	...	...	...	Rājput, Janwār
Sultānpur	58,146	166,001	...	...	700	...	Janwār
Fakhrpur, has a brick fort	191,720	3,157,876	56,035	150	2,000	...	Raikwar
Firozābād, ditto ..	108,601	1,933,079	4,107	200	7,000	...	Rājput or Tanwār
Fort of Nawagarh ..	417,601	2,140,858	...	50	1,000	...	Various
Kharonsa, has a brick fort	28,489-17	1,315,051	2,628	100	1,000	...	Bais

* A tribe of Rajputs in Sihonda and Simauni of Bundelkhand: Rasulābād and Bithur of Cawnpore, and in Kutiya Gunir of Fatehpur.

Sarkār of Khairābād.

Containing 22 *Mahals,* 1,987,700 *Bighas,* 6 *Biswas. Revenue,* 43,644,381 *Dāms* in money. *Suyurghal,* 171,342 *Dāms.* Castes various. Cavalry 1,160. Infantry 27,800.

	Bighas Biswas	Revenue D.	Suyurghāl D.	Cavalry	Infantry	Elephants	Castes
Baror Anjnah	79,670-9	4,325,437	107,079	50	2,000	...	Rājput, Brāhman
Baswah, has a brick fort	135,119	3,545,643	107,916	30	1,000	...	Rājput, Bāchhal
Pāli	144,627	1,849,270	37,945	30	1,000	...	Asnin ?

Sarkār of Khairābād—(contd.)

	Bighas Biswas	Revenue D.	Suyurghāl D.	Cavalry	Infantry	Elephants	Castes
Bāwan	56,156	1,161,235	26,488	20	1,000	...	Ditto.
Basrah	60,063	...	...	...	300	...	Various
Bhurwārah, has a brick fort	8,971-18	43,543	...	50	2,500	...	Ahnin
Basārā	21,740	276.066	...	...	200	...	Bachhal
Pilā	981-14	48,202	...	...	200	...	Ahnin
Chhatyāpur	64,706	1,765,641	41,094	50	700	...	Rājput Gaur
Khairābād with suburban District, 2 Mahals, has a brick fort ..	159,072	2 161,234	174,191	50	2,000	...	Brāhman
Sāndi, has a brick fort	211,804	3,055,339	195,106	20	2,000	...	Sombansi
Sarah	68,832	2,091,983	8,666	60	500	...	Chauhān
Sadrpur	120,698	831,175	15,581	20	500	...	Janwār Bāchhal
Gopāmau, has a brick fort	107,368,5	5,620,466	562,037	100	3,000	...	Rājput Kuār
Kheri, do. do. ..	260,168	3,250 522	50,522	60	1,500	...	Bisen, Rājput, Janwār
Khairigarh, one of the most important fortresses in Hindustān. There are 6 forts of brick and mortar, at a short distance from it	43,052-7	1,829,328	...	300	1,500	...	Bais, Bisen, Bachhal, Kahnah
Kharkhelā	15,815-16	473,727	...	20	500	...	Asin ?
Khānkhat Mau ..	3,058-11	235,656	...	...	400	...	Various
Lāharpur	208,288	3,029,479	209,079	50	1,000	...	Brāhman
Machharhatta	71-069	2,112,176	2,430	30	2,000	...	Rājput, Bachhal
Nimkhār, has a brick fort	58,775-18	3,566,055	66,055	100	1,500	...	Ahir
Hargarāon	66,952	200,000	26,385	20	500	...	

Sarkār of Lucknow.

Containing 55 *Mahals,* 3,307,426 *Bighas,* 2 *Biswas.* Revenue 80,716,160 *Dāms* in money. *Suyurghāl,* 4,572,526 *Dāms.* Castes various. Cavalry 2,680. Elephants 36. Infantry 83,450.

	Bighas Biswas	Revenue D.	Suyurghāl D.	Cavalry	Infantry	Elephants	Castes
Amethi, has a brick fort	117,381	3,076,480	300,217	300	2.000	20	Ansāri
Unām, has a brick fort	61,045	2,012,372	253 747	50	4,000	...	Sayyid
Isauli, has a brick fort on the Gumti ..	1,670,093	4,208,046	240,846	50	2,000	...	Rājput, Bachgoti

Sarkār of Lucknow—(contd.)

	Bighas Biswas	Revenue D.	Suyurghāl D.	Cavalry	Infantry	Elephants	Castes
Asiyun	57,726	830,625	63,421	10	500	...	Bais, Chandel
Asoha	25,027	509,901	...	...	400	...	Ahnin
Unchahgāon	33,122	417,957	...	1000	2,000	...	Bais
Bilgrāon, has a brick fort	192,800	5,124,113	356,892	20	1,000	...	Sayyid, Bais
Bangarmau Ditto ..	242,291	3,802,122	151,481	...	2,000	...	Rājput, Ghelot
Bijlaur [*v.* Bijnor] ..	80,581	2,505,047	193,961	30	1,000	...	Chauhān
Bāri	80,590	1,284,799	51,560	30	1,000	...	Bais
Bharimau	19,409-3	591,406	...	20	500	...	Bais
Pangwān	34,727	420,732	12,730	...	500	...	Bais
Betholi	8,736	340,191	8,194	...	200	...	Rājput, Jāt
Panhan	8,945	267,809	...	...	300	...	Bais
Parsandan	9,111	237,537	...	...	200	...	Rājput, Kumbhi
Pātan	5,621	214,256	...	...	400	...	Brāhman, Kunbi
Bārāshakor	9,357	168,584	...	...	300	...	Brāhman
Jahalotar	61,774	1,123,176	21,441	20	2,000	...	Chandel
Dewi, has a brick fort	88,637	1,938,837	174,207	30	2,000	...	Rājput
Deorakh	13,340-9	689,586	...	100	1,500	...	Bais
Dadrah	10,796	73,737	...	50	...	...	Rājput
Ranbarpur, has a brick fort	75,490	2,425,885	79,225	100	2,000	...	Bais, Brāhman
Rāmkot, Ditto ..	9,790	268,099	...	...	200	...	Rājput
Sandilah, Ditto ..	393,700	10,623,901	837,245	100	5,000	...	Ghelot, Bāchhal
Sāipur	39,083-15	2,625,388	28,836	40	1,000	...	Rājput, Chandel
Sarosi	2,571	1,239,767	1,567	20	1,000	...	Chandel, Rājput
Sātanpur	60,600	1,028,800	10,192	50	2,000	...	Bais, Brāhman
Sahāli	13,065	694,707	130,216	10	500	...	Rājput
Sidhor*	35,794	1,692,281	313,022	100	1,000	...	Afghān, Rājput
Sidhpur	9,371-4	505,018	...	150	1,500	...	Bais
Sandi	7,856-9	392,313	13,792	...	1,000	...	Rājput
Saron	5,576	210,316	2,858	...	100	...	Rājput, Shaikhzādah,
Fatehpur, has a brick fort	198,300	3,161,440	261,440	200	2,000	5	Kunbi Rājput
Fatehpur Chaurāsi ..	105,952	909,176	6,594	10	500	...	Rājput, Chandel
Garh Anbhatti (Amethi) has a brick fort ..	47,356	1,800,000	...	250	5,500	8	Rājput, Bahman Goti
Kursi, has a brick fort	80,817	1,693,844	62,919	20	2,000	3	Rājput
Kākori, Ditto ..	31,584	1,134,432	14,430	30	500	...	Rājput, Bisen
Khanjrah	22,300	818,472	...	100	2,000	...	Bais

* *Var.* Sayyidpur, Seopur, Sheopur. G. Seedhore.

Sarkār of Lucknow—(contd.)

	Bighas Biswas	Revenue D.	Suyur-ghāl D.	Cavalry	Infantry	Elephants	Castes
Ghātampur	27,390	552,561	...	...	500	...	Brāhman
Kachhandan	22,066	430,596	4,460	...	500	...	Chandel
Gorandā	4,803	334,769	...	...	200	...	Brāhman
Konbhi	5,940	267,089	...	...	400	...	Rājput
Lucknow with suburban district	91,722	1,746,771	241,195	200	3,000	...	Shaikhzādah, Brāhman, Kāyath
Lashkar	16,894	168,529	...	...	4,000	...	Bais
Malihābād, has a brick fort	169,269	4,479,250	108,545	30	1,000	...	Bais
Malāwah	83,022	3,598,713	222,038	30	2,000	...	Bais
Mohān has a brick fort	60,990	1,996,673	198,484	30	2,000	...	Rājput, Bais
Morāon has a brick fort	68,847	1,698,444	4,806	150	2,000	...	Rājput, Bais
Madiāon	49,422	1,136,213	32,900	30	500	...	Barkhalā*
Mahonāh	50,895	977,860	8,805	50	2,000	...	Rājput
Manawi, has a brick fort	29,455	771,372	13,767	...	2,000	...	Mussalmān, Rājput
Makrāed	17,959	576,200	5,247	...	1,000	...	Rājput, Bais
Harha, has a brick fort	163,226	2,450,522	6,509	100	1,500	...	Bais
Hardoi	11,734	359,748	6,026	...	300	...	Brāhman
Hanhār	13,109	329,735	...	80	500	...	Bais

* Here a word illegible, Barkalā is an inferior class of Rājputs found in Western and Central *parganahs* of Bulandshahr.

The Subah of Agra, the Royal Residence.

It is situated in the second climate. Its length from Ghātampur on the Allahabad side to *Palwal* on that of Delhi is 175 *kos.* In breadth it extends from *Kanauj* to *Chanderi* in *Mālwah.* On the east lies *Ghātampur;* to the north, the *Ganges;* to the south *Chanderi,* and to the west, *Palwal.* It possesses many rivers, of which the principal are the *Jumna* and the *Chambal.* The former flows down from the northern mountains, the latter rises at *Hāsilpur* in *Mālwah* and unites with the *Jumna* at *Kālpi.* Ranges of hills lie scattered to the south. The excellence of its climate is almost unrivalled. Agriculture is in perfection. Fruits and flowers of all kinds abound. Sweet-scented oil, and betel-leaf of the first quality are here obtained, and its melons and grapes rival those of Persia and Transoxiana. *Agra* is a large city and possesses a healthy climate. The river *Jumna* flows through it for five *kos,* and on either bank are delightful villas and pleasant stretches of meadow. It is filled with people from all countries and is the emporium of the traffic of the world. His Majesty has built a fort of red stone, the like of which travellers have never recorded. It contains more than five hundred buildings of masonry after the beautiful designs of Bengal and Gujerat which masterly sculptors and cunning artists of form have fashioned as architectural models. At the eastern gate are two elephants of stone with their riders graven with exquisite skill. In former times Agra was a village dependent on *Biānah*. Sultan Sikandar Lodi made it his capital, but his present Majesty embellished it and thus a matchless city has arisen. On the opposite side of the river is the *Chār Bāgh*, a memorial of Bābar.* It was the birth-place of the writer of this work, and the last resting-place of his grandfather and his elder brother. Shaikh Ālāu'ddin Majzub, Rafiiu'ddin Safawe and many other saintly personages also repose there.

Near the city on the banks of the river Jumna is a village called *Rangtah*, a much frequented place of Hindu worship.

Fatehpur was a village formerly one of the dependencies of *Biānah*, and then called *Sikri*, situated twelve *kos* distaut from Agra. After the accession of his Majesty, it rose to be a city of the first importance. A masonry fort was erected and two elephants carved in stone at its gate inspire astonishment. Several noble buildings also rose to completion and although the royal palace and the residences of many of the nobility are upon the summit of the hill, the plains likewise are studded with numerous mansions and gardens. By the command of his Majesty a mosque, a college and a religious house were also built upon the hill, the like of which few travellers can name. In the neighbourhood is a tank, twelve *kos* in circumference and on its embankment his Majesty constructed a spacious courtyard, a *minār*, and a place for the game of *Chaugān;* elephant fights were also exhibited. In the vicinity is a quarry of red stone whence columns and slabs of any dimensions can be excavated. In these two cities under his Majesty's patronage carpets and fine stuffs are woven and numerous handicraftsmen have full occupation. *Biānah* in former

* The old Agra of the Lodi dynasty lay on the left bank of the river where traces of its foundations still exist. The modern city is on the right bank and is the work of Akbar. The fort was built in A.D. 1566. Babar's garden later called *Hasht Bihisht*, or *Nurafshān* Gardens, now called the **Rām Bāgh.**

times was a large city. It possesses a fort containing many buildings and cellars, and people at the present day still find therein weapons of war and copper utensils. There is also a lofty tower. Fine mangoes grow here, some of them more than two pounds in weight. Sugar of extreme whiteness is also manufactured. Here too is a well, with the water of which mixed with white sugar, they make cakes weighing two pounds more or less which they call *kandaurah* (with no other water will they solidify) and these are taken to the most distant parts as a rarity. Indigo of finest quality is here to be obtained, selling at ten to twelve rupees per *man* weight. Excellent *hinna* (*Lawsonia inermis*) is also to be found, and here are the tombs of many eminent personages.

Todah Bhim is a place at a distance of three *kos*, from which is a pit full of water, the depth of which none has sounded. Mines of copper and turquoise are said to exist, but the expense of working them exceeds their income.

Mathura (Muttra) is a city on the banks of the *Jumna*: it contains some fine temples, and is one of the most famous of Hindu shrines. *Kālpi* is a town on the banks of the *Jumna*. It is the resting-place of many saintly personages. Excellent sugarcandy is here manufactured. In the time of the *Sharqi* princes, it was tributary to Delhi. When Qādir Khān affecting the airs of sovereignty proclaimed his independence, Sultān Hoshang marched from Mālwah and having chastised him, reinstated him in the government. Sultān Muhmud of the *Sharqi* dynasty, however, seized it in turn from Nasir Khān, the son of Qādir Khān.

Kanauj was in ancient times the capital of Hindustān.

Gwalior is a famous fortress and an elephant carved in stone at its gate fills the beholder with astonishment. It contains some stately edifices of its former rulers. Its climate is good. It has always been noted for its exquisite singers* and lovely women: here is an iron mine.

Alwar (Ulwar) produces glass and woollen carpets.

Bairāt possesses a copper mine, so profitable that from a *man* weight of ore, they obtain 35 *sers* of metal. A silver mine is also said to exist but it does not pay to work it. [A dependency of Narnol, but now in Jaipur.]

Near the hill of *Nārnol* is a well at which the Hindus worship and when the *tithi* of *Amāwas* falls on a Friday,

* According to the *S. ul M.* the famous Tānsen was one of these. See Vol. I, pp. 611 of the Āin.

it overflows at sunrise and water can be drawn without the aid of a rope.

At *Singhānah, Udaipur* and *Kotputli* are mines of copper. In the town of *Kānori* are many cold and hot springs.

The *Subah* contains thirteen *Sarkārs,* two hundred and three *Parganahs* (fiscal subdivisions). The measured lands are 2 *krors,* 78 *lakhs,* 62,189 *bighas,* 18 *biswas.* The revenue is 54 *krors,* 62 *lakhs,* 50,304 *dāms.* (Rs. 13,656,257-9-6). Of this, 1 *kror,* 21 *lakhs,* 5,703½ *dāms* (Rs. 302,642-9)are *Suyurghāl.* The provincial force consists of 50,681 cavalry, 577,570 Infantry and 221 elephants.

Sarkār of Agra.

Containing 33 *Mahals,* 91,007,324 *Bighas.* Revenue 191,819,265, *Dāms* in money. *Suyurghāl* 14,566,818 *Dāms.* Castes various. Cavalry 15,560. Infantry 100,800.

	Bighas Biswas	Revenue D.	Suyurghāl D.	Cavalry	Infantry	Elephants	Castes
Agra with suburban district	891,990-5	44,956,458	8,824 454	3000	1,5000	...	Gaur,* Jat, Lodh, &c.
Etāwah, has brick fort on the Jamna	284,106	10,739,325	151,362	2000	1,5000	...	Chauhān, Bhadauriya, Brāhman
O'l [=*Ao,* near Dig.]	153,377-9	5,509,477	81,542	1000	1000	...	Rājput, Brāhman
Oudehi, (Elliot Odhi)	274,067	2,884,365	78,165	20	500	...	Rājput, Brāhman, &c.
Ud [Udai]	203,505	1,003,848	36,870	100	500	...	Shaikhzādah
Bijwārah has a stone fort ..	663,236	10,966,560	...	1500	5000	...	...
Biānah with suburban dist. has a stone fort ..	235.442	7,110,104	562,205	50	100	...	Ahir, Jat
Bāri	276,964	5,064,158	57,414	300	7000	...	Rājput, Panwār
Bhosāwar	303,509	5,505,460	255,460	50	1500	...	Rājput of various castes
Banāwar [?Bhandor]	12,880	155,360	...	30	400	...	Bargujar

* A Surajbansi tribe of Rajputs. *Lodh,* a widely spread tribe, chiefly fishermen. *Bhadauriya* is a branch of the Chauhan Rājputs. For *Oudehi* I suggest *Uchen* and for *Bhaskar* either *Pahesar* or *Bisawar.* [J. S.]

Sarkār of Agra—(contd.)

	Bighas Biswas	Revenue D.	Suyurghāl D.	Cavalry	Infantry	Elephants	Castes
Todah Bhim ..	264,103-11	3,737,075	13,361	100	1000	...	Rājput, Thatthar[1]
Bhaskar	43,009	2,891,100	15,325	20	700	...	Rājput, Brāhman, Ahir
Jalesar, has a brick fort	904,733	6,835,400	412,080	400	5000	...	Ghelot, Suraj Bānkrah
Chandwar, has a brick fort on the Jumna	407,652	11,442,250	60,342	200	7000	...	Chauhān
Chausath [Chaumuha] ..	974,34	4,182,048	674,315	50	1000	...	Rājput, Brāhman, Jat, Ahir
Khānwah	5,334	2,912,495	222,628	30	4000	...	Rājput, Jat
Dholpur, has a brick fort on the Chambal	284,087	9,729,311	255,747	200	4000	...	Sikarwār[2]
Rāpri, has a brick fort	477,201-11	13,508,035	173,407	200	4000	...	Chauhān, descendants of Rāwat-Bāhan
Rajhohar [?Rajakhera]	318,285	1,694,208	48,023	20	300	...	Rājput
Songar Songri ..	90,599	985,700	7,822	70	500	...	Rājput, Chauhān
Fatehpur, has a stone fort ..	202,723-17	8,494,005	597,346	500	4000	...	Shaikhzādah, Chishti, Rājput, Sankarwāl
Kotumbar	96,760	745,951	...	50	300	...	Rājput, Jat
Mahāwan, has a brick fort ..	290,703	6,784,780	284,787	200	2000	...	Sayyid, Brāhman
Mathurā, do. ..	37,347	1,155,807	69,770	...	...	...	...
Maholi	66,690	1,501,246	...	30	500	...	Rājput, &c.
Mangotlah [Mangtai]	74,974	1,148,075	79,355	20	400	...	Do.
Mandāwar	10,190	132,500	...	150	800	...	Chauhān
Wazirpur	71,328	2,009,255	9,255	20	300	...	Rājput
Hindaun	482,930	9,049,831	301,980	100	1000	...	Rājput, Brāhman, Jat
Hatkānt, has a brick fort	606,991-12	5,693,807	43,231	2000	20,000	...	Chauhān, Bhadauriya
Hilak	137,421	2,789,494	30,531	20	500	...	Rājput of various castes.

[1] Gujars converted to Islam. Elliot, I, 101.
[2] Sikarwār, a branch of the Bargujar Rajputs.

Sarkār of Kālpi.

Containing 16 *Mahals,* 300,023 Bighas, 9 Biswas, Revenue, 49,356,732 *Dāms* in money. *Suyurghāl* 278,290½ *Dāms.* Castes various, Cavalry 1,540. Elephants 30. Infantry 34,000.

	Bighas Biswas	Revenue D.	Suyur-ghāl D.	Cavalry	Infantry	Elephants	Castes
U'lai [? Urai] ..	95.677-18	1,297,379	72 213	20	500	...	Rājput
Bilāspur	126 888-14	3,714,547	13.110	100	50,000	...	Kachhwāh
Bhudekh	72 930-14	1 260,199	3 414	50	2000	...	
Derāpur	103,085	1,760,750	4,221	50	2000	...	Shaikhzādah
Deokali [?Churki] ..	109,652	1,466,985	1,700	200	2000	10	Brāhman
Rāth, has a brick fort	510,970-16	9,270,894	270,894	70	3000	9	Afghan, Turkoman
Rāepur	43,166-8	120,000	...	...	500	10	Rājput,
Suganpur [?Jagmanp]	...	1,507,877	58 664	60	1000	...	Rājput, Bais
Shāhpur	...	8,848,420	245,747	300	3000	6	Chauhān, Malikzādah
Kālpi, with suburban district	...	4,871,053	203,909	4000	5000	10	Various
Kanār [? Karmār] ..	...	4,943,096	6,085	100	2000	1	Sengar*
Chandaut	...	3,027,917	27,121	50	4000	...	Parihār
Khandelah, (Elliot Khurela)	86,053-11	871,733	15,008	20	1000	...	Rājput
Muhammadābād ..	184,080	1,617,257	4,260½	50	1000	...	Rājput Kumbi
Hamirpur	404,797-6	4,803,828	182,245	200	2000	...	Kumbi

Sarkār of Kanauj.

Containing 30 *Mahals,* 2,776,673 *Bighas,* 16 *Biswas.* Revenue 52,584,624 *Dāms.* *Suyurghāl,* 1,184,655 *Dāms.* Castes various. Cavalry 3,765. Infantry 78,350.

	Bighas Biswas	Revenue D.	Suyur-ghāl D.	Cavalry	Infantry	Elephants	Castes
Bhongāon, has a fort and near it a tank called Somnāt full of water extremely sweet	337,105	4,577.010	53 316	1000	10,000	...	Chauhān
Bhojpur	150,974-13	3,446 737	104 705	150	3000	...	**Kharwār**
Tālgrāon	74,100-10	3,387,076	128,558	20	1000	...	Rājput, Mussalmān

* *Sengar,* a branch of the Agnibansi Rājputs.

Sarkār of Kanauj—(Contd.)

	Bighas Biswas	Revenue D.	Suyurghāl D.	Cavalry	Infantry	Elephants	Castes
Bithur	175,042-11	2.921 389	...	300	5000	...	Chandel
Bilhaur	63,773-14	2 828 347	216 741	20	1000	...	Rājput
Patiāli	158,634-14	1,877,600	45,656	100	2000	...	Rājput, Chauhān
Pati Alipur	38.418-11	1,153 682	8,060	20	500	...	Rājput
Pati Nakhat [?Agath]	49 261-18	566 997	2,497	50	500	...	Sengar
Barnah	34,736-14	450,000	...	10	200	...	Rājput of various castes
Bārā	8,739-14	400,000	...	10	300	...	Chauhān
Phapund	111.546	5 482 391	19,313	300	2 000	...	Sengar
Chhabrāmau	76,318-7	1,522,028	22,128	20	500	...	Rājput, Chauhān
Deohā	11,950-12	483,171	79,045	20	300	...	Chauhān Bais, Dhākar[1]
Saket	132,955-9	3 230.752	158,310	100	3000	...	Chauhān
Sonj [=Sonkh] ..	64,070-6	1 200 000	...	200	3000	...	Dhākar
Sahāwar	78,574-9	252 245	21,969	20	500	..	Gāuruah[2]
Sheoli	12 523	623 473	...	10	300	...	Rājput
Sakatpur	22 561	623 441	...	300	4000	...	Rājput, Bais
Sakrāon	19 817-10	549 050	2 253	10	500	...	Rājput
Sahār	25,195-8	846,553	1,640	30	500	...	Chauhān,
Saurikh	10,089-5	465,328	7,138	20	400		Chauhān, Dhākar
Sikandrapur Udhu ..	4,964.14	276,918½	22,624	10	200	...	Gauruah, Brāhman
Saror [Barour] ..	20,121-16	447,563	2,044½	10	300	...	Chauhān, Sengar
Sikandarpur Atreji ..	36,084-17	269,622	6.511	5	150	...	Rājput
Shamsābād, has a fort on the Ganges ..	718,577-7	7,138,452	19,603	400	2000	...	Rāthor
Kanauj, with suburb. dist. has a brick fort : one of the great capitals of Hindustān ..	126,255-12	2,470,743	222,036	200	10,000	...	Shaikhzādah, Farmuli, Afghān, Chauhān
Kampil	139,803-6	1,651,586	30,370	100	200	:	Rājput, Chauhān, Panwār
Kurāoli	40,445-6	1,409.988	...	20	1000	..	Rājput
Malkusah	30,229-14	1,500,000	...	300	15,000	...	Rājput, Ghelot
Nānāmau[3]	3,329-5	136,921	...	200	200	...	Rājput, Brāhman

[1] *Dhākar*, a Rajput tribe scattered over Agra, Mathura, Etawa and Rohilkhand. Elliot, I. 78.

[2] *Gauruah*, an inferior clan of Rājputs often confounded with Gaurāhars but quite distinct. Elliot, I. 115.

Sarkār of Kol, (Koil).

Containing 21 *Mahals,* 2,461,730 *Bighas.* Revenue 54,992,940 *Dāms* in money, *Suyurghāl* 2,094,840 *Dāms.* Castes various. Cavalry 4,035. Infantry 78,950.

	Bighas Biswas	Revenue D.	Suyurghāl D.	Cavalry	Infantry	Elephants	Castes
Atrauli	320,569	5,454,459	5400,459	500	9500	...	Rājput, Chauhān, Afghān
Akbarābād	118,389	3,003,409	23,060	500	5000	...	Rājput, Pundir[1]
Ahār, has a brick fort on the Ganges ..	45,764	2,106,554	87,140	20	400	...	Musalmān, Brāhman
Pahāsu	55 060	2 502 562	...	100	2000	...	Bargujar
Bilrāon	111,878	2,131,765	56,561	50	1000	...	Afghān Chauhān
Pachlānā	39.128	624,825	...	200	5000	...	Rajput, Gaurāhar
Tappal, has a brick fort	163.046	1,802.571	2,571	100	8000	...	Chauhān
Thānah Fāridā [=Pharihā]	63 847	112,750	...	20	500	...	Rajput, Bāchhal
Jalāli	145.801	2,957,910	86,352	500	6000	...	Rājput, Pundir
Chandaus	42 469	1 749 238	36,662	100	2000	...	Chauhān
Khurjah	89,726	3,703,020	583,056	200	5000	...	Bargujar
Dibhāi, has a brick fort	48 539	2,169.939	72,869	50	1000	...	Do.
Sikandrah Rāo, has a brick fort	83,480	4,412,331	290,458	400	4000	...	Afghān, Pundir
Soron, has a brick fort	40.656	875.016	16,900	20	400	...	Sayyid, Rājput
Sidhupur	70,567	989,458	...	200	2500	...	Rājput Surki
Shikārpur	44,830	1,974,827	50,291	250	2000	...	Sayyid, Shaikhzādah, Bargujar
Kol, has a brick fort ..	548,655	10,412.305	445	450	29,050	...	Chauhān, Janghārah[2]
Gangeri	53,545	372,050	31,849	25	200	...	Afghān, Rājput
Marahrah	205 537	3,679 582	156 095	200	2000	...	Chauhān
Malakpur	30,845	1,446,132	2,288	50	400	...	Pundir, Chauhān
Nuh, has a brick fort, (Elliot, Noh) ..	139,299	1,311,955	29,160	100	3000	...	Rājput, Jat, Afghān

[1] Pundir is one of the numerous branches of the Gujar clan. Elliot, I. 19.
[2] A turbulent tribe of Rājputs of the Tuar clan in the S. E. Rohilkhand. Elliot, I, 141.

Sarkār of Gwālior.

Containing 13 *Mahals,* 1,146,465 *Bighas,* 6 *Biswas.* Revenue 29,683,649 *Dāms* in money. *Suyurghāl* 240,350 *Dāms.* Castes various. Cavalry 2,490. Infantry 43,000.

	Bighas Biswas	Revenue D.	Suyurghāl D.	Cavalry	Infantry	Elephants	Castes
Anhon, has a fort ..	106 899-14	2,277,947	...	200	4000	...	Tonwar
Badrhattah, Do. ..	63,914-18	696,800	...	300	5000	...	Do., Rājput
Chinaur Do. ..	140.140-16	1,051,341	35.930	100	4000	...	Brāhman
Jhalodā [Jakhoda] fort	32 677-15	219 306	...	100	2000	...	Gujar
Dandroli	197,316-11	1,807,207	...	50	1000	...	Rājput Tonwar
Rāepur	87 797-17	1,017,721	...	40	700	...	Tonwar
Sirseni [Sirsi] ..	94 243	832 128	...	200	5000	...	Sikarwāl
Samauli [Silauli] ..	46,284-8	2,001,344	...	50	700	...	Bāgri
Sarbandah, has a brick fort	22,124-17	267,497	...	200	6000	...	Sikarwāl
Alāpur, has a fort; during Sultān Alāuddin's time it was called Akhār[1] ..	211,229	5,128,766	...	50	500	...	Brāhman
Gwālior with suburban district	345,657	12 483.072	138,740	1000	2000	...	Rājput, Tonwar
Khatoli, has a fort ..	198,270	3,105,315	6,450	200	4000	...	Jat

Sarkār of Irij.

Containing 16 *Mahals,* 2,202,124 *Bighas,* 18 *Biswas.* Revenue 37,780,421 *Dāms* in money. *Suyurghāl* 456,493 *Dāms.* Castes various. Cavalry 6,160. Elephants 190. Infantry 68,500.

	Bighas Biswas	Revenue D.	Suyurghāl D.	Cavalry	Infantry	Elephants	Castes
Irij	625,597	2,922,436 in money.	101,661	100	5000	10	Kāyath
Parhār,[2] has a brick fort	752,791	5,237,096	172,380	940	20500	59	Rājput
Bhānder	257 042-18	2,533,449	100,638	50	2000	5	Afghān, Kāyath
Bijpur [Bijawar] ..	30,635	1,391,097	...	3000	5000	...	Tanwar
Pāndor [Pandwaha] ..	8,951	464 111	...	100	2000	5	Parihār

[1] Var. Akhar, Kahār, Sahār.
[2] Probably *Panwārī.*

Sarkār of Irij—(contd.)

	Bighas Biswas	Revenue D.	Suyurghāl D.	Cavalry	Infantry	Elephants	Castes
Jhatra, 4 mahals, has a brick fort ..	...	11,787,904	...	4000	15000	70	Rājput
Riābānah[1], has a fort ..	12,072	500,000	...	50	2000	...	Kachhwāhah
Shāhzādapur	21,257	450,781	...	...	...	...	...
Khatolah &c. 3 mahals, has a fort	...	3,000,000	...	100	5000	20	Gond
Kajhodah [?Gahrauli]	...	750,200	...	...	...	...	...
Kidār	...	120,000	...	...	...	...	...
Kunch, has a fort ..	155,320	1,851,802	27,712	50	2000	...	Kumbi
Khakes,[3] has a fort ..	89,233	1,343,073	7,673	50	1000	...	Kachhwāhah
Kānti	...	240,000	...	20	5000	10	Gond
Khāerah, [Khārela] has a brick fort ..	222,557	4,776,357	46,729	200	5000	10	Kachhwāhah
Maholi	26,581	502,102	...	100	10000	10	Parihār

Sarkār of Bayānwān.

Containing 27 *Mahals*, 762,014 *Bighas*. Revenue 8,459,296 *Dāms*. *Suyurghāl* 82,662 Dāms. Castes various. Cavalry 1,105. Infantry 18,000.

	Bighas Biswas	Revenue D.	Suyurghāl D.	Cavalry	Infantry	Elephants	Castes
Antri, yields excellent quality of betel leaf from which the revenue is chiefly derived	906,140	...	...	10	100	...	Various
Amwāri [Amola] ..	223,000	...	...	Entered under Ratangarh.			Mārwār Gauruah
Atiwan [Araon] ..	35,958	165,165	54,114	15	200	...	Gond, Gauruah
Autelah	29,444	32,455	1,257	...	100	...	Brāhman
Bayānwān	86,241	801,275	20,169	320	3000	...	Pundir, Panwār
Banwār	17,329	457,439	6,558	20	300	...	Brāhman, Khidmatiyah
Parānchah [Paraich] ..	89,784	396,193	21,541	20	500	...	Bundela

[1] *Riābānah* = ? *Rebai* of map.
[2] Kedpur.
[3] Khankes. Khakesh. Ganges. Khaksen,

Sarkār of Bayānwān—(*contd.*)

	Bighas Biswas	Revenue D.	Suyurghāl D.	Cavalry	Infantry	Elephants	Castes
Badnun [Bardun] ..	...	275,000	...	10	200	...	Bundela
Bhāsandā	...	169,040	...	10	300	...	Panwar
Chinaur, has a fort ..	50,973	548,631	3,800	10	200	...	Ahir, Brāhman
Jarhali	19,865	144,055	...	10	300	.	Panwār
Jagtān [?=Jignā] ..	...	123,680	...	...	150	...	Various
Dahāilah,* here a large lake, full of water-lilies	13,127	17,306	...	20	350	...	Brahmān, Gujar
Ruchādah [Ruchera] ..	94,223	472,839	15,702	10	200	...	Kāyath, Brāhman
Ratangarh, has a fort	70,523	855,995	...	200	4000	...	Jat
Roherah	2 309	1,017,682	...	50	500	...	Gujar
Sohandi, has a brick fort [? Suchendi] ..	81,655	896,959	...	300	5000	...	Panwār
Kanaulah [Karaia] ..	11,764	364,968	...	10	200	...	Gujar, Jat
Karharah	...	277,000	...	...	...	...	Mentioned under Ratangarh
Kaheod,† has a fort in the mountains ..	27,290	196,804	...	...	200	...	Brāhman
Khandhā	17,403	162,661	3,036	...	200	...	Ahir, Jat
Khand Bajrah the greater	33,782	138,934	...	25	300	...	Bundela, Jat
Do. the lesser ..	1,602	68,470	...	10	200		Minā, Gujar
Kherihāt	24,318	112,079	...	...	800	...	Do.
Kajhārah, has a stone fort on a hill ..	17,269	82,291	...	5	300	..	Gujar
Kadwāhah	7,169	43,296	...	50	300	...	Ahir
Mau, has a fort ..	59,070	850,429	5,189	50	1000	...	Ahir

* *Dahailah* [*Ind. Atlas*. 51 *S.E.*], 16 m. due east of Narwar, on the way to Antri, has a very large lake. It was 2 miles to the west of this place, according to T. that Abul Fazl lost his life in the ambuscade set for him by the Bundelā Chief Bir Sing. *Dabra* in the maps 13 miles south of Antri and 42 m. n. of Jhansi, has no lake, and cannot be this mahal.

† Prob. *Kāmod* of map.

Sarkār of Narwar.

Containing 5 *Mahals,* 394,353 *Bighas.* Revenue 4,233,322 *Dāms. Suyurghāl* 95,994 *Dāms.* Castes, Rajput Tonwar. Cavalry, 500. Infantry, 20,000.

	Bighas Biswas	Revenue D.	Suyur-ghāl D.	Cavalry	Infantry	Elephants	Castes
Baroi, has a fort; some of the villages near the Saklā are of great productive value	88,085	638,700	...	...	...	...	...
Bauli (? Paori), has a fort on the Saklā ..	242,456	141,915	...	...	...	...	...
Seopuri, has a stone fort	24,975	1,250,000	...	...	...	..	...
Kolāras has 2 forts, one near the village of Barwā. There is a small hill with a waterfall. It is a place of Hindu worship	133,10	764,380	14,882	...	...	...	...
Narwar with suburb: dist. has a stone fort. In certain parts of the fort are ancient Hindu temples of stone	25,522	438,025	81,312	...	...	...	

Sarkār of Mandrāel.

Containing 14 *Mahals.* 65,642 *Bighas.* Revenue 3,738,084 *Dāms.* Castes Rājput, Jādon. Cavalry 4,000. Infantry 5,000.

	Bighas Biswas	Revenue D.		Bighas Biswas	Revenue D.
Untgar, has a stone	7,674	493,978	Dungri	902	54,126
fort on a hill and	6,413	359,706	Ratanbalāhar ..	1,215	82 098
below it flows the	6,866	324,091	Samarthalah ..	9.160	526,330
river Chambal ..	4,382	261,746	Kamukherah ..	1,938	116,168*
Bijaipur	..	...	Kharnun	820	54,074
Balāoli	769	38,498	Kahtoni	1,925	51,944
Bākhar (=Manākhur) ..			Mandrāel, has a fort		
Bagrond			on a hill and the		
Jhakwār (=Jakoda) ..			river Chambal on the		
Dāng Makhori ..	7,812	493,978	north	15,745	697,794

* Var. 1310 and 764,380 for the area and revenue.

Sarkār of Alwar.

Containing 43 *Mahals,* 16,62,012 *Bighas.* Revenue 39,832,204 *Dāms. Suyurghāl* 699,212 *Dāms.* Cavalry 6,504. Infantry 42,020.

	Bighas Biswas	Revenue D.	Suyurghāl D.	Cavalry	Infantry	Elephants	Castes
Alwar, has a stone fort on a hill	85,084	2,679,820	350 056	10	1,500	...	Khānzādah of Mewāt, descendants of Bahādur Khān
Anthlah Bhābru ..	24,956	850,731	...	20	500	...	Kachhwāhah
Umran	39,762	642,153	1,043	20	1,000	...	Baqqāl
Ismāilpur	28,988	503,840	2,266	40	500	...	Khānzādah of Mewāt
Bairāt, has a stone fort (Parāt, p. 103) ..	23,522	7,201,791	1,796	50	1,000	...	Baqqāl
Bihrozpur	119,015	2,621,958	9,317	350	2,000	...	Khānzādah of Mewāt
Bahādurpur	60,451	1,950,000	95,000	500	2,000	...	Do. Do.
Bharkol	74,281	678,733	...	50	1,000	...	Do. Do.
Balhār (? Bairohar) ..	58,654	443,612	...	40	500	...	Bargujar, Rājput
Barodah Fateh Khān ..	16,074	201,059	1,059	30	300	...	Mewāt Khānzādah o
Panāin	28,726	195,680	...	5	50	...	Khānzādah and Meo.
Baroda [Bagar] Meo ..	13,062	153,045	619	50	300	...	Do.
Bhudah Thal	30,606	146,000	...	5	50	...	
Bhiwāi	14,918	122,088	...	5	50	...	Various
Basānah (=Baswa) ..	20,789	100,356	...	5	50	...	Do.
Bajherah	2,663	104,890	...	10	50	...	Khānzādah and Meo.
Balheri (Bālhattah) ..	6,565	183,507	...	30	500	...	Bargujar
Jalālpur	46,340	893,599	10,665	...	...	...	Khānzādah and Meo.
Hasanpur Badohar ..	20,353	947,871	3,020	100	300	...	Do.
Hasanpur Kori, (Gori)	47,740	1,259,659	...	120	300	...	Do.
Hājipur, has a stone fort ..	26,439	456,779	3,120	500	1,000	...	Chauhān
Deoli Sājari ..	83,188	1,600,000	...	150	1,000	...	Bargujar
Dadekar ..	27,051	695,262	7,312	150	1,000	...	[1] Meo.

[1] Mentioned in Elliot as in ancient times a well-known lawless plundering race, driven out of the Etawah tract by the Senghers and Chauhāns. According to Sherring (III, 90) they are an indigenous tribe converted to Islām, but retaining a good many Hindu customs; now an agricultural people divided into 12 clans.

Sarkār of Alwar—(*contd.*)

	Bighas Biswas	Revenue D.	Suyurghāl D.	Cavalry	Infantry	Elephants	Castes
Dharā	12,338	512,613	5,015	100	508	...	Khānzādah and Meo.
Rāth	6,030	229,741	3,744	10	100	...	Meo.
Sakhān	18,790	804,262	...	100	700	...	Chauhān
Khohari Rana ..	2,208	4,359,272	96,919	900	5,000	...	Khānzādah of Mewāt, A'mā and Duar (obscure text)
Khelohar	58,276	1,459,048	14,088	125	1,000	...	Meo
Kol [=Gol] Dhoār ..	33,956	627,100	...	30	500	...	Rājput
Kiyārah	307	600,000	...	100	1,000	...	Minā
Khirali	26,746	465,640	23,150	100	500	...	Sayyid, Gujar
Ghāt Sudan (or Seon) has a fort	16,494	357,110	...	...	...	...	
Kohrānā [=Ghosrana]	3,565	166,666	...	300	1,000	...	Māhat (?)
Mandāwar, has a brick fort	100,322	1,889,097	5,608	500	1,000	...	Chauhān
Maujpur	44,140	639,858	12,022	300	500	...	Abbāsi
Mubārakpur [Māra..pur]	18,636	514,198	...	50	300	...	Khānzādah
Mongonā [Mangwar] ..	38,112	475,260	...	100	700	...	Do.
Mandāuar	17,800	27,051	...	4	20	...	Chauhān
Naugāon (Nowgong) ..	23,771	2,056,512	34,296	70	500	...	Khānzādah
Nāhargarh	35,452	604,194	...	20	200	...	Do.
Harsoli	11,800	227,096	...	10	100	...	Meo
Harpur	16,944	686,605	3,255	20	4,000	...	Jat
Harsānā	4,025	208,281	...	40	500	...	Meo

Sarkār of Tijārah.

Containing 18 *Mahals.* 740,001 *Bighahs.* 5½ *Biswas.* Revenue 17,700,460 *Dāms.* *Suyurghāl* 701,761½. Cavalry 1,227. Infantry 9,650.

	Bighas Biswas	Revenue D.	Suyurghāl D.	Cavalry	Infantry	Elephants	Castes
Indri, has fort on a hill	134,150	1,995,216	26,096	400	3,000	...	Khānzādah of Mewat
Ujinah [Uchaira] ..	33,926	428,347	22,796	45	150	...	Khānzādah, Thathar

Sarkār of Tijārah—(*contd.*)

	Bighas Biswas	Revenue D.	Suyurghāl D.	Cavalry	Infantry	Elephants	Castes
Umrā Umri	8,107	307,037	...	10	100	...	Thathar, Meo
Bisru	35,703	215,800	5,354	10	200	...	Khānzādah, Meo
Pur	2,476	540,645	1,559	10	200	...	Thathar
Pinangwān, has a stone fort	75,148	1,329,350	34,312	20	300	...	Meo
Bhasohrā, has stone fort	57.778	1.416 715	25,471	30	400	...	Do.
Tijārah, has a fort ..	131,960	3,603,596	204,419	500	2,000	...	Do.
Jhimrāwat, has a stone fort on a hill ..	22,632-11	496,202½	31,283½	50	300	...	Do.
Khānpur	9,893	195,620	...	20	150	...	Do.
Sākras	12,106	460,088	50,411	14	150	...	Do.
Sānthādāri	7,712-11	406.811	267,470	200	...	...	Do.
Firozpur, situated on the skirt of a hill in which there is an ever-flowing fountain with an image of Mahadeo set up; a Hindu Shrine ..	64,150	3,042,642	69,044	50	1,000	...	Do.
Fatehpur Mungartā ..	43,700	1,135,140	12,955	10	200	...	Do.
Kotlah, has a brick fort on a hill on which there is a reservoir 4 *kos* in circumference	71,265	1,552,196	7,017	30	700	...	Khānzādah, Gujar
Karherah, (Ghāserah, Elliot)	9,785	330,076	...	10	200	...	Meo
Khora ka Thānah. So in MSS., but Elliot Khawā)	7,945	168,719	...	10	250	...	Do.
Naginān [Noganwa] ..	7,215-19	377.257	3,572	100	150	...	Do.

Sarkār of Nārnol.

Containing 16 *Mahals.* 2,080,046 *Bighas.* Revenue 50,046,703 *Dāms.* *Suyurghal* 775,103 Dāms. Castes various. Cavalry 7,520. Infantry 37,220.

	Bighas Biswas	Revenue D.	Suyurghāl D.	Cavalry	Infantry	Elephants	Castes
Bārh	146,754	2,060,662	...	100	1,000	...	Chauhān, Rājput, Musalmān, Khandār. (*Var.* Kedār).

Sarkār of Nārnol—(contd.)

	Bighas Biswas	Revenue D.	Suyur-ghāl D.	Cavalry	Infantry	Elephants	Castes
Bābāi, has a stone fort and a coppermine; hills adjacent ..	78.426	920,170	...	400	3,000	...	Parihār.
Barodah [Bahora] Rāna	47,266	592,995	...	300	2,000	...	Chauhān.
Chālkaliānah ..	517,540	7,744,027	56,164	200	5,000	...	Jat of the Sangwān clan.
Jhojeun [Jhajlai], has a stone fort on the skirt of a hill ..	95,331	2,329,069	...	2000	3,000	...	Kiyām-Khāni.*
Singhānah Udaipur, has a coppermine and mint for copper coinage	...	11,881,629 in money.	3,351	400	1,000	...	Tonwar, Parihār.
Kānodah, in the village of Zerpur in this Parganah, a large Hindu temple	10,723	4,356,189	91,577	1000	4,000	...	Rājput, Musalmān, Hālu. [Jat]
Kotputli, has a stone fort and in the village of Bhāndhārah is a copper mine in working	170,674	4,266,837	29,425	700	4,000	...	Tonwār Rājput, Gond.
Kanori [?Kanti), has 3 forts in three villages	150,297	2,721,126	...	1000	5,000	...	Tonwār.
Khandelā	...	1,300,000 in money.	...	200	2,000	...	Rājput, Kachhwāhah.
Khodāna [or Konodana]	18,493	808,109	...	20	700	...	Jat.
Lapoti [=Pataudi] ..	88,281	1,512,470	16,000	100	500	...	Chauhān.
Villages at the foot of the mountain where is a copper mine. In that of Rāepore is a copper mine and a mint and the stream there is polluted by it	176,650	274,350	...	100	2,000	...	Narbān.
Nārnol, has a stone fort	214,218	5,913,228	549,161	500	2 000	...	[Chauhan]
Narhar [?Narera] do. ..	356,293	4,262,837	29,405	500	2,000	...	Ahir. Kiām Khāni, Afghan, Mākar. (?)

* Called Kāim Khāni by Elliot and Sherring. They are Chauhāns converted to Islam. Their ancestors fought against Bāber in 1528.

Sarkār of Sahār.

Containing 7 *Mahals*. 763,474 *Bighas*. Revenue 5,917,569 *Dāms*. *Suyurghāl* 109,447 *Dāms*. Castes various. Cavalry 265. Infantry 1,000.

	Bighas Biswas	Revenue D.	Suyurghāl D.	Cavalry	Infantry	Elephants	Castes
Pahāri	106,422	1,228,999	26,045	20	700	...	Meo, Thathar
Bandhauli	25,980	441,840	6,840	10	300	...	Jat &c.
Sahār, has a fort ..	385,895	2,489,816	21,678	200	7,000	...	Bāchhal, Gujar, Jat, Kachhwāhah.
Kāmah	90,500	505,724	1,229	10	300	...	Meo, Jat Ahir
Koh Mujāhid [Q. Kho]	23,769	170,365	...	4	200	...	Meo, Jat,
Nunherah	50,816	618,115	17,515	...	...	...	Ahir, Jat, Meo
Hodal	78,500	462,710	33,140	10	200	...	Jat &c.

THE SUBAH OF MĀLWA.

It is situated in the second climate. Its length from the extreme point of *Gaṛha* (*Māndla*) to *Bānswārah* is 245 *kos*. Its breadth from *Chanderi* to *Nandarbār* is 230 *kos*. To the east lies *Bāndhun* [Rewa]; to the north *Narwar;* to the south *Baglānah;* to the west *Gujarāt* and *Ajmer*. There are mountains to the south. Its principal rivers are the *Narbadah*, the *Siprā*, the *Kāli Sind*, the *Betwa*, and the *Godi*.* At every two or three *kos* clear and limpid streams are met on whose banks the willow grows wild, and the hyacinth and fragrant flowers of many hues, amid the abundant shade of trees. Lakes and green meads are frequent and stately palaces and fair country homes breathe tales of fairyland. The climate is so temperate that in winter there is little need of warm clothing, nor in summer of the cooling properties of saltpetre. The elevation of this province is somewhat above that of other areas of the country and every part of it is cultivable. Both harvests

* The *Godi* is a tributary of the Narmada.

are excellent, and especially wheat, poppy, sugarcane, mangoes, melons and grapes. In *Hāsilpur* the vine bears twice in the year, and betel leaves are of fine quality. Cloth of the best texture is here woven. High and low give opium to their children up to the age of three years. The peasants and even grain dealers are never without arms. *Ujjain* is a large city on the banks of the Sipra. It is regarded as a place of great sanctity and wonderful to relate, at times the river flows in waves of milk. The people prepare vessels and make use of it, and such an occurrence brings good fortune to the reigning monarch.

In the 43rd year of the Divine Era when the writer of this work was proceeding to the Deccan by command of his Majesty, a week before his arrival at *Ujjain*, on the 16th of the Divine month of *Farwardin* (March) four *gharis* of the night having elapsed, this flow occurred, and all conditions of people, Musalman and Hindu alike talked of it.*

In the neighbourhood are 360 places of religious worship for Brāhmans and other Hindus. Close to this city is a place called *Kāliyādah*, an extremely agreeable residence where there is a reservoir continually overflowing yet ever full. Around it are some graceful summer dwellings, the monuments of a past age.

Garha† is a separate State, abounding with forests in which are numerous wild elephants. The cultivators pay the revenue in mohurs and elephants. Its produce is sufficient to supply fully both Gujarāt and the Deccan.

Chanderi was one of the largest of ancient cities and possesses a stone fort. It contains 14,000 stone houses, 384 markets, 360 spacious caravanserais and 12,000 mosques.

Tumun is a village on the river *Betba* (Betwā) in which mermen are seen. There is also a large temple in which if a drum is beaten, no sound is heard without.

In the Sarkār of *Bijāgarh* there are herds of wild

* Another reading adopted by Gladwin is "partook of it." Gladwin while rejecting this fable, suggests a sudden impregnation of the river with chalk.

† It was the ancient capital of the Gond Dynasty of Garha Māndla and its ruined keep known as the Madan Mahal still crowns the granite range along the foot of which the town stretches for about 2 miles. *I. G.*

elephants. *Mandu* is a large city; the circumference of its fort is 12 *kos*, and in it there is an octagonal tower. For some period it was the seat of government and stately edifices stili recall their ancient lords. Here are the tombs of the Khilji Sultāns. A remarkable fact is that in summer time water trickles from the domed roof of the mausoleum of Sultān Hoshang and the simpleminded have long regarded it as a prodigy, but the more acute of understanding can satisfactorily account for it. Here the tamarind grows as large as a cocoanut and its kernel is extremely white.

Learned Hindus assert that a stone is met with in this country which when touched by any malleable metal turns it into gold, and they call it *Pāras*. They relate that before the time of Bikramājit, there reigned a just prince named Rājā Jai Sing Deva who passed his life in deeds of beneficence. Such a stone was discovered in that age, and became the source of vast wealth. The sickle of a straw cutter by its action was changed into gold. The man, not understanding the cause, thought that some damage had occurred to it. He took it to a blacksmith by name Māndan to have it remedied, who divining its properties, took possession of it, and amassing immense wealth, garnered a store of delights. But his natural beneficence suggested to him that such a priceless treasure was more fitted for the reigning prince, and going to court he presented it. The Rāja made it the occasion of many good deeds, and by means of the riches he acquired, completed this fort in twelve years, and at the request of the blacksmith, the greater number of the stones with which it was built, were shaped like an anvil. One day he had a festival on the banks of the Narbadah, and promised to bestow a considerable fortune on his Brāhman priest. As he had somewhat withdrawn his heart from worldly goods, he presented him with this stone. The Brāhman from ignorance and meanness of soul, became indignant and threw the precious treasure into the river to his subsequent and eternal regret. Its depth there prevented his recovering it, and to this day that part of the river has never been fathomed.

Dhār is a town which was the capital of Rājā Bhoja and many ancient princes. The vine here bears twice in the year when the sun first enters Pisces (February) and Leo (July), but the former of these two vintages is the sweeter.

In the Sarkār of *Handiah* are numerous wild elephants.

In *Nandurbār* good grapes and melons are obtainable.

This *Subah* contains 12 *Sarkārs*, subdivided into 301 *Parganahs*. The measured land is 42 *lakhs*, 66,221 *Bighas*, 6 *Biswas*. The gross revenue is 24 *krors*, 6 *lakhs*, 95,052 *Dāms*. (Rs. 6,017,376,-4-15). Of this 11 *lakhs*, 50,433 *Dāms* (Rs. 28,760-13) are *Suyurghāl*. The Provincial force consists of 29,668 Cavalry, 470,361 Infantry and 90 Elephants.

Sarkār of Ujjain.

Containing 10 *Mahals*. 925,622 *Bighas*. Revenue 43,827,960 *Dāms* in money. *Suyurghāl*, 281,816 *Dāms*. Castes various. Cavalry 3,250. Infantry 11,170.

	Bighas Biswas	Revenue D.	Suyurghāl D.	Cavalry	Infantry	Elephants	Castes
Ujjain with suburban district, has fort of stone below and of brick above ..	289,560	1,888,035	55,323	760	2,000	...	Ujjainia, Rāthor
Unhel	56,841	2,801,972	20,935	130	500	...	Rājput, Ujjainia, Dhakarah
Badhnāwar has a stone fort	60,096	3,056 195	1,095	500	3,000	...	Rāthor, &c.
Pānbihār	36 567	1,937 596	29,400	100	500	...	Ujjainia
Dipālpur	95,706	6,000,000	...	500	1,000	...	Rājput, Ujjainia
Ratlām	94,466	4,421,540	21,548	500	1,000	...	Rājput Mehtar, Soriah
Sānwer	46,694	2,418,375	133,156	150	300	...	Rājput, Magwar
Kampil has a fort partly stone, partly brick	59 802	2,907,817	2,344	150	400	...	Rājput
Khāchrod	66,626	2,651,044	...	60	1,200	...	Rājput, Deora [Chauhan], Dharar or Dhur (?)
Nolāi has a brick fort on the banks of the Chambal [? Naulāna]	126,264	3,851,886	18,015	400	1,200	...	Bais, Jādon, (Yadu)

Sarkār of Rāisin.

	Bighas Biswas	Revenue D.	Suyurghāl D.	Cavalry	Infantry	Elephants	Castes
Asapuri &c. 6 *Mahals* ..	3,238	...	173,064	170	945	...	
Bhilsah	40,816	6,094,970	...	480	1,000	...	Rājput
Bhori (? Bamari) ..	5,970	316,017	...	...	100	...	
Bhojpur	4,097	220,592	...	115	1,000	...	
Bālābahat	...	215,122	...	265	500	...	
Thānah Mir Khān ..	...	735,315	...	200	500	...	Rājput
Jājoi (Khajuri ?) ..	...	215,122	...	15	100	...	
Jhatānawi	3,404	184,750	...	10	150	...	
Jalodā	250	13,290	...	2	5	...	
Khiljipur	775	41,060	...	2	150	...	
Dhāmoni (=Dharoli) ..	13,007	788,389	...	5	400	...	
Digwār	4,932	292,313	...	75	520	...	Rājput
Dilod	1,974	144,000	...	35	100	...	
Diwatia [?or Dhānia]	...	21,502	...	20	170	...	
Raisin, with suburb, district has a stone fort on a hill, one of the famous fortresses of Hindustān ..	17,497	934,739	...	80	425	...	Rājput, Solankhi
Siwāni	10,975	580,828	...	80	945	...	
Sarsiah (? Bersia) ..	5,557	279,346	...	70	500	...	
Shāhpur	1,673	89,067	...	5	40	...	
Khimlāsah	11,720	645,665	...	40	100	...	Rājput
Kherā	10,534	560,037	...	30	320	...	
Kesorah	8,375	473,267	...	40	100	...	
Kham-Khera	7,102	378,460	...	50	100	...	
Kargarh	6,907	365,707	...	70	500	...	
Korai	.	145,566	...	50	100	...	
Laharpur	...	32,267	...	30	100	...	
Māhsamand (Dhamand)	814	43,024	...	50	140	...	

*Sarkār of Garha.**

Containing 57 *Mahals.* Revenue 10,077,080 *Dāms.* Castes Gond. Cavalry 5,495. Infantry 254,500.

	Bighas Biswas	Revenue D.	Suyurghāl D.	Cavalry	Infantry	Elephants	Castes
Amodgarh has a brick fort on a hill ..	...	239,000	...	...	...	...	Gond
Bāri and Bangar, 2 mahals	...	485,000	...	5	200	...	Do.

* Clearly printed in the Persian text as *Garha,* but misread by Jarrett as *Kanauj.* [J. S.]

Sarkār of Garha—Contd.

	Bighas Biswas	Revenue D.	Suyurghāl D.	Cavalry	Infantry	Elephants	Castes
Bhutgāon	...	400,025	...	50	1,000	...	Gond
Bārh, Sānā and Jhāmāhar, 3 mahals ..	...	395,000	...	200	4,000	...	Do.
Biāwar and Nejli, 2 mahals	...	300,000	...	...	...	...	Do.
Bakhrah	...	238,000	...	100	10,000	...	Do.
Banākar, Amrel, 2 mahals, has a stone fort	...	140 000	...	150	10,000	...	Do.
Babai	...	82,000	...	100	10,000	...	Do.
Bairagarh has a strong fort	...	45,000	...	15	200	...	Do.
Chāndpur, Chanderi, 2 mahals	...	39,000	...	5	...	...	Do.
Jetgarh, Bhaldewi and suburb, district, 3 mahals	...	12,000	...	400	30,000	...	Do.
Jethā (v. Chetia) ..	...	12,000	...	100	1,000	...	Gond Brāhman
Damodah	...	1,355,000	...	10	500	...	Gond
Dhāmeri (=Dhamari) and Dhamerā, 2 mahals	...	49,000	...	10	200	...	Do.
Deogāon	...	25,000	...	20	1,000	...	Do.
Deohār, Hurbhat, 2 mahals	...	18,000	...	20	1,000	...	Do.
Darkarah	...	18,000	...	10	200	...	Do.
Ratanpur and Parhar, 2 mahals	...	613,000	...	10	...	...	Do.
Rāngarh	...	400,000	...	200	10,000	...	Do.
Rāngarh and Sārangpur (? Singarpur) 2 mahals	...	1,055 000	...	10	200	...	Do.
Rasuliyā	...	12.000	...	200	5,000	...	Do.
Sitalpur	...	75,000	...	...	...	...	Gond mentioned under Garha
Shāhpur, Chaurāgarh, 2 mahals, has a strong fort	...	350,000	...	100	1,000	...	Gond
Garha with suburb. district has a strong fort	...	1,857,000	...	500	8.000	...	Do.
Kedārpur &c. 12 mahals	...	121 000	...	500	50 000	...	Do.
Khatolah	...	1,626,000	...	500	10,000	...	Do.
Lānji, Karolah, Dungarolah, 3 mahals ..	...	1,000,000	...	200	20,000	...	Do.
Mandlā	...	352,000	...	100	1,000	...	Do.
Harariya(Deogarh, 2 mahals, has a wooden fort on a hill ..	...	900,000	...	1500	50,000	...	Do.

Sarkār of Chanderi.

Containing 61 *Mahals.* 554,277 *Bighas.* 17 *Biswas.* Revenue 31,037,783 *Dams.* *Suyurghāl* 26,931 *Dāms.* Castes various. Cavalry 5,970. Infantry 66,085. Elephants 90.

	Bighas Biswas	Revenue D.	Suyurghāl D.	Cavalry	Infantry	Elephants	Castes
Udaipur has a stone fort	35,995	832,086	...	2000	10,400	...	Bāgri, Bakkāl
Aron	...	216,000	...	10	40	...	Khāti
Eran	1,759	1,759	...	10	100	...	Dāngi (Bundelas)
Itāwa	2,315	80,000	...	15	50	...	Ahir &c.
Bhorāsa has a stone fort on the Betwa ..	6,783	755,000	...	40	150	...	Brāhman
Bandarjhalā	2,750	720,000	...	25	600	...	Brāhman, Jat, Bāgri
Bāra &c. 5 mahals. Each of the 5 Parganahs has a fort of which 4 are stone and that of Māl (?) brick	12,074	635,500	...	500	5,000	...	Bundela, Kāyath
Badarwās and Ahak, 2 mahals	4,951	304,800	...	10	170	...	Ahir
Bajhār (? Pachar) has a brick fort and a large tank and small hill are adjacent ..	2,600	174,000	...	20	300	...	Brāhman
Beli [=Bijli]	1,253	70 000	...	10	170	...	Ahir
Tāl Baroda [Barwa Sagar]	18,619	1,090,000	...	60	3,000	...	Musalmān
Tumun, on the Betwa: the residents there say that mermen inhabit the river. There is also a temple ..	6,704	312,504	...	15	120	...	Brāhman
Thatābariyār (? Manohar Thāna)	403-17	22,500	...	5	10	...	
Thanwāra, Lalatpur &c. 3 mahals, has a stone fort	10,977	619,987	...	80	2,000	...	Rājput Sāhti

Sarkār of Chanderi—Contd.

	Bighas Biswas	Revenue D.	Suyurghāl D.	Cavalry	Infantry	Elephants	Castes
Chanderi* with suburban district, 2 mahals, has a stone fort	23,021	1,186,388	...	95	1,350	...	Ahir
Jhājhon, Deohari the smaller, 2 mahals ..	6,468	387,480	...	80	900	...	Chauhān &c.
Jorsingār &c. 5 mahals	9,568	448,000	...	30	100	...	Mākhāti
Chirgāon has a fort ..	5,096	200,000	...	15	150	...	Khāti
Joāsah	2,550	144,000	...	15	40	...	Rājput, Khāti
Deohari, the greater, on the river Sindh ..	16,466	857,998	...	65	200	...	Do.
Dub Jākar has a stone fort	8,875	580 500	...	500	5.000	...	Khichi
Daurāhal &c. 4 mahals	2,600	147,282	...	310	5,000	...	Various
Ranod has a stone fort and near it a large reservoir which is a Hindu shrine ..	5,833	364,000	...	15	6C	...	Baqqāl
Rodahi &c. 5 mahals, has a stone for above the *bandar* where there is also a large temple ..	3,652	206,000	...	20	700	...	Rājput, Gond
Rāgah (? Rāghogarh) has a stone fort ..	1,487	84,000	...	50	150	...	Rājput, Us Karor
Saronj, white muslin of the kind called Mahmudi is here manufactured	186,427	11,065,765	26,931	100	2,500	...	Rawāthansi karer (?)
Sahjan &c. 3 mahals ..	70,221	3,976,700	...	150	20,000	...	Dandar (?)
Shādora near this town is a small hill ..	5,840	334,290	...	50	1.000	...	Makhāti
Gunā has a brick fort ..	18,615	1,092,062	...	15	250	...	Khichi &c.
Garanjiyab has a stone fort on the Betwa ..	8,837	468,000	...	30	200	...	Dingi
Koroi (=Korwai) on the Betwa	4,196	252,000	...	25	150	...	Brāhman
Kāngrah has a stone fort on the Sind ..	4,670	239,990	...	35	100	...	Musalman
Kādrola has a stone fort	2,970	168,000	...	20	400	...	Dingi

* Emendations suggested by J. S.—Deohari (=Dehri), Kangra (=Kanjit), Kadrala (=Kadwana), Kojan (=Kanjia), Bandarjhala (=Bandrāila), Bārah (=Barāgāon), Thanwara (=Tahrauli), Jhājhon (=Jaklou), Joāsa (=Churāra), Kalakot (=Kālapāhar), Laroala (=Ladhaura), Rāgah (may also be Raksa)—all found in the Survey of India maps.

Sarkār of Chanderi—Contd.

	Bighas Biswas	Revenue D.	Sayurghāl D.	Cavalry	Infantry	Elephants	Castes
Kolakot, has a stone fort on a hill ..	2 771	156 459	...	150	1,500	...	Gujar.
Kojān, on the Betwa ..	1,224	69,152	...	10	20	...	
Laroālah, on the Betwa	3,140	168,000	...	10	20	...	Bakkāl.
Mungāoli, has a brick fort	29,756	1,440,000	...	70	700	...	Kāyath.
Miānah, 3 kos from it is a high hill ..	12,196	668,600	...	60	3,000	...	Rājput Khātri.
Mahadpur	561	144,000	...	...	140	...	Khātri.

Sarkār of Sārangpur.

Containing 24 *Mahals.* 706,202 *Bighas.* Revenue 32,994,880 *Dāms.* *Suyurghāl* 324,461 *Dāms.* Castes various. Cavalry 3,125. Infantry 21,710.

	Bighas Biswas	Revenue D.	Sayurghāl D.	Cavalry	Infantry	Elephants	Castes
Ashtah	48,502	800,790	790	230	1,500	...	Chauhān, Dodhi, (Dodhia).
Akbarpur	30,094	170 610	...	45	150	...	Various.
Āgra	7,852	472,362	...	100	2,000	...	Chauhān.
Bajilpur produces the finest quality of betel leaf	11,590	647,544	...	140	560	...	Khichi.
Paplun	11,180	610 544	...	160	700	...	Rathor.
Bhorāsah	4,147	259,777	...	30	100	...	Various.
Bajor (? Pachor) ..	1,100	65,820	...	10	200	...	Do.
Bāniān	721	40 841	...	25	100	...	Do.
Beāwar	2,505	156,740	...	60	700	...	Kāyath.
Talain	48,056	1,800,700	27,826	150	500	...	Chauhān.
Khiljipur	113	6,027	...	100	200	...	Various.
Zirapur	6,047	377,352	...	40	300	...	Various. nil. Khichi.
Sārangpur, with suburb. district 2 mahals, has a brick fort ..	21,800	1,294,321	47,559	120	2,000	...	Chauhān.
Sahār Bābā Hāji .	20,263	1,093,049	...	150	1,000	...	Dhandel.

Sarkār of Sārangpur—Contd.

	Bighas Biswas	Revenue D.	Sayurghāl D.	Cavalry	Infantry	Elephants	Castes
Sandarsi	9,443	434,989	...	105	2,000	...	Chauhān.
Sosner	121	54,876	...	25	300	...	Various.
Shujāapur	133,433	8,017 124	238,212	500	3 000	...	Chauhān.
Karhali (Karapli) ..	17,179	7,447,906	80,506	500	2,000	...	Do.
Kāyath (=Kāoti) ..	33.938	1,193 396	10,368	110	700	...	Do.
Kānhar (Khātar) ..	26,045	1,097,047	15,318	...	...	...	
Karhari	288	17,252	...	25	200	...	Various.
Muhammadpur ..	47,704	1,981,182	...	170	1,000	...	Aljiyah, Dharar, Rāthor, Dudmā. (?)
Naugām	69,472	2,755,433	4,882	200	1,500	...	Chauhān.

Sarkār of Bijāgarh.†

Containing 29 *Mahals.* 283,278 *Bighas,* 13 *Biswas.* Revenue 12,249,121 *Dāms.* Castes various. Cavalry 1,773. Infantry 19480.

	Bighas Bighas	Revenue D.	Sayurghāl D.	Cavalry	Infantry	Elephants	Castes
Anjari (=Amjad), situated near the Narbada	13,713	1,707,093	...	...	...	...	Bhil, included in seorānah.
Un, Sanāwads, here a temple to Mahadeo	5,321	290,348	...	300	1,000	...	Sohar, Rajput.
Amlāta, here a lake called by the Hindus Saman (? Biman) ..	4,919	226,677	...	...	...	...	Rājput, Sohar, included in Balakwarah.
Bāmangāon	15,679	781,014	...	5	100	...	Bersiya Brāhman.
Balakwāra, famous for fine sweet musk melons	9,268	407,014	...	500	1,000	...	Sohar, Rājput.
Barodara	5,452	369,898	...	5	50	...	Brāhman.

† South of the Narmada and south of Mandaleshwar.

Sarkār of Bijāgarh—Contd.

	Bighas Biswas	Revenue D.	Sayurghāl D.	Cavalry	Infantry	Elephants	Castes
Bikhangāon, has a stone fort; here good horses are procurable	12,580	223,816	...	50	215	...	Rājput, Sohar.
Balkhar, near the Narbada; adjacent are small hills ..	5,584	223,616	...	included in Balakwārah		...	Rājput.
Bāsniyah	9,870-13	85,000	...	...	50	...	As above mentioned.
Badriya (? Beria) ..	3,839	84,293	...	...	50	...	Rājput, Sohar.
Bangelah, forest adjacent where elephants are hunted	2,185	52,939	...	5	800	...	Bhil.
Biror (=Barur) ..	7,477	391,333	...	5	500	...	Do.
Tikri, on the Kodi; here a large temple to Mahādeo, and a small hill	14,771	645,245	...	included in Seorānah		...	Rājput, Bhil, &c.
Jalālābād, with suburb. district has a stone fort	9 285	414,268	...	34	1,470	...	Bhil, Bāhal.
Chamāri, has a stone fort	17,916	543,994	...	100	500	...	Rājput, Sohar.
Deolā Khatiā (Dival) ..	6,430	392,080	...	...	...	...	Rājput, Sohar, included in Balakwārah.
Deolā Narhar (?Dhaoda)	3,286	98,569	...	5	500	...	Bhil.
Seorānah, near the Narbadah, and a large temple there ..	13,074	627,207	...	300	2,025	...	Bhil, &c.
Sindhawā, good hunting ground for elephants	9,974	353,819	...	24	550	...	Koli.
Silwārah, has a brick fort	9,628	325,544	...	350	9,000	...	Bhil.
Sāngori (=Sangvi) ..	4,607	170,210	...	5	250	...	Nahal, Karhah.
Kasrāod, on the Narbadah, has a large tank and a small hill	20,490	1,150,569	...	under Balakwārah.			Sohar.

Sarkār of Bijāgarh—Contd.

	Bighas Biswas	Revenue D.	Sayurghāl D.	Cavalry	Infantry	Elephants	Castes
Khargon, has a fort, stone below, brick above	14,526	753,194	...	50	500	...	Rājput, Sohar, Kanārah (Khatri ?)
Kānapur	5,358	126,846	...	under Balakwaīah.			Do. do.
Khudgāon	2,738	85,082	...	5	20	...	Rājput, Kanāri.
Lahrpur, commonly Muhammadpur ..	6,792	205,743	...	5	400	...	Rājput, Kahiri.
Lowārikoh	2,476	50,000	...	5	300	...	Bhil.
Mandawara, here a large temple ..	15,948	777,881	4,187	under Seoranah			Do.
Mahoi (Mohipur), near the Narbada	8,318	395,206	...	5	50	...	Bhil, &c.
Morāna (Mardāna) has a stone fort ..	9,211	355,902	...	5	70	...	Rājput, Sohar.
Nāwari (Newali), has a stone fort	9,779	408,164	...	...	...	...	Bhil.
Nangalkādi	9,057	370,208	...	5	500	...	Bāhal.

Sarkār of Mando.

Containing 16 *Mahals.* 229,969 *Bighas,* 15 *Biswas.* Revenue 13,788,994 *Dāms. Suyurghāl* 127,732 *Dāms.* Castes various. Cavalry 1,180. Infantry 2,526.

	Bighas Biswas	Revenue D.	Sayurghāl D.	Cavalry	Infantry	Elephants	Castes
Amjhera	...	395,400	3,806	60	...	...	
Barodah	27,370-19	1,307,760	3,936	80	150	...	
Betmān	7,780-12	656,556	8,750	60	100	...	
Choli Mahesar ..	18,183	968,370	10,500	70	200	...	
Hāsilpur, the vine here bears twice a year, and fine cloth of the kind *Amān* and *Khāsah* are manufactured	4,805-13	210,000	...	40	85		
Dhār, anciently a large city	38,660	2,079,306	36,364	120	150	...	

Sarkār of Mando —Contd.

	Bighas Biswas	Revenue D.	Sayur-ghāl D.	Cavalry	Infantry	Elephants	Castes
Dikhtān	17,643	958,986	...	70	200	...	
Dharmagāon	3,018-11	916,442	...	...	...	...	
Sāgor	12,807-14	683,084	...	50	150	...	
Sanāsi	70,670	3,097,190	29,696	800	600	...	
Kotra	...	2,393,871	385	165	300	...	
Mando, with suburb. district, 2 mahals ..	540-17	48,398	...	10	50	...	
Manāwara	2,048-10	102,164	...	20	50	...	
Nalchah	9,949-7	545,952	34,105	70	200	...	
Nawāli	...	224,608	...	45	100	...	

Sarkār of Handiah.

Containing 23 *Mahals*. Land under special crops 20 *Mahals*. 89,573-18 *Bighas*, 18 *Biswas*. Amount of revenue in cash from crops charged at special rates and from land paying the general *bigah* rate. 11,610,969 *Dāms*. *Suyurghāl* 157,054 *Dāms*. Castes various. Cavalry 1,296. Infantry 5,921.

	Bighas Biswas	Revenue D.	Sayur-ghāl D.	Cavalry	Infantry	Elephants	Castes
Unchod	59,495	2,037,877	10,825	200	500	...	
Angalgāon	414	422,947	...	150	200	...	
Amondah	392	21 834	...	7	20	...	
Bijnolā	606	44,418	...	25	100	...	
Punāsa	873	25,251	...	10	100	...	
Balahri (? Bhilakheri)	...	825	...	...	15	...	
Chakhodā	2,319	158,876	13,324	20	80	...	
Champāner	317	20,350	...	20	100	...	
Dewās	188,249	6,718,000	42,837	375	2,000	...	
Rājorā	383	25,641	...	7	20	...	
Satwās	971	89,080	7,504	45	150	...	
Samarni [? Timurni] ..	775	52,115	...	5	40	...	
Siyāmgarh	160	20.494	...	111	550	...	
Seoni	...	2,250	...	50	600	...	
Khandohā Islāmpur ..	22,632	1,298,581	6,400	120	500	...	
Mundi	367	19,443	...	7	20	...	
Mardānpur	...	450	...	50	500	...	
Nimāwar	18,207	946 467	...	25	100	...	
Naugāon	1,187	79,264	...	30	120	...	
Niman (=Nimanpur) ..	1,160	75,152	...	14	56	...	
Hāndah (=Harda) ..	2,954	146,044	...	30	100	...	
Handia, with suburb. district, has a stone fort on the Narbada on a level plain ..	5,154-15	350,051	76,160	40	150	...	

Sarkār of Nandurbār.

Containing 7 *Mahals*. 2,059,604 *Bighas*. Revenue 50,162,250 *Dāms*. *Suyurghāl* 198,478 *Dāms*. Castes various. Cavalry 500. Infantry 6,000.

	Bighas Biswas	Revenue D.	Sayur-ghāl D.	Cavalry	Infantry	Elephants	Castes
Bhāmber (Bhamer) ..	212,830	69,244,355	...	...	...	...	
Sultānpur	995,993	28,119,749	159,744	...	...	...	
Khāer (or Jahur ?) ..	868	53,310	...	...	...	...	
Nandurbār, with sub. district	203,007	14,252,191	38,734	...	...	...	
Ner	15,253	722,760	...	...	...	...	
Namorhi	1,645	89,585	...	...	...	...	

Sarkār of Mandesor.

Containing 17 *Mahals*. Revenue 6,861,396 *Dāms*. *Suyurghāl* 23,387 *Dāms*. Castes various. Cavalry 1,194. Infantry 4,280.

	Bighas Biswas	Revenue D.	Sayur-ghāl D.	Cavalry	Infantry	Elephants	Castes
Ringnod	...	716 355	...	80	250	...	Sisodiā.
Ujenwās	...	170 953	...	60	200	...	Ahir, Gond.
Basād	...	515,400	...	80	250	...	Sisodiā.
Budha ..	...	255,062	...	65	300	...	Rājput, Dodia. (Bodhia.)
Tharod	...	109,220	...	74	250	...	Ahir.
Barāudah	...	106.703	...	50	200	...	Ahir, Gond.
Baraltah	...	90 970	727	30	100	...	Chauhān.
Bhathpur (? Bhanpur)	...	63.104	...	16	250	...	Rājput. Dodia.
Tāl	...	1,600 000	...	160	250	...	Do. do.
Titrod	...	500 000	...	80	220	...	Do. do.
Jamiāwara	...	619,759	...	80	200	...	Sisodiā.
Sukhera	...	46 090	...	50	300	...	
Ghiyaspur	...	138 890	...	60	800	...	Gond, Ahir.
Qiyāmpur .. .	...	175,350	...	110	300	...	Deorā.
Kotri	...	303	...	50	500	...	
Mandesor, with suburb. district, 2 mahals ..	....	1,651,920	28,660	100	400	...	Rājput.

Sarkār of Gāgron.

Containing 12 *Mahals.* 63,529 *Bighas.* Revenue 4,535,794 *Dāms.*

	Bighas Biswas	Revenue D.	Sayurghāl D.	Cavalry	Infantry	Elephants	Castes
Urmāl	...	502,774 in money.	...	...	...	...	
Akbarpur	...	62,500	...	...	...	...	
Panch Pahār	21,399	1,573.560	...	...	...	...	
Chechat	...	222,640	...	...	...	...	
Khairābād	17,136	646.000	...	...	...	...	
Rāepur	9,716	28,730	...	...	...	...	
Sonel	9,638	281,909	...	...	...	...	
Sendar (=Sandhara) ..	695	81,929	...	...	...	...	
Ghāti	...	600,046	...	...	...	...	
Gāgron, with suburb. district, has a stone fort	...	19,781 in money.	...	...	...	...	
Nimthor	4-945	608,834	...	...	...	...	

Sarkār of Kotri Parāwa.

Containing 10 *Mahals.* 190,039 *Bighas.* Revenue 8,031,920 *Dāms.* Castes various. Cavalry 2,245. Infantry 6,500.

	Biswas	Revenue D.	Sayurghāl D.	Cavalry	Infantry	Elephants	Castes
Alot (*missp.* Āsop) ..	42 220	1,733 927	250	700		...	...
Ājigarh	4,553	855 612	350	200		...	Rajut, Deora.
Āwar	9 204	532,056	...	80	300	...	
Barod	20,224	923,667	...	160	400	..	Rajput, Sondhia.
Dāgdudhālia	13.881	458,144	...	125	400	...	Do. do.
Soyat	13 381	693,585	...	240	500	...	Do. Deora.
Kotri Parāwa, 2 mahals with suburb. dist. ..	46,046	1,856,566	...	770	1,800	...	Kayath.
Gangrār	200,615	1,066,683	...	200	700	...	Rajput, Sondha.
Ghosi (? Gadguchi) ..	2,597	116,380	...	60	200	...	Sondhia.

Princes of Mālwa.

I.

Five Rājahs of this dynasty reigned in succession,
387 years, 7 months, 3 days.
(Dates from Prinsep.)

		Ys.	Ms.	Ds.
B. C. 840.	Dhanji, (Dhananjaya, a name of Arjun, about 785 before Vikramaditya), ...	100	0	0
,, 760.	Jit Chandra, ...	86	7	3
,, 670.	Sālivāhana, ...	1	0	0
,, 680.	Nirvāhana, ...	100	0	0
,, 580.	Putrāj, (Putra Rājas of Vansāvalis without issue), ...	100	2	0

II.

Eighteen princes of the Ponwār caste reigned
1,062 years, 11 months, 17 days.

		Ys.	Ms.	Ds.
B. C. 400.	Aditya Panwār, (elected by nobles. [Co-temp. Sapor, A. D. 191. Wilford.	86	7	3
,, 390.	Brahmarāj, (reigned in Vidarbhanagar), ...	30	7	3
,, 360.	Atibrahma, (at Ujain, defeated in the north), ...	90	0	0
,, 271.	Sadhroshana, (Sadasva Sena. Vāsudeva of Wilford, Basdeo of Ferishta, A. D. 390, father-in-law of Bahrām Gor. revived Kanauj dynasty), ...	80	0	0
,, 191.	Hemarth, (Heymert, Harsha Megha, killed in battle), ...	100	0	0
,, 31.	Gandharb,* (Gardabharupa, Bahrāmgor of Wilford), ...	35	0	0
B. C. 56.	Bikramjit, (Vikramaditya. Tuār caste, 3rd of Wilford), ...	100	2	3

* Under power of a curse, in consequences of a crime, he was changed into an ass resuming his human form only at night. Hemar I, notwithstanding, gave him his daughter in marriage and she gave birth to Vikramaditya.

		Ys.	Ms.	Ds.
A. D. 44.	Chandrasen of the same race (possessed himself of all Hindustān), ...	86	3	2
,, 135.	Kharagsen, (Surya Sena, w. 676),	85	0	0
,, 215.	Chitarkot, ...	1	0	0
,, 216.	Kanaksen, (cōnquered Saurashtra [Surāt and Gujerāt] founder of the Mewār family, ancestry traced by Jain Chronicles consulted by Tod, to Sumitra, 56th from Rāma), ...	86	0	0
,, 302.	Chandrapāl of the same race, ...	100	0	0
,, 402.	Mahendrapāl, ...	7	0	0
,, 409.	Karamchand of the same race, ...	1	0	1
,, 410.	Bijainand, (Vijyananda), ...	60	0	0
,, 470.	Munja, (killed in the Deccan, reigned A. D. 993, according to Tod).			
,, 483.	Bhoja, (by Tod 567 A. D. The other two Rājās Bhoja, Tod fixes in 665 [from Jain MSS.] and 1035, the father Udāyati. Kālidās flourished), ...	100	0	0
,, 583.	Jayachand, (put aside in favour of the following), ...	10	0	2

III.

Eleven princes of the Tonwar, (Tuar) caste reigned 142 years, 3 days.

A. D. 593.	Jitpāp, ...	5	0	0
,, 598.	Rānā Rāju, ...	5	0	0
,, 603.	Rānā Bāju, ...	1	0	3
,, 604.	Rānā Jaj Jalu, *var,* and U. T.), ...	20	0	0
A. D. 620.	Rāna Chandra, ...	30	0	0
,, 654.	Rāna Bahadur, ...	5	0	0
,, 659.	Rāe Bakhmal, (Bakhtmal), ...	5	0	0
,, 664.	Rāe Sukanpāl, ...	5	0	0
,, 669.	Rāe Kiratpāl, ...	5	0	0
,, 674.	Rāe Anangpāl, (rebuilt and peopled Delhi 791, Tod.), ...	60	0	0
,, 734.	Kunwarpāl, ...	1	0	0

IV.

Eleven princes of the Chauhān caste reigned 140 years.

			Ys.	Ms.	Ds.
A. D.	735.	Rājā Jagdeva, ...	10	0	0
,,	745.	Jagannāth, his nephew, ...	10	0	0
,,	755.	Hardeva, ...	15	0	0
,,	770.	Bāsdeva, ...	16	0	0
,,	786.	Srideva, ...	15	0	0
,,	801.	Dharmdeva, ...	14	0	0
,,	815.	Baldeva, ...	10	0	0
,,	825.	Nānakdeva, ...	9	0	0
,,	834.	Kiratdeva, ...	11	0	0
,,	845.	Pithurā, ...	21	0	0
,,	866.	Māldeva, (conquered by Shaikh Shāh father of Ala u'd din), ...	9	0	0

V.

Ten princes reigned 77 years.

A. D.	1037.	Shaikh Shāh, (from Ghazni), ...	70	0	0
,,	1037.	Dharmrāja Sud, (Vizier during minority of, ...	20	0	0
,,	1057.	Ālā u'd din, son of Shaikh Shāh, put the Vizier to death, ...	20	0	0
,,	,,	Kamāl u'd din, (murdered by, ...	12	0	0
,,	1069.	Jitpal Chauhān, (Jaya Sing of Delhi and Lahore? 977, a descendant of Mānikya Rai?)'	20	0	0
,,	1089.	Harchand, ...	20	0	0
,,	1109.	Kiratchand, ...	2	0	0
,,	1111.	Ugarsen, ...	13	0	0
,,	1124.	Surajchand, ...	12	0	0
A. D.	1136.	Birsèn, (dispossessed by the following), ...	10	0	0

VI.

Eight princes reigned 205 years.

A. D.	1146.	Jalāl u'd din, (an Afghan), ...	22	0	0
,,	1168.	Ā'alam Shah, (killed in battle by, ...	24	0	0

		Ys.	Ms.	Ds.
A.D. 1192.	Kharagsen, son of Birsen (Birsen, emigrated to Kāmrup, married the king's daughter, succeeded to the kingdom and regained Malwah), ...	8	0	0
,, 1200.	Narbāhan. { Udayādityadeva, Naravarmadeva, Yasovarmadeva, Jayavarmadeva, Lakhan,* ...	20	0	0
,, 1220.	Birsāl, ...	16	0	0
,, 1236.	Puranmal, ...	39	0	0
,, 1268.	Haranand, ...	62	0	0
,, 1330.	Sakat Sing, (killed at the invasion of the following), ...	60	0	0

VII.

Eleven princes reigned 142 years, 2 months 4 days.†

		Ys.	Ms.	Ds.
A. D. 1390.	Bahādur Shāh, (king of Deccan, killed at Delhi), ...	some ms.		
,, 1390.	Dilāwar Khān Ghori, (viceroy of Mālwah assumed sovereignty), ...	20	0	0
,, 1405.	Hoshang Shāh, ...	30	0	0
,, 1432.	Muhammad Shāh, (Ghizni Khān, poisoned), ...	some ms.		
,, 1435.	Sultān Mahmud, uncle of Hoshang, (Rānā of Chitor Kumbho, presents *tankas* coined in his own name, 1450), ...	34	0	0

---

* These five reigned A.D. 1137—1143 according to the Ujjain inscription.

† Correct list of Malwa Sultans—

Dilawar Kh. Ghuri	A.H. 794/1932 A.D.
Hushang Sh.	808/1405
Muhammad Sh. (Ghazni Kh.)	838/1435
Ma'sud	839/1436
Mahmud I.	839/1436
Ghiyās-ud-din	873/1469
Nāsir-ud-din	905/1500
Mahmud II.	916-937/1510-31

		Ys.	Ms.	Ds.
A.D. 1469.	Sultān Ghiyās u'd din, ...	32	0	0
,, 1500.	,, Nāsir u'd din, (his son Shahāb u'd din revolts),	11	4	3
,, 1512.	,, Mahmud II, (younger son, last of the Khiljis),	26	6	11
,,	Qādir Shāh, ...	6	0	0
,,	Shujāat Khān, known as Shujāwal Khān, ...	12	0	0
,,	Bāz Bahādur.			

In 1534 Malwah was incorporated with Gujerāt kingdom; in 1568 as a province of Akbar's empire.

It is said that two thousand, three hundred and fifty-five years, five months and twenty-seven days prior to this, the 40th year of the Divine Era [761 B.C.] an ascetic named *Mahābāh*, kindled the first flame in a fire-temple, and devoting himself to the worship of God, resolutely set himself to the consuming of his rebellious passions. Seekers after eternal welfare gathered round him, zealous in a life of mortification. About this time the Buddhists began to take alarm and appealed to the temporal sovereign, asserting that in this fire-temple, many living things were consumed in flaming fire, and that it was advisable that Brahmanical rites should be set aside, and that he should secure the preservation of life. It is said that their prayer was heard, and the prohibition against the said people was enforced. These men of mortified appetites resolved on redress, and sought by prayer a deliverer who should overthrow Buddhism and restore their own faith. The Supreme Justice brought forth from this fire-temple, now long grown cold, a human form, resplendent with divine majesty, and bearing in its hand a flashing sword. In a short space, he enthroned himself on the summit of power, and renewed the Brahmanical observance. He assumed the name of *Dhananjaya* and coming from the Deccan, established his seat of government at Mālwah and attained to an advanced age.

When Putrāj, the fifth in descent from him. died without issue, the nobles elected Aditya Ponwār his successor, and this was the origin of the sovereignty of this house. On the death of Hemarth in battle, Gandharb, the chosen, was raised to the throne. The Hindus believe that he is the same as Hemarth whom the Supreme Ruler introduced among the celestials in the form of a *Gandharb*[1] and then clothed in human shape. Thus he became universally known by this name and prospered the world by his justice and munificence. A son was born to him named Bikramājit who kept aflame the lamp of his ancestors and made extensive conquests. The Hindus to this day keep the beginning of his reign as an era and relate wonderful accounts of him. Indeed he possessed a knowledge of talismans and incantations and gained the credulity of the simple. Chandrapāl obtained in turn the supreme power and conquered all Hindustān. Bijainand was a prince devoted to the chase. Near a plant of the Munja[2] he suddenly came upon a new-born infant. He brought him up as his own son and called him by the name of Munja. When his own inevitable time approached, his son Bhoja was of tender age. He therefore appointed Munja his successor, who ended his life in the wars of the Deccan.

Bhoja succeeded to the throne in the 541st year of the era of Bikramājit and added largely to his dominions, administering the empire with justice and liberality. He held wisdom in honour, the learned were treated with distinction, and seekers after knowledge were encouraged by his support. Five hundred [*correctly* nine] sages, the most erudite of the age, shone as the gathered wisdom of his court and were entertained in a manner becoming their dignity and merit. The foremost of these was Barruj [Vararuchi], a second was Dhanpāl [Dhanwantari] who have composed works of great interest and left them to intelligent seekers of truth, as a precious possession. At the birth of Bhoja, either through a grave miscalculation of the astrologers or some inadvertence on the part of those who cast his horos-

---

[1] A class of demigods who inhabit the heaven of Indra and form the celestial choir at the banquets of the deities. He appears in the lists as *Gandhapāla,* fostered by an ass, *Gandha-rupa* or *Harshamegha,* epithets of the same animal. According to Wilford the Pandits who assisted Abul Fazl disfigured the chronology of the supplement to the *Agni-purana.* Of Salivahana and Naravahana they made two distinct persons as well as of Bahrām with the title of Gor in Persian and Himār, or the Ass in Arabic. Thus they introduced Himār or Hemarth and Gor or Gandharb.

[2] *Saccharum munja,* a rush or grass from the fibres of which a string is prepared of which the Brahmanical girdle is properly formed. Munja wrote a geographical description of the world or of India which still exists under the name of *Munja-prati-desa-vyvasthā* or state of various countries. It was afterwards corrected and improved by Rājā Bhoja, and still exists in Gujerāt. Munja transferred the capital from Ujjain to Sonitpura in the Deccan called after him *Munja-pattana* on the Godaveri.

cope, the learned in the stars in consultation announced a nativity of sinister aspect. They prognosticated hazard to the lives of such as sympathised with him, and these to save their own, cast this nursling of fortune in the dust of destitution and exposed him in an inhospitable land. He was there nourished without the intervention of human aid. The sage Barruj, who at that time was not accounted among the learned, having recast his horoscope after profound investigation, foretold the good tidings of a nativity linked to a long life and a glorious reign. This paper he threw in the way of the Rājā, whose heart on reading it, was agitated with the impulse of paternal love. He convened an assembly of the astrologers, and when the nativity was scrutinised, and it was ascertained where the error lay, he went in person and restored Bhoja to favour and opened the eyes of his understanding to the strangeness of fortune. They relate that when the child was eight years old, the short-sighted policy of Munja impelled him to desperate measures and he contemplated putting the innocent boy to death. He entrusted him to some of his trusty followers to make away with him secretly, but these ministers of death spared him, and concealing him, invented a plausible tale. On his taking leave, he gave them a letter telling them to read it to the Rājā in case he should inquire regarding him. Its purport ran as follows :—"How doth darkness of soul in a man cast him out of the light of wisdom, and in unholy machinations stain his hands in the blood of the innocent! No monarch in his senses thinks to carry with him to the grave his kingdom and treasures, but thou by slaying me seemest to imagine that his treasures perpetually endure and that he himself is beyond the reach of harm." The Rājā on hearing this letter, was aroused from his day-dream of fancied security and brooded in remorse over his crime. His agents, when they witnessed the evidences of his sincerity revealed to him what had occurred. He gave thanks to God, welcomed Bhoja with much affection and appointed him his successor.

When his son Jayachand's[1] reign was ended, none of the Ponwār caste was found worthy to succeed. Jitpal of the Tonwar caste, who was one of the principal landowners was elected to the throne, and thus by the vicissitudes of fortune the sovereignty passed into this family.

[1] Jayananda according to Wilford, who gives the next name as Chaitra or Jytepāl and identifies or comounds him with Chandrapala.

When Kunwarpāl died, the royal authority passed into the hands of the Chauhāns. During the reign of Maldeva, Shaikh Shāh came from Ghazni and acquired possession of Mālwah and lived to an advanced age. At his death his son Alā u'd din was a minor, and his chief minister Dharm Rāj Sud occupied the throne. As soon as Alā u'd din came of age, he rose in arms to assert his rights and put to death the disloyal usurper. Jitpal Chauhān, a descendant of Mānik Deva Chauhān, who was in the service of Kamāl-u'd-din, under the impulse of malice and in pride of wealth compassed the destruction of his master and in the hope of gain, acquired for himself eternal perdition. Under the rule of Tipparsen, an intriguing Afghān, getting together some desperate characters as his abettors, laying an ambush for the Rājā, slew him while hunting, and assumed the sovereignty with the title of Jalāl u'd din. Tipparsen had married his son Kharagsen into the family of the Rājā of Kāmrup. The Rājā, for his eminent services, appointed this adopted son his heir, and when the Rājā died, Kharagsen ascended the throne and to avenge his wrongs marched an army against Mālwah and Aālam Shāh was killed in battle.

In the reign of Sakat Singh a prince named Bahādur Shāh advanced from the Deccan and having put the Rājā to death, marched against Delhi and was taken prisoner while fighting against Sultān Shahāb u'd din.

From the time of Sultān Ghiyās u'd din Balban (A.D. 1265) to that of Sultān Muhammad son of Firoz Shāh (A.D. 1387) no serious weakness in the imperial authority betrayed itself, but on his death the empire of Delhi became a prey to distractions. Dilāwar Khān Ghori who had been appointed by him to the government of Mālwah, assumed independence. The Sultān bestowed the government of four provinces upon four individuals who had been faithful to him in his adversity. To Zafar Khān[1] he gave Gujerāt; Khizr Khān was appointed to Multān; Khwājah Sarwar to Jaunpur and Dilāwar Khān to Mālwa. After his death, the time being favourable, each of the four assumed independence. [Persian text confused.]

Alp Khān the son of Dilāwar Khān was elected to the succession under the title of Hoshang. It is said that his father was poisoned by his order whereby he has gained

[1] Zafar Khān took the title of Muzaffar Shāh.

everlasting abhorrence. Sultān Muzaffar of Gujerāt marched against him and took him prisoner and left his own brother Nasir Khān in command of the province. But as he was tyrannous in conduct and ignored the interests of his subjects, Musa, cousin of Hoshang, was raised to the throne. Sultān Muzaffar released Hoshang from confinement and despatched him to Mālwa in company with his own son Ahmad Khān, and in a short time he was restored to power. On the death of Muzaffar, he perfidiously marched against Gujerāt, but meeting with no success, returned. On several subsequent occasions he attacked Sultān Ahmad of Gujerāt but was shamefully defeated.

On one occasion cunningly disguised as a merchant, he set out for *Jājnagar*.[1] The ruler of that country accompanied by a small retinue visited the caravan. Hoshang took him prisoner and hastened back. While journeying together, Hoshang told him that he had been induced to undertake this expedition in order to procure a supply of elephants and added that if his people attempted a rescue, the prince's life should pay the penalty. The prince therefore sending for a number of valuable elephants, presented them to him and was set at liberty.

Hoshang was engaged in wars with Mubārak Shāh son of Khizr Khān viceroy[2] of Delhi, with Sultān Ibrahim of the Jaunpur dynasty, and with Sultān Ahmad of the Deccan.[3] On his death, the nobles, in accordance with his bequest, raised his son Nasir Khān to the throne under the

---

[1] Jājpur on the Baitarani river in Orissa, capital of the province under the Lion Dynasty, the Gajpati or Lords of Elephants. This story occurs in the Tab. Akbari, p. 537, and in Ferishta, Vol. II, p. 236. (Briggs, IV, 178). Ferishta's account is that in A.H. 825 (1421—2), Hoshang with a 1,000 picked cavalry disguised as a merchant set out for Jājnagar, one month's journey from Mālwa and took with him a number of cream-coloured horses, much sought after by the ruler of Orissa and stuffs of various kinds, his object being to exchange these for elephants the better to meet Sultān Ahmad of Gujerāt in the field. On his arrival near Jājnagar he sent to inform the Rājah of the presence of his caravan and the prince arrived with a number of elephants to barter for the horses, or ready to pay in coin, as the need arose. The horses were caparisoned and the stuffs laid out for inspection, when a storm of rain came on and the lightning frightening the elephants, they trampled on the goods and caused great damage. Hoshang tore his hair and swore that life was no longer worth having and at a signal, his men mounted and attacked the Rājā's guard, and put them to flight. Capturing the Rājā, Hoshang discovered himself and excused his action on the ground of destruction of his property. He then stated his object. The Rājah admired his audacity and 75 elephants purchased his own release. Hoshang carried him as far as the frontier and set him at liberty.

[2] He never assumed the royal title but styled himself viceroy of Timur in whose name the coin was minted and the *Khutbah* read.

[3] Ahmad Shah Wali of the Bahmani dynasty (1422—35)

title of Muhammad Shāh. Mahmud Khān, cousin of Sultān Hoshang, basely bribed his cup bearer and that venal wretch poisoned the Sultān's wine. The generals of the army kept his death secret hoping to place his son Masaud Khān upon the throne and they sent to confer with Mahmud Khān. He replied that worldly affairs had no longer any interest for him but that if his presence in council were necessary, they must come to him. They foolishly went to his house and were placed in confinement, and by the aid of some disloyal mercenary partisans, he seized upon the sovereignty of Mālwa and was proclaimed under the title of Sultān Mahmud (Khilji). Upon such a wretch,[1] in its wondrous vicissitudes thus did Fortune smile and the awe he inspired secured him the tranquil possession of power. He waged wars with Sultān Muhammad son of Mubārak Shāh, king of Delhi, with Sultān Ahmad, king of Gujerāt, with Sultān Hussain Sharqi of Jāunpur, and with Rānā Kumbha of Mewār.

Khwājah Jamāl u'd din Astarābādi[2] was sent to him as ambassador by Abu Said Mirza with costly gifts which greatly redounded to his glory. Mahmud II (1512 A.D.) through his ungenerous treatment of his adopted followers[3] fell into misfortune but was again reinstated in power by the aid of Sultān Muzaffar Shāh (II) of Gujerāt (A.D. 1511-26). Through his reckless bravery in battle he was taken prisoner by the Rānā (Sanga)[4] who treated him with generosity and restored him to his kingdom. He was again captured in action against Sultān Bahādur of Gujerāt and conveyed to the fortress of Chāmpāner. He was killed (A.D. 1526) on his way thither and Mālwa was incorporated with Gujerāt until it was conquered by Humayun. When this monarch returned to Agra, one of the relations of Sultān Mahmud, by name Mallu, seized on the government of Mālwa under the title of Qādir Khān.

---

[1] He proved notwithstanding, the ablest and most chivalrous of all the Mālwa princes.

[2] This ambassador arrived with presents from Mirza Sultān Said 3rd in descent from Tamerlane who reigned over Transoxiana and held his court at Bokhārā—grandfather of Bāber. He returned with presents of elephants, singing and dancing girls, Arab horses and an ode in the vernacular composed by Mahmud himself which Abu Said valued above all the other gifts. Ferishta II, 254.

[3] The reference is to his dismissal of his Hindu minister Medni Rāe and the Rājput troops to whom he owed his kingdom when deserted by his nobles at the beginning of his reign.

[4] Rana Sanga (A.D. 1508—1529) under whom Mewār reached its highest prosperity, fought Babar in 1526.

During the supremacy of the usurper Sher Khān the control of the province was invested in Shujāat Khan, who rebelled under the reign of Salim Khān and assumed independence under Mubāriz Khān.

On his death, his eldest son Bāyizid succeeded under the title of Bāz Bahādur until the star of his Majesty's fortune arose in the ascendant and this fertile province was added to the imperial dominions.

May the robe of this daily-widening empire be bordered with perpetuity, and its inhabitants enjoy to their hearts' fill a prosperity that shall never decay.

SUBAH OF DĀNDES.

This flourishing country was called *Khāndes*, but after the capture the fortress of *Asir* (1600 A.D.) and when this province fell under the government of prince Dānyāl, it was known as *Dāndes.*[1] It is situated in the second climate. Its length from *Borgāon* which adjoins *Handiah* to *Lalang* which is on the borders of the territory of *Ahmadnagar* is 75 *kos*. Its breadth from *Jāmod* adjoining *Berār* to *Pāl* which borders *Mālwa* is 50, and in some parts only 25 *kos*. On its east is *Berār;* to the north, *Mālwa;* to the south, *Gālnah* (Jālna)* : to the west, the southern chain of the mountains of *Mālwa*. The rivers are numerous, the principal being the *Tāpti* which rises between *Berār* and *Gondwāna,* the *Tabi* which has its source from the same quarter and which is also called the *Purna,* and the *Girna* near *Chāpra*. The climate is pleasant and the winter temperate.

Jowāri is chiefly cultivated, of which, in some places, there are three crops in a year, and its stalk is so delicate and pleasant to the taste that it is regarded in the light of a fruit. The rice is of fine quality, fruits grow plentifully and betel leaves are in abundance. Good cloth stuffs are woven here : those called *Siri Sāf* and *Bhiraun* come from *Dharangāon*.

Asir is the residence of the governor. It is a fortress on a lofty hill. Three other forts encompass it which for strength and loftiness are scarcely to be equalled. A large and flourishing city is at its foot. *Burhānpur* is a large city three *kos* distant from the *Tapti*. It lies in latitude 21° 40′, and is embellished with many gardens and the sandal-wood also grows here. It is inhabited by people of all countries and handicraftsmen ply a thriving trade. In the summer, clouds of dust fly which in the rains turns to mud.

Aādilābād is a fine town. Near it is a lake, a noted place of worship, and the crime of Rājā Jasrat (Dasarath)[1]

---

* *Galna* is 20 m. S.W. of Dhulia in W. Khandesh, while *Jalna* is far to the south of E. Khandesh, beyond the Ajanta range.

[1] Dasarath's crime was committed in his youth when he unwittingly killed the hermit's son in the forests by the banks of the river Sarayu in Oudh. The story is told in Rāmāyan, Bk. II, Sec. 63 (see Griffith's translation, Vol. II, p. 243). He was cursed by the bereaved father and fated to be similarly agonised for the loss of his son in after years.

was expiated at this shrine. It is full all the year round and it irrigates a large area of cultivation.

Chāngdeo is a village near which the *Tapti* and the *Purnā* unite, and the confluence is accounted a place of great sanctity. It is called *Chakra Tirth.* Adjacent to it is an image of *Mahādeo.* They relate that a blind man carried about him an image of Mahādeo which he worshipped daily. He lost the image at this spot. For a time he was sore distressed, but forming a similar image of sand, he placed it on a little eminence and adored it in a like spirit. By a miracle of divine will, it became stone and exists to this day. Near it a spring rises which is held to be the Ganges. An ascetic by the power of the Almighty was in the habit of going to the Ganges daily from this spot. One night the river appeared to him in a dream, and said, "Undertake these fatigues no longer; I myself will rise up in thy cell." Accordingly in the morning it began to well forth and is flowing at the present time.

Jāmod is a rich *parganah.* In its neighbourhood is a fort on a high hill called *Pipaldol. Dhāmarni* is a prosperous town. Near it is a tank in which a hot spring perpetually rises and which is an object of worship.

Choprah is a large flourishing town, near which is a shrine called *Rāmesar* at the confluence of the *Girna* and the *Tapti.* Pilgrims from the most distant parts frequent it. Adjacent to it is the fort of *Malkāmad* [=Malkheda].

Thālner was for a time the capital of the *Fāruqi* princes. The fort though situated on the plain is nevertheless of great strength.

This *Subah* contains 32 *parganahs.* Scarce any land is out of cultivation and many of the villages more resemble towns. The peasantry are docile and industrious. The provincial force is formed of *Kolis, Bhils* and *Gonds.* Some of these can tame lions, so that they will obey their commands, and strange tales are told of them.

Its revenue is 12,647,062, *Berāri tankahs* as will appear in the statement. After the conquest of Asir, this revenue was increased by 50 per cent. The *tanka* is reckoned at 24 *dāms.* The total is therefore, 455,294,232 Akbari *dāms.* (Rs. 11,382, 355-12-9).

Sarkār of Dāndes.

Containing 32 *maḥals.* Revenue in money 12,647,062 Tankas.

	Tankahs		Tankahs
Asir, north of Burhanpur ...	1,060,221	Chāndsir, south	198,900
Atrāl, south	264,249	Jalod, south [Jalam?] ...	317,205
Erandwel, east, by south ...	543,328	Chopra, west	730,965
Amalnerā	2,406,180	Dāngri, south	315,325
Warangāon, east by south ...	215,504	Dāmri, west	325,300
Pāchorah, west	206,728	Rāver, west	883,655
Purmāl, west	162,830	Renpur, east [? Ratanpur]	820,971
Bodwad, south-west ...	183,540	Sāvdā, south	430,008
Names omitted in all MSS ...	58,511 246,112	Shendurni, between E. and W.	104,754
Bāhil, south	290,311	Aādilābād, east by south ...	527,223
Bhadgāon, south	256,331	Laling, south	352,644
Betāwad, south	320,782	Lohārā, south	247,965
Bāer [Bhāmer], west by south	595,968	Mānjrud, east [Mānjal] ...	104,965
Thālner, west by south ...	594,239	Nasirābād, south	824,925
Jāmod, east	175,844	Name omitted in all MSS. ...	316,338
Jāmner, midway between E. and W.	470,042		

In ancient times this country was a waste and but few people lived about the fortress of Asir. The locality was traditionally connected with *Ashwatthāmā** and established as a shrine. It is related that *Malik Rāji* from whom *Bahādur*[1] is the ninth in descent, under stress of misfortune came from *Bidar* to these parts and established himself in the village of *Karondā*,[2] a dependency of *Thālner*, but being molested by the natives, he repaired to Delhi and took service under Sultān Firoz. The king admired his skill as a huntsman, and his reward being left to his own choice, he received a grant of that village and by judicious policy acquired possession of other estates and reclaimed much waste land. In the year 784 A.H. (A.D. 1382), he made *Thālner* his seat of government, assumed the title of Aādil Shāh and reigned for 17 years. He was succeeded by his son Ghizni Khān under the title of Nasir Shāh, after which this province became known as Khāndes. He reigned 40 years, 6 months, and 26 days. On his death his son Mirān Shāh administered the State. By some he is called Aādil Shāh. He occupied the throne 3 years, 8

* Son of Drona, a hero of the *Mahābhārat*.

[1] Bahādur Khān Fāruqi, 1596 A.D. last of the dynasty.

[2] According to T., his father was Khān Jahān one of the ministers in the court of Alā-ud-din Khilji and of Muhammad Tughlaq. He claimed descent from the Caliph Omar called by Muhammad "al Fāruq" or the discriminator, on the day that he publicly professed his conversion, because on that day "Islām was made manifest and truth distinguished from falsehood." See as Suyuti's *Hist. of the Caliphs*, Jarrett's translation, p. 118. Karonda= *Karwand*, 12 m. n. of Thalner.

months and 23 days. He was followed by his son Mubārik Shāh Chaukandi Sultān during 17 years, 6 months and 29 days. His son Aādil Shāh Aynā whose name was Ahsan Khān, had a prosperous reign of 46 years, 8 months and 2 days. He removed to *Burhānpur* and made himself master of Asir. Sultān Ahmad of Gujerāt, the founder of Ahmedābād, gave him his daughter in marriage. At his death, his brother Dāud Shāh reigned for 7 years, 1 month and 17 days. Aādil Shāh (II) son of Hasan took refuge in Gujerāt. Sultān Māhmud Bigarah Rāji gave him in marriage *Ruqayya* the daughter of Sultān Muzaffar, (his son) and accompanying him to *Khāndes*, restored him to his kingdom and returned to his own. He reigned 13 years. He left two sons, Mirān Muhammad Shāh and Mubārik Shāh. Sultān Bahādur of Gujarāt being on terms of friendly alliance with the first-named[1] made him his heir, and guadian to his nephew Mahmud and his own brother Mubārik. Mirān Shāh from a sense of their deserts, and with political sagacity did them no injury and contenting himself with the kingdom of Khāndes, restored Mahmud to the sovereignty of Gujerāt. He reigned 16 years, 2 months and 3 days. When the measure of his days was full, the nobles raised his son Rāji to the throne. Mirān Mubārik wrested it from him and reigned in succession to his brother, administering the government for 31 years, 6 months and 5 days. He was succeeded by his son Mirān Muhammad who reigned 9 years, 9 months and 15 days. When he died, his younger brother Rāja Ali Khān[2] was elected and assumed the title of Aādil Shāh. His administration was conducted with ability and he was killed in the

[1] His sister being mother of Mirān Shāh.
[2] He married a sister of Abul Fazl.

Khandesh Muslim rulers—

Malik Rājā, Rājā Ahmad	A.H. 784/1382 A.D.
Nasir Khan	801/1399
Adil Kh. I.	840/1437
Mubārak Kh. I, Chaukanda	844/1441
'Adil Kh. II, Ainā	861/1457
Dāud Kh.	907/1501
Ghazni Kh.	914/1508
Hasan Kh.	914/1508
'Alam Kh. (usurper)	914/1508
'Adil Kh. III. ('Alam Kh.)	914/1509
Mirān Muhammad Sh. I.	926/1520
Ahmad Sh.	943/1537
Mubārak Sh. II.	943/1537
Muhammad Sh. II.	974/1566
Hasan Sh.	984/1576
'Adil Sh. IV. (Rājā 'Ali Kh.)	985/1577
Bahādur Sh. (Qadr Kh.)	1006-1009/1597-1601

wars of the Deccan fighting on the side of his Majesty's victorious troops. He was buried at Burhānpur, after a successful reign of 21 years, 3 months and 20 days. At his death the succession devolved on Khizr Khān, his son, who took the name of Bahādur Shāh. But the star of his destiny was obscure and in the 45th year of the Divine era, he was deprived of his kingdom as has been recorded in its proper place.

SUBAH OF BERĀR.

Its original name was *Wārdātat,* from *Wārdā,* the river of that name and *tat,* a bank. It is situated in the second climate. Its length from *Baithalwādi* to *Biragarh* is 200 *kos,* its breadth from *Bidar* to *Handia* 180 *kos.* On the east lies *Biragarh* adjoining *Bastar;* to the north is *Handia;* to the south *Telingāna;*[1] on the west *Mahkarābād.* It is a tract—situated between two hill-ranges having a southerly direction. One of these is called *Bandah* upon which are the forts of *Gāwilgarh, Narnāla* and *Melgarh.* The other is *Sahia,* where rise the forts of Mahur and Rāmgarh.

The climate and cultivation of this province are remarkably good. There are many rivers, the principal of which is called *Ganga Gautami* called also the *Godavari.* As the Ganges of Hindustān is chiefly connected with the worship of Mahādeo, so is this river with (the *Rishi*) *Gautama.* Wonderful tales are related regarding it and it is held in great sanctity. It rises near *Trimbak*[2] in the *Sahia* range and passing through the country of *Ahmadnagar,* enters *Berār* and flows into *Telingāna.* When Jupiter enters the sign Leo, pilgrims flock from all parts to worship.[3] The *Tāli* and *Tapti* are also venerated. Another river the *Purnā* rises near *Dewalgāon,* and again the *Wardā*

---

[1] As this province corresponds geographically with the ancient *Tri-Kalinga,* Gen. Cunningham thinks Telingana to be probably, a slight contraction of Tri-Kalinga. See *Anc. Geo. Ind.,* p. 519.

[2] In the Nāsik District, about 50 miles from the Indian Ocean. At this spot is an artificial reservoir, reached by a flight of 90 steps, into which the water trickles drop by drop from the lips of an earthen image shrouded by a canopy of stone.

[3] Once in every 12 years, a great bathing festival called *Pushkaram,* is held on the banks of Godaveri, alternately with the other eleven sacred rivers of India. The most frequented spots are the source at Trimbuk, Bhadrāchalam on the left bank about 100 miles above Rājāmahendri, the latter itself, and the village of Kotipāli. *I. G. Tāli,* variants *Pāli, Pāti.*

issues forth ten *kos* higher up than the source of the *Tāli*. The *Napta** also rises near *Dewalgāon*.

In this country the term for a *Chaudhri* [village headman] is *Desmukh*, for a *Qānungo*, *Des Pāndia;* the *Muqaddam* is called *Patil* and the *Patwāri*, *Kulkarni*.

Elichpur is a large city and the capital. A flower violet in colour is found here and is very fragrant. It is called *Bhui champah*[1] and grows close to the ground.

At the distance of 7 *kos* is *Gāwil*, a fortress of almost matchless strength. In it is a spring at which they water weapons of steel.

Panār is a strong fort on an eminence which two streams surround on three sides.

Kherla is a strong fort on a plain. In the middle of it is a small hill which is a place of worship. Four *kos* from this is a well, into which if the bone of any animals be thrown it petrifies, like a *cowrie-shell* only smaller. To the east of this resides a *Zamindār* named *Chātwāi* (=Jātibā) who is master of 2,000 cavalry, 50,000 foot and more than 100 elephants. Another such *Zamindār* is named *Dādhi Rāo* who possesses 200 cavalry, and 5,000 foot. To the north is *Nāhar Rāo* a chief whose force consists of 200 horse and 5,000 foot. Formerly in this neighbourhood, was a *Zamindār* named *Hatiā*, but now his possessions are under other subjection and the whole race are *Gonds*. Wild elephants are found in this country. The chiefs were always tributary to the kings of Mālwa; the first, to the governor of *Garha*, and the others to the government of *Handia*. *Narnālah* is a strong fortress on a hill, containing many buildings. *Bija Rāo* is a *Zamindār* in the neighbourhood who has a force of 200 cavalry and 5,000 foot. Another is *Dungar Khān* with 50 horse and 3,000 foot: both of the *Gond* tribe. Near *Bālāpur* are two streams, about the borders of which are found various kinds of pretty stones, which are cut and kept as curiosities. Six *kos* distant was the head-quarters of Prince Sultān Murād which grew into a fine city under the name *Shahpur*.

Near *Melgarh* is a spring which petrifies wood and other substances that are thrown into it.

---

* *Napta*—doubtfully written in Persian. The great *Penganga* is evidently meant, but only one small feeder of it rises here; NPTA=PNNA.

[1] The *S. ul M.* calls it *Bhuin Champa* and adds "it grows also in Bengal; it shoots from the gronnd with leaves like the ginger-plant and till the rainy season it continues in growth and is green. In the winter it withers away and disappears altogether." The word is properly *Bhum Champak*, "The ground Champak", and is the Kœmpferia Rotunda.

Kallam (Kalamb), is an ancient city of considerable importance; it is noted for its buffaloes. In the vicinity is a *Zamindār* named *Babjeo* of the *Gond* tribe, more generally known as *Chāndā* : a force of 1,000 horse and 40,000 foot is under his command. *Birāgarh* which has a diamond mine and where figured cloths and other stuffs are woven, is under his authority. It is but a short time since that, he wrested it from another chief. Wild elephants abound.

About *Bāsim* is an indigenous race for the most part proud and refractory called *Hatkars* : their force consists of 1,000 cavalry and 5,000 infantry. *Banjāra* is another *Zamindāri*, with 100 horse and 1,000 foot. At the present time it is under the authority of a woman. Both tribes are Rājputs.

Māhur is a fort of considerable strength situated on a hill. Adjacent is a temple dedicated to *Durgā*, known in this country as *Jagadathā* [=Jagatdhātri]. Here the buffaloes are of a fine breed and yield half a *man* and more of milk. The *Zamindār* is a Rājput named *Indradeo* and is entitled *Rānā*. He commands 100 horse and 1,000 foot.

Mānikdrug is a remarkable fort on a hill surrounded by extensive forests. It is near *Chandā*, but up to the present is independent territory.

Jitanpur is a village in the Sarkār of *Pāthri*, where there is a thriving trade in jewels and other articles of value.

Telingānah was subject to *Qutb ul Mulk*[1] but for some time past has been under the authority of the ruler of Berār.

In *Indur* and *Nirmal* there exist mines of steel and other metals. Shapely stone utensils are also carven here. The breed of buffaloes is fine and, strangely enough, the domestic cocks are observed to have bones and blood of a black colour.* A *Zamindār* called *Chanāneri*,[2] is *Desmukh*, a man of the most distinguished character, who has a force of 300 horse. *Rāmgir* is a strong fort on a hill, enclosed by forests. Wild elephants are numerous. It has not as yet been annexed to the empire.

---

[1] *Warangal* was the ancient capital of this kingdom founded by the Narapati Andhras which was also considered to include the coast territory from the mouth of the Ganges to that of the Kistnā known as Kalinga. After the invasion of Alā u'd din in 1303, it continued with some interruptions under Hindu rule till its remains were incorporated in the dominions of Quli Qutb Shāh the founder of the Qutb Shāhi dynasty, in 1512 with Golconda as its capital.

* See Constable's ed. of Bernier, p. 251, note.

[2] *Var. Jayaberi.*

Lonār is a division of *Mehkar*, and a place of great sanctity. The Brahmans call it *Bishan Gayā*. There are three *Gayās*, where the performance of good works can be applied as a means of deliverance to the souls of deceased ancestors; namely, *Gayā* in *Behār* which is dedicated to *Brahma*, *Gayā* near *Bijāpur* dedicated to *Rudra*, and this one. Here is also a reservoir, having a spring in it of great depth, and measuring a *kos* in length and in breadth, and surrounded by lofty hills. The water is brackish, but when taken from the centre or at its sides, it is sweet. It contains the essential materials for the manufacture of glass and soap, and saltpetre is here produced and yields a considerable revenue.

On the summit of a hill is a spring at the mouth of which is carved the figure of a bull. The water never flows from this spring to the other, but when the 30th lunar day (conjunction) falls on a Monday, its stream flows into the large reservoir. In the neighbourhood is a *Zamindār* called *Wāilah* of the Rājput tribe, commanding 200 horse and 2,000 foot. Another is called *Sarkath*, also a Rājput, and possesses 100 horse and 1,000 foot.

Batialah is a fort of considerable strength on a hill, of which *Pātāl Nagari* is a dependency. In the sides of the hill twenty-four temples have been cut, each containing remarkable idols. The *zamindar is Medni Rāo*, a Rajput, with 200 horse and 1,000 foot. Another is *Kāmdeo*, a Rājput having under him 100 horse and 1,000 foot.

This *Subah* contains 16* *sarkārs* and 142 (should be 242) *parganahs*. From an early period the revenues were taken by a valuation of crops, and since the *tankah* of this country is equal to 8 of Delhi, the gross revenue was 3½ *krors* of *tankahs* or 56 *krors* of *dāms*[1] (Rs. 14,000,000). Some of the Deccani princes increased the revenue to 37,525,350 *tankahs*. In the time of Sultān Murād a further

* But only 13 Sarkars are named in the detailed statement given in the following pages.

[1] This makes 16 *dāms* to the *tankah*. In the revenue statement of Khandesh, the *tankah* is reckoned at 40 *dāms*. That of Gujerāt = two-fifths of a *dām* or 100 to the rupee of 40 *dāms*. Bayley *Hist. of Gujerāt*, p. 6. If Prince Murād's increase be added to that of the Deccani princes, the total gives 40,162,804 *tankahs*. This sum multiplied by 16 results in 642,604,864 *dāms*. As 40 Akbari *dāms* are equivalent to a rupee, the above total represents 16,065,121 rupees. Under Akbar, according to the I. G. the land tax of Berār was Rs. 17,376,117. Under Shāh Jahan, Rs. 13,750,000, and under Aurangzeb, 15,350,625, but the latter amount, taken by Mr. E. Thomas from Manucci, is given by Tieffenthaler from the same authority as 10,587,500. See his dissertation on the apparent inaccuracies of calculation in the registers of the empire and their cause. Vol. I, p. 65.

addition of 2,637,454 Berāri *tankahs* was made. The total amounted to 40,162,704 Berāri *tankahs*. The original amount and the additional increase were thus tabulated, the whole reaching the amount of 642,603,272 Delhi *dāms*.

Eight *parganahs* of the *Sārkar* of *Kallam* (Kalamb) were annexed to *Chāndā*, the revenue of which is not included, nor those of 22 *parganahs* of the *Sarkār* of *Kherla*, held by Chātwā (Jātibā) and some few other *Zamindārs*.

Sarkār of Gāwil.

Containing 46 *parganahs*. Revenue 134,666,140 *dāms*. *Suyurghāl* 12,874,048 *dāms*.

	Revenue D	Suyurghāl D		Revenue D	Suyurghāl D
Sub. dis. of Ellichpur, has a fort of stone and brick on the plain ..	14,000 000	2,800,000	Thugāon	5,600,000	...
Ashti	4,800,000	...	Chakhli, (Banjārās) and Gonds, 400 Cav. 2,500 Inf.) ..	2,400,000	...
Aron	3 200 000	...	Daryāpur	6,400 000	...
Anji	1,600 000	...	Dhāmori	2,718,540	1,118,540
Anjangāon	3,200,000	...	Ridhpur	6,400,000	...
Karyāt Bāhil ..	604,000	...	Sarasgāon	5,296,000	496,000
,, Bāri ..	114,368	82,368	Qasbah Serālā ..	1,835 390	1,015,390
Bhādkali	3 200,000	...	Sarson	4,800,000	...
Basrauli	1,280 000	...	Sālor	340,000	...
Beāwadā	700,000	60,000	Karyāt Sherpur ..	48 000	...
Palaskher	960,000	...	Karhātha Kuram ..	2,400,000	...
Karyāt Pālā, (100 Cav., 2,000 Inf. Gonds)	800,000	....	Kholāpur	4,870,114	70,114
Baror	1,280,000	...	Kāranja, Badhonā, 2 mahals	4,800,000	...
Qasbah Baligāon ..	817,350	177,350	Karanjgāon, Qasbāh Kherah, 2 mahals	523,200	...
,, Postah ..	814,416	594,460	Kumargāon ..	640 000	...
Radharāmani ..	1,825,300	1,625,300	Kāranjā Bibi ..	4 200 000	1,400,000
Tivsā	800,000	...	Kurha	4,800 000	...
Maner	800,000	...	Mane	4,800,000	...
Mānjarkher ..	6,400,000	...	Nandgāon Pith ..		
Mālkher	480,000	...	Nandgāon	6,633,826	233,826
Manglor, (Mangrol)	2,800,000	...	Parganah Nir ..	3,220,000	...
Murjhi [Mojhri] ..	4,800,000	...	Hātgāon	3,200,000	1,600,000
				1,600,000	...

Sarkār of Panār.

Containing 5 *Parganas*. Revenue 13,440,000 *Dāms*.

	Revenue D.		Revenue D.
Sub. dist. of Panār, has a lofty stone fort, surrounded on 3 sides by water ...	4,000,000	Kheljhari, 100 horsemen, 400 foot, Rājput	2,400,000
Sewanbārhā, Kānt Barhā ...	640,000	Māndgāon Karar, 25 horse, 400 foot, Rājput [=Nandgaon Qazi of map] ...	4,800,000
Shelu, 10 horsemen, 400 foot	1,600,000		

Sarkār of Kherla.

Containing 35 *Parganahs.* Revenue 17,600,000 *Dāms.*

	Revenue D.		Revenue D.
Atner, has a stone fort on the plain. Rājput, 100 horse, 2,000 foot	3,200,000	Suburb. dist. of Kherla, Rājput, Lohāri, Goṇd, 50 horse, 2,000 foot ...	3,200,000
Āshta	160,000	Sātner, Atner, 2 mahals. Gond, 100 horse, 2,000 foot	1,600,000
Patan	1,200,000	Sāinkherah	2,000,000
Bhesdahi, Rājput, 100 horse, 2,000 foot	1,600,000	Qasbah Jaror ...	480,000
Baror, Chandji Māli (?) 20 horse, 500 foot	2,800,000	Mundavi, Brahman, Gond, 10 horse, 100 foot ...	480,000
Bāsad, (Māsod), Brahman, Gond, 10 horse, 100 foot ...	480,000	Multāi	
Pauni, Rājput, 40 horse, 500 foot	400,000	Durgah	
		Nārangwari [?Maramjhiri]	
		Mālābil	
Māloi		Bāri	
Mangah		Wāigāon	
Sewah		Deo-thānah	
Jāmkher		Bāri	
Belwali		Saloi	
Sirāi		Rāmjok	
Chakhli		Janābak [? Halbatak] ...	
Khāwar [? Kenaur] ...		Jomār [? Chopar] ...	
Wāldah		Habiyāpur	

Sarkār of Narnāla.

Containing 34 *Parganas.* Revenue 130,954,476 *Dāms.*
Suyurghāl 11,038,422 *Dāms.*

	Revenue D	Suyurghāl D		Revenue D	Suyurghāl D
Ankot	6,470,066	70,066	Dhāror	1,200,000	...
Ādgāon, Dogar, Gond, 50 horse, 2,000 foot ..	8,000,000	...	Dhendā	5,600,000	...
Amner and Jalpi, 2 mahals	4,800,000	...	Rohankher ..	2,000,000	...
Āngolah	11,200 000	...	Rājor	1,000,000	520,000
Bālapur	22 000 000	3,300.000	Sheolā	640,000	...
Panjar	2,000 000	...	Sherpur	48,000	...
Bārsi Tānkli ..	2,864,000	...	Karankher	2,400,000	800,040
Pigalgāon	2,400,000	...	Kothal	1,409,000	209,000
Pātar Shaikh Bābu	3,700 000	500 000	Kothil	640.000	...
Qasbah Bārigāon ..	1,600,300	640 000	Mangāon	4,800,000	...
Pātarra	3,342 500	1,262 500	Mahen	600 000	280,000
Bānbahar	1.568 000	668 000	Malkāpur	11,200,000	...
Badner Bhuli ..	2,764,450	364 452	Melgarh, (from proceeds of road tolls or safe-conduct passports) ..	94,360	...
Badner Kānka ..	4 813 700	13 800	Karyāt Rājor ..	400,000	170,356
Jalgāon	10,000,000	2,000,000	Nādura, (Nandura)	1,200 000	...
Jaipur	400 000	...	Qasbah Hatgāon ..	1,500,000	300,000
Chāndor	4,887,000	87,000			

Sarkār of Kallam (Kalamb).

Containing 31 *Parganahs.* Revenue 32,828,000 *Dāms* in money.

	Revenue D.		Revenue D.
Indori [Undri]	1,200,000	Qasba Kallam	500,000
Amrāoti	1,200,000	Kelāpur	1,200,000
I'ni [Anjni]	1,600,000	Lādkher	1,600,000
Punah [? Pusda]	3,600,000	Nāigāoṅ	960,000
Bori	1,200,000	Nachangāon	640,000
Belur	2,800,000	Yunt Lohārā [? Noni L.)]	128,000
Tālegāon	100,000	Barkhonda or Tark Chanda (in the possession of a *Zamindār*)	
Talegaon, Waigāon ...	4,800,000		
Dungar	1,600,000		
Rālegāon	200,000	Malbori	
Sālod	3,200,000	Chandur	
Kurha	960,000	Lahubāti [? Lohagarh] ...	

Sarkār of Bāsim.

Containing 8 *Parganahs.* Revenue 32,625,250 *Dāms* in money. *Suyurghāl* 1,825,250.

	Revenue D	Suyurghāl D		Revenue D	Suyurghāl D
Aunda	4,864,000	64,000	Chār Thāna ..	4,800 000	1,600,000
Suburb. dist. of Bāsim, Rājput, 100 horse, 1,000 foot ..	8,161,250	161,250	Kalambuh Nāri ..	3 200,000	
			Karari and Bāmni ..	1,200 000	
			Manglur	3,200 000	
Bāthi [Pathri] ..	2,400,000	...	Narsi	4,800,000	

Sarkār of Māhur.

Containing 20 *Parganahs.* Revenue 42,885,444 *Dāms* in money. *Suyurghāl* 97,844 *Dāms.*

	Revenue D.		Revenue D.
Ansing	960,000	Pusād	4,000,000
Amar Kher	6,400,000	Tāmsā	2,177,844
Chikni	3,200,000	Seoli	64,000
Chincholi	2,400,000	Giroli	3,200,000
Suburb. dist. of Māhur, with Qasbah, of Surah, *Suyurghal* 97,844	3,680,000	Khenot	1,300,000
		Korath [Korandh]	480,000
		Metth [Mantha]	2,400,000
Dhārwah	2,400,000	Mahāgāon	1,600,000
Dhānki [Dhamni]	320,000	Nāndāpur	2,000,000
Shevālā	2,400,000	Hald Badhonā	

Sarkār of Manikdrug.

Containing 8 *Parganahs.* Revenue 14,400,000 *Dāms* in money.

	Revenue D.		Revenue D.
Papal	3,400,000	Rājor	2,400,000
Bhān	2,000,000	Karath	2,000,000
Chāndor	2,400,000	Nair	1,600,000
Jāir [? Jaora]	1,600,000		

Sarkār of Pāthri.

Containing 18 *Parganahs.* Revenue 80,805,954 *Dāms* in money. *Suyurghāl* 11,580,954 *Dāms.*

	Revenue D	Suyurghāl D		Revenue D	Suyurghāl D
Ardhāpur	1,600,000	...	Jahri [Jherree]	1,600 000	400,000
Suburban district of Pathri	25,114.740	5,014,740	Shevli	3 600,000	1,200,000
Parbani	8,000 000	...	Kosri	3,200 000	...
Pānchalgāon	2,000,000	...	Lohgāon	4,800,000	1,600,000
Balhor [Valur]	2,400 000	...	Makat Mādhkher	2,400 000	...
Basmat	11,200,000	...	Mātargāon [? Mānegaon]	480,000	160,000
Bārad	160,000	...		6,871 203	471,209
Tākli	640,000	...	Nander	400,000	...
Jintor	3,600,000	1,200,000	Wasā	1,200,000	240,000
			Hātā		

Sarkār of Telingāna.

Containing 19 *Parganahs.* Revenue 71,904,000 *Dāms* in money. Suyurghāl 6,600,000 *Dāms.*

	Revenue D.		Revenue D.
Indur	4,800,000	Qaryāt Khudāwand Khān	640,000
Ullah	800,000	Dhakwār [? Deglur]	96
Bodhan, *Suyurghāl* 4,400,000	8,000,000	Rājor, *Suyurghāl* 800,000	1,600,000
Bāsar, *Suyurghāl* 400,000	1,600,000	Kotgir, *Suyurghāl* 1,000,000	2,200,000
Bhaisa	6,400,000	Kharki	6,400,000
Bālkondā	6,400,000	Kosambet	664,000
Bimgal [Potangal]	2,400,000	Luhgāon	11,200,000
Bānorā [Banauli]	3,200,000	Mudhol	6,400,000
Bhukar	1,600,000	Nirmal	6,400,000
Tamburni	1,600,000		

Sarkār of Ramgarh [=Rāmgir]

Containing 5 *Parganahs.* Revenue 9,600,000 *Dāms* in money.

	Revenue D.		Revenue D.
Bal Arab	800,000	Khandwah [? Khandar]	2,240,000
Subub. dist. of Rāmgir	2,560,000	Mul Marg	800,000
Chinur	3,200,000		

Sarkār of Mehkar.

Containing 4 *Parganahs.* Revenue 45,178,000 *Dāms* in money. *Suyurghāl* 376,000 *Dāms.*

	Revenue D.		Revenue D.
Suburban district of Mehkar, 7 divisions ...	... 2,560,000	Dewalgāon ...	... 5,600,000
Tamurni [? Samarni]	... 7,200,000	Sakkar Kherla, *Suyurghāl* 376,000	... 6,776,000

Sarkār of Baithalwādi.

Containing 9 *Parganahs.* Revenue 19,120,000 *Dāms.* *Suyurghāl* 4,800,000 *Dāms.*

	Revenue D.		Revenue D.
Undangāon ...	... 400,000	Dahād [=Dhār] ...	... 4,800,000
Anāwān [Anva] ...	... 40,000	Dhāwer [=Dhāora]	... 2,600,000
Baithal-wādi ...	... 1,200,000	Seoni	... 640,000
Chāndor [=Chāndol]	... 1,280,000	Sānolad Bārah [? Shilod Barud]	... 1,600,000
Chikhli	... 2,000,000		

This province was dependent on the ruler of the Deccan. During the reign of Sultān Mahmud, five *Sardārs* rebelled and kept him under restraint, and the sovereignty was assumed by Fath-ullah who had held the office of Imād-ul-Mulk.[1] He ruled but four years. At his death,

---

[1] Imād-ul-Mulk one of the oldest of the Bahmani ministers had been appointed to the government of Berār by Muhammad Shāh II of the Bahmani dynasty (A.D. 1463—1482) under the advice of his prime minister Mahmud Gawan, to whom this dynasty owed its splendour, and which perished at his death. Mahmud II (A.D. 1482—1518) for a period of 37 years was content with the nominal sovereignty leaving the real power in the hands of Qasim Barid and his son Amir, the founder of the Barid Shāhi dynasty of Ahmadābād. The Bahmani kingdom was now broken up into five independent sovereignties, *viz.*, the Barid Shāhi, the Adil Shāhi of Bijāpur, the Nizām Shāhi of Ahmadnagar, the Qutb Shāhi of Golconda and the Imād Shāhi of Berār. Imād-ul-Mulk, in the general anarchy seized the government which had been entrusted to him and declared his independence in A.D. 1484. The succession is thus given in the U. T.

1484. Fath u'l lah Bahmani, governor of Berār, became independent.
——. Alā u'd din, Imād Shāh, fixed his capital at Gāwel.
1528. Darya Imād Shāh, married his daughter to Hasan Nizām Shāh.
——. Burhān Imād Shāh, deposed by his ministers.
1568. Tufal, whose usurpation was opposed from Ahmadnagar and family of Imād Shāh and Tufāl was extinguished. In the appendix to Elphinstone's Hist of India, (Edit. Cowell 1866) the dates are as follows :—

	A.D.
Fatah Ullah	1484
Alā u'd din	1504
Derya (about)	1529
Burhān (perhaps)	1560

During the minority of Burhān, his prime minister, Tufāl usurped the government and the State merged in that of Ahmadnagar in A.D. 1572.

his son Alā-ud-din, took the same title and reigned 40 years. His son Daryā Khān succeeded, and enjoyed the government for 15 years. After him, his son, Burhān, a minor, was raised to the throne, but the nobles perfidiously usurped the administration, till Murtaza Nizām-ul-Mulk conquered and annexed the country to Ahmadnagar.

SUBAH OF GUJARAT.

It is situated in the second climate. Its length from *Burhānpur* to Jagat [*i.e.*, Dwārkā in Kathiawar] is 302 *kos;* its breadth from *Jālor* to the port of *Daman* 260 *kos,* and from *Idar* to *Kambhāyat* (Cambay) 70 *kos.* On the east lies *Khāndes;* to the north *Jālor* and *Idar;* to the south, the ports of *Daman* and *Kambhāyat,* and on the west, *Jagat* which is on the seashore. Mountains rise towards the south. It is watered by noble rivers. Besides the ocean, there are the *Sābarmatti* (Savarnamati), the *Bātrak,* the *Mahendri,* the *Narbadah,* the *Tapti,* the *Saraswati,* and two springs called *Ganga* and *Jamna.* The climate is temperate and the sandy character of the soil prevents it from turning into mud in the rainy season. The staple crops are *Jowāri,* and *Bājra,* which form the principal food of the people. The spring harvest is inconsiderable. Wheat and some food grains are imported from *Mālwa* and *Ajmer,* and rice from the Deccan. Assessment is chiefly by valuation of crops, survey being seldom resorted to. The prickly pear is planted round fields and about gardens and makes a goodly fence, for this reason the country is difficult to traverse. From the numerous groves of mango and other trees it may be said to resemble a garden. From *Pattan*[1] to *Baroda* which is a distance of a 100 *kos,* groves of mango yield ripe and sweet fruit. Some kinds are sweet even when unripe. Fine figs grow here and musk-melons are delicious in flavour both in summer and winter, and are abundant during two months in both seasons. The grapes are only moderate in quantity : flowers and fruit in great plenty. From the thick growth of forest sport is not satisfactory. Leopards[2] abound in the wilds.

The roofs of houses are usually of tiles and the walls of burnt brick and lime. Some prudently prepare the foundations of stone, and of considerable breadth, while the walls have hollow spaces between, to which they have secret access. The usual vehicles are two-wheeled drawn by two oxen. Painters, seal-engravers and other handicraftsmen

---

[1] I. G. Anhilwāra Pattan, lat. 23° 51′ 30″ N., long. 72° 10′ 30″ E. on the Saraswati, one of the oldest and most renowned towns of Gujarāt.

[2] The term *yuz* is employed in *Āin* 27 and 28 Vol. I, (Book II) for leopards generally including the hunting leopard, (F. Jubata), being used indifferently with the common name for the latter, *chitā.*

are countless. They inlay mother-o'-pearl with great skill and make beautiful boxes and inkstands. Stuffs worked with gold thread and of the kinds *Chirah, Fotah,*[1] *Jāmahwār, Khārā,* and velvets and brocades are here skilfully manufactured. Imitations of stuffs from Turkey, Europe, and Persia are also produced. They make likewise excellent swords and daggers of the kinds *Jamdhar*[2] and *Khapwah,* and bows and arrows. There is a brisk trade in jewelry and silver is imported from Turkey and Irāq.

At first *Pattan*[3] was the capital of the province, next *Champāner* and at the present day, *Ahmadābād.* The latter is a noble city in a high state of prosperity, situated on the banks of the *Sābarmatti.* It lies in latitude 25°.[4] For the pleasantness of its climate and its display of the choicest productions of the whole globe it is almost unrivalled. It has two forts, outside of which are 360 quarters of a special kind which they call *Pura,*[5] in each of which all the requisites of a city are to be found. At the present time only 84 of these are flourishing. The city contains 1,000 stone mosques, each having two minarets and rare inscriptions. In the *Rasulābād Pura* is the tomb of *Shāh Aālam Bokhāri. Batwah*[6] is a village 3 *kos* from

---

[1] See p. 52, (note II) Vol. II, Book III, and pp. 93—95 of Vol. I, B. I. *Chirah* is a parti-coloured cloth used for turbans. *Jāmawār,* is a kind of flowered woollen stuff, well known, *Khārā* an undulated silk cloth.

[2] See p. 110, Vol. I, Book I.

[3] Of successive dynasties of Rājput kings from 746 to 1194 A.D. *Champāner* was taken by Mahmud (Bigārah) of Ahmadābād after a siege, it is said, of 12 years and was made his capital and continued to be that of the Gujarāt kings till about 1560 A.D. I. G.

[4] Lat. 23° 1′ 45″ N., long. 72° 38′ 30″ E. The Emperor Aurangzeb had a different opinion of its climate and called it among other abusive epithets, Jahannumābād or the Abode of Hell. See Bayley, p. 91.

[5] A quarter or ward of a town, having its own gateway. The I. G. has *pol* and describes it as a block of houses varying in size from small courts of 5 or 10, to large quarters of the city containing as many as 10,000 inhabitants. The larger blocks are generally crossed by one main street with a gate at each end and subdivided into smaller blocks each with its separate gate branching off from the chief thoroughfare.

[6] The text has *Patwah,* the variant *Batwah* being relegated to the notes, but the best authorities concur in the latter reading. For Qutb-i-Aālam, see Bayley, p. 128, and Briggs' Cities of Gujarashtra, p. 292. Regarding the lithoxyle over the tomb, Briggs writes that one of the legends given him concerning it is that Qutb-i-Aālam on a journey to his masjid tripped against a stone and picking it up, said, "Can this be stone, wood or iron?" and the combination ensued. A visitor who had preceded Briggs on a visit to this place wrote to him as follows: "The size mentioned by Abul Fazl is correct. The stone is not now on the sepulchre but deposited in the chief Said's house. Great reverence is paid to it and on such occasions as visitors desire to see it, it is produced under a covering of brocade. It appears to be petrified wood; the barky part gives it the appearance of iron oxydised; that portion where it has been chipped by the hand of Akbar when he visited Batwa (according

Ahmadābād where are the tombs of *Qutb-i-Aālam* father of *Shāh Aālam,* and of other eminent personages. In the vicinity are fine gardens. Over the tomb is suspended a covering of about the measure of a cubit, partly of wood, partly of stone and a part also of iron, regarding which they relate wonderful stories. At a distance of three *kos* is the village of *Sarkhech* (Sarkhej) where repose *Shaikh Ahmad Khattu,*[1] *Sultān Ahmad* after whom, *Ahmadābād* is named, and many other princes. Indigo of good quality is here grown and exported to Turkey and other countries.

Twelve *kos* from Ahmadābād is *Mahmudābād* a city founded by *Sultan Mahmud,* in which are beautiful buildings extending to an area of 4 *kos* square. The whole is surrounded by a wall and at every half *kos* is a pleasure house and a preserve in which deer and other kinds of game are at large.

The chief of *Idar* is a *Zamindār* named *Narāin Dās,* and of such austere life that he first feeds his cattle with corn and then picks up the grains from their dung and makes this his food, a sustenance held in much esteem by the Brāhmans. He is regarded as the head of the *Rāthor* tribe and has a following of 500 horse and 10,000 foot.

The ports of *Ghoga* and *Kambhāyat* (*Cambay*) are included in this (Gogo) *Sarkār.* The latter is a large city where merchants of divers kinds reside and wherein are fine buildings and much merchandise. Vessels sail from and trade to *Ghogah.* The cargoes are put into small ships called *Tawari* which transport them to *Kambhāyat.*

In *Kari* are fine oxen, a pair being worth 300 rupees, and according to their shapeliness, strength and speed fetching even a larger price.

Jhālāwār was formerly a separate principality containing 1,200 villages. Its length is 70 *kos* and its breadth 40. It furnished 10,000 horse and the same number of infantry. Now it possesses but 2,000 horse and 3,000 foot. Its ruler was subject to the king of Gujarāt. It formed four divisions, the inhabitants mostly of the *Jhāla* tribe of Rājputs.

---

to the Abbot of the community) shews the fibre or vein of the wood; and upon the opposite side, where it seems to have been ground crosswise, it bears the appearance of stone."

[1] See Bayley's *Hist. of Gujarāt,* pp. 90 and 130. A description of these mausoleums will be found in Messrs. Hope and Fergusson's *"Architecture of Ahmedābād."* London Murray, 1866. Khattu is one of the towns in the Sarkār of Nāgor. Cf. Briggs' *Cities of Gujarashtra,* p. 275.

At the present day it is accounted a *Pargana* of Ahmadābād, and its villages and districts are summarized in the following table.

Great Jhālāwār contains *Birāmgāon* residence of the chief, *Halod, Wadhwān, Koha, Daran Gadra, Bijānā, Pātri* which has a salt-pit, *Sahālā, Baroda, Jhinjhuwārā, Sanjān,* (? Sanand), *Dhulhar, Mandal.*

Parganahs of *Machhukhantā* contain *Morbi, Rāmpur, Tankārā, Khanjariā, Malia, Kazor,* in the vicinity of which pearls are found, *Dhansar, Amrol* (Amreli).

Parganahs of Jāmbuji contain Jāmbu, Limri, Siāni.

Parganahs of *Chaubisi,* chief seat of the *Parmār* tribe contain *Morbi,* with 36 villages and *Chotilā* with 55 villages. Now *Morbi* with 7 districts is included in *Sorath.*

Pattan has two forts, one of stone and one of brick. It lies in long. 117° 10′, lat. 23° 30′. It produces fine oxen that will travel 50 *kos* in half a day. Good cotton cloths are here woven and are taken to diṣtant parts as gifts of value.

Sidhpur is a town on the Sarsuti and a great place of pilgrimage.

Barnagar [Vadnagar] is a large and ancient city and containing 3,000 pagodas, near each of which is a tank; it is chiefly inhabited by Brāhmans.

Chāmpāner is a finely situated fort on a crag of great height[1]; the approach to it for two *kos* and a half is extremely difficult. Gates have been posted at intervals. At one place a cutting about 60 yards long has been made across which planks are laid which can be removed when necessity arises. Fine fruits abound.

Surat is a celebrated port. The river *Tapti* runs by it and at a distance of 7 *kos* thence, falls into the sea.

Rānder on the opposite side of the *Tapti* is a port dependent on *Surat;* it was formerly a large city. The ports of *Khandewi* and *Balsār* also are a part of the Surat division. Numerous fruits abound especially the pine apple, and oils of all kinds and rare perfumes are obtainable. The followers of Zoroaster coming from Persia, settled here. They follow the teaching of the Zend and the Pāzend, and erect funeral structures. Thus through the wide tolerance of His Majesty every sect enjoys freedom. Through the negligence of the ministers of state and the commanders of the frontier pro-

[1] Tieffenthaler states that the fortress on the summit of the hill is called *Pauagarh* and the town at its foot Chāmpāner.

vinces, many of these *Sarkārs* are in the possession of European nations, such as *Daman, Sanjān,*[1] *Tārāpur, Māhim* and *Base* (Bassein) that are both cities and ports.

Bharoj (Broach) has a fine fort. The *Narbada* flows past it in its course to the ocean. It is accounted a maritime town of first rate importance, and the ports of *Kāwi, Ghandhār, Bhābhut and Bhankorā* [Bhakora] are its dependencies.

Near the town of *Hānsot* is a game preserve 8 *kos* in length by 4 in breadth, full of deer and other animals. The cover is rich and fresh with verdure, being situated on the banks of the *Narbada* and is perfectly level.

The *Sarkār* of *Sorath*[2] was an independent territory, having a force of 50,000 cavalry and 100,000 infantry, the ruling tribe being *Ghelot*. Its length from the port of *Ghogo* (Gogo) to that of *Arāmdāe*[3] is 125 *kos;* its breadth from *Sardhar* (? *Sadra,* n. of Ahmadabad) to the seaport of *Diu,* 72 kos. On the east it is bounded by *Ahmadābād;* on the north by the State of Kachh (Cutch); on the south and west by the (Indian) Ocean. Its climate is healthy, its fruits and flowers numerous and grapes and melons grow here. This territory is divided into 9 districts each inhabited by a different tribe, as follows :—

Parganahs of new Sorath.

Junahgarh with suburban district, *Sultānpur, Barwa* [Bantva], *Hānsāwar, Chaura Rāmpur, Kandolnā, Hast Jati, Und, Bagsarā, Mahandrā* [Mandurda], *Bhāntror* [Ghantwar], and others.

Parganahs of old Sorath, called Nāghar.

Pattan Somnāth, Aunah, Delwārah, Manglor, Korinār, Mul Mahādeo, Chorwār, Diu, &c.

Parganahs of Gohelwārah.

Lāthi, Luliyānah, Bhimpur, Jasdhom, Māndwi, Birāi, Sehor.

---

[1] A small village in Thānā (Tanna) Dist., where the Parsis first landed in India, known to the Portuguese and long after their time as St. John. I. G.

[2] The old name for Kāthiawār, or Saurāshtra and Prakritised in that of Sorath which is to this day the name of a large district 100 miles in length in the south-west.

[3] *Aramda,* near port Okha, n. of Jagat Dwarka.

Parganahs of Wālā.

Mahwah, Talājā, Pālitānah, &c.

Parganahs of Bādhelah.

Jagat (called Dwārkā), *Arāmdāe, Dhārhi* (? Sankudhār).

Parganahs of Barrā. (Berda ?)

Barrā, Gumli, &c.

Parganahs of the Bāghela[1] *tribe.*

Sordhār, Gondal, Rāyet, Dhānak, &c.

Parganahs of the Wāji in the uncultivated tracts.

Jhānjhmer.

Parganahs of the Timbel tribe.

Not assigned in any of the MSS.

The first district known as New *Sorath* had remained unexplored on account of the impenetrable nature of the forests and the intricate windings of the mountains. A recluse by chance found his way into it and through him a knowledge of it was gained. Here is the celebrated stone fortress of *Junahgarh* which Sultān Māhmud,[2] I, captured by force of arms and at the foot of it built another fort of stone. At a distance of 8 *kos* is the fort of *Osam* on the summit of a hill; it has now fallen into decay, but is worthy of restoration. There is also another stronghold on the summit of the hill of *Girnār* in which are many springs, a place of worship of the *Jains*. Adjacent is the port of *Kondi Kolidyā*,[3] which derives its name from two villages at a distance of one *kos* from it. In the rear of *Junahgarh* is an island called *Siālkokah* 4 kos in length by 4 in breadth,

---

[1] The I. G. (I. 550) calls this clan Wāghelā tribe of Rājputs, a remnant of the Solānki race who fled from Anhilwārah when that kingdom was destroyed by Alā u'd din, in A.D. 1297.

[2] Bigarah of Gujarāt. One derivation of this name is its supposed meaning of two forts (garh) because Mahmud's army conquered on one day Chāmpāner and Junahgarh, Vol. I, p. 506, n. According to T. Junahgarh signifies the ancient fort, because it was long concealed in the dense forest and discovered by a wood cutter. The legend runs that 1500 years elapsed from its discovery to the time of Māndalik from whom Mahmud wrested the fortress. See Bayley's Hist. of Gujarāt, pp. 161—182, for the derivation of the name.

[3] *Var.* and G. Kondi or Gondilakiyāt. [Can it be *Kodinar*?]

adjacent to which is a forest, 3 *kos* square, where wild fruits grow and where there is a settlement of *Kolis*. This tract is called *Gir*. Near the village of *Tunkagosha,*[1] the river *Bhādar* falls into the ocean. Its fish are so delicate that they melt when exposed to the sun. Good camels are here obtainable and a breed of horses somewhat larger than the Gunth.

In the second district is *Pattan,* a city on the seashore possessing a stone fort. This they call *Pattan Somnāth*. It is both a capacious harbour and a town having nine[2] stone towers on the plain, within an area of three *kos* on the seashore. Good swords are made here, there being a well in the vicinity the water of which gives them a keen edge.

The ports of *Manglor,*[3] *Diu, Purbandar, Korinār, Ahmadpur* and *Muzaffarābād* are about this coast. A spring of the Sarsuti (Saraswati[4]) rises near *Somnāth*. The Brahmanical shrines are numerous, but among these *Somnāth, Parānchi,* and *Korinār* are accounted among the most sacred. Between the rivers *Haran* and *Sarsuti* about 4,000 years ago, 560,000,000 of the *Yadu* race while engaged in sport and merriment, fell to fighting and all of them perished in that field of death, and wonderful are the legends that they relate. Two and a half *kos* from *Pattan Somnāth* is *Bhāl ka Tirth*[5] (or the shrine of the Arrow). In this place an arrow struck Sri Kishn and buried itself under

---

[1] A note says *Tunkragosā,* in the maps. There are two rivers of the name of Bhādar; one rises in the Māndav hills and flowing S. W. falls into the sea at Nawi-Bandar after a course of 115 miles. Another from the same hills, flowing E. falls into the Gulf of Cambay. The Kolis are a predatory tribe and their distribution is not confined to a single province. They were spread over the country between Cambay and Ahmadābād and the well-wooded country afforded them a refuge from attack.

[2] Gladwin has turned these words into a name which mistranslation I notice as it has been adopted by Count von Noer in his monograph on Akbar, p. 98. (Mrs. Beveridge's Trans.). The Diwān of Junagarh, Haridās Viharidās, has courteously given me the benefit of his local knowledge. The new temple and the ruins of the old are within the fort which was inhabited chiefly by the attendants of the shrine, the population living in the environs forming the town. Pattan is said to have had three walls and hence named *Trigadhi*. The length of the present walls covers nearly two miles. The fort had or has 10 towers or bastions of which 8 are existing and two are in ruins.

[3] The I. G. gives Mangrol. The text unites Diu and Purbandar (elsewhere Porbandar) in one name, as Somnāth is called Deo Pattan, but it is probable that the port of Diu was intended by Abul Fazl.

[4] The river rises in Mount Abu and enters the Runn of Cutch, though a part of its course near Sidhpur and Patan towns, is said to be subterranean.

[5] Apparently the *Bhāt Kund* of the I. G. Yudhisthira after the slaughter of the 56 tribes of the Yadu race on the field of Kurukshetra and the death of Duryodhana, in grief at the loss of so many kinsmen, placed Parikshita on the throne of Indraprastha, and retired with Krishna and Baldeo to Dwarka. They were attacked by the Bhils and Krishna was slain. Baldeo founded the city of Patalibotra or Patna.

a *pipal* tree on the banks of the *Sarsuti*. This they call *Pipal sir,* and both these spots are held in great veneration. An extraordinary event occurs at the town of *Mul Mahādeo* where there is a temple dedicated to Siva. Every year on a certain day before the rainy season, a bird called *Mukh*[1] appears. It is somewhat smaller than a pigeon, with a coarser beak and pied in colour. It alights on the temple, disports itself for a while, and then rolls over and dies. On this day, the people of the city assemble and burn various kinds of perfume and from the proportions of black and white in the plumage of the bird, they calculate the extent of the coming rainfall, the black portending rain, the white, drought. In this tract, there are three crops of *jowar* annually. At *Unah* there are two reservoirs, one of which is called *Jamna,* the other *Ganga.* The water bubbles up and forms a stream and the fish of these two springs have three eyes, the third eye being in the forehead.

Between *Manglor* and *Chārāwār* is a tract into which the sea enters. On a certain day of the year the water is sweet. It is related that in ancient times a certain person was in need of Ganges water. A recluse made a sign to the expanse and sweet water came forth. Ever since, upon that day this wonder is repeated to the astonishment of all.

In both of these districts the *Ghelot* tribe of Rājputs prevail and the ruling power in this country is in their hands. At the present time the force (of the first district) consists of 1,000 horse and 2,000 foot. There is also a settlement of Ahirs called *Bābriyas.*[2] Tne force (of the second district) is 2,000 horse and 3,000 foot.

In the third district at the foot of the *Satrunjah* (Satrunjaya) hill,[3] is a large fort and on its summit, the fort of *Pālithānah.* Though in ruins, it deserves restoration. It is in great veneration with the *Jains.* The port of *Ghoga* (Gogo) is a dependency of this district. The island of *Biram* (Perim) was formerly the residence of the governor; it is 9 *kos* square and is a low rocky island in

---

[1] Or *Makh.* In a work called *Haqiqat-i-Hindustān,* the word is *Sakh* or *Sukh.* See Bayley, p. 197, who records this event and places it in the village of Madhopur.

[2] The name of one of the old territorial *prants* or districts into which Kāthiawār was divided, was called Bābriawār, a hilly tract on the S.E.

[3] The hill is sacred to Adināth the deified priest of the Jains. The description of Pālitāna in the I. G. taken from Mr. Burgess' "Notes of a visit to Satrunjaya Hill," gives an interesting sketch of this temple hill. Perim (the Baiones of the *Periplus*) is in the Gulf of Cambay, 8 miles S. of Gogo.

the midst of the sea. The *Zamindār* is of the *Gohel*[1] tribe. This district possesses 2,000 horse and 4,000 foot.

In the fourth district, are the ports of *Mohwah* and *Talājā,* inhabited by the *Wali* clan. The local force consists of 300 men and 500 foot.

In the fifth district is *Jagat,* called also *Dwārkā. Sri Krishna* came hither from Mathura (Muttra) and here died. It is a great Brahmanical place of worship. The island of *Sankudhār* [Bait] 4 *kos* square is reckoned within this district. Near *Arāmdāe* is an island 70 *kos* in length and breadth. An area of half a *kos* of this land is for the most part stony and if an excavation is made salt-water pours in on all sides. *Malik Ayāz*[2] *Khās Khel,* of Sultān Mahmud I of Gujerāt, had, one-fourth of it dug up. The port of *Arāmdāe* is superior to most of its class. The inhabitants are of the *Bādhel* tribe. It musters 1,000 horse and 2,000 foot.

In the sixth district *Barra,*[3] the country is so hilly, the forests so impenetrable and the defiles so extensive that it is impassable for troops. The *Jaitwah* clan inhabit it. It furnishes 1,000 horse and 2,000 foot.

In the seventh district are the *Baghelahs.* It furnishes 200 horse and the same number of foot. The *Kāthis*[4] are numerous in this tract; they are of the *Ahir* caste and are skilful in the management of horses. The military force is 6,000 cavalry and 6,000 infantry. They are said by some to be of Arabian origin. Cunning but hospitable, they will eat of the food of people of every caste, and are a handsome race. When any *Jagirdar* comes amongst them they make it a condition that there shall be no account

---

[1] The Gohels came from the north in the 13th century, and retreating before the tide of Muhammadan conquest conquered for themselves new seats in the decadence of Anhilwāra. They are now in E. Kāthiawār.

[2] See Bayley's Hist. of Gujarāt, p. 233 et seq. Khās Khel represents the position of a royal equerry combined with high command. Ferishta calls him the *ghulām-i-khās* or confidential attendant of Mahmud. He was premier noble (Amir u'l Umarā) and commander in chief of the army, fought and defeated the Portuguese fleet at Chaul and sank the admiral's flagship valued at a *kror* of rupees. (A.H. 913—A.D. 1507).

[3] I have no doubt that this is Bardā (or Jaitwār) of the I. G.; a division of Kāthiawār lying between 21° 11′ and 21° 57′ N. lat., and 69° 30′ and 70° 7′ E. long., bounded N. and N.-E. by Hallār; E. by Sorath, and S.-W. by the Arabian Sea. The Barda hills are from 12 to 18 miles distant from the coast and formed a favourite refuge for outlaws.

[4] The name of Kāthiawār, was formerly given to a tract to the E. of the centre of the peninsula; from having been overrun by the Kāthis who entered from Cutch in the 13th and 14th centuries, it was extended to the whole country by the Mahrattas who had come into contact with them in their forays.

taken of the incontinence of any of their people. In the vicinity of the *Kāthis* on the banks of the river *Dondi*, there is a sept of *Ahirs* called *Porechas*. Their force is 3,000 horse and the same number of foot. They are perpetually at feud with the *Jāms*.[1]

In the eighth district Jhānjhmer is a maritime port. The *Wāji* tribe prevail. There are 200 horse and 2,000 foot.

In the ninth district is the Chāran tribe. Mahadeva formed a man from the sweat of his brow and gave him the charge of his own bull. He spoke in rhythmic sentences and sang the divine praises and revealed the past and the future. His descendants are known by his name. They chiefly recite panegyrics and genealogies and in battle chant deeds of valour and animate the warriors and some of them reveal future events. There are few of the nobles of Hindustān who have not some of these in their retinue. This district furnishes 500 horse and 4,000 foot. The tribe called *Bhāt* resemble this caste in their panegyrics, their powers, their battle-chants, and genealogical recitations, and although in some of these respects they surpass them yet the *Chārans* are better swordsmen. Some pretend that the *Chārans* were called into life by the mere volition of the divinity, and the *Bhāts* from *Mahādeva*.

Between *Jhālwāra* in the *Sarkār* of *Ahmadābād*, and *Pattan* and *Sorath* is a low-lying tract, 90 *kos* in length by 7 to 30 in breadth, called the *Ran*[2] (the Runn). Before the rainy season, the sea rises and covers this area and falls as the rains cease. A considerable part dries up and is covered with salt, the duties of which are collected in the *pargana* of *Jhālwāra*. *Ahmadābād* lies to the east of this tract. On the west is a large separate territory called *Kachchh* (Cutch) 250 *kos* in length by 100 *kos* in breadth. *Sind* lies to the

[1] The Jāreja [R]ājputs, to which branch the Rao of Cutch belongs, are descended from the Summa (Sama!) tribe and came originally from the north. They are said to have emigrated from Sind about the 15th century under the leadership of Jā Lākha, son of Jāra from whom the tribe derive their name. Till 1540 the Jāms ruled over Cutch in three branches. About that year Khengār succeeded in making himself head of the tribe and master of the province. His uncle Jām Rāwal fled to Kāthiawār and founded the present reigning house of Nawanagar, the rulers of which are still called Jāms. See Jām under the account of Sind.

[2] The word in Hindi signifies a waste or wilderness. There are two, the northern or larger Runn, 150 by 80 miles has an area of about 7,000 square miles. The eastern or smaller Runn, 70 miles from E. to W., covers an area of 2,000 square miles. Except a stray bird, a herd of wild asses, or an occasional caravan, no sign of life breaks the desert loneliness. *I. G.*

west of Cutch. The physical aspect of the country is barren and sandy. There is an excellent breed of horses believed to be of Arabian race, and there are good camels and goats. The chief of this country is of the *Yadu*[1] race and his tribe is now known as *Jārejas*. The military force of this clan is 10,000 cavalry and 50,000 infantry. The men are handsome, tall in stature and wear long beards. The residence of the chief is *Bhuj*, which has two strong forts *Jhārah* and *Kantkot*. On the Gujarāt side towards the south is a *Zamindār* of note whom they call *Jām*, a relative of the ruler of the above-mentioned state. Sixty years ago, Jām Rāwal, after a war of two months, was driven out of the country, and settled in *Sorath* between the territories of the *Jaitwah*, *Bādel*, *Chāran*, and *Tumbel* tribes. He posssessed himself of other parts and founded the city of *Nawanagar* and his country received the name of *Little Cutch*. *Sattarsāl* the present Rājah, is his grandson. There are many towns and the agricultural area is extensive. The residence of the chief is at *Nawanagar* and his force consists of 7,000 cavalry and 8,000 infantry. The camels and goats are of good breeds. For a considerable period the prime ministers of these two states have been of the Muhammadan religion.

In the vicinity of *Morā* and *Mangrej* is a state called *Pāl*[2] through which runs the river *Mahendri* towards the Gujarāt side. It has a separate ruler who resides at *Dungarpur*. On the Mālwa side is Bānswāra and that too has a separate chief. Each of them has a force of 5,000 horse

[1] The lunar race established by the Scythian Budh, expanded into fifty-six branches and filled nearly the whole of northern India. Yadu 4th in descent from Budh gave his name to the royal line which closed in Krishna and Balrāma. While the solar race was confined to a narrow strip of land between the mountains and the Ganges, the Yadus had spread over the whole country. Yadu, says Elliot, (Races of the N.-W. P., Vol. I, 128) is the patronymic of all the descendants of Buddha, the ancestor of the Lunar race, of which the Bhatti and the Jāreja are now the most conspicuous, but the title of *Jādon* is now exclusively applied to that tribe which appears never to have strayed far from the limits of the ancient Suraseni, and we consequently find them in large numbers in that neighbourhood. The tract south of the Chambal called after them Yaduvati is in the possession of the Gwalior Mahrattas and the state of Kirauli on the Chambal is now their chief independent possession.

[2] *Pāk* in the text, with the emendation *Pāl* by the Editor. There are two of the name, one within Māhi Kānta on its N. E. frontier. The other one of the petty states in Hallār, Kathiawār. The former must here be meant, as Dungarpur lies in lat. 23° 52′ N., long. 73° 49′ E. It is now a separate native state. The early history of the ruling family is not known with certainty; they paid tribute to the Mughal Empire and did military service, and on the fall of the Empire became tributary to the Mahrattas. I. G. The name *Pāl* says Bayley, seems to have been given to a congeries of petty hill states of which the rulers were Hindus. They appear to have included Dungārpur, Bijanagar and others.

and 10,000 foot, and both are of the *Sisodia* clan. The rulers were of the Rānā's family, but for some time past it has been otherwise.

Adjoining the *Sarkār* of Pattan is a state, the chief town of which is *Sirohi* and which possesses a force of 2,000 horse and 5,000 foot. On the summit of a hill is the strong fortress of *Abugarh* (Mount *Ābu*) about which are 12 flourishing villages. Pasturage is plentiful.

There is also a territory having *Nandurbār* on the east, *Mandu* on the north, *Nandod* on the south and *Chāmpāner* on the west. Its length is 60 *kos,* and its breadth 40. The chief is a Chauhān and his residence is the town of *Āli Mohān.* Wild elephants are numerous. The force consists of 600 horse and 15,000 foot.

Between *Surat* and *Nandurbār* is a mountainous but flourishing tract called *Baglāna,* the chief of which is a *Rathor,* commanding 3,000 cavalry and 10,000 infantry. Fine peaches, apples, grapes, pineapples, pomegranates, and oranges grow here. It possesses seven remarkable forts, among which are *Mulher*[1] and *Salher.*

Between the *Sarkārs* of Nandod and Nandurbār is a hilly district 60 *kos* in length by 40 in breadth, which the *Gohel* tribe of Rājputs inhabit. At the present day a Brāhman named *Tewāri* has the management of affairs, the titular Rajah being of no account. He resides at *Rājpipla* or *Khulu,* and has a force of 3,000 horse and 7,000 foot. The water of this tract is very unwholesome. Rice and honey of the finest quality are here produced.

This *Subah* embraces 9 *Sarkārs* and 198 *Parganahs,* of which 13 are ports. The revenue is 43 *krors,* 68 *lakhs,* 22,301 *dāms* (Rs. 10,920,557-8-0) and one *lakh,* 62,028¾ *Mahmudis*[2] as port dues.

The measured land (except Sorath which is paid in money by estimate) is 1 *kror,* 60 *lakhs,* 36,377 *bighas,* 3 *biswas,* out of which 4 *lakhs,* 20,274 *dāms* are *Suyurghāl.* The local force is 12,440 cavalry, and 61,100 infantry.

---

[1] Both these lie in the Navasari (Nosari) district of the Baroda territory, the latter in the S. E. corner. Songarh and Rupgarh are two other forts. The former 43 miles E. of Surat, and Rupgarh 10 miles S. of Songarh. The hills must refer to the Rājpipla range, there being no other in the whole territory.

[2] Mr. E. Thomas (*Numismatic Chronicle,* Vol. III, 3rd series) quotes Sir T. Herbert as saying about 1676 A.D. "A mahmudi is twelve pence, a rupee two shillings and three pence." See Bayley's *History of Gujarāt,* p. 16. The relative value of coin varied according to time and locality. The Changezi Mahmudi is variously valued at half and two-thirds of a rupee and at half a crown, French money. *Ibid,* pp. 12 and 16.

Sarkār of Ahmadābād.

Containing 28 *Mahals.* 8,024,153 *Bighas.* Revenue 208,306,994 *Dāms.* *Suyurghāl* 6,511,441 *Dāms.* Castes various. Cavalry 4,120. Infantry 20,500.

	Bighas Biswas	Revenue D.	Suyurghāl D.	Cavalry	Infantry	Castes
City of Ahmadābād ...	...	15,000,073	144,680	100	300	
Suburb. dist. of Ahmadābād	370,087	23,999,371	4201,783	...	...	
Rurdhu Matar (*mis.* Arhar M.) on the river Baroli	145,384	9,662,753	160,938	100	200	Chauhān.
Ahmadnagar has a stone fort faced with *chunam*	54,370	1,770,912	50,774	500	5,000	Solanki.
Idar, [revenue by estimate of crops]	...	1,616,000	...	1000	5,000	Garāsiah[1]
Bahiel	375,675	6,988,920	...	100	200	Rājput.
Bārah Sewah [Bāla Sinor]	84,960	2,814,124	5.608	50	100	Bhodia Rājput, Lodiah.
Birpur [? Pithapur] has a stone fort on the Mahendri	173,385	1,778,300	...	300	600	Rājput, Kharbā and Bonah.
Paplod [Palod]	39,930	1,493,249	...	50	100	Rājput.
Parāntij	159,273	2,076,574	...	100	200	Ol.
Bandar Solah [?Bhadarwa] (revenue in money) ...	...	600,000	...	...	...	
Petlād	...	771,960	128,990	...	...	
Thāmanah [? Thawad] (rev. in money) ...	...	600,000	...	...	...	
Chhala-Babra, has a brick fort, somewhat dilapidated, saltpetre obtained here	43,283	34,903,220	232,860	200	10,000	Koli.
	579,877	4,825 392	5,627	50	200	Jhālāwār.
Dholqa, the Sābarmati flows adjacent	834,606	1,650,000	188,160	50	100	Ponwār.
Dhandhok, has a masonry fort of *chunam* ...	403,523	113077044[5]	...	500	4,000	Do.
Sirnāl	80,646	2,528,632	...	100	300	Garāsiah, Mehtar.
Kari	936,837	30,125,778[6]	394,963	300	1,000	Ol. etc.
Kambhāyat	336,813	22,147,986	160,405	100	200	Rājput, Bārah.
Kapadbhanj, a masonry fort of *chunam* ...	...	30,125,778	27,309	100	500	Koli.
Mandwa	...	22,147,978	301,320	50	500	Do.
Modāsa, has a brick fort	507,370	423,510	16,062	100	200	Do.
Mahmudābād, has a temple to Mahādeva ...	45,590	1,748,080	160,088	...	...	Chauhān.
Masaudābād, has a brick fort	213,805	1,400,000	...	...	...	Ol (Koli)
Mangrej, has a masonry fort of *chunam* ...	76,629	121,762	...	100	300	Chauhān.
Nāriād	202,062	8,103,098	49,478	entered under Siruāl		Garāsiah.
Hasol	200,020	752,202	...	20	100	Koli.

[1] The Rājputs are here divided into two classes. (1) Garāsiahs or land-owners (see Bayley's *History of Gujarāt*, p. 98, for the derivation of this term), and (2) Cultivators. The former live a life of idleness on their lands and are greatly given to opium. *I. G.*

Sarkār of Pattan, north.

Containing 16 *Mahals*. 38,500,015 *Bighas*. Revenue 600.325,099 *Dāms*. *Suyurghāl*, 210,627 *Dāms*. Castes various. Cavalry 715. Infantry 6,000.

	Bighas Biswas	Revenue D.	Suyurghāl D.	Cavalry	Infantry	Castes
Pattan, has two forts ...	...	957,462	143,862	150	3,000	Rājput, Koli, Kumbi.
Bijāpur	290,554	6,001,832	2,832	200	500	Koli.
Pāthanpur	...	528,611	3,600,000*	50	500	Do.
Badnagar, has a stone fort	37,600-13	1,844,324	1,749	under Bijapur		Do.
Visalnagar	13,281	674,348	...	20	100	Rājput, Jādun.
Therād, has a brick fort ...	240,052-11	4,000,000	...	50	200	Rājput, Bārhah.
Tervāda do. ...	294,516-17	2,130,000	...	50	1,000	Koli.
Suburb. dist. of Pattan ...	14,787-50	20,054,045	862,104	under Pattan		
Rādhan [-pur], has a brick fort	257,709-6	4,000,000	...	100	200	Koli.
Sami, has a shrine much venerated in Hindustan	107,298[2]	1,266,498	...	20	100	Do.
Santalpur	34,267	287,340	...	...	...	
Kherālu	101,946-17	4,000,000	...	...	...	
Kākrej	112,338	1,312,590	...	under Tehrār		
Munjpur	51,814-11	909,630	...	25	100	Do.
Morvāda	47,777	320,020	...	...	200	Do.
Disah, has a brick fort ...	288,270	1,600,000	...	50	200	Do.

* So the MSS, but I apprehend these figures should be reversed, the larger coming under revenue, as G. has it.

Sarkār of Nandod—north.

Containing 12 *Mahals*. 541,817 *Bighas*, 16 *Biswas*. Revenue 8,797,596 *Dāms*. *Suyurghāl* 11,328 *Dāms*.

	Biswas Bighas	Revenue D.		Bighas Biswas	Revenue D.
Amreli	15,548-16	148,620	Jamungāon ...	21,444	412,093
Avidhā	4,290	17,076	Kahāar ...	14,903	80,307
Barsāi, (*Suyurghāl* 11,328)	158,696	2,061,368	Marghadrah	15,028	62,328
			Māndun ...	5,402	16,000
Badāl [?Bhadli] ...	40,663	272,645	Nāndod with suburb dist. ...	128,021	3,929,330
Tilakwāda ...	55,859	1,595,525			
Tahwā [Tankhala] ...	73,263	165,500	Natrang ...	15,188	40,798

Sarkār of Baroda, south.

Containing 4 *Mahals.* 922,212 Bighas. Revenue 41,145,895 *Dāms. Suyurghal* 388,358 *Dāms.* Castes various. Cavalry 900. Infantry 5,800.

	Bighas Biswas	Revenue D.	Suyurghāl D.	Cavalry	Infantry	Castes
Baroda with sub. dist. has a brick fort	500,920	20,403,485	...	200	400	Ponwār, &c Rājput.
Bahādurpur, has a brick fort	1,680,920	6,243,280	...	500	5.000	Rājput.
Dabhoi, has a stone fort ...	167,090	9,252,550	4,562	500	500	Rājput, Bahrāh.
Sinor, the Narbada, in its course from the north, passes under the town ...	148,150	5,746,580	...	500	5,000	Rājput, ,following name illegible).

Sarkār of Broach, south.

Containing 14 *Mahals.* 349,771 *Bighas.* Revenue 21,845,663 *Dāms. Suyurghal* 141,820 *Dāms.* Castes various. Cavalry 990. Infantry 8,600.

	Bighas Biswas	Revenue D.	Suyurghāl D.	Cavalry	Infantry	Castes
Olpād	186,420	1,659,877	...	...	...	
Anklesar	138,376	558,010	...	...	...	
Atlesar [Amalsari] ...	90,333	307,737	...	50	280	Gwāliā.
Broach, has a brick fort, on the Narbada; here is a Hindu shrine ...	64,660	456,230	...	500	5,000	Rājput,
Tarkesar	8,752	5,651	...	...	...	
Chharmandvi	44,821	122,795	...	...	...	
Suburban dist. of Broach	52,975	7,022,690	64,516	...	...	
Dehej Bārhā [Vagra] ...	42,664	1,174,540	...	...	...	
Kāri [Kareli]	177,939	4,275,000	12,650	20	300	Rājput, Barhāh.
Kala [Ghalha]	15,181	353,670	...	...	300	Rājput, Garāsiah.
Gandhār, a port frequented by vessels	...	240,000	...	...	...	

Sarkār of Broach, South—Contd.

	Bighas Biswas	Revenue D.	Suyurghāl D.	Cavalry	Infantry	Castes
Lorakh [?Luhara], on the seashore	31,760	1,287,230	...	...	...	
Maqbulābād, on the seashore. Salt here obtained	81,750	1,912,040	...	20	100	Rājput. Musalmān.
Hānsot, one of the ports of this district ...	77,560	2,439,158	...	400	3,000	Rājput Bāghelah.

Sarkār of Chāmpaner.

Containing 9 *Mahals.* 80,337 *Bighas.* 11 *Biswas.* Revenue 15,009,884 *Dāms.* *Suyurghāl* 173,730 *Dāms.* Castes various. Cavalry 550. Infantry 1,600.

	Bighas Biswas	Revenue D.	Suyurghāl D.	Cavalry	Infantry	Castes
Arwārah	19,129	48,209	...	...	...	
Chāmpāner, with sub. dist. has two stone forts, one on a hill called Pāwah, and the second at its foot	159,590	1,429,649	173,730	500	1,000	
Chandāwārah	27,323-8	21,530	...	...	...	
Chaurāsi	107,713	2,215,275	...	...	...	
Dohad, has a stone fort ...	68,249	1,283,300	...	...	...	
Dhol [Derol]	32,014	172,992	...	...	...	
Dilāwarah	18,129	48,628	...	...	...	
Sonkherah	240,313	2,995,696	...	...	...	
Sānwes, has a strong stone fort	120,391-1	2 300,000	...	50	100	Rājput.

Sarkār of Surat.

Containg 31 *Mahals.* 1,312,815 *Bighas.* 16 *Biswas.* Revenue 19,035,180 *Dams.* *Suyurghāl* 182,370 *Dāms.* Castes various. Cavalry 2,000. Infantry 5500.

	Bighas Biswas	Revenue D.	uyurghāl D.	Cavalry	Infantry	Castes
Ambhel, has a stone fort	6,581	424,355	...	...	...	
Pārchol [=Parujan] ...	55,920	1,508,000	...	...	...	

Sarkār of Surat—Contd.

	Bighas	Revenue D.	Suyurghāl D.	Cavalry	Infantry	Castes
Balsār, on the sea ...	74,702	1,281,420	59,785	100	500	
Balesar	86,400	1,013,045	15,035	...	...	
Beāwarah, has a stone fort near Tapti	58,659	554,320	...	2000	5,000	Rājput.
Balwārah, has a stone fort, and a shrine with a hot spring [?Palsana] ...	41,650	478,620	...	...	...	
Bhesrot [Bhestan] ...	21,170	425,055	...	...	...	
Pārnera	54,460	277,475	...	...	...	
Bhutsar	12,075	146,230	...	...	...	
Bālor [?Kadod] ...	21,435	592,180	...	...	...	
Tilāri [Taori]	85,095	917,890	90,835	...	...	
Timbā	51,029-19	263,390	2,040	...	...	
Chikhli, on the sea, has an iron mine	337,613	389,320	...	...	...	
Dhamori, on the river Timi ? (Kim ?) ...	40,994-19	767,520	...	...	...	
Rander	5,523	63,692	13,092	...	...	
Surat with suburb. dist. has a stone fort ...	50,733	5,530,145	...	...	...	
Supā	37,594	73,151	8,720	...	...	
Sarbhun	64,127	601,257	...	...	...	
Khoblori [?Kumbharia] ...	4,024	026,760		...	...	
Ghandevi	4,524	835,330	7,310	...	...	
Kharka [Kharsawa], on the Timi	42.019	629,310	...	...	...	
Karodah [Kathodra] ...	000,704	383,240	24,550	...	...	
Kāmrej	68,044	328,205	...	...	...	
Kos [-amba], has a stone fort	9,771	228,390	...	...	... ...	
Lohari	5,928	85,280	...	...		
Maroli, on the sea ...	17,044	370,410	...	...	...	
Mahwah (Moha ?) on the sea	15,016	100,290	...	...	...	
Nārolī	1,620	65,220	...	...	...	
Nosari, with a manufactory of perfumed oil, found nowhere else ...	17,353	297,720	...	...	...	
Nariād, on the sea ...	7,290	130,700	...	...	...	

Sarkār of Godhrā.

Containing 12 *Mahals*. 535,255 *Bighas*. Revenue 3,418,624 *Dāms*. Castes various. Cavalry 1,000. Infantry 5,000.

	Bigha	D.		Bigha	D.
Audhā [Aradrā]	17,877	184,935	Bera [Bariya] ...	37,318	257,202
Atlawara [?Atar Sunba] ...	46,704	63,460	Jadnagar* ...	46,690	120,660

* *Jadnagar*—either Jambughoda or Chandpur.

Sarkār of Godhrā—Contd.

	Bigha	D.		Bigha	D.
Jhālod [Halol] ...	92,409	794,654	Kohāna [Kadana]	20,858	785,360
Dhānbod [Dhanpur] ...	17,082		Marāl [Marwa]	46,755	525.975
Shehera ...	35,702	146,322	Mahadwārah	19,285	10,826
Godhra with sub. dist. ...	150,250	785,660			

Sarkār of Sorath (Kathiawad).

Containing 12 *Mahals,* of which 13 are ports. Revenue 63,437,366 *Dāms.* Cavalry 17,000. Infantry 365,000.

	Revenue D.		Revenue D.
Una	7,620,388	Dharwār [Dholarwa] ...	59,792
Aivej	780,500	Dhāntror	252,048
Amreli	1,784,160	Dhāri	644,270
Apletah	1,214,592	Rānpur	16,127
Pattan Deo [Somnath] ...	4,453,912	Rālgan	113,280
Bānwāra [?Wadhwan] ...	2,049,340	Rāmot	28,320
Belkhā	140,000	Siyor	42,480
Bālsar	509,760	Sarii	4,936
Beri [? Baori]	145,600	Sultānpur	424,800
Barwa [? Baroda] ...	50,664	Gariadhar	623,040
Bandah	84,960	Korinār	4,538,560
Bāndor [Wanod] ...	14,060	Ghogah (Gogo), exclusive of port	
Bhimrād	28,320	Kianābanāerā	42,480
Pālitana	240,592	Kathar	127,480
Bagsra [? Digsar] ...	56,340	Garidhari	598,704
Barar	734,790	Gondal	56,640
Barwārā [? Wasawad] ...	74,792	Kotiānā (Katiana) ...	1,797,256
Bādli	14,160	Kandolnā	198,432
Talāja	2,435,520	Luliānā	1,423,080
Chokh [Charkha] ...	453,120	Lemorā Batwā	487,576
Jaitpur		Lāthi	296,152
Jagat [Dwarka] ...	803,200	Malikpur	995,048
Chorwād (Charadwa) ...	936,960	Mohwah, (Mowa) ...	2,051,136
Chaurā	97,288	Mandwi	127,440
Jetwad	1,071,660	Manglor	16,689,472
Jasdhon (Jasdān ...	98,560	Medarah	2,208,160
Suburban dist. of Sorath	932,000	Morbi	2,603,326
Daulatābād	357,424	Miānah	14,106
Dāng	4,410	Nāgsari	755,376
Dungar	760,400	Hatasni (?)	1,012,592

Port duties.

	Revenue Mahmudis		Revenue Mahmudis
Port of Manglor ...	27,000	Port of Mohwah (Mowa)	1,000
„ Pattan Deo ...	25,000	„ Meykor ? ...	3,000
„ Korinār ...	1,000	„ Dungar ...	1,000
„ Nāgsari ...	10,000	„ Talājā, 4 *Mahals*	7,000
„ Porbandar ...	27,228	„ Una	15,000

Princes of Gujarāt.

Seven princes reigned in succession 196 years.

	Years.
Bana-rāj Chauhan[1]	60
Jog Rāj	35
Bhimrāj	52
Bhor	29
Bahr Singh	25
Ratnādat (*var.* Rashādat)	15
Sāmant	7

* *Sorath* corresponds to mod. Junagad. The following emendations are suggested from Hamilton's *E. I. Gazetteer* and the Survey of India *Atlas*: Dhantror (=Dhamnagar), Dhari (=Darwa), Rālgaon (=Ranigaon), Siyor (=Sihor), Sarii (=Sarya), Korinar (=Kauri Nagar, 10 m. N. of Diu point), Kathar (=Kantharia), Kandolna (=Kadorna), Luliana (=Lilaola), Una =Una-Delwara).—*J. Sarkar.*

[1] The following table is from the *U. T.* taken from the *Ain-i-Akbari,* and collated with the Agni Purāna of Wilford.

A.D.
696. Saila Deva, living in retirement at Ujjain found and educated.
745. (S. 802) Banarāja, son of Samanta Sinh (Chohān) who founded Anhalpur, called after Anala Cohān.
806. Jagarāja.
841. Bhira Rājā, (Bhunda Deva. Wilford).
866. Bheur.
895. Behersinh.
920. Reshadat, (Raja Adity W.).
935. Samanta, (dau. married son of Delhi Raja). The total of years of reigns in the A. A. makes 223 instead of 196. G. and T. give Bhimrāj 25 instead of 42, and thus correct the error.

Ten princes of the Solanki race reigned 224 years.[1]

	Yrs.	Ms.
Mulrāj Solanki	56	0
Chāmand	13	0
Balabha	0	6
Durlabha, his nephew	11	6
Bhim, his nephew	42	0
Karan	31	0
Jai Singh, called also Sudhrāj	50	0
Kumārpāl, grandson of his uncle	23	0
Ajaipal, his nephew	8	0
Lakhmul	8	0

Six princes of the Bāghelah tribe reigned 126 years.[2]

	Yrs.	Ms.	Ds.
Hardmul Bāghelah	12	5	0
Baldeva	34	6	10
Bhim, his nephew	42	0	0
Arjun Deva	10	0	0
Sārang Deva	21	0	0
Karan	6	10	15

[1] The totals give only 238 years. The *U. T.* runs as follows :—

A.D.
910. Mula Rāja, usurped the throne.
1025. Chāmund, invaded by Sultan Mahmud (Samanta. W.).
1038. Vallabha (ancient line restored).
1039. Durlabha (Dabisalima Ferishta) usurped the throne.
1050. Bhima Rāja.
Kaladeva (Karan. A. A.) Carna Rajendra or Visaladeva, (W.) who became paramount sovereign of Delhi.
1094. Siddha or Jayasinha, an usurper. Kumārapal, poisoned (by Ajayapala, son of Jayasinha).

[2] The *U. T.* give the following :—

The Bhāghela tribe.

Mula (Lakhmul. A. A. Lakhan Raya. W.) without issue.
Birdmul } Baluca—Mula, W. of Bhāghela tribe.
Beildeva }

A.D.
1209. W. Bhima Deva, or Bala Bhima Deva, same as last W.
1250. Arjun Deva, } A. A.
1260. Saranga Deva, }
1281. Karan }
Karna the Gohila fled to the Deccan when in the year 1309 Gujarāt was annexed to Delhi by Alā ud din.

Fourteen (Muhammadan) princes* reigned about 160 years.

A.D.		Yrs.	Ms.	Ds.
1391.	Sultān Muzaffar Shāh, ...	3	8	16
1411.	Sultān Ahmad, I, his grandson (builds Ahmadābād and Ahmadnagar), ...	32	6	20
1443.	Mahammad Shāh, his son, ...	7	9	4
1451.	Qutb ud din Ahmad Shāh (opposes Malwa King and Chitor Raja Kombha), ...	7	0	13
1459.	Dāud Shāh, his uncle, (deposed in favour of)	0	0	7
1459.	Mahmud Shāh I, son of Muhammad Shāh (Begarrā : two expeditions to Deccan), ...	55	1	4
1511.	Sultān Muzaffar, his son, (war with Rājā Sangrām), ...	14	9	0
1526.	Sultan Sikandar, his son, (assassinated), ...	0	10	16
1526.	Sultan Nasir Khān, his brother, (Mahmud Shāh II, displaced by), ...	0	4	0
1526.	Sultan Bahādur, son of Sultān Muzaffar, (invades Mālwa : murdered by Portuguese), ...	11	9	0
1536.	Muhammad Shāh, sister's son, (Fāruqi of Mālwa), ...	0	9	0
1536.	Sultān Mahmud, grandson of Muzaffar, ...	18	2	some days.
1553.	Sultān Ahmad (II) a descendant of Sultān Ahmad, (spurious heir set up by ministers), ...	8	0	0

* List of Gujrat Muslim rulers :

Muzaffar I	A.H. 798/1396 A.D.
Ahmad I	814/1411
Md. I. Karim	846/1442
Qutbuddin	855/1451
Dāud	862/1458
Mahmud I	862/1458
Muzaffar II	917/1511
Sikandar	932/1526
Mahmud II	932/1526
Bahādur	932/1526
Muhammad II	943/1537
Muhammad III	943/1537
Ahmad II	961/1554
Muzaffar III	969-980/1562-1572

A.D.		Yrs. Ms. Ds.
1561.	Sultān Muzaffar III, (Habbu, a supposititious son of Mahmud), ...	12 & odd.
1583.	Gujarāt becomes a province of Akbar's Empire.	

The Hindu chronicles record that in the year 802 of Bikramājit, corresponding with A.H. 154 *Sarāj* kindled the torch of independence and Gujarāt became a separate state. Rājā Sri Bhor Deva ruler of Kanauj put to death one of his dependants, named Sāmant Singh for his evil disposition, disloyalty and disorderly conduct, and seized his possessions. His wife was pregnant at the time, and urged by distress, she fled to Gujarāt and in an uninhabited waste gave birth to an infant. It happened that a Jain devotee named Saila Deva passing that way took compassion on the child and committed it to the charge of one of his disciples who took it to Rādhanpur, and brought it up with tender solicitude. When he grew to manhood, associating with wicked reprobates, he fell to outrage and highway robbery and a gang of free-booters was formed. He plundered the Gujarāt treasure on its way to Kanauj, and through the good fortune that attended him, he was joined by a grain merchant[1] called Chāmpā. Wisdom guided his sword and from works of evil he inclined to deeds of goodness till in the fiftieth year of his age, he acquired the sovereignty of the state, and founded Pattan. It is said that he long deliberated regarding the site of his capital and was diligent in search of a suitable place. A cowherd called Anhil informed him that he knew an excellent site which he would show on condition that the king would call the city after his name. His offer being accepted, he directed them to a wooded spot where a hare, he narrated, had grappled with a dog and by sheer strength of limb had got away. The Rājā founded the city there and named it Anhilpur. Astrologers have predicted that after the lapse of 2,500 years, 7 months, 9 days, and 44 *gharis,* it shall be in ruins. Through the corruption of language and syllabic change it came to be called Nahrwālah, but as in the tongue of that country 'chosen' is rendered 'Pattan,' it became universally distinguished by that name.

Rājā Sāmant Singh gave his daughter in marriage to Sri Dandak Solanki, a descendant of the Delhi princes.

[1] A trade in favour, apparently, with Gujarāt kings. One was the intimate friend and counsellor of Sultān Muhammad. See Bayley, pp. 132 and 188.

She died when on the point of giving birth, but a son was by a surgical operation taken from her womb. The moon at the time was in the sixteenth[1] mansion termed by the Hindus *Mul,* and hence he was named *Mulrāj.* Rājā Sāmant Singh adopted him as his own son and watched over his education. When he grew up, he entered into a conspiracy with some evil-disposed persons. The Rājā in a fit of drunkenness abdicated in his favour, but on becoming sober recalled his promise which so infuriated this miscreant that he slew his benefactor and assumed the sovereignty. During the reign of Rājā Chāmand A.H. 416 or 1064 of the era of Bikramājit,[2] Sultān Mahmud of Ghazni conquered this country, but on leaving, he found no fitter person on whom he might confer the government than a descendant of the royal line, and having arranged for the annual payment of a tribute, he returned by way of Sind. What is remarkable is that at the desire of this prince he carried with him captive another scion of the same family. After a time, either through fear or foresight, the captive's restoration was solicited by the same prince who went out to meet him as he approached his territory in order that intriguers might not secure his favour. On the day that they were to meet, the Rājā fell asleep for a short space under a tree, when an animal of prey tore out an eye. At that time a blind man being incapacitated from reigning, the ungrateful soldiers substituted the captive prince in his place and placed the Rājā in confinement.[3]

Kumārpāl Solanki through fear of his life lived in retirement, but when the measure of Jai Singh's days became full, he came forth from the wastes of disappointed ambition and seated himself on the throne and considerably enlarged his dominions. Ajaipāl wickedly poisoned his sovereign and for a fleeting gratification has acquired eternal abhorrence.

Lakhmul having no issue, the worthiest representative of the Baghelah tribe was chosen as sovereign.

---

[1] Variously taken as the 17th, 19th and 24th lunar asterism, containing 11 stars, apparently those in the tail of Scorpio and said to be unlucky. In the dissertation on Astronomy that follows in a subsequent book, Mul is counted as the 19th mansion.

[2] 1064 A.B. is equivalent to A.D. 1007 and A.H. 416 to A.D. 1025. It was in Sept. 1024 A.D. that Mahmud set out from Ghazni in his expedition against Somnāth.

[3] The story is related at greater length from the *Mirat i Ahmadi* in Bayley's Hist of Gujarāt, pp. 29-34 and its probability defended in a discursive note.

During the reign of Karan, the troops of Sultān Alā u'd din overran Gujarāt. Karan, defeated in the field, fled to the Deccan. Although previous to this time Muizz u'd din Sām[1] and Qutb u'd din Eibak had made expeditions into the country, it was not until the reign of Alā u'd din that it was formally annexed to Delhi.

In the reign of Muhammad, son of Firuz Shāh, Nizām Mustakhrāj, called also Rāsti Khān,[2] was appointed to the government of Gujarāt, but his injustice becoming oppressive, he was removed and the viceroyalty was conferred on Zafar Khān son of Wajih u'l Mulk Tānk. The former governor disloyally rebelling, was killed in the field. The events of this time may be gathered from the history of the Delhi sovereigns. His son Tātār Khān was a man of base character and in whom wickedness was ingrained. At this period after the death of Sultān Muhammad when the throne of Delhi devolved on Sultān Mahmud, considerable anarchy prevailed. Zafar Khān withdrew from affairs and Tātār Khān assumed the royal state and marched against Delhi, but was poisoned at the instigation of his father[3] who coming forth from his retirement had the *Khutbah* read and the coin struck in his own name, and was proclaimed under the title of Sultān Muzaffar. (1407.) Gujarāt thus became an independent kingdom and the government of the province was established in the *Tānk* family. The father of Zafar, Wajih u'l Mulk had been a Brahman and was converted to Islām. Ahmad the son of Tātār Khān conspired against the life of his grandfather and took possession of the throne thus garnering eternal perdition. Ahmadābād was founded by him. With deep design and meditated hypocrisy he withdrew himself from all worldly pageantries till at a festival when all suspicion was laid asleep in the midst of universal enjoyment, he put to death twelve of his uncles. Subsequently he applied himself with earnestness to the

---

[1] Otherwise Shahāb ud din Ghori.

[2] Malik Mufarrah Sultāni, who afterwards obtained the title of Farhat ul Mulk Rāsti Khān. Zafar Khān was appointed to succeed him on the 2nd Rabia I, 793 A.H. (21st Feb. 1931) (Bayley *Hist. of Guj.*), p. 58. Wajih ul Mulk was a Hindu called Sadhāran, converted to Islam and belonged, says the *Mirat i Sikandari,* to the Tānk caste, an outcast branch of the Khatris. One of them was expelled for his use of strong drinks and the name is said in Hindi to signify an outcast. The derivation is asserted to rest on some form of the Sanskrit *tyāga,* meaning separation, divorce. See Bayley's note. *Ibid,* p. 67. Baber calls the race *Tang. Memoirs,* Erskine, p. 311.

[3] It is commonly believed, says the *Mirat i Sikandari* that Tātār Khān placed his father in confinement and seated himself on the throne under title of Mhd. Shāh, whence the reprisal. *Ibid.,* p. 81-82.

duties of his government and was filled with continual remorse, and to his last breath set himself to a just and capable administration of the state.

When Dāud Khān was deposed on account of his incapacity, Fath Khān son of Muhammad Shāh was raised to the throne and was proclaimed as Sultān Mahmud (I). He distinguished himself by his recognition of merit[1] and by his justice, and girt himself with the fence of munificence and liberality. Malik Shabān who held the title of Imād u'l Mulk was of the utmost service to him.[2] In the beginning of his reign some of the wealthy favourites conspired against the life of their lord and in the first instance plotted the overthrow of this judicious and sincere counsellor. Like intriguers as they were, they conveyed false allegations to the king, and as the worldly-minded are suspicious of each other, he imprisoned this peerless denizen of the world of faith and purposed putting him to death. He was on the point of being condemned when Malik Abdu'llah the superintendent of the elephants who had the royal ear, revealed the innocence of his faithful minister and the designs of the conspirators. The king skilfully contrived his escape and, the veil of their pretence being rent asunder, the miscreants took to arms. The royal guard and the slaves together with the officers in charge of the elephants made a stand against them, and the elephants themselves proved of service in chastising the rebels. Disgracefully routed, these disloyal subjects met with just retribution.. At Mahmud's death, his son Muzaffar Shāh, with the assistance of the nobles, ascended the throne and assumed the title of Sultān Muzaffar (II). His reign was beneficent. Shāh Ismail of the Sufi dynasty of Persia sent him as presents the choicest goods of Irāq[3] and he in turn courteously reciprocated his acknowledgments. On his decease, his son succeeded him under the title of Sultān Sikandar. In a short time he was wickedly done to death by Imād u'l Mulk who raised his brother Nasir Khān to the throne. The nobles plotted to

[1] And likewise by his enormous appetite. His daily allowance of food was one *man Gujarāt* weight (equal to 15 Bahloli *seers*). He put aside 5 *seers* of boiled rice and before going to sleep, placed half on one side of his couch and half on the other, so that on whichever side he awoke, he might find something to eat. This was followed in the morning by a cup of honey, a cup of butter and 100 to 150 plaintains. After this, Abul Fazl's appetite sinks into insignificance. *His* allowance was 22 *seers* daily.

[2] The whole account will be found in Bayley under this monarch's reign. The reader is referred to that work for details of this historical synopsis.

[3] A turquoise cup of great value, a chest full fo jewels, many valuable tissues and 30 Persian horses. Bayley, p. 244.

displace him. The king appealed for succour to His Majesty Bāber and engaged to surrender to him the port of *Dib* (Diu) with its dependencies and several *krors* of *tankahs,* if he would advance in aid with his victorious troops. On account of his former ungrateful conduct, his offer was refused.[1] At this juncture, Bāhadur the son of Sultān Muzaffar came from Delhi at the invitation of the Bābriyas[2] and the nobles joined his standard. During his father's reign he was unable to remain at court through the envy borne towards him by his brother (Sikandar). He, therefore, betook himself to Sultān Ibrahim Lodi at Delhi and was received with favour. The nobles of Jaunpur invited him to be their king, and his intentions were inclined that way, when at this time his partisans wrote to him from Gujarat and entreated his acceptance of the throne. He willingly set out for the capital and being successful, he made his administration prosperous by his justice and liberality. Carried away by the intoxication of worldly success, he imprudently engaged in a war with Humayun, and being defeated, sullenly withdrew in discomfiture.[3]

At his death, Mirān Muhammad ruler of Khāndesh, his nephew, whom during his lifetime he had constituted his heir, was in his absence proclaimed in the *khutbah* by the nobles, but died shortly before reaching Gujarāt. Mahmud, grandson of Sultān Muzaffar, who was then in confinement, succeeded him. A miscreant called Burhān with some of his adherents put him to death[4] and under pretence of

[1] Ferishta says (Bayley, p. 319) that this letter never reached Bāber, the Rājah of Dungarpur having intercepted it.

[2] See Bayley, p. 35, n.; and for his adventures after leaving Gujarāt, p. 321 *et seq.*

[3] Baber says of him that he acted rightly in enforcing the law of retaliation by putting to death Imād Mulk who had strangled his brother Sikandar, but besides this, he slew a number of his father's Amirs and gave proof of a blood-thirsty and ungovernable nature.

[4] Bayley, p. 445, *et seq.* Burhān who had been a low favourite of the king, poisoned and stabbed his master and sallied forth from the palace in the pomp of royalty when he was met and slain by Shirwān Khān Bhatti, adopted son of Afzal one of the murdered nobles. Ferishta's account is that on the death of the king becoming known, Itimād Khān with Changiz Khan, Ulug Khān, Habshi and others, came out to oppose him. Burhān was thrown at the first charge and killed by Shirwān Khān. His feet were tied to a rope and he was dragged throughout the city. The *Mirat-i-Sikandari* gives the name of Razi ul Mulk to one of the nobles who was sent to bring the new king, Ahmad, to the capital, but Ferishta expressly states that this descendant of Ahmad Shāh was named Razi ul Mulk and was raised to the throne as Ahmad Shāh II. He continues, that disgusted with his nominal sovereignty, after a 5 years' tutelarge he took refuge with Mirān Mubārak Shāh one of the principal nobles on whose death in the field, an accommodation was again effected with Itimād Khān, but having expressed himself too openly as desirous of death of that minister, he himself was found dead the next day,

establishing a rightful succession, massacred twelve of the nobles. Itimād Khān prudently absented himself on the occasion, and next morning collecting his followers, attacked him and put him to the death he deserved. He then set up one Razi u'l Mulk by name a descendant of Sultān Ahmad, I, under the title of Sultān Ahmad (II) as a nominal sovereign and took the government into his own hands. But when the boy grew to manhood, he altered his purpose and carrying him to the house of one of his adherents, he slew him and then leading some unknown minor by the hand, swore upon oath that he was the son of the last Sultān Mahmud (II). By fraudful allegations, he bestowed on him the sovereign authority and giving him the title of Sultān Muzaffar, he himself assumed the reins of power, until his present Majesty threw the shadow of justice over the province and annexed this prosperous country to the imperial dominions.

May it ever be adorned with perpetuity and high and low enjoy unfading blessings.

---

near the river opposite the house of Wajih ul Mulk and it was given out that, caught in a love intrigue in that nobleman's house, he had been unwittingly slain. The *Mirat-i-Sikandari* tells the story more in detail. On his death, Itimād Khān produced a boy (not named in Ferishta nor, I think, in the *Mirat*) whom he swore to be the son of Mahmud Shāh II, his mother's pregnancy not having been discovered till the 5th month when too late to check it. For Mahmud had unnaturally interdicted the fertility of his wives to avoid a disputed throne. The nobles accepted or feared to oppose the pretension, and the boy was placed under the control of Itimad Khān. The subsequent history may be read in Ferishta, or in Brigg's free but generally faithful rendering, but the events of his worthless life—it cannot be called a reign—are lost in the contests of the nobles for their share of short-lived power till the incorporation of the kingdom with the empire on the 24th Rajab A.H. 890 (Nov. 20th, 1572). Bayley's translation concludes with the death of Mahmud Shāh IV, but his original continues the history of Gujarāt to 1001 A.H. (1592-3) and the death by his own hand of the last of its sovereigns.

SUBAH OF AJMER

It is situated in the second climate. Its length from the village of Pokhar (*Bhakar*—Pushkar) and dependencies of *Amber* to Bikaner and *Jaisalmir* is 168 *kos*. Its breadth from the extreme limits of the *Sarkār* of *Ajmer* to *Bānswārah* is 150 *kos*. To the east lies *Agra* : to the north the dependencies of *Delhi:* to the south *Gujarāt:* to the west *Dipālpur* and *Multān*. The soil is sandy, and water obtainable only at great depth, whence the crops are dependent on rain. The winter is temperate, but the summer intensely hot. The spring harvest is inconsiderable. *Jowāri, Lahdarah* and *Moth* are the most abundant crops. A seventh or an eighth of the produce is paid as revenue, and very little in money. The people dwell in tent-shaped bamboo huts. To the south are the (Aravalli) mountains of which the passes are difficult to traverse.

This Subah is formed of *Mewār, Marwār* and *Hadauti.*[1] The former possesses 10,000 (troops) and the whole of the *Sarkār* of *Chitor* is dependent on it. Its length is 40 *kos* by 30 in breadth. It has three famous fortresses, *Chitor* the residence of the governor, *Kombhalmer*[2] and *Māndal.* In the village of *Jāwar,*[3] one of the dependencies of *Chainpur* is a zinc mine. In *Chainpur* and other dependencies of *Māndal* are copper mines, which are extremely profitable.

The chief of the state was formerly called *Rāwal,* but for a long time past has been known as *Rānā.*[4] He is of the Ghelot clan and pretends a descent from Noshirwān the Just.[5] An ancestor of this family through the vicissitudes of fortune came to Berār and was distinguished as the chief of *Narnālah.* About eight hundred years previous to the present time, *Narnālah* was taken by an enemy and many were slain. One *Bāpā,* a child, was carried by his mother

---

[1] Harowtee or Hārāoti, a tract formed of the territory of Kotah and Bundi, and named after a dominant tribe of Rājputs.

[2] Komulmir is a pass that runs through a series of rugged ravines in the Aravalli ranges and is defended by a fortress. In art. Udaipur, it is spelt Kumalmer.

[3] *Jāwar,* 24 miles S. of Udaipur, is said to have possessed zinc mines now unworked.

[4] The foundation of the Ghelot dynasty in Rājputāna was effected by Bappa Rawal who is said to have established himself in Chitor and Mewār in 728 A.D. *I. G.*

[5] It is asserted that a daughter of Noshirwān, whose queen was a daughter of Maurice of Constantinople married into the Udaipur royal family.

from this scene of desolation to *Mewār,* and found refuge with *Rājah Mandalik,*[1] a *Bhil.* When he grew up to man's estate he followed the pursuit of a shepherd and was devoted to hunting in which his daring was so conspicuous that he became in favour with the Rājā and a trusted minister of state. On the death of the Rājā, his four nephews disputed the succession, but they eventually decided to resign their pretensions in favour of *Bāpā* and to acknowledge his authority. *Bāpā,* however, declined their offer. It happened one day that the finger of one of these four brothers began to bleed, and he drew with the blood the ceremonial mark of installation on the forehead of Bāpā, and the others concurred in accepting his elevation. He then assumed the sovereignty. To this day the custom continues of making with human blood this sign of investiture on any *Rāna* who succeeds to the throne. The ungrateful monarch put the four brothers to death.. On a former occasion while passing through the wilds, mistaking one *Marich* [Rishi], a hermit, for a wild animal, he fitted an arrow to his bow. The hermit intuitively prescient of this action through his purity of heart, made himself known, and the Rājā repentantly excused himself and humbly visited him with assiduity. The hermit one day predicted his elevation, and marvellous tales are told regarding him. Having made his head quarters at *Sisodā,* the tribe is called *Sisodiah* and as a Brāhman, at the beginning of their history nurtured their house, they are accounted as belonging to this caste.

When *Rāwal Rattan Si* died, a relative named *Arsi* was raised to the throne and entitled Rānā from whom the present *Rāna Umrā* is tenth in descent, thus; *Hamir, Kaitā, Lākha, Mokul, Kombhā, Rāemal, Sangā, Udai Singh, Partāb, Umrā.*

Ancient chronicles record that Sultān Alā ud din Khilji king of Delhi had heard that *Rāwal Rattan Si* prince of *Mewār* possessed a most beautiful wife. He sent to demand her and was refused, upon which he led an army to enforce compliance and laid siege to *Chitor.* After a long persistence in beleaguering the place in vain, he had recourse to artifice and proposed terms of peace and friendship. The Rājā readily acquiesced and invited him to an entertainment. The Sultān entered the fort with his chosen followers and the meeting took place amid festivity and mirth, and finding

[1] Rao Mandalik says Bayley (*Hist. of Gujarāt*) is the title assumed by all the chiefs of Girnār.

his opportunity he seized the Rājā and carried him off. It is said that the Sultān's retinue consisted of a hundred men and 300 picked soldiers dressed as attendants. Before the Rājā's troops could assemble he was hurried away to the camp amidst the wailing of his people. The king kept the Rājā in close confinement with a view to extort compliance with his desire. The faithful ministers of the Rājā implored the king not to injure him and promised to deliver up to him not only the object of his love but other suitable partners of his harem. They also sent a forged letter purporting to come from the virtuous queen and lulled his suspicions to sleep. The king was delighted and not only refrained from personal violence but treated the Rājā with cordiality. It is related that 700 of the choicest troops dressed as women were placed in litters and set out for the king's camp and it was given out that the Rāni with a large number of her attendants was on the way to the royal pavilion. When they approached the camp, word was sent that the Rāni wished to have an interview with the Rājā previous to entering the king's quarters. Lapped in his illusive dream of security the king granted the interview, during which the soldiers seizing the opportunity, threw off their disguise and bore off their prince. Time after time the Rājputs stood to face their pursuers fighting manfully and many were slain before the Rājā had gone far. At length the Chauhāns, *Gaurā* and *Bādal* made a stand fighting to the death enabling the Rāwal to reach Chitor in safety amidst universal acclamation. The king having endured great hardships during the siege and finding it to no purpose, returned to Delhi. After an interval, he set his heart again on the same project but returned discomfited. The Rāwal wearied with these assaults, conceived that an interview with the king might result in an alliance and that he would thus escape this state of continual strife. Guided by a traitor he met the king at a place 7 *kos* from *Chitor* where he was basely slain. His relative *Arsi,* after this fatal event, was raised to the throne. The Sultān returned to the siege of *Chitor* and captured it. The Rājā was slain fighting and all the women voluntarily perished by fire.

Hamir his son betook himself to the adjacent mountains. *Sultān Muhammad Khuni*[1] made over the govern-

[1] "The murderer," the special title to fame of Muhammad Tuglak, but this monopoly of the epithet is scarcely fair to many other members of the royal houses of Delhi.

ment of Chitor to Māldeva Chauhān ruler of Jālor. As this prince was unable to bring the province into order, he summoned *Hamir,* made him his son-in-law, and through his means restored its prosperity. At his death, Hamir made away with his sons and raised the standard of independence.

The present local militia consists of 16,000 cavalry and 40,000 infantry, but Mewār formerly controlled much more extensive territories, so much so that Rājah Sanka (Sanga) possessed a force of 180,000 cavalry and a numerous infantry.

Mārwār is 100 *kos* in length by 60 in breadth, and it comprises the *Sarkārs* of *Ajmer, Jodhpur, Sirohi, Nāgor,* and *Bikaner.* It has long been the head quarters of the Rāthor tribe. When Muizz ud din Sām had terminated his campaign against *Pithurā* (Prithwi Rājā, A.D. 1191-93), he resolved to turn his arms against *Jaichand* king of *Kanauj.* The Rājah in his flight was drowned in the Ganges.[1]. His brother's son Siha, who resided in *Shamsābād* was slain with a large number of troops. His three sons *Sutik, Ashwatthama* and *Aj* set out for Gujarāt, and on their way rested at *Pāli* near *Sojhat.* In this city dwelt a number of Brāhmans who were much molested by the *Minah* tribe, some of whom at this period made a raid on the town. The exiles came out, attacked them valorously, and put them to flight. The Brāhmans gave them great honour and treated them with every consideration and thus alleviated in some degree their distress of heart. As they acquired the means of worldly success they grew bolder and seized *Kher* [Kumbher] from the *Gohel* tribe and thus advanced their condition. *Sutik* independently wrested *Edar* from the *Minahs,* and *Aj* setting out for *Baglānah,* took that district by force from the *Kolis.* From that time their descendants have inhabited the country. The descendants of *Ashwatthamā* who remained in *Mārwār* gradually gained credit till eventually *Maldeva* his sixteenth descendant waxed so powerful, that Sher Khān nearly lost his life in his campaign against him.[2]

---

[1] Other accounts assert that he was slain by an arrow from the bow of Qutb-uddin the favorite general of the Muhammad Ghori, and the founder of the Dynasty of the Slave Kings. It is historical that his body was found and recognised by his false teeth, "a circumstance," says Elphinstone in the solitary instance of humour in his solemn history, "which throws grave light on the state of manners." One result of this defeat was the retreat of the greater part of the Rahtor clan from Kanauj to Mārwār.

[2] Sher invaded Mārwār in A.D. 1544 and his camp was surprised by an atttack of 12,000 Rājputs who so nearly put an end to his campaigning that he declared he had nearly lost the empire of India for a handful of millet,

This territory contains many forts, but the most important are *Ajmer, Jodhpur, Bikāner, Jaisalmir, Amarkot, Abugarh* and *Jālor.*

Hādāoti is called also the *Sarkār* of Nāgor. It is inhabited by the *Hādā* (Hara) tribe.

This *Subah* comprises 7 *Sarkārs* and 197 *parganahs.* The measured land is 2 *Krors,* 14 *lakhs,* 35,941 *bighas,* 7 *Biswas.* The revenue in money is 28 *krors* 84 *lakhs,* 1,557 *dāms,* (Rs. 7,210,308-14-9) of which 23 *lakhs,* 26,336 *dāms* (Rs. 51,158-6-5) are Suyurghal. The local force is 86,500 cavalry, 347,000 infantry.

Sarkār of Ajmer.

Containing 28 *Parganahs,* 5,605,487 *Bighas.* Revenue in money, 62,183,390 Dāms. *Suyurghāl* 1,475,714 *Dāms.* Tribes, *Kachhwāhah, Afghān, Chauhān.*

	Bighas.	Revenue D	Suyurghāl D.
Ajmer with dist. its fort on a hill, one of	795,335	6,214,731	D.
the most important in India	1,135,095	12,256,297	802,440
Amber, has stone fort on a hill ...	179,573	1,755,960	...
Arāin	279-295	2,200,000	...
Parbat [-sar]	90,488	486,161	...
Phāgi	349,774	1,400,000	...
Bhināi	68,712	271,256	...
Bharāna [Baghera]	168,712	749,733	...
Bawāl [? Borach]	81,914-11	600,000	...
Bāhal [Barl]	15,522	435,664	15,674
Bāndar Sindri	24,220	270,000	
Bharondā	351,779-12	3,300,090	...
Tusinā [? Tilonia]	138,718	241,442	...
Jobner	27,092-18	501,844	...
Jhāk	49,065	1,200,000	...
Deogāon [Baghera]	76,548	692,512	...
Koshanpur [? Kishanpur]	194,064	9,649,947	277,537
Sāmbhar, has a stone fort	245,136	1,616,825	...
Sarwār, has a brick fort	72,098	1,270,000	16,027
Sithlā [Setholao]	147,923	1,860,016	...
Kekri	50,640	1,808,000	...
Kherwah	71,356	7,020,347	...
Mārot	252,871	5,756,402	...
Muzābād	251,973	1,459,577	...
Masaudābād [Masuda]	14,361	1,587,990	...
Narāina	266,614	2,660,159	260,100
Harsuli, has a brisk fort	163,273	1,200,926	926

Sarkār of Chitor.

Containing 26 *Parganahs,* 1,678,800 *Bighas,* 17 *Biswas.* Revenue, 30,047,649 *Dāms. Suyurghāl,* 360,737 *Dāms.* Tribes, Rājput Sesodia, Cavalry, 22,000. Infantry, 82,000.

	Bighas	Revenue D	Suyurghāl D.
Islāmpur, known as Rāmpura ...	101,526	7,000,000	...
Udaipur, here a large lake about 16 *Kos* in circumference; by its means wheat crops are grown	...	1,120,000 in money	...

Sarkār of Chitor—contd.

	Bighas	Revenue	Suyurghāl D.
Uparmāl	27,805	280,000	...
Arnod	44,720	200,000	...
Islāmpur, known as Mohan	...	126,600 in money	...
Badnor, has a stone fort	113,265	4,311,551	59,815
Phuliā do.	257,481	2,843,470	43,470
Banerā	58,038	3,296,200	244,000
Pur	199,209	2,601,041	13,452
Bhainsror, has a stone fort	...	1,200,000	...
Bāgor (Bāgol)	1,744-17	39,550	...
Begun	234,804	1,175,729	...
Barsi [? Patti] Hājipur, has a stone fort	35,098	1,375,000	...
Chitor, with sub. dist. 2 mahals, has a stone fort, and is a frontier of Hindustān proper	451,118	800,000	...
Jiran	39,218	1,985,250	...
Sānwārghāti	...	470,294	...
Sādri, has a stone fort	5,991	400,020	...
Sembal [?Sanwad] with the cultivated tracts	...	100,000 in money	...
Kosiānah [? Gosunda]	52,713	263,812	...
Māndalgarh, has a stone fort on a hill ...	...	3,384,750 in money	...
Māndal has a brick fort	18,848	447,090	...
Mandāriyā [Madri]	...	160,000 in money	...
Nimach &c. 3 mahals	21,416	719,202	...

Sarkār of Rantambhor.

Containing 73 Mahals. 6,024,196 *Bighas,* 11 *Biswas.* Revenue, 89,824,576 *Dāms.* *Suyurghāl,* 181,134 *Dāms.* Rājput Hādā (Ḥara). Cavalry, 9,000. Infantry, 25,000.

	Bighas	Revenue D.	Suyurghāl D.
Alanpur	18,481	1,562,239	20,209
Unārā	57,308	1,237,169	...
Atādā [?Etawa]	45,349	770,525	...
Āton	14,584	600,000	...

Sarkār of Rantambhor—contd.

	Bighas	Revenue D.	Suyurghāl D.
Islampur [=Aligarh]	5,191	77,500	...
Amkhorah	...	160,000	...
Antardah	166,173	in money	...
Awān Bosamir	25,747	1,500,000	...
Bundi, has a stone fort on a hill	33,161	1,200,000	...
Baonli, has a stone fort	151,430	2,622,747	22,747
Baroda	267,326	4,571,000	...
Jarwāra	163,226	1,969,776	...
Pātan [Kesorai]	139,280	2,800,000	...
Bhadlāon	96,895	2,686,389	...
Baklānt	149,087	1,200,000	...
Palāita	29,302	1,400,000	...
Bhosor	40,677	600,000	...
Banahta	21,257	524,356	...
Bilona	31,615	456,479	...
Bijari	15,594	334,800	...
Bālākhatri	33,930	300,000	...
Bhori Bhāri (Bari Pahar)	16,845	110,000	...
Bārān	242,107	880.000	...
Tonk	502,402	7,500.000	...
Toda	443,028	5,859.006	...
Todri	400,768	5,456,840	...
Talād	32,509	423.288	...
Jetpur	23,014	928.500	...
Chātsu	516,525	7,536.829	...
Jhalāwa (Jhalāi)	13,180	500,000	...
Jhāin	37,753	475.000	...
Khilchipur	30,813	1,209.886	...
Dhari (? Darah)	97,861	1,800,000	...
	54,668	409,260	
Dablāna	...	733,400	9,260
		in money	
Rantambhor with sub. dist	371-19	156,795	
Rawanjna (Dungar)	49,745	430,354	1,505
Sheopur	494,070	5,041,306	6,292
Sārsop	36,636	1,058,876	...
Sahansāri	28,575	300,000	...
Kotā, has a stone fort on a hill, near which the Chambal flows	360,378	3,000.000	...
Khāndar, has a stone fort on a hill	90,246	400,000	...
Khankra	220,350	1,511,994	...
Kheri	35,443	528,178	11,994
Khātoli	2,389	200,000	26,744
Gendawar	6,930-12	188,095	...
Karor, has a stone fort on a hill	6,377	200.000	...
Lākheri do.	3,523	800,000	...
Londa	17,400	250.000	...
Loharwāra	20,334	250,000	...
Luāwad	3,678	125,000	...
Mau-maidana, 16 *Mahals*		4,100,000	...
Malārna	172,693	3,299,241	...
Mangrol	140,799	1,004,348	
Nawai	33,927	930,000	
Nāgar (Nāgor)	33,900	1,000,000	

Sarkār of Jodhpur.

Containing 22 *Mahals.* Revenue 14,528,750 *Dāms.* Tribe, Rāthor, Cavalry 15,000. Infantry, 50,000.

	Revenue D.		Revenue D.
Āsop has a brick fort ...	8,000,000	Jetāran, has a small fort on a hill	3,000,000
Indrāoti	8,000	Dunārā, has a stone fort	100,000
Phalodi, has a stone fort	640,000	Sojat, has a stone fort on a hill	2,812,750
Palpārah [Pipar] ...	1,463,000	Sāalmer do. ...	560,000
Bilara	314,000	Siwānā do. one of the most important strongholds in India ...	',200,000
Pāli &c., 3 *Mahals,* has a small stone fort ...	250,000	Kherwā	220,000
Bahila	180,000	Khimwasar, has a stone fotr	172,000
Podhah has a stone fort	46,003	Gundoj do. ...	90,000
Bhadrārjun, has a stone fort on a plain ...	800,000	Mahewah	960,000
Jodhpur with sub, dist. has a stone fort on a hill	280,000		

Sarkār of Sirohi.

Containing 6 *Mahals.* Revenue 4,2,077,437 *Dāms.* Tribes, Rājput, Ghelot, Afghān. Cavalry, 8000. Infantry, 3,800.

	Revenue D.	Cavalry	Infantry	Tribe
Abugarh and Sirohi, 2 *Mahals;* the latter has a strong stone fort ...	12,000,000	3,000	15,000	Rājput.
Bānswārah, a delightful country; has a stone fort	8,000,000	1,500	20,000	Do.
Jālor, Sānchor, 2 *Mahals;* has a very strong stone fort ...	14,077,437	2,000	5,000	Afghān.
Dungarpur	8,000,000	1,000	2,000	Rājput Ghelot.

Sarkār of Nāgor.

Containing 31 *Mahals.* 8,037,450 *Bighas,* 14 *Biswas.* Revenue, 40,389,830 *Dāms. Suyurghāl,* 30,805 *Dāms.* Castes various. Cavalry, 4,500. Infantry, 22,000.

	Bighas Biswas	Revenue D.	Suyurghāl D.	Cavalry	Infantry	Castes
Amarsar	849,809	7,029,370	...	4000	20,000	Kachhwāhah.
Indāna	262,302	1,313,006	479	...	...	

Sarkār of Nāgor—contd.

	Bighas Biswas	Revenue D.	Suyurghāl D.	Cavalry	Infantry	Castes
Bhadāna	544,340	2,271,960	70460	...	...	...
Baldu	87,947	570,000	...	...	...	...
Patoda	141,370	322,816	...	...	...	...
Baroda	2,620	220.363	...	...	...	...
Bārah Kāin	230,379	58,000	...	...	...	...
Jāel	293,069	955,273	3200	...	...	...
Jārodah	141,592	874,284	2147	...	...	...
Jakhara, surrounded by a waste of sand ..	...	137,757	...	...	...	...
Khārij Khattu, has a stone fort, and a quarry of white marble* ..	77,577	348,814	...	...	...	...
Didwāna, has a brick fort	36,581	4,586,828	15215	...	...	...
Dronpur	219,698	780,085	...	...	...	...
Rewāsā	801,117	1,995,824	...	...	...	...
Run	615,212	913,251	...	...	...	...
Rasulpur	114,985	704,306	...	...	...	...
Rahot	45,269	188,137	...	...	...	...
Sādela	153,032	1,262,930	...	...	...	...
Fatehpur Jhunjhunu, has a stone fort	152,200	1,233,222	...	500	2000	Qiyām Khāni.
Kāsli	28,740	1,587,157	...	...	...	...
Khāela	114,955	558,560	..	...	...	...
Kuchera	270,490	466,890	...	...	...	...
Kolewa [Kolia]	12,748	352,805	...	...	..	...
Kumāri	469,881	435,604	3220	...	...	...
Kheran	26,033	57,160	...	...	...	...
Lādnu	149,760	780,842	4837	...	...	...
Merta, has a stone fort ..	2,114,773	7,701,522	45,433	...	...	...
Manoharnagar	129,895	2,903,386	...	...	...	...
Nokhā	83,096	380,756	...	...	...	...
Nāgor with sub. dist. has a brick fort	57,755-14	813 581	114,440	...	...	...

* *Khatu* is 38 miles s.e. of Nāgor.

Sarkār of Bikaner.

Containing 11 *Mahals*. Revenue 4,750,000 *Dāms*. Tribe, Bhāti. Cavalry, 12,000. Infantry, 50, 000.

	Tribe		Tribe
Bikampur	...	Bikaner	Rāthor.
Barsalpur	...	Jaisalmir	Bhāti.
Bāharmel (Barmer) ...	...	Chhotan	...
Pungal	...	Kotrā	...
Barkal	...	Dewādawar	...
Pokharan	...		

SUBAH OF DELHI.

It is in the third climate. Its length from *Palwal*[1] to *Ludhianah* on the bank of the *Satlej* is 165 *kos*. Its breadth from the *Sarkār* of *Rewāri* to the *Kumāon* hills is 140 *kos*, and again from *Hisār* to *Khizrābād* is 130 *kos*. On the east lies[2] the capital, Agra; on the north-east it marches with *Khairābād* in the *Subah* of *Oudh;* to the north are mountains; on the south the *Subahs* of *Agra* and *Ajmer;* on the west is Ludhiānah. The chief rivers are the *Ganges* and the *Jumna,* and both these take their rise in this *Subah*. There are besides numerous other streams, amongst them the *Ghaghar*. The mountains principally to the north. The climate is nearly temperate. Much of the land is subject to inundation and in some places there are three harvests. The fruits of Irān, Turān and Hindustān are here grown and abundant flowers of various kinds. Lofty buildings of stone and brick delight the eye and gladden the heart, and it is scarce equalled for the choice productions of every clime.

Delhi is one of the greatest cities of antiquity. It was first called *Indrapat* and is situated in long. 114° 38′, lat. 28° 15′. Although some consider it as the second climate, making the southern mountainous system begin from this region they are certainly mistaken as the latitude shows. Sultāns *Qutbuddin* (1206-10), and *Shamsuddin* (Altmish, 1210-35) resided in the citadel of Rajah *Pithura* (Prithwi). Sultān *Ghiyāsuddin Balban* erected another fort, intending it as a (royal) cemetery. He also built a handsome edifice in which if any criminal took sanctuary, he was absolved from retribution. *Muizz ud din Kai Kubād* (1286-9) founded another city on the banks of the *Jumna* called *Kelukhari*. *Amir Khusrau* in his poem the *'Qirānu's Sadain'*[3] eulogises this city and its palace. It is now the last resting-place of

[1] A town of undoubted antiquity, supposed to figure in the earliest Aryan traditions under the name of *Apelava*, part of the Pāndava kingdom of Indraprāstha.

[2] The word *'Khāwar'* like *'Bākhtar'* is often misapplied and the two are interchangeably and incorrectly used for E. and W. alike. Abul Fazl, however, invariably uses *"Bakhtar"* for W. and *Khāwar* for E., though with a southing tendency, as may be seen from his delimitations of other provinces. Hence Agra is certainly E. of Delhi in longitude, but it is almost south of it. See Cunnningham's explanation of the anomalous use of *'Khāwar'* and *'Dakkhin'* in his *Anc. Geog. of India*, p. 94.

[3] See *Journ. As. Soc. Bengal*, 1860, p. 225, and Elliot, iii, 524.

Humāyun where a new and splendid monument has been erected. Sultān *Alā ud din* (1295-1316) founded another city and fort called *Siri*. *Tughlaqābād* is a memorial of *Tughlaq Shāh* (1321-24). His son *Muhammad* (1324-51) founded another city and raised a lofty pile with a thousand columns of marble and constructed other noble edifices. *Sultān Firoz* (1351-88) gave his own name to a large town[1] which he founded and by a cutting from the *Jumna* brought its waters to flow by. He likewise built another palace at a distance of 3 *kos* from *Firozābād*, named *Jahānumā* (*the world-view*). Three subterranean passages were made wide enough to admit of his passing along in mounted procession with the ladies of his harem; that towards the river, 5 *jaribs* in length; the second towards the *Jahānumā*, 2 *kos*, and the third to old Delhi, 3 *kos*. Humāyun restored the citadel of *Indrapat* and named it *Dinpanāh* (*asylum of the faith*). Sher Khān destroyed the Delhi of *Alā ud din* and built a separate town. Although the monuments of these cities are themselves eloquent and teach us the highest moral lessons, yet even is this latest Delhi now for the most part in ruins. The cemeteries are, however, populous. *Khwājah Qutb ud din Ushi* lies here and *Shaikh Nizām ud din Aulia*, and *Shaikh Nasir ud din Mahmud*, the Lamp of Delhi, and *Malik Yār-i-Pirān*, and *Shaikh Salāh*, and *Mālik Kabir-i-Aulia*, and *Maulanā Muhammad*, and *Hāji Abdul Wahhāb* and *Shaikh Abdullah Quraishi*, and *Shaikh Shams Tark-i-Biyābāni*, and *Shaikh Shams-i-Autād* and *Amir Khusrau*[2] with many other servants of God instructed in Divine knowledge who in this spot repose in their last sleep. Here too lie Sultān *Shahāb ud din Ghori*, and *Sultān Shams ud din*, and *Nāsir ud din Ghāzi*, and *Ghiyās ud din*, and *Alā ud din* and *Qutb ud din*, and *Tughluq*, and *Muhammad Aādil*, and *Firoz* and *Bahlol*, and *Sikandar Lodi*. Many now living, likewise, have laid out pleasant spots and groves for their final resting-place—to the introspective a source of blissful ecstasy, to the wise an incentive to watchfulness.

In the hill of *Islāmābād* is a very deep spring called *Prabhās Kund* from which warm water continually bubbles up, and which is a great place of worship.

---

[1] It is supposed to have occupied the ground between Humāyun's tomb and the Ridge. *I. G.*

[2] Of these personages the last is sufficiently famous. The second and third and last on the list will be found in Ferishta's lives of the saints at the close of his History. Also *Ency. Isl.*

Biswamitra Rikhesar [Rishishwar] made a deep excavation of three *bighas* of this hill and devoted it to purposes of worship, and to this day it testifies to the antiquity of this construction.

Badāon is conspicuous amongst ancient cities and a great many holy religious are there buried.

A part of the northern mountains of this *Subah* is called *Kumāon*. Here are mines of gold, silver, lead, iron, copper, orpiment and borax. Here also are found the musk-deer and the *Qutās* cow,[1] as well as silk-worms, hawks, falcons and game of various kinds, and honey in abundance and the species of horse called *Gut* (Gunt).

There is game in plenty in the *Sarkār* of Sambal (Sambhal), where the rhinoceros is found.[1] It is an animal like a small elephant, without a trunk, and having a horn on its snout with which it attacks animals. From its skin shields are made, and from the horn, finger-guards for bow-strings and the like. In the city of Sambal is a temple called *Hari Mandal* (the temple of Vishnu) belonging to a Brāhman, from among whose descendants the tenth avatār will appear in this spot. *Hānsi* is an ancient city, the resting-place of *Jamal* the successor of Shaikh Farid-i-Shakar-ganj.

Near the town of *Sahnah** is a hot spring on the summit of a hill, the peculiarity of which is undoubtedly due to a sulphur mine.

Hisār (Hissār) was founded by Sultan *Firoz* who brought the waters of the *Jumna* to it by means of a cutting. A holy devotee predicted his accession to the throne and at his request the canal was made. Strange to say, it enters a pool named *Bhadrā* near the town of *Sirsā*, and there loses itself. Wonderful stories are related regarding it. There are few rivers in this district, and wells have to be dug to a considerable depth.

---

[1] Visvamitra is the name of a celebrated Kshatriya deriving his lineage from an ancestor Kusik of the lunar race : he was king of Kanyā-Kubjā or Kanauj. His famous quarrel with the rival sage Vasishtha to perform the great tribal sacrifice, runs through the Rig Veda and he succeeded in raising himself to the rank of a Brāhman by long and plainful austerities. According to the Rāmāyan he became the companion and counsellor of the young Ramachandra. He was the father of Sakuntalā by the nymph Menakā whom the gods, jealous of his increasing power, sent to seduce him from his passionless life

* *Sohna*, 15 miles S. of Gurgaon City.

Sahrind (Sirhind) is a city of note. Here are the gardens of *Hāfiz Rakhnah,* the delight of all beholders.

Thanesar is accounted one of the most sacred places of pilgrimage. The *Saraswati* flows near it for which the Hindus have great veneration. Near it is a lake called *Kurukshetra,*[2] which pilgrims from distant parts come to visit and where they bathe, and bestow charitable offerings. This was the scene of the war of the *Mahābhārat* which took place in the latter end of the *Dwāpar Yug.*

In the city of *Hastinapur* reigned *Rājā Bharat* who by his justice and consideration for his people gathered a fitting reward of happiness, and his virtues and good deeds confirmed for a long period the succession in his family, and fortune favoured son after son. The eighth in lineal descent from him was *Rājā Kuru* from whom *Kuru-Kshetra* received its appellation. After six intermediate progenitors, an heir was born named *Vichitravirya,*[3] who had two sons, one of whom was *Dhritarāshtra.* He was the father of 101 children, the eldest of whom was *Rājā Duryodhana,* and they are called the *Kauravas.* The other was *Pandu.* Although the first mentioned was the elder son yet on account of his blindness, the succession fell to his brother who obtained the sovereignty. His sons are called the *Pāndavas.* They were five, namely, *Yudishtir, Bhimsen, Arjuna, Nakul and Sahadev.* On *Pāndu's* death the kingdom reverted to Dhritarashtra, but although the nominal sovereignty was his, the real power was possessed by *Duryodhana.* Since to crush their enemies is the way of the princes of the earth, *Duryodhana* was ever in fear of the *Pāndavas* and sought their destruction. When *Dhritarāshtra* observed the growing feud, he resolved to establish his nephews in the city of Vāranāvatra, and sent skilled artisans with instructions to build their residences. The

---

[1] Genl. Cunningham says (p. 145) that the name of Sarhind or 'frontier of Hind' was popularly given to the city at an early period when it was the boundary town between the Hindus and the later Muhammadan kingdom of Ghazni and Lahore, but the name is probably much older as the astronomer Varāha Mihira mentions the *Sairindhas* immediately after the Kulutas or people of Kullu and just before Brahmapura which was the capital of the hill country N. of Hardwār.

[2] It is an oblong sheet of water, 3,546 feet in length by 1,900. During eclipses of the moon, the waters of all other tanks are believed to visit this, so that the bather is blessed by the concentrated virtues of all other ablutions. The right ankle of Durga is said to have fallen here on her being cut to pieces and her limbs scattered over the earth by Vishnu.

[3] He died childless, but at the request of his mother Satya-vati, the *Rishi* Dwaipāyana raised up three children to him, viz., Dhritarāshtra, Pāndu and Vidura. *Vishnu Purāna.*

workmen at the instigation of *Duryodhana* constructed a secret chamber of lac and pitch, in order that at a fitting opportunity the *Pāndavas* might be destroyed in a flaming conflagration. But whom the Lord defends by his protection, what avails against him the striving of the impotent? When the *Pāndavas* accepting their exile, settled in this spot, they became aware of the design. By chance a woman with five sons dwelt hard by. The *Pāndavas* set the house on fire and set out for the wilds with their mother, while their neighbours were consumed in the flames.

Duryodhana believing that the *Pāndavas* were destroyed, held a festival of rejoicing. The *Pāndavas* after many adventures came forth from the wilds to the inhabited country and settled in the city of *Kampilā* [Panchāl]. In a short time, the fame of their valour, skill and open-handed munificence filled the world, but none knew their name or lineage, till *Duryodhana* himself awaking from his dream of security suspected that the burning of the *Pāndavas* was a fable. After prosecuting inquiries, his suspicions were confirmed, upon which he had recourse to entreaty, and recalled them with protestations of friendship, hoping thus to secure his aim. He bestowed *Delhi* (Indraprastha) upon them with half his kingdom and retained *Hastinapur* with the other half. *Yudhishthira* by his prudence and good fortune aided by the divine favour rose to greatness and his administration advanced his power. The *Kauravas* flocked to his service, and in a short space he acquired universal sway. The other brothers likewise reduced many princes to their obedience. *Duryodhana* was beside himself at the sight of their sovereign splendour, and the pangs of envy drove him more distraught. With deceptive intent, he held a restival and invited the *Pāndavas* and proposed a game of *chaupar,* playing himself, with cogged dice. By this means he won all they possessed. The last stake was made on the condition that if the *Pāndavas* won, they should recover all that they had lost, but if otherwise, they were to quit the royal dominions and wander in the wilds for twelve years in the garb of mendicants after which they might return to civilised life for a year, and so conduct themselves that none should know them. If this last particular were infringed, they would have to pass a similar period of twelve years in the forests. Unsuspecting foul play, their uprightness brought them to ruin. Elated by the success of his device, *Duryodhana* was lulled into the slumber of a false security while the *Pāndavas* under the divine direction accomplished their part of the agreement. *Duryodhan* now began to treat them with severity. Much altercation followed till the *Pāndavas* consented to accept five villages if peacefully surrendered to them. *Duryodhana* in his pride refused and rose in arms. The scene of the conflict was in the vicinity of *Kuru-kshetra*. But as the end of the fraudful is disaster, *Duryodhana,* and his companions were totally destroyed and *Yudhishthira* was victorious after eighteen days of successive engagements.

Towards the close of the *Dwāpar Yug,* 135 years before the beginning of the *Kali Yug,* and 4,831 years anterior to this the 40th of the Divine Era,* this event rose into fame and was left to posterity as a record of portentous warning.

It is said that in this mighty war, the army of the *Kauravas* consisted of 11 *achhauhini,* and that of the *Pandavas* of 7. An *achhauhini* consists of 21,870 men mounted on elephants, the same number in chariots, and 65,610 cavalry; and 109,350 infantry. Marvellous to relate but 12 individuals of both armies survived this war. Four of the army of *Duryodhana,* escaping with their lives took refuge with *Yudhishthira, viz., Kripāchārya* Brahman who had been preceptor to both families and was renowned for wisdom and valour; *Ashwatthāmān* who was celebrated for the same qualities; *Kritvarmān* Yadu, a brave champion; and *Sanjaya* who, together with his reputation for wisdom, acquired renown as the charioteer of *Dhritarāshtra*. On the side of the Pandavas, eight survived,[1] *viz.,* the 5 brothers; *Satyaki Yadu* famous for his bravery and sagacity; *Yuyutsa* brother of *Duryodhana* by another mother, and *Krishna*. After this *Yudhishthira* reigned supreme for 36 years, and his happy destiny and virtuous disposition discovering to him the vanity of mundane things, he sought retirement and resolutely forsook a world that oppresses the weak. Together with his brethren he chose the path of renunciation and played the last stake of his life.

This great war has been related in the *Mahābhārata* with numerous episodes in a hundred thousand couplets, and has been translated into Persian by command of His Majesty under the title of *Razmnāma* (History of the War).

---

* See p. 15 where it is stated that from the era of Rāja Yudhishthira to the 40th of Akbar's reign (A.H. 1003, commencing 5th Dec. 1594 and ending 25th November, 1595 A.D.) there had elapsed 4,696 years, making the commencement of the Kali Yuga 3,101 B.C. To this period an addition of 135 brings the figure to 4,831.

It is set forth in eighteen *Parba* or books. The *first* part is an account of the *Kauravas* and *Pandavas* and a list of contents. The *second; Yudhishthira* sends his brethren to conquest—his supreme monarchy—the gambling feast held by the *Kauravas*, &c. *Third,* the departure of the *Pandavas* into the solitude of their exile and other events. *Fourth,* the coming of the *Pandavas* from the wilds to the city of *Virāta* and remaining unknown. *Fifth,* the *Pandavas* discover themselves; the mediation of *Krishna* and his rejection; the gathering at *Kura-kshetra* and disposition of the armies. *Sixth,* the opening of the combat, the wounding of *Bhishma,* the slaughter of many of the sons of Dhritarāshtra, and the events of the ten days' engagement. *Seventh,* the council of war held by *Duryodhana;* the appointment of *Drona* to the general command, his death and other events during five days. *Eighth,* description of the two days' battle; *Duryodhana* names *Karna* to the command, his exploits—the flight of *Yudhisthira* before him—the death of *Karna* at the hand of *Arjuna* on the second day. *Ninth, Shalya* is appointed general on account of his heroism—his death—*Duryodhana* conceals himself in a tank—his end and that of many champions. *Tenth,* the conclusion of the war, the coming of *Kritvarmān, Ashwatthāmān,* and *Kripāchārya* to *Duryodhana* on the field of battle while still breathing and his advice of a night attack &c. *Eleventh,* the lamentations of the women on both sides—Gāndhāri mother of *Duryodhana* curses *Krishna. Twelfth,* account of *Yudhishthira* after the victory—his desire to resign his kingdom. *Byās* and *Krishna* comfort him by their counsel. *Bhishma* delivers many admirable and instructive maxims setting forth the duties of sovereign administration. *Thirteenth,* the advice tendered by *Bhishma.* In my judgment, the 12th and 13th books should be comprised in one as they both contain the counsels of *Bhishma,* and the 9th divided into two, the one dealing with the episode of *Shalya* and the other with the death of *Duryodhana. Fourteenth,* the great horse-sacrifice (ashwa-medh). *Fifteenth,* the retirement to a hermitage of *Dhritarāstra, Gāndhāri,* and *Kunti* mother of *Yudhishtira. Sixteenth,* the destruction of the *Yadu* tribe. *Seventeenth, Rāja Yudhishtira* retires with his brethren who all perish in a snow-drift. *Eighteenth, Yudhishtira* in his own body mounts to the upper world; the dissolution of the mortal remains of his brethren. The conclusion called *Haribans,* contains the history of the *Yadus.*

In this work, although there are numerous extravagant tales and fictions of the imagination, yet it affords many instructive moral observations, and is an ample record of felicitous experience.

This *Subah* contains 8 *Sarkārs* subdivided into 232 *parganahs**—the measured land consists of 2 *krors*, 5 *lakhs* and 46,816 *Bighas* 16 *Biswas*. The revenue is 60 *krors*, 16 *lakhs* 15,555 *Dāms* (Rs. 15,040,388-14) of which 3 *krors*, 30 *lakhs*, 75,7 9 are *Suyurghāl* (Rs. 8,26,893-7-7). The local force is 31,490 Cavalry, 242,310 Infantry.

* The eight Sarkārs comprise 232 *mahals*, if we omit the five unsettled *mahals* of Kumaon. The Suyurghāl total is incorrect, because by adding together the *Suyurghāl* for 7 Sarkārs only (that of Kumaon not being given), we get a totalof 3,31,75,437 *dāms*. [J. S.]

Sarkār of Delhi.

Contains 48 *Mahals,* 7,126,107 *Bighas,* 17 *Biswas.* Revenue 123,012,590 *Dāms.* *Suyurghāl* 10,990,260 *Dāms.* Castes various. Cavalry, 4,000. Infantry 23,980.

	Bighas Biswas	Revenue D.	Suyur-ghāl	Cavalry	Infantry	Castes.
Islāmābād Pākal, has a stone fort on a hill ..	970,67-19	1,779,407	31,462	50	1000	Rājput Sānd
Adhah [?Odhan] ..	14,912-8	513,081	45,420	20	200	Ahir
Pānipat, has a brick fort	568, 444	10,756,647	3,540,632	100	2000	Afghān, Gujar, Ranghar
Pālam	245,240	5,726,787	1,231,880	70	1000	Jat
Baran, has a brick fort on the *Kāli Nadi* ..	171,160	3,907,928	153,190	20	300	...
Bāghpat, on the Jumna, between two streams	200,515	3,582,868	180,159	20	200	[Brāhman Chauhān
Palwal,[1] has a brick fort and it stands on a mound	234,783	1,769,493	218,225	25	500	Rājput, Gujar
Barnāwah	145,000	1,879,125	50,759	25	200	Shaikhzādah
Pāth, has a brick fort	48,191	621,749	7,243	60	600	Tonwar (Tuar)
Beri Dobaldhan ..	119,002-19	1,404,225	...	40	800	Jat
Tilpat, has a brick fort	119,578	3,077,913	92,583	40	400	Brāhman, Rājput, Gujar
Tāndah Phugānah on the Jumna	51,669	1,289,306	11,366	25	200	Afghān Jat
Tilbegampur	14,237-7	370,374	15,754	10	100	
Jhajhar	128,417	1,422,451	306,461	60	1000	
Harsia, has a stone fort in the village of Dhānah (*cor. Dhaulri*) built by Sultān Firoz on the banks of the Hindan	87,923	3,605,.28	376,079	60	600	Badgujar
Jewar	133,746	1,878,378	85,439	40	400	Rājput, Chhokar
Jhinjhānah	57,923-16	1,700,250	100,250	20	300	Jat
Chaprauli, stands between two streams ..	32,701-12	1,138,759	5,719	20	300	Do.
Jalālābād, stands between two streasm amid much forest ..	96,189	1,333,711	9,099	50	600	Do.
Jalālpur Barawat, much forest	42,061-17	1,001,875	1,775	20	400	Do.

[1] *Palwal.*—This mound stands to this day considerably above the surrounding lēvel and consists entirely of ancient remains crumbling to decay. It is a town of undoubted antiquity and supposed to figure in the earliest Aryan traditions under the name of Apelava, part of the Pandava Kingdom of Indraprastha. *Baran* is the mod. Bulandshahar.

Sarkār of Delhi—Contd.

	Bighas Biswas	Revenue D.	Suyurghāl D.	Cavalry	Infantry	Castes
The old suburban district	128,417	1,422,451	306,460	10	40	Jat, Chauhān.
The new do. do. ..	36,447	3,635,315	595,984	25	300	Gujar, Jat, Ahir.
The metropolis of Delhi	971	736,406	18,783	135	1,500	...
Dasna between Ganges and Jumna	282,777	4,933,310	162,535	60	300	Ghelot (here some illegible words).
Dādri Tāhā	179,789	4,326,059	118,577	20	400	Afghān, Jat.
Dankaur, on the Jumna	128,523	1.016,682	4,840	20	200	Gujar.
Rohtak, has a brick fort	636,835	8,599,270	428,000	100	2,000	Jat.
Sonipat (Sonpat) has a brick fort	283,299	7,727,323	775,105	70	1,000	Afghān, Jat.
Safidun, has a brick fort	81,730	1,975,596	99,647	60	600	Rājput Ranghar, Jat.
Sikandarābād ..	66,907-15	1,259,190	17,844	50	400	Bhāti, Gujar etc.
Sarāwa, has a brick fort	42,387-12	1,583,899	31,914	40	300	
Santha	39,147-9	854,191	48,207	30	300	Chauhān.
Siyāna, between two streams	166,407-17	849,090	4,959	50	400	Taga.*
Shikarpur	52,139	2,111,996	780,305	70	200	Chauhān.
Karnāl, the stream Sānjauli flows below the town	540,444	5,678,242	207,999	50	800	Ranghar Chauhān.
Ganaur, has a brick fort	40,990-16	1,718,792	33,390	20	400	Tagā.
Garh Muktesar, has a brick fort on the Jumna, a Hindu place of pilgrimage ..	101,340-10	1,591,492	41,490	40	400	Rājput, Musalmān, Hindu.
Kutāna	91,706-13	1,423,779	892	20	150	Jat.
Kāndhla	68,934-5	1,374,430	37,930	20	30	Gujar.
Kāsna, on the Jumna	104,021-19	1,522,315	149,250	40	400	Do.
Kharkhanda ..	51,895-15	1,105,856	4,958	50	600	Afghān, Jat.
Gangeru Kherah, has a brick fort between two streams ..	11,062-15	316,405	13,830	40	300	Sayyid.
Loni, has a brick fort between two streams	75,363	3,278,878	148,445	20	200	

* Sir H. Elliot has an interesting discussion on the Gaur *Tagas*, an important tribe of Brahmanical descent in the N.-W. of India extending over a great part of upper Rohilkhand, the upper Doāb and the Delhi territory. Sherring's *Hindu Tribes and Castes* should be consulted in elucidation of the doubtful readings of the text.

Sarkār of Delhi—Contd.

	Bighas Biswas	Revenue D.	Suyur-Suyur-D.	Cavalry	Infantry	Castes
Mirath (Meerut) has a brick fort between two streams	610,422	4,391,996	331,096	100	300	Tagā, Ranghar, Chandrāl.
Māndāuthi, the autumn harvest abundant: near the town a tank which is never dry throughout the year	90,464	2,858,223	2,984	30	500	Jat.
Masaudābād, has an old brick fort ..	89,478	2,809,156	269,315	30	30	Do.
Hastināpur, on the Ganges: an ancient Hindu settlement ..	176,340	4,466,904	36,291	20	300	Tagā.
Hāpur, on the Kāli Nadi between two streams	239,845	2,103,589	5,229	4	300	Do.

Sarkār of Badāon.

Containing 13 *Mahals.* 8,093,850 *Bighas,* 10 *Biswas.* Revenue 34,817,063 *Dāms. Suyurghāl* 457,181 *Dāms.* Castes various. Cavalry, 2,850. Infantry, 26,700.

	Bighas Biswas	Revenue D.	Suyurghāl D.	Cavalry	Infantry	Castes
Ajāon [Rajwan] ..	82,467-17	1,362,867	...	500	3000	Chauhān.
Aonla	14,701	690,620	...	50	400	Kānwar [?Tuar]
Badāon with suburban district	658,320-5	7,357,571	287,986	50	5000	Shaikhzādah, Kāyath.
Bareli	661,227	12,507,434	91 320	1000	10,000	Rājput.
Barsar [? Paraur] ..	196,700	2,147,824	6,754	50	500	Kāyath.
Paund [Elliot Punar] ..	5,749	260,840	...	50	300	Kahor
Talhi (Balhati)	25,982	1,077,811	1,505	50	1000	Tagā, Brāhman.
Sahiswan	253,120	2,493,898	15,444	100	2000	
Sanās Mandah (B. Satāsi Mundiyā)	58,110	795,815	3,471	50	500	Tagā, Brāhman.

Sarkār of Badāon—Contd.

	Bighas Biswas	Revenue D.	Suyurghāl D.	Cavalry	Infantry	Castes
Suneyā	29,753	1,315,725	...	50	500	Ulus ?
Kānit [=Känt]	55,584	2,439,369	48,444	300	2000	Bāchhal.
Kot Sālbāhan has a fort	227,500-8	1,219,165	...	50	500	Kanwār.
Golah	24,540	1,136,931	4,257	100	1000	Dewak, Bāchhal.

Sarkār of Kumāon.

Containing 21 *Mahals*. The revenue of 5 *Mahals* undetermined. 16 *Mahals*, in money. 40,437,700 *Dāms*. Castes various. Cavalry, 3,000. Infantry, 50,000.

	Revenue D.		Revenue D.
Āudan [?Adon] ...	400,000	Jakrām	5,000,000
Bhuksi and Bhāksā, 2 Mahals	400,000	Jariyah	3,000,000
Bastwah	200,000	Jāwan	2,500,000
Pachotar	400,000	Chaulī, Sahajgar, Guzarpur, Dwārakhot [Kot Dwara]*	
Bhikan Diwār	200,000	Malwārah	
Bhakti	11,000,000	Malāchor, Sitachor, Kemus, 3 Mahals ...	
Bhuri, undetermined ...	...		
Ratilā [? Balila] ...	10,025,000		
Chanki [Chauki-ghal3 ...	400,000		

* Sahajgar is now *Jaspar*, Guzarpur is *Gadarpura;* Malwara may be *Talwara.*

Sarkār of Sambhal.

Containing 47 *Mahals*. 4,047,193 *Bighas*, 2 *Biswas*. Revenue 66,941,431 *Dāms*. *Suyurghāl* 2,892,394 *Dāms*. Castes various. Cavalry, 4,375. Infantry, 31,550. Elephants, 50.

	Bighas Biswas	Revenue D.	Suyurghāl D.	Cavalry	Infantry	Elephants	Castes
Amrohah	820,654	6,342,000	993 358	1000	5000	50	Sayyid.
Āazampur	55,467	2,889,478	137,544	30	300	...	Tagā.
Islāmpur Bharu ..	66,096	1,370,640	12,133	100	200	...	Baishnavi.

Sarkār of Sambhal—Contd.

	Bighas Biswas	Revenue D.	Suyurghāl D.	Cavalry	Infantry	Elephants	Castes
Ujhāri	125,221	697,609	2,788	20	300	...	Jat.
Akbarābād	53,790-14	640,264	27,860	50	200	...	
Islāmpur Dargu ..	11,217-10	429,675	675	20	200	...	
Islāmābād	25,261-10	346,348	6,394	50	500	...	Jat.
Bijnaur	60.362	3,855,465	18,154	60	500	...	Tagā, Brāhman.
Bachharāon	115,226-12	828,322	8,632	50	200	...	Tagā.
Biroi	15,027-12	150,000	...	25	100	...	Kohi
Bisārā	8,008-7	200,000	...	25	100	...	Khasia.
Chāndpur	87,278	431,071	259,959	50	200	...	Tagā, Jat, &c.
Jalālābād	49,398	1,470,072	12,263	25	100	..	Jat.
Chaupalah	1,016,199	1,340,812	...	100	500	...	Gaur.
Jhālā	26,795	237,809	34,916	50	400	...	Jat.
Jadwār	76,757-19	828,846	...	50	200	...	Badgujar.
Suburban district of Sambhal	206,450	3,322,448	148,739	100	500	...	Tagā, Brāhman &c.
Deorah	96,965	1,924,887	...	25	200	...	
Dhaka	130,158-16	670,364	6,487	25	200	...	Rahes.
Dabhārsi	82,692-11	280.306	...	25	200	...	
Dudilah	80,180-15	210,000	...	20	100	...	Kohi
Rājpur	189,390	700,000	...	50	400	...	Rājput.
Rājabpur	40,346-9	612,977	2.288	25	100	...	Kokar, Shaikhzādah
Sambhal, has a brick fort	42,400	850,953	63,404	50	400	...	Khokhar.
Seohārah	27,945	1,833,732	1,418	50	800	...	Tagā.
Sirsi	52,400-11	958,769	152,814	20	200	...	Sayyid, &c.
Sahanspur	54,844-10	944,804	1,038	50	400	...	Tagā.
Sursāwah	37,502	808,065	...	15	400	...	Kaurawah.
Sherkot	19,870	4,921,051	218,157	100	1000	...	
Shāhi	80,417	500,496	478	20	200	..	Gaur.
Kundarki	86,164	674.936	74,936	50	400	...	Kāyath.
Kiratpur	80,973	2,410,609	166,218	100	500	...	Tagā, Jat.
Kachh	99,868	1,248,995	5,765	20	200	...	
Gandāur	18,576-17	751,520	34,270	30	200	...	Tagā.
Kābar	83,232-7	566,339	16,019	50	400	...	Chauhān.
Ganaur	51,005-1	267,919	17,719	10	100	...	Musalmān.
Khānkari	31,546-7	200,000	...	10	100	...	
Lakhnor	246,440	2,499,208	82,983	1000	5000	...	Gaur.
Liswah	1,871	100,000	...	10	100	...	
Mughalpur	168,374	3,580,800	80,800	100	500	...	Tagā.
Majhaulah	142,461	1,737,556	6,970	400	8000	...	Badgujar.
Mandāwar	65,710	1,256,995	20,455	25	300	...	Bais.
Nagina	99,233	2,647,242	284,368	50	500	...	Ahir.

Sarkār of Sambhal—Contd.

	Bighas Biswas	Revenue D.	Suyurghāl D.	Cavalry	Infantry	Elephants	Castes
Nahtaur, in this *parganah,* the mulberry grows in great perfection of size and sweetness—a span in length*	95,974-12	1,788,160	4,675	50	300	...	Tagā.
Neodhanah	209,620-10	904,675	...	100	500	...	Gaur.
Naroli	181,621	1,408,093	48,212	50	400	...	Badgujar.
Hatamnah	5,706-14	250,000	...	50	400	...	Kodar.

* Probably, according to Dr. King, the *Morus laevigata,* a long thin berry with a mawkish, sweet taste.

Sarkār of Sahāranpur.

Containing 36 *Mahals.* 3,530,370 *Bighas,* 3 *Biswas.* Revenue, 87,839,659 *Dāms.* *Suyurghāl* 4,991,485 *Dāms.* Castes, various. Cavalry, 3,955. Infantry, 22,270.

	Bighas Biswas	Revenue D.	Suyurghāl D.	Cavalry	Infantry	Elephants	Castes
Indri, has a brick fort near the Jumna ..	143,900-28	7,078,326	691,903	50	1000	...	Ranghar, Tagā.
Ambihta	17,764	324,560	...	20	300	...	Gujar, Aawān?
Budhāna	155,633	3,698,041	131,780	40	300	...	Tagā, Jat.
Bidauli	111,226	3,115,125	1,400,255	...	...	...	Sayyid
Bhatkanjāwar ..	173,471	2,676,407	146,749	50	500	...	Tagā, Bārhah.
Bhogpur, has a brick fort on the Ganges, a Hindu place of worship	94,428	2,338,120	6,941	100	1000	...	Rājput
Purchapār	86,949	2,191,460	120,438	20	200	...	Sarir.
Bhumah	67,451	2,135,490	28,453	2000	7000	...	Sayyid.
Baghrā	50,390	1,918,196	74,840	20	200	...	Jat.
Bhanāth	49,288	1,321,440	8,650	20	200	...	Tagā.
Thānah Bhim ..	281,377	3,578,540	317,260	20	500	...	Rājput, Sadbār.

Sarkār of Sahāranpur—Contd.

	Bighas Biswas	Revenue D.	Suyurghāl D.	Cavalry	Infantry	Elephants	Castes
Tughlaqpur	81,856	222,277	128,853	20	30	...	Jat.
Jaurāsi	211,751	2,471,277	71,297	20	200	...	Bidar.
Jauli	45,653	1,310,057	152,396	...	...	...	Sayyid (Cavalry entered under Sarot).
Charthāwal	35,916	1,668,882	68,872	20	200	...	Tagā.
Suburban district of Sahāranpur, has a brick fort, cloths of the kinds *Khasa* and *Chautār* (Vol. I, p. 94) are here made in perfection	212,335-16	6,951,545	706,448	100	800	...	Afghān. Kulāl Tagā.
Deoband, has a brick fort	335,861	6,477,977	641,946	60	800	...	Gujar, Tagā.
Rāmpur	79,419	1,777,908	78,597	50	400	...	Sadbār, Tagā.
Rurki	2,768	1,628,860	8,361	25	200	...	Rājput, Sadbār, Tagā, Brāhman.
Rāepur Tātār ..	4,688-8	369,080	...	10	200	...	Tagā.
Sikri Bhukarheri ..	188,211	3,008,611	110,611	40	200	...	Jat.
Sarsāwah, has a brick fort	106,800	2,516,125	16,165	80	200	...	Tagā.
Sarot	90,617	2,207,779	51,571	50	1000	...	Do.
Sardhana	113,780	1,590,606	43,842	30	800	...	Tagā, Ahir
Sambalherā	31,963	1,011,078	11,078	...	...	...	Sayyid (Cav. entered under Bhona).
Soranpalri	10,648	574,320	22,628	40	250	...	Jat.
Khatauli	104,747	3,624,588	190,919	40	800	...	Tagā, Kulāl
Khodi	85,618	2,514,673	58,906	50	400	...	Jat, Tagā.
Kairāna	71.245	2,025,238	223,579	20	200	...	Gujar.
Gango	52,137	2,029,032	322,515	800	2000	...	Turkomān.
Lakhnauti	79,694	1,796,058	76,602	300	2000	...	Do.
Muzaffarābād ..	81,305-15	4,074,064	71,899	20	200	...	Ranghar, Sander (?Pundir).
Manglaur, has a brick fort	60,987	2,850,311	197,216	40	800	...	Brāhman, Badgujar.
Malhaipur	81,010	2,244,070	23,077	100	500	...	Afghān, Tagā, Brāhman.
Nakor	65,612-10	1,887,070	26,104	40	800	..	Afghān, Brāhman.
Nānauta	29,224	724,150	18,684	40	800		Afghān.

Sarkār of Rewāri.

Containing 12 *Mahals.* 1,155,011 *Bighas,* 10 *Biswas.* *Suyurghāl,* 739,268 *Dāms.* Revenue† * * * Cavalry, 2,175. Infantry, 14,600.

	Bighas Biswas	Revenue D.	Suyurghāl D.	Cavalry	Infantry	Castes
Bāwal	110,375	4,114,753	16,274	100	2001	Rājput, Ahir, Jat.
Pātaudhi	61,970	2,270,080	5,260	50	500	Do. Do.
Bhoharah (E. Bhorah) ..	38,547	755,543	345	100	1000	Ahir.
Tāoru, has a brick fort ..	35,858	986,228	11,573	50	500	Musalmān, Khaildār(?)
Rewāri with sub. dist., has a brick fort	405,108	11,906,847	404,100	400	2000	Thathar, Ahir, Jat.
Ratāi Jatāi	52,120	289,603	523	...	400	
Kot Qāsim Ali	80,410	3,357,930	110,330	25	400	Rājput, Ahir.
Ghelot	27,270-10	656,688	...	700	2000	Rājput, Thatar.
Kohāna	15,264	421,440	...	50	500	Do. Do.
Suhna, has a stone fort on a hill; here a hot spring and Hindu shrine	251,738	3,928,364	150,563	200	2000	Do. Do.
Nimrāna, has a stone fort on a hill	35,047	682,259	...	500	4000	Various.

† By deducting the revenues of the other 7 Sarkārs from the total revenue of the Subah (given on p. 290), we get 35,222,658 *dāms* as the revenue of Rewāri. [J. S.]

*Sarkār of Hisār Firozah.**

Containing 27 *Mahals.* 3,114,497 *Bighas.* Revenue, 52,554,905 *Dāms.* *Suyurghāl,* 1,406,519 *Dāms.* Castes, various. Cavalry, 6,875. Infantry, 60,800.

	Bighas Biswas	Revenue D.	Suyurghāl D.	Cavalry	Infantry	Castes
Agrowa (var. Agrohah). Game of all kinds abounds. Sport chiefly hawking	45,717	1,748,970	6,654	200	2000	Jātu, Jat.
Ahroni	19,537	857,357	160,038	100	1000	Gujar, Jat.

* Called after the Emperor Firoz Shāh Tughlaq who founded the town of that name about 1354 A.D.

Sarkār of Hisār Firozah—Contd.

	Bighas Biswas	Revenue D.	Suyurghāl D.	Cavalry	Infantry	Castes
Atkhera, has a brick fort, and a Hindu temple called Govardhan	82,991	1,576,200	...	200	2000	Jat, Tonwār.
Bhangiwāl	...	1,800,000	...	200	2000	Rājput, Rāthor, Jat, Punya (Jat).
Puniyān	...	1,200,000	...	150	8000	Jat, Punyan
Bhārangi	...	880,882	...	200	2000	Rāthor, Jat.
Barwāla	136,799	1,097,807	109,052	100	1500	Sayyid, Malikzādah, Bakkāl.
Bhatu	...	440,280	...	50	1000	Jat.
Barwā	6,254	64,680	...	25	300	Jātu, Jat.
Bhatner, has a brick fort	15,688	933,042	...	500	10,000	Rāthor, Rājput.
Tohānah, Do. ..	180,744	4,694,354	150,680	400	3000	Afghān, Lohāni.
Toshām	511,075	1,068,548	2,686	200	1000	Rāthor, Rājput, Jat.
Jind, 3 miles from the town in the village of Pandārah, is a Hindu temple	281,584	5,401,749	128,080	500	4000	Sālār, Rājput, Jātu.
Jamālpur, the Ghaggar flows through several villages here	142,455	4,277,261	81,461	700	400	Tonwar, Jat
Hisār (Hissār) with sub. dist. has 2 forts, one of brick, one of stone ..	176,512-18	4,039,895	183,879	500	2000	Jātu, Ranghar, Sowārān (Sheoram), Sāngwān.
Dhātarat, has a brick fort	29,207-18	978.027	45,556	100	2000	Jāt, Afghān.
Sirsā, Do. ..	258,355	4,361,368	163,104	500	5000	Junah (note Johiya).
Seorān	...	400,000	...	100	1000	Jat, Seorān (Sheoram).
Sidhmukh, soil mostly sand	..	171,872	...	50	100	Rājput, Rāthor, Jat.
Sewāni	48,512	76,750	...	100	1000	Rājput, Jātu
Shānzdah Dihāt (sixteen villages)	29,740	960,111	12,586	200	1500	Rājput, Tonwar.

Sarkār of Hisār Firozah—Contd.

	Bighas Biswas	Revenue D.	Suyurghāl D.	Cavalry	Infantry	Castes
Fathābād, has a brick fort	83,661	1,184,392	81,867	200	3000	Rājput, Rāthor, Gujar, Jat.
Gohāna	68,951	2,876,115	16,146	300	8000	Jat, Dādbalāsa Duhna ?
Khānda, here a large tank in which the Hindus think it auspicious and holy to bathe	19,438	1,119,364	47,978	100	2000	Jat, Gadi (var. Kari).
Muhim, has a brick fort ..	188,080	4,958,613	84,202	700	2000	Rājput, Tonwar, Jat.
Hānsi, has a brick fort ..	886,115	5,434,438	180.056	500	7000	Rājput, Multāni, Jātu, Jat.

Sarkār of Sirhind.

Containing 33 *Mahals*. 7,729,466 *Bighas*, 7 *Biswas*. Revenue, 160,790,549 *Dāms*. *Suyurghāl*, 11,698,330. Castes, various. Cavalry, 9,225. Infantry, 55,700.

	Bighas Biswas	Revenue D.	ghāl D.	Cavalry	Infantry	Castes
Ambāla	154,769	4,198,094	321,488	100	1000	...
Banor	420,337	12,549,953	1,087,209	700	8000	Ranghar, Afghān.
Pāel, has a brick fort ..	525,932	7,322,260	162,267	200	2000	Ranghar, Jat.
Bhader	86,877	3,103,269	1,406,106	50	700	Jat, *Dāhsurati* ?
Bhatinda	...	3,125,000	...	400	2000	Bhatti.
Pāndri	34,190	686,870	47,152	20	300	Ranghar.
Thāra, has a brick fort on the Sutlej	273,866	7,850,809	2,869.841	1500	1,000	Munj (or Shaikh). Jat.

Sarkār of Sirhind—Contd.

	Bighas Biswas	Revenue D.	Suyur-ghāl D.	Cavalry	Infantry	Castes
Thānesar, has a brick fort	228,988-17	7,850,808	2,069,841	50	1500	Ranghar, Jat.
Chahat on the Ghaggar ..	158,739	750,994	49,860	650	1100	Afghān, Rājput.
Chark	63,683	1,538,090	21,619	20	300	Jat.
Khizrābād, has a brick fort	332.489	12,059,918	528,170	200	3000	Bhatti, Jat.
Dorāla	65,768	2,188,443	86,710	50	300	Ranghar.
Dhota	71,357	1,601.346	1,346	800	1500	Rājput.
Deorāna	12,339	580,985	17,385	20	200	Jat.
Rupar, has a brick fort ..	66,144	5,005,549	26,084	200	1000	Rājput &c.
Sirhind with sub. dist. has a brick fort	828,458	12,082,680	603,536	1700	2000	Rājput, Barāh, Khauri, Dādah (Dādu ?), Jat.
Samāna	904,261	12,822,270	782,000	700	2000	Barāh, Jat.
Sunām, has a brick fort ..	988,562	7,007,696	7,696	500	2000	Ranghar.
Sadhuna, has a brick fort	34,361	4,298,064	278,265	400	5000	Chauhān, Ranghar.
Sultānpur Bārha	13,736	427,085	82,759	20	100	Do. Rājput.
Shāhābād	184,146	6,751,468	761,587	200	1500	Chauhān, Rājput, Brāhman.
Fathpur	50,931	684,370	15,440	25	400	Rājput, Pundir.
Karvāt Rāe Samu ..	28.099	1,220,090	5,874	40	900	Ranghar, Jat, Barāh, (var. Bārah).
Kaithal, has a brick fort : here Hindu shrines ..	918,025	10.688,630	309,146	200	3000	Rājput.
Guhrām, Do. ..	188,574	6,188,630	1,058,982	50	100	Ranghar, Jat, Khauri.
Ludhiāna, has a brick fort on the Sutlej	43,469	2,294,688	44,683	100	700	Awān,* Khauri, Ranghar.
Mustafābād	271,399	7,496,691	570,976	200	1000	Chauhān, Ranghar.
Masengan	204,377	7,058,259	626,690	200	1000	Jat.
Mansurpur	116,242	1,830,025	326,690	200	1000	Ranghar.
Māler	103,444	260,583	26,176	100	500	Munj.
Māchhiwāra, has a brick fort	17,272	250,556	250,552	100	500	Khauri, Wāh (var. Wārah)
Hāpari	93,756	1,145,118	...	80	300	Ranghar, Jat.

* See—Elliot, I, 113. Extract from Cunningham who gives the possession of Taxila to this people before Alexander's invasion.

Sovereigns of Delhi.

I.

Twenty princes reigned 437 years 1 month 28 days.*

	Ys.	M.	D.
Anangpāl, Tonwar	18	0	0
Bāsdeva	19	1	18
Ghangnu (var. Khanku, Kanakpāl Gangu)	21	3	28
Pirthimal (var. Pirthipāl)	19	6	19
Jaideva	20	7	28
Nirpāl (var. Hirpāl)	14	4	9
Adrah (var. Andiraj and 26-8-15) ...	26	7	11
Bichhrāj	21	2	13
Bik, (Anangpāl, Anakpāl)	22	3	16
Raghupāl	21	6	5
Nekpāl (Rekhpāl)	20	4	4
Gopāl	18	3	15
Sulakhan	25	2	2
Jaipāl	16	4	13
Kanwarpāl	29	9	11
Agnipāl	29	6	18
Bijaipāl. (var. Tajpāl)	24	1	6
Mahipāl	25	2	13
Aknepāl [Anangpāl]	21	2	15
Prithiraj	22	3	16

II.

Seven princes reigned 94 years and 7 months.

	Ys.	M.	D.
Bildeva Chauhān	6	1	4
Amr Gangu	5	2	5
Khirpāl	20	1	5
Sumer	7	4	2
Jāhir	4	4	8
Nāgdeva	3	1	5
Pithaura (Prithwi Rāe)	49	5	1

* This number does not accord with the totals. It would be as unprofitable as it is hopeless to attempt to digest or reconcile the order, number and length of these reigns among various authorities, when dates are unknown or conjectural, the names of the princes disputed and their existence mythical. After this, the minute exactness of their duration of reigns would be ridiculous.

III.

Eleven princes of the Ghori dynasty reigned 96 years 6 months and 20 days.

A.H.	A.D.					
588	1192	Sultān	Muizzu'ddin Muhammad Sām Ghori ...	14	0	0
602	1206	,,	Qutbuddin Eibak ...	4	0	0
607	1210	,,	Ārām Sāh, his son ...	1	0	0
607	1210	,,	Shamsuddin Altmish ...	26	0	0
633	1235	,,	Ruknu'ddin Firoz Shāh, his son	0	6	28
634	1236	,,	Raziah, his sister ...	3	6	6
637	1239	,,	Muizzu'ddin Bahrām Shāh, his brother ...	2	1	15
640	1242	,,	Alāu'ddin Masaud Shāh, his nephew ...	4	1	1
643	1245	,,	Nāsiru'ddin Mahmud Shāh, his uncle ...	19	3	0
664	1265	,,	Ghiyāsu'ddin Balban ...	20 and some months		
685	1286	,,	Muizzu'ddin Kaikubād, his grandson ...	3	Do.	

IV.

Thirteen princes of the Khilji dynasty reigned 129 years 10 months and 10 days.

A.H.	A.D.			Ys.	Md.	D.
688	1289	Sultan	Jalālu'ddin Khilji ...	7	some months	
695	1295.	..	Alāu'ddin Khilji, his nephew ...	20	some months	
716	1316	,,	Shahabu'ddin Omar, his son	0	3 some days	
717	1317	,,	Qutbu'ddin Mubārak Shāh his elder brother	14	4	0*

* All the MSS. concur in this glaring error, an evident slip of a copyist of 14 for 4. He was raised to the throne on the 7th Muharram A.H. 717 (22nd March 1317) and was killed 5th Rabii I, A.H. 721 (5th April 1321).

721	1321	,,	Nāsiru'ddin Khusrau Khān	0	6	0
721	1321	,,	Ghiyāsu'ddin Tughlaq Shāh	4	some months	
725	1324	,,	Muhammad, his son ...	27	0	0
752	1351	,,	Firoz Shāh, son of his paternal uncle ...	38	some months	
790	1388	,,	Tughlaq Shāh, his grand-son	0	5	3
791	1389	,,	Abu Bakr Shāh, son of his paternal uncle ...	1	6	0
793	1391	,,	Muhammad Shāh, his paternal uncle ...	6	7	0†
796	1393	,,	Ala'uddin Sikandar, his son	0	1	11
796	1393	,,	Mahmud, his brother ...	20	2	0

V.

817	1414		Khizr Khān of the Sayyid Dynasty ...	7	2	2
824	1421		Mubārak Shāh	13	3	16
837	1433		Muhammad Shāh	10	some months	
850	1446		Sultān Alā'uddin Aālam Shāh	7	do	
854	1450	,,	Behlol Lodi ...	38	8	8
894	1488	,,	Sikandar, his son ...	28	5	0
923	1517	,,	Ibrahim, his son ...	7	some months	
		,,	Bābar	5	0	0
		,,	Humayun	9	8	1
947	1540	,,	Sher Khān Sur ...	5	0	0
952	1545	,,	Salim Khān, his son ...	8	and odd	
960	1552	,,	Mubāriz Khān Adali.			
961	1553	,,	Ibrahim	some months		
962	1554	,,	Sikandar		do.	
		,,	Humāyun	1	3	0

† Thus in all MSS., but Ferishta discovers the method of computation by dating this reign from the abdication of his father Firoz Shāh in his favour on the 6th Shabān 789 A.H. (21st August 1387) to his death on the 17th Rabii I 796 (20th January 1393) disregarding the two intermediate reigns.

In the year 429 of the era of Bikramājit (A.D. 372) Anangpāl[1] of the Tonwar tribe reigned with justice and founded Delhi. In the year 848 of the same luni-solar era (A.D. 791) in the vicinity of that renowned city, a hotly contested battle was fought between Prithirāj Tonwar and Bildeva Chauhān, and the sovereignty was transferred to this latter tribe. During the reign of Rājā Pithaura (Prithwi Rājā) Sultān Muizzu'ddin Sām made several incursions into Hindustān without any material success. The Hindu chronicles narrate that the Rājā engaged and defeated the Sultān in seven pitched battles. In the year 588 A.H. (A.D. 1192), an eighth engagement took place near Thānesar and the Rājā was taken prisoner. One hundred renowned champions (it is related) were among his special retainers. They were severally called *Sāmant*[2] and their extraordinary exploits cannot be expressed in language nor reconciled to experience or reason. It is said that at this battle none of these champions was present, and that the Rājā kept to his palace in selfish indulgence, passing his time in unseemly pleasure, heedless of the administration of the state and of the welfare of his troops.

The story runs that Rājā Jaichand Rathor, who held the supremacy of Hindustān was at this time ruling at Kanauj, and the other Rājās to some extent acknowledged his authority and he himself was so liberal-minded that many natives of Irān and Turān were engaged in his service. He announced his intention of celebrating the great sacrifice symbolic of paramount supremacy and set about its preparations. One of its conditions is that all menial service should be performed by princes alone, and that even the duties of the royal scullery and the kindling of fires are directly a part of their office. He likewise promised to bestow his beautiful daughter on the bravest of the assembled chivalry. Rājā Pithaura had resolved to attend the festival, but a chance speech of some courtier that while the Chauhān sovereignty existed, the great sacrifice could

---

[1] Another name for Raya-Sena. Wilford says that he was called Anangpāla or befriended by love probably for his success in his amours, which he displayed by carrying off his brother's wife. Tieffenthaler calls him Rasena and credits him with the building of Delhi, which is confirmed by the *Agnipurāna*.

[2] I learn from Professor Cowell that the primary meaning attached to this term in the St. Petersburg Dict. is 'neighbour', and the second signification, 'vassal', in which sense it often occurs in Sanskrit poetry. Monier Williams defines it as "a neighbouring king—a feudatory or tributary prince" and adds a third meaning 'a leader, general, champion' which applies to the text.

not legitimately be performed by the Rathor chief, inflamed his ancestral pride and he held back. Rājā Jaichand proposed to lead an army against him, but his counsellors representing the duration of the war and the approach of the appointed assembly, dissuaded him from the enterprise. To carry out the integrity of the festival, a statue of Rājā Pithaura was made in gold and placed in the office of porter at the royal gates. Roused to indignation at this news, Rājā Pithaura set out in disguise accompanied by 500 picked warriors and suddenly appeared at the gathering and carrying off the image, he put a great number to the sword and hastily returned. The daughter of Jaichand, who was betrothed to another prince, hearing of this adventurous deed, fell in love with Pithaura and refused her suitor. Her father, wroth at her conduct, expelled her from her chamber in the palace and assigned her a separate dwelling. Pithaura, distracted at the news, returned with a determination to espouse her, and it was arranged that Chāndā a bard, a rival in skill of Babylonian* minstrelsy, should proceed to the court of Jaichand on the pretence of chanting his praises, while the Rājā himself with a body of chosen followers should accompany him as attendants. Love transformed the intention into act, and by this ingenious device and the spell of valour, he carried off his heart's desire, and after prodigies of bravery and heroism reached his own kingdom. The hundred *Sāmants* (above mentioned) accompanied him under various disguises. One after the other they covered his retreat and defeated their pursuers. Gobind Rāe Gehlot made the first stand and bravely fighting, fell. Seven thousand of the enemy sank engulfed in death before him. Next Narsingh Deva, Chāndā, Pundir, and Sārdul Solanki, and Pālhan Deva Kachhwāha with his two brothers, during the first day's action, after performing feats of astonishing heroism sold their lives dearly, and all these heroes perished in the retreat.

The Rājā, with the bard Chāndā and two of his brothers, brought his bride to Delhi amid the admiration of a wondering world.

Unfortunately the prince was all engrossed by his affection for his beautiful wife and neglected all other affairs.

---

* The text here is corrupt, and the variants printed give no help. Jarrett made the above translation with the warning that he was not satisfied with it. I suggest the emendation—"Chand the bard, who was a clever confidant [of Prithvi Rāj]," *āz damsāzān-i-māhir-ash ast.* [J. Sarkar.]

After a year had thus passed, Sultān Shahābu'ddin by reason of the above events, formed an alliance with Rājā Jaichand, and assembling an army, invaded the country and captured many places. But no one dared even to represent, not to say, remedy this state of affairs. At last, the principal nobles meeting together, introduced Chāndā through the seven gates of the palace, who entering the women's apartments, by his representations somewhat disturbed the Rājā's mind. But in the pride of his former victories, he marched to battle with but a small army. As his brave champions were now no more, his kingdom fallen from its ancient renown, and Jaichand his former ally, reversing his past policy, in league with the enemy, the Rājā in this contest was taken prisoner and carried by the Sultān to Ghazni, Chāndā in his fidelity and loyalty hastened to Ghazni, entered the Sultān's service and gained his favour. By his address, he discovered the Rājā and comforted him in his prison. He proposed that he should praise his dexterity with the bow to the Sultān who would desire to witness it, and that then he might use his opportunity. The proposal was carried out and the Rājā pierced the Sultān with an arrow. His retainers fell upon the Rājā and Chāndā and cut them to pieces.

The Persian historians give a different account and state that the Rājā was killed in battle.

Fate discloses many such events from its treasure-house of wonders. But where—and blessed is he—who will take warning thereby and act on the lesson?

When the Chauhān dynasty fell, the choicest portion of Hindustān passed into the hands of Sultān Muizzu'ddin Ghori. Leaving Malik Qutbu'ddin (Eibak) who was one of his slaves, at the village Guhrām, [Ghuram in Patiala] he himself returned to Ghazni, laying waste the hilly country on his northern march. Qutbuddin in the same year possessed himself of Delhi and many other places and followed up his successes with remarkable ability. On the death of Muizzu'ddin, Ghiyāsu'ddin Mahmud son of Ghiyasu'ddin Muhammad sent from Firozkoh (his capital) the umbrella and insignia of royalty to Malik Qutbu'ddin. Qutbu'ddin was enthroned at Lahore and exalted his reputation by his justice, munificence and valour. He lost his life while playing at *chaugan* [polo.]

The nobles raised his son Arām Shāh to the throne, but a strong faction set up Malik Altmish, who had been a purchased slave, and was the son-in-law and adopted heir of Qutbu'ddin. Arām Shāh was defeated and retired into obscurity, and Altmish assumed the title of Shamsu'ddin. It is said that his father was chief of some of the Turkish tribes. His brethren and cousins distracted by envy, sold, like Joseph, this nursling of intelligence, into slavery. Through the vicissitudes of fortune, he had various changes of masters until a merchant brought him to Ghazni. Sultān Muizzu'ddin Sām proposed to purchase him, but his owner chaffered for his value and placed an exorbitant price on him. The Sultān enraged, forbade any one to purchase him. Qutbu'ddin on his return to Ghazni after the conquest of Gujrāt, having obtained permission, bought him for a large sum and adopted him as a son. Khwājah Qutbu'ddin Ushi* was his contemporary and edified the world by his outward demeanour and the sanctity of his interior life. When Altmish died, his son (Ruknu'ddin Firoz Shāh) succeeded him who regarded wealth as a means of self-indulgence and thought little of winning the affections of his people. He made over the control of affairs to his mother Shāh Turkān. The nobles withdrawing their allegiance raised Raziah the daughter of Sultān Shamsu'ddin to the throne. The Sultān himself had previously made her his heir. Some of his courtiers asked him the reason of his doing so while he had sons still living. He replied that his sons, addicted to drinking were unfitted for the dignity. During the reign of Muizzu'ddin Bahrām Shāh, the Mughal troops devastated Lahore. A disloyal faction imprisoned the king and put him to death. In the reign of Sultān Alāu'ddin Masud Shāh occurred an irruption of the Mughals into Bengal, entering by way of China or Tibet, but his troops defeated them. Another body advanced from Turkistān to Uch. The Sultān set out to engage them, but on reaching the banks of the Biāh, intelligence reached him that the enemy had retreated. He returned to Delhi and there affected the company of low and base flatterers and ended his days in prison.

Nāsiru'ddin Mahmud ruled with capacity and munificence. In his time also, the Mughals entered the Panjāb but retreated on hearing of his approach.

---

* Ush is in Transoxiana and his birthplace. He is also known as Kāki from the miraculous production of bread cakes of the kind called in the vernacular *kāk* applied by the prophet Khizr for the needs of his family whose sustenance his meditations gave him no leisure or occasion to provide.

The *Tabaqāt i Nāsiri* takes its name from him. He had many excellent qualities. Ghiyasu'ddin Balban who had been the slave and son-in-law of his father, he raised to the rank of chief minister and gave him the title of Ulugh[1] Khān. This minister filled his high office worthily and sought the divine favour in watchfulness over his people.

Nāsiru'ddin dying without children, the faithful minister was raised to the sovereignty. Clemency and solid gravity of character added fresh lustre to his dignity, and far from spending his precious hours in unworthy pursuits, he gladdened his kingdom by his appreciation of merit, his knowledge of men and his devotion to God. Those of ill repute and the wicked were banished into obscurity, and the good happily prospered under his encouragement. He conferred the government of the Panjāb on his eldest son Muhammad, commonly known as *Khān i Shahid*[2] through whose valour and vigilance the province rested in security. Mir Khusrau and Mir Hasan were in his suite. He was returning from a visit to his father unprepared for hostilities, when he encountered some Mughal troops between Dipālpur and Lahor and lost his life in the action. Mir Khusrau was taken prisoner but contrived to escape. The province of Bengal had been bestowed by Ghiyāsu'ddin on his youngest son Bughra Khān.

On the death of Ghiyāsu'ddin, the nobles despatched Kai Khusrau the son of Khān i Shahid, who had been nominated heir, to (his father's government of) Multān, and bestowed the title of Sultān Muizzu'ddin Kaikubād on the son of Bughra Khān who thus acquired the sovereignty of Delhi. His father in Bengal, assuming the title of Nāsiruddin marched to Delhi whence Kaikubād advanced with a force to encounter him. The armies met on the banks of the Sarju (Gogra) near the town of Ajodhya, and through the conspiracy of disloyal and evil counsellors, the father after the interview returned to Bengal and the supreme sovereignty rested with the son. It is strange that Amir Khusrau should have chosen such a subject as this interview for encomium in his poem the *Qirān us Sa'dain.*

---

[1] *Ulugh* is a Tartar word and signifies 'great', and used often as a proper name as in the case of Ulugh Beg grandson of Timur.

[2] Or the martyred prince. Abul Fazl's assertion of the prince's unpreparedness is not confirmed. It was in the pursuit of the flying Mughals that he was surprised by an ambush while he halted by the banks of a stream to drink and to return thanks to God for his victory. Amir Khusrau alludes to his escape in his well-known poem, the *Khizr Khāni.*

The fortunes of this thankless unfilial son through his insobriety fell into decay. A faction set up his son, under the title of Shamsu'ddin to remedy the disorder, and the body of the wretched Kaikubād was flung into the waters of the Jumna. Shamsuddin was set aside and the sovereignty, by assent of the ministers, conferred on the Khiljis.

Jalālu'ddin who was paymaster of the Imperial forces, ascended the throne and by his simplicity of character lent no favour to the designs of the factious. His nephew Malik Alāu'ddin who had been brought up under his care, went from Karrah to the Deccan and having amassed great booty was inflated by its possession and proved rebellious. The Sultān by the persuasion of intriguers advanced from Delhi to Karrah, where the traitor slew him and assumed the title of Sultān Alāu'ddin. Thus by a marvel of Fate did the empire devolve on this miscreant, yet he accomplished some excellent reforms. On several occasions he encountered and defeated the Mughals. Mir Khusrau dedicated to him his *Khamsah*[1] and the story of Dewal[2] Rāni to his son Khizr Khān. Unfortunately he abandoned his usual prudence and fell under the influence of a eunuch (Kāfur) on whom he conferred the conduct of the administration. Through the suggestions of that wretch, his three sons Khizr Khān, Shādi Khān and Mubārak Khān were imprisoned, and on his own death, by the same instrumentality the youngest son was raised to the throne under the title of Shahābuddin. He destroyed the sight of two of his brothers, but Mubārak Khān providentially escaped. A few days later the wretch (Kāfur) was himself assassinated and Mubārak Khān who was in prison became chief minister.

---

[1] Or *five* poems, *viz.*, the Hasht Bihisht, Sikandar Nāmah, Panj Ganj, Laila wa Majnum, and Shirin wa Khusrau.

[2] The story will be found in Briggs, Vol. I, pp. 327-366. Kaunla Devi her mother, the wife of Karan Rāe of Nahrwāla had been taken captive in the wars against that prince (1297) and placed in the royal harem. In 1306 an expedition proceeding to the Deccan under Kāfur, Kaunla Devi represented to the king that she had borne two daughters to her former husband, that one had died, but the other Dewal Devi was still alive and she desired to recover her. Passing through Mālwah, Kāfur demanded her of Karan Rae without success. Shankar Deva Rāe, prince of Deogarh had long sought to obtain her hand, but the proud Rajput had hitherto refused his daughter to the upstart Mahratta. The desire to gain his aid in the war against the king's troops secured his consent and he despatched her under an escort which fell in accidentally with a body of Muhammadan troops near the caves of Ellora. An engagement resulted in the capture of the princess and her despatch to her mother at Delhi. Her beauty won the heart of Khizr Khān the king's son and the rough course of their love with its hapless termination is celebrated in the Khizr Khāni. When they first met these prococious lovers were respectively ten and eight years of age.

Subsequently he deposed his younger brother, and assumed the title of Sultān Qutbuddin. He reduced Gujarāt and the Deccan. Through his incapacity and licentious disposition he chose a favourite of the lower orders named Hasan for the comeliness of his person, and bestowed on him the title of Khusrau Khān. Although the faithful ministers of the Crown represented the man's unworthiness and infamy, the king regarded their honest advice as the suggestions of envy, till Khusrau Khān, plotting secretly, dared to assassinate his master and assumed the sovereignty under the title of Nāsiru'ddin. He put to death the surviving members of the family of Alāu'ddin and perpetrated the greatest cruelties. Malik Ghāzi who was one of Alāu'ddin's chief nobles, defeated and slew him and with the concurrence of the nobles, ascended the throne with the title of Sultān Ghiyasu'ddin Tughlaq Shāh. After settling the affairs of Bengal, he returned to Delhi. His son Muhammad Khān erected a pavilion at the distance of 3 *kos* from Delhi, in the space of three days and with much entreaty invited the king to enter it. The roof of the building fell in and the king perished in the ruins. Although (Ziāuddin) *Barni*[1] endeavours to substantiate the innocence of Muhammad Khān, the haste with which the pavilion was erected, and the eagerness to entertain the king therein, have all the appearance of guilty design.

When Sultān Muhammad died, Firoz the son of (Sālār) Rajab his paternal uncle was, according to the will of Muhammad, raised to the throne. He ruled with capacity and prudence and left many useful works as memorials of his reign. At his death anarchy to some extent prevailed in the empire. A faction set up his grandson (Ghiyāsuddin) Tughlaq Shāh (II) but in a short space he was sent to his last sleep by the hands of traitors and Abu Bakr[1] another grandson succeeded him.

In the reign of Sultān Mahmud, the direction of affairs devolved on Mallu Khān who received the title of Iqbāl Khān, but his incapacity and ill-fortune were unequal to the burden of state guidance. Internal disorders arose. A grandson of Firoz Shāh was acknowledged by some, under the title of Nasrat Shāh and increased the anarchy. Constant struggles took place in the vicinity of Delhi till in the

[1] The well-known author of the *Tarikh i Firoz Shāhi*.
[1] Son of Zafar Khān, son of Firuz Shāh.

year 801 A.H. (A.D. 1398) Timur invaded the country. Sultān Mahmud fled to Gujarāt and every competitor for power was crushed.

When Timur was on his return march, he left Khizr Khān, whom he had met during his invasion, in the government of Multān and Dipālpur. For two months Delhi was a waste. Nasrat Shāh who had fled into the Doāb, took possession of the throne. Iqbāl Khān then marched on Delhi and seized it and the other fled to Mewāt. Mahmud Khān now came from Gujarāt and Iqbāl Khān feigned acceptance of his service. One night the Sultān, in desperation of his affairs departed alone to the court of Sultān Ibrahim of the Sharqi dynasty (of Jaunpur) but met with no encouragement nor assistance. He was compelled therefore to return and Iqbāl Khān now opposed him but without success, and subsequently was taken prisoner in an action against Khizr Khān and was slain. Sultān Mahmud now took possession of Delhi, and was for some time occupied in hostilities, till he was carried off by an illness, and the Khilji dynasty terminated with him.

For a short period allegiance was paid to Daulat Khān (Lodi) *Khāsah Khail,* till Khizr Khān marched from Multān and took possession of Delhi. Malik Mardān Khān, one of the nobles of the Court of Sultān Firoz, had adopted Sulaimān the father of Khizr Khān as his son who subsequently, in default of recognised heirs, succeeded to his government.[1] Khizr Khān in gratitude (to Timur) did not[2] assume the regal title but styled his Court "The Sublime Standards," and adorned the *Khutbah* with the name of that illustrious monarch and afterwards with that of Mirzā Shāh Rukh, but it concluded with a prayer for himself. His son Mubārak Shāh succeeded him in accordance with his will. Sultān Ibrahim Sharqi and Hoshang (of Mālwah) being engaged in hostilities, Mubārak intended an attack

[1] The obscurity of this sentence in the original lies in the eliptical style of Abul Fazl. The sense I have given is in accordance with the facts of Ferishta who says that Malik *Marwān* Daulāt had adopted Sulaimān, and being himself appointed to the government of Multān, was succeeded at his death by his own son Malik Shaikh. The latter dying, made way for Sulaimān who was in turn succeeded by his son Khizr Khān. Ferishta makes the name Marwān and not Mardān.

[2] The MSS. omit the negative, but the text supplies it. Ferishta is clear on the point. "He did *not* take the name of king nor assume any regal epithet." The title in the text is not mentioned by him, which, however, is somewhat analogous to the Ottoman style of the 'Babi Aāli' or Sublime Porte, though in the latter it is absolute, and in the former vicarious.

on Kālpi and the adjacent territories, but he was perfidiously set upon by a band of traitors and slain.[1] Muhammad Shāh, who according to some was the son of Farid the son of Khizr Khān, while another account makes him the son of Mubārak, was raised to the throne. Sultān Alāu'ddin (his son and successor) possessed no share of rectitude and abandoned himself to licentious gratifications.

Bahlol (Lodi) now aspired to greatness. He was the nephew of Sultān Shāh Lodi of the Shāhu Khel tribe (of Afghāns). His father Bahrām in the time of Sultān Mahmud, came with five sons from the borders of Balot to Multān and subsisted with some difficulty by traffic. Sultān Shāh[2] obtained service under Khizr Khān. He received the title of Islām Khān, and the revenues of Sirhind were assigned to him. Bahlol, the son of his nephew on his brother's side was prospering ill in Sirhind, but was received into favour by him and adopted as a son. Bahlol was born in Multān and during the month in which his birth was expected, a beam of the house fell and killed his mother. He was extracted by the Caesarean operation and his destiny proved fortunate. Although he allowed his sovereign (Alāu'ddin) who lived in retirement (at Badāon) to retain nominal power, he boldly assumed the supreme authority.[3] His reign showed some capacity and his conduct was marked by intelligence and recognition of merit. He was carried off by an illness in his 80th year. It is said that he once happened to meet with a darvesh, having at the time with him but a trifling sum of money. The spiritually enlightened recluse called out, "Who will buy the kingdom of Delhi for such a sum of money?" His companions laughed in mockery at the man, but Bahlol frankly gave him all he had, and paid him reverence and eventually fulfilled the prediction. He carried on wars with the Sharqi kings which continued with varying successes, until he took Jaunpur and this dynasty was overthrown. He left his son, Bārbak at Jaunpur and returned to Delhi. As he was returning to Delhi from an

---

[1] He had laid the foundations of the city of Mubārakābād on the Jumna and was in the habit of visiting it to inspect the progress of the buildings. It was in one of these that he was assassinated at the instigation of the Wazir Sarwar ul Mulk on the 9th Rajab 837 (A.D. 1433). Ferishta.

[2] His eldest son, the others were Malik Kālā, Malik Firoz, Malik Muhammad and Malik Khwājah. Ferishta.

[3] Removing the name of Alāu'ddin from the *Khutbah*, and assuming the insignia of royalty. Ferishta.

expedition against Gwalior he died near the town of Saketh.[1] His son Nizām Khān with the concurrence of the nobles, assumed the sovereignty and was styled Sultān Sikandar. He ruled with sagacity and appreciation of character and transferred the capital to Agra. In the year A.H. 911 (A.D. 1505), a great earthquake occurred and many lofty buildings were levelled. Sikandar was of comely person and mild disposition and popular from his liberality and open-handedness.

On his death, his son Sultān Ibrahim ascended the throne of Delhi and his authority was recognised as far as the confines of Jaunpur, the nobles conferring upon Jalāl Khān, another son of Sikandar's, the sovereignty of Jaunpur. Dissensions followed between the brothers, and Jalāl Khān abandoned his government and took refuge with the governor of Gwalior, but meeting with no success, fled to the court of Sultān Mahmud of Mālwa and succeeding as little there, he set out for Gondwāna. There the royal partisans seized him and carried him to the king by whom he was put to death. During his reign various chiefs revolted, such as Daryā Khān Lohāni viceroy of Behār, and his son Bahādur Khān had the *Khutba* read and the coin minted in his own name. Daulat Khān Lodi fled at Kabul and sought protection at the court of Babar, whom he led to the conquest of Hindustān while affairs resulted in a prosperous issue.

---

[1] Suketa or Saketa according to the *I. G.* is one of the classical names borne by Ajodhya, the ancient capital of Oudh. Abul Fazl places *Saketh* in the Sarkār of Kanauj.

SUBAH OF LĀHOR.

It is situated in the third climate. Its length from the river *Satlaj* (Sutlej) to the *Sind* river is 180 *kos*. Its breadth from *Bhimbar* to *Chaukhandi* one of the dependencies of *Satgarah*,[1] 86 *kos*. It is bounded on the east by *Sirhind;* on the north by *Kashmir;* on the south by *Bikaner* and *Ajmer;* on the west by *Multān*. It has six principal rivers which all flow from the northern mountains.

(1.) The *Sutlej* the ancient name of which is *Shattudar*[2] and whose source is in the *Kāhlor* hills. *Rupar, Māchhiwārah* and *Ludhiānah* are situated on its banks, and it receives the Biāh at the *Bauh*[3] ferry.

(2.) The *Biāh* (Beās) was anciently called *Bipāsha,* (Sansk. Vipasa Gr. Hyphasis). Its source is named *Biahkund* in the *Kullu* mountains in the vicinity of which the town of *Sultānpur*[4] stands above the river.

(3.) The *Ravi*, the ancient *Irawati,*[5] rises in the *Bhadrāl*[6] hills. Lahor the capital, is situated on its banks.

(4). The *Chenāb*, anciently *Chandarbhāgā*. From the summit of the *Kishtawār*[7] range issue two sweet water streams, the one called *Chandar,* the other *Bhāgā* which unite near *Khatwār* and are known by the above name whence they flow by *Bahlolpur, Sudharah* and *Hazārah*.

---

[1] Satgarha is situated 13 miles east of Gugaira on one of the projecting points of the high bank which marks the limits of the windings of the Ravi on the east. The name means 'seven castles' but these no longer exist. There is an old brick fort and several isolated mounds which mark the site of an ancient city. Cunningham, p. 212.

[2] The Sydrus or better reading, Hesidrus of Pliny. It rises like the Indus on the slopes of the Kailās mountains, the Siva's paradise of ancient Sanskrit literature, with peaks 22,000 feet high. The twin lakes of Mānasarowar and Rakas-tal, united with each other, are its direct source. See *I. G.*

[3] In the maps, according to the text note, *Baupur*. The junction is at the south boundary of the Kaparthala state.

[4] It is in Kullu proper on the right bank of the Beas in lat. 30° 58′ N., and long. 77° 7′ E., at an elevation of 4,092 feet above sea level. It is perched on a natural eminence, once surrounded by a wall. Only two gateways remain of the ancient fortifications. *I. G.*

[5] Hydraotes of Arrian.

[6] Var. Bhadrā. It rises in the northern half of the Bangāhal valley in Kangra dist.

[7] The *I. G.* places *Kistawār* in the Kashmir state, lat. 33° 18′ 30″ N., long. 75° 48′ E. near the left bank of the Chenab which here forces its way through a gorge with precipitous cliffs 1,000 feet high. The Chenāb is called Sandabad by Ptolemy but the Greek historians of Alexander named it *Akesines* because its proper name was of ill omen, from its similitary thinks Bishop Thirlwall to *Alexandron-phagos* 'devourer of Alexander.' *Ladak,* pp. 118, 352.

(5.) The *Bihat* (Jhelum), anciently called *Bidasta*,[1] has its rise in a lake in the *parganah* of *Ver* in *Kashmir*, flows through *Srinagar* and enters Hindustān. *Bherah* lies on its (left) bank.

(6.) The source of the *Sindh* (Indus) is placed by some between *Kashmir* and *Kāshghar*, while others locate it in China. It flows along the borders of the *Sawād* territory by *Atak Benares*[2] and *Chaupārah* into *Baluchistān*.

His Majesty has given the name of *Beth Jālandhar* to the valley between the *Biāh* and the *Satlaj*; of *Bāri*, to that between the *Biāh* and the *Rāvi*; of *Rechna* to that between between the *Rāvi* and the *Chenāb*; of *Jenhat*[3] to the valley of the *Chenāb* and the *Bihat*, and *Sindh Sāgar* to that of the *Bihat* and *Sindh*. The distance

between the Satlaj and the		Biāh	is	50	*kos*.
,, ,, Biāh	,,	Rāvi	,,	17	,,
,, ,, Rāvi	,,	Chenāb	,,	30	,,
,, ,, Chenāb	,,	Bihat	,,	20	,,
,, ,, Bihat	,,	Sindh	,,	68	,,

This province is populous, its climate healthy and its agricultural fertility rarely equalled. The irrigation is chiefly from wells. The winter though not as rigorous as in Persia and Turkestān, is more severe than in any other part of India. Through the encouragement given by His Majesty, the choicest productions of Turkestān, Persia and Hindustān are to be found here. Musk-melons are to be

[1] Bidasta and Bihat are corruptions of Sansk. *Vitasta*, the Hydaspes of Horace, and the more correct Bidaspes of Ptolemy. The pool of Vira Nāg was walled round by Jahangir, but the true source of the river is more to the S.-W. in N. lat. 33° 30′ and E. long. 75° 25′. Bherah is in the Shāhpur dist. lat. 32° 29′ N., long. 72° 57′ E. The ruins of the original city known as Jobnāthnagar are identified by Genl. Cunningham with the capital of Sopheites, contemporary of Alexander the Greeat.

[2] It is so called by the Muhammadan historians in contradistinction to Katak Benares in Orissa at the opposite extremity of the empire. *I. G.* On his return from Kābul, on the 14th Safar 989 A.H. (20th March 1581), Akbar crossed the Indus at Attock and ordered the building of the fort, of mortar and stone in order to control that part of the country and called it Atak which signifies in the vernacular 'hindrance' or 'prohibition', it being forbidden to the Hindus to cross the Indus. Ferishta. The Swāt territory is here meant, the river of that name, the *Swastos* of the Greeks (Sansk. *Suvastu*) rising on the east slopes of the mountains which divide Panjakora from the Swāt country, receives the drainage of the Swāt valley and entering the Peshawar dist. north of Michni, joins the Kābul river at Nisatha. The course of the Indus has there a somewhat parallel direction.

[3] Under list of *Sarkārs* Chenhat, more commonly known as the *Jech* or Jechnā Doāb.

[4] Tieffenthaler quotes other measurements besides these, giving the reason for the variations in the differences of route, the incapacity of travellers and the universal ignorance of geometry.

had throughout the whole year. They come first in season when the sun is in Taurus and Gemini, (April, May, June), and a later crop when he is in Cancer and Leo (June, July, August). When the season is over, they are imported from Kashmir and from Kābul, Badakhshān and Turkestān. Snow is brought down every year from the northern mountains. The horses resemble the Irāq breed and are of excellent mettle. In some parts of the country, they employ themselves in washing the soil whence gold, silver, copper, *rui*,[1] zinc, brass and lead are obtained. There are skilful handicraftsmen of various kinds.

Lāhor is a large city in the *Bari Doāb*. In size and population it is among the first. In ancient astronomical tables it is recorded as *Lokāwar*. Its longitude is 109° 22′, lat. 31° 50′. During the present reign the fortifications and citadel have been strengthened with brick masonry and as it was on several occasions the seat of government, many splendid buildings have been erected and delightful gardens have lent it additional beauty. It is the resort of people of all countries whose manufactures present an astonishing display and it is beyond measure remarkable in populousness and extent.

Nagarkot is a city situated on a hill : its fort is called *Kāngrah*. Near the town is the shrine of *Mahāmāyā*[2] which is considered as a manifestation of the divinity. Pilgrims from distant parts visit it and obtain their desires. Strange it is that in order that their prayers may be favourably heard, they cut out their tongues : with some it grows again on the spot, with others after one or two days. Although the medical faculty allow the possibility of growth in the tongue, yet in so short a space of time it is sufficiently amazing. In the Hindu mythology, *Mahāmāyā* is said to be the wife of Mahādeva, and the learned of this creed represent by this name the energizing power of the deity. It is said that on beholding the disrespect (shown to her husband, Siva) she cut herself in pieces and her body fell in

[1] This metal is defined at p. 41 Vol. I. as being composed of 4 *sers* of copper to ½ of lead, and in India called *Bhangār*.

[2] The Great Illusion, or the illusory nature of worldly objects divinely personified, an epithet of the goddess Durgā. The earlier name Hardwār, *Māyāpur*, represents the ancient worship of this supreme energy and 'by her, whose name is Maya", says the *Bhagavata* "the Lord made the universe." His temple still exists in Hardwar, and is described in Cunningham's *Anct. Geog.*

four places; her head and some of her limbs in the northern mountains of Kashmir near *Kāmrāj*, and these relics are called Shāradā; other parts fell near *Bijāpur* in the Deccan and are known as *Tuljā Bhawāni*. Such portions as reached the eastern quarter near *Kāmrup* are called *Kāmākhyā*, and the remnant that kept its place is celebrated as *Jālandhari* which is this particular spot.[1]

In the vicinity torch-like flames issue from the ground in some places, and others resemble the blaze of lamps.[2]

---

[1] Read with variation of detail the preface to the *Gopatha Brāhmana* published in Nos. 215-252 of the Bibl. Ind., pp. 30-35. It occurs in the 2nd Book in the germ which afterwards developed into the Puranic tale of *Daksha's great sacrifice*. This mind-born son of Brahmā and father of Uma or Durga assisted at a Visrasrig sácrifice celebrated by his father in which discourtesy was shown to Siva. A quarrel broke out between Daksha and Siva, resulting in the exclusion of the latter from the great sacrifice to which the whole Hindu pantheon was bid. Uma seated in her blissful mansion on the crest of the Kailāsa mountain, saw the crowds proceeding to her father's court to which she repaired and learning the exclusion of her husband, upbraided her father for his injustice and refused to retain the body she had inherited from him. Covering herself up with her robe, she gave up her life in a trance of meditation. The wrath of Siva incarnate in a giant form pursued the feasters and created stupendous havoc. *Vishnu* unable to pacify Siva and knowing that his fury was kindled by the sight of his dead wife, cut the body to pieces bit by bit with his discus and threw it about the earth and thus calmed the irate and oblivious deity who thereupon restored the killed and wounded to life and soundness. Daksha's head having been burnt in the melee, it was replaced by that of a goat which happened to be at hand, apparently without remonstrance from the reanimated demigod or even his consciousness of the substitution. The *Tantra Chudāmani* is able fortunately to detail the portions of the body and to identify the places where they fell. As these are said to be still held in high veneration, I record them for the instruction of the curious or the devout.

1. The crown of the head at Hingulā (Hinglaj). 2. The three eyes at Sarkarāra. 3. The nose at Sugandhā. 4 The top of the neck at Kāsmira. 5. The tongue at Jwālamukhi. 6. Right breast at Jālandhara. 7. Heart at Vaidyanātha. 8. Knees at Nepāla. 9. Right hand at Mānasa. 10 Navel at Ukala. 11. Right cheek at Gondaki. 12. Left arm at Vahulā. 13. Elbow at Ujjayani. 14 Right arm at Chāttola, Chandrasekhara. 15. Right foot at Tripurā. 16. Left foot at Trisrota. 17. *Yoni* at Kāmagiri (Kāmākhyā). 18. Right great toe at Yugādyā. 19. Other right toes at Kālipitha (Kalighāt). 20. Fingers at Prayāga. 21. Thighs at Jayanti. 22. Earrings at Vārānasi. 23. Back of the trunk at Kamyāsrama. 24. Right ankle at Kurukshetra. 25. Wrists at Manivedaka. 26. Back of the neck at Srisaila. 27. Backbone at Kānchi. 28. One hip at Kālamādhara. 29. Other hip at Narmadā. 30. Left breast at Rāmagiri. 31. Hairs of the head at Vrindāvana. 32. Upper row of teeth at Suchi. 33. Lower ditto at Panchasāgara. 34. Left *talpa* (shoulder-blade) at Karatoyā. 35. Right ditto at Sripārvatta. 36. Left ankle at Vibhāsha. 37. Belly at Prabāsha. 38. Upper lip at Bhairavaparvata. 39. Chin at Jala-sthala. 40. Left cheek at Godavari. 41. Right shoulder at Ratnāvali. 42. Left shoulder at Mithila. 43. Legbone at Nalāpāti. 44. Ears at Karmāta. 45. Mind(?) at Vakresvara. 46. Palm at Jasora. 47. Lower lip at Attahasa. 48. Necklace at Nandipura. 49. Anklets at Lankā. 50. Toes of left foot at Virāta. 51. Right leg at Magadha.

[2] See Hugel's *Travels in Kashmir*, p. 42, for this phenomenon. The text has *pilsuj*, which is a lamp in the shape of a platter, three feet in height from the base, and about 6 inches diameter at the top; having in the middle a small tube with two holes through which the wick is fed by oil or grease kept in liquefaction by the flame. This shrine is the famous *Jwālāmukhi* (mouth of Flame) distant two days' journey from Kāngra.

There is a concourse of pilgrims and various things are cast into the flames with the expectation of obtaining temporal blessings. Over them a domed temple has been erected and an astonishing crowd assembles therein. The vulgar impute to miraculous agency what is simply the effect of a mine of brimstone.

In the middle of *Sindh Sāgar* near *Shamsābād* is the cell of Bālnāth Jogi which they call *Tilah Bālnāth.*[1] Devotees of Hindustān regard it with veneration and Jogis especially make pilgrimage to it. Rock-salt is found in this neighhood. There is a mountain 20 *kos* in length from which they excavate it, and some of the workmen carry it out. Of what is obtained, three-fourths is the share of those that excavate and one-fourth is allotted to the carriers. Merchants purchase it at from half to two *dāms* a *man* and transport it to distant countries. The landowner takes 10 *dāms* for every carrier and the merchant pays a duty of one rupee for every 17 *mān* to the state. From this salt artificers make dishes, dish-covers, plates and lamp-stands.

The five *Doābs* of this province are subdivided into 234 *parganahs.* The measured land is one *kror, 61 lakhs,* 55,643 *Bighas,* and 3 *Biswas.* The gross revenue is 55 *krors,* 94 *lakhs,* 58,423 *dāms.* (Rs. 1,39,86,460-9-2). Of this 98 *lakhs,* 65,594 *dāms* (Rs. 246,639-13-7) are *Suyurghāl.* The local force consists of 54,480 Cavalry and 426,086 Infantry.

For traditions regarding the four *pithas* and the number of the *pithas,* vide the *Sakta Pithas* by Dr. D. C. Sarkar in the *J.R.A.S.B.,* Vol. XIV, 1948, pp. 11-15, 17-31. According to Dr. Sarkar, the *Hevajra Tantra* of the Buddhists contains the earliest tradition about the *Four Pithas* which are :—(1) Jalandhara, (2) Odiyāna (Uddiyan in the Swat valley), (3) Purnagiri and (4) Kāmrupa. The same is echoed in the Kālikā Purāna which mentions Odrā in the place of Uddiyāna. This corresponds, barring Uddiyana, to Abul Fazl's enumeration of the *pithas.*

[1] General Cunningham (*Ancient Geog. of India,* p. 164) says that the Tila range, 30 miles in length, occupies the west bank of the Jhelum from the east bend of the river below Mangala to the bed of the Bunhar river, 12 miles north of Jalālpur. The full name is *Goraknāth ka Tila,* the more ancient, *Bālnath ka Tila,* both derived from the temple on the summit dedicated to the sun as Bālnath, but now devoted to the worship of Goraknath, a form of Siva.

Sarkār of the Bet Jālandhar Doāb.

Containing 60 *Mahals,* 3,279,302 *Bighas,* 17 *Biswas.* Revenue 124,365,212 *Dāms* in money. *Suyurghāl* 2,651,788 *Dāms.* Castes, various. Cavalry, 4,155. Infantry 79,436.

	Bighas Biswas.	Revenue D	Suyurghāl	Cavalry	Infantry	Castes.
Islimābād	2,735	458,122	...	15	200	Afghān.
Pati Dhuniat ...	57,866	3,601,678	80,607	30	400	Nāru.
Bhungā	51,089-13	2,760,530	10,232	20	300	Do. (var. Barar).
Bajwāra	12,363	2,425,813	689	30	200	Khori Wāhah.
Bhalon, has a stone fort	32,761	1,305,006	...	70	1000	Dhāhwāl.
Barwa	13,611	668,000	...	...	...	
Pālakwā	4,532	200,000	...	...	...	
Bachheru	4.215	160,000	...	...	...	
Besāli and Khattah, 2 *Mahals*	11,405	566,366	...	...	...	
Talwan	201,450	6,780,337	804,889	70	700	Main.
Tatārpur, has a stone fort	3,458	170,388	...	...	...	
Jālandhar, has a brick fort	474,308	14,751,626	773,167	100	1000	Afghān. Lodhi, and Lohāni, and Ranghar tribes.
Chaurāsi	96,330	5,463,913	255,516	50	1000	Afghān.
Jeora	48,124	2,474,854	23,527	50	300	Bhatti.
Jason Bālākoti, has a stone fort	15,054	600,000	...	500	3000	Jaswāl, called also Bikaner.
Chanor	...	313,000	...	100	2000	Sombansi.
Hājipur Sāriyāna ...	59,255	2,693,874	...	...	...	
Dādrak [Dārdak] ...	497,202-11	9,707,993	92,153	150	4000	Khori Wāhah.
Dasuya, has a brick fort	157,962	4,474,950	67,249	...	...	Khokhar.
Dadial, has a stone fort	34,150	1,650,000	...	300	4005	Sasahwāl.
Dādah, Do. ...	30,218	1,200,000	...	...	...	
Darparah	26,444	900,000	...	...	...	
Dardhi	15,054	600,000	...	100	1000	Sombansi.
Dunnāgor	11,490	455,870	...	...	...	
Dhankali	1,880	72,000	...	...	...	
Rahimābād	8,790	2,480,689	13,613	80	200	Khori Wāha.

Sarkār of Bet Jālandhar Doāb—Contd.

	Bighas Biswas	Revenue D.	Suyurghāl D.	Cavalry	Infantry	Castes
Rājpurpatan, has a stone fort	...	1,800,000	...	...	...	...
Sultānpur, has a brick fort	101,865	4,020,232	405,830	200	1000	Bhatti.
Sānkarbanot	59,952	2,533,225	16,485	50	500	Khori Wāhah.
Suket Mandi, has copper and iron mines ...	42,150	1,680,000	...	100	8000	Sombansi.
Sopar	24,583	1,000,000	...	...	2000	Sasahwāl.
Siba, has a stone fort ...	8,114-18	800,000	...	200	2000	Do.
Sorān	213,333	...	...	...	...	...
Shaikhpur	97,173	4,722,604	52,639	150	2000	Bhatti.
Shergarh	3,640	194,294	...	...	...	...
Isāpur	...	346,667	...	...	...	...
Kothi	116,286	5,546,661	30,670	30	400	Jat.
Garh Diwāla	58,083	2,670,087	4,530	20	200	Jat.
Kotla	42,152	1,680,000	...	300	4000	Jasrotiah.
Kotlehar, has a stone fort	32,932-16	1,310,847	...	200	3000	Kotlahariah.
Kharakdhār	42,043-12	48,000	...	...	...	...
Kheunkherā, has a stone fort	6,021-16	240,000	...	under Nakroh		Jaswāl.
Gangot, has a stone fort ...	6,021-16	240,000	...	...	...	Do.
Khera	6,021-16	240,000	...	20	4000	Surajbansi.
Ghawāsan (var. and G. Ghawās)	14,742-14	586,906	...	...	...	...
Loidheri	15,959-8	536,414	17,810	...	...	...
Lālsingi	5,937	236,850	...	...	...	...
Miāni Nuria	68,229	21,061,565	6,156	20	400	Bhatti.
Melsi	54,653-17	1,823,559	1,217	20	3000	Ranghar, Jat.
Muhammadpur	38,231	1,802,558	10,553	100	1000	Ranghar, Main.
Mānsawāl	6,668	286,667	...	...	...	...
Malot	6,412	4,603,620	...	...	...	...
Mandhota [Mamdot] ...	13,280	426,367	...	...	...	...
Nakodar	78,731	3,710,756	9,757	20	1000	Main.
Nangal	4,808	267,270	...	...	...	...
Nakrota	32,642	1,300,061	...	500	5000	Jaswāl.
Nonangal	46,180	2,315,368	...	30	300	Baloch, Jat.
Nandon	133,439	5,300,000	...	100	1500	Nagarkotiah.
Harhana [Hariana] with Akbarābād, 2 *Mahals* ...	626,889	6,032,032	49,650	40	406	Nāru.
Hadiābād	17,126	519,467	2,067	...	...	...

Sarkār of the Bāri Doāb.

Containing 52 *Mahals.* 4,580,002 *Bighas,* 18 *Biswas.* Revenue 142,808,183 *Dāms* revenue in cash from crops charged at special rates and from land paying the general *bīgah* rate. *Suyurghāl,* 3,923,922 *Dāms.* Castes, various. Cavalry, 31,055. Infantry, 129,300.

	Bighas Biswas	Revenue D.	Suyurghāl D.	Cavalry	Infantry	Castes
Anchhara	...	500,000	...	50	500	Khokhar.
Andora	20,781	1,193,739	7,624	...	...	...
Abhipur	...	168,000	...	...	...	...
Udar [Utar]	...	9,600	...	...	...	...
Lahore city Balda ...	...	2,912,600	...	5000	4000	...
Phulwāri	4,727-10	452,694	143,955	20	100	...
Phulrā	106,463	2,413,268	13,268	20	100	Sadhāl, Bhalar
Panchgrāmi [Panjgiran] ...	65,557	1,461,630	73,177	15	1000	Khokhar.
Bharli	17,967	4,060,507	209,789	...	...	
Bhilwāl	62,875	3,181,699	225,408	20	400	Jat.
Pati Haibatpur	1,576,633	28,395,380	284,647	700	10,000	Jat.
Batāla	515,479	16,820,998	256,853	200	5000	Bhatti, Jat.
Pathān [-kot], has a brick fort	199,872	7,297,015	97,015	250	2000	Brāhman.
Paniāl	65,789	4,266,000	276,091	150	400	Jat Khatiān.
Biāh	60,523	3,822,255	8,976	200	2000	Bhatti.
Bahādurpur	11,489	447,750	...	...		...
Talwāra	6,334	514,666	10,364	20	200	Bakkāl.
Thandot	25,222	610,064	3,234	20	500	Afghān.
Chandrāu	7,194-10	263,568	...	20	100	Jat, Sindhu.
Chārbāgh Barhi	213	58,502	...	...	...	...
Chamiāri	250,614	8,813,140	309,090	200	2000	Khokhar.
Jalālābād	152,058	5,163,119	20,456	300	4000	Afghān, Jat, Bhatti.
Chhat and Ambālah, 2 *Mahals*	...	2,300,000	...	50	500	Rājput, Sombansi.
Jatgarh	...	45,600	...	...	...	...
Khānpur	...	280,038	...	30	600	Khokhar.
Dābhawāla	121,495	6,282,139	57,674	100	3000	Jat.
Dhameri (now Nurpur) ...	...	1,600,000	...	60	1300	...
Darwa	...	240,000	...	50	500	Rājput, Sombansi.
Darwa, Digar	...	24,000	...	...	...	...
Sankhā Arwal	10,874	544,145	91,413	10	100	Arwal.
Sindhuwān	263,402	5,854,649	12,700	200	400	Jat Sindhu.
Lahore suburbs	11,401	674,053	202,300	...	...	...
Shāhpur	42,399	2,382,235	126,720	...	...	...
Sherpur	...	480,000	...	...	...	...
Ghurbatrāwan	7,391-13	411,985	63,103	20	100	Jat Sindhu.
Kasur	259,456	3,915,506	23,124	300	4000	Bhatti.
Kalānur	286,052	8,329,111	447,639	150	1500	Jat, Bakkāl.
Kunhewan	63,608	3,511,499	127,665	50	500	Khokhar, Bakhās.
Khokhowāl	75,194	3,475,510	3,510	20	500	Jat.
Goler	66,239	2,643,000	3,000	100	3000	Rājput Sombansi.

Sarkār of Bāri Doāb—Contd.

	Bighas Biswas	Revenue D.	Suyurghāl D.	Cavalry	Infantry	Castes
Kāngra, has a stone fort	...	2,400,000	...	2400	29,000	Sombansi.
Kotla	...	182,518	...	...	...	...
Karkārāon	...	16,000	...	...	...	...
Malik Shāh	28,684-9	1,475,562	52,283	10	100	Bhandāl, (var. Bhadāl).
Mau and Nabā [≐Omba], 2 *Mahals*	...	2,400,000	...	300	...	Rājput.
Mahror	...	24,000	...	...	...	...
Hoshiār Karnāla ...	22,225	489,372	...	20	400	Jat.
Pālam, } These four *parganahs*, are now abandoned.	...	9,600	...	...	...	...
Patiyār,	...	...	...	...	...	...
Bhatti,	...	...	...	...	...	...
Jarjiya	...	...	...	...	...	...

Sarkār of the Rechnāu Doāb.

Containing 57 *Mahals.* 4,253,148 *Bighas,* 3 *Biswas.* Revenue, 172,047,691 *Dāms.* *Suyurghāl,* 2,684,134 *Dāms.* Castes, various. Cavalry, 6,795. Infantry, 99,652.

	Bighas Biswas	Revenue D.	Suyurghāl D.	Cavalry	Infantry	Castes
Amrāki Bhatti	70,752-8	1,942,606	8,673	50	1000	Bhatti.
Lands of Bāgh Rae Bocha	2,683	52,837	...	...	...	...
Eminābād, has a brick fort	515,675-4	24,853,006	498,480	500	5000	Khokhar, Chimah &c.
Panchnagar	31,741.	1,181,266	27,879	50	500	Jat.
Parsaror	509,858-4	27,978,583	486,551	200	4000	Jat, Bājoh Telah &c.
Badubhandāl	23,752-18	1,611,882	46,979	...	...	...
Pati Zafarwāl, has a fort	6,108,148	3,697,338	150,865	50	2000	Jat, Bholron.
Pati Tarmali	29,056	525,953	...	20	400	Kolrā.
Bhalot	20,312-10	818,182	...	100	2000	Manhās.
Bhadrān, situate on a hill	...	240,000	...	50	4000	Do.
Balāwarah	6,021-6	240,000	...	50	3000	Balāwariāh.
Bhutiyāl	2,407,18	96,000	...	30	1000	Bhutiyālah.
Ban	1,346-19	48,000	...	100	4000	Manhās.
Tāral	38,669-8	2,144,945	8,400	150	2000	Jat, Tāral.
Talwandi	95,698-17	1,578,207	3,792	30	300	Jat.
Chima Chata	95,698	5,878,691	26,439	100 50	1000	Chimah Chatah.
Chandanwarak, (var. darak)	81,426-6	4,128,313	30,571		150	Jat, Warak.
Chhotādhar	22,858-5	1,391,692	...	...	...	...
Jabudhadi	12,474	815,587	31,135	...	...	...
Chiniwot, has a brick fort	154,154	2,806,369	190,052	500	5000	Jat Jabuhar.

Sarkār of Rechnāu Dāab—Contd.

	Bighas Biswas	Revenue D.	Suyurghāl D.	Cavalry	Infantry	Castes
Jammu, situate at the foot of a hill, and a stone fort above it*	19,329-11	3,956,000	...	1000	20,000	Manhās.
Jasrotā (in one MS.)	150,430	...	...	400	5000	Malanhās.
in another	430-19	1,150,000	...	...	...	...
Chari Champā [Chamba]	6,021-6	240,000	...	100	1000	Gwāleri.
Hāfizābād	169,499	4,548,000	48,000	150	150	Jat Balhan (Bhalar).
The lands of Khānpur ...	402	27,028	...	...	...	...
Daulatpur	4,779-10	115,050	...	...	...	...
Dāud Bhandāl Barhi ...	23,142	1,725,089	237,082	...	...	...
Daulatābād	14,368	241,740	...	10	100	Jat Salah, (var. Sad).
Rupnagar	6,705	410,513	...	...	...	...
Rinhā	58,850-8	275,550	5,461	...	...	Brāhman, Bāghbān.
Rechnā	130,207	8,680,742	442,082	700	7000	...
Sāhumali	152,391	5,574,764	18,353	40	1200	...
Sidhpur	108,923	3,127,212	79,972	100	2000	Jat, Marāli.
Siālkot, is situate on the edge of a ridge on the banks of the Aik torrent, has a brick fort ...	102,035	22,090,792	184,305	500	7000	Jat, Ghaman and Chimah.
Sahajrāo	5,627-7	362,326	4,803	100	1000	Chimah.
Sohdra, on the Chenāb, has a high brick minaret	121,721-1	7,096,710	99,731	100	1000	Do.
Shānzdah Hinjrāo ...	64,140	1,536,480	...	50	1000	Jat, Hinjrāo.
Shou [-kot?]	107,347	2,278,940	5,061	1000	5000	Jat, Langāh, Sanāwal (Sahāwal).
Fattu Bhandāl Barhi ...	7,826-7	613,917	5,842	...	...	
Fazlābād	2,115-7	136,528	...	...	...	
Gobindwāl	55,069	1,253,957	194,622	50	300	Orak and Jat.
Kāthohā	126,598-12	5,888,254	...	20	10,000	Kāmwāl (var. Kāhwāl).
Gujrān Barhi	2,631-14	670,936	11,787	...	...	
Kālāpind	2,801-19	203,964	21,702	...	...	
Kārnari, commonly called Sāniā	27,665-4	1,500,000	...	100	300	
Kharli Tarli	...	768,000	...	...	...	
Lakhnor	17,169-1	681,818	...	...	...	
Mangtanwāla	131,583	3,819,690	57,788	50	300	Jat.
Muhammad Bari Dukrāo	16,561-6	1,127,903	3,367	...	...	Jat.
Mahror	102,586-4	3,005,602	6,602	5	500	Brāhman.
Mengri	62,293	1,475,225	5,748	20	1000	Silhariyā and Gujar.
Mankot, includes 4 towns each with a stone fort	1,312	85,119	...	30	1200	Manhās.
Wan	140,234	371,553	20,278	50	1000	Jārak Silhar.
Haminagar	141,063	8,391,082	59,541	30	1000	Jat.
Hantiyāl (var. Hatiyāl) ...	6,201-6	240,000	...	30	200	Hatiyālah.

* The town and palace stand on the south bank of the river Tāvi a tributary of the Chenab; the fort overhangs the left or east shore at an elevation of 150 feet above the stream, *I. G.*

Chenhat (Jech) Doāb.

Containing 21 *Mahals,* 2,633,210 *Bighas,* 5 *Biswas.* Revenue 64,502, 394 *Dāms.* *Suyurghāl* 511,070 *Dāms.* Castes, various. Cavalry, 3,730. Infantry, 44,200.

	Bighas Biswas	Revenue D.	Suyurghāl D.	Cavalry	Infantry	Castes
Andarhal	31,070	485,418	...	—	...	Gakkhar (see Vol. I. 546).
Akhandor Ambāran ...	9,866-5	392,000	...	300	3000	Manhās.
Bhera, on the banks of the Bhimbar[1]	912,107-7	19,910,000	53,560	700	10,000	
Bahlolpur, on the banks of the river Chenab ...	170,607	3,830,575	10,583	100	500	Jat.
Bolet	8,748	400,080	...	50	300	
Bhimbar, situated on the banks of the stream ...	28,668	1,200,000	...	...	...	
Bhadu	4,717	192,000	...	30	1200	Jat, Bhandwāl.
Buhati	2,874	57,222	...	10	100	Mangharwāl.
Sāilā and Dudiyāl, 2 *Mahals*	27,421	735,741	...	200	800	Khokhar.
Shorpur	169,874	3,121,546	8,497	100	1000	Jat, Khokar, Jander.
Shakarpur	7,684	1,050,819	...	...	...	
Gujrāt	285,094	8,266,150	...	120	1000	
Kariyāli	57,818	2,643,270	6,633	100	2000	
Khokhar, has a brick fort	92,826	2,320,594	58,410	100	1000	Khokar.
Ghari, on the river Bihat	20,176	1,505,241	...	20	2000	Do.
Lolor, separated from Khushāb	192,253	3,746,166	11,290	200	2000	Khokhar and Mikan.
Mangli	2,839	432,000	...	400	2000	Manhās.
Malot Rāe Kedāri, situate on a hill	17,007	370,549	...	40	400	Mangharwāl.
Hareo	247,878	9,150,828	76,321	300	3000	Tat, Barwānji ?
Hazāra, has a brick fort	270,392	4,689,136	219,536	700	3000	Jat, Khokar Bāranij ?

[1] Bherah is on the left bank of the Jhelum. The Bhimbar torrent rising in the second Himalayan range, flows within 4 miles N. W. of Gujrāt and eventually joins the Jalālia *nālā* a branch of the Chenab. *I. G.*

Sindh Sāgar Doāb.

Containing 42 *Mahals,* 1,409,929 *Bighas.* Revenue, 51,912,201 *Dāms.* *Suyurghāl,* 4,680 *Dāms.* Castes, various. Cavalry, 8,553. Infantry, 69,700.

	Bighas Biswas	Revenue D.	Suyurghāl D.	Cavalry	Infantry	Castes
Akbarābād Tarkheri ...	204,381	5,491,738	...	2000	15,000	Gakkhar.
Atak Benares (Attock) ...	5,418	3,202,216	...	1000	5000	Khatar, called also Salāsah.
Awān, here are horses of good breed	10,096	415,970	...	50	500	Awān. (See Vol. I, 456, n. and I.G. under Hazāra).
Paharhāla, has a stone fort, below the fort runs the river Sowāri (=Sohān) ...	192,247	5,158,109	...	...	...	
Bel Ghāzi Khān ...	17,426	320,000	...	100	1500	Jānohah (Janjuah).
Bālā Khattar	5,825	1,000,040	...	20	100	Khattar.
Paru Khattar	1,195	48,000	...	...	...	
Balokidhan	7,679	1,316,801	...	100	500	Gakkhar.
Tharchak Dāmi	6,082	250,575	...	100	1000	Do.
Suburban dist. of Rohtas,* has a stone fort, beneath which flows the Kuhān stream	120,884	60,403,140	67,052	500	3000	Gakkhar. Bagiyāl.
Khushāb, situate near the river Bihat (Jhelum) the greater part is jungle ...	73,086	2,702,509	...	500	7000	Afghān Niyazi and Isā Khel.
Dān Gari [D. Gali] ...	147,647	3,301,201	...	1500	10,000	Gakkhar,
Dhānkot [Dinkot], on the banks of the river Mihran, *viz.,* Indus, has a salt mine	8,927	480,000	...	150	4000	Awān.

* The fort built by Sher Shāh as a check on the Gakkhar tribes, now in picturesque ruin. It is situated in the Salt Range on a gorge overlooking the Kuhān Nadi 11 miles north-west of Jhelum town. The walls extend for three miles and encircle the rocks which command the entrance of the pass. Some parts have a thickness of from 30 to 40 feet. One gateway still remains in excellent preservation. *I. G.*

Sindh Sāgaṛ Doāb—Contd.

	Bighas Biswas	Revenue D.	Suyurghāl D.	Cavalry	Infantry	Castes
Darband, (here two unintelligible words)	...	3,100,000 in money	...	20	500	Janohāh (Janjuah).
Dhrāb	2,330	96,000	...	20	150	Do.
Dudwat	2,830	96,000	...	20	300	Do.
Reshān	1,195	92,496	...	10	200	Awān.
Shamsābād	24,664	7,034,503	...	50	500	Gakkhar (var. Khokhar).
Patālā	11,146	624,000	...	100	1500	Jānohah.
Fatehpur Kālauri (var. Kanauri and T.)	157,042	4,261,881	...	500	10,000	Gakkhar.
Kalbhalak	40,913	2,883,253	18,176	30	200	Baloch.
Gheb (var. Khet, Khes, Khep)	16,961	934,161	...	300	1200	Khattar (sic).
Khār Darwāzah ...	4,316	24,541	...	50	300	Jānohah.
Girjhāk[1]	21,491	961,755	...	100	1500	Do.
Kachākot, one *kos* distant from this *parganah* is the spring of Hasan Abdāl[2]	5,825	340,000	...	50	2000	Rāwalah, Tarin, Afghān.
Kāhwān, has a stone fort	4,660	192,000	...	10	200	Jānohah.
Kambat	2,330	96,000	...	...		
Langahtiyār (var. G. Siyār)	2,330	96,000	...	10	100	
Mākhiāl, has a stone fort on a hill—there is scarcity of water—has a salt mine and a shrine ...	9,320	834,000	...	100	1500	Jānohah.

[1] Said by Cunningham, (*Anct. Geog.*, p. 163 and pronounced *Girjhak*) to be the Hindu name for Jalālpur, the probable site of the famous city of Bukephala built in memory of Alexander's horse.

[2] This well-known village lies on the road between Rawal Pindi and Peshawar which with its ruins, says the I. G., forms part of a group of ancient cities lying round the site of the ancient Taxila. Hwen Thsang the Chinese Buddhist pilgrim of the 7th Century A.D. visited the tank of the Serpent King, Elapatra, identified with the spring of Bābā Wali (Kandahāri) or Panja Sāhib. The fountain is hallowed by legends of Buddhist, Brahman, Moslem and Sikh. The shrine of Panja Sāhib crowns a precipitous hill about one mile east of the town, and at its foot is the holy tank, a small square reservoir, full of fish. Delapidated brick temples surround the edge and on the west side the water gushes out from beneath a rock made with the representation of a hand, ascribed by the Sikhs to their founder Bābā Nānak. The scenery is extremely picturesque; the river Haroh hard by affords excellent fishing, and on its near shore two ancient cypresses are the only epitaph above the tomb of one of Akbar's wives. For *Kachakot*, see Cunningham, *Anct. Geog.*, p. 116.

Sindh Sāgar Doāb—Contd.

	Bighas Biswas	Revenue D.	Suyurghāl D.	Cavalry	Infantry	Castes
Marāli, at the foot of a mountain	5,825	240,000	..	15	500	
Malot, has a stone fort on a hill	3,236	133,233	...	10	200	Janohah.
Nandanpur, has a brick fort on a hill	40,997	24,110	4,110	20	150	Do.
Nilāb, (Indus) land included under (Attock) Benares	8,787	481,305	...	...	...	
Nārwi, on the Sind ...	997	38,091	...	under Akbarābād		Gakkhar.
Nokosiral Khattar ...	926	38,096	...	10	50	Khattar.
Hazāra Qarlug	214,932	1,805,342	5,342	100	500	Dālāzāk Afghān.
Haliyār Lang	7,281	300,000	...	...	...	Bhakar barkhatri (with illegible variants).
Hazāra Gujrān	6,575	280,896	...	under Akbarābād		
Himmat Khān Karmun ...	165	48,000	...	Do.		Gakkhar.

*Beyond the Five rivers (Birun i Panjnad).**

	Bighas Biswas	Revenue D.	Suyurghāl D.	Cavalry	Infantry	Castes
Belot	...	322,740	...	100	10,000	Baloch.
Sahlor	...	1,700,000	...	40	700	Chandel and others.
Kahlor, (Punjāb Hill State)	...	1,800,000	...	50	1000	Do.

* The valley of the Jhelum takes the name of *Trimāb* (Three rivers) after its junction with the Chenāb and the Rāvi and that of *Panjnad* (Five rivers) after receiving the united waters of the Beās and Sutlej. *I. G.* This restricted signification cannot here apply. Certain outlying portions beyond the limits of the Punjāb Proper were evidently attached to the *Subahs* of Lahor and Multān and to the *sarkar* of Dipalpur and were denominated—*Birun i Panjnad.*

SUBAH OF MULTĀN

It is situated in the first, second and third climates simultaneously. Before *Tattah* was comprised in this province, its length from *Firozpur* and *Sewistān*, was 403 *kos* and its breadth from *Khatpur*[1] to *Jaisalmir*, 108 *kos*, but since its inclusion, it measures to *Kach* (Gandāvā) and *Mekrān*, 660 *kos*. On the east, it marches with the *Sarkār* of Sirhind; on the north with *Shor;* on the south, with the *Subah* of *Ajmer*, and on the west, with *Khach* and *Mekrān*. 660 *kos*. On the east, it marches with the *Sarkār* of Sirhind; on the north with *Shor;* on the south, with the *Subah* of *Ajmer*, and on the west, with *Khach* and *Mekrān*. For facility of reference, the two territories are separately described. Its principal rivers are the six already mentioned. The *Bihat* (Jhelum) joins the *Chenāb* near the *parganah* of *Shor* and after a course of 27 *kos*, they unite with the Ravi at *Zafarpur* and the three flowing collectively in one stream for 60 *kos*, enter the *Indus* near *U'ch*. Within 12 *kos* of *Firozpur*, the *Biāh* joins the Sutlej which then bears several names, *viz.*, *Har, Hāri, Dand, Nurni*,[2] and in the neigh-

---

[1] Khatpur is placed by Abul Fazl in the Rachna Doāb and by Tieffenthaler as the first stage in a journey from Lahor to Multān.

[2] The text diffidently forms two names of these four, viz.. Harhāri, Dandnurni, but the authority of the two best MSS. (relegated to the notes) divides them. One at least of these names, Dand, still lives in the local designation of a former bank of the Sutlej, whose shifting course has modified the aspect of the country. One ancient bed, forming the base of the segment where the Sutlej after its junction with the Beās curves round to the south-west is called the Sukhar Nai (*I. G.*) which crosses the district east to west and joins the modern channel near the borders of Sirsa. The Danda bank points to a still more ancient course crossing the south-west corner 35 miles east of the present stream, traceable as far as Moodkee and thence at intervals to the Sutlej 15 miles farther north. The old beds of the Rāvi and Beās which formerly united their waters much lower down, at present may be traced through a great part of the Bāri Doāb. (*I. G.*) See the ancient courses of these rivers in Cunningham's *Ancient Geography of India*, p. 220, *et seq*. General Cunningham bases his discussion on Gladwin's translation, *viz.*, 'For the distance of 17 *kos* from Feerozpoor, the rivers Beyah and Seteluj unite: and then again as they pass along, *divide* into 4 streams, *viz.*, the Hur, Haray, Dund and the Noorny: and near the city of Multān these 4 branches join again," and says that these beds still exist but their names are lost. Now Abul Fazl does not say that the Sutlej divides into 4 streams, but that it bears several names. Abul Fazl is describing the rivers watering the Multān Subah. He says they are the six previously mentioned, *viz.*, under Lahor. He first speaks of the Jhelum and the Chenāb and follows them to their junction with the Rāvi and then to their meeting with the Indus. Here are four. He now turns to the Beās and Sutlej which join near Firozpur and the stream after bearing several names becomes confluent with "those four" near Multān, not, I consider, with the four local

bourhood of *Multān,* confluent with the former four, their accumulated waters unite. Every river that discharges itself into the Indus takes its name of *Sindh.* In *Tattah,* they call it *Mihrān.*[1]

To the north are the mountains. Its climate is similar to that of Lahor which it resembles in many aspects, but in Multān, the rainfall is less and the heat excessive.

Multān is one of the oldest cities of India: Long. 107° 35′; Lat. 29° 52′. It has a brick fort and a lofty minaret adds to its beauty. *Shaikh Bahā-u'ddin Zakariyā* and many other saints here repose.

Bhakkar (Bhukkur) is a notable fortress; in ancient chronicles it is called *Mansura.*[2] The six rivers united roll beneath it, one channel passing the southern face of the fort, the other the northern. The rainfall is inconsiderable, the fruits excellent.

Between *Siwi*[3] and *Bhakkar* is a vast desert, over which for three months of the hot season the simoom blows.

---

names, even were they separate beds, but with the four that complete the six. The doubt arises why he should place the junction near Multān instead of Uch, but this is not surprising to any one accustomed to his obscure and vague style of narrative. Moreover the passage in the text resembles a notice of these six rivers in Baber's *Memoirs* to which Abul Fazl was much indebted in the preparation of this third book of the Ain. The passage is as follows: I use the translation of Erskine. "To the north of Sehrend, six rivers, the Sind, the Behat, the Chenāb, the Rāvi, the Biāh, and the Setlej, take their rise in these mountains, and all uniting with the Sind *in the territory of Multān,* take the common name of Sind, which flowing down to the west, passes through the country of Tatta, and disembogues into the sea of Oman." Further the division of the Sutlej into the four local streams does not alter its point of junction with the Chenāb for at p. 222, Cunningham says that Abul Fazl's measurements of distances from the confluence of the Chenāb and Jhelum to that of the Chenāb and Rāvi and the Chenāb and Indus agree with the *later* state of these rivers.

[1] The main stream of the Indus. See its course and the names of its channels in Cunningham's *Ancient Geography of India,* pp. 252, 272, 286, 298, &c.

[2] After the decline of the Arab power in Sind about A.D. 871, two native kingdoms raised themselves at Multān and Mansura. The former comprised the upper valley of the Indus as far as Alor; the latter extended from that town to the sea and nearly coincided with the modern province of Sind. Alor, or Aror, the capital, almost rivalled Multān and had an extensive commerce. *I. G.* Genl. Cunningham (*Ancient Geog.*) gives the name of Mansura to the town founded, according to Masaudi, by Jamhur, the Moslem governor of Sindh, and named after his own father Mansur, so close to Brahmanābād as to be regarded as the same place. His learned discussion depends too much on analogies of sound in names, to be quite convincing. See, also Mansura in Elliot's *Arabs in Sind,* p. 50, *et seq.*

[3] Siwi, Sewistān, and Sehwān are constantly confounded or mistaken as Elliot remarks without, however, himself determining the position of the first which is a town or the geographical limits of the second which is a province. Siwi is somewhat south of the direct line between Dera Ghazi Khān and Quetta, now well known as Sibi. Vol. I, p. 362, *Sewe.*

The river *Sind* (Indus) inclines every few years alternately to its southern and northern banks and the village cultivation follows its course. For this reason the houses are constructed of wood and grass.

This *Subah* comprises three *Sarkārs* of 88 *parganahs*, all under assessment for crops paying special rates. The measured land is 3,273,932 *bighas*, 4 *biswas*. The gross revenue is 15 *krors*, 14 *lakhs*, 3,619 *dāms*. (Rs. 37,85,090-8-0), of which 30 *lakhs*, 59,948 *dāms* (Rs. 76,498-11-2), are *Suyurghāl*. The local militia consists of 18,785 Cavalry and 165,650 Infantry.

Sarkār of Multān. Four Doābs.

Containing 47 *Mahals*, 558,649 *Bighas*, 4 *Biswas*. Revenue, 53,916,318 *Dāms*. *Suyurghāl*, 5,494,236 *Dāms*. Cavalry, 8,965. Infantry, 90,650.

Bet Jālandhar Doāb.

Containing 9 *Mahals*, 52,090 *Bighas*. Revenue, 17,240,147 *Dāms*. Cavalry, 1,410. Infantry, 17,100.

	Bighas Biswas	Revenue D.	Ṣuyurghāl D.	Cavalry	Infantry	Castes
Ādamwāhan	5,386	369,445	...	30	700	Hasar.
Jalālābād	5,000	299,798	...	10	200	Bhim.
Dunyapur	27,889	1,876,862	11,998	50	400	Uki, Rānu.
Rājpur	1,368	90,397	...	20	300	Junah.
Shergarh	75,000	5,741,200	...	400	4000	Kachhi, Junah, Bikānah, Malāh.
Fathpur	61,797	4,008,661	24,596	500	5000	Junah.
Kahror	47,695	305,856	40,931	100	2000	Junah.
Khāibuldi	80,411	594,233	...	200	...	Jat and another name illegible.
Ghalu Khārah	19,820	1,201,086	...	100	2000	Kalu, Jat.

Bāri Doāb.

Containing 11 *Mahals,* 137,629 *Bighas,* 13 *Biswas.* Revenue, 9,863,341 *Dāms.* *Suyurghāl,* 207,382 *Dāms.* Cavalry 775. Infantry, 14,550.

	Bighas Biswas	Revenue D.	Suyur ghāl D.	Cavalry	Infantry	Castes
Islāmpur, has a brick fort	23,085	1,550,896	60,894	1000	3000	Bhim, Maral.
Ismailpur	900	49,932	...	5	50	Maral.
Multān town, has a brick fort	2,324	1,719,168	88,980	50	1000	Bhim, Shaikh-zādah.
Tulamba	19,310	1,200,778	15,766	300	5000	Sohu.
Villages of the *parganah* of Chaukhandi ...	2,927	191,054	...	...	...	
Suburban dist. of Multān	35,925	2,288,354	37,463	...	...	Bhim.
Villages of *parganah* of Khatpur	2,487	149,578	...	...	...	
Do. Do. Deg.* Rāvi	897-14	50,146	...	...	...	
Shāh Aālampur	24,121	1,555,563	1,180	200	4000	
Villages of *parganah* of Khāibuldi	7,584-19	460,654	...	...	...	
Matila	2,068	608,418	3,598	20	500	Jat.

* The Degh (*I. G.*) is the chief tributary of the Rāvi, which it receives after entering Montgomery District on its north-west bank and then passes into Multān District.

Rechnāu Doāb.

Containing 6 *Mahals,* 83,229 *Bighas,* 18 *Biswas.* Revenue, 5,113,883 *Dāms.* Cavalry, 770. Infantry, 9,500.

	Bighas Biswas	Revenue D.	Suyur-ghāl D.	Cavalry	Infantry	Castes
Irajpur and Deg Rāvi ...	37,230	2,377,300	...	100	2000	Kharal.
Chaukhandi	7,620	215,830	...	100	2000	Do.
Khatpur	8,387	505,398	...	500	3000	Jat, Sindh.
Dalibhati	3,768-18	256,569	...	20	500	Kharal.
Kalbah	16,208	958,786	...	50	2000	Jat, Sohu.

Sind Sāgar Doāb.

Containing 4 *Mahals,* 34,812 *Bighas.* Revenue, 2,178,192 *Dāms. Suyurghāl,* 13,399 *Dāms.* Cavalry, 220. Infantry, 2,000.

	Bighas Biswas	Revenue D.	Suyurghāl D.	Cavalry	Infantry	Castes
Villages of Islāmpur ...	5,775	378,357	...	...	...	
Rangpur	22,907	1,410,737	10,737	200	2000	Jat.
Raepur Kanki	5,550	306,068	2,662	20	500	Bhim.
Miscellaneous villages, 1 *Mahal*	600	38,030	...	...	...	

Beyond the Five, Rivers. (*Birun i Panjnad.*)

Containing 17 *Mahals,*[1] 205,893 *Bighās,* 13 Biswas. Revenue, 18,820,255 *Dāms. Suyurghāl,* 38,688 *Dāms.* Cavalry, 5,800. Infantry, 57,600.

	Bighas Biswas	Revenue D.	Suyurghāl D.	Cavalry	Infantry	Castes
Ubaura	11,320	915,256	4,684	30	500	Dhar.
Uch	29,056	1,910,140	...	100	400	Shahibzadah, Bukhari, Sayyid.
Bhurtiwāhan, (var. and G. Dāman)	16,696	1,336,029	13,564	200	2000	Rājput, Lodhi.
Jamsher	4,334	348,037	...	150	2000	Baloch, Bholdi and Nardi.
Dudāi, has a brick fort ...	40,520-11	2,400,000	...	4000	30,000	Dudāi.
Diwār i Awwal, (Cunningham. Dirāwal) ...	2,718	140,000	...	50	500	Rājput, Kotwāl.
Dud Khān	17,890	1,440,000	...	...	...	
Villages of Rājpur ...	452	29,854	...	...	...	
Rupari	12,075	1,080,000	...	...	...	
Sitpur	44,538-8	4,608,000	...	1000	20,000	Afghān.
Seorāhi	5,124	28,800	...	20	100	Dhar.
Villages of Fatehpur ...	5,224	330,779	...	...	...	
,, ,, Kaharor ...	1,384	87,289	...		...	
Majlol Ghāzipur ...	40,521	2,400,000	...	...	...	
Mauh, has a brick fort. (Cunningham Moj.) ...	9,083	707,069	20,440	50	1000	Kuraishi.
Marot, do. ...	5,456	204,000	...	200	1000	Bhatti.
Mahand	9,336-12	8,014,000	...	200	1000	

[1] Of these Cunningham can identify but Uch, Dirāwal, Moj and Marot, which he places, east of the Sutlej. The limits of the province of Multān in the time of Hwen Thsang included the north half of the Bhawalpur territory in addition to the tract lying between the rivers, the north frontier extending from Derah Din Panāh on the Indus to Pāk Pattan, a distance of 150 miles; on the west, the frontier line of the Indus to Ekānpur, 160 miles; on the east from Pāk Pattan to the old bed of the Ghager, 80 miles: on the south from Khānpur to the Ghagar, 220 miles, p. 220.

Sarkār of Dipālpur.

Containing 29 *Mahals,* 1,433,767 *Bighas,* 8 *Biswas.* Revenue, 129,334,153 *Dāms.* *Suyurghāl,* 2,079,170 *Dāms.* Cavalry, 5,210. Infantry, 53,300.

Bet Jālandhar Doāb.

Containing 10 *Mahals,* 710,946 *Bighas,* 10 *Biswas.* Revenue, 88,808,855 *Dāms.* *Suyurghāl,* 1,481,564 *Dāms.* Castes, various. Cavalry, 2,400. Infantry, 20,400.

	Bighas Biswas	Revenue D.	Suyurghāl D.	Cavalry	Infantry	Castes
Pattan, (Pāk Pattan) has a brick fort	49,014	2,628,928	599,989	100	2000	Bhil, Dhokar.
Dipālpur Lakhi, has a brick fort	242,344-11	13,514,059	499,535	502	7000	Jat, Khokhar, Kasu, Bhatti.
Dhanakshāh, has a brick fort	60,676-1	3,484,375	87,152	...	400	
Deotir	40,730	2,489,850	23,400	50	1000	Jat.
Rahmatābād	38,285	1,825,009	...	100	2000	Baloch, Khokhar.
Qabula, has a brick fort	86,615-12	4,808,817	...	1000	2000	Jusah Rumi.
Qiyāmpur Lakhi, has a brick fort	54,678-19	2,008,274	88,855	300	2000	Bhatti, Jat.
Kalnāki Lakhi	55,243-3	2,385,969	93,809	50	1000	Do. do.
Khokarāin Lakhi ...	21,130	1,011,715	35,383	150	1000	Khokhar.
Lakhi Losqāni	61,519-16	3,156,759	5,940	100	2000	Bhatti, Khilji.

Bāri Doāb.

Containing 6 *Mahals,* 193,495 *Bighas,* 9 *Biswas.* Revenue, 1,175,393 *Dāms.* Castes, various. Cavalry, 1,100. Infantry, 14,000.

	Bighas Biswas	Revenue D.	Suyurghāl D.	Cavalry	Infantry	Castes
Bahrapāl	18,717-9	1,175,393	...	50	500	Bhatti.
Bābā Bhoj, has a fort ...	39,385	2,020,256	20,256	150	2000	Sayyid, Jat.
Chahni	25,993	1,200,600	600	50	2000	Sayyid, &c.
Rahimābād	24,329	1,182,714	...	50	500	Kharal, Baloch.
Sadkharah [?Satgarh] ...	59,447	3,551,630	20,976	300	4000	Do.
Mandhāli	25,624	2,708,429	...	500	5000	Bhim.

Rechnāu Doab.

Containing 7 *Mahals,* 142,856 *Bighas,* 2 *Biswas.* Revenue, 8,534,915 *Dāms.* *Suyurghāl,* 5,808 *Dāms.* Castes, various. Cavalry, 710. Infantry, 6,300.

	Bighas Biswas	Revenue D.	Suyurghāl D.	Cavalry.	Infantry.	Castes
Khānpur	19,599-18	1,285,740	80,380	30	500	Kharal.
Dalchi Chandhar ...	9,153-12	605,557	1,620	50	1000	Chandhar.
Shahzādah Baloch ...	12,749-12	789,741	...	100	1000	Baloch.
Aābidi Ābād	5,975	843,932	...	10	300	Jat.
Faryādābād	18,708	1,098,694	...	20	1000	Jat.
Kharal	33,782	1,907,069	2,800	300	2000	Khari.
Mahes	42,944	2,509,182	...	200	500	

Beyond the Five Rivers (Birun i Panjnad).

Containing 6 *Mahals,* 386,470 *Bighas,* 7 *Biswas.* Revenue, 20,580,771 *Dāms.* *Suyurghāl* 549,972 *Dāms.* Cavalry, 1,000. Infantry, 12,300.

	Bighas Biswas	Revenue D.	Suyurghāl D.	Cavalry.	Infantry.	Castes
Jalālābād	34,475-7	1,789,289	...	50	1000	Ranghar, Bhatti (or Latti), Jat.
Jangal	18,012	653,516	...	300	4000	Bhatti.
Aālampur	31,008-10	1,579,558	...	50	1000	Ranghar, Jat.
Firozpur	217,710-17	11,479,404	199,404	500	3000	Afghān, Ranghar.
Villages of Lakhi Qabula	29,185	1,636,550	...	...	...	
Muhammadwat	56,614-13	3,492,454	350,568	100	3600	Bhatti, Khokhar.

Sarkar of Bhakkar (Bukkur).

Containing 12 *Mahals,* 282,013 *Bighas.* Revenue, 18,424,947 *Dāms. Suyurghāl,* 600,419 *Dāms.* Cavalry, 4,600. Infantry, 11,100.

	Bighas Biswas	Revenue D.	Suyur-ghāl D.	Cavalry	Infantry	Castes
Alor, has a fort	143,700	1,132,150	20,550	200	500	Dharejah.
Bhakkar, has a strong fort	...	74,362	...	200	1000	Mehar and Rahār.
Jāndola	57,847	3,102,709	85,064	400	800	Jahna.
Jatoi	179,821-14	2,346,878	156,841	400	800	
Darbela	121,146	1,262,761	68,872	200	500	Bhatti.
Sankar	100,818	1,808,628	32,332	500	1000	Sahejah.
Siwi	...	1,381,930	...	500	1500	
Fathpur	8,050-10	477,859	...	200	1000	Saheja, Dhārejah.
Khajāna	10,063	645,205	...	200	1000	Jāman.
Khāra Kākan	154,151	2,732,331	138,608	500	1000	Dhārejah.
Kākhari, (var. Kākri) ...	178,338-16	2,106,431	63,208	500	1000	Mankrerah.
Mānhalah	128,078	1,353,713	28,944	500	1000	Dhārejah (var. Hārejah).

*Kings of Multān.**

	Years.
Shaikh Yusuf, reigned	2
Sultān Mahmud† (var. Muhammad Shāh) ...	17
,, Qutbu'ddin, his son	16
,, Husain, his son	30

* This province, says the *U. T.*, was first conquered by Mahomed Kāsim at the end of the first century Hejira. It was recovered by the Hindus on the decline of the Ghazni power. After Mahomed Ghori's subjugation it remained tributary to Delhi until

A.H.	A.D.	
847.	1443.	Shaikh Yusuf established an independent monarchy.
849	1445.	Rav Sehra, or Kutbu'ddin Hosen Langa I expelled the Shaikh.
908.	1502.	Mahmud Khān Langa; his minister Jam Bayezid.
931.	1524.	Hosen Langa II, overcome by Shāh Hosen Arghun. Under Humayun, becomes a province of the empire.

† This name is altogether omitted by Ferishta who describes Qutbu'ddin's intrigue and succession, in his history of Multān. The name of Qutbu'ddin was Rāe Sahra and he was governor of Sewi and the adjacent territory and the head of the Afghān clan of Langāh. He died in A.H. 874 (A.D. 1469), Husain Shāh in 904 or 908 (1498 or 1502) and Mahmud in 931 (1524).

Sultān Firoz, his son 1
,, Husain, a second time.
,, Mahmud, son of Sultān Firoz ... 27
,, Husain II, son of Sultān Mahmud ... 1
Shāh Husain, (Arghun), ruler of Sind.
Mirzā Kāmrān.
Sher Khan.
Salim Khān.
Sikandar Khān.

At one period the province was subject to the sovereigns of Delhi : at another it was under the control of the rulers of Sind, and for a time was held by the princes of Ghazni. After its conquest by Muizzu'ddin Sām (Ghori), it continued to pay tribute to Delhi. In the year A. H. 847 (A. D. 1443) when Sultān Alāu'ddin reigned at Delhi, and constituted authority fell into contempt, every chief in possession of power, set up a pretension to independence. A noisy faction raised Shaikh Yusuf Quraishi, a disciple of Shaikh Bahāu'ddin Zakariya, to supremacy. He was subsequently deposed and proceeded with haste to the court of Sultān Bahlol at Delhi. The sovereignty now devolved upon one of the Langāh family, who assumed the title of Sultān Mahmud Shāh. It is related that this chief had given his daughter in marriage to Shaik Yusuf, and on the strength of this connection, used frequently to visit her alone, till one night by a successful intrigue he accomplished his design on the throne. During the reign of Sultān Qutbuddin, Sultān Mahmud Khilji advanced from Mālwah against Multān but returned without effecting anything. Some maintain that the first of the Langāh family who was raised to the throne was Qutbu'ddin. In the reign of Sultān Husain, Bahlol sent (his son) Barbak Shāh with a force to reinstate Shaikh Yusuf, but they returned unsuccessful. Sultān Husain becoming old and doting, placed his eldest son upon the throne under the title of Firoz Shāh, and withdrew into retirement. His Wazir Imadu'l Mulk, poisoned him in revenge for the murder of his own son and Sultān Husain a second time resumed the sceptre and appointed Mahmud Khān, son of Sultān Firoz, his heir. On the death of Sultān Husain, after a reign of 30 or 34 years [908 A.H.], Sultān Mahmud ascended the throne. During his reign several incursions were made by the Mughals who, however, retired discomfited. Some malicious intriguers through jealousy created a misunderstanding between the Sultān and Jām Bayazid who had long held the office of prime minister, and misrepresentations cunningly made in a roundabout way, brought them into open conflict. The minister withdrew from Multān to Shor and read the *khutbah* in the name of Sultān Sikandar Lodi. On the death of Sultān Mahmud, his infant son was raised to the throne as Sultān Husain (II). Mirzā Shāh Husain (Arghun) marched from Tattah and took Multān and entrusted its charge to Langar Khān. Mirzā Kāmrān dispossessed him of it and after him Sher Khān, Salim Khān and Sikandar successively held it till the splendour of Humayun's equal administration filled Hindustān with its brightness and secured its peace. At the present day under the just sway of His Majesty his subjects find there an undisturbed repose.

Sarkār of Tattah.

During a long period this was an independent territory but now forms part of the imperial dominions. Its length from Bhakkar to *Kach* and *Mekrān* is 257 *kos,* its breadth from the town of *Budin* to *Bandar Lāhari,*[1] 100 *kos,* and again from the town of *Chāndo* one of the dependencies of *Bhakkar,* to *Bikaner* is 60 *kos.* On the east lies *Gujarāt*: to the north *Bhakkar* and *Sewi*:[2] to the south, the ocean, and to the west *Kach* and *Mekrān.* It is situated in the second climate and lies in Longitude 102° 30′ Lat. 24° 10 .

The ancient capital was *Brāhmanābād,*[2] a large city. Its citadel had 1,400 towers, at an interval of a *tanāb,* and to this day there are many traces of its fortifications. *Alor*[3] next became the metropolis and at the present day it is *Tattah,* also called *Debal.* The mountains to the north

---

[1] "Lahari Bandar" in Cunningham's account of Sindh. (*Ancient Geography*).

[2] Identified by Cunningham with Harmatelia, (a softer pronunciation of Brāhmathala, or Brahmanasthala) of Diodorus and placed on the east branch of the Mihrān or Indus, 47 miles north-east of Haidarābad 28 miles east of Hāla and 20 miles west of the eastern channel of the Indus known as Nāra. He gives the number of bastions as 140 on the authority of the MSS. but both Gladwin and Blochmann concur in 1,400, and there is no variant reading. His conclusion is, that the place known now as *Bambhra ka thul* represents the ruined city of Mansura and the neighbouring mound now called Dilura, Brahmanabād.

[3] The ruins of *Alor,* or more correctly Aror, are situated to the south of a gap in the low range of limestone hills stretching from Bhakar to the south for about 20 miles until it is lost in the broad belt of sand hills bounding the Nāra or old bed of the Indus. On the west, Cunningham regards it as the capital of the Musicani of Curtius. He disputes the assertion of Abul Fazl that Debal and Tattah are the same. Sir H. Elliot places Debal at Karāchi, General Cunningham prefers a site between Karāchi and Tattah.

form several branches. One of them trends towards *Qandahār,* and another rising from the sea coast extends to the town of *Kobhār,* called *Rāmgar,* and terminates in Sewistān and is there known as *Lakkhi.*[1] This tract is inhabited by an important Baloch tribe called *Kalmāni,* [? Kirmāni] consisting of twenty thousand cavalry. A fine breed of camels is here indigenous. A third range runs from *Sehwān* to *Sewi* and is called *Khattar* [Kirthar], where dwells a tribe named *Nohmardi* that can raise a force of 300 horse and 7,000 foot. Below this tribe, there is another clan of the *Baloch* known as *Nazhari* with a force of a thousand men. A good breed of horses comes from this tract. A fourth mountain chain touches Kach (Gandāvā) on one side, and on the other the *Kalmāni* territory, and is called *Kārah* inhabited by 4,000 *Balochis.*

In the winter season there is no need of *poshtins* (fur-lined coats) and the summer heats are moderate except in Sewistān. Fruits are of various kinds and mangoes are especially fine. In the desert tracts, a small kind of melon grows wild. Flowers are plentiful and camels are numerous and of a good breed. The means of locomotion is by boats of which there are many kinds, large and small, to the number of 40,000. The wild ass is hunted, and game, such as, hares, the *kotah pāchah*[2] and wild boars; fishing likewise is much pursued.

The assessment of the country is made on the system of division of crops, a third being taken from the husbandman. Here are salt-pits and iron mines. *Shāli* rice is abundant and of good quality. Six *kos* from *Tattah* is a mine of yellow stone, large and small slabs of which are quarried and used for building. The staple food consists of rice and fish. The latter is smoked and loaded in boats, and exported to the ports and other cities, affording a considerable profit. Fish-oil is also extracted and used in boat building. There is a kind of fish called *palwah* which comes up into the *Indus* from the sea, unrivalled for its fine and exquisite flavour. Milk-curds of excellent quality are made and keep for four months. [*Palo,* Bengali *hilsā.*]

[1] The Lakhi range is an offshoot from the Kirthar which separates Sind from Beluchistān. *I. G.*

[2] Literally 'short legged'. It is thus described in Babar's *Memoirs,* "Its size may be equal to that of the white deer. Its two fore-legs as well as its thighs are short, whence its name. Its horns are branching like those of the gawezin but less. Every year too it casts its horns like the stag. It is a bad runner and therefore never leaves the jungle." These characteristics seem to point to the hog-deer, (*Cervus porcinus*).

Near *Sehwān* is a large lake, two days' journey in length called *Manchur,* in which artificial islands have been made by fishermen who dwell on them.

But the greatest of all wonders is the *Liver-eater* (*Jigar Khwār*), an individual who by glances and incantations can abstract a man's liver. Some aver that under certain conditions and at certain times, he renders the person senseless upon whom he looks, and then takes from him what resembles the seed of a pomegranate, which he conceals for a time in the calf of his leg. During this interval the person whose liver is stolen remains unconscious, and when thus helpless, the other throws the seed on the fire which spreads out like a plate. Of this he partakes with his fellows and the unconscious victim dies. He can convey a knowledge of his art to whomsoever he wills, by giving him a portion of this food to eat and teaching him the incantation. If he is caught in the act and his calf be cut open and the seed extracted and given to his victim, the latter will recover. The followers of this art are mostly women.

They can convey intelligence from long distances in a brief space of time and if they be thrown into the river with a stone tied to them, they will not sink. When it is desired to deprive one of these of this power, they brand both sides of his head and his joints, fill his eyes with salt, suspend him for forty days in a subterraneous chamber, and give him food without salt, and some of them recite incantations over him. During this period he is called *Dhachrah.* Although his power then no longer exists, he is still able to recognize a Liver-eater, and these pests are captured through his detection. He can also restore people to health by incantation or administering a certain drug. Extraordinary tales are told of these people that are beyond measure astonishing.

This country is the fourth *Sarkār* of the *Subah* of Multān. From the confines of *Uch to Tattah* towards the north are rocky mountain ranges inhabited by various Baloch tribes, and on the south from *Uch* to *Gujarāt* are sandhills in which region are the *Ahshām Bhatti*[1] and other

[1] According to Cunningham, the early Arab geographers place a strong fort called Bhātia between Multān and Alor, which, from its position has a claim to be identified with the city built by Alexander among the Sogdi, but he mentions no tribe of the name, neither have any of the Bhatti Rajputs mentioned by Elliot any such prefix as *Ahshām* [=warriors]. The Sodahs have been identifiedd by Tod with the Sogdoi. *Ancient Geography,* pp. 253-254.

numerous clans. From *Bhakkar* to *Nasirpur* and *Umarkot* are the *Sodah, Jārejah* and other tribes. This *Subah* contains 5 *Sarkārs* subdivided into 53 *parganahs*. The revenue is 6,615,393 *dāms*.* (Rs. 165,384-13-2.)

Sarkār of Tattah.

Containing 18 *Mahals*. Revenue, 25,999,891 *Dāms*.

	Revenue D.		Revenue D.
Lāhari Bandar	5,521,419	Sankurah[3]	2,108,097
Batorā [1]	4,932,286	Sirsi Jām	142,641
Bahrāmpur	1,311,612	Karhar, (var. and K. Karkar)	3,328,476
Bori	434,305	Lekin Kherah	535,795
Jakār [Jarak][2]	348,462	Maljah	1,105,606
Jārā	82,390	Mānjar	1,221,752
Darak, (var. Durg) ...	2,970 441	Nizāmpur	352 724
Dankari, (var. Dekri) ...	315,921		
Ratnah	842,144		

* This is incorrect. Adding together the revenues of the five sarkārs, we get a total revenue of 6 62,51,393 dāms (Rs. 16,56,284-13-2).

[1] Var. Patora, Batwār, Banwār.

[2] *Jarak*, midway between Haidarābad and Tatta.

[3] See Elliot, *Arabs in Sind*, p. 230.

Sarkār Hājkān.

Containing 11 *Mahals*. Revenue 11,784,586 *Dāms*.

	Revenue D.		Revenue D.
Bāgh Fath	340,173	Karori	529,937
Belah	656,317	Laundā	1 119,973
Hajkān	555,699	Mandni, (var. and G. Mandri)	694,269
Jaun	3,165,418	Madui	2,352,605
Rahbān	742,973	Nubiyar, (var. and G. Napiyār)	1,280,439
Detached villages[1] ...	436,783		

[1] *Qariyāt-i-mazkuri*, the term *mazkuri*, being applied in old revenue accounts to small and scattered estates not included in the accounts of the districts in which they were situated and of which the assessments were paid direct to Government.

Sarkār of Sewistān.

9 *Mahals*. Revenue, 15,546,808 *Dāms*.

	Revenue D.		Revenue D.
Bātar, (var Pātar G. Palar)	2,020,884	Khat	1,329,923
Baghbānān	1,948,152	Sub. dist. of Sewistān, has a strong fort	1,669,732
Batan (var. and T. Patan)	1,902,033	Kāhān	1,640,764
Busikān (var. and G. Bustkān, T. Lusigān) ...	1,825,190	Lakhāwat (var. Lakiāwat)	1,231,776
Janjah	1 978,953		

Sarkār of Nasirpur.

7 *Mahals*. Revenue, 7,834,600 *Dāms*.

	Revenue D.		Revenue D.
Umarkot	1,057,802	Kāsār	401,738
Talsarah	326,104	Mārkandan	623 936
Samāwāni, (var. and G. Samādāni)	3,031,530	Nasirpur	1,878,126
Kidāl, (var. Kandāl) ...	515,904		

Sarkār of Chakarhālah.

8 *Mahals*. Revenue, 5,085,408 *Dāms*.

	Revenue D.		Revenue D.
Arpur	731,190	Tewāri (var. Lawāri) ...	571,073
Chakarhālah	747,175	Khari Junah	508,152
Siyār	719,207	Burkah Manāwali ...	490,368
Ghāzipur	983,655	Barhi	333,588

Princes of Tattah.[1]

1. The family of Tamim Ansāri during the ascendancy of the House of Umayyah.

2. The Sumra (Rājput) line of 36 princes, reigned 500 years, (according to Ferishta—100—their names unrecorded).

3. Of the Samma dynasty,

	Years	Months	D.
Jām Unar, reigned	3	6	0
,, Junā, his brother	4	0	0
,, Banhatiyah	15	0	0
,, Tamāchi, his brother ...	13 and some months.		
,, Salāhuddin	11 and	do.	
,, Nizāmuddin, his son ...	2 and a fraction.		
,, Ali Sher Tamāchi	6 and some months.		
,, Karān, son of Tamāchi ...	0	0	$1\frac{1}{2}$
Fateh Khān, son of Sikandar ...	11 and some months.		
Tughlaq, his brother	28	0	0
Mubarāk, the chamberlain ...	0	0	3

---

[1] The following list is from the *U. T.*

A.H.	A.D.	
87.	705.	Belochistān invaded by Hijaj, governor of Bassora, and Md. Qāsim.

The *Ansaries*, the *Sameras*, and the *Samanas* or *Jams*, successively gain the ascendancy, then a Delhi governor (1205?) Nasir ud din Qabbacha, becomes independent, drowned.

The *Jami* Dynasty of Sumana, originally Rājputs.

A.H.	A.D.	
737.	1336.	Jām Afra; tributary to Toghlak Shāh.
740.	1339.	,, Choban.
754.	1383.	,, Bang; asserted his independence.
782.	1367.	,, Timaji, his brother.
783.	1380.	,, Salāhu'ddin, convert to Islām.
793.	1391.	,, Nizamu'ddin.
796.	1393.	,, Aly Sher.
812.	1409.	,, Giran, son of Timaji.
812.	1409.	,, Fatteh Khān.
827.	1423.	,, Toghlak, invaded Gujerat.
854.	1450.	,, Sikandar.
856.	1452.	,, Sangar, elected.
864.	1460.	,, Nandā or Nizām-u'ddin, cot. of Hasan Langa.
894.	1492.	,, Feroz; the Turkhan family became powerful, 1520.
927.	1520.	Shāh Beg Arghun, occupies Sind.
930.	1523.	Shāh Hosein Arghun.
962.	1554.	Mahmud of Bhakar.
982.	1572.	Akbar annexes Sind. (Ferishta, 1001 = 1592).

The title of Jām, Ferishta pronounces, is a boast of their supposed descent from Jamshid, but commonly given to their head or chief to preserve the tradition of this fabulous lineage. The lineage of the Sumra and Samma dynasties is discussed in Appendix P. of Elliot's Arabs in Sind. The latter name may be traced in the Sambastæ and Sambus of Alexander's historians. Sambus occurs as Sabbas in Plutarch, Saboutas in Strabo, Ambigarus in Justin and Ambiras in Orosius.

	Years	Months	D.
Sikandar, b. Fath Khān	1	6	0
Sanjar, commonly called Rādhan (var. and G. Rādman	8 and some months.		
Jām Nizāmuddin, known as Jām Nandā, (see Vol. I, p. 362) ...	60 and some months.		
Jām Firoz, his son.			
,, Salāhuddin, a relation of Firoz.			
,, Firoz, a second time.			

In former times, there lived a Rājā named *Siharas*[1] whose capital was Alor. His sway extended eastwards, as far as Ḳashmir and towards the west to Mekrān, while the sea confined it on the south and the mountains on the north. An invading army entered the country from Persia, in opposing which the Rājā lost his life. The invaders contenting themselves with devastating part of the territory, returned. Rāi Sāhi, the Rājā's son, succeeded his father, by whose enlightened wisdom and the aid of his intelligent minister *Rām*, justice was universally administered and the repose of the country secured. A Brāhman named *Jach* [Chach] of an obscure station in life, attached himself to the minister's service and by flattery and address made himself of much consequence and was advanced to a post of dignity, and on the death of the minister, was chosen to succeed him. He basely and dishonourably carried on an intrigue with the Rājā's wife, which the Rājā, notwithstanding its disclosure to him by the ministers of State, refused to credit. During the Rājā's illness, the wicked wretch, in collusion with this shameless paramour, sent for the generals of the army separately, on pretence of consulting them and set them apart, and by seductive promises won over the several enemies of each to accomplish their death. When they were put out of the way and the Rājā too had breathed his last, he assumed the sovereignty.

The pursuers of worldly interests attached themselves to his cause and he took the *Rāni* to wife, thus garnering eternal perdition, but he laboured for the prosperity and increase of his dominions and seized upon *Kach* (Gandāvā), and *Meḳrān.*

[1] Of the Rai dynasty whose capital was Alor. The *Tuhfatul Kirām* makes *Siharas* the son and successor of *Rāi Diwāij*, followed by *Rāi Sāhasi*, the first, second and third of that name. It was under the latter that Chach rose to power.

During the Caliphate of Omar (b. u'l) Khattab, Mughirah Abu'l Aās advanced by way of *Bahrain* to *Debal*, but the troops there opposed him and he was killed in the engagement. In the Caliphate of Othmān an intelligent explorer[1] was sent to ascertain the condition of Sind, and an army of invasion was under orders. The messenger, however, reported that if a large force were sent, supplies would fail, and a small one would effect nothing and he added many dissuasive representations. The Prince of the Faithful, Ali, despatched troops that occupied the borders of Debal but on hearing of the death of the Caliph they withdrew in haste to Mekrān. Muāwiyah twice despatched an army to Sind and on both occasions many of the troops perished.

Chach died after a prosperous reign of 40 years, and his youngest son *Dāhir* succeeded him on the throne. In the Caliphate of Walid b. Abdul Malik, when Hajjāj was governor of Irāq, he despatched on his own authority Muhammad Qāsim his cousin and son-in-law to Sind who fought Dāhir in several engagements.[2] On Thursday, the 10th of Ramazān A.H. 99, (17th April 717) the Rājā was killed in action and the territory of Tattah became subject to the invaders. The two daughters of Rājā Dāhir, who had been made captive were sent with some valuable presents to the Caliph. In a spirit of revenge, they deceitfully represented to the Caliph that Muhammad Qasim had dishonoured them. He therefore abstained from visiting them, and in a fit of fury gave orders that Qāsim should be stuffed into a raw hide and despatched to his presence. The commands of the Caliph reached him when he was about to march against Hari Chand, king of Kanauj, and he obediently submitted to them. When he was thus

[1] Hākim, b. Jabala al Abdi was sent to explore Sejistān and Mekrān and the countries bordering on the Indus valley by Abdu'llah Amar, a cousin of the Cāliph, who succeeded Abu Musa Ashari in the government of Basra. His report was as follows: "Water in that country is of a dark colour, flowing only drop by drop, the fruits are sour and unwholesome, rocks abound and the soil is brackish. The thieves are intrepid warriors, and the bulk of the population dishonest and treacherous. If the troops sent there are few in number, they will be exterminated, if they are numerous, they will perish of hunger." Elliot. The expeditions of Ali and Muāwiyah and the progress of the Arab conquests in Sind may be read in the succeeding pages. Elliot's conclusion that Debal was taken in A.H. 93 is confirmed by As Suyuti in his biography of Al Walid, b. Abdu'l Malik, in which year Kirah, or Kiraj as Ibn ul Athir calls it, was also captured. (See translation of As Suyuti's *History of the Caliphs*, p. 229). Elliot thinks this probably situated in, if not named from Kachh.

[2] Described in Elphinstone, p. 308, and in Briggs' Ferishta, IV, p. 417.

carried to the court, the Caliph exhibited the spectacle to the two princesses who expressed their gratification in viewing the slayer of their father in this condition. This decision of the Caliph excites astonishment inasmuch as it was pronounced without deliberate investigation. It is the duty of just princes not to be swayed by the representation of any one individual, but to be circumspect in their inquiries, since truth is rare and falsehood prevalent, and more especially in regard to the recipients of their favour, towards whom the world burns with envy without just cause of resentment. Against the outwardly plausible and inwardly vicious they should be particularly on their guard, for many are the wicked and factious who speciously impose by their affected merit and by their misrepresentations bring ruin on the innocent.

After Muhammad Qāsim's death, the sovereignty of this country devolved on the descendants of the Banu Tamim Ansāri.* They were succeeded by the *Sumrah* race who established their rule and were followed by the *Sammas* who asserted their descent from *Jamshid,* and each of them assumed the name of *Jām.* In the reign of *Jām Bānhatiyah*[1] Sultān Firoz Shāh on three occasions led an army from Delhi against that prince, and obtained some conspicuous successes. On the third occasion, he took him prisoner and carried him to Delhi, leaving Sind under charge of his own officials. Subsequently being satisfied with his good will and capacity he reinstated him in his government. On the death of *Jām Tughlaq,* the chamberlain *Mubārak* succeeded him through the efforts of a vain and seditious faction, and was followed by Sikandar the son of *Jām Fath Khān.*

During the reign of *Jām Nandā, Shāh Beg Arghān* made a descent from Qandahār and took *Sewi* and leaving the command of it to his brother Sultān Muhammad, returned to Qandahār. The Jām marched a force against

---

* Several of this tribe were at various periods sent to Sind. Under the Caliphate of Yazid b. Abd u'l Malik, Halāl a't Tamimi was sent in pursuit of the Banu Muhallab. About 107 A.H. Tamim b. Zaid al Utbi succeeded Junaid in the government of that province and died near Debal. Under the Abbassides Musa b. Kab a't Tamimi, drove out Mansur b. Jamhur the Umayyad governor. Abdu'r Razzāk the first Ghaznevide governor of Sind, about A.H. 417, (1026) found the descendants of old Arab settlers of the tribes of Thakifi, Tamimi, Asad etc.

[1] Māni according to Ferishta who says that the expedition of Firoz Tughlaq took place in 763 A.H. (A.D. 1320).

Muhammad who was killed in action. Shah Beg made a second incursion and took possession of *Sehwān* and a considerable part of Sind and leaving his conquests in charge of his own people, withdrew.

In the reign of Jām Firoz, a relative of his named Salāhu'ddin rose in rebellion and failing in his attempt, took refuge with Sultān Mahmud of Gujarāt who received him graciously and assisted him with an army; Daryā Khān the prime minister of Jām Firoz espoused his cause and the kingdom of Sind fell under his power without a blow. Subsequently the said Daryā Khān determined to restore Jām Firoz who had withdrawn into private life, but who thus recovered his kingdom. Salāhu'ddin a second time advanced from Gujarāt with a force furnished by the Sultān and occupied Sind. Firoz retired to Qandahār and Shāh Beg supplied him with troops, and an engagement took place near *Sehwān* in which Salāhu'ddin and his son were slain. Thus Firoz was again established in his kingdom. In the year A.H. 929 (A.D. 1522-3) Shāh Beg took possession of Sind and Jām Firoz retired to Gujarāt, gave his daughter in marriage to Sultān Bahādur and was attached to the Court in the ranks of its nobles. Sind was now subject to Shāh Beg. This prince was the son of Mir Zu'n Nun Beg, the commander-in-chief of Sultān Husain Mirzā, who received the government of Qandahār. He fell fighting bravely against Shaibak Khān Uzbek who was engaged in hostilities with the sons of Sultān Husain Mirzā. His eldest son succeeded to the government of Qandahār, a prince of distinguished valour and versed in the learning of his age. At his death, his son Shāh Husain ascended the throne and wrested Multān from Sultān Mahmud. After him Mirzā Isā son of Abdu'l Ali Tarkhān[1] succeeded, followed by Muhammad Payandah[2] but his prince being subject to fits of mental estrangement, did not

---

[1] *Tarkhān* was originally a rank among the Mughals and Turks, but in the time of Baber it had come to belong to a particular family. The ancient Tarkhān was exempt from all duties and could enter the royal presence without asking leave and was to be pardoned nine times be the fault what it would. He had perfect liberty of speech and might say what he pleased before royalty. The name constantly occurs in the early portion of Baber's *Memoirs*.

[2] He has omitted the succession of Muhammad Bāqi son of Isā Tarkhān to whom Ferishta gives a prosperous reign of 18 years. The genealogical tree of Mirzā Jāni Beg and the subsequent history of this family will be found at pp. 361-2, Vol. I of this work. Ferishta altogether omits Muhammad Payandah and gives the succession to Jāni Beg immediately after Muhammad Bāqi.

personally administer the government. Mirzā Jāni Beg, his son assumed the direction of affairs till His Majesty's victorious troops advanced into the country and reduced it to order, and Mirzā Jāni Beg was enrolled in the ranks of his nobility.

SUBAH OF KABUL.

It is situated in the third and fourth climates, and comprises *Kashmir, Pakli, Bimbar, Swāt, Bajaur, Qandahār* and *Zābulistān.* Its capital was formerly *Ghaznah,* but now *Kābul.*

KASHMIR.

(*Editor's Note.*)

The notes on the subah of Kashmir in this revised edition of Jarrett's translation have been entirely prepared by Prof. Nirod Bhusan Roy, after a minute study of A. Stein's *Memoir on Maps of Ancient Kashmir* (Asiatic Society of Bengal, 1895) and *Rajatarangini: a Chronicle of the Kings of Kashmir* (2 vols. 1901),—which are cited here under the respective titles of *Stein, J.A.S.B.* and *Stein, Chron.* In addition, Prof. Roy has consulted Drew's *Jummo and Kashmir Territories* (1875), Bates' *Kashmir Gazetteer,* Rose's *Glossary of Punjab Tribes and Castes* (3 vols., 1914), and the *Travels* of Vigne and Moorcroft.

Abul Fazl devoted more space to the description of the places of note in Kashmir than in any other subah, because he looked upon it as a holy land full of sacred places, hermits' retreats and quiet natural scenes,—"appropriate to be the retired abode of the recluse", as he himself says. This Sufi's paradise is said to contain a temple of liberal broad-minded worshippers of God, for which he wrote a charming inscription printed by Blochmann at the end of his life of Abul Fazl in the first volume of his translation (pp. xxxii-xxxiii).

But when Abul Fazl compiled his *Ain-i-Akbari,* Mughal rule was not yet firmly in the saddle in this recently conquered province, and full and correct reports on Kashmir had not begun to reach the imperial chancellory at Delhi. Hence its statistics are less accurate than those of the longer-settled subahs of Akbar's empire, which formed the basis of his *Imperial Gazetteer.* The Persian text of the chapter on Kashmir is vitiated by too many errors in proper names and topographical data, which may have been due to Abul

Fazl's clerks as well as to later transcribers of his book. The hopeless confusion thus created was first removed by the publication of Stein's two works cited above.

In the present edition, copious extracts have been made from these scholarly sources by Prof. N. B. Roy and the obsolete or useless notes of Jarrett have been deleted. *The new topographical notes are given in one place at the end of Abul Fazl's account and not at the foot of each page.—Jadunath Sarkar.*

Stein's remark on A. F.'s account of Kashmir.

"Abul Fazl's detailed description of Kashmir, is in many respects valuable to the historical student, but it is particularly in connection with topographical search that we must feel grateful to the author for having, like his great master, caught some of the enthusiasm of the valley.

The account of Abul Fazl presents for us an authentic survey of all the Kashmirian *tirthas* that were well known and popular at the end of the 16th century. . . Abul Fazl's notes have enabled me to trace in more than one instance the position of ancient *tirthas* or particular features regarding them which have since his time been wholly forgotton." Stein, *Chron.* II, 382-83.

A NOTE ON THE LANGUAGE OF KASHMIR.

Kashmiri or Koshiru.

The Kashmiri language is the language of the Valley of Kashmir. In a dialectic form it has spread south-west into the Valley of Kashtawar (Kishtwar), and to the south it has flowed over the Pir Pantsal Range into the lower hills lying north of the River Chinab, where it reappears in a number of mixed dialects.

The word 'Kashmiri' is Persian or Hindi, and is derived from the Sanskrit Kasmirika. It is not the name used by the people of Kashmir itself. There the country is called Kashiru, and the language Koshiru.

Kashmiri has one true dialect,—Kashtawari, spoken in the Valley Kashtawar (commonly known as Kishtwar), lying to the south-east of the Valley of Kashmir. Kashmiri has also overflowed the Pir Pantsal Range into the Jammu Province of the State, and in the valleys between the southern hills of the range, between the water-shed and the valley of the Chinab, there are a number of mixed dialects, such as Poguli, Siraji of Doda, and Rambani. The first two of these represent Kashmiri merging into Dogri. Farther east, over the greater part of the Riasi District of the State, there are more of these mixed dialects, about which nothing certain is known, except that the mixture is rather between Kashmiri and the Chibhali form of Lahnda.

In the standard Kashmiri of the Valley, there are minor differences of language, which, however, are not sufficient to entitle us to divide it out into further separate dialects. For instance, the Kashmiri spoken by Musalmans differs from that spoken by Hindus. Not only is the vocabulary of the former more filled with words borrowed from Persian, but also there are slight differences of pronunciation.

Kashmiri belongs to the Dard group of the Dardic languages. It is most nearly related to Shina. It has, however, for many centuries been subject to Indian influence, and its vocabulary includes a large number of words derived from India. Its speakers hence maintain that it is of Sanskritic origin, but a close examination reveals the fact that, illustrious as was the literary history of Kashmir, and learned as have been its Sanskrit Pandits, this claim of Sanskrit origin cannot be sustained for the vernacular of the latter. Kashmiri is a very old language. Three words in it are quoted by Kalhana (circ. 1150 A.D.) in his *Rajatarangini,* and these are not very different from the language of the present day. [Grierson, *Linguistic Survey of India,* Vol. 8, part II, pp. 233-235.]

Sarkār of Kashmir.

It lies in the third and fourth climates. Its length from *Qambar Ver* to *Kishan Ganga* is 120 *kos,* and its breadth from 10 to 25 *kos.* On the east are Paristān and the river Chenāb : on the south-east *Bānihāl* and the *Jammu* mountains : on the north-east, Great Tibet : on the west, Pakli and the Kishan Ganga river : on the south-west, the Gakkhar country : on the the north-west, Little Tibet. It is encompassed on all sides by the Himalayan ranges. Twenty-six different roads lead into Hindustān but those by *Bhimbar* and *Pakli* are the best and are generally practicable on horseback. The first mentioned is the nearest and it has several routes of which three are good, *viz.*, (1) *Hasti Bhanj*[1] which was the former route for the march of troops; (2) *Pir Panjāl,* which His Majesty has thrice traversed on his way to the rose garden of Kashmir. If on these hills an ox or a horse be killed, storm clouds and wind arise with a fall of snow and rain[2]; (3) *Tangtala.*

The country is enchanting, and might be fittingly called a garden of perpetual spring surrounding a citadel terraced to the skies, and deservedly appropriate to be either the delight of the worldling or the retired abode of the recluse. Its streams are sweet to the taste, its waterfalls music to the ear, and its climate is invigorating. The rain and snow-fall are similar to that of Turkestān and Persia and its periodical rains occur at the same season as in Hindustān. The lands are artificially watered[3] or dependent on rain for irrigation. The flowers are enchanting and fill the heart with delight. Violets, the red rose and wild narcissus cover the plains. To enumerate its flora would be impossible. Its spring and autumn are extremely beautiful. The houses are all of wood and are of four stories and some of more, but it is not the custom to enclose them. Tulips[4] are grown on the roofs which present a lovely sight in the spring time. Cattle and sundry stores are kept in the lower storey, the second contains the family apartments, and in the third and fourth are the household chattels. On account of the

---

[1] The three different routes into Kashmir are thus described. The first runs almost in a straight line passing through Nowsherah, Rajori, the Pir Panjāl pass and Shupiyon. The second deviating from Rajori runs to the Punch river and on to Punch and crossing the Hāji Pir, joins the Murree road near Uri. The third, parting from Samani Sarai, passes through Kotli and Sera to Punch and unites with the second. The route by Shupiyon is the Pir Panjāl. The second is Tangtala which name, however, is no longer known and is probably a misscript. The third is believed to be the Hasti Bhanj, for it is the only one by which elephants can travel. *Cf.* Vigne's *Kashmir and Ladāk,* I. 147 in which 20 passes into Kashmir are mentioned and described.

[2] The superstition regarding the tempest of wind and snow and rain, appears to be connected with that of the *Yedeh* or rain-stone frequently alluded to by Baber, the history of which is given by D'Herbelot. It is of Tartar origin and the virtues of the stone are celebrated in Yarkand and attested by authorities who have never witnessed them. It is said to be found in the head of a horse or a cow, and if steeped in the blood of an animal with certain ceremonies, a wind arises followed by snow and rain.

[3] The terms are *Abi, Lalmi.* The first signifies in the N.-W. P., land watered from ponds, tanks, lakes and watercourses, in distinction to that watered from wells, and as being liable to fail in the hot season, is assessed at a lower rate. The second is a Pushtu word (Raverty) and means growing spontaneously and applied to crops wholly dependent on rain for irrigation or spring crops. The next term *Chalkhai* in the text has a variant *Jalkhāya* signifying parched land that has absorbed its moisture.

[4] Dr. King takes this to be probably the *Fritillaria Imperialis,* though there is nothing against the plant being a real tulip. The *T. stellata* is common in many parts of the N. W. Himalayas.

abundance of wood and the constant earthquakes, houses of stone and brick are not built, but the ancient temples inspire astonishment. At the present day many of them are in ruins. Woollen fabrics are made in high perfection, especially shawls which are sent as valuable gifts to every clime. But the bane of this country is its people, yet strange to say, notwithstanding its numerous population and the scantiness of the means of subsistence, thieving and begging are rare. Besides plums and mulberries, the fruits are numerous. Melons, apples, peaches, apricots are excellent. Although grapes are in plenty, the finer qualities are rare and the vines bear on mulberry trees. The mulberry is little eaten, its leaves being reserved for the silk-worm. The eggs are brought from *Gilgit* and *Little Tibet*, in the former of which they are procured in greater abundance and are more choice. The food of the people is chiefly rice, wine, fish and various vegetables, and the last mentioned they dry and preserve. Rice is cooked and kept overnight to be eaten. Though *shāli* rice is plentiful, the finest quality is not obtainable. Wheat is small in grain and black in colour, and there is little of it, and little consumed. Gram (chick-pea) and barley are nowhere found. They have a species of sheep[1] which they call *Hāndu*, delicate and sweet in flavour and wholesome. Apparel is generally of wool, a coat of which will last for some years. The horses are small, strong, and traverse difficult ground. There are neither elephants nor camels. The cows are black and ill-shaped, but give excellent milk and butter. There are artificers of various kinds who might be deservedly employed in the greatest cities. The bazār system is little in use, as a brisk traffic is carried on at their own places of business. Snakes, scorpions and other venomous reptiles are not found in the

---

[1] According to Cunningham (*Ladak*, p. 210) the Ladāki sheep are of two kinds, the tall black-faced *Huniya* used chiefly for carrying burdens and the pretty diminutive sheep of *Purik* used only for food. The common sheep is the *Huniya* which with the exception of the *Purik* breed is almost the only kind of sheep to be found throughout Tibet. It is much larger than any of the Indian breeds, the height averaging from 27 to 30 inches. Nearly the whole of the traffic is transported on these sheep which are food, clothing and carriage and are the principal wealth of the country. Drew (*Jummoo and Kashmir*, p. 288) gives the average weight carried by them at from 24 to 32 lbs. The *Purik* sheep when full grown is not larger than a south-down lamb of 5 or 6 months, and is said by Moorcroft to equal in the fineness and weight of its fleece and flavour of its mutton any race hitherto discovered. The oxen are the yāk or chauri-taled bull and the yāk cow, Brimo or Dimo, and they reproduce with the common cattle. The yāk is kept chiefly for loads, being generally too intractable for the plough. The cow is kept only for milk. The most valuable hybrids are the *Dso* bull and *Dsomo* cow, the produce of the male yāk and common cow.

cities. There is a mountain called *Mahādeva* and in any spot whence its summit can be seen, no snake exists, but fleas, lice, gnats and flies are very common. From the general use of pellet-bows which are fitted with bow-strings, sparrows are very scarce. The people take their pleasure in skiffs upon the lakes, and their hawks strike the wild-fowl in mid-air and bring them to the boats, and sometimes they hold them down in the water in their talons, and stand on them, presenting an exciting spectable.

Stags and partridges likewise afford sport and the leopard too is tracked. The carriage of goods is effected by boat, but men also carry great loads over the most difficult country. Boatmen and carpenters drive a thriving trade. The Brāhmaṇ class is very numeorus.

Although *Kashmir* has a dialect[1] of its own, their learned books are in the Sanskrit language. They have a separate character which they use for manuscript work, and they write chiefly on *Tuz*[2] which is the bark of a tree, worked into sheets with some rude art and which keeps for years. All their ancient documents are written on this. Their ink is so prepared as to be indelible by washing. Although, in ancient times, the learning of the Hindus was in vogue, at the present day, various sciences are studied and their knowledge is of a more general character. Their astrological art and astronomy are after the manner of the Hindus. The majority of the narrow-minded conservatives of blind tradition are *Sunnis*, and there are some *Imāmis* and *Nur Bakhshis*,[3] all perpetually at strife with each

[1] The languages of Kashmir are divided into 13 separate dialects. Of these Dogri and Chibali which do not differ much from Hindustāni and Panjābi, are spoken on the hills and the Punch and Jammu country. Kashmiri is mostly used in Kashmir proper and is curiously and closely related to Sanskrit. Five dialects are included in the term *Pahāri*: two are Tibetan spoken in *Baltistān, Ladakh* and *Champas,* and three and four varieties of the Dard dialects of Aryan origin in the North-West. The thirteen dialects are enumerated and discussed by Drew (*Jummoo and Kashmir*).

[2] *Tuz* in the *Burhān i Qāti* is said to be the bark of a tree used to wrap round saddles and bows. Dr. King identifies it with the well-known birch, Betula Bhojpattra, Wall. *Bhojpattra* he states is the current vernacular name.

[3] As the account of this sect in Ferishta has been almost entirely passed over by Briggs in his translation, the omission may be here made good and will serve the double purpose of supplementing his version and elucidating the present text. With the following note may be compared a monograph on the Roshaniyah sect by Dr. Leyden in the XIth Vol. Asiatic Researches.

Mirzā Haidar (Doghlāt) in his work the *Kitab i Rashidi* says that formerly all the inhabitants of Kashmir were of the Hanifi sect. In the time of Fath Shāh, a man named Shamsu'ddin came from Irāq and declared himself to be a follower of Mir Muhammad Nur Bakhsh. He introduced a new form of religion which he called *Nurbakhshi,* which accords neither with the Sunni or Shia belief. And the followers of this sect, like heretics, consider it their duty to revile and abuse the three Caliphs and Ayesha, but unlike the Shias,

other. These are chiefly from Persia and Turkestān. Their musicians are exceedingly many and all equally monotonous, and with each note they seem to dig their nails into your liver. The most respectable class in this country is that of the Brāhmans, who notwithstanding their need of freedom from the bonds of tradition and custom, are true worshippers of God.

They do not loosen the tongue of calumny against those not of their faith, nor beg nor importune. They employ themselves in planting fruit trees, and are generally a source of benefit to the people. They abstain from flesh-meat and do not marry. There are about two thousand of this class.

The *Tolah* in this country is 16 *māshās*, each *māshā* being equal to 6 *surkhs.*[1] The gold mohur weighs 16 *dānis*, each *dāni* equalling 6 *surkhs*, being 4 *surkhs* more than the ordinary mohurs of Delhi. *Rop Sāsnu* is a silver coin of 9 *māshas*. The *panchhu* is of copper, equal to the fourth of a *dām* and is called *kaserah*. One-fourth of this is the

---

they regard Amir Sayyid Muhammad Nur Bakhsh as the Mahdi and Apostle of his time, and they do not believe as the Shias do in saints and holy persons, but consider them to be Sunnis.

"I compelled many men of Kashmir who were much disposed to this heresy, to accept willingly or otherwise the true religion and I put others to death. Some of these men saved themselves by adopting mystic doctrines and called themselves Sufis."

Before these people, there lived in Kashmir a sect of Sun-worshippers who were called Shammāssin. Their creed was that the sun's light owed its existenc to their purity of faith, and that they themselves existed through the light of the sun, and that if they rendered their faith impure, the sun would cease to be. [Jarrett.] *Nur-bakhshiya* in *Encyclopaedia of Islam*, iii. 961-962. Elias & Ross, *Tarikh-i- Rashidi*, 435-437. *Shammāsi* in Elias & Ross, 436. For Hindu sun-worship, Hastings, *Encyclopaedia of Religion and Ethics*, xii. 83, ii. 483-484; Panjab Sun Creed, ix. 604. Babylonian *Shamash*, *ibid.*, ii. 311. [J. Sarkar.]

[1] The *Surkh* is the common red and black bead, *Abrus precatorius*, and is equal to a *rāti* in weight.

The Kashmiri mohur = 16 *dāni* or *dānāqs* 1 D = 6 S } = 96 *surkhs*.

The 96 *ratis* or *surkhs* in a *tolah* exactly represent the 96 carat grains in the old assay pound. [Jarrett.]

With reference to the monetary system of Kashmir, Stein indicates the connection between the terms used by Abul Fazl for the various denominations of coins and their modern equivalents in Kashmir. Thus *Panchuhu* is the same as *Puntsa*, (Skr. *Panchabimsati*), *hāth* unchanged (Skr. *sata*), *Sansu* same as *Sasun* (Skr. thousand). According to Abul Fazl *Bahagani*, (*bārakani*) is equal to ¼ *Panchuhu*. Stein corrects it and says that the above denomination represented one-half of the *Panchuhu*. The term *bah* in Kashmir means twelve and *bahabeni* as a twelver. All the terms used above with only one exception are stated to have survived in Kashmir to this day in the popular system of reckoning, notwithstanding the repeated changes which the currency of the State has undergone since Akbar's time. Stein, *Chronicle*, Vol. II, 312. [J. S.]

bahgani, [*barakani*], of which again one-fourth is called *shakri*.

4 *kaserahs* = 1 *rāhat*.
40 *kaserahs* = 1 *sāsnu*.
1½ *sāsnu* = 1 *sikkah*.
100 *sikkahs* = 1 *lakh* which, according to the imperial estimate, is equal to one thousand *dāms*.

The whole country is regarded as holy ground by the Hindu sages. Forty-five shrines are dedicated to *Mahadeva*, sixty-four to *Vishnu*, three to *Brahmā*, and twenty-two to *Durga*. In seven hundred places there are graven images of snákes which they worship and regarding which wonderful legends are told.[1]

Srinagar is the capital and is 4 *farsakhs* in length. The rivers *Bihat*, *Mār*, and *Lachmahkul*[2] flow through it. The last-mentioned runs occasionally dry : the second, at times, becomes so shallow that boats cannot pass. This has been a flourishing city from ancient times[3] and the home of artificers of various kinds. Beautiful shawls are woven, and they manufacture woollen stuffs (*Saqarlāt*) extremely soft. *Durmah*, *pattu* and other woollen materials are prepared but the best are brought from Tibet. *Mir Sayyid Ali Hamadāni*[4] resided for some time in this city, and a monastery founded by him still preserves his memory. To the east is a high hill known as the *Koh i Sulaimān*, and adjoining the city are two large lakes always full of water, and it is remarkable that their water will not deteriorate in good savour and wholesomeness for any length of time provided that their free exit is undisturbed.

---

[1] Serpent-worship, according to Genl. Cunningham, has been the prevailing religion in Kashmir from time immemorial. A full account of Hindu serpent-worship in Hastings' *Encyclo.*, xi. 411-419 (Kashmir on p. 412). J. S.

[2] The Jhelum, which nearly intersects the valley is formed, says the *I. G.*, by the junction of three streams, the *Arpat*, *Bring* and *Sandaram*, and receives in its course numerous tributaries. It mentions the *Tsont i Kul*, or apple-tree canal connecting the *Dal* or city lake, with the Jhelum which it enters opposite the palace and the *Nalli Mār* which flows into the Sind near *Shādipur* connecting the *Auchar* with the *Dal*. The Dudganga, a stream of good volume joins the river on the left bank at the city of Srinagar.

[3] Srinagari, the old capital, prior to the erection of Pravarásenapura is stated in the *Raja Tarangini* to have been founded by Asoka, who reigned between B.C. 273—232. It stood on the site of the present Pāndrethān, and is said to have extended along the bank of the river from the foot of the *Takht i Sulaimān* to *Pāntasok*, a distance of more than three miles.

[4] This monastery is built entirely of wood. It is still extant and known as the Khānqāh i Muālla, on the right bank of the Bihat above Zenu Kadal the fourth bridge of the town of Srinagar.

Near the town of *Brang* [Bring] is a long defile in which is a pool seven yards square and as deep as a man's stature. It is regarded as a place of great sanctity. Strange to say it is dry during eleven months, but in the Divine month of Urdi-bihisht (April), water bubbles forth from two springs. First in one corner of it is a cavity like a mortar called *Sendh brāri* : when this becomes full, the spring rises in another corner called *Sapt rishi.* From these two sources the pool runs over. Sometimes it boils up for three hours, and at times for only a second. Then it begins to decrease till not a drop remains. At three periods of the day, *viz.*, morning, noon and evening, this rise occurs. Various flowers are thrown in as offerings to either spring, and after the reflux of the water, the flowers of each votary are found in their respective springs.[1]

But this, like the divining cup is a contrivance of the ancients to secure the devotion of the simple.

In this vicinity also is a spring, which during six months is dry. On a stated day, the peasants flock to worship and make propitiatory offerings of a sheep or a goat. Water then flows forth and irrigates the cultivation of five villages. If the flush is in excess, they resort to the same supplications, and the stream subsides of its own accord. There is also another spring called *Kokar Nāg,* the water of which is limpid, cold and wholesome. Should a hungry person drink of it, his hunger will be appeased,[2] and its satisfaction in turn renews appetite. At a little distance, in the midst of a beautiful temple, seven fountains excite the wonderment of the beholder. In the summer time self-immolating ascetics here heap up a large fire around themselves, and with the utmost fortitude suffer themselves to be burnt to ashes. This they consider a means of union with the Deity. There is also a spring which produces touchstone, and to the north of it a lofty hill which contains an iron mine.

The village of *Vij Brāra,* one of the dependencies of *Aneych* is a place of great sanctity. It was formerly a large

---

[1] Tieffenthaler ascribes the cause of the phenomenon to the melting of the mountain snows under the influence of the sun which descending along hollows or by subterranean passages reach this cavern and boil up within it. The later ebullitions he conceives, are due either to the shade of the trees or the declining force of the sun on the snows. Bernier's opinion is somewhat the same. *Voyages,* II, 293.

[2] Vigne (I, 339) on the contrary bears testimony to its being provocative of appetite. The spring, situated about 2½ miles from the iron works at Sof Ahan, forms a stream equal in volume to that of Vernag and far superior in the quality of its water.

city[1] and contained wonderful temples. In the vicinity is an upland meadow called *Nandimarg,* of which I know not whether most to praise its level sweep of mead, the loveliness of its verdure and flowers, or the bountiful virtues of its streams and its air. In the village of *Pampur,* one of the dependencies of Vihi, there are fields of saffron[2] to the extent of ten or twelve thousand *bighas,* a sight that would enchant the most fastidious. At the close of the month of March and during all April, which is the season of cultivation, the land is ploughed up and rendered soft, and each portion is prepared with the spade for planting, and the saffron bulbs are placed in the ground. In a month's time they sprout and at the close of September, it is at its full growth, shooting up somewhat over a span. The stalk is white, and when it has sprouted to the height of a finger, it begins to flower one bud after another in succession till there are eight flowers in bloom. It has six lilac-tinted petals. Usually among six [3]filaments, three are yellow and three ruddy. The last three yield the saffron. When the flowers are over, leaves appear upon the stalk. Once planted it will flower for six years in succession. The first year, the yield is small: in the second as 30 to 10. In the third year it

---

[1] The principal ancient cities of Kashmir are the old capital of Srinagari and the new, Pravarasenapura which was lost in the former name: Khagendrapura and Khanamusha, identified with Kākapur on the left bank of the Bihat, ten miles to the south of the Takht i Sulaimān, and Khunamoh, four miles north-east of Pāmpur: Vijipara and Pantasok. The former twenty-five miles south-east of the capital: the latter three miles from the Takht i Sulaimān; Surapura the modern Sopur, mentioned in the Kashmir chronicles as Kambuca: Kanishkapura, corrupted to Kāmpur: Hushkapura probably Baramula: Jushkapura now Zukru or Zukur four miles north of the capital: Parihasapura built by Lalitaditya (A.D. 723—760): Padmapura now Pampur: and Avantipura, now only a small village, Wantipur, seventeen miles south-east of the present capital. Cunningham, pp. 95, 103.

[2] See Vol. I, p. 84 where the method of cultivation of this plant is explained somewhat differently.

[3] I am indebted to Dr. King fcr the following note:

"There are three stamens and three stigmas in each flower. The latter yield the saffron. The style divides at the level of the anthers into three yellow drooping branches which hang out of the flower and become gradually thickened and tubular upward, stigmas dilated, notched and often split down one side, dark orange coloured. The mode of collection and preparation of saffron varies in different countries, but it consists essentially in removing the stigmas with the upper part of the style from the other parts of the flower and afterwards drying the parts detached. A not uncommon adulteration of saffron is made by intermixing the dyed stamens of the saffron crocus. It takes from 7,000 to 8,000 flowers to yield 17½ ounces of fresh saffron which by drying is reduced to 3½." *Medicinal Plants* by Bentley and Trimen, IV, 274. In the Waqiāt i Jehāngiri, it is asserted that in an ordinary year, 400 maunds or 3,200 Khurasāni maunds are produced. Half belongs to Government, half to the cultivators and a ser sells for about 10 Rs. A note states that one good grain of saffron contains the stigmata and styles of 9 flowers; hence 4,329 flowers yield one oz.

reaches its highest point and the bulbs are dug up. If left in the same soil, they gradually deteriorate, but if taken up they may be profitably transplanted.

In the village of *Zewan* are a spring and a reservoir which are considered sacred, and it is thought that the saffron seed came from this spring. When the cultivation begins, they worship at this fount and pour cow's milk into it. If as it falls it sinks into the water, it is accounted a good omen and the saffron crop will we plentiful, but if it floats on the surface, it will be otherwise.

In the village of *Khriu* 360 springs refresh the eye and each of these is accounted a means of divine worship. Near this is an iron mine.

Maru Adwin[1] adjoins *Great Tibet* where the *Handu* is found of the best breed and large in size, and carries heavy burdens. Near this is a hill called *Chatar Kot* on the summit of which snakes are so numerous that no one can approach it. There is also a high hill difficult of ascent, on which is a large lake. It is not every one that can find his way to it, for it often disappears from sight. At the foot of the mountain in different places images of *Mahādeva* fashioned of a stone like crystal are found and are a source of wonder.

In the neighbourhood of *Achh Bal,* one of the dependencies of *Khattār* is a fountain which shoots up to the height of a cubit, and is scarce equalled for its coldness, limpidity and refreshing qualities. The sick that drink of it and persevere in a course of its waters, recover their health.

In the village of *Kotihār* is a deep spring, surrounded by stone temples. When its water decreases, an image of *Mahādeva* in sandal-wood appears. The quality of this spring does not alter.

In the vicinity of *Wular* is a lofty mountain, containing a salt spring. The Kashmir stag[2] is here found in numbers.

Matan [Martand] stands upon a hill and once possessed a large temple. There is a small pool on the summit, the water of which never decreases.* Some suppose this to be

---

[1] Mare Wurdwun according to Vigne.

[2] The Bārā Singha or Kashmir stag, (*Cervus Cashmerianus*).

* Martand, situated on the highest part of the *Karewah* or raised plain between Islāmābād and the higher mountains. The temple is described by Hügel as "Korau Pandau," the beautiful ruins of which are the finest in Kashmir. Vigne inverts the order as Pandu Koru. At 150 yards distance as the Chāh i Bābil or well of Hārut and Mārut whose story does not need repetition. The spring referred to in the following paragraph is that of

the *Well of Babylon,* but at the present day there is no trace of anything but an ordinary pit.

On the slope of the hill is a spring, at the head of which a reservoir has been constructed, full of fish. The sanctity of the place preserves them from being touched. By the side of it is a cave, the depth of which cannot be ascertained.

In *Khāwarpārah* is a source, whose waters tumble headlong with a mighty roar.

In the village of *Aish*[1] is the cell of *Bābā Zainu'ddin Rishi.* It is in the side of a hill. It is said that in ancient times the hill held no water, but when he took up his abode there, a spring began to flow. For twelve years he occupied this cell and at length closed its mouth with a large stone and never went forth again, and none has ever found trace of him.

The town of *Dachchhinpārah* is on the side of a mountain bordering *Great Tibet* and is fed by the waters of the above-mentioned spring. Between *Great Tibet* and the above-mentioned *parganah* is a cave in which is an image in ice called *Amar Nāt.*[2] It is considered a shrine of great sanctity. When the new moon rises from her throne of rays, a bubble as it were of ice is formed in the cave which daily increases little by little for fifteen days till it is somewhat higher than two yards, of the measure of the yard determined by His Majesty; with the waning moon, the image likewise begins to decrease, till no trace of it remains when the moon disappears. They believe it to be the image of *Mahādeva* and regard it as a means (through supplication) of the fiulment of their desires. Near the cave is a rill called *Amrāoti,* the clay of which is extremely white. They account it auspicious and smear themselves with it. The snows of this mountainous tract nowhere melt, and from the

---

Bawan, one of the holiest in Kashmir, swarming, says Vigne, (I, 359) with Himalayan trout. Hügel gives the legend of the caves one of which he was assured extended 10 kos, and that no one who ever entered, had been known to return. He penetrated to the end of it in a few minutes. Matan is the name of the *Karewah* at the end of which, according to Moorcroft, the Martand temple stands (II, 255) ascribed like most of the architectural remains to the Pāndus.

[1] The village of Aish Maqām or the abode of pleasure, holds in a long building situated conspicuously on the left bank of the Lidar, the shrine of the saint. He directed that a tomb should be erected where his staff should be found, as his body would disappear. It is still missing. See Vigne, II, 6.

[2] The Amarnāth cave is marked in Drew's map, south-east of Baltal and Sonamarg, near the sources of the Sind river. Its history and ceremonies are told by Vigne, II, 8. The ice bubble was doubtless a stalactite. See Moorcroft, II, 252.

extreme cold, the straitness of the defiles and the rough inequalities of the road, they are surmounted with great toil.

In the village of *Dākhāmun* is a spring, and whenever its water boils up and becomes turbid its surface is covered with particles of straw and rubbish, the dust of dissension arises in the country. A quarry of Solomon's stone[1] is in the vicinity of which utensils are fashioned.

About the *parganah* of *Phāk* grow a variety of herbs and plants. Adjoining is a large lake called *Dal*. One side of it is contiguous to the city and on its surface a number of floating islands[2] are constructed which are cultivated, and fraudulent people will at times cut off a piece and carry it away to a different position. *Sultān Zainul Abidin* constructed in this lake a causeway (*sad*) of clay and stone one *kos* in length from the city to this *parganah*. In the vicinity also is a spring of which the sick drink and are restored to health.

In the village of *Thid,* is a delightful spot where seven springs unite : around them are stone buildings, memorials of bygone times. There is also a source which in winter is warm and in summer cold.

In the village of *Bāzwāl* is a waterfall from the crest of *Shāhkot*. It is called *Shālahmār*. Here fish are caught in numbers. A streamlet is caged at two ends and when the water is carried off, the fish between are taken.

In *Ishibāri* is a spring held sacred by the people of Hindustān, called *Suryasar,* surrounded by stone temples. *Shakarnāg* is a spring which is dry all the year, but should the 9th day of any month happen to fall on a Friday, it bubbles up and flows from morn till eve, and people flock to partake of its blessings.

In the village of *Rambal* are a spring and a pool. Those who have special needs throw in a nut, if it floats, it is an augury of success; if it sinks, it is considered adverse.

In *Bānihal* is a temple dedicated to *Durgā*. If any one desires to learn the issue of a strife between himself

---

[1] Applied indiscriminately to both agate and onyx. Tieffenthaler describes a stone of their country, as green with white streaks which is worked with diamond powder and made into phials, saucers, hafts of daggers and the like. It is probably a kind of jade.

[2] Cucumbers and melons are commonly grown on them. Their construction is described by Moorcroft (II, 138) with the thoroughness which characterizes his observations. The causeway is called by Vigne, (II, 99) *Sad i Chodri* and is carried entirely through the lake to the village of Isha Bryri, four miles on the opposite side.

and his enemy, he fills two vessels with boiled rice, the one representing his own fortunes, the other those of his foe, and places them in the temple and closes the doors. On the following day the devotees present themselves to learn the result. In whose vessel roses and saffron are found, his undertaking will prosper, and that which is full of straws and dirt, portends the ruin of the person it represents. Stranger still, in a dispute where it is difficult to discover the truth, each party is given a fowl or a goat and sent to the temple. They then poison each of these animals and severally rub them with their hands. His animal whose cause is just recovers, and the other dies.

In the *Ver* tract of country is the source of the *Bihat.* It is a pool measuring a *jarib* which tosses in foam with an astonishing roar, and its depth is unfathomable. It goes by the name of *Vernāg*[1] and is surrounded by a stone embankment and to its east are temples of stone. In the village of *Kambar* is a spring called *Bawan Sendh* which during two months of the spring time is in agitation. It is always full and its water never decreases.

In *Devsar* in the village of Balau is a pool called Balau Nāg 20 yards square in which the water is agitated : it is embosomed in delightful verdure and canopied by shady trees. Whosoever is desirous of knowing the prospects of the harvest, or whether his own circumstances are to be prosperous or unfavourable, fills an earthen vessel with rice, writes his name on its rim, and closing its mouth, casts it into the spring. After a time the vessel of its own accord floats on the surface, and he then opens it and if the rice be fragrant and warm, the year will be prosperous and his undertakings successful, but if it be filled with clay or mud and rubbish, the reverse will be the case.

Veshau is the name of a stream which issues picturesquely from an orifice in a mountain, and at the same place is a declivity down which the waters tumble from a height of 20 yards with a thundering roar. Hindu devotees throw themselves down from its summit and with the utmost fortitude sacrifice their lives, in the belief that it is a means of securing their spiritual welfare.

Kuthār[2] is a spring which remains dry for eleven years, and when the planet *Jupiter* enters the sign of *Leo,* it flows

[1] *Ver* is the old name of Shahābād. A description of this celebrated fountain may be read in Vigne's *Kashmir,* I, 332, and in Moorcroft, II, 250.

[2] This appears to be the Kosah Nāg of Vigne which he says is pronounced *Kausar* by the Muhammadans after the fountain in Paradise.

on the following Thursday and during the succeeding seven days is again dry and once more fills on the Thursday next following, and so continues for a year.

In the village of *Matalhāmah* is a wood in which is a heronry,[1] the feathers are taken for plumes, and the birds are here regularly fed.

Near *Shukroh* is a low hill on the summit of which is a fountain which flows throughout the year and is a place of pilgrimage for the devout. The snow does not fall on this spur.

In *Nāgām* is a spring called *Nilah Nāg,* the basin of which measures 40 *bigahs.* Its waters are exquisitely clear and it is considered a sacred spot, and many voluntarily perish by fire about its border. Strange to relate omens are taken by its means. A nut is divided into four parts and thrown in, and if an odd number floats, the augury is favourable, if otherwise, the reverse. In the same way if milk (thrown in) sinks, it is a good omen, and if not, it is unpropitious. In ancient times a volume, which they call *Nilmat,* arose from its depths, which contained a detailed description of *Kashmir* and the history and particulars of its temples. They say that a flourishing city with lofty buildings is underneath its waters, and that in the time of *Badu Shāh,*[2] a Brāhman descended into it and returned after three days, bringing back some of its rarities and narrated his experiences.

In the village of *Biruwā* is a spring and in its water lepers bathe early on the first day of the week and are restored to health. In the vicinity is a plateau, a pasture ground for cattle, the grass of which has peculiar fattening properties.

In the village of *Halthal* of the *parganah* of *Yech* is found a quivering tree.[3] If the smallest branch of it be shaken, the whole tree becomes tremulous.

Lār borders on the mountins of *Great Tibet.* To its north is a lofty mountain which dominates all the surrounding country, and the ascent of which is arduous. At its foot are two springs, two yards distant from each other, the waters of one being extremely cold and those of the other

[1] The word is pronounced *Oukar* or *Okar* and signifies a heron. See Vigne, I, 306. The heronries are strictly guarded.

[2] Badu Shāh is Zainul Abidin (Vigne, II, 73).

[3] Dr. King informs me that the Aspen (*Populus tremula*) occurs wild in the N. W. Himalaya. The *P. Euphratica* of which the leaves are as tremulous as the aspen, is also common in many parts.

exceedingly hot. They are considered sacred and the bones of bodies are here reduced to ashes: the bones and ashes of the dead are cast into a large lake on the mountain and this ceremony is regarded as a means of union with the Divinity. If the flesh of an animal fall into it, a heavy fall of snow and rain ensues. The river called *Sind* which rises in *Tibet,* is wholesome to drink, and is so clear that the fish in it are visible. They strike them with iron spears and catch them also in other ways. *Shahāb-u'ddinpur* is on the banks of the *Bihat,* and about it are large plane trees which is a favourite resort. The *Sind* joins the Bihat at this point.

In *Tulmulā* is an area of about 100 *bighas* in extent which is flooded during the rains, and remains somewhat moist even after the waters have dried up. The people plunge in sticks of a yard in length, more or less, and work them about, and thrusting their hands into the holes pull out fish of four pounds weight and more, but commonly of small size.

In *Satpur* is a pool, the depth of which cannot be fathomed. It is held in great veneration and is a place of worship. *Bhutesar* is a temple dedicated to *Mahādeva.* Whoever approaches to pay his devotions, hears the sounds of ceremonial worship and no one can tell whence they proceed.

In *Khoihāma* which adjoins *Little Tibet* is a large lake called the Wular twenty-eight *kos* in circumference. The *Bihat* flows into it and its course is somewhat lost to the eye. Here *Sultān Zainul Abidin* built a large palace called *Zain Lanka.*[1] Boats full of stones and branches of trees are sunk in the lake and pulled up by ropes after the lapse of three or four months, and many fish are taken that have homed there. The capture of water-fowl here affords considerable sport, and in the village of *Ajas,* stags are chased down to the lake and taken. Near *Māchhāmu* is an island covered with trees which when shaken by the wind, cause the island also to quake.

Saffron is also cultivated in *Paraspur.* It formerly held a lofty temple which when destroyed by *Sikandar* father of *Sultān Zainul Abidin,* a copper tablet was discovered on which was inscribed in *Sanskrit,* that after the

[1] See Vigne, II, 153. The legend of the Lanka islet is given in Muhammad Aāzam's *Hist. of Kashmir* translated by me in the *A. S. Journal,* XLIX, Part I, 1880.

lapse of eleven hundred years, one Sikandar would destroy it and gather for himself exceeding great chastisement.[1]

In the *Parganah of Kamrāj*[2] at the village of *Trahgām* the residence of the *Chaks* is a fountain of sweet water called *Chatarnāg* and in the middle is a stone building of great age. The fish grow to great size but whosoever touches them, is afflicted by some calamity.

Near *Kargon* is a defile called *Soyam*[3] where an area of ten *jaribs* of land becomes so hot at the time of the conjunction of Jupiter and Leo that trees are burnt up and a vessel of water if left on the ground will boil. A flourishing little town stands here. From *Kamrāj* is a defile, one end of which touches *Kāshghar* and on the west lies *Pakli*, where gold is obtained in the following manner. The skins of long-haired goats are spread in the fords of this river, with stones placed round them that the current may not bear them away. They are taken up after three days and left in the sun. When dry, they are shaken, yielding their three *tolahs* weight of gold dust. *Gilgit* is the name of another pass which leads to *Kāshghar*. Gold is there obtained by soil washings.

At two days' distance from *Hāehāmun* is the river named *Padmati* which flows from the *Dārdu*[4] country. Gold is also found in this river. On its banks is a stone temple called *Sāradā* dedicated to *Durgā* and regarded with great veneration. On every eighth *tithi* of *'Shuklapaksha*, it begins to shake and produces the most extraordinary effect.

---

[1] Cunningham alludes to this at p. 102 and adds, 'The same story is told by Ferishta with the addition of the name of the Rāja whom the translator calls *Balnāt* (a mistake for *Lāldit*, the contracted form of *Lalitaditya* among the Kashmiris).

[2] Kamrāj and Merāj were two large districts into which Kashmir was divided from the earliest times, the former being the north half of the valley below the junction of the Sind with the Jhelum, and the latter the south half, above that junction. Cunningham, p. 94. Vigne calls the village Tāragāon (II, 139) the village of the stars. The remains of ancient masonry round a fine spring were still to be seen, some of the blocks little inferior in size to those of Martand.

[3] Suhoyum in Vigne, (II, 281) who states that it lies near the village of Nichi Hama in the Parganah of Machiapora at the north-west end of the valley, and that 36 years before his visit an intense heat was found to issue from the spot. The phenomenon has several times occurred, a white smoke being occasionally seen to issue from the ground, but without sulphurous smell or fissures in the soil.

[4] Few people can be traced through so long a period in the same place as these whom H. H. Wilson (Moorcroft, II, 266, n.)identifies as the *Dāradas* of Sanskrit geography, and *Daradræ* or *Daradæ* of Strabo. He supposes them to be the Kāfirs of the Muhammadans, though now nominally converted to Islam. The auriferous region of the Dāradas is mentioned by Humboldt (*Cosmos* II, p. 513. E. C. Otté) who places it either in the Thibetian highlands east of the Bolor chain, west of Iskardo, or towards the desert of Gobi described also as auriferous by Hewen Thsang.

The system of revenue collection is by appraisement and division of crops, assessments for crops paying special rates and cash transactions not being the custom of the country. Some part of the *Sair Jihāt* cesses, however, are taken in cash. Payments in coin and kind were estimated in *kharwārs* of (*Shāli*) rice. Although one-third[1] had been for a long time past the nominal share of the State, more than two shares was actually taken, but through His Majesty's justice, it has been reduced to one half. According to the assessment of Qāzi (Ali)* the revenue was fixed at 30 *lakhs,* 63,050 *kharwārs,* 11 *tăraks,* each *kharwār* being 3 *man,* 8 *sers Akbarshāhi.* A weight of two *dāms* is called a *pal,* and ½ and ¼ of this weight are also in use.

Seven and a half *pals* are considered equivalent to one *ser,* two sers are equal to half a *man,* and four *sers* to a *tarak,* and sixteen *taraks* to one *kharwār.* A *tarak,* according to the royal weights (of Akbar) is eight *sers.* Taking the prices current for several years, the *Qāzi* struck an average of the aggregate, and the *kharwār* (in kind) was ascertained to be 29 *dāms,* and the *kharwār* in money was fixed according to the former rate of $13\frac{8}{25}$ *dāms.* The revenue, therefore, amounted to 7 *krors,* 46 *lakhs,* 70,411 *dāms.* (Rs. 1,866,760-4-5), out of which 9 *lakhs,* 1,663 *kharwārs* and 8 *taraks* were paid in money, equivalent to 1 *kror,* 20 *lakhs,* 22,183 *dāms.* (Rs. 300,554-9-2). The revenue fixed by Āsaf Khan, was 30 *lakhs,* 79,443 *kharwārs,* of which 11 *lakhs,* 11,330½ *kharwārs* were in money.

---

[1] The immemorial tradition in Kashmir considered the whole of the land as the property of the ruler. Of some portions of the *khālsa* lands the sovereigns divested themselves by grants in *jagir* for various periods. The Sikhs made a general resumption, ousted the possessors of grants and reduced thousands to destitution. In Moorcroft's time (II, 125) the *khālsa* lands were let out for cultivation. Those near the city as Sar Kishti, head or upper cultivation, those more remote Pai-Kishti, or foot and lower. When the grain was trodden out, an equal division took place formerly between the farmer and the government, but the latter advanced its demands till it appropriated ⅞ of the Sar-Kishti and ¾ of the P. K. crop. The straw fell generously to the share of the cultivator who was also permitted to steal a portion of his own produce by the overseer,—for a consideration. In the time of Zainu'l Aābidin, the rice crop (the staple) is said to have been 77 lakhs of *kharwārs.* In Moorcroft's day it was 20, at from 2½ to 6½ Rs. a *kharwār.* His weight-measures differ from those of Abul Fazl, a *kharwār* being 16 *taraks,* a *tarak* 6 *sers,* a *ser* 20 *pals,* a *pal* 3½ Mahomed Shahi rupees, which (the rupee being 173·3 grains) should make the *ser* nearly 2 pounds. The actual *ser* was, however, not above one pound avoirdupois, and a *kharwār* or ass-load was therefore 96 pounds. A horse-load equalled 22 *taraks.*

* See pp. 347 and 411 of Vol. I, where further information is given regarding the revenue system, its exactions and the disturbances which led to the Qāzi's murder.

The cesses *bāj and Tamghā,*[1] were altogether remitted by His Majesty, which produced a reduction of 67,824½ *kharwārs,* equivalent to 898,400 *dāms.* (Rs. 22,460). For the additional relief of the husbandman, five *dāms* on the price of a *kharwār,* were thrown in. Although the revenue, in *kharwārs,* of *Āsaf Khān* was in excess of that of Qāzi Ali by 16,392 *kharwārs,* yet calculated by money the receipts are less, after deducting the remissions, by 860,034½ *dāms* (Rs. 21,500-13-7), because he estimated the *kharwār* in money which is of lower relative worth, above its value.

In the revenue returns forwarded by *Qāzi Ali* to the Imperial Exchequer, forty-one *parganahs* are taken while the return submitted by *Āsaf Khān* contains but thirty-eight, there being thirty-eight in point of fact. For Qāzi Ali on a review of the question separated the two villages *Karnā* and *Dārdu,* of the *parganah* of *Kamrāj,* and dividing the *parganah* of *Sāir i Mawāzi* into two, constituted these into two *parganahs.* In former times certain selected towns of each *parganah* were denominated *Sāiru'l Mawāzi* (village-group) and were held as *Khālisa.*[2] *Qāzi Ali* united forty villages of the *Marāj* side under the name of *Parganahi Hāveli* and retained eighty-eight villages of *Kamrāj* according to the former distribution, as *parganah* of *Sāiru'l Mawāzi.*

The whole kingdom was divided under its ancient rulers into two divisions, *Marāj* on the east, and *Kamrāj* on the west.

At the present day that a great part of the army in Kashmir has been withdrawn, the local militia consists of 4,892 cavalry and 92,400 infantry.

Sarkār of Kashmir.

Containing 38 *Mahals.* Revenue 3,011,618 *kharwārs,* 12 *taraks,* being equivalent to 62,113,040½ *dāms.* (Rs. 1,552,826); out of which 9,435,006 *kharwārs,* 14 *taraks* is

[1] *Tamghā* has been already defined at p. 63 of this Volume, as being a demand in excess of the land revenue and *bāj* is simply a toll or tax and must here have a somewhat similar application, but there were various other taxes in excess of land revenue, such as *Jihāt, Sāir Jihāt, Farua'āt* and others whose nature is defined at p. 63. Elliot discusses the value of the terms at p. 6, Vol. II, of his *Races of the North-West Provinces.*

Tamghā occurs later under Kabul, signifying inland tolls.

[2] Lands of which the revenue was the pooperty of the government, not being made over in grants or gifts, *Jāgir* or *Inām* to any other parties. Also lands and villages held immediately of government and of which the State is the manager or holder. Wilson, *Gloss.*

paid in money, equivalent to 12,501,880 *dāms*. (Rs. 312,547). Castes, various. Cavalry, 3,202. Infantry, 27,725.

The Marāj Tract.

Containing 22 *Mahals*. Revenue 1,792,819 *kharwārs*, equivalent to 35,796,122½ *dāms*, (Rs. 894,903), of which 670,551 *kharwārs*, 12 *taraks* are paid in money, equivalent to 8,885,248 *dāms*, (Rs. 222,131-3-2). Cavalry, 1,620. Infantry, 4,600.

City of *Srinagar*. Revenue 342,694 *kharwārs*, 12 *taraks*, in money, 342,996 *kharwārs*, 8 *taraks*; in kind, 1,698 *kharwārs*, 4 *taraks*.

Parganahs east of Srinagar, 3 *Mahals*.

	In kind		In money		Cavalry	Infantry	Castes
	Khar-wārs	*Taraks*	*Khar-wārs*	*Taraks*			
Yech	144,102	0	62,034	4	5	50	Khamash ? and Zinah.
Brang	78,834	4	8,769	8	68	1000	
Vihi	209,632	8	161,968	8	12	400	Bahtā, Brāhman.

Parganahs, north-east, 7 *Mahals*.

	In kind		In money		Cavalry	Infantry	Castes
	Khar-wārs	*Taraks*	*Khar-wārs*	*Taraks*			
Wular	128,656	4	12,605	8	20	200	Dardah and Shāl.
Phāk	71,111	12	17,402	8	...	...	
Dachhinpār	75,153	0	6,902	12	20	100	Khān.
Khāwarpār ..	45,226	8	3,575	8	100	500	Khāwar.
Khattār	37,479	4	3,221	12	15	300	Dard.
Maru Adwin (Maru Wardwun, Vigne)	...		5,041	0	200 half bow-men	200	
Matan	190,43½		18,62½		20	100	Bhāt.

Parganahs, south-east, 11 *Mahals.*

	In kind		In money		Cavalry	Infantry	Castes
	Khar-wārs	*Taraks*	*Khar-wārs*	*Taraks*			
Ādwin	101,432	4	14,815	16*	1	100	Dard.
Yech	98,369	0	14,377	4	6	30	Brāhman.
Banihāl	6,435 40 horseloads		...		400	4000	Sihar.
Bātu	3,515 besides transit duties remitted	0	4,235	8	50	300	Nāik.
Devsar	85,644	8	822	8	300	000	Zinah.
Zinahpur	15,875	4	1,799	1	20	...	
Soparsaman ..	6,133 besides dues on firewood		2,003	4	70	200	Kamboh.
Shādarah	39,167	0	8,550	12	...	...	Thakur.
Shukroh	45,224	0	12,757	8	20	...	Ashwār.
Nāgām	189,770	12	22,576	4	15	100	Bhāt.
Ver	12,270	8	838		500	5000	Sahsah.[1]

* This must be a mistake for 12, as 16 *taraks* make a *kharwār*: in the Arabic numerals the 2 and 6 are easily confounded. A horse load is 22 *taraks*.

[1] Var. Sahah, Sansah, Nakhah.

Kamrāj Tract.

Containing 16 *Mahals*. Revenue 1,218,799 *kharwārs*, 12 *taraks*, equivalent to 26,316,918 *dāms*. (Rs. 657,922-15-2). In money, 272,954½ *kharwārs*, equivalent to 3,616,632 *dāms*. (Rs. 90,415-12-9). Cavalry, 1,590. Infantry, 16,965.

Parganahs, north-west.

	In kind		In money		Cavalry	Infantry	Castes
	Khar-wārs	*Taraks*	*Khar-wārs*	*Taraks*			
Zinahkar	13,253	0	32,55½	0	50	100	Bhāt, Musalmān.
Khoihāma	83,670	12	15,522	0	50	1000	Zinah.[2]

[2] Var. Ahir.

Parganahs, south-west.

	In kind		In money		Cavalry	Infantry	Castes
	Khar-wārs	*Taraks*	*Khar-wārs*	*Taraks*			
Indarkol	9,553	4	7,238	0	...	...	Bhāt.
Paraspur	18,830	12	3,352	8	...	...	Siyāhi.
Patan	4,799	4	523	0	30	110	Bhāt, Musalmān
Bānkal	115,233	12	20,280	4	200	500	Bākri.
Barwi	57,098	12	13,383	0	35	30	Kahār.
Telkām	15,415	12	4,435	4	...	30	Pandit.
Dinsu	53,219½		17,038½		150	400	Doni.
Dachhin Khāwarah ..	36,222	4	20,653	0	25	300	Khasi, Kanku, Zinah.
Sāir u'l Mawāzi ..	192,641	4	18,553	12	...	...	
Khoi	12,945	0	370		...	15	Rawer.
Kamrāj	342,844	4	103,725	4	1000	10,000	Chak.
Karohan	115,474	0	29,779	12	...	110	

SOVEREIGNS OF KASHMIR.

Fifty-three princes reigned during 1266 *years.*

I.

Ugnand.
Damodar, } his sons.
Bāl, }
Thirty-five princes succeeded whose names are unknown.

II.

Lavah, (var. Lava.)
Kishen, his son (var. Kish.)
Kahgandra, his son.
Surandra, his son.
Godhara, of another tribe.
Suran, his son.
Janaka, his son.
Shachinar, (var. Hashka, Bishka).
Asoka, son of Janaka's paternal uncle.
Jaloka, his son.
Damodar, descendant of *Asoka.*
Hashka, }
Zashka, } three brothers. Buddhists.
Kaniska, }
Abhiman.

III.

	Y.	M.	D.
Rājā Ganand (Gonerda III) reigned ...	35	0	0
,, Bhikan (Vibhishana), his son ...	53	0	0
,, Indrajita, his son	35	6	0
,, Rāwana, his son	30	0	0
,, Bhikan II, his son	35	6	0
,, Nara, (also called Khar), his son ...	39	9	0
,, Sidha, his son	60	0	0
,, Utpalāchah, his son	30	6	0
,, Hiranya, his son	37	7	0
,, Hirankal, his son	60	0	0
,, Abaskaha, his son	60	0	0
,, Mihirkal, his son	70	0	0
,, Baka (Vaka), his son	63	0	13
,, Khatnanda, his son	30	0	0
,, Vasunanda, his son	52	2	0
,, Nara, his son	60	0	0
,, Aja (Aksha), his son	60	0	0
,, Gopāditya, his son (MSS. Kopārat) ...	60	0	6
,, Karan, his son	57	0	11
,, Narendraditya, his son	36	3	10
,, Yudishthira, his son	48	0	10

IV.

Six princes reigned 192 *years.*

Pratapāditya, said to be a descendant of Vikramāditya	32	0	0
Jaloka, his son	32	0	0
Tanjir, (Tunjina) his son	36	0	0
Bijai, relation to above	8	0	0
Jayandra, (var. Chandra), his son ...	37	0	0
Ārya Rāj	47	0	0

V.

Ten princes reigned 592 *years,* 2 *months,* 1 *day.*

	Y.	M.	D.
Meghavāhana, a descendant of Judishthira	34	0	0
Srishtasena, his son	30	0	0
Hiran, his son	30	2	0
Mātrigupta, Brāhman	4	9	1
Pravarasena, a descendant of Meghavāhana	63	0	0
Judishthira, his son	39	3	0
Lakshman, called also Nandradit ...	13	0	0
Ranāditya, his younger brother ...	30	0	0
Vikramāditya, his son	42	0	0
Bālāditya, his younger brother, no issue ...	36	0	0

Seventeen princes reigned 257 *years,* 5 *months,* 20 *days.*

	Y.	M.	D.
Durlabhavardhan, son-in-law of Bālādit ...	36	0	0
Pratapāditya, grandson of his daughter ...	50	0	0
Chandrapira, his eldest son	8	0	8
Tārāpira, his brother	4	0	24
Lalitāditya, another brother	36	7	11
Kuvalayāpirā, his son	1	0	15
Vajrāditya, his brother	7	0	0
Prithivyāpirā, his son	4	1	0
Sangrāpirā, grandson of Lalitāditya by a son	7	0	0
Jayāpira, ditto	31	0	0
Jajja, his brother-in-law	some months		
Lalitāpira, his son	12	0	0
Sangrāmapira, his brother	37	0	0
Brihaspati, son of Lalitāpira	12	0	0
Ajitāpira, or Ajayāpira, son of Prabhubāpira	36	0	0
Anangāpira, son of Sangrāmapira ...	3	0	0
Utpalāpira, son of Ajayāpira.			

VI.

Fifteen princes reigned 89 *years,* 1 *month,* 15 *days.*

	Y.	M.	D.
Avanti Varmā, of the Chamār caste ...	28	3	3
Sankar Varmā, his son	18	7	19
Gopāl Varmā	2	0	0
Sankat, said to be his brother	0	0	10

	Y.	M.	D.
Sugandhā Rāni, mother of above-mentioned Gopāl	2	0	0
Pārtha, son of Sukh Varmā	15	0	10
Mārjit Varmā, son of Sukh Varmā, his brother	1	1	0
Chakra Varmā	10	0	15
Sura Varmā, his brother	1	0	0
Pārtha, son of Mārjit	1	4	0
Chakra Varmā, second time	0	6	0
Sankar Vardhana, son of Mir Vardhana ...	3	0	0
Chakra Varmā, third time	3	0	0
Unmatt Avanti Varmā, son of Rājā Pārtha	2	2	0
Surma (Sura) Varmā, second time, last of the Chamār princes	0	6	0

VII.

Ten princes reigned 64 *years,* 3 *months,* 14 *days.*

	Y.	M.	D.
Jasasra (Jasaskar) Dev, a peasant ...	9	0	0
Buranit, an uncle's descendant ...	0	0	1
Sangrāma Deva, son of Jasaskar ...	0	6	7
Parva Gupta, one of his subjects ...	1	4	0
Khema (Kshema) Gupta	8	6	0
Abhiman, his son	14	0	0
Nanda Gupta, his son	1	1	9
Tribhuvana	2	0	7
Bhimā Gupta, son of Abhiman ...	4	3	20
Diddā Rāni, mother of Abhiman ...	23	6	0

Twenty-seven princes reigned 351 *years,* 6 *months,* 17 *days.*

	Y.	M.	D.
Sangrāma, son of Adirāj, nephew of the Rāni	24	2	0
Harirājā, his son	0	0	22
Ānanta, his son	5	5	0
Kalasa Deva, his son	26	0	0
Utkarsā, his son	0	0	22
Harsha, son of Kalasa	12	0	0
Uchal, grandfather of Harsha	10	4	2
Riddha, son of Siddha, one of the murderers of Uchal	[one night and 3 hours		
Salhan, brother of Uchal	0	3	27

	Y.	M.	D.
Susalha, brother of Salhan	7	10	0
Bhekhyājar, son of Haras	0	6	12
Rājā Susalha, second time	2	3	0
Jaya Singh, son of Susalha	27	0	0
Parmānak, son of above	9	6	10
Dati (var. and G. Danji Deva), his son ...	9	4	17
Jas Deva, his younger brother ...	18	0	13
Chag (Jag) Deva, son of above ...	14	2	0
Rājā Deva, his son	23	3	7
Sangrāma Deva, his son	16	0	10
Rāma Deva, his son	21	1	13
Lachhman (Lakshman) Deva, son of a Brāhman	13	3	12
Sinha Deva, chief of Labdar of Daskhinpārah	14	5	27
Sinha Deva, brother of above	19	3	26
Rinjan of Tibet, a native of that country ...	10	some months	
Adin Deva, relation of Sinha Deva ...	15	2	10
Rāni Kotā Devi, wife of Adin Deva ...	0	6	15

Thirty-two princes reigned 282 *years,* 5 *months,* 1 *day.*

A.H.	A.D.		Y.	M.	D.
715	1315	Sultān Shamsu'ddin, minister of Sinha Deva ...	2	11	25
750	1349	,, Jamshid, his son ...	1	10	0
752	1351	,, Alāu'ddin, son of Shams-uddin	12	8	13
765	1363	,, Shahābu'ddin ...	20	0	0
785	1386	,, Qutbu'ddin, son of Hasan-uddin	15	5	2
799	1396	,, Sikandar, his son whose name was Sankār ...	22	9	6
819	1416	,, Ali Shāh, his son ...	6	9	0
826	1422	,, Zainul Abidin, younger brother of Ali Shāh ...	52	0	0
877	1472	,, Hāji Haidar Shāh, his son	1	2	0
878	1473	,, Hasan Khān, his son ...	12	0	5
891	1486	,, Muhammad Shāh, his son	2	7	0
902	1496	,, Fath Shāh, son of Ādam Khān, son of Sultān Zainul Abidin ...	9	1	0

			Y.	M.	D.
911	1505	Sultān Muhammad Shāh, a second time	0	9	9
		,, Fath Shāh, a second time	1	1	0
		,, Muhammad Shāh, a third time	11	11	11
		,, Ibrahim, his son ...	0	8	25
942	1535	,, Nāzuk Shāh, son of Fath Shāh, (*Ferishta,* "son of Ibrahim, son of Muhammad Shāh") ...	1	0	0
		,, Muhammad Shāh, a fourth time	34	8	10
		,, Shamsi, son of Muhammad Shāh	0	2	0
		,, Ismāil Shāh, his brother ...	2	9	0
		,, Nāzuk Shāh, a second time	13	9	0
		,, Ismāil Shāh, a second time	1	5	0
948	1541	Mirzā Haidar Gurgān ...	10	0	0
		Sultān Nāzuk Shāh, a third time	1	0	0
		Ghāzi Khān, son of Kāji Chak ...	10	6	0
971	1563	Husain Chak, his brother ...	6	10	0
		Ali Chak, brother of Husain Chak	8	9	0
986	1578	Yusuf Shāh, his son ...	1	0	20
		Sayyid Mubārak Shāh, one of his nobles	0	1	25
		Lohar Chak, son of Sikandar, son of Kāji Chak	1	2	0
		Yusuf Shāh, a second time ...	5	3	0
		Yāqub Khān, his son ...	1	0	0

Thus this series of 191 princes, reigning throughout a period of 4,109 years, 11 months and 9 days, passed away.

When the Imperial standards were for the first time borne aloft in this garden of perpetual spring, a book called *Rāj Tarangini* written in the Sanskrit tongue containing an account of the princes of Kashmir during a period of some four thousand years, was presented to His Majesty. It had been the custom in that country for its rulers to employ certain learned men in writing its annals. His Majesty who was desirous of extending the bounds of knowledge appointed capable interpreters in its translation which in a short time was happily accomplished. In this work it is stated that the whole of this mountainous region was submerged under water and called *Sati Sar*. *Sati* is the name of the wife of *Mahādeva,* and *Sar* signifies a lake. One day of *Brahmā* comprises 14 *manvantaras*. Up to the 40th year of the Divine Era, of the seventh *manvantara,* at which time Kashmir began to be inhabited, 27 (*kalpas*) each of four cycles (*yug*) as before mentioned, have elapsed and of the twenty-eighth three cycles, and of the fourth cycle, 4,701 solar years. And when, according to the legend which they relate, the waters had somewhat subsided, *Kasyapa*[1] who is regarded as one of the most sublime amongst ascetics, brought in the Brāhmans to inhabit the new region. When men began to multiply they sought to have a just ruler over them, and experienced elders, solicitous of the public weal met together in council and elected to the supreme authority one who was distinguished for his wisdom, his large understanding, his comprehensive benevolence and his personal courage. From this period dates the origin of their monarchical government which proceeded thus to the time of *Ugnand* 4,044 years prior to this the 40th year of the Divine Era.[2] Ugnand fell by the hand of *Balbhadra,* the elder brother of *Kishan* in the battle fought at *Mathurā* between Kishan and *Jarāsandha* rājā of Behār. *Dāmodara* (his son), to avenge his death marched against some of the relations of Kishan who were hastening to a marriage festival in Qandahār, and was killed fighting on the banks of the *Sind*. His wife being then pregnant and the astrologers foretelling that it would prove a son, Kishan bestowed on him the government of the province. Thirty-five princes succeeded, but through their tyranny their names are no more remembered. When *Lavah* ascended the throne, justice was universally administered and deeds met their just recognition. He founded in *Kamrāj* the great city of *Lavapur* the

---

[1] According to Tieffenthaler, he was called *Cashapmir,* from Cashapa grandson of Brahmā and *mer,* a mountain or habitation. Bāber mentions in his Memoirs that the hill country along the upper course of the Indus was formerly inhabited by a race called *Kās* from whom he conjectures that Kashmir received its name. The *Kasiă regio* of Ptolemy applies to the race and seems to confirm his conjecture. Kasyapa was the son of Marichi the son of Brahmā, and was father of Vivaswat the father of Manu. His name signifies a tortoise which form he assumed as Prajapati, the father of all, and had a large share in the work of creation. He was one of the seven great Rishis.—Dowson.

[2] As the 40th year of Akbar's reign is A.H. 1003, commencing 5th Dec. 1594 and ending 25th Nov. 1595 A.D. the date of Ugnand would be B.C. 2449.

ruins of which are still to be traced. It is said to have held 800,000,000 houses. As the sage of *Ganjah*[1] well says:

House linked to house from Ispahan to Rai
Like jointed canes, I've heard, stretch countlessly,
So that a cat might trace the distant span
From roof to roof twixt Rai and Ispahan ;
But if the tale my credit doth belie,
The teller is its surety, faith not I.

When the succession devolved on *Asoka* the son of *Janaka's* paternal uncle, he abolished the Brahmanical religion and established the *Jain* faith.* His personal virtues adorned his reign, and his son *Rājā Jaloka* was distinguished for his justice, and his conquests were limited only by the ocean. On his return from *Kanauj,* then the capital of Hindustān, he brought with him a number of learned and enlightened men and of these his sagacity and perception of worth selected seven individuals. To one of them he entrusted the administration of justice; to another the revenue department; to a third the finances; to a fourth the superintendence of the troops; the fifth took charge of the department of commerce; the sixth controlled the material resources of the state, and the seventh interpreted the mysteries of the stars. He had also a knowledge of alchemy. It is said that a huge serpent ministered to his commands, mounted upon which he could descend below water for a long space. Sometimes he appeared as an old man, and at other times, as a youth, and marvellous tales are related of him. Buddhism became prevalent about this time.

Damodar (II) is said by some to have been one of the descendants of *Asoka.* He was a pious devout prince but was transformed into a snake through the curse of an ascetic. In the reign of *Rājā Nara* the Brāhmans prevailed over the Buddhists and levelled their temples to the ground. *Rājā Mihirkal* was a shameless tyrant, but by the strange freaks of fortune he made extensive conquests. As he was once returning homewards by the pass of *Hastibhanj,* an elephant lost its footing, and its screams and manner of falling caused him such amusement that he ordered a hundred ele-

---

[1] Shaikh Nizāmi, who was born in that town. The lines occur in the *Haft Paikar,* one of the *Khamsah* or Five poems of Nizāmi.

* See Thomas's *Jainaism or the Early Faith of Asoka* for this theory, which modern scholars have rejected.

phants to be precipitated in a similar manner. From this circumstance the pass received its name, *hasti* signifying *elephant*, and *bhanj*, *injury*. During his reign, a large rock blocked up the ferry of a river, and, however much it was cut away, it yet increased again during the night to its ordinary dimensions. Remedies were proposed in vain. At length a voice came forth intimating that if touched by the hand of a chaste woman, the rock would displace itself. Time after time it was touched by women in succession, and when no effect was produced, he ordered the women to be put to death for incontinence, the children for bastardy, and the husbands for consenting to the evil, until three *krors* of human beings were massacred. The miracle was at length effected by the hand of a chaste woman, a potter by trade and caused great wonder. The Rājā being afflicted by various diseases, burnt himself to death.

Rājā Gopadit possessed considerable learning and his justice increased the extent of his sway. The slaughtering of animals was forbidden throughout his dominions and high and low abstained from eating flesh. The temple which now stands on *Solomon's Hill* was built by his minister.

Rājā Judishthira in the beginning of his rule administered the state with an impartial hand, but in a short space through his licentious conduct and intimacy with base associates, his subjects became estranged from him, and the kings of Hindustān and Tibet were arrayed against him. The chiefs of Kashmir threw him into prison.

During the reign of *Rājā Tanjin* (Tunjin) snow fell when the sun was in Leo (July, August). The crops were destroyed and a terrible famine threw the country into disorder.

Rājā Jayandra possessed a minister wise, loyal and virtuous, and void of levity and dissimulation. His equals bore him envy, and the wicked at heart but specious in appearance, sought his ruin and undermined his influence by underhand misrepresentations. As princes are on these occasions apt to err and do not investigate closely, forgetful of former experiences of what envy can effect, the minister was overthrown, and banished in disgrace. His strange destiny, however, did not deprive him of his composure. He allowed not grief to encompass him, but gladdened his days with cheerfulness of heart. His wicked enemies represented him as aiming at the throne, and the Rājā, ignorant of the real facts, ordered him to be impaled. After some time had elapsed, his spiritual preceptor happened to pass that way and read on the frontal bone of his skull that he was destined to disgrace and imprisonment and to be impaled, but that he should again come to life and obtain the sovereignty. Amazed at learning this, he took down the body and secretly kept it and continued in supplication to the Almighty. One night the spirits gathered round and by their incantations restored the corpse to life. In a short time he succeeded to the throne, but his experience of life soon induced him to withdraw into retirement.

Meghavāhan was renowned for his virtues and gave peace and security to Hindustān as far as the borders of the ocean. After the death of *Rājā Hiran* without issue, the chiefs of Kashmir paid allegiance to *Rājā Bikramājit* the ruler of Hindustān. *Rājā Mātrigupta* was a learned Kashmiri Brāhman. Bikramājit profited by his wisdom but did not advance his temporal interests. He, however, gave him a sealed letter to convey to Kashmir and furnishing him with a small sum of money for his expenses as he started, despatched him on his mission. The Brāhman set out with a heavy heart. On his arrival in Kashmir, the letter was opened. It ran thus. 'The bearer has rendered important services at my Court and has experienced many reverses of fortune. On the receipt of this letter, let the government of the country be entrusted to him, and be this mandate obeyed under fear of the royal displeasure.' The chiefs met in council and yielded their submission.

Rājā Pravarasena had withdrawn from the country and lived in retirement in Hindustān. A devout and enlightened servant of God predicted to him the good tidings of his future elevation to a throne. On the faith of this, he went to Nagarkot and possessed himself of that place. On hearing of the death of Bikramājit, *Mātrigupta* abdicated and setting out for Benares lived in seclusion. *Pravarasena* was universally distinguished for his justice and liberality. He founded *Srinagar*[1] the capital of the country and

[1] The old capital previous to the erection of Pravarasenapura is stated to have been founded by Asoka (*Rāj Tarangini,* i, 104), (B.C. 263—226). It stood on the site of the present *Pāndrethān* and is said to have extended along the bank of the river from the foot of the *Takht i Sulaimān* to *Pāntasok,* a distance of more than three miles. It was still the capital in the reign of Pravarasena I, towards the end of the 5th century when the king erected a famous symbol of the god Siva, named after himself *Pravareswara.* The new capital was built by Pravarasena, II, in the beginning of the 6th century. *Anct. Geog. India,* 97.

rendered it populous during his reign with 600,000 houses. With surpassing munificence he sent to *Mātrigupta* the aggregate of eleven years' revenue of Kashmir which that personage bestowed upon the indigent. *Rājā Ranāditya* was a just prince and made many conquests. In the neighbourhood of Kishtawār near the river Chenāb, he entered a cave with all his family and many of his courtiers, and was seen no more; many strange legends are related regarding him. *Rājā Balāditya* invaded Hindustān and extended his dominions to the borders of the sea.

In the reign of *Rājā Chandrapira* the wife of a Brāhman appeared to him claiming justice, saying, that her husband had been killed and the murderer was undiscovered. He asked her if she suspected any one, to which she replied that her husband was of an amiable disposition and had no enemy, but that he often had disputations on points of philosophy with a certain person. This man was brought up but strenuously denied the accusation, and the complainant would not accept an ordeal by fire or water lest the man should employ some supernatural means of escaping it. The Rājā in his perplexity could neither eat nor sleep. An enlightened sage appearing to him in a vision taught him an incantation to be uttered over rice-meal scattered about, upon which the suspected person was to walk. If the footsteps of *two* people were observed as he passed over it, he was not to be suffered to escape. Through this suggestion the truth was discovered and punishment duly meted out. But as a Brāhman could not be put to death, an iron image of a man without a head was made and his forehead branded therewith.

Rājā Lalitāditya devoted himself to the prosperity of his kingdom and in the strength of the divine aid overran Irān, Turān, Fārs, Hindustān, Khata, and the whole habitable globe, and administered his dominions with justice. He died in the mountains of the north, and it is said that he was turned into stone by the curse of an ascetic, but others relate the story differently.

Rājā Jayāpira reached a lofty pitch of glory and his conquests were extensive. Ninety-nine thousand nine hundred and ninety-nine horses were bestowed by him in charity at Benares, and his gifts to the poor were on the same munificent scale. He asked of the elders whether the army of his grandfather Lalitāditya or his own were the larger. They answered that his contained but 80,000 litters, whereas 125,000 of such conveyances were arrayed under his grandfather's standard, by which proportion he might judge of the numerical strength of his other retinue. When he had proceeded some distance on his march of conquest, his brother-in-law, *Jajja,* who was in Kashmir disputed the throne. The nobles of the king, in anxious fear for their wives and children, betrayed him and preferred their outward reputation before their true honour. The Rājā hastened alone to Bengal, and with the aid of troops from that country, repossessed himself of his kingdom, Jajja being slain in battle.

Rājā Lalitāpira took low companions into favour and associated with buffoons, and his wise councillors withdrew from the court. His minister finding remonstrance of no avail, retired from office.

Rājā Sankar Varmā conquered Gujarāt and Sind, and overran the Deccan, but left it in the possession of its ruler. Although in the beginning of his reign he followed a virtuous course, he lacked perseverance. The intoxication of worldly prosperity plunged him into every vice.

During the reign of *Rājā Jasaskardeva,* a Brāhman lost a purse of a hundred gold *mohurs.* Under the impulse of violent grief he resolved to make away with himself. The thief hearing of this, asked him how much he would be satisfied to take, if he discovered the purse. The Brāhman answered, "Whatever you please." The thief offered him ten *mohurs.* The Brāhman, sore at heart, appealed to the Rājā who inquired into the case, and sending for the thief ordered him to restore ninety *mohurs,* intending by this, that the amount the thief desired to keep for himself, should be the portion of the Brāhman.

In the reign of *Sinhadeva,* a Muhammadan named Shāh Amir who traced his descent to Arjun the *Pandava* was in the royal service. About this time Dalju the chief commander under the king of Qandahār, attacked and plundered the kingdom. The Rājā took refuge in the mountain passes and levied forcible contributions on the people, and sent them to him and entreated him as a supplicant. The invader withdrew, dreading the severity of the weather, and many of his troops perished in the snow. About the same time also, *Rinjan,* the son of the ruler of Tibet invaded the country which was reduced to great distress. On the death of the Rājā, the sovereignty devolved on *Rinjan* who was distinguished for his munificence. He appointed *Shāh Mir* his minister whose religion, through intimacy and association with him, he eventually adopted.

When *Rājā Adindeva* died, the aforesaid Shāh Mir by specious flattery and intriguing, married his widow. In the year 742, A.H. (1341-2, A.D) he caused the *khutbah* to be read, and the coin to be minted in his own name and assumed the title of *Shamsu'ddin* and levied a tax of one-sixth on all imports into Kashmir. It had been revealed to him in a dream that he would obtain the sovereignty of the kingdom.[1]

Sultān Alāu'ddin issued an ordinance that an unchaste woman should not inherit of her husband.

Sultān Shahābu'ddin encouraged learning and proclaimed an equal administration of the laws. Nagarkot, Tibet and other places were overrun by him.

During the reign of *Sultān Qutbu'ddin* Mir Sayyid Ali Hamadāni arrived in Kashmir and was received with great favour.

Sultān Sikandar was a rigid follower of religious tradition and a bigot. He overthrew idolatrous shrines and persecuted people not of his faith. During his reign, Timur invaded Hindustān and sent him two elephants. *Sikandar* desired to pay his homage to that conqueror, but on his road to the interview he learnt that it was reported in Timur's camp that the sovereign of Kashmir was bringing with him a present of a thousand horses. Concerned at the untruthfulness of this rumour he returned and sent his excuses. Ali Shāh appointed (his brother) Zainul Abidin regent in his stead and set out for Hijāz. By the persuasion of foolish and evil advisers[2] and through inconstancy of purpose, he returned with the view of recovering his authority in Kashmir and aided by the Rājā of Jammu he took possession

---

[1] Such is the literal translation according to the punctuation of the text which I suspect is in error. Ferishta states that Shamsu'ddin abolished the exactions of his predecessors and having repaired the ruin, caused by the invasion and exactions of *Dalfu*, by written orders fixed the revenue at 1/6th of the produce. The text as corrected runs as follows: "Assumed the title of Shamsu'ddin and fixed the revenue at one-sixth of the produce. Before his arrival in Kashmir, it had been revealed to him in a dream that he would obtain &c."

[2] These, states Ferishta, were his father-in-law the *Jammu Rājā*, and the chief of *Rajauri*.

of the kingdom. Zainul Abidin set out for the Panjāb and joined Jasrat of the Khokhar[1] tribe. Ali Shāh collecting a large army advanced into the Panjāb and a great battle took place in which Ali Shāh was defeated and fell into obscurity while *Zainul Abidin* recovered the sovereignty of Kashmir. Jasrat leaving Kashmir advanced against Delhi but defeated by Sultān Bahlol Lodi retreated to Kashmir and with the assistance of an army from its monarch, conquered the Panjāb.

Zainul Abidin overran *Tibet* and *Sind*. He was a wise prince, devoted to philosophical studies and it was his fortune to enjoy universal peace. He was regarded by high and low as a special servant of God and venerated as a saint. He was credited with the power of divesting himself of his corporeal form, and he foretold that under the dynasty of the *Chaks*, the sovereignty of Kashmir would be transferred from that family to the monarchs of Hindustān, which prediction after a period of years was accomplished. His benevolence and love of his people induced him to abolish the capitation tax (*levied on other than Muslims*) and to prohibit the slaughtering of cows, as well as penalties and presents of all kinds. He added somewhat to the measure of the *Jarib*. His private revenues were drawn from copper mines. He often personally administered medicinal remedies[2] and resolved all difficult undertakings with ease. Robbers were employed in chained gangs on public works. His gentleness of disposition dissuaded men from the pursuit of game, and he himself ate no flesh or meat. He caused many works to be translated from the Arabic, Persian, Kashmiri and Sanskrit languages. During his reign musicians from Persia and Turkestān flocked to his court; among them Mulla Uudi the immediate pupil of the famous Khwājah Abdu'l Qādir arrived from Khurāsān, and Mulla Jamil who in singing and painting was pre-eminent among his contemporaries. Sultān Abu Said Mirzā sent him presents of Arab horses and dromedaries from Khurāsān

---

[1] According to Ferishta *Jasrat Shaikha Ghakar* imprisoned by Timur in Samarkand, escaped and founded or acquired a principality in the Panjāb. Zianu'l Aābidin with his aid defeated Ali Shāh who, according to one account was taken prisoner by Jasrat, and to another was expelled from Kashmir by his successful brother. This freebooter gave considerable trouble to the Sayyid dynasty and held his own against Bahlol Lodi when that chief governed Multan under Sayyid Muḥammad. See Vol. I, 456, n. for the Gakkhars (as it is there spelt) and the reference to Delmerick's history of this tribe.

[2] Ferishta says that for the encouragement of the study of medicine, he specially favoured *Sri Bhat* an eminent physician, by whose advice, the Brāhmans, expelled under Sikandar the Iconoclast, were recalled.

and Bahlol Lodi king of Delhi and Sultā Mahmud of Gujarāt were in friendly alliance with him.

Sultān Hasan, collecting an army invaded the Panjāb and encountering Tārtār[1] Khān (Lodi) in several actions devastated the country.

In the reign of *Fath Shāh,* Mir Shamsu'ddin one of the disciples of Shāh Qāsim Anwār,[2] came from Irāq and promulgated the *Nur Bakhshi* doctrines, from which period date the dissensions between *Sunnis,* and *Shias* in this country.

During the third reign of *Muhammad Shāh* when he recovered the kingdom by the help of Sultān Sikandar (Lodi of Delhi), Bābar invaded Hindustān.

During *Sultān Ibrāhim's* domination, Abdul Mākri[3] represented to Sultān Bābar that Kashmir might be conquered with little difficulty. Shaikh Ali Beg, Muhammad Khān and Mahmud Khān were therefore despatched to that country and obtained some success, but the intrigues of the people prevented a settlement and they returned with gifts and presents and *Nāzuk Shāh* succeeded to the government. Under the reign of *Muhammad Shāh* for the fourth time, the emperor Humāyun ascended the throne of Delhi, and when Mirzā Kāmrān[4] was at Lahor, the officers formerly despatched to Kashmir (Ali Beg and Muhammad Khān) persuaded him that Kashmir could be taken with little trouble. The Mirzā therefore, despatched Mahram (Beg) *Kokah* with a body of troops to that country which they occupied. Massacres were frequent and their intolerable tyranny drove the people to rise till the Mughal chiefs sued for terms and withdrew. In the year A.H. 930, (1523-4) by command of Sultān Said Khān of Kāshghar, his son

[1] The Delhi governor of the Punjāb and the country at the foot of the hills.

[2] Ferishta places the accession of Fath Shāh in A.H. 894 (A.D. 1488-9), about which time occurred the arrival of Shāh Qāsim son of Sayyid Muhammad *Nur Bakhsh,* and the establishment of his doctrines as the prevailing creed. All religious grants and places of worship were made over to this sect, among the most illustrious converts to which were the Chak tribe.

[3] He was the son of Ibrahim Mākri who was minister in chief to Muhammad Shāh during his second reign. Abdāl Mākri his son played a considerable part in the stirring events of this time and was eventually driven from court by the intrigues of the minister Malik Kāji. He went to India and incited Bābar to the conquest of Kashmir. Fearing that the inhabitants would be opposed to the foreign rule of the Mughals, the enthronement of Nāzuk the son of Ibrāhim was adopted as a pretext to conciliate the Kashmiris, who, on his instalment in authority, dismissed the troops of Bābar with conciliatory gifts.

[4] Brother of the Emperor, governor of Kabul and Qandahār, to whom Humāyun had ceded the government of the Panjāb and the Indus frontier.

Sikandar Khān and Mirzā Haidar advanced into Kashmir at the head of 10,000 troops by way of Tibet and Lār, and taking an enormous booty retired after a short time under terms of peace. In the year A.H. 948 (1541-2) Mirzā Haidar, by command of Humāyun a second time entered Kashmir, guided by some of the natives of that country, as has been related in former accounts, and took possession of a part of Great Tibet. Kāji Chak came to Hindustān and bringing with him the aid of an army from Sher Khān, engaged Mirzā Haidar but was defeated. The Mirzā won over the Kashmiris by peaceful and conciliatory measures, so that he succeeded in having the *Khutbah* read and the coin minted in the name of Humāyun, the Kashmiris having previously read the *Khutbah* in the name of Nāzuk Shāh.

At the present time under the sway of His Imperial Majesty it is the secure and happy abode of many nationalities, including natives of Persia and Turkestān as well as of Kashmir.

CORRECT LIST OF RULERS OF KASHMIR.*

Historical Kings of Kashmir.

Asoka	C 260 B.C.
Jalauka.	
Kanishka.	
Gananda III.	
Mihir Kula. ...	
Karkota dynasty.	
Durlabha Vardhana ...	627-649 A.D.
Pratāpāditya II or Durlabhaka. ...	
Chandrapida	713, 720.
Tārāpida.	
Lalitāditya Muktapida ...	736, 747.
Kuvalayapida	
Vajrāditya	Kalhana's *Chronicle* unattested by coin or other evidence.
Bāppiyaka	
Prithivyapida	
Samgrāmapida	
Jayapida	end of the 8th Century.
Cippata Jayapida ...	826-838.

* *Camb. Hist. of India*, iii. 277-293.

Ajitapida	... ...	850/1.
Anangapida		
Utpalapida		
Line of Utpala	... ...	855/856—939 A.D.
Utpala	... ...	died 853.
Sukhavarman	... ...	r. 855-56.
Avantivarman	... ...	856-883.
Sankaravarman	...	883-902.
Gopālvarman	... ...	902-904.
Sankata	... ...	rule for 10 days in 904
Sugandhā, Gopālvarman's widow	... ...	defacto ruler 904-'6.
Pārtha	... ...	906-921.
Pangu	... ...	921-923.
Chakravarman	... ...	923-933, 935-937.
Suravarman I	... ...	933-934.
Unmattāvanti	... ...	937-939.
Suravarman II	... ...	939.
Line of Viradeva	... ...	939-949.
Yasaskaradeva	... ...	939-948.
Sangrāmadeva	... ...	948-49.
Line of Abhinava	... ...	949-1003.
Parvagupta	... ...	949-950.
Kshemagupta(Diddā-Kshemā)		950-958.
Abhimanyu	... ...	958-972.
Nandigupta	... ...	973.
Tribhuvana	... ...	973-975.
Bhimagupta	... ...	975-980.
Diddā	... ...	980-81—1003.
Lohara dynasty	... ...	1003-1171.
Sangrāmarāja	... ...	1003-1028 A.D.
Harirāja	... ...	Rule for 22 days.
Ananta	... ...	1028-1063 A.D.
Kalasa	... ...	1063-1089.
Utkarsa	... ...	1089.
Harsa	... ...	1089-1101.
Period of civil war and internecine strife	... ...	1101-1339.
Uccala	... ...	1101-11.
Salhana	... ...	1111-12.
Sussala	... ...	1112-28.
Jayasinha	... ...	1128-1155.
Paramānuka	... ...	1155-1165.
Vantideva	... ...	1165-1171,

Line of Buppādeva	...	1171-1286.
Buppādeva ...	...	1171-1180.
Jassaka ...	...	1180-98.
Jagadeva ...	...	1198-1212-13.
Rājadeva ...	...	1212-13-1235.
Sangrāmadeva ...	...	1235-52.
Rāmadeva ...	...	1252-73.
Laksmandeva ...	...	1273-86.
Sinhadeva ...	...	1286-1301.
Tibetan dynasty		
Rinchana ...	...	1320-23.
Udyāndeva ...	...	1323-38.
Kotadevi ...	...	1338.
Muslim Sultans of Kashmir.		
Shamsuddin Shah	...	1346-1349.
Jamshed ...	...	1349-1350.
Alauddin ...	...	1350-59.
Shihābuddin ...	...	1359-1378.
Qutbuddin ...	...	1378-1394.
Sikandar ...	...	1394-1416.
Ali Shah ...	...	1416-1420.
Zain-ul-ābidin ...	...	1420-1470.
Haidar Shah ...	...	1470—Dec. 1471 or Jany. 1472.
Hasan Shah ...	...	1472-1489.
Muhammad Shah	...	1489, 1497, 1499-1526, 1529-1534.
Fath Shah ...	...	1489-1497, 1498-99.
Ibrāhim Shah, I	...	1526-27.
Nāzuk Shah ...	...	1527-29, 1540, 1551-52.
Shamsuddin Shah	...	1534-1540.
A new line.		
Mirza Haidar Shah	...	Nov. 1540-1551.
Ibrāhim Shah ...	...	1552-55.
Ismail Shah ...	...	1555-57.
Habib Shah ...	...	1557-61.
Ghāzi Shah ...	...	1561-1563, 64.
Nāsiruddin Husain Shah	...	1564-1569-70.
Ali Shah ...	...	1570-1579.
Lohar Chakk ...	...	1579-80.
Yusuf Shah ...	...	1579, 1580-86.
Yaqub Shah ...	...	1586-89

Peoples of Kashmir.

Bakhri—a clan claiming Rajput origin, found in several districts of the Panjab, converted to Islam by Bahauddin Zakariya, Rose, *Glossary of Panjab tribes and castes,* II, 39.

Khasa—Khasaka tribe, mod. Khakhas, Stein, *Chron.* II, 519.

Khawar—Var. *Kahu*,—*Either* Kahoi, a Jat clan found in Amritsar and Multan, *or* Kahut, another Jat clan found in Gujrat and Rawalpindi districts, Rose, 245.

Khamash—Rose mentions a Jat clan *Khamah,* resident in Multan, *ibid,* 491.

Bat, Bhat, or Bhatta,—Jarrett's classification of them as Muhammadans is not tenable, for there are Hindu Bhats as well, Rose, *ibid,* 94-101.

Kambah—Kamboh, "one of the finest cultivating tribes" found also in the Panjab, claiming descent from Raja Karan and saying that their ancestor fled to Kashmir. They belong to different religious pursuasions. Rose, II, 442-446.

Doni—*Either* Dhunia, a weaver caste *or* Dun, so called from Duhna to milk, hence milkman, Rose, II, p. 251.

Chak—*Either* a Kamboh clan *or* a sept of Jats, Rose, II, p. 146.

Shal—conjectured *Chahal,* Rose, III.

Siyahi—Sahi ?, sometimes pronounced Chhahi in Ludhiana, a Jat tribe claiming descent from Solar Rajputs, Rose, III, p. 342. *Shahiya* ?

Rawar—is it Rayar, a Jat clan of Amritsar ? Rose, III, 332.

Sahasu—Sahasni ?, a Jat clan of Amritsar, Rose, III, 342.

Thakur—representing the high-caste population of Kashmir, Rose, III, p. 326-329.

NOTES ON PLACES IN KASHMIR.

(*Compiled by Prof. N. B. Roy*)

P. 351. Qambar Ver—possibly the hill of Kamelana Kotta (anc. *Kramavarta*), a watch-station on the Pir Pantsal range. Stein, *Chron.* II, 292.

P. 352. Hasti Bhanj—Stein (*Chron.* Book I, n. 302) derives the name from Sanskrit *hasti,* elephant and W. Panjabi *vanj* to go. He describes this route in *J.A.S.B.*, 1895, pp. 376 sq., *Chron.* II, 394.

Tangtalah—5 miles n. of Pir Pantsal pass. For details Stein (*Chron.* II, 398).

P. 356. *Behat*—Vyath or Vitasta, embodiment of Parvati. Stein, Bk. I, 29, its legendary origin and course above Srinagar. *Chron.* II, 411, 415. *Cam. Hist. Ind.*, III, 286.

Mar—ancient name *Mahasarit.* (Stein, *Chron.* ii. 416). This stream drains the Dal lake to the east of the city of Srinagar, and carries off the surplus waters of the lake towards the Vitasta (Jhelum).

Lacham-Kul—canal of Srinagar (Stein, *Chron.* II, 457).

Sayyid Ali Hamadoni,—For anecdotes about him, Vigne, I, 82-83; shrine, Moorcroft, II, 120, Percy Brown, II, 83.

P. 357. *Brang*—modern *Bring.*

Sendhbrar—mod. *Sundbrar.* Stein identifies it with the spring of the goddess *Samdhya.* The spring flows during uncertain periods in the early summer, three times in the day and three times in the night. (*Chron.* I, note 33. *Chron.* II). Sendhbrar—Vigne writes about this tirtha saying,—on the 15th of Har (corresponding to 13th June), several thousand people are assembled, nearly naked—and wait for the rising of the water; those who are nearest to it, shaking peacock's feather over it as an act of enticement and veneration. When the basin perceptibly begins to fill, the immense multitude exclaim Sondi, Sondi, (it appears), and then they fill their brazen water-vessels, drink and perform their ablutions and return towards their home. Read Bernier's description, *Travels,* Brock's ed., II, p. 153.

P. 357. Kokar Nag—a *tirtha* in the Bring valley, situated a mile above the village of Bidar. The seven fountains inside the temple, mentioned by Abul Fazl, are the spring now known as *Sweda Nag*. (Stein, 1899, *J.A.S.B.*, 181, *Chron.* II, 469.

Iron mine—Located by Vigne, I, 337, he describes the route from Shahabad to Sof-ahun where the principal or in fact the only iron works of the valley are to be seen.

Vej Brar—modern Vija-brar, one of the most famous *tirthas* of Kashmir, so called from the ancient shrine of Siva Vijayeshwar. The place being situated on the way to Martand and Amarnath, is much frequented even at the present day. (Stein, *J.A.S.B.*, pp. 173-175. *Chron.* II, 463).

P. 358. *Nandi-marg*—a beautiful mountain down situated on the eastern slopes of the Pir Pantsal range, about 12 miles s.e. of Supyan, 33. 34 N. 75 E. Bates, *Kashmir Gazetteer,* 287. Vigne, I, 299.

Pampur—mod. Pampar, ancient Padma-pur, the chief place of the Vihi pargana. Stein, *Chron.* II, 450; Stein, *J.A.S.B.*, 167.

P. 359. Zewan—mod. Zevan, ancient *Jaya-van,* in the Vihi pargana. Here is a pool sacred to Takshaka, the lord of snakes, which is visited annually by pilgrims. (Stein, *J.A.S.B.*, 166, *Chron.* Bk. I, 220 *note,* 166).

Khriu—mod. *Khruv,* ancient *Khaduvi.* Stein noted an abundance of fine springs in and about Khruv, and a mystical diagram called Sayambhu chakra, above the village which is held sacred to Jvalamukhi Durga, *Chron.* II, 459.

Maru Adwin—*Madivād-van* valley situated along the range that forms the eastern frontier of Kashmir, running from the Zoji-la almost due south towards Kastawar. (Stein, *Chron.* II, 435). Vigne (*Travels,* i. 354) noticed here a tank, 100 yards square.

Achh Dal—misreading for *Achabal,* a short distance from Sundabrar. Here was formerly a country-house of the kings of Kashmir, and then of the Mughal Emperors. See Bernier's *Travels*.

Khattar—mod. *Kutahar,* in the valley of Arapath or Harsapath which opens to the east of Islamabad. Stein derives the word from *Kapateshwar,* a *tirtha* on the southern side of the valley close to the village of *Kother.* (Stein, *J.A.S.B.*, 179, *Chron.* II, 467).

Kotihar—mod. *Kother,* near Achabal. Here is the deep spring of *Pāpa-sudan* (or Remover of sin), mentioned by Kalhan. Siva is believed to have shown himself here in the disguise of pieces of wood floating on the water.

(Stein, *J.A.S.B.*, 179). The route to this *tirtha* is described fully by Vigne (i. 351).

Wular—*Vular,* ancient Holada. It is situated in the pargana of the same name, comprising the valley opening to the n.e. of the Vitasta, between Dachunpor and Vihi. (Stein, Chron. I, Bk. I, note 306, II, 460, *J.A.S.B.* p. 168).

Matan—Martand *tirtha,* situated in the eastern portion of the Lidar valley, at a distance of about 2 miles from Islamabad. For a description of its most famous temple, Vigne (i. 385-391), Moorcroft (ii. 255-256), Percy Brown (*Ind. Arch.* i. 181), Stein (*J.A.S.B.*, 176-178).

P. 360. Well of Babylon—The reference is to the imprisonment of two angels, Harut and Marut, in a well in Demavand for their submission to sin and temptation. (*Encyclo. Islam,* ii. 272). Vigne says that at a distance of 150 yards from the temple there was the residence of a faqir whose duty was to superintend the existence of a well called the *Chah-i-Babul.* (*Travels,* I, 361).

Kharwar-para—mod. Khovur-pur. The source mentioned here is a small river that feeds the northern branch of the principal tributary of the Behat. (Stein, *Chron.* II, 465).

Dachchhin-para—mod. Dachunpor, a district situated east of the confluence of the Vitasta and the Gambhira, and comprising the whole western side of the Lidar valley, and also the low-lying tract between the Vitasta and the lower course of the Visoka. (Stein, *J.A.S.B.*, 170, Stein, *Chron.* II, 461).

Amarnath—Situated north of the Lidar valley but south of the high peak, (about 10 miles east-south of Zoji-La) that marks the eastern boundary of Kashmir. For a description of this tirtha which is the most popular of Kashmirian *pilgrimage places,* read, Stein, *J.A.S.B.*, p. 94, 163-4, *Chron.* Vigne, II, 7-8, Moorcroft, II, pp. 252-53.

P. 361. Dāl lake—Situated east of Srinagar, and forming one of the most favoured spots of the Srinagar valley. The floating gardens which covered its surface in Abul Fazl's time are described by Stein, *J.A.S.B.*, 105, *Chron.* II, 417, Moorcroft, II, 115, 137-140, Vigne, II, 90-91, Drew, *Jammu and Kashmir,* 186.

Thid—ancient Thed which was adorned by king Aryaraja with *mathas,* divine images and lingas. Stein, *Chron.* II, 135. The seven springs mentioned by Abul Fazl still exist, but other remains do not, Stein, *J.A.S.B.*, 1879, *Chron.* II, 454.

Shalamar—Shalimar, this *bagh* along with *Nishat* and *Nasim,* form the three most delightful places on the Dal lake, Drew, *History of Jammu and Kashmir,* 187, described by Vigne, *Travels,* Vol. II, 100-101, Stein, *Chron.* II, 456 fn.

Ishibari—mod. Isabar, lying a short distance from the Nishat garden and Suresvari Ksetra, still sacred to Durga-Suresvari who is worshipped on a high crag to the east of the village. Of the several springs in and about Isabar, two are mentioned by Abul Fazl,—Suryasar and Shakarnag, one of them might be what is stated by Stein to be *Gupta-ganga,* forming the chief attraction of the place and filling an ancient stone-lined tank in the centre of the village, Stein, *J.A.S.B.*, p. 161, Stein, *Chron.* II, 455.

Rambal—mod. *Ranyal,* anc. Hiranyapur, north of Srinagar, situated at the foot of the ridge running down to the opening of the Sindh Valley. Stein mentions the existence of a spring to the south of the village. Stein, *J.A.S.B.*, 163, *Chron.* II, 456.

P. 362. Banihal—anc. Bansala. Stein says nothing about the temple of Durga mentioned by Abul Fazl, but he refers to a group of peaks sacred to Brahma, Vishnu and Siva. (Stein, *J.A.S.B.*, 71, *Chron.* II, 393). The pass of the same name has always been a convenient route of communication towards the Upper Chenab valley and the eastern Panjab hill states, *Chron.* II, 392.

Ver—Old name of Shahabad pargana, comprising the valley of the Sandran river (Stein, *Chron.* II, 469).

Vernag—Situated in the Sandran valley. The stone temples of Abul Fazl's time have disappeared; their materials having been partly used for the construction of a fine stone enclosure which Jahangir built around the spring. (Stein, *J.A.S.B.*, 182, *Chron.* II, 411, 469. Vigne, *Travels,* i. 332. Moorcroft, ii. 249).

Kambar—Bates mentions a village Kammar in the Shahabad valley, near the left bank of the Sandran river. Below this village lies at present the ziarat of Qadam Rasul. *Kas. Gaz.*, 223, nothing is said about the spring.

Devsar—mod. *Devasar,* anc. *Deva-saras,* drained by the Visoka. (Stein, *J.A.S.B.*, 183, *Chron.* II, 470).

Balau—probably anc. Bilava, about 4 miles north-east of Drabgam, Stein, *Chron.* II, 473.

Veshau—mod. *Visoka.* Stein refers to a place named Gudar where a small stream called the Godavari falls down the hill, as a *tirtha* of some repute (*J.A.S.B.*, 184).

Kuthar—Jarrett suggests Kausar-nag, a lake two miles long described by Stein (*J.A.S.B.*, 71). Stein, *Chron.* II, 393.

P. 363. Shukroh—Jarrett's identification with *Zuyru* (4 m. n. of the capital) is far-fetched. Stein identifies it with the modern *Sukru,* where the ancient *tirtha* of Kalyanpur (mod. *Kalampur*) still stands, on the high road from Pir Pantsal to Srinagar. The fountain of the *Ain* is that at the mod. *Buda-brar* (anc. Bheda-giri). (Stein, *J.A.S.B.*, 186).

Nila-nag—situated in a valley between two spurs descending from the Pir Pantsal range. Stein points out that Abul Fazl has here made the mistake of transferring to this spring the legends of the famous Nila-nag at Vernag. (Stein, *J.A.S.B.*, 190, *Chron.* II, 475).

Biruwa—mod. *Biru* (anc. *Bahurupa*), situated west of Dunts and towards the Pir Pantsal range. (Stein, *J.A.S.B.*, 192).

Halthal—Halathal in Yech. Stein took it for *Salasthal* (*Chron.* II, 475).

Lar—anc. *Lahara,* comprises the whole of the valleys drained by the Sind and its tributaries. (Stein, *Chron.* II, 488).

P. 364. Shahab-ud-dinpur—*Shadipur,* at the confluence of the Vitasta and the Sindhu, (Stein, *Chron.* II, 379).

Tulmula—mod. *Tulamul* (anc. *Tulamalya*) situated in the midst of the Sind delta. According to Stein, the spring here is still held sacred. (Stein, *J.A.S.B.*, 210, *Chron.* II, 488).

Satpur—

Bhutesar—in the narrow gorge of the Kankanai river, which flows past the south foot of the spur. Two miles above Vāngath are found the ruins of some 17 temples of various size and dimension. These ruins were identified by Stein with the temple of Bhutesar. (Stein, *J.A.S.B.*, 211).

Khoihama—mod. *Khuyahom* (anc. *Khuyasrama*) stretching in a semi-circle round the north shore of the Volur lake. (Stein, *Chron.* II, 488, *J.A.S.B.*, 209).

Volur lake—anc. Mahāpadmasaras, 12 *kos* n.w. of Srinagar, a most striking physical feature in the western portion of Kashmir. For details, Stein, *Chron.* II, 423, Moorcroft, II, 111.

Zain Lanka—built by Sultan Zain-ul-abidin, in the midst of the Volur lake. (Stein, *Chron.* II, 423). Described by Moorcroft, II, 224.

Machhamu—Stein suggests that the village of *Ratasum* represents it, though there is a pargana of the name *Manchahom.* (*Chron.* II, 477).

Paraspur—anc. *Parihaspur,* the capital of Lalitaditya. The plateau on which it stood, is "about two miles from north to south and its greatest breadth is not much over a mile." The Badrihel canal bounds it on the north. In the S.W. part are the ruins of two large temples, much decayed but still showing dimensions which considerably exceed those of the great temple of Martand. On that part of the Udar which lies to the n.e. and towards the Badrihel *nala,* there is a whole series of ruined structures. The four great temples of Vishnu Parihasa-Keshava, Mukta-Keshava, Mahavaraha, and Govardhan-dhara, as well as the Rajvihar with its colossal image of Buddha, must all be looked for among the ruins. Extremely decayed condition." (Stein, *Chron.* II, 477, sec. iv, 194-204).

P. 365. Kamraj—anc. *Krama-rajya,* as distinguished from *Maraj* (*Madhya-rajya*). In modern times it designates only the parganas to the west and north-west of the Volur lake (Stein, *Chron.* II, 436).

Trahgam—anc. *Tri-gami,* mod. *Trigam,* 1½ miles n.e. of the Paraspur ruins. (Stein, *Chron.* II, 329, 479).

Kargon—Kherigam, a short way from Sardi (Stein, *Chron.* II, 282).

Soyam—(derived from *Swayambhu*) half a mile south-west of the village of Nichahom, in the Machipur pargana, where volcanic phenomena are observed in a shallow hollow formed between banks of clay and sand. Hot vapours issue from fissures in the ground. (Stein, *Chron.* I, Bk. I, note 34).

Haehamun—mod. *Hayahom,* on the pilgrim route to Sarada (Stein, *Chron.* II, 280, 486).

Padmate—miswritten for *Madmati* (=Madhumati). Stein suggests that Abul Fazl here confuses the Madhumati with the Kishanganga, which (latter) alone flows from the Dard country. The notice of gold being found in the river, clearly refers to the Kishanganga, which drains a mountain region still known as auriferous. (Stein, *Chron.* II, 247).

Dardu—mod. Dard.

Sarada tirtha—situated on a small hill above the junction of the Kishanganga and the Madhumati. (Stein, *Chron.* I, Bk. I, note 37, for temple ii. 284-287).

P. 368. Phak—comprising the tract lying between the east shore of the Anchiar, the range towards the Sind valley and the hills which enclose the Dal on the east and the south.

Khattar—Kutahar pargana, comprising the valley Arupath or Harsapatha opening to the east of Islamabad. Stein, *Chron.* Vol. II, p. 467.

Matan—comprising the plateau on which the temple of Martand stands. Stein, *Chron.* Vol. II, 466.

P. 369. Adwin—Adavin, lies north of Divasar, reaching from the western end of Khur-Naravao to the lower course of the Visoka. Stein, *Chron.* Vol. II, 471.

Itch = Yech—anc. Iksika, comprises the tract to the immediate vicinity of Srinagar. Stein, *Chron.* II, 475.

Batu—Bot, adjoining Adavin on the north-east, Stein, *Chron.* II, 472.

Devsar—Divasar, adjoins the pargana of Shahabad Ver on the west and comprises the tract of alluvial plain drained by the Vesau, Stein, *Chron.* II, 470.

Zinahpur—Zainapur, comprising the northernmost portion of Adawin, Stein, *Chron.* II, 471.

Soparsaman—Suparsamun, comprising the villages lying at the foot of the spurs descending into the plain west and north-west of Supiyan. Stein, *Chron.* II, 472.

Nagam—(anc. Nagram), situated north of Chrath Pargana, Stein, *Chron.* II, 474.

Zinahkar—Zaingir, comprises the fertile Karewa tract between the Volur and the left bank of the Pohur River, Stein, *Chron.* II, 487.

Khoihama—Khuyahom, stretches in a semi-circle round the north shore of the Volur lake. Stein, *Chron.* II, 488, Bates, 233.

P. 370. Indarkol—Mod. Andarkoth, (anc. Jayapura) comprises the marshy tract south of the Volur. Stein, *Chron.* II, 480).

Paraspor—comprising the well-defined little tract lying between the marshes on the left bank of the Vitasta immediately to the south-west of Shadipur. Stein, *Chron*. II, 300. According to Stein, the Paraspor Udar, until some sixteen years ago, continued to form a separate pargana, *ibid*, p. 333.

Patan—Anc. Samkarapur, situated on the direct road between Srinagar and Baramula. Stein, *Chron*. Vol. II, 481.

Bankal—Bangil, anc. Bhangila, situated between Firozpur and Patan, sloping down from the mountains to the morass on the left bank of the Jhelum.

Telkam—Tilgama, a very small pargana, adjoins Patan.

Dinsu—Dunts, west of Vech and close to Srinagar. Stein, *Chron*. II, 470.

Sair-ul-Mawazi—lying on the left bank of the Vitasta with Chrath. Stein, *Chron*. II, 474.

Khoi—Khuhy, north of Patan and Tilagam.

Karohan—Karnav, anc. Karnaha, north-west of Kashmir lying between the Kishanganga and the Kajanāg range. Stein, *Chron*. II, 405.

P. 378. Solomon's Hill—mod. Takht-Sulaiman, anc. Gopadri. The temple referred to is the shrine of Siva Jyesthesvara, built on the summit by Gopāditya; for the description of this tirtha, Stein, *Chron*. II, 159.

Sarkār of. Pakli.

Its length is 35 and its breadth 25 *kos*. It is bounded on the east by *Kashmir*, on the north by *Kator*,[1] on the south by the territory of the *Gakhars*, and on the west by *Atak Benāres*. Timur left a few troops to hold this tract, and their descendants remain there to this day. Snow lies perpetually on these mountains and at times falls on the plains. The period of winter is longer than the summer. The rainfall is somewhat similar to Hindustān. It is watered by three rivers, the *Kishan Ganga*, the *Bihat* and the *Sindh*. The language of the country differs from that of Kashmir, Hindustān or Zābulistān. Vetches and barley are the principal crops. Apricots, peaches and walnuts grow wild, it not being the custom to plant fruit trees. Game and horses, camels and buffaloes are of middling account: goats and poultry, plentiful. The rulers of this district generally paid tribute to Kashmir.

Sarkār of Sawād (Swāt).

It comprises three districts, those of *Bimbar*, *Swāt* and *Bajaur*. The first is 16 *kos* long by 12 broad and is bounded by *Pakli* on the east, *Kator* and *Kāshghar*[2] on the north, *Atak Benāres* on the south and *Swāt* on the west. Two roads approach it from Hindustān, *viz.*, the *Sherkhāni* pass and the *Balandari Kotal;* although both routes are difficult to traverse, the first is the more rugged.

The second district (Swāt) is 40 *kos* in length by 5 to 15 in breadth. On the east lies *Bimbar;* to the north *Kator* (Kunar) and *Kāshghar;* to the south *Bigrām*[3] and on the west *Bajaur*. It possesses many defiles. Near the *Damghār* pass which leads to *Kāshghar* is the town of *Manglor*[4] the

---

[1] Ferishta says (p. 144) that Kattor or Katār is a place of note in the Kafiristān country, but in the maps Kunar occupies a corresponding position.

[2] By Kāshghar cannot be meant the well-known town of E. Turkestān which is too far removed, but Chitral or Kāshkar, which, according to Erskine, (*Bābar's Memoirs*) is a corruption of Kāshghar with the territory of which it was long included. The *Kasia* or *Akhassa regio* of Ptolemy beyond Mount Imaus has perhaps given its name to both Kāshghar and Kashmir.

[3] *Bigrām* is said by Cunningham (p. 29) to signify "the city" *par excellence* and is applied to 3 other ancient sites near Kābul, Jalālābād and Peshāwar. Masson derives the name from the Turki *bi* or *be* "chief" and the Hindi *grām*.

[4] *Manglaur* was the capital of Udyāna, the Sanskrit name for the modern districts of Panjkora, Bajaur, Swāt and Buner. It is mentioned by Hwen Thang as Mung-kie-li or Mangalu.

residence of the governor. It is entered by two routes from Hindustān, *viz.*, the passes of *Malkand Baj* [Malakand] and *Sherkhānah*. It has no extremes of heat or cold, and though snow falls, it does not lie in the plains for more than three or four days; in the mountains it is perpetual. It is springtime here during the periodical rains of Hindustān. Rainfall occurs and the spring and autumn are very delightful. Its *flora* are those of Turkestān and India, wild violets and narcissus covering the meadows, and various kinds of fruit trees grow wild. Peaches and pears are excellent, and fine hawks and falcons are obtained. It also possesses an iron mine.

The third district (Bajaur) is 25 *kos* in length by 5 to 10 in breadth. On the east lies *Swāt*, on the north *Kator* and *Kāshghar*, on the south *Bigrām*, and on the west *Kuner* (and) *Nurkil*.[1] Numerous passes lead from Kābul.

An ancient mausoleum[2] exists here, and there is a strong fortress which is said to be the residence of the governor. Amir Sayyid Ali Hamadāni died here and his body was conveyed to *Khutlān* by his last testament. Its climate is similar to that of Swāt, but the extremes of cold and heat are greater. It has only three roads, one from Hindustān called *Dānishkol*, and two from Kābul, one called *Samaj* and the other *Kuner* and *Nurkil*, the easiest of these being *Dānishkol*. Adjoining this and between the mountains and the Indus and Kabul rivers, is a plain, 30 *kos* in length by 20 to 25 *kos* in breadth.

The whole of this tract of hill and plain is the domain of the *Yusufzai* clan. In the time of *Mirzā Ulugh Beg* of Kābul, they migrated from Kābul to this territory and wrested it from the Sultāns who affected to be descended from a daughter of Alexander Bicornutus. It is said that this monarch left some of his treasures in these parts with a few of his kindred and to this day the descendants of this band dwell in these mountains and affect to show their genealogical descent from Alexander.[3]

---

[1] Erskine states that *Kuner* and *Nurgil* form another Tumān situated in the midst of Kafiristān which forms its boundary. Nurgil, says Bāber, lies on the west and Kuner on the east of the Cheghān sarāi or Kāmeh river, p. 143.

[2] The text is here confused, and the translation has been made after correction from Babar's *Memoirs*.

[3] See Elphinstone's *Cabul*. App. C, p. 617.

Under the present ever-during Imperial sway, of the lawless inhabitants of this country, some have been put to death, others imprisoned, while some happily dwell under their tribal rule.

Sarkār of Daur, Banu and Isakhel.

This territory is to the south-east of *Kābul*, and is inhabited entirely by Afghāns. It is the principal settlement of the Shirāni, Kararāni and Waziri tribes.

Sarkār of Qandahār.

It is situated in the third climate. Its length from *Qalāt Banjārah* to *Ghor* and *Gharjistān*[1] is 300 *kos* : its breadth from *Sind* to *Farah* is 260 *kos*. On its east lies *Sind* ; to the north *Ghor* and *Gharjistān;* on the south *Siwi*, and on the west *Farah; Kābul* and *Ghaznin* on the north-east. Its mountains are covered with perpetual snow which seldom falls in the city.

Eighteen *dinārs* make a *tumān*, and each *tumān* is equivalent to 800 *dāms* [=Rs. 20]. The *tumān* of Khurāsān is equal in value to 30 rupees and the *tumān* of Irāq to 40.*

Grain is for the most part taken in *kharwārs*, the *kharwār* being equivalent to 40 Qandahāri *man*, or 10 of Hindustān.

The capital of the district is *Qandahār*. Its longitude is 107° 40′, and the latitude 33° 40′. It has two forts. The summer heats are extreme and the cold in winter is inconsiderable, but the ice-pits are filled in December and January. Once in three or four years a fall of snow occurs and is hailed with delight. Flowers and fruits are in abundance. Its wheat is extremely white, and is sent as a present of value to distant countries. At a distance of five *kos* is a hill called *Azhdarkoh* (the Dragon Hill) in which is a wonderful cave known as the *Cave of Jamshid*. People

---

[1] Its limits are defined by Erskine, (p. 152), within Herat on the west, Farah on the south and Ghor on the east. *Encyclo. Islam,* ii. 141, gives "Ghardjistan, a tract on the upper valley of the Murghāb in Afghan Turkistan, . . . the country now occupied by the Firoz Kohis." [J. S.]

* *Tumān. Encyclo. Islam,* iv. 836. In the period of Mongol dominion, the *tumān* was 10,000 *dinars*=60,000 *dirhems*. Value varied from country to country.

enter with lighted lamps, but the oppression of its atmosphere prevents exploration of its extent. Eight *kos* from *Qālāt* is a large mountain in the side of which is a huge cave called *Ghār i Shāh* (the King's Cave). Within it are two natural columns, one of which touches the roof of the cave and is 30 yards high. Water flows down it and enters a basin at its foot. The other is 11 yards in height. The waters of the *Hirmand* (Helmand) which rises between Balkh, and Kābul, flow in this direction along the skirts of the mountains. The meaning of *Hirmand* is 'abounding in blessings'. *Maulānā Muinu'ddin* in his history of Kurāsān records that it feeds a thousand streams. At a distance of 16 *kos* is a mountain, at the base of which is an area of land called *Natil* [Tānil], formerly full of watercourses, where melons are grown in great quantity and perfection. The mountain has several clear springs. There is also an iron-mine, and at the foot of the mountain is an iron-foundry for the smelting of the ore, a work of ancient times.

West of Qandahār is a long torrid tract of country, (*Garmsir*) through which flows the *Hirmand*. One side of it touches the *Dāwar*[1] territory, and on the other *Sistān* There are many forts and much cultivation on both sides of the river. In this neighbourhood once stood a large city, the residence of the Sultāns of Ghor, and many ruins still exist of the palaces of its ancient kings.

Between the *Hirmand* and Qandahār is the well-known city of *Maimand*, described in old astronomical tables.

Wheat and barley are called *Safedbari*.[1] The *jarib* of sixty (square) yards is used for measurements, but they reckon 30 yards of this according to the *Hijāzi jarib*, each yard of 24½ digits, the *gaz* there in use; equal altogether to 54 *gaz* of Qandahār. In the exchequer, out of every ten *kharwārs*, two are taken for the minister of finance on account of revenue and *jihāt* cesses. Cultivation is reckoned under seven heads. In the registers, the best kind of land is marked with an *'Ain* [Arabic letter] and calculating the

---

[1] *Dāwar* or *Zamin Dāwar*, lies west of the Helmand, below the hills, in S.W. Afghanistan.

[2] Var. and G. *safedtari*. I am disposed to think the marginal reading correct and that it signifies *white crops* in contradistinction to the *sabzbari* or *green crops* that follow lower down, though it is not easy to see why rice should be relegated to the green, rather than the white class. There are, however, two kinds of *shāli* rice, the white requiring deep water and the red needing only a moist soil.

produce of each *jārib* at 3 *kharwārs*, 24 *man* are taken as revenue. Thus :

No.	Kind of land.	Distinguishing Marks. Arabic letter.	Produce in *Kharwārs*.	Revenue in *mans*
1	Best.	'ain	3	24
2	Best and Medium.	toi 'ain	2½	20
3	Medium.	toi	2	16
4	Medium and Poor.	dal toi	1½	12
5	Poor.	dal	1	8
6	Poor and Poorest.	dal-dal, dal	30 *man*.	6
7	Poorest.	dal-dal	8	4

But if the husbandman is incapable of sustaining this class of assessment, the produce is divided into three heaps, two of which are taken by the tenant, and the third is again subdivided into three shares, two of which go to the revenue department and the third is charged to incidental expenses.

The revenue from grapes also is taken by agreement and by paying a special rate. In the latter case experts appraise the average outturn of the vineyard and exact 4 *bābaris* for each *kharwār*. Under the reigns of Bābar and Humāyun the rate was fixed at 2 *bābaris* and 4 *tangahs*. The *babari* is one *miskāl* weight and 2½ are equivalent to the rupee. Besides these three (wheat, barley, grapes), upon nine other articles called *sabzbari*, 7½ *bābaris* are taken for every *jarib*, formerly rated at 5 *bābaris*, *viz.*, rice (Shāli), musk-melons, water-melons, cucumbers, onions, turnips, carrots and lettuce. On other crops than these, two *bābaris* were formerly taken, the Turkomāns exacting three.

In the torrid tract (above-mentioned, between Dāwar and Sistan), the *safedbari* crops are divided into three heaps according to the Qandahār custom and all crops paying special rates are registered under the *'Ain* and *Toi* class (No. 2), and for every *jarib*, 50 *man* of the torrid tract (*Garmsir*) equalling 20 *man* of Qandahār, are taken. The *kharwār* of this district is 100 *man*, equivalent to 10 *man* of Hindustān. Grapes are treated in the same manner as at Qandahār. All articles under *Sabzbari*, pay two *babaris* on each *jarib*.

In the *Dāwar* tract, produce under *safedbari* is apportioned in three heaps as described above and the exchequer receives for every 4 *jaribs*, one *kharwār* weight of *Dāwar*, which is equavalent to one *kharwār* and ten *man* of Qandahār, and for other produce, one *kharwār* on three *jaribs*.[1]

Sarkār of Qandahār.

Containing 24 *Mahals*. Revenue 8,114½ *tumāns*, 39,600 *dinārs*; 45,775 *sheep*; 45 Balochi horses; 3,752,977 *kharwārs* of grain; 420 *man* of rice; 2 *kharwārs* of flour; 20 *man* of clarified butter. It furnishes 13,875 Cavalry and 25,260 Infantry. Qandahār city—5,270 *tumāns* in cash; 35,120 *kharwārs* of corn; 550 horse; 1,000 foot.

Dependencies east of Qandahār.

Territory of Duki,[1] has a fort of unbaked brick. 6 *tumāns* in money; 1,800 *kharwārs* of grain; 12,000 sheep; 15 Balochi horses; Afghāns of the *Tarin* and and *Kākar* tribes; 500 horse, and 1,000 foot.

,, *of Pashang;* has an old fort of unbaked briek. 33 *tumāns* in money; 3,200 sheep; 500 *kharwārs* of grain; 1,500 horse and 1,500 foot.

,, *of Shāl,* has a mud fort; 4½ *tumāns* in money; 940 sheep; 780 *kharwārs* of grain; Afghāns of *Kāst* and *Baloch;* 1,000 horse, and 1,000 foot.

,, *of Mashtang*, (Mastang) has a mud fort; 10 *tumāns* and 8,000 *dinārs* in money; 470 *kharwārs* in grain. Afghāns of *Kasi*, and *Baloch* 100 horse and 500 foot.

,, *of Khelgari*, 12 *tumāns* in money; 415 *kharwārs* of grain; 200 horse, 300 foot.

Tribe of Pani, 60 sheep, an Afghān clan, 1,000 horse, 1,000 foot.

[1] Under the Caliphs, the land-tax was usually rated at 2/5 of the produce of wheat and barley if the fields were watered by public canals; 3/10 if irrigated by wheels or other artificial means; and 1/4 if altogether unirrigated. If arable land were left uncultivated, it seems to have paid 1 *dirhem* per *jarib* and 1/10 of probable produce. Of dates, grapes, garden produce, 1/3 was taken either in kind or money; and 1/5 of the yield of wines, fishing, pearls and generally of products not derived from cultivation, was to be delivered in kind or paid in value even before the expenses had been defrayed. The customs and transit dues, for which unbelievers paid a double rate, and the taxes on trades, manufactures and handicrafts were also sources of public revenue. Sir H. Elliot. (*Arabs in Sind*, p. 78). For Aurangzib's revenue regulations, based on Islamic orthodox doctrines, see J. Sarkar's *Mughal Administration*, Ch. XI.

Tribe of Abdāli, formerly paid revenue 1,000 sheep; fixed in the time of the *Qāzilbāshis*[2] at 100 *tumāns,* 400 horse, 600 foot.

,, *of Abdāli,* 2,800 sheep, 5 *kharwārs* of butter. Afghāns 2,000 horse, 3,000 foot.

,, *of Jamandi,* responsible for 11 *tumāns* and 4,000 *dinārs.* Afghāns, 30 horse, 20 foot.

Surkh Rābāt i Balochān, revenue included under city of Qandahār. 50 horse, 50 foot.

Dependencies south of Qandahār.

Qalāt Banjārah, has a strong mud fort. 30 Balochi horses, 30 camels,—Baloch—500 horse, 500 foot.

Shorābak, 1,200 sheep. Afghans. 200 horse, 100 foot.

Tribe of Bisakh, 225 sheep. Afghans. 200 horse, 300 foot.

,, *of Mirkhāni,* 9 *tumāns* in money, 3,250 sheep. Afghans. 200 horse, 400 foot.

,, *of Maswāni,* 200 sheep. 7 *man* of butter. Afghans. 50 horse, 100 foot.

Dependencies north of Qandahār.

Territory of Qalāt Tartuk [? Barluk] has a very strong mud fort. 520 *tumāns,* 9,600 *dinārs* in money. 4,346 sheep; 1,171 *kharwārs* (of grain?) 1 *man* of butter; 1 *kharwār* of rice. Ghilzai Afghāns. 2,200 horse, 3,820 foot.

Hazārah Dahlah, [*Dahna*] 1,454 sheep; 20 *kharwārs* of grain; 200 horse, 500 foot.

Hazār Banjah Banji, [?] 160 sheep; 15 horse, 50 foot.

Territory of Tarin, has a strong fort. 15,000 sheep; 1,000 *kharwārs* of grain. Hazārah tribe. 1,500 horse, 3,000 foot.

---

[1] *Duki* signifying a hill in the language of the country, and may be opposed to *Deshi,* or plain. Erskine's *Bāber,* p. 164.

[2] This name (*Qizil,* red, *bāsh,* head) was given to the seven Turkish tribes, descendants of the captives released by Timur at the request of Safiu'ddin ancestor of Shaikh Ismail the first of the Suffavean monarchs. To the gratitude of these Carmanian captives the *Safi,* (*Anglice* Sophy) dynasty of Persia owed its elevation to the throne. See the XIVth Chapter of Malcolm's *History of Persia.* Round the red cap was twisted a turban in 12 plaits to the memory and in honour of the 12 Imāms. D'Herbelot. The term is applied generally to the Persians, and is so employed by Bāber, p. 181.

Dependencies west of Qandahār.

Territory of the torrid tract (*Garmsir*). 602 *tumāns*, and 8,000 *dinārs* in money; 12,000 *kharwārs* of grain. 200 horse, 2,000 foot.

,, *of Zamin Dāwar*, 1,200 horse, 1,000 foot.

Tribe of Siāhkhānah, 42 *tumāns*; 30 horse, 70 foot.

Fort of Kushk Nakhod, has a mud fort, revenue included under city of Qandahār.

Sarkār of Kābul.

It is situated in the third and fourth climates. Its length from *Atak Benāres* on the Indus to the *Hindu koh* is 150 *kos*; its breadth from *Qarābāgh*[1] of *Qandahār* to *Cheghān Serā*, 100 *kos*. It is bounded on the east by Hindustān; on the north-west by the mountains and Ghor; between to the north lies *Anderāb* of Badakshān, the *Hindu koh* intervening; on the south by *Farmul* and *Naghr*. Adequate praise of its climate is beyond the power of pen to express, and although its winter is severe rather than moderate, it occasions no distress. The torrid and cold belts are so contiguous that the transition may be made from one to the other in a single day. Such approximation of summer and winter pasturage in an inhabited country is uncommon. Snow falls both in the plains and on the mountains; in the former from November and on the latter from September : Bāber states that the snowfall in the direction of Hindustān does not pass the crest of the *Bādām Cashmah*.[2] This doubtless was the case in those days, but at the present time it extends to the crest of the *Nimlah*, and indeed as far as the *Khaibar* pass. Even in summer

---

[1] According to Tieffenthaler 11 royal miles from Ghazni (about 19½ common miles) on the road to Qandahār, I, 21. The greater part of the account of this province is taken without acknowledgment by Abul Fazl from the *Memoirs of Bābar*, which should be in the hands of the reader for comparison and illustration of this brief sketch. Chenghānserāi contains one village only, according to Bābar, and lies in the entrance of Kafiristān. The large river known as the Chenghānsarāi river comes from the north-east behind Rajaur. Another smaller stream from the west after flowing through Pich, a district of Kāfiristān, falls into it. Naghr is sometimes written Naghz. It is now unknown but Erskine conjectures it to have been on the upper course of the Kurram, and Farmul probably Urghun where the Persian race of Farmulis still exist. Niamatu'llah (Dorn's *History of the Afghāns*, p. 57) says that Farmul was originally the name of a river running between the borders of Kābul and Ghazni and the dwellers on its banks were called Farmulis. See Elphinstone's *Cābul*, p. 315 for a fuller account of this division of the Tājiks.

[2] The pass of Bādām Chashmah lies south of the Kābul river between Little Kābul and Bārikāb. Erskine.

time covering is needed during the nights. There are various delightful fruits, but the melons are not so good.[1] Agriculture is not very prosperous. The country is surrounded on all sides by lofty mountains, so that the sudden invasion of an enemy is attended with extreme difficulty.

The *Hindu koh* separates Kābul from Badakshān and Balkh, and seven routes are employed by the people of Turān in their marches to and fro. Three are by the *Panjhir*[2] (valley), the highest of which is over the *Khawāk* pass; below this is *Tāl,* and the next lower in succession, *Bāzārak.* The best of these is *Tul* but it is somewhat long as its name implies. The most direct is over the heights of *Bāzārak.* Between the high range and *Parwān* are seven other heights called *Haft Bachah* (*the Seven Younglings*). From *Anderāb* two roads unite at the foot of the main pass and debouch (on Parwān) by the *Haft Bachah.* This is extremely arduous. Three other roads lead by Parān up the *Ghorband* valley. The nearest route is by the pass of *Yangi-yuli,*[3] (the new road) which leads down to *Waliyān* and *Khinjān;* another is the *Qibchāk pass,* also somewhat easy to traverse, and a third is the *Shibertu.* In the summer when the rivers rise, it is by this pass that they descend by way of *Bāmiān* and *Tālikān,* but in the winter the *Abdarah* route is chosen, for at this season, all other routes but this are closed.

---

[1] Bābar confirms or originates this fact, and adds that those raised from seed brought from Khurāsān are tolerable. He praises those of Bokhāra, but pronounces those of Akhsi, a district north of the Jaxartes, to be beyond comparison the best.

[2] The word is so written by Bābar, but, according to Cunningham, (p. 32), the true name is *Panchir,* the Arabs writing *j* for the Indian *ch.* The modern spelling is *Panjshir.*

[3] I have corrected the inaccuracies of the text by the true readings in Bāber. Bāber himself passed through Bāmlān and by the Shibertu Kotal on his march from Khorasan to Kabul in February 1507. Three of these roads, the τριοδον of Strabo, leading to Bactria parted at Opiān near Charikār, the Hupiān of Bāber, identified with Alexandria Opiana by Cunningham who gives the routes as follows :

1. The north-east road, by the Panjshir valley, and over the Khāwak pass to Anderāb.

2. The west road by the Kushān valley, and over the Hindu Kush Pass to Ghori.

3. The south-west road up the Ghorband valley and over the Hājiyak (Hājigak) Pass to Bāmiān.

The first of these roads, he continues, was taken by Alexander on his march into Bactriana from the territory of the Paropamisadæ, and by Timur on his invasion of India. The second road, he supposes Alexander to have followed on his return from Bactriana, as Strabo mentions the choice of another and shorter route over the same mountains. The third was taken by Changiz Khān after his capture of Bāmiān; by Moorcroft and Burnes on their journey to Bokhara.

There is also a road leading from *Khurāsān* to *Qandahār* which is direct and has no mountain pass.

From Hindustān five roads* are practicable. 1. *Karapah,* which after traversing two defiles, leads to Jalālābād. This route is not mentioned by Bāber and doubtless was not used in his time. 2. *Khaibar,* this was formerly somewhat difficult, but by the command of His Majesty it has been made easily practicable for wheeled conveyance, and at the present time travellers from Turān and India take this route. 3. *Bangash* which is reached by crossing the Indus at the Dhankot ferry. 4. *Naghr.* 5. *Farmul,* by which the Indus must be crossed at the *Chaupārah* ferry.

Eleven languages are spoken in this province, each nationality using its own, *viz.,* Turkish, Mughal, Persian, Hindi, Afghāni, Pushtu, Parāchi, Geberi, Bereki, Lamghāni and Arabic.[1] The chief tribes are the *Hazārahs* and *Afghāns,* and the pasturage of the country is in the hands of these two clans. The *Hazārahs* are the descendants of the Changhatai army, sent by *Manku Qāān* to the assistance of *Hulāku Khān.* These troops were sent to these parts under the command of his son *Nikodār Oghlān.* Their settlements extend from Ghazni to Qandahār and from Maidān to the confines of Balkh. They number more than 100,000 families,[2] and the third part of which consists of cavalry. They possess horses, sheep and goats. They are divided into factions, each covetous of what they can obtain, deceptive in their common intercourse and their conventions of amity savour of the wolf.

The Afghāns consider themselves the descendants of the *Israelites.* They assert that their remote progenitor, named *Afghān,*[3] had three sons, *viz., Saraban* to whom the *Sarabani* clan trace their lineage; the second, *Ghurghusht* from whom the *Ghurghustis* claim descent, and the third *Batan* to whom the pedigree of the *Batani* tribe is ascribed. From these three branches they developed into their several

---

* The best account of the passes between India and Kābul is C. R. Markham's paper on "The Mountain Passes on the Afghan Frontier of British India", in the *Journal* of the Royal Geographical Society, 1879. Also Holdich.

[1] Bābar adds Pashāi; Gabri is said in the Khulāsatu'l Ansāb, to be a place in Bajaur. Dorn, p. 131.

[2] Lit. houses; the Tartars reckon the numbers of their families by households, tents and sometimes by kettles. Erskine's *Bāber.*

[3] In Dorn, Abdur Rashid, surnamed Pathān. Rose's *Glossary of Punjab Castes and Tribes,* for more accurate information.

clans, each distinguished by its eponymous tribarch. The following septs unite in SARABAN, *viz.*, *Tarin*, *Baraich*, *Miyānah*, *Kharshin*, *Shirāni*, *Urmar*, *Kāsi*, *Jamand*, *Kheshgi*, *Katāni*,[1] *Khalil*, *Mohmandzai*, *Dāudzai*, *Yusufzai*, *Kaliyāni*,[2] and *Tarkalāni*. From GHURGHUSHT spring the *Surāli* (var. Surāni), *Jilam*, *Orakzai*, *Afridi*, *Jagtāni*, *Khattaki*, *Kararāni*, *Bāwar*, *Mansub*, *Kākar*, *Nāghar*, *Bāni*, *Maswāni*, *Pani*, and *Tāran*. To BATAN are ascribed the *Ghilzai*, *Lodi*, *Niyāzi*, *Lohāni*, *Sur*, *Bani*, *Sarwāni* and *Kakbor*.

It is said that *Mast Ali*[3] *Ghori* whom the Afghāns call *Mati* had illicit intercourse with one of the daughters of Batan. When the results of this clandestine intimacy were about to become manifest, he preserved her reputation by marriage, and three sons were born to him, *viz.*, *Ghilzai*, *Lodi*, and *Sarwāni*.

Some assert the Afghāns to be *Copts*, and that when the Israelites came to Egypt from Jerusalem, this people passed into Hindustān. The tradition is too long to be condensed within narrow limits, but it is noticed in passing as a fanciful digression.

There are many wild tribes, such as the *Khwājah Khizri*, *Qāqshāl*, *Maidāni*, *Uzbek*, *Kalatki*, *Parānchi*, *Nilpurchi*, *Bakderi*, *Bahsudi*, *Sidibāi*, *Tufakandāz* (matchlockmen), *Arab*, *Gilahbān* (shepherds) and *Tuqbai* but not as numerous as the first mentioned, and most of them at the present time have become settled colonists.

The *City of Kābul* is situated in the fourth climate. Its longitude is 104° 40′, and its latitude 34° 30′. It is one of

---

[1] According to the *Khulāsat-u'l Ansāb* (Dorn, p. 127) the Ka'tānis possess no territory but are scattered in single families. From Niāzi descend the Musakhail, Isakhail, Sambal Saharangh, conjointly called Niāzis: they reside about the town of Makhad on the banks of the Indus as far as Dera Ismail Khān. The descendants of Pani reside about Shikārpur. Another account places them, after their expulsion from their country, about Jeypur and Jodhpur where they subsist by traffic and carry merchandise to the Deccan. Nāghar's descendants reside about Dera Ghāzikhān, and Kākaris near Qandahār. The word 'zai' or 'zacy' as Raverty writes the word, signifies son', and answers to Mac, Fitz, and O. Suffixed to the tribal name, it means 'a man' of the particular clan.

[2] Probably a misscript for Gagiyāni.

[3] According to Dorn, Shāh Husain, Prince of Ghor, (pp. 46, 48, Part II). Matu was the name of Shaikh Patni's daughter and Shāh Husain not being of Afghān extraction, his descendants were called by the maternal name of Mati. The name of Ghilzai was given on account of the clandestine amour, '*ghil*' signifying thief, and '*zai*' born, a son.

the finest of ancient[1] cities, and is said to have been founded in the time of *Pashang*. It possesses a double earthwork fortress of considerable strength. To the south-west of the fortified town is a low hill which is a source of much beneficence, called *Shāh Kābul*,[2] doubtless with reference to an edifice erected upon it by one of its former kings. Upon its summit stands the citadel, and there was a separate ridge named *Aqābain*. As it somewhat overlooked the fort, it was included within its precincts by royal command. Skirting its base are fair embankments, pleasure-gardens and delightful groves, amongst which the *Shahr Ārā* (Pride of the City) are especially beautiful. The city is watered by two streams. One of these, called the Jui Khatibān, enters from *Lalandar* and flowing through the *Shahr Ārā* passes by the city; the other, the *Jui Pul Masṭān*,[3] more wholesome and limpid than the former, from the narrows of the *Deh i Yaqub* winds past the Delhi Gate and runs on to *Deh i Mamurah*. Near this a canal called *Mahum Anagah*[4] has been brought, which is of extreme convenience, and adjacent is the *Gulkanah* quarter fair to the eye and dear to the heart. From the hill (of Shāh Kābul) flow three streams citywards; at the head of one is the shrine of Khwājah Hamu [Shams]; the second, according to popular belief, had been visited by the prophet *Khizr;* the third is over against (the tomb of) *Khwājah* Abdu's Samad known as *Khwājah Roshanāi*. The wise of ancient times considered

---

[1] It was the old capital of the country, says Cunningham, before the Macedonian conquest, and Ibn Haukal states that inauguration at Kābul was a necessary qualificaiton for government in a king. Tieffenthaler names 4 gates, *viz., Lahor, Kābul, Nalbandi* and *Fatouhi*, adding that near this last was an ancient castle with mud walls. It was pulled down by Ahmed Abdāli, and the houses in front of the Fatouhi gate razed to the ground. A new fort was then erected of brick work 'sur un lieu elevé', and its garden laid out by the governor.

[2] Erskine says that there is a hill *south* of Kābul on which Qābil (Cain) the founder, is said to have been interred, but the only hill south-west is that known as Bābar Badshāh where Bābar himself was interred, and is the great holiday resort of the people. Bābar's description is as follows: "There is a small ridge which runs out from the hill of Shāh Kābul and is called Aqābain, and there is besides another small hill on which stands the citadel. The fortified town lies on the north of the citadel." Erskine identifies Aqābain with that now called Ashikān Arifān, which connects with Bābar Bādshāh. The Bālā Hissār is on the same ridge further east and south-east of the town. The beneficence of the Shāh Kābul mentioned in the text, is due to three streams that issue from it, two of which are in the vicinity of the shady and retired Gulkanah, the scene, as Bābar not regretfully notes, of many a debauch. The position of the citadel and of the conjoined hills, has been carefully described by Forster, Travels, p. 73.

[3] It is a canal derived from the river Logar as it enters the plains of Shevaki and has a course of about five miles. *I. G.*

[4] The name of Akbar's nurse (Anagah) who attended him from his cradle and exercised a backstair influence that affected many political fortunes.

Kābul and Qandahār as the twin gates of Hindustān, the one leading to Turkestān and the other to Persia. The custody of these highways secured India from foreign invaders, and they are likewise the appropriate portals to foreign travel.

In Kābul as well as in Samarqand and Bokhāra, a *parganah* which comprises towns and villages is called a *Tumān*. The *Tumān of Bigrām* is called *Parashāwar*, the spring season of which is delightful. Here is a shrine greatly venerated called *Korkhatri*,[1] visited by people especially *yogis* from distant parts.

The *Tumān of Neknihāl*[2] is one of the dependencies of *Lamghān*. The residence of the governor was formerly at *Adinahpur* but is now at *Jelālābād*. There is here no snowfall and the cold is not so severe. Nine streams irrigate the cultivated lands; the pomegranates have no seed-stones. Near Jelālābād is the *Bāgh i Safā*[3] (*The Garden of Purity*) a memorial of Bābar, and adjacent to *Adinahpur* is the *Bāgh i Wafā* (*The Garden of Fidelity*) another relic of the same monarch. To the south lies the stupendous range of the *Safed koh* (*The White Mountain*) with its perpetual snows from which it derives its name. In this neighbourhood is a low hill[4] where when it snows in Kābul, a similar snowfall occurs.

---

[1] This shrine, is mentioned by Bābar as one of the holy places of the Hindu jogis who came from great distances to cut off their hair and shave their beards at this spot. He rode out to Bigrām to see the great tree but was not shown the shrine in 1505. Fourteen years later his curiosity was gratified. Gor Khatri was once a Buddhist monastery, (*I. G.*) then rebuilt into a Hindu temple, and now used as a *sarāi*.

[2] In the *I. G. Nangnihār* and by Bābar Nangenhār or Nekerhār, the district south of the Kābul river in the province of Jelālābād, that on the north, bounded on the west and east by the Alingār and Kunar rivers, being Lamghān. It lies along the Kābul river on the south, and the name is said to mean 'nine rivers'. The *I. G.* affirms it to be a distortion of the ancient name of *Nagarahāra*, identified by Lassen with the *Nagara* of Ptolemy regarded by Cunningham as identical with Jelālābād. Adinahpur is south of the Kābul river.

[3] A garden of this name was planted by Bābar at Keldeh-Kehār (Kuller Kaher) near Pind Dādan Khān, eleven years after that of the Bāgh i Wafā near Adinahpur south of the Kābul river. It was situated 10 *kos* from Bahrah in the middle of the hill of Jud on a level plot of ground in the centre of which was a lake which received the water of the surrounding hills and was about five miles in circumference. *Bahrah* or *Bhira* is marked in the maps 20 *kos* from Kuller Kaher, but the name is said to be common in the district.

[4] Bābar is more explicit. 'On the south of the fort of Adinahpur is the *Surkh-rud* (runs into the Kābul river between Jagdalik and Gandamak). On the north is a detached mass of mountain dividing Nangenhār and the Lamghānāt. Whenever it snows at Kābul, the snow falls also on the top of this mountain by which means the people of the Lamghānāt can tell when it snows at Kābul.

The *Tumān of Mandrāur* : monkeys here abound. The *Alishang* river uniting with the Alingār joins the *Bārān,* while the *Cheghān Sarāi* river flowing through the north-east quarter enters *Kator.*[1]

The *Tumān of Alishang* is surrounded by lofty mountains covered with snow in which is the source of the *Alishang* river. The inhabitants are called *Kāfirs.* In the vicinity is a tomb asserted by the people to be that of *Lām* the father of Noah, called also Lamek (Lamech). The people here pronounce the *kāf* like a *ghain,* and hence the currency of the name (Lamghān).

The mountainous *Tumān of Najrāo*[2] also is peopled by the *kāfirs.* Instead of lamp they burn the *chilghozah.*[3] There is also an animal called the *Flying Fox,*[4] which flies upward about the height of a yard. There is also a rat which exhales the smell of musk.

Charkh is a village of the *Tumān of Loghar* which gives its name to *Maulana Yaqub Charkhi. Sajāwand* is also one of the well-known villages of this *Tumān.*

The mountains of the *Tumān of Badrāo* (?) are the home of *kāfirs* and wild Hāzarahs and Afghāns.

The *Tumān of Alsā*[5] is situated intermediately between the torrid and cold belts. Birds cross this tract about the beginning of spring and good sport is had.

---

[1] Bābar's words are : 'The river of Cheghansarāi, after passing through Kaferistān from the north-east, unites with the river Bārān, in the *Baluk* of Kāmeh and then passes onwards to the east.'

[2] It lies north-east from Kābul in the hill country according to Bābar, who adds that their inhabitants are wine drinkers, never pray, fear neither God nor man, and are heathenish in their usages.

[3] The seed of the *Pinus gerardiana;* the cone, which is as big as a man's two fists, and also the tree itself, said to be derived from *chihal* 'forty' and *ghoza* a 'nut'.

[4] Copied from Bābar whose account is as follows : "It is an animal larger than a squirrel with a kind of leathern web stretching between its fore and hind feet like a bat's wing. It is said that they can fly a bowshot from a higher tree to a lower one. I myself have never seen them fly, but have let one go beside a tree which it quickly clung to and ascended, and when driven away, expanded its wings like a bird and came to the ground without injury." This must be the flying squirrel, which does not fly though wing-handed, but is supported by its membrane as it leaps.

[5] Bābar, *Alah-sāi,* which Erskine says is now called Tugow. "It lies two or three farsangs east of Najrāo from which you advance straight towards Alah-sāi." Bābar places it between the cold and warm belts, and says that the birds take their flight across in the spring. Fowlers sit behind, scream and raise nets as the flights of fowl approach and intercept them. In the winter season the birds come down to the skirts of the hills and if in their flight they happen to pass over a vineyard they are no longer able to fly and are caught. A similar story is told of some fields near Whitby. (Notes to *Marmion*). The pomegranates of Alah-sāi are famous in the country, and are sent to Hindustān.

The *Tumān of Bangash*[1] furnishes 7,000 Cavalry and 87,800 Infantry, *viz.* :—

	Cavalry	Infantry
Mohmand	500	500
Khalil	500	6,500
Dāudzai	3,000	37,000
Gagiyāni	500	4,500
Muhammadzai	400	4,000
Sini	100	1,400
Utmānkhail	50	850
Ghilzai	100	2,900
Khizrkhail	30	950
Sherzād	20	1,400
Kharguni [Khar Kuli] ...	10	200
Khattaki	200	4,000
Abdu'r Rahmāni ...	100	2,500
Afridi	500	10,500
Oruk, (Orakzai) ...	500	5,500
	6,510	82,700

The *Tumān of Gardez*[2] has a strong fort. The houses are for the most part three and four stories high.

Ghaznin is situated in the third climate, and is also known as *Zābul*, and was the capital of Sultān Mahmud, Sultān Shahābu'ddin and several other monarchs.

This territory was formerly called Zābulistān, and some reckon Qandahār as included within it. Here is the last resting-place of *Hakim Sanāi*[3] and many other saintly personages. The winter season is said to resemble that of Samarqand and Tabriz. A river runs from north to south which waters all the arable tracts. The cultivators are put

---

[1] Occupies the lower grounds from Gardez to Kohāt. Bābar says it is infested by Afghān robbers such as the Khugiāni, Khirilchi, Buri and the Linder.

[2] Upwards of sixty-five miles south-east from Kābul. Bābar says that the Daroghā of the Tumān of Zurmat, south of Kābul and south-east of Ghazni, resides at Gardez which is not named as a separate Tumān. Next follows the Tumān of Farmul omitted by Abul Fazl. It is notable only in the fact that the Shaikhzādahs, who were treated, as Bābar says, with such distinguished favour in Hindustān during the time of the Afghāns, were all of Farmul and descended from Shaikh Muhammad Musalmān.

[3] This tomb is mentioned by Elphinstone, *Cābul*, 433. He was a mystic of high authority and repute whom the great Sufi Maulanā Rum looked up to as his master. He flourished under Bahrām Shāh, son of Masaud Shāh of Ghazni (A.D. 1118-52) to whom he dedicated his *Hadiqat ul Haqāiq*. He left also the usual Diwān which is necessary to every Persian poet's fame or ambition. He is said to have died in 1131 at the age of 62. *Encyclo. Islam*, iv. 146; Browne, *Lit. History of Persia*, ii. 317.

to great trouble as fresh soil has to be supplied each year to fertilize the land and it becomes then more productive than that of Kābul. The metal called *ruin*[1] is here abundant and is imported into Hindustān. In the time of Bābar there was here a tomb which shook whenever the praises of Muhammad were recited. The investigations of acute observers discovered that this was effected by fraud of relic-mongers.[2] There is also a spring into which if any filth be thrown, a thunderstorm ensues with a fall of snow and rain.

The *Tumān of Dāman i koh*[3] has a profusion of flowers and its spring and autumn are matchless in beauty.

In the *Tumān of Ghorband* the variety of floral hues is beyond expression. Three and thirty species of tulips here bloom and one kind named the *rose-scented tulip* breathes the fragrance of the blush-rose.[4]

Mines of silver and lapis-lazuli are also found. Near the mountains is a sandy tract called *Khwājah Reg i Rawān*[5] and from this quicksand, the sound as of drums is heard in the summer time.

In the *Tumān of Zohāk* and *Bāmiān*, the fortress of *Zohāk* is a monument of great antiquity, and in good preservation, but the fort of Bāmiān is in ruins. In the mountain-side caves have been excavated and ornamented with plaster

---

[1] Composed of four *sers* of copper to 1½ of lead. See Vol. I, p. 41.

[2] Albiruni in his *Chronology*, Chap. XIII alludes to the "famous well in the mountains of Farghāna" which causes rain if contaminated and adduces several similar traditions. Bābar says that he made strict inquiry for the well, but no one could give him the slightest information about it. The discovery of the fraud at the tomb is due to his observation. A scaffolding had been erected over it, so contrived, that it could be set in motion when any one stood upon it, so that a lookeron imagined it was the tomb that moved. He directed the persons who attended the tomb to come down from the scaffolding, after which no number of prayers or praises could persuade it to stir.

[3] The beautiful plain is better known as *Koh Dāman*, the *hill skirt* of the Paghmān range. The gardens of Istalif at its north extremity, gay with flowers, its limpid ice-cold streams, the Arghwān trees with their vivid blossoms of scarlet and yellow seen in no other part of the country its groves of oak and spreading plane trees have excited the eloquent admiration of Bābar.

[4] It is needless to say that the nomenclature of native flora by Persian or Indian writers is extremely unscientific and vague, and beyond a few well-known kinds, the rest are indiscriminately expressed by a shuffling of the few botanical terms they possess, and the same name does duty for more than one flower. The etymology of Ghorband is given by Bābar from *band*, a steep hill pass, and *ghor*, the country to which it mainly leads.

[5] This is mentioned by Bābar. The name of Khwājah *Reg i rawān* (Khwājah quicksand) appears in the margin of Elphinstone's Turki copy of Bābar's *Memoirs* as that of one of three personages known as the *Seh Yārān* or Three Friends who have given this name to a fountain in the *Koh Dāman* (Khwājah Seh Yārān) mentioned by Bābar. The other two are Khwājah Maudud Chashti and Khwājah Khawend Said, p. 147.

and paintings. Of these there are 12,000 which are called *Sumaj* and in former times were used by the people as winter retreats. Three colossal figures are here : one is the statue of a man, 80 yards in height; another that of a woman 50 yards high, and the third is that of a child measuring 15 yards. Strange to relate, in one of these caves is placed a coffin containing the body of one who reposes in his last sleep.[1] The oldest and most learned of antiquarians can give no account of its origin, but suppose it to be of great antiquity. In days of old the ancients prepared a medicament with which they anointed corpses and consigned them to earth in a hard soil. The simple deceived by this art, attribute their preservation to a miracle.

The territory of Kābul comprises twenty *Tumāns*. The Emperor Bābar in his Memoirs sets down the revenue at twenty *lakhs* of *Shahrukhis,* inclusive of *Tamgha*[2] imposts, equivalent to three *lakhs* and twenty thousand *Akbar Shāhi* rupees, the rupee being reckoned at forty *dāms*.

At the present time notwithstanding the remission of various taxes, by the blessing of this ever-during rule, the revenue has reached the amount of six *krors,* seventy-three *lakhs,* six thousand, nine hundred and eighty-three *dāms*. (Rs. 1,682,674-9). The increase is to be attributed to the improved state of the cultivation, and also that *Parashāwar* and *Ashtaghar*[3] were not included in the former account, and lastly, that the revenue officers of that time were not as capable as they are at present.

Sarkār of Kābul.

Containing 22 Mahals : Revenue 80,507,465 *Dāms* in money : *Suyurghāl* 137,178 *Dāms*. Cavalry, 28,187. Infantry, 212,700.

---

[1] The punctuation in the text is clearly misplaced.

[2] Inland tolls. See Vol. I, 189, but Bābar's words are : "The amount of the revenue of Kābul, whether arising from *settled lands or raised from the inhabitants of the waste,* is eight *lakhs of Shāhrukhis.*" The word 'twenty' *bist* must be a copyist's error for *hasht* eight, as the Akbar Shāhi rupee being equal to 2½ Shāhrukhis, the whole would give exactly three *lakhs* and twenty thousand rupees. Erskine notes *tamgha* as the stamp tax. All animals, goods, clothes &c. brought into the country are stamped or marked and a tax collected.

[3] A corruption of Hashtnagar, now a *tahsil* of the Peshāwar district. The "eight towns" of which it was composed were Tangi, Shirpao, Umrzai, Turangzai, Usmānzai, Rajur, Chārsada and Parāng. The last two are seated close together in a bend of the Kābul river and the sites of all are shown in Map IV. of Cunningham's *Anct. Geog.*, p. 46.

City of Kābul—Revenue, 1,275,841 *Dāms*. Cavalry, 7,000 Infantry, 15,000.

Dependencies east of Kābul.

	Revenue. D.	Suyurghāl. D.	Cavalry.	Infantry.	Tribes.
Tumān of Bigrām	9,692,410	...	...		...
,, Neknihāl (Nangnihār)	11,894,003	1,224	200	5,000	...
Buluk i Kāmah (not recorded)	...	...	...		...

North.

	Revenue. D.	Suyurghāl. D.	Cavalry.	Infantry.	Tribes.
Tumān of Mandrāur ...	2,684,880	...	50	500	...
,, Alishang ...	3,701,150	1948	50	5000	Alishang.
,, Alingār ...	1,544,670	...	500	1000	Lamghāni.
Buluk Najrāo	2,045,451	...	3000	3000	Kāfir.
Tumān of Loghar	3,193,214	22,960	50	500	...
,, Badrāo	413,885	...	50	500	...
,, Alsāi	600,000	...	...	5000	Dilazāk.
,, Panjhir (Panjshir)	461,940	...	...	35,000	Pani.

South.

	Revenue. D.	Suyurghāl. D.	Cavalry.	Infantry.	Tribes.
Tumān of Bangash	3,332,347	...	7,087	87,800	Afghān.
,, Kohat, (var. Kohast, Karbast) ...	701,620	...	300	5000	Orakzai &c.
,, Naghr (var. Naghz)	854,000	...	1000	7000	Afghān, Banukhail.*
,, Gardez	2,030,002	...	200	1000	Afghān.
,, Maidān	1,606,799	1,864	2000	...	Hazārah Maidāni.
,, Ghaznin	3,768,642	1,076	1000	5000	...

* Variant, *Shahu Khail.*

West.

	Revenue. D.	Suyurghāl. D.	Cavalry.	Infantry.	Tribes.
Tumān of Farmul	325,712	...	1000	5000	...
,, Dāman i koh ...	16,461,785	...	5000	30,000	...
,, Ghorband ...	1,574,760	...	3000	5000	Hazārah and Turkomān.
,, Zohāk Bāmiān ...	861,750	...	200	1000	...

In the year 77 of the Flight (A.D. 696-7) Abdu'l Malik b. Marwān removed Umayyah b. Abdu'l Malik from the government of Khurasān and conferred it upon Hajjāj b. Yusuf of the tribe of Thakif, and sent Abdu'llah b. Abu Bakr to Sistān, who levied an army, marched against Ranthel, king of Kābul. The latter unable to withstand him took refuge in the depths of the mountains. Abdu'llah not realising the difficulties of his undertaking eagerly pursued. The mountaineers barricading the passes with stone breastworks, blocked his road. The invading force was hard-pressed and reduced to extremity through want of provisions. Abdu'llah was therefore compelled to purchase a retreat with the sum of 700,000 *dirhams*, equivalent in present money value to 3,00,000 rupees. Shuraih b. Hāni in indignation at the compact advanced to an engagement notwithstanding his being stricken in years, and fell bravely fighting. Hajjāj on hearing of the event, reprimanded Abdu'llah and removed him from his command. In the year 80 (A.D. 699) he appointed Abdu'r Rahmān b. Muhammad Ashath to conduct the war against Ranthel and bestowed on him the government of Sistān and the adjacent territory. Abdu'r Rahmān on his arrival in Kābul adopted the former tactics, but prudently occupied each defile with his pickets and performing prodigies of valour, secured a large booty. The difficulties of the country, however, prevented its permanent occupation. Hajjāj disapproving his retreat sent him a severe reprimand in the following terms : "Although your exertions during the present year have been strenuous, the retribution demanded by your dishonourable retreat is that immediately on the receipt of this letter, you take possession of the country. Should you, through persistence in your own opinions or through fear of the consequences to yourself, refuse to comply and defer operations till the coming year, you are removed from your command, are hereby required to look upon Ishāq b. Muhammad as your commander and to place yourself under his orders." Abdu'r Rahmān, confiding in the strength of possession, disloyally formed a compact with his officers and refusing submission, made peace with the king of Kābul and marched against Hajjāj. The conditions of peace were that Abdu'llah if victorious should altogether withdraw from Kābul and in no way molest it, but if defeated, the king should on his part afford him protection and assistance. Hajjāj was enraged at this rebellious conduct, and gave him battle outside the walls of Tustar.[1] Abdu'r Rahmān was victorious, and Hajjāj retreated to Basrah. A second engagement took place in which the rebel was defeated and took refuge in the fortress of Bast [in Luristan] which was held by one of his lieutenants. This accursed of God and man, with a view to ingratiate himself with Hajjāj, seized him with the intention of surrendering him to Hajjāj. The king of Kābul, on being informed of the circumstance, set out with the greatest expedition and releasing him, returned with him to Kābul. On several subsequent occasions, with the assistance of the king, he continued the war but without success. In the lunar year 84, (A.D. 703) Ranthel overcome by the persuasion and seductive promises of Hajjāj, sent Abdu'llah to him as a prisoner. The latter resenting the dishonour, whilst on the road, threw himself from a precipice and was killed.

In A.H. 107 (A.D. 725-6) under the caliphate of Hishām b. Abdu'l Malik, Amin b. Abdu'llah Qashari, governor of Khurasān conquered Ghor, Gharjistān, the territory of Nimroz[2] and Kābul and made (the latter) his capital. From that time continuously under the dynasties of Umayyah and Abbās, it was held by the governor of Khurasān, until under the Sāmānis, Alptegin a slave of that House, withdrew from their obedience, took possession of Ghaznin and Kābul and asserted his independence. On his death Sabuktegin father of the great Mahmud succeeded to the kingdom, and it continued under the House of Ghazni. From this it passed to that of Ghor and thence into the pos-

[1] Now *Shuster* in Khuzistān. It was first conquered in A. H. 20 in the Caliphate of Omar.

[2] Usually applied to Sejestān. Elliot. *Arabs in Sind*. p. 172.

session of their slaves, one of whom was Tāju'ddin Eldoz. The kings of Khwārizm succeeded, yielding in turn to the Great Qāān Changiz Khān. From him it reverted to Timur and is held by his descendants. May its fortune, through the enduring justice, unstinted clemency and ever increasing wisdom of the Imperial House, be blessed by an unfading prosperity.

AIN 16.

The Karoh or Kos.

The system of survey and measurement, as promoting the interests of civilization having deeply engaged the attention of His Majesty, directions were issued for the ascertainment of distances and their determination by the standard measure of the *kos*. The *kos* was fixed at 100 *tanābs*,[1] each consisting of 50 *Ilāhi gaz*, or of 400 poles (*bāns*) each pole of 12½ *gaz*. Both of these measurements give 5000 *gaz* to the *kos*.

Whenever His Majesty travels, the distances are recorded in pole-measurements by careful surveyors, and their calculations are audited by the superintendent and inspector.

Sher Khān fixed the *kos* at 60 *jaribs*, each of 60 *Sikandari gaz* which measurement is employed in the *Delhi* country. In *Mālwah* it consists of 90 *tanābs* of 60 *gaz* each and in *Gujarāt* is called the *cow kos*, that is, the greatest distance at which the ordinary lowing of a cow can be heard, which is put by experts at 50 *jaribs*. In *Bengal* it is called

---

[1] See p. 61 of this Volume. This subject is discussed by Elliot. (*Races, N.-W.* p. II. 194). Cunningham (*Anct. Geog. of Ind.* App. B. p. 571) and Tieffenthaler (I. 23). To the measurements of Abul Fazl, I may add the length of the *kos*, as fixed by Bābar. On Dec. 19th, 1526 he gave orders, as his Memoirs record, to have the distance measured between Agra and Kābul; that at every 9 *kos*, a *minār* should be raised 12 *gaz* in height surmounted by a pavilion; that at every 10 *kos*, a post-house for 6 horses should be placed. The *kos* was fixed in conformity with the *mil* according to the following verse in Turki.

Four thousand paces are one *mil*
Know that the men of Hindustān call it a *kuroh*.
This pace is a cubit and a half ;
Every cubit is six hand-breaths;
Each hand-breadth is six inches; and again each inch
Is the breadth of six barleycorns. Know all this.

The measuring *tanāb*, was to consist of 40 *gaz* or paces, each measuring one and a half of the cubit that has been mentioned and so equal to nine hand-breadths, and 100 of these *tanābs* were to go to one *kos*.—Erskine adds that the larger *gaz* or pace was 9 hand-breadths; the smaller or cubit, 6 hand-breadths.

dhapiyah,[1] which is the distance that a fast runner can traverse at one breath. Some assert that it is the distance within which a green leaf placed on the head of one who walks rapidly, will become dry.

In ancient tables of measurement by *farsakh* of distances and magnitudes, it is recorded that the circumference[2] of the globe according to the method of the old geographers, was 8,000 *farsakh,* but 6,800 of the modern school, while all agree in defining a *farsakh* as three *kos.* The former made the *kos* 3000 *gaz,* each *gaz* of 32 digits. The latter fixed it at 4000 *gaz,* each of 24 digitis. The digit with both was the breadth of six ordinary barley-corns placed front to back in succession, and the breadth of each barley corn was equal to the thickness of six hairs of the mane of a Turki horse. To short-sighted superficial observers, it would appear that these two systems differ in their estimate of the *kos,* but it is clear to the perspicacity of the far-seing that their conclusion is the same, and the apparent difference is caused by the variance in the number of the digits as may be proved by the rule of proportion. This consists of four numbers, the first bearing the same ratio to the second, as the third does to the fourth, as for instance, two is to four as eight is to sixteen. Of the properties of this relation one is this that the product of the extremes is equal to the product of the means, as is evident from the example above mentioned. The proof is given in the 19th proposition of the 7th book of Euclid[3] where the apparent contradiction is removed. The ratio of 3000 to 4000 is the ratio of 24 to 32. Although the four numbers are here

---

[1] The word is Hindi and means a short run according to Wilson's *Glossary,* about ¼ of a *kos* or half a mile.

[2] The circumference of the earth, according to our calculations is 24,897 miles and the *farsakh* is about 3¾ English miles; there are of course many local variations. Hamdu'llah Mustaufi, the author of the *Nuzhat'ul Qulub,* says that the *farsakh* under the Kaianian dynasty contained 3 miles of 12,000 feet; that of Khwarizm was 15,000 yards; in Azarbijān and Armenia, 12,000 yards, while in the two Ira'ks and the neighbouring provinces it was reckoned at 6000 yards, and in some other places at 8000.

[3] The *Elements* of Euclid were restored to Europe by translations from the Arabic which were begun to be made under the Caliphs Harun and Mamun at a time when the very name of that geometrician had disappeared from the West. Nasiru'ddin Tusi (see p. 4, n. 4 of this Volume) in the preface to his Arabic Edition of the thirteen books of the Elements, describes their original composition by Euclid and the subsequent addition of two books by Hypsicles. From it I transcribe the enunciation of the proposition referred to in the text.

"When four numbers are proportionals, the product of the 1st and 4th = the product of the 2nd and 3rd, and if the product of the 1st and 4th = the product of the 2nd and 3rd, the ratio of the 1st is to the 2nd as the ratio of the 3rd to the 4th."

severally distinct, the product of 3000 and of 32 which are the extremes, is equal to the product of 4000 and of 24 which are the means, namely, 96,000. Thus the result in both is the same, and the discrepancy in the number of yards is through the difference in the number of digits. Each *farsakh* therefore consists of 12,000 *gaz* (of 24 digits) according to the measure of the moderns or of 9000 (of 32 digits) according to the *gaz* of the ancients. The properties and virtues of these proportional numbers are manifold. Among them are the following: If one of the extremes be unknown, multiply the means together and divide by the known extreme, and the quotient is the unknown extreme. For instance in the given example, if 2, the first extreme, be unknown, by multiplying the means together which are 4 and 8, we get 32. Dividing this by 16, the quotient (2) is the unknown extreme. In the same way, if the other extreme, which is 16, be unknown, by dividing the product of the means by 2, the known extreme, the quotient is 16. Again, if the unknown quantity be one of the means, we divide the product of the extremes by the known mean, and the quotient is the unknown mean. For example, if 4, the first mean, be unknown, by dividing the product of the extremes, which is 32, by the known mean which is 8, the quotient is 4. And if the second mean, 8, be unknown, by dividing the product of the extremes by 4, the quotient is 8.

By the same means the distance and altitude from the base of a given object can be ascertained. A staff of a given height is fixed upright. Its shadow and that of the elevate object are measured. The ratio of the shadow of the staff to the staff is proportional to the ratio of the shadow of the object-height to the height itself. Again, a staff is fixed in the ground in the same line with the height to be measured and regarded from such a point that the line of vision may pass over the top of the staff to the summit of the object-height; the ratio of the distance from the standpoint of vision to the base of the staff is to the height of the staff as the ratio of the distance from the same point to the base of the object is to the height of the object. And if the altitude of an object be measured in a mirror or water and the like, a position must be taken whence the incident line of vision may strike the summit of the (reflected) object-height. The ratio of the distance of the reflected summit from the foot of the spectator is to his height as the ratio of the distance of the same point from the base of the object is to the height of the object. And if it be required to find the depth of a well, the observer must stand where his line of vision traversing the brink of the well touches the level bottom of the well on the side opposite to him. The ratio of the distance of the brink of the well from the foot of the observer is to his height as the breadth of the well is to its depth.*

Some take the *barid* as the standard measure of length and make.

1 *barid*	equal to	3 *farsakh*.
1 *farsakh*	,,	3 *mil*.
1 *mil*	,,	12,000 *bāa* (pole).
1 *bāa*	,,	4 *gaz*.
1 *gaz*	,,	24 digits.
1 digit	,,	6 barleycorns.
1 barleycorn	,,	6 hairs of a mule's tail.

According to the Hindu philosophers—

8 barleycorns stripped of husks and laid breadth-ways	make	1 digit (*angusht*).
24 digits	,,	1 *dast* (cubit).
4 *dast*	,,	1 *dand* (pole or perch) or *dhanuk*.
2000 *dand*	,,	1 *karoh* or *kos*.
4 *karoh*	,,	1 *yoojana*.

Some measure by the steps of a woman with a water-jar on her head and carrying a child in her arms, reckoning a thousand such steps to a *kos*.

Praise be unto God that the institutes of imperial administration have been completed and a general survey of the Empire, by the aid of divine grace, placed upon record. The numbers of the tribal contingents and the chronology of the ancient kings with some other particulars have cost considerable labour, and from the conflicting accounts received, I was well nigh relinquishing the task, but the decrees of fate cannot be resisted. I have set down what has best commended itself to my judgment, hoping that it may win lustre from the light of public acceptance and its errors escape the carping of illiberal criticism.

END OF VOLUME II.

* This method of calculating distance and altitudes is more scientifically given with illustrations in the *Siddhanta Stromani* of Pundit Bapu Deva.

Inhalt

Einführung

Hallo, App-Programmierer der Zukunft!

Einfach nur vorgegebene, fertige Apps nutzen ist dir zu wenig? Du willst selbst Apps erstellen? Du hast aber noch nie programmiert?

Dann bist du hier genau richtig!

In diesem Buch lernst du Schritt für Schritt, wie du mit dem MIT App Inventor 2 ganz ohne Vorkenntnisse *Apps für dein Android-Smartphone* erstellen kannst.

Über den MIT App Inventor 2

Das Programm, mit dem du Apps für dein Smartphone entwickeln kannst, heißt: *MIT App Inventor 2*. MIT steht dabei für Massachusetts Institute of Technology, was eine große und ziemlich berühmte amerikanische Universität ist. App Inventor heißt auf Deutsch übersetzt »App-Erfinder«.

Der MIT App Inventor 2 hat einige tolle Eigenschaften. Das Programm ...

- ist extra für *Einsteiger* entwickelt worden,
- *kostet nichts*,
- muss *nicht installiert* werden, da es im Browser läuft,
- ist ganz *einfach zu bedienen*, da es fertige Puzzle-Bausteine für deine App zur Verfügung stellt und
- es gibt einen *Emulator*, ein Fenster am Computer, das ein Smartphone nachbildet, sodass du nicht unbedingt ein eigenes Smartphone brauchst (mit einem echten Smartphone macht es aber noch mehr Spaß 😉).

Der App Inventor wurde ursprünglich von Google entwickelt und steht seit 2010 App-Entwicklern in der ganzen Welt zur Verfügung. 2012 wurde der App Inventor von Google an das MIT übergeben und heißt seitdem MIT App Inventor. Die aktuelle Version heißt *MIT App Inventor 2*.

Weltweit erstellen (programmieren) wahnsinnig viele Menschen, hauptsächlich Informatikerinnen und Informatiker, kleine und auch große Programme für den

Computer oder auch Apps für das Smartphone. Darum sind die meisten Programme dazu in Englisch und es ist sehr gut, wenn auch du schon ein wenig Englisch sprechen bzw. lesen kannst. Aber keine Sorge, bei neuen oder schwierigen Wörtern helfen wir dir, indem wir die Begriffe für dich übersetzen. Das sieht dann zum Beispiel so aus: »book« (auf Deutsch »Buch«) oder auch einfach nur (»Buch«). Du kannst den App Inventor auch auf eine andere Sprache stellen (bisher 21 Sprachen). Dort kannst du auch Deutsch auswählen. Da aber die meisten Texte automatisch übersetzt wurden und deshalb nicht alles fehlerfrei ist, empfehlen wir dir lieber gleich bei Englisch zu bleiben.

Über dieses Buch

Wir – Nadine und Thiemo – wollen dir mit diesem Buch zeigen, wie einfach du selbst Apps erstellen kannst und vor allen Dingen, wie viel Spaß das macht.

Da man – wie so oft – am Anfang etwas mehr Hilfe braucht, werden wir gemeinsam die ersten Schritte gehen. Dazu werden wir als Erstes …

- erforschen, was *Smartphones* und *Apps* sind und was sie von Computern und Computerprogrammen unterscheidet,
- gemeinsam ein *Google-Konto* einrichten, falls du oder deine Eltern noch kein Google-Konto haben, oder den App Inventor **ohne** *Google-Konto* nutzen, und
- eine erste einfache *App erstellen*.

Danach hast du mehrere Möglichkeiten. Wir haben für dich Anleitungen zu unterschiedlich schwierigen Apps erstellt. Du kannst also wählen zwischen …

- Apps für Einsteiger: *Das mähende Schaf* und *Dein eigenes Malprogramm*,
- Apps für Fortgeschrittene: *Maulwurf-Jagd* und *Pinguin-Lagesteuerung* und
- Apps für Profis: *Durchblick im Supermarkt*, *Smalltalk mit dem Smartphone*, *Wo bin ich?*, *Sicher ist sicher* und vieles mehr.

Wenn du dich noch nicht so genau einschätzen kannst, empfehlen wir dir, bei den Apps für Einsteiger zu beginnen und dich dann zum App-Experten hochzuarbeiten.

Übrigens bieten wir dir auf der Webseite des Verlags einige Illustrationen und zwei Sound-Dateien an, mit denen du deine Apps gestalten kannst, und Musterlösungen: www.wiley-vch.de/ISBN9783527722853 oder www.downloads.fuer-dummies.de.

Über dich

Du musst für dieses Buch nicht programmieren können! Was du benötigst:

- einen *Computer* oder Laptop,
- *Internetzugang*,
- grundlegende *Englischkenntnisse*,
- wenn möglich ein *Smartphone* oder *Tablet* (aber es geht auch ohne) und
- *Lust* auf App-Programmierung.

Vermutlich hast du schon öfter am Computer gearbeitet und weißt, wie man Dinge (zum Beispiel Bilder) speichert. Wenn du unsicher bist, frage bitte immer deine Eltern oder jemand anderen um Hilfe.

Über die Symbole, die wir in diesem Buch verwenden

Dir werden in diesem Buch öfter verschiedene Symbole begegnen. Damit wollen wir dir besonders wichtige Sachen mitteilen oder auch Tipps mitgeben:

Dieses Symbol zeigt dir an, dass nun ein wichtiger Tipp *kommt. Wenn du also einmal nicht mehr weiterweißt, suche nach einem solchen Tipp.*

Der Elefant weist dich auf Informationen hin, die du dir am besten gut merkst, da du sie noch öfter brauchen wirst. Der Elefant steht also für Erinnerung.

Dieses Symbol steht für Warnung. *Hier findest du ganz wichtige Informationen, die du unbedingt lesen und auch beachten solltest.*

Hervorgehobene Textteile lenken deine Aufmerksamkeit auf eine Abbildung.

Damit du dich in größeren Abbildungen zurechtfindest, gibt es noch ein weiteres Symbol, nämlich die *Lupe*. Diese zeigt dir jeweils an, wo die wichtigen Stellen im Bild sind.

Kapitel 1
Smartphone-Apps

Was sind eigentlich Smartphone-Apps? Die Wörter *Smartphone* und *App* begegnen dir ja eigentlich jeden Tag, aber bei den vielen ähnlichen Begriffen ist es manchmal schwierig, den Überblick zu behalten. Dabei wird dir dieses Kapitel helfen.

Nach diesem Kapitel wirst du wissen, …

- » was der Unterschied zwischen einem *Smartphone*, einer *Smartwatch* und einem *Tablet* ist,
- » was das alles mit dem *Computer* zu tun hat,
- » wie die *Apps* auf das Smartphone kommen und
- » was ein *Betriebssystem* ist.

Was ist ein Smartphone?

Fangen wir mal ganz vorne an. Was bedeutet eigentlich Smartphone? Das Wort »Smartphone« kommt aus dem Englischen und besteht aus zwei Teilen – nämlich dem Wort »smart« und dem Wort »phone«.

» *Smart* bedeutet schlau, klug, intelligent oder pfiffig.

» *Phone* bedeutet einfach Telefon.

Ein Smartphone ist also ein *intelligentes Telefon*. Auch mit einem klassischen Telefon oder Handy kannst du telefonieren, aber ein Smartphone kann noch einiges mehr.

Typische Eigenschaften von Smartphones sind:

» ein *Touch-Display*,

» kleine Programme (*Apps*) und

» viele *Sensoren*.

Ein **Touch-Display** ist ein Bildschirm (auf Englisch »Display«), der auf Berührungen (»Touch«) reagiert. Das macht es möglich, dass du das Smartphone mit deinen Fingern bedienen kannst.

Die **Apps** werden wir uns im nächsten Abschnitt genauer ansehen.

Die **Sensoren** machen das Smartphone aber erst wirklich smart. Ein Smartphone hat viele Sensoren. Die Sensoren, die alle Smartphones haben, sind der Beschleunigungssensor, der Lagesensor, der Lichtsensor und der GPS-Empfänger.

Die vier Sensoren können verschiedene Dinge registrieren und dies an die Recheneinheit (praktisch so etwas wie das Gehirn) des Smartphones weitergeben. Hier findest du eine kleine Auflistung über die Fähigkeiten der Sensoren.

» **Beschleunigungssensor**: Mit diesem Sensor kann das Smartphone messen, wie schnell es gerade beschleunigt wird. Damit kannst du zum Beispiel messen, ob das Smartphone geschüttelt wird oder ob du gerade rennst oder gehst.

» **Lagesensor**, auch **Orientierungssensor** genannt: Dieser Sensor funktioniert ähnlich wie eine Wasserwaage. Das Smartphone kann mithilfe dieses Sensors zum Beispiel registrieren, ob es auf einem Tisch liegt oder ob du es gerade zum Telefonieren an dein Ohr hältst.

» **Lichtsensor**: Vielleicht ist dir schon einmal aufgefallen, dass der Bildschirm des Smartphones ausgeht, wenn du es beim Telefonieren an dein Ohr hältst, und dass er auch wieder angeht, wenn du es vom Ohr wegnimmst. Das macht der Lichtsensor, indem er die Helligkeit misst.

» **GPS-Empfänger**: Der berühmteste Sensor des Smartphones ist der GPS-Empfänger. Durch diesen kann das Smartphone seine Position auf der Erde auf ein bis drei Meter genau bestimmen. Aber nur solange es im Freien ist, da der Sensor dazu Signale von Satelliten empfangen muss. (Mehr zu diesem Sensor erfährst du im Kapitel 5 in einer der Profi-Apps.)

Was ist der Unterschied zu einem Tablet?

Ein *Tablet* ist größer als ein Smartphone und du kannst mit einem Tablet auch meistens nicht telefonieren. Das Wort »Tablet« bedeutet aus dem Englischen übersetzt Notizblock oder Schreibtafel.

Ein Tablet besitzt meist die gleichen Sensoren wie ein Smartphone. Ein Tablet wird aufgrund seines größeren Bildschirms häufig dazu verwendet, Texte zu lesen oder Videos zu schauen. Auch das Betrachten von Internetseiten geht mit einem größeren Bildschirm viel besser. Zum Telefonieren müsstest du dir aber das ganze Tablet ans Ohr halten. Da das unhandlich ist und auch ziemlich lustig aussieht, haben viele Tablets keine Telefonfunktion.

Smartphones und Tablets gibt es in ganz vielen verschiedenen Größen. Welche Smartphonegröße für dich die richtige ist, hängt davon ab, wofür du das Smartphone benutzt.

Da Smartphones und Tablets ganz viele Gemeinsamkeiten haben und beide Geräte auf die gleiche Art mit dem App Inventor programmiert werden können, verwenden wir in diesem Buch das Wort »Smartphone« und meinen damit genauso auch Tablets.

Und was ist eine Smartwatch?

Eine *Smartwatch* hast du bestimmt schon einmal gesehen. Das sind kleine Geräte, die man genau wie eine Uhr um das Handgelenk trägt. Eine Smartwatch kann auch die Uhrzeit anzeigen, aber sie kann noch viel mehr, da sie ja auch »smart« ist. Das Wort *Watch* bedeutet Uhr. Eine Smartwatch ist also eine *intelligente Uhr*. Auch auf einer Smartwatch können Apps laufen und mit manchen Smartwatches kann man sogar schon telefonieren, sodass sich eine Smartwatch von einem Smartphone kaum noch unterscheidet. Leider kann man mit dem App Inventor momentan noch keine Apps für Smartwatches programmieren. Aber dies wird bald bestimmt auch möglich sein.

Unterschiede zu Computern und Laptops

Smartphones und Tablets hast du kennengelernt. Was haben diese aber jetzt mit *Computern* und *Laptops* zu tun? Ziemlich viel. Smartphones und Tablets sind praktisch kleine Computer. Smartphones, Tablets und Laptops sind einfacher mitzunehmen als klassische Computer, da sie einen eingebauten *Akku* haben. Schließlich willst du sie auch unterwegs nutzen und nicht ständig an einer Steckdose hängen. Der Akku von Tablets hält in der Regel wesentlich länger als der von Smartphones, was leicht nachvollziehbar ist, da im Gehäuse mehr Platz ist. Klassische Computer werden hauptsächlich am Schreibtisch (auf Englisch »Desktop«) benutzt und daher auch Desktop-Computer genannt.

Computer und Laptops sind in erster Linie zum Arbeiten, manchmal auch zum Spielen gedacht. Mit beiden kannst du meist nicht telefonieren. Dafür sind sie in der Regel *leistungsstärker* und haben mehr *Speicherplatz*. Somit sind sie besser für größere Programme oder das Verarbeiten von großen Datenmengen geeignet.

Ein weiterer wichtiger Unterschied sind die *Eingabegeräte*. Smartphones, Smartwatches und Tablets kannst du direkt mit deinen Fingern auf dem Display bedienen, Computer und Laptops bedient man meist mit einer Tastatur und einer Maus. Ein klassischer Computer besteht dabei aus mehreren Einzelteilen. Er hat einen Monitor, der mit Kabeln an den Computer angeschlossen wird.

Da sowohl Computer als auch Smartphones ihre Vor- und Nachteile haben, gibt es immer mehr Geräte, sogenannte Convertibles, die eine Mischform aus Tablet und Laptop darstellen.

Apps – die kleinen Mini-Programme

Apps machen dein Smartphone zu etwas Besonderem. Ohne die Apps kannst du mit deinem Smartphone meist nur telefonieren und SMS schreiben. Die kleinen Mini-Programme, die Apps genannt werden, können auf alle Sensoren des Smartphones zugreifen und diese benutzen, um Spiele oder andere Programme spaßig oder nützlich zu gestalten. Zum Beispiel gibt es Apps, die dir den Weg nach Hause zeigen oder dafür sorgen, dass du morgens nicht verschläfst.

Hier in diesem Buch wirst du viele tolle Ideen und Anleitungen finden, was für Apps du für dein Smartphone entwickeln und wie du die eingebauten Sensoren nutzen kannst. Neben dem, was deine App kann, also der *Funktionalität*, wird auch das *Aussehen* (*Design*) deiner App eine wichtige Rolle spielen.

Woher bekommst du Apps?

Apps bekommst du auf zwei Arten. Entweder du erstellst dir selbst Apps (wie du es im nächsten Kapitel tun wirst) oder du kannst dir Apps aus dem *App Store* (also auf Deutsch »App-Geschäft«) deines Smartphones herunterladen. Auch kannst du Apps von Webseiten herunterladen und installieren. Das wird aber fast nie gemacht, weil die Apps aus dem App Store viel sicherer sind. Der App Store, auf Android-Geräten heißt er *Play Store* und auf Apple-Geräten einfach *App Store*, ist selbst auch eine App, die dir eine Übersicht über alle Apps anzeigt, die es für dein Smartphone gibt. Die Apps, die schon auf deinem Smartphone vorhanden sind, siehst du, wenn du dein Smartphone startest.

Für manche Apps muss man bezahlen, aber sehr viele sind auch kostenlos. Bei den kostenlosen Apps ist es so, wie du es aus dem Fernsehen kennst: In einer kostenlosen App wird häufig Werbung eingeblendet. Wenn du dir die Werbung ansiehst oder auch draufklickst, verdient der App-Entwickler Geld.

Wenn du eine tolle App entwickelt hast, kannst du dir also überlegen, ob du direkt Geld damit verdienen willst, indem du deine App zu einem bestimmten Preis verkaufst, oder ob du Werbung in deiner App einblenden willst, um damit etwas zu verdienen. Du kannst deine App aber natürlich auch einfach kostenlos und ohne Werbung anderen Leuten zur Verfügung stellen.

Was hat es mit dem kleinen Roboter und dem Apfel auf sich?

Wenn du dich mit der Entwicklung von Apps für Smartphones und Tablets weiter beschäftigen wirst, werden dir vor allem zwei Logos immer wieder begegnen – ein kleiner grüner Roboter und ein angebissener Apfel. Sie stehen für zwei verschiedene Smartphone-Betriebssysteme.

Was ist denn ein *Betriebssystem*? Wie der Name es schon verrät, ist das Betriebssystem dafür da, dass das Smartphone überhaupt funktionieren kann. Das Betriebssystem ist das erste Programm, was startet, wenn du dein Smartphone einschaltest, und alle anderen Programme dürfen nur das tun, was das Betriebssystem ihnen erlaubt. Auch Laptops und Computer arbeiten mit einem Betriebssystem, diese sind noch ein wenig umfangreicher als die für Smartphones und Tablets.

Der kleine grüne Roboter heißt »Android Robot«. An ihm erkennt man, dass das Smartphone oder Tablet mit dem Betriebssystem *Android* der Firma Google läuft.

Die Apps, die du hier in dem Buch entwickeln wirst, funktionieren nur auf einem Smartphone mit dem Betriebssystem Android. *Halte also nach dem Android-Roboter Ausschau, wenn du ein Smartphone suchst, um deine Apps auszuprobieren.*

Die meisten Smartphones laufen momentan mit dem Betriebssystem der Firma Google. Es gibt aber auch Smartphones, die mit dem Betriebssystem der Firma Apple laufen. »Apple« bedeutet eigentlich »Apfel« und deshalb ist das Logo der

Firma auch ein angebissener Apfel. Das Betriebssystem der Firma Apple heißt *iOS* (gesprochen ei-os) und die Smartphones heißen *iPhone*. Es gibt auch noch andere Betriebssysteme (zum Beispiel Sailfish OS), aber die kommen eher selten vor.

Was haben Betriebssysteme mit Süßigkeiten zu tun?

Alle Betriebssysteme werden regelmäßig verbessert. Da häufig neue Fähigkeiten zum Betriebssystem hinzukommen, hat man zur besseren Unterscheidung eine Nummer hinter den Namen des Betriebssystems geschrieben. Zum Beispiel heißt das erste Android-Betriebssystem, das auf einem Smartphone war, Android 1.0. Von da an hat man immer weiter hochgezählt, wenn etwas Neues zum Android-Betriebssystem dazu kam. Bei kleinen Änderungen hat man die Zahl hinter dem Punkt erhöht, zum Beispiel Android 1.5, und bei größeren Änderungen die Zahl vor dem Punkt. Als dieses Buch gedruckt wurde, hatte die allerneueste Android-Version die Nummer 15.0. Bei Apples iOS ist es genauso. Die aktuelle iOS-Version ist die Nummer 17.0.

Da sich aber Nummern nur schwer merken lassen, hat jede neue Android-Version mit einer höheren Zahl vor dem Punkt zusätzlich eine Süßigkeit als Namen bekommen. Android 13.0 trägt den Namen »Tiramisu« und Android 15.0 heißt »Vanilla Ice Cream« also Vanilleeis.

Kapitel 2
Deine erste App

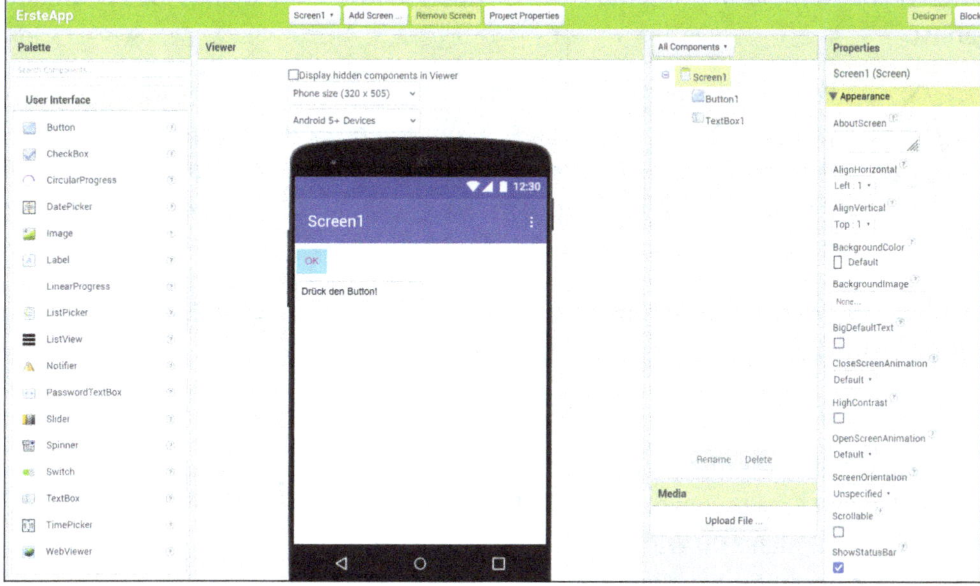

Aller Anfang ist schwer ... Aber dafür begleiten wir dich auf jedem Schritt bis zu deiner ersten App! Also App geht's!

Code merken oder Account anlegen

» Du hast *kein Google-Konto*? Kein Problem, wir zeigen dir in diesem Kapitel, wie du den App Inventor ohne Konto nutzen kannst oder wie du ein Konto einrichtest.

» Du hast schon *ein Google-Konto*? Super, dann kannst du die Einrichtung des Kontos überspringen und direkt mit der Anmeldung im App Inventor weitermachen.

Um deine Apps beim App Inventor speichern zu können, musst du dir entweder einen Code aufschreiben oder die Apps werden mit deinem Google-Konto verbunden und damit gespeichert. Der App Inventor wird zwar heute vom MIT, einer berühmten amerikanischen Universität, betrieben, er wurde aber ursprünglich von der Firma Google entwickelt. Durch das Konto ist sichergestellt, dass nur du durch deine Anmeldung (mit Mailadresse und Passwort) auf deine Apps zugreifen kannst.

Wenn du 13 Jahre oder älter bist, kannst du dir ein eigenes Konto anlegen. Wenn du jünger als 13 Jahre alt bist, dann hole dir bitte Hilfe bei deinen Eltern, damit diese sich für dich anmelden. Bitte beachte: Ein eigenes Google-Konto darfst du dir erst einrichten, wenn du mindestens 13 Jahre alt bist.

Öffne zuerst deinen Internetbrowser (Chrome, Firefox oder Edge) und gehe auf die Webseite: https://code.appinventor.mit.edu/login/

Du siehst jetzt die App Inventor-Begrüßungsseite.

Du hast jetzt drei Möglichkeiten, dich beim App Inventor anzumelden. Welche du wählst, liegt daran, ob du dir ein Konto bei Google einrichten willst oder ob du dir lieber einen Code aufschreibst.

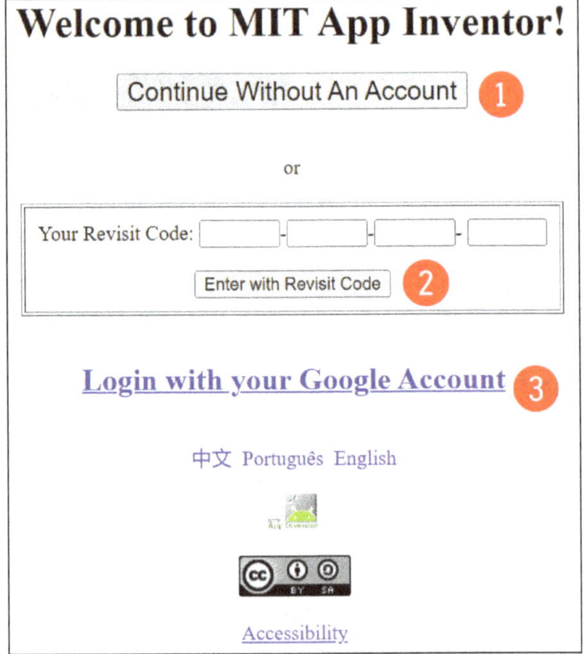

1 **Klicke auf den Button Continue Without An Account, wenn du kein Google-Konto erstellen willst. Das bedeutet auf Deutsch »Weiter ohne einen Account«.**

Wenn du kein Google-Konto hast oder keins anlegen möchtest, dann ist dieser Weg der richtige. Klickst du auf den Button, dann bekommst du einen Code angezeigt, den du dir aufschreiben musst, damit du deine erstellten Apps auch wiederfinden kannst.

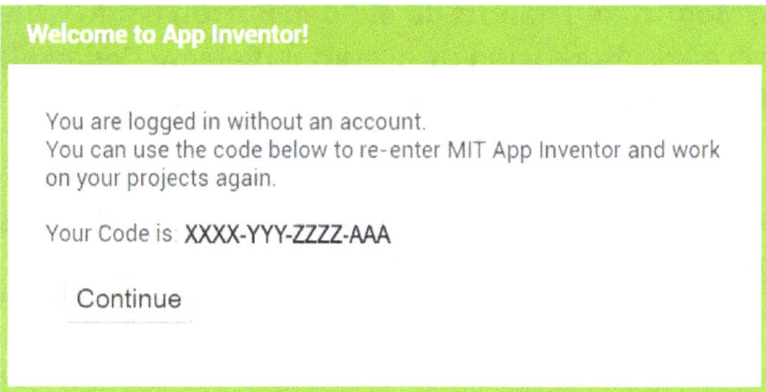

Du findest deinen geheimen Code hinter dem Text Your Code is: angezeigt. Dies bedeutet auf Deutsch »Dein Code ist«. Dahinter siehst du dann deinen Code, der aus einer Reihe von Buchstaben besteht. Es werden zufällig zwischen 2 und 4 Buchstaben zwischen den Strichen erzeugt und dir angezeigt. Auf dem Bild haben wir als Beispiel den Code XXXX-YYY-ZZZZ-AAA angegeben. Deiner hat andere Buchstaben.

Solltest du den Code verlieren, kannst du deine Apps nicht mehr wiederfinden. Da der Code so gemacht wurde, dass es ganz viele Möglichkeiten gibt, wie der aussehen kann (genau genommen 64.509.974.703.297.150.976), sind das über 64 Trillionen Möglichkeiten. Wenn du jede Sekunde einen Code eingeben würdest, bräuchtest du mehr Zeit als es die Erde gibt, um alle Codes auszuprobieren.

2 **Hast du früher schon einmal einen Code erstellt, dann kannst du diesen bei Your Revisit Code eintragen und auf den Button Enter with Revisit Code klicken. Das bedeutet auf Deutsch »Mit einem Wiederholungscode anmelden«.**

Mit einem Wiederholungscode werden dir alle Apps angezeigt, die du früher schon mal erstellt hast. Du verlierst auf diese Weise nie deine erstellten Apps.

3 **Als dritte Möglichkeit kannst du auf den Button Login with your Google Account klicken, um dich, statt mit einem Code, mit einem Google Account anzumelden oder eins zu erstellen.**

Wenn du dich für diesen Weg entscheidest, dann werden alle Apps mit deinem Google-Konto verknüpft. Du musst dir dann aber das Passwort für dein Google-Konto aufschreiben oder merken.

Wenn du dich für die Möglichkeiten 1 oder 2 entschieden hast, dann kannst du direkt zur Anmeldung beim App Inventor springen (siehe Kapitel »Jetzt geht es wirklich looooos«.

Ein Google-Konto erstellen

Falls du oder deine Eltern schon ein Google-Konto besitzen, könnt ihr direkt eure Google-Mailadresse zum Anmelden verwenden. Dann kannst du die nächsten Schritte überspringen und direkt mit der Anmeldung im App Inventor weitermachen.

Hast du kein Google-Konto, dann klicke auf Konto erstellen.

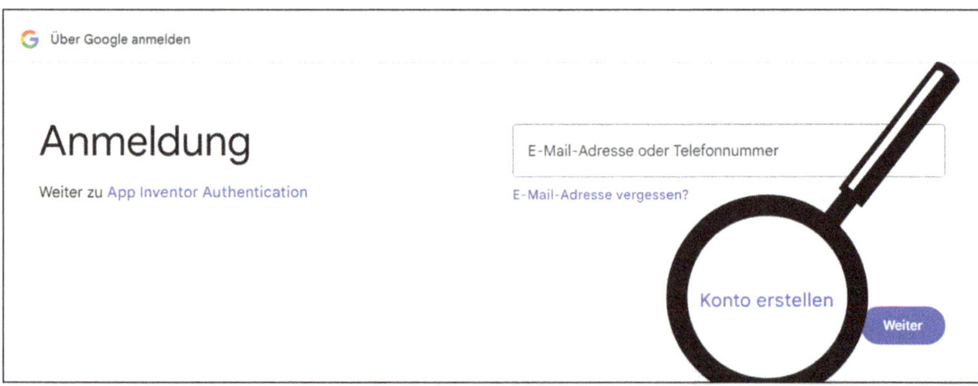

Daten für ein Google-Konto eingeben

Auf dem Bildschirm, der jetzt erscheint, musst du nur die markierten Felder ausfüllen. Alle anderen Felder kannst du ausfüllen, musst du aber nicht.

1 **Trage einen Namen ein und klicke danach auf Weiter.**

Du kannst deinen richtigen Namen eintragen, musst es aber nicht.

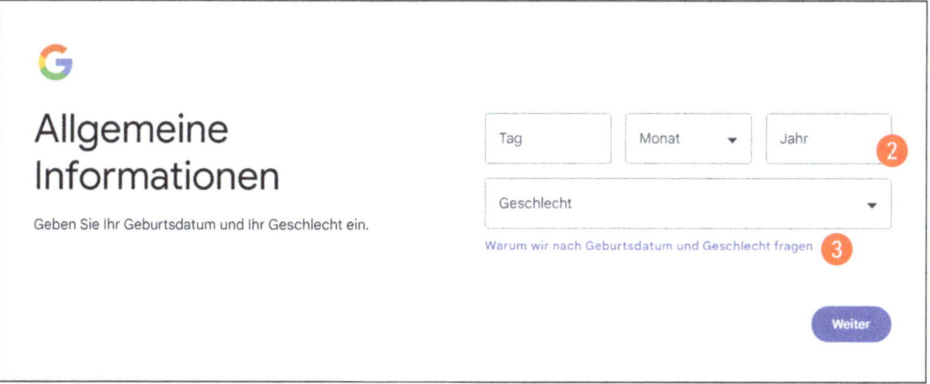

2 **Bestätige mit deinem Geburtsdatum, dass du mindestens 13 Jahre alt bist.**

Denk daran, dass du dir nur dann ein Google-Konto selbst erstellen darfst, wenn du mindestens 13 Jahre alt bist. Ansonsten müssen deine Eltern für dich ein Konto einrichten. Damit kannst du natürlich genauso gut Apps erstellen.

3 **Gib dein Geschlecht an.**

Du kannst frei auswählen, was du angeben möchtest, wenn du nicht dein richtiges Geschlecht angeben willst.

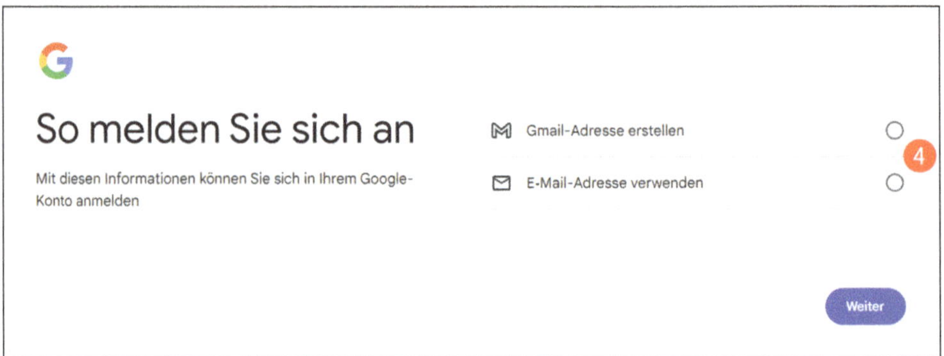

4 **In diesem Schritt kannst du dir zur Anmeldung beim App Inventor eine neue Gmail-Adresse erstellen oder eine vorhandene nutzen.**

Wir zeigen dir hier den Weg, wenn du eine neue Mailadresse nutzen möchtest.

5 **Suche dir eine Mailadresse aus den Vorschlägen aus oder klicke auf Gmail-Adresse erstellen, wenn dir die Vorschläge nicht gefallen. Klicke dann auf Weiter.**

Google überlegt sich hier Vorschläge aufgrund des Namens, den du angegeben hast. Viele Mailadressen werden schon von anderen Menschen genutzt und die kannst du dann nicht mehr aussuchen. Für die Mailadresse kannst du Buchstaben, Zahlen und Sonderzeichen (das sind zum Beispiel: !, ?, # oder auch -) verwenden.

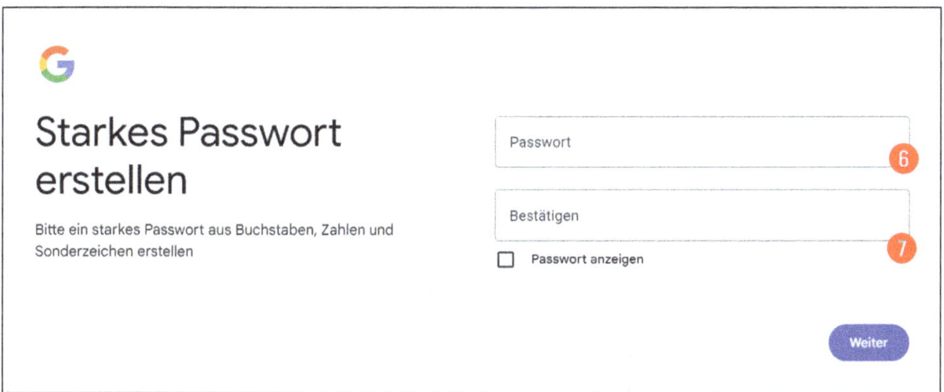

6 **Trage ein Passwort ein.**

Dein Passwort muss aus mindestens 8 Zeichen bestehen. Es sollte nicht zu leicht sein. Wenn dein Passwort zu leicht zu erraten ist, dann zeigt dir die Webseite das an.

Ein Passwort dient dazu, deine eigenen Daten, Dateien (zum Beispiel Fotos) oder auch deine eigene Arbeit (im App Inventor deine selbsterstellten Apps) zu schützen. Daher solltest du ein Passwort immer so wählen, dass es niemand anderes erraten kann. Das Passwort »Anna123« ist zum Beispiel nicht so sicher wie das Passwort »K73fh"9!hcq0«.

7 **Gib dein Passwort noch einmal ein.**

So wird sichergestellt, dass du dich nicht beim ersten Mal vertippt hast.

Gehe bei der Eingabe deiner Daten sorgfältig vor und schreibe dir wichtige Dinge wie deinen Benutzernamen und dein Passwort auf.

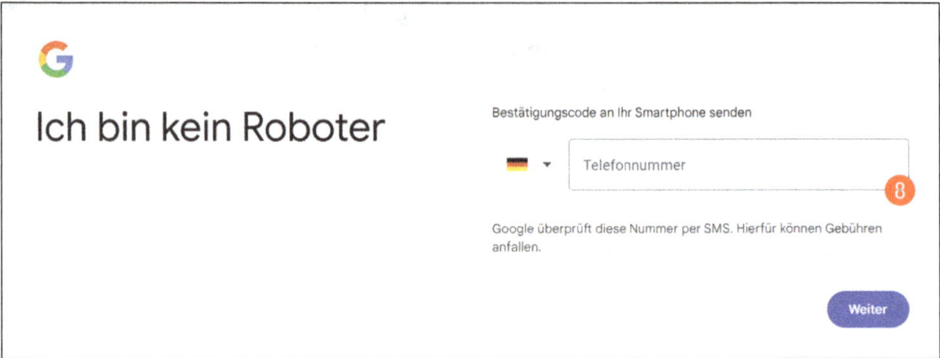

8 Gib deine Handynummer ein und drücke auf Weiter.

Damit du zeigen kannst, dass du kein Roboter bist, brauchst du ein Smartphone. Wenn du die Handynummer eingibst, dann bekommst du eine SMS mit einem Code. Den kannst du dann wieder am Computer eingeben und zeigen, dass du kein Roboter, sondern ein Mensch bist.

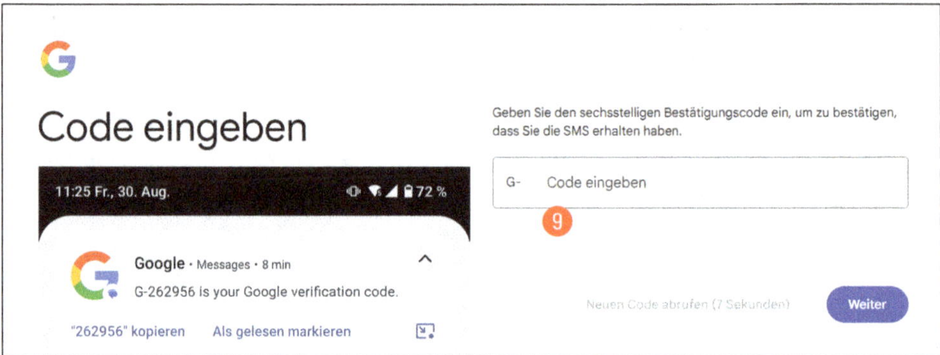

9 Gib den Code, den du in der SMS bekommen hast, ein und klicke auf Weiter.

Super, du hast es geschafft. Alle wichtigen Dinge sind eingetragen. Bei den nächsten Eingaben holst du am besten deine Eltern dazu. Da geht es vor allem darum, welche Daten die Firma Google von dir speichern und verwenden darf. Du kannst hier alles ablehnen. Es hat keine Auswirkungen auf den App Inventor. Der Erklärung zum Datenschutz musst du aber zustimmen.

Für die Benutzung des App Inventors wird dein Name, deine Mailadresse, deine Spracheinstellung und dein Profilbild gespeichert. Alle anderen Daten werden ignoriert.

Jetzt solltest du die Anmeldung zum App Inventor von Google sehen. Wir haben uns die E-Mail-Adresse kuckumu4@gmail.com erstellt. Auf deinem Bildschirm steht an dieser Stelle deine eigene E-Mail-Adresse.

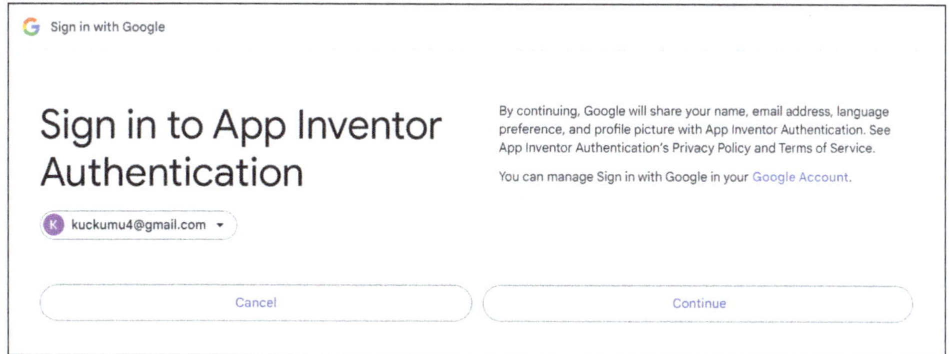

10 Klicke auf Continue, um dich beim App Inventor anzumelden.

Geschafft! Herzlichen Glückwunsch, du bist nun im App Inventor angemeldet und solltest jetzt den Startbildschirm sehen.

Developer: *Dieser Begriff bedeutet ins Deutsche übersetzt Entwickler. Er bezeichnet alle Menschen, die Programme (Code) für Computer, Smartphones oder andere technische Geräte schreiben. Mit diesem Buch wirst auch du zum Developer.*

Console: *Dieses Wort heißt auf Deutsch ganz ähnlich, nämlich Konsole. Es meint hier aber keineswegs eine Spielekonsole, sondern ein Fenster zur Erstellung von Computerprogrammen.*

Im App Inventor anmelden

Falls du die vorherigen Schritte übersprungen hast, weil du dich mit dem Wiederholungscode anmelden willst oder du schon ein Google-Konto hast, ist dies die richtige Stelle, um wieder einzusteigen!

Vielleicht wird noch ein anderes, kleines Fenster eingeblendet. Hier werden dir verschiedene Möglichkeiten vorgestellt, wie du deine spätere App testen kannst. Wie das geht, werden wir dir im Abschnitt »Schritt für Schritt zum Test-Ziel« alles ganz genau erklären. Du kannst also ein Häkchen setzen bei Do Not Show Again *(»Nicht wieder anzeigen«) und dann auf* Continue *(»Fortfahren«) klicken. Anschließend erscheint ein weiteres Fenster. Dort wirst du gefragt, ob du an einer Umfrage zum App Inventor teilnehmen oder dir Beispiele ansehen möchtest. Da du den App Inventor noch gar nicht kennst, drückst du am besten auf* CLOSE *(auf Deutsch »schließen«).*

Jetzt geht es wirklich looooos!

Lege dein erstes Projekt an.

1. **Klicke auf New project (»Neues Projekt«).**

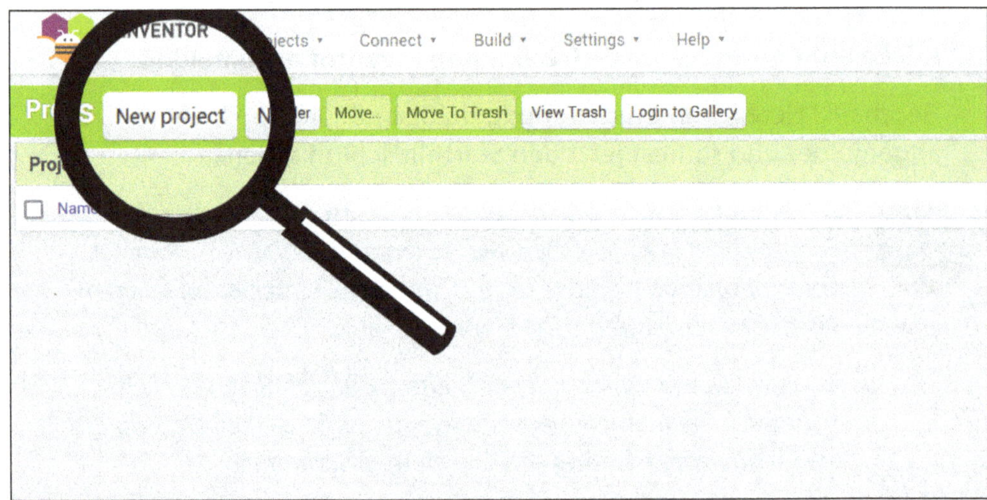

2. **Gib hinter Project name (»Projektname«) in das Textfeld `ErsteApp` ein und klicke auf OK.**

Projektnamen dürfen, wie auch einige andere Benennungen im App Inventor, keine Umlaute (also ä, ü, ö, ß) oder Leerzeichen enthalten und müssen mit einem Buchstaben beginnen.

Jetzt ist alles vorbereitet und deine erste App kann entstehen!

Der erste Eindruck – das Design

Deine erste App, jetzt ist es so weit! Stück für Stück wirst du jetzt eine App zusammenbauen, die schon einige tolle Dinge kann:

- Deine App wird einen *Text* (auf Englisch: »Text« oder »Label«) und einen *Knopf* (auf Englisch: »Button«) haben.
- Der Text wird sich verändern, wenn du auf den Knopf drückst.
- Auch ein Bild wird zu sehen sein. Dieses kannst du dir später selbst aussuchen.
- Wenn du dann auf das Bild klickst, wird ein lustiges Geräusch ertönen. Welches Geräusch das sein wird, bestimmst auch du selbst!

Beim Programmieren sind sehr viele Begriffe auf Englisch. Am Anfang ist das nicht immer leicht. Bei neuen Wörtern hilft dir die Übersetzung in diesem Buch, die du hinter den Begriffen in Anführungszeichen (» «) findest. Du wirst außerdem merken, dass sich die Wörter wiederholen und man sich ganz schnell daran gewöhnt.

Was du zum Start wissen musst: Es gibt zwei Ansichten im App Inventor:

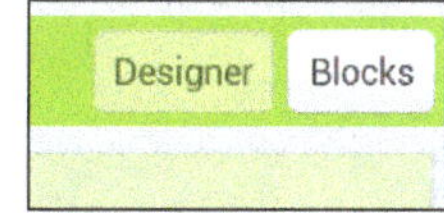

- Die erste Ansicht ist der *Designer*. Hier legst du das Design (»Aussehen«) deiner App fest. Du kannst zum Beispiel Farben auswählen oder bestimmen, welcher Text angezeigt wird.
- Die zweite Ansicht heißt *Blocks*. Hier programmierst du die Funktionalität deiner App, also was passiert, wenn du auf einen Button (»Knopf«) drückst.

Du startest in der Designer*-Ansicht des App Inventors. Oben rechts kannst du immer sehen, wo du gerade bist, und zwischen den beiden Ansichten wechseln.*

Schau dir als Erstes die Palette am linken Bildschirmrand an. Hier findest du viele tolle Dinge, die du in deiner App gebrauchen kannst. Zuerst ist der Unterpunkt User Interface wichtig. User Interface heißt übersetzt: »Oberfläche, die der Benutzer (»User«) sieht«.

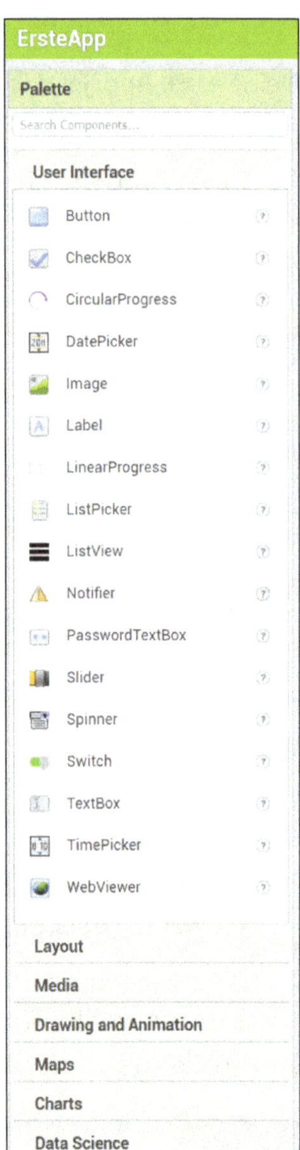

Für deine erste App brauchst du zwei verschiedene Dinge:

- **Button**: Buttons sind dir sicherlich schon einmal begegnet, zum Beispiel auch bei der Anmeldung zum App Inventor. Buttons sind die Knöpfe auf dem Bildschirm, mit denen man bestimmte Aktionen auslösen oder bestätigen kann.
- **TextBox**: Durch die TextBox kannst du Text auf dem Bildschirm anzeigen lassen. Damit kannst du jemandem, der deine App benutzt, zum Beispiel erklären, wie deine App funktioniert.

Schaue dir den Viewer in der Mitte des App Inventors an. Dies ist das Vorschaubild für deine App. Deine App wird auf einem Smartphone so aussehen, wie es im Viewer angezeigt wird.

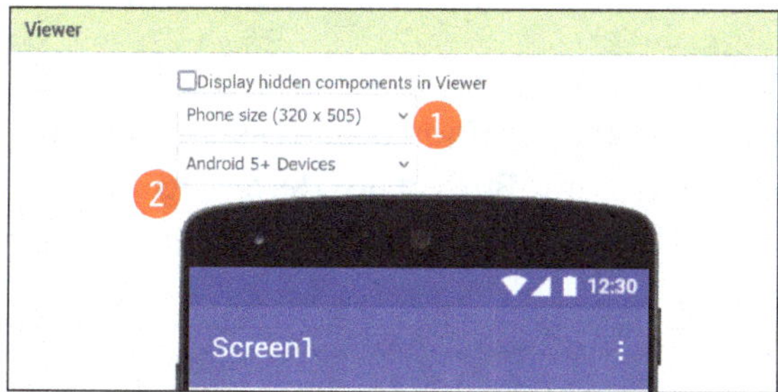

Du siehst noch zwei Auswahlmöglichkeiten. Damit kannst du das Aussehen der Vorschau anpassen:

1. **Unter Phone size kannst du die Größe der Vorschau anpassen. *Phone size (320 x 505)* ist normalerweise ausgewählt und beschreibt die Größe eines Smartphones. Du kannst hier noch auf *Tablet size (480 x 675)* (»Tabletgröße«) oder *Monitor size (768 x 1024)* (»Bildschirmgröße«) umstellen.**
2. **In der zweiten Auswahl bestimmst du das Design der Vorschau. Ausgewählt ist die Ansicht *Android 5+ Devices*. Also Geräte die das Betriebssystem Android 5 oder neuer haben. Du kannst hier auch auf eine ältere Ansicht oder die iPhone-Ansicht umstellen, wenn du magst.**

Du wechselst hier nur die Ansicht der Vorschau! Du kannst diese immer wieder ändern, wenn du magst. Das ändert nichts an deiner App und wie diese später auf deinem Gerät oder auf anderen Geräten aussieht. Du kannst dir das hier nur einfach schon einmal anschauen.

Wir bleiben hier im Buch bei der vorausgewählten Ansicht, die hier abgebildet ist. Jetzt bist du dran, es kann losgehen!

Ein Button für die App

1 **Ziehe einen Button von der Palette in den Viewer, indem du mit der Maus zum Button in der Palette gehst, die linke Maustaste drückst und gedrückt hältst und dann mit der Maus den Button in das weiße Feld des Viewers ziehst.**

Du siehst, dass du an der richtigen Stelle bist, wenn im Viewer eine blaue Linie erscheint. Falls dir der Button auf dem Weg zum Viewer verloren geht, ist das gar nicht schlimm. Du kannst es jederzeit noch einmal versuchen.

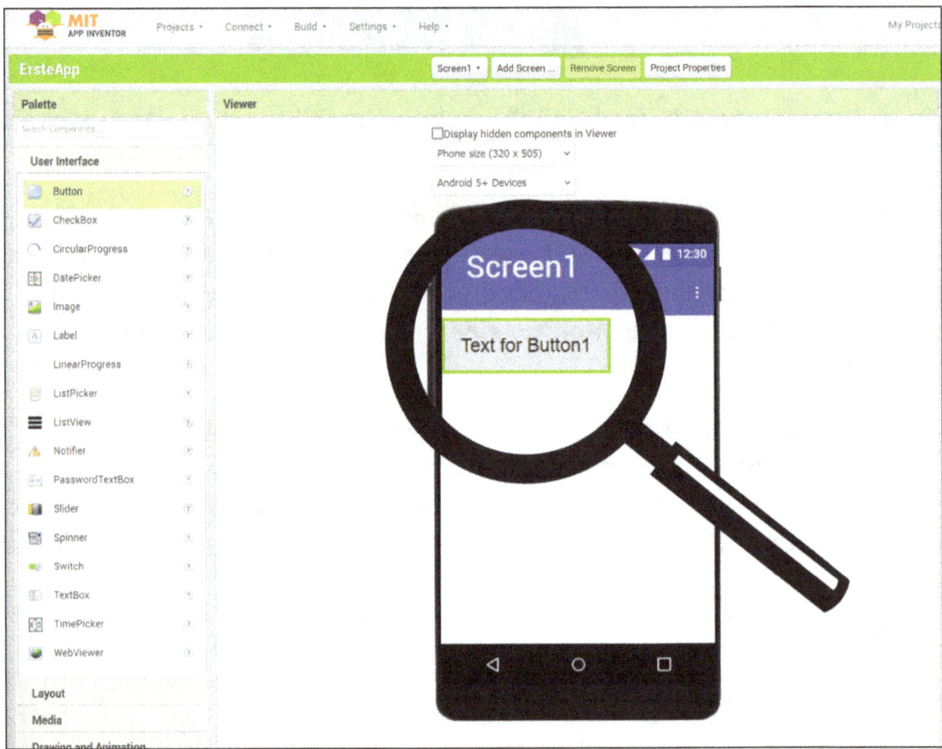

Zwei Dinge haben sich auf deinem Bildschirm geändert, als du den Button in den Viewer gezogen hast:

- In den Components (Komponenten) rechts vom Viewer ist unter Screen1 (dies ist dein »Bildschirm«) der Button1 aufgetaucht. Er gehört damit zum Screen1 und wird später in deiner App angezeigt.

- Zweitens haben sich die Properties (»Eigenschaften«) geändert. Hier findest du jetzt die Eigenschaften des Buttons. Und die kannst du ändern! Das Properties-Feld findest du ganz rechts auf deinem Bildschirm.

2 Wähle für deinen Button eine neue Hintergrundfarbe (BackgroundColor).

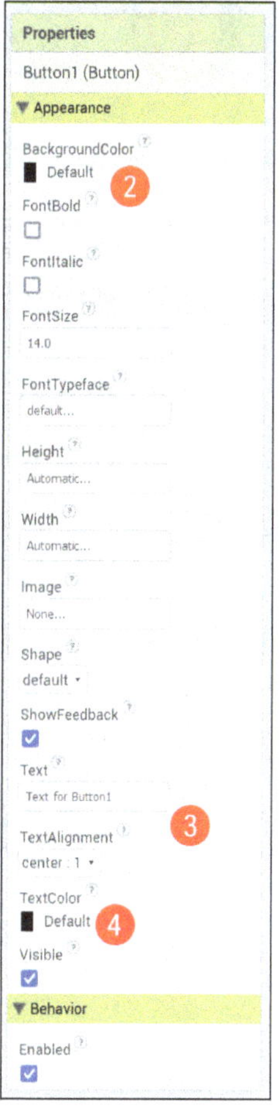

Klicke dazu in den Properties auf das schwarze Kästchen. Wähle eine Farbe aus, indem du sie anklickst.

Super! Jetzt hast du die Farbe des Buttons verändert. Probiere ruhig die Farben einmal durch, bis du deine Lieblingsfarbe gefunden hast.

Wenn du neben dem Button in den Viewer klickst, werden dir rechts nicht mehr die Eigenschaften des Buttons, sondern die des Screen1 (also des gesamten Bildschirms) angezeigt. Mit einem Klick auf den Button (im Viewer oder unter Components) kannst du wieder zurück zum Button wechseln.

3 Ändere den Text des Buttons in OK.

Schaue dir die Properties einmal ganz genau an. Dort findest du eine Stelle, an der Text steht. In dem Feld darunter steht genau das, was auch auf deinem Button im Viewer zu sehen ist. Hier kannst du den Text verändern. Probiere verschiedene Varianten aus. Na, klappt alles?

Wie du bestimmt schon gemerkt hast, ändert sich die Ansicht im Viewer automatisch. Du musst also nicht speichern, das passiert alles automatisch. Wenn Änderungen von dir nicht direkt im Viewer zu sehen sind, dann klicke mit der Maus einmal neben das Eingabefeld, dann sollte es klappen.

4 Passe auch die Farbe der Schrift (TextColor) nach deinen Wünschen an.

Die Textfarbe soll zur Farbe des Buttons passen.

Toll! Jetzt hast du schon die Farbe und den Text des Buttons geändert sowie auch die Textfarbe.

Was passiert eigentlich, wenn die Farbe des Buttons und die Farbe des Textes auf dem Button gleich sind? Probiere es aus!

Eine Textbox für die App

Jetzt wird es Zeit, eine TextBox zum Screen hinzuzufügen.

1 **Ziehe eine TextBox aus der Palette in deinen Screen unter den Button.**

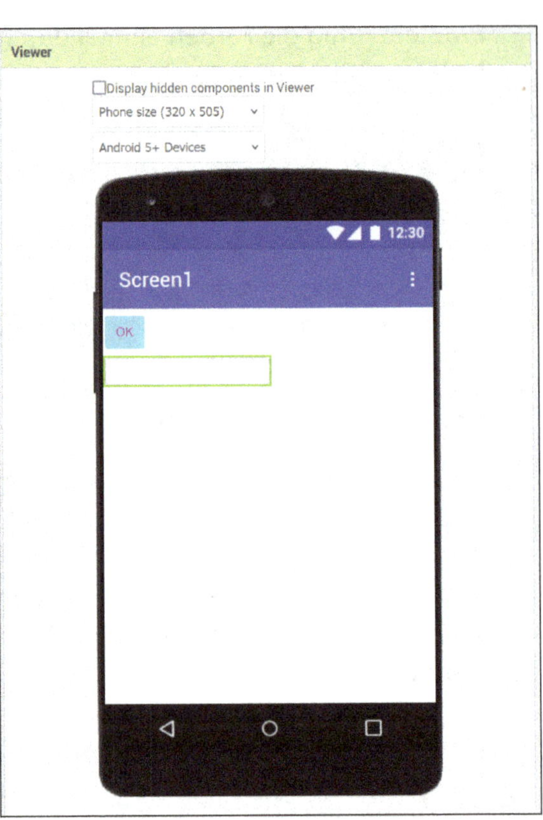

Deine App sieht dann in etwa so aus wie in der Abbildung. Nur ein bisschen anders, da du vermutlich andere Farben ausgewählt hast. Die Properties zeigen jetzt die Eigenschaften deiner TextBox an und unter Components ist die TextBox1 aufgetaucht.

Mit einem Klick auf ein Element (im Viewer *oder unter* Components*) kannst du dir jederzeit seine Eigenschaften anzeigen lassen.*

2 **Verändere den Text der TextBox zu `Drück den Button!`.**

Dies kannst du genauso machen, wie du schon den Text auf dem Button geändert hast. Schaffst du das schon alleine?

Ansonsten kommt hier noch einmal ein Tipp: Klicke in das Feld unter Text (das diesmal noch leer ist), schreibe den Text hinein und klicke mit der Maus neben das Eingabefeld.

Das Aussehen, oder, wie es die Developer sagen, das Design ist jetzt fertig. Jetzt geht es ans Programmieren, denn bisher sieht deine App zwar schick aus, aber noch kann sie nichts.

Nicht vergessen, das Ziel ist, dass sich der Text verändert, wenn man auf den Button klickt.

Aussehen ist nicht alles – die Funktionalität

Jetzt wird programmiert!

1 Wechsel in den Blocks-Editor, indem du auf den Button Blocks in der Ecke rechts oben drückst.

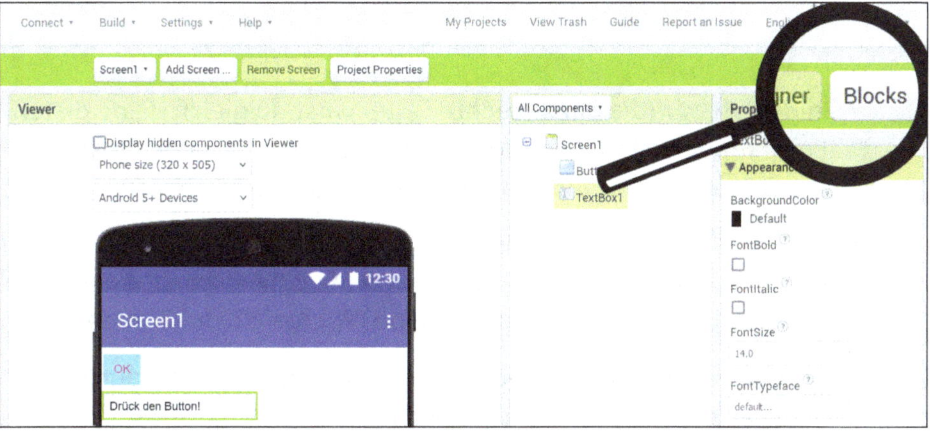

Jetzt siehst du die zweite Ansicht, den Blocks-Editor. Hier füllst du deine App mit Leben. Bis eben hast du dich ausschließlich mit dem Design, also dem Aussehen deiner App beschäftigt. Jetzt wirst du der App sagen, was sie tun soll. Dazu schaust du dir zuerst den Blocks-Editor genauer an.

- In den Blocks (linke Seite) findest du alle Programmbausteine, die du zum Programmieren deiner App brauchst. Auch alle Dinge, die du im Designer auf deinen Screen geschoben hast, findest du dort wieder.

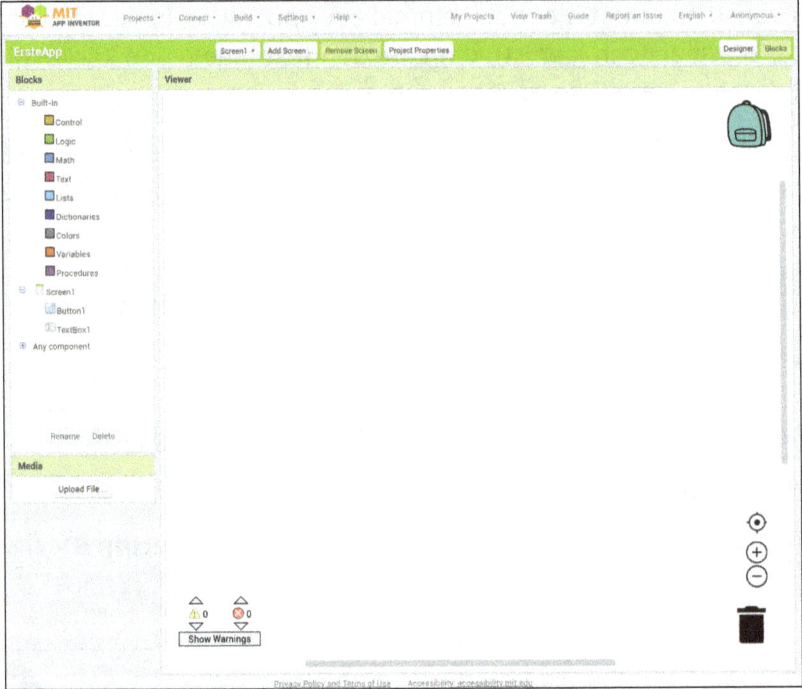

- In den Viewer (die ganze rechte Seite) wirst du gleich deine ersten Programmbausteine einfügen, indem du diese aus den Blocks in den Viewer ziehst. (Das funktioniert hier genau wie im Designer.)
- Falls du dich einmal mit einem Block vertan hast, kannst du diesen einfach in den *Mülleimer* unten rechts ziehen und damit löschen. Wenn du gleich mehrere Bauteile löschst, kommt eine Abfrage, ob du dir auch sicher bist.
- Falls du Programmteile auch in anderen Projekten oder auch für andere Screens (dazu später mehr) verwenden möchtest, kannst du sie in den *Rucksack* packen und an anderer Stelle wieder rausholen.

Drückst du oben rechts auf Designer, kommst du wieder zurück zum Designer. So kannst du immer zwischen dem Aussehen deiner App und den Funktionen deiner App hin- und herwechseln.

2 In den Blocks findest du den von dir erstellten Screen1 wieder und direkt darunter taucht auch dein Button1 auf. Klicke diesen an.

In dem neuen Fenster siehst du alle Programmbausteine, die du zum Programmieren deines Button1 benutzen kannst.

3 **Klicke den ersten Programmbaustein mit der Beschriftung when Button1.Click do an und halte die Maustaste gedrückt, bis nur noch der angeklickte Programmbaustein im Viewer zu sehen ist.**

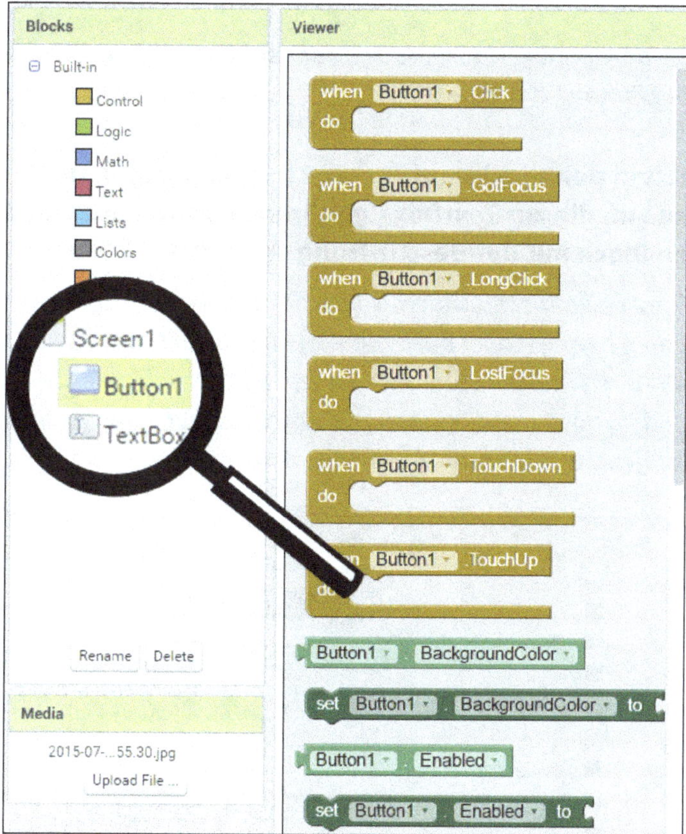

Jetzt befindet sich der Programmbaustein im Viewer.

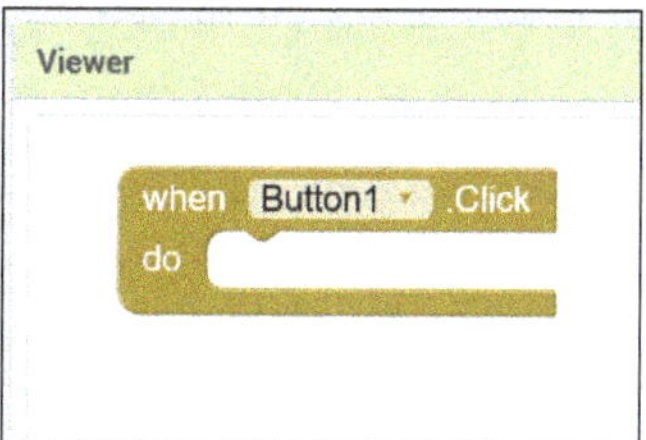

Schaue dir den Programmbaustein einmal genauer an. Hier eine kleine Übersetzungshilfe:

- when bedeutet »wenn«,
- Button1 ist dein eingefügter Button,
- Click bedeutet »wird angeklickt« und
- do bedeutet »dann tue etwas«.

Also bedeutet dieser Programmblock übersetzt »Wenn Button1 angeklickt wird, dann tue etwas«.

Was dann getan werden soll, kommt jetzt hinter das do.

Deine Aufgabe ist es, dass sich der Text deiner App ändert, wenn man auf Button1 drückt.

4 **Klicke jetzt in den Blocks auf TextBox1. Jetzt tauchen die Programmbausteine auf, die zur TextBox1 gehören. Scrolle durch die Liste und suche den Block mit der Beschriftung set TextBox1.Text to.**

Scrollen kannst du, indem du den Scrollbalken rechts nach oben oder unten bewegst oder auch das Rad an deiner Maus drehst, falls du eine Maus mit Rad benutzt. Du wirst sehen, dass sich die Liste dann bewegt und du noch mehr Programmbausteine sehen kannst. Dies geht immer, wenn ein Balken am Rand zu sehen ist.

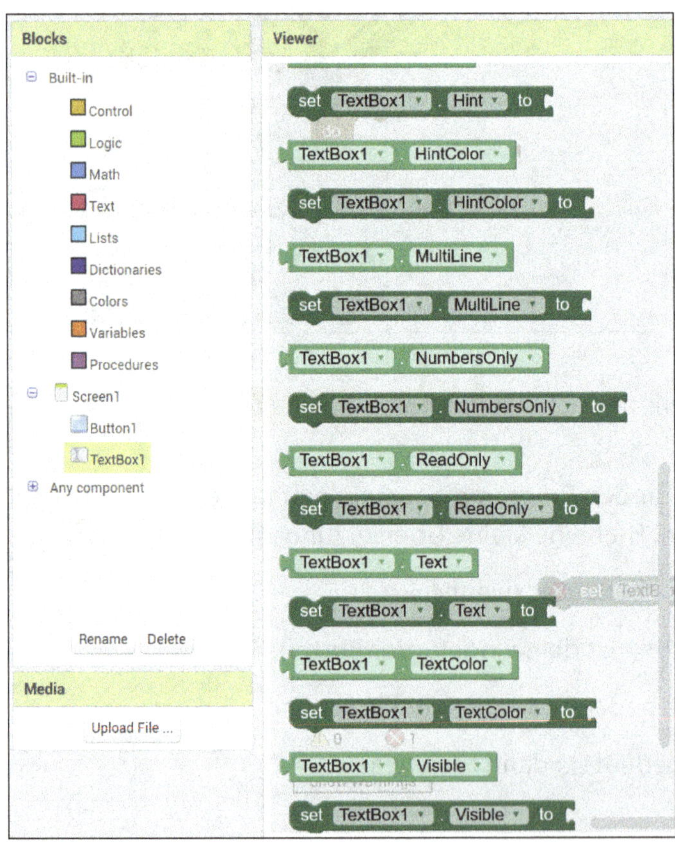

5 **Toll, du hast den Programmbaustein gefunden! Klicke ihn an und lege ihn im Viewer ab, indem du die Maustaste wieder loslässt.**

Jetzt liegen die zwei Programmbausteine in deinem Viewer.

6 **Füge die beiden Programmstücke zusammen, indem du das grüne Programmstück hinter das do in die Lücke ziehst.**

Dieses muss dort einrasten, dann ist das grüne Programmstück in dem orangenen eingefügt.

Es ist ganz wichtig, dass die Programmbausteine richtig einrasten. Wenn du den grünen Baustein an die richtige Stelle ziehst, bekommt die kleine Beule an dem orangenen Bauteil eine gelbe Umrandung. Dann kannst du den Baustein loslassen.

Schaue dir das eingefügte Programmstück genau an. Wieder eine kleine Hilfe zum Übersetzen der englischen Wörter:

- set bedeutet hier »verändere«,
- TextBox1 ist deine TextBox, die du im Designer in deine App hinzugefügt hast,
- Text ist der Text der TextBox1 und
- to bedeutet »zu«.

Zusammen mit dem Programmstück von eben, hast du also folgenden Satzanfang zusammengesetzt: »Wenn Button1 angeklickt wird, dann setze in der TextBox1 den Text auf …«.

Wenn du dir den Viewer genau anschaust, fallen dir bestimmt zwei Dinge auf.

- Zum einen ein kleines gelbes und ein kleines rotes Warndreieck.
- Zum anderen, dass der Satz noch nicht beendet ist. Rechts ist ja noch ein offenes Puzzleteil zu sehen. Du musst der App noch sagen, wie der neue Text lauten soll. Dies gehört hinter das to.

Das gelbe Warndreieck und das rote Kreuz geben an, dass in deinem Programm noch etwas fehlt. Kontrolliere dann alle deine Programmbausteine ganz genau, da deine App sonst nicht richtig funktioniert. Wenn du auf Show Warnings *(auf Deutsch »Zeige Warnungen«) klickst oder direkt auf die roten Kreuze, wird dir angezeigt, wo genau das Problem liegt.*

7 Suche unter Blocks die Auswahl »Text«, klicke diese an und ziehe direkt den obersten Programmbaustein (er stellt ein leeres Textfeld dar) in den Viewer.

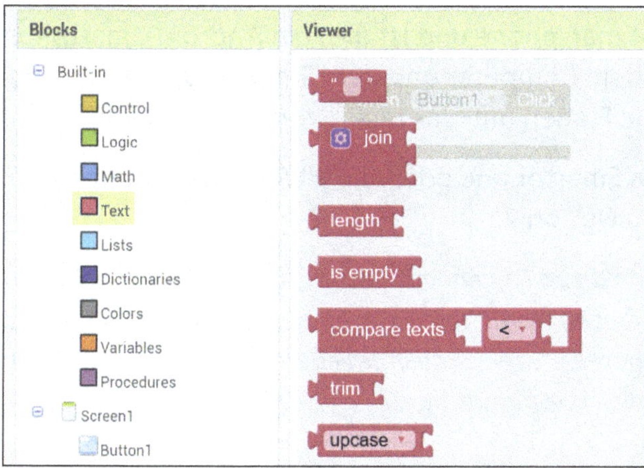

8 Baue den Programmbaustein hinten an den grünen Baustein an.

when Button1 .Click
do set TextBox1 . Text to " "

9 Klicke in die Mitte des neu angelegten Programmstücks zwischen die beiden Anführungszeichen. Tippe `Super!` ein.

when Button1 .Click
do set TextBox1 . Text to " Super! "

Als *Programmcode* hast du jetzt eingegeben: »when Button1.Click do set TextBox1.Text to "Super!"«. Übersetzt bedeutet das: »Wenn Button1 angeklickt wird, dann setze in der TextBox1 den Text auf "Super!"«.

Prima! Du hast deine App programmiert. Jetzt wird es Zeit, deine App zu testen.

Schritt für Schritt zum Test-Ziel

Du hast zwei Möglichkeiten, deine App auszuprobieren. Wir helfen dir zuerst einmal herauszufinden, welche Möglichkeit für dich die bessere ist. Beantworte dafür die folgenden Fragen:

» Hast du ein Smartphone und ist dies ein Android-Smartphone? Bist du zu Hause und dein Computer und dein Smartphone sind beide im WLAN? Wenn du alle Fragen mit »Ja« beantwortet hast, dann wähle Option 1.

» Du hast kein Smartphone oder das WLAN funktioniert nicht? Dann blättere weiter bis zu Option 2.

Wenn du im Folgenden etwas nicht verstehst, solltest du dir Hilfe bei deinen Eltern holen. Am Ende jeder Option findest du eine Internetadresse zu einer ausführlicheren Anleitung, die allerdings nur in Englisch verfügbar ist.

Option 1: Die App auf dem eigenen Smartphone testen

Auf deinem Smartphone musst du Folgendes erledigen:

1. **Öffne die App Play Store (Android) oder App Store (Apple) auf deinem Smartphone.**
2. **Gib in das Suchfeld `MIT APP Inventor` ein.**
3. **Installiere die App MIT AI2 Companion auf deinem Smartphone.**
4. **Starte die App.**

Auf deinem Computer sind folgende Schritte zu tun:

1 Klicke im App Inventor auf Connect und anschließend auf AI Companion.

Unter Your Code is: wird dir nun ein Code aus sechs Buchstaben angezeigt. Dieser Code ändert sich bei jeder Verbindung, sodass bei dir dort andere Buchstaben stehen werden.

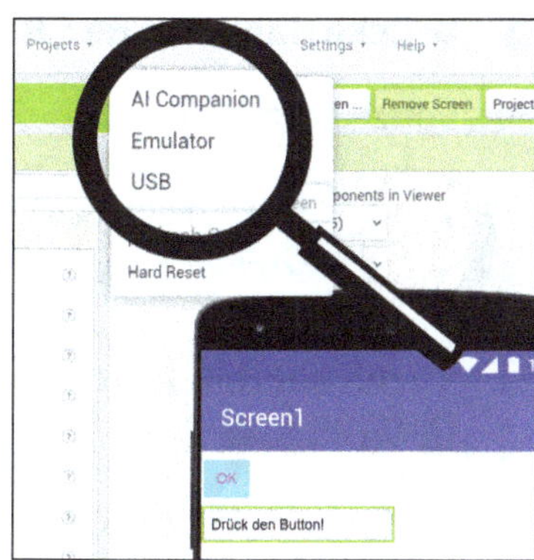

2 Gib deinen Code in das weiße Textfeld auf deinem Smartphone ein.

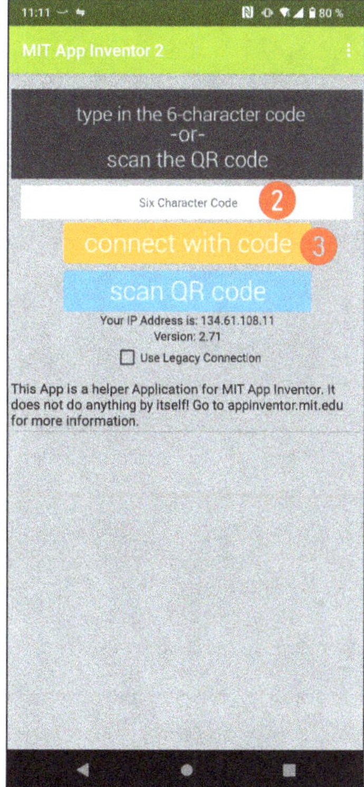

3 **Drücke dann auf den Button connect with code.**

Spitze, jetzt solltest du deine App in deinem Smartphone sehen.

Es kann ein wenig dauern, bis deine App auf dem Smartphone erscheint. Habe etwas Geduld.

4 **Klicke auf den Button und schaue, ob deine App auch richtig funktioniert.**

- Sieht deine App beim Starten so aus wie in der Abbildung links?
- Sieht sie nach dem Drücken auf den Button aus wie in der Abbildung rechts?

Falls du deine App nicht auf deinem Smartphone sehen kannst, dann besuche mit deinen Eltern diese Webseite: http://appinventor.mit.edu/explore/ai2/setup-device-wifi.html. Dort findest du viele Tipps zur Installation des MIT AI Companion und zur Verbindung deines Computers mit dem Smartphone.

Option 2: Die App mit dem Emulator testen

Der Emulator sieht aus wie ein Smartphone, ist aber nur ein Fenster auf deinem Computer. Er wird von deinem Computer erstellt und kann fast alles, was auch ein echtes Smartphone kann. Aber es existiert nur im Computer, damit du deine App auch ohne Smartphone testen kannst.

1 **Installiere den Android Emulator auf deinem Computer.**

Den Download und auch eine Anleitung dazu gibt es auf der Webseite: http://appinventor.mit.edu/explore/ai2/setup-emulator.html

Bitte für diesen Schritt unbedingt deine Eltern um Hilfe, damit du auch die passende Version des Programms installierst.

Auf deinem Computer findest du jetzt ein Programm mit dem Namen aiStarter.

2 **Starte das Programm, indem du es anklickst.**

3 **Wechsel nun wieder in den App Inventor (in deinem Internetbrowser).**

4 **Drücke auf Connect und anschließend auf Emulator.**

Jetzt startet der Emulator, der genau das anzeigt, was auch auf einem Smartphone angezeigt werden würde. Du solltest also deine App auf dem Bildschirm des Emulators sehen.

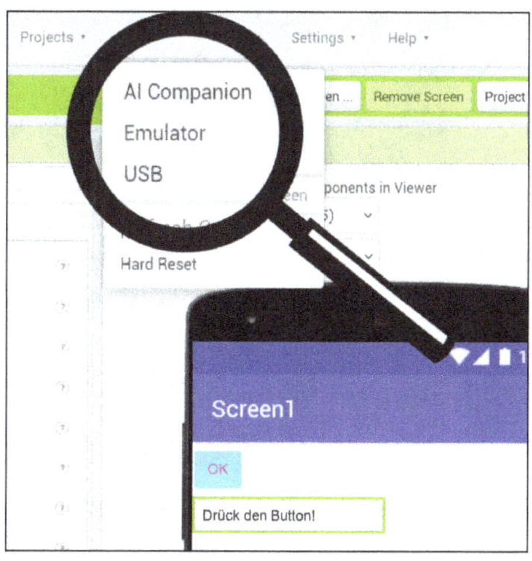

5 Klicke auf den Button und schaue, ob deine App auch richtig funktioniert.

- Sieht deine App beim Starten so aus wie in der Abbildung links?
- Sieht sie nach dem Drücken auf den Button aus wie in der Abbildung rechts?

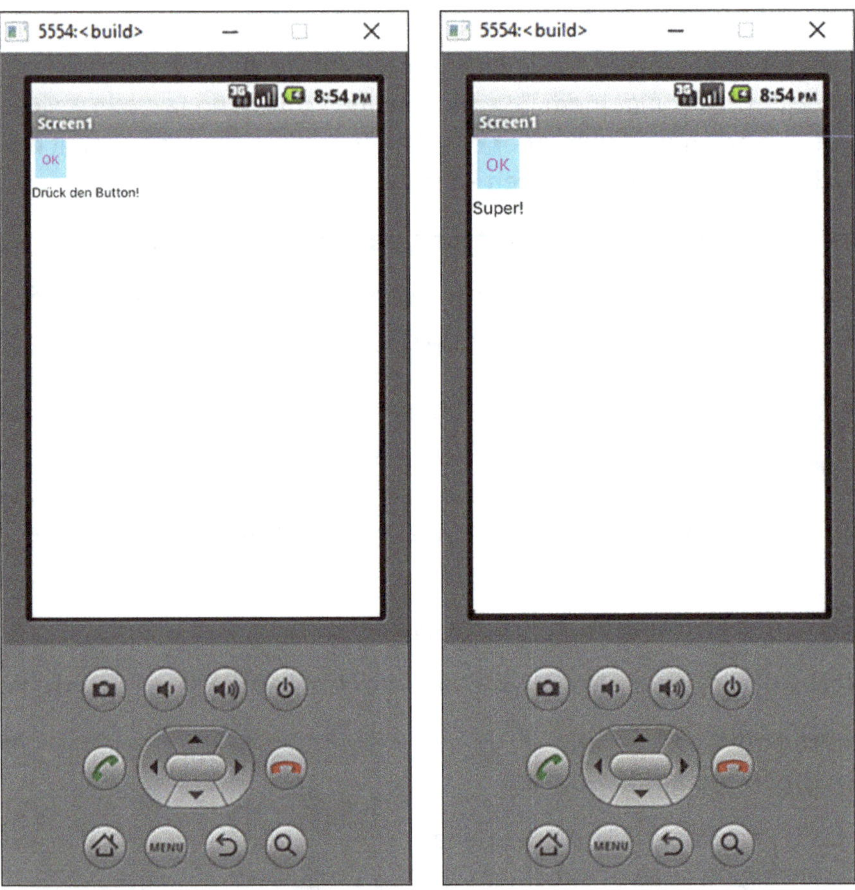

Falls du den Emulator nicht installieren konntest oder falls du deine App nicht im Emulator sehen kannst, dann besuche mit deinen Eltern diese Webseite: http://appinventor.mit.edu/explore/ai2/setup-emulator.html. Dort findest du viele Tipps zur Installation des Emulators.

Herzlichen Glückwunsch, du hast deine erste echte Smartphone-App programmiert! Das hast du super gemacht.

Übers Ziel hinaus – noch mehr Möglichkeiten

In den nächsten Kapiteln findest du Anleitungen zu zahlreichen Apps, die ganz unterschiedlich sind und unterschiedliche Elemente (zum Beispiel besondere Sensoren) verwenden. Diese sind nach den drei Schwierigkeitsstufen geordnet:

- Anfänger
- Fortgeschrittene
- Profis

Wir empfehlen dir, mit den einfacheren Apps zu starten und dich Schritt für Schritt zum Profi-App-Entwickler hochzuarbeiten. Wenn dich eine App ganz besonders interessiert, kannst du natürlich dahin vorblättern, musst aber unter Umständen wieder zurückblättern, wenn du eine bestimmte Sache (zum Beispiel das Anordnen von Elementen auf dem Screen) übersprungen hast.

Wir wünschen dir viel Spaß bei den weiteren Apps, also »APP geht's!«.

Kapitel 3
Einsteiger-Apps

Jetzt hast du deine erste App erfolgreich gemeistert und kannst es wahrscheinlich nicht erwarten, weitere Apps zu programmieren. In dem Kapitel »Einsteiger-Apps« lernst du, deine Apps bunt und laut werden zu lassen, indem du Bilder einfügst und Töne abspielen lässt.

Die zwei Apps für Einsteiger sind:

- *Das mähende Schaf*
- *Mein eigenes Malprogramm*

Das mähende Schaf

Wie der Name der neuen App *Das mähende Schaf* schon vermuten lässt, werden wir ein Schaf als Bild in die App einfügen und dieses dann mähen lassen, so oft wir wollen.

Deine Aufgaben sind:

- *einen* Button *mit der Beschriftung* `Mähhh` *einzufügen,*
- *ein* Image *(»Bild«) eines Schafes vom Computer in die App zu übertragen und*
- *einen* Sound *zur App hinzuzufügen.*

Bevor es losgeht, musst du ein neues Projekt erstellen, das zum Beispiel `Schaf` heißen könnte. Auch kannst du schon den App Inventor mit deinem Smartphone oder Tablet verbinden, falls du eines hast.

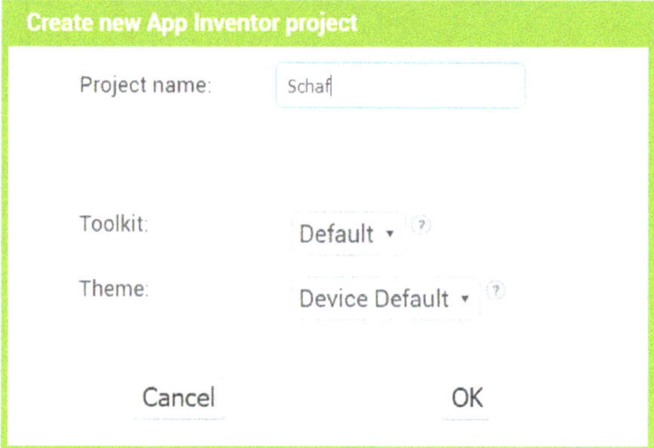

Falls du dich nicht mehr daran erinnerst, wie du ein Projekt anlegst, dann schaue doch noch einmal in Kapitel 2, »Deine erste App«, nach, da wurde das ganz genau erklärt.

1 **Ziehe einen Button von der Palette in den Viewer.**

Unter Components ist der Button1 aufgetaucht und die Properties des Button1 sind verfügbar.

2 **Ändere in den Properties den Text des Button1 auf `Mähhh`.**

3 **Ändere die Width (»Breite«) des Buttons auf 320 Pixel.**

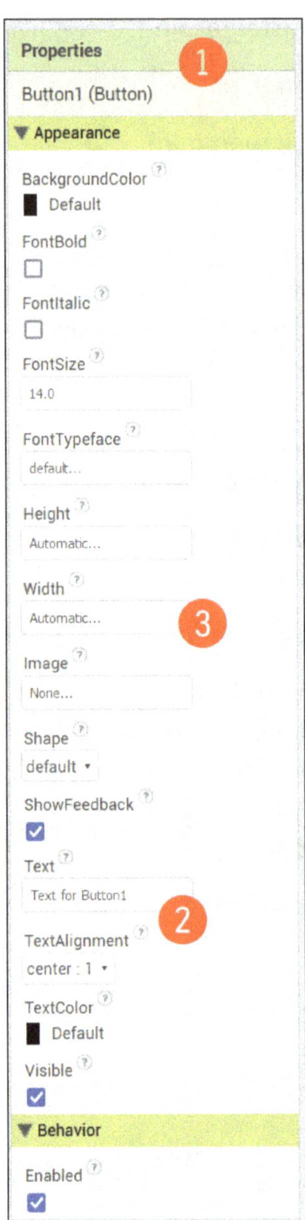

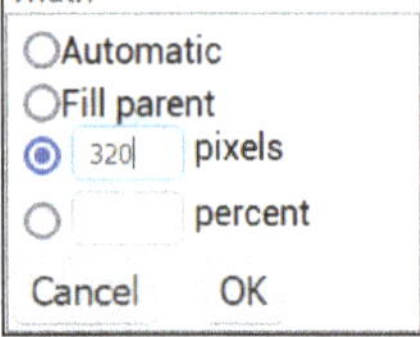

App mit Bild

Jetzt wollen wir ein Bild hinzufügen.

1 Ziehe ein Image vom User Interface in deinen Screen1.

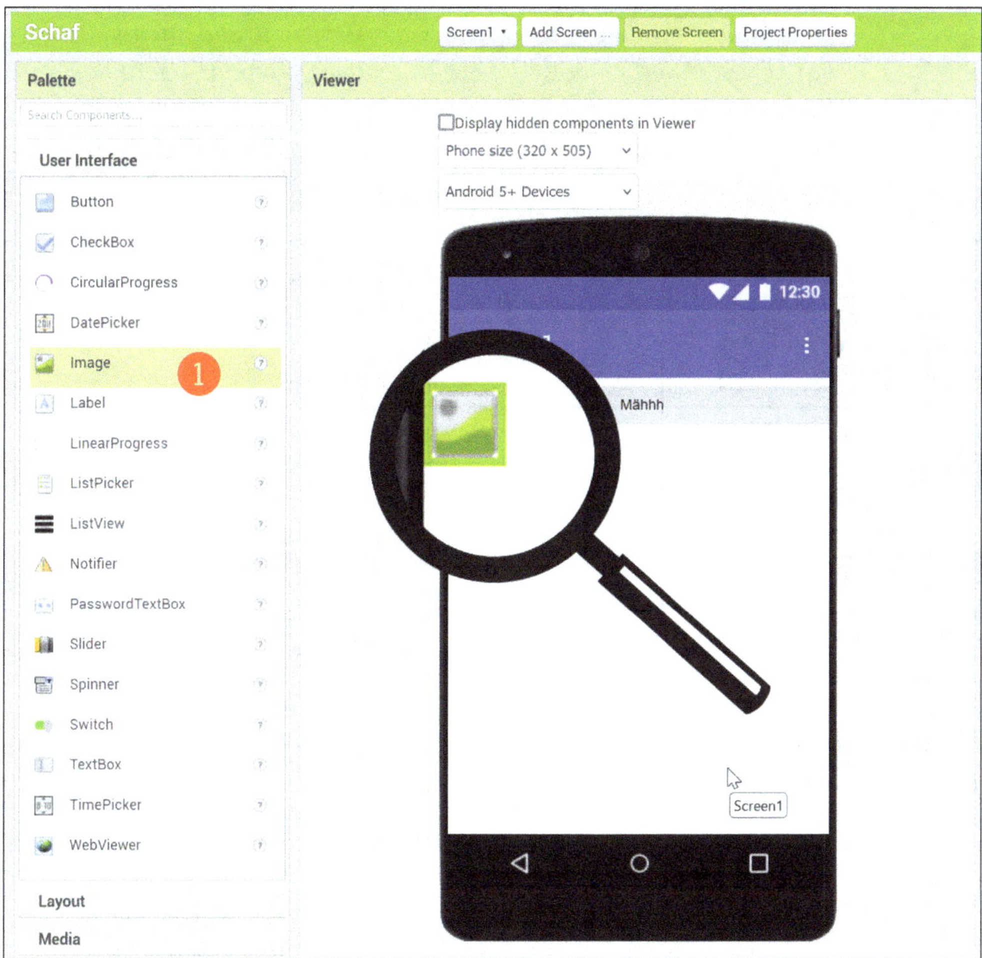

Image ist das englische Wort für »Bild«. Du kannst damit jedes Bild, das du auf dem Computer hast, in deine App einbauen. Falls du kein passendes Bild auf deinem Computer findest, kannst du auch eines aus dem Internet herunterladen.

Wenn du Bilder verwendest, die du nicht selbst erstellt hast, musst du das Urheberrecht beachten. Dies bedeutet, dass du die Erlaubnis des Urhebers, also des Künstlers oder des Fotografen, brauchst, wenn du das Bild verwenden oder gar verändern willst. Du denkst, jetzt ist dein Projekt gestorben? Glücklicherweise gibt es an manchen Bildern im Internet Markierungen, die dir sagen, was du mit dem Bild tun darfst. Am weitesten verbreitet ist dabei die Creative Commons-Lizenz (kurz CC-Lizenz), von der es verschiedene Stufen gibt. Die unkompliziertesten findest du in der Tabelle. Achtung: Es gibt noch mehr CC-Lizenzen und es ist gar nicht so leicht, sie richtig zu verstehen!

Icon	Abkürzung	Erklärung
PUBLIC DOMAIN	CC 0	Keinerlei Einschränkungen
CC BY	CC-BY	Der Name des Urhebers muss genannt werden.
CC BY NC	CC-BY-NC	Der Name des Urhebers muss genannt werden. Das Bild darf nur genutzt werden, wenn mit dem Produkt, in dem es erscheint, kein Geld verdient wird.
CC BY ND	CC-BY-ND	Der Name des Urhebers muss genannt werden. Das Bild darf nicht verändert werden.

Es gibt spezielle Webseiten, die Bilder anbieten, die man einfach so verwenden kann. Einige Grafiken, die wir für die hier vorgestellten Apps verwenden, kommen von den Webseiten https://pexels.com/ und https://openclipart.org/. Dort siehst du für jedes einzelne Bild die Lizenzangabe. Für dieses Buch verwenden wir nur Grafiken der CC-0-Lizenz.

Unter dem Button1 ist jetzt ein kleines Rechteck zu erkennen. Das Rechteck zeigt an, dass hier Platz für ein Bild ist. Das Bild selbst müssen wir noch hinzufügen.

In den Components findest du unter dem Button1 jetzt auch das Image1.

2 **In den Properties hast du nun die Möglichkeit, genauso wie beim Button die Eigenschaften des Bildes zu ändern. Füge ein Bild hinzu, indem du auf das Feld unter Picture klickst.**

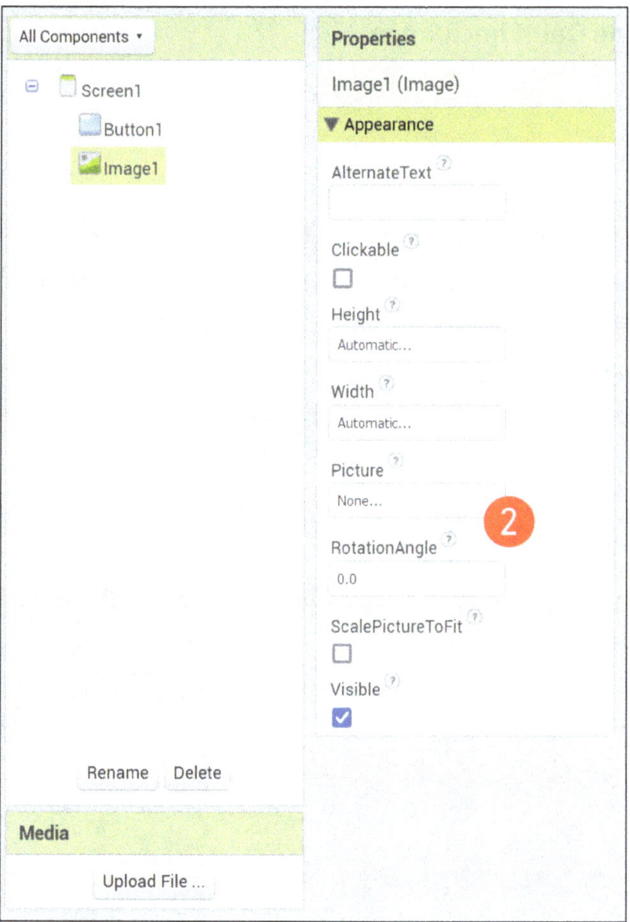

Falls du kein passendes Bild zur Verfügung hast, kannst du ein Bild in den Online-Materialien zu diesem Buch oder unter https://openclipart.org/ finden. Du kannst dort auch Bilder in hoher Auflösung herunterladen, aber das ist gar nicht nötig, denn für Smartphone-Apps reichen auch die kleinen Bildgrößen aus.

3 In dem kleinen Fenster, das aufgeht, siehst du das Wort None markiert. Dies bedeutet, dass noch kein Bild vorhanden ist. Damit du eins von deinem Computer hochladen kannst, klickst du auf Upload File ... (»eine Datei hochladen«).

4 Jetzt kannst du ein Bild von deinem Computer auswählen, indem du auf Durchsuchen... klickst.

5 Klicke anschließend auf OK.

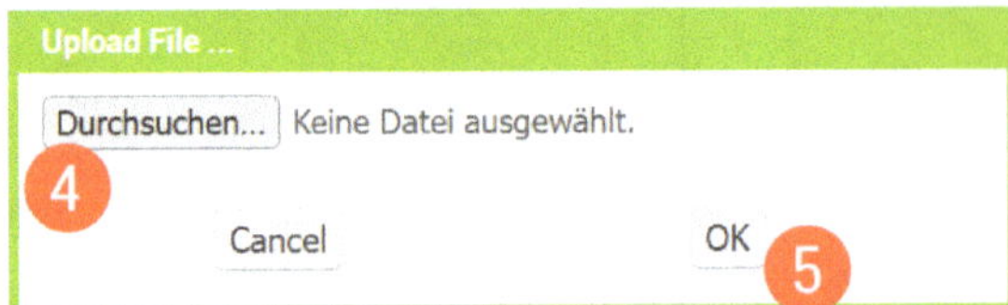

6 Je nachdem, welches Bild du ausgewählt hast, passt es nicht auf den Screen1.

7 **Setze in den Properties die Width (»Breite«) des Bildes auf die Breite des Buttons (320 Pixel).**

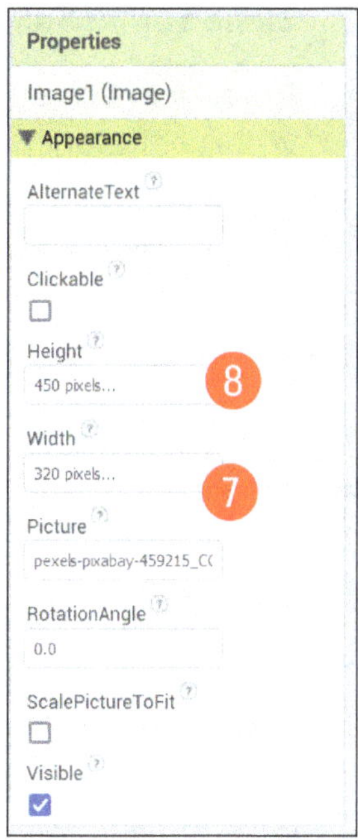

8 **Damit auch die Höhe des Bildes passt, setze Height (»Höhe«) auf 450 Pixel.**

Hurra! Jetzt passt das Bild auf den Screen1 und deine App sieht super aus.

App mit Ton

Jetzt musst du dich aber noch um den Ton kümmern, denn das Schaf soll ja auch wirklich »Mäh« machen, wenn du auf den Button drückst. Also los geht es!

1 **Auf der Palette klickst du auf Media. Hier findest du alle Dinge, die mit Sound oder Videos zu tun haben.**

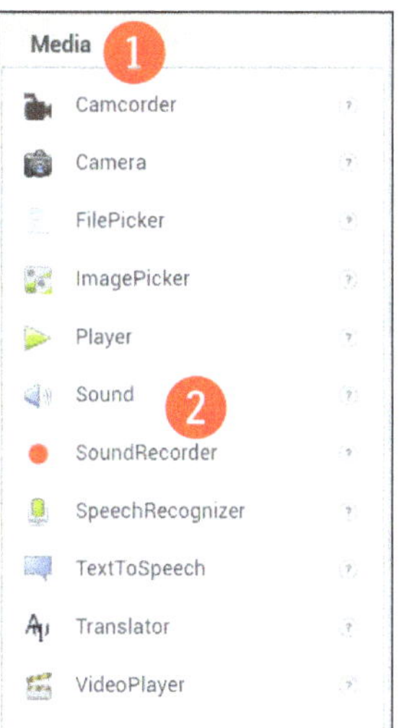

2 Ziehe Sound auf deinen Screen1.

Unter dem Screen1 taucht jetzt der Sound1 auf und darüber steht Non-visible components (»nicht sichtbare Komponenten«).

Das bedeutet, dass der Sound nicht sichtbar ist (in Englisch »non-visible«), er gehört aber zu deiner App und deinem Screen.

3 **Jetzt kannst du auch die Properties des Sound1 verändern. Und genauso, wie du es beim Bild gemacht hast, kannst du jetzt einen Sound hochladen, indem du im Feld Source auf Upload File klickst und dann einen Sound von deinem Computer auswählst.**

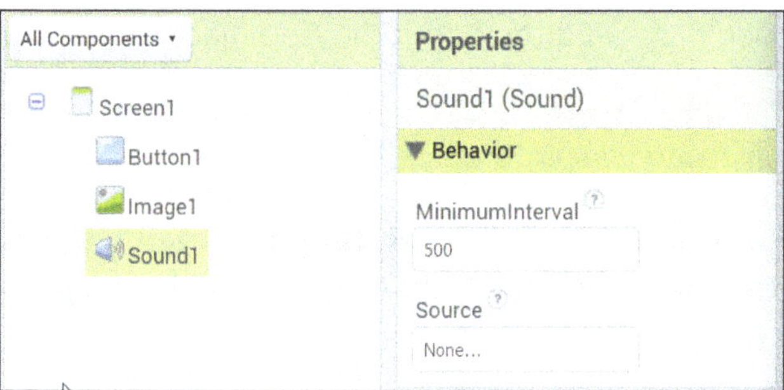

Deine Sounds sollten erst einmal eher kurz sein. Wenn du noch keine Sounds auf deinem Computer hast, kannst du entweder selbst Sounds aufnehmen oder solche von Webseiten wie https://www.freesound.org herunterladen. Freesound gibt es leider nur auf Englisch. Du musst dir einen Account anlegen, um die Töne kostenfrei herunterzuladen. Den Mähhh-Sound findest du auch in den Online-Materialien zu diesem Buch.

Falls dein Bild oder der Button nicht ganz genau in den Bildschirm passt, wie hier auf der Abbildung, ist das kein Problem. Es gibt viele verschiedene Größen von Bildern und Geräten, sodass es überall ein wenig anders aussieht. Passe einfach die Breite und Höhe an, bis es passt.

Super, das Schaf sieht doch schon sehr glücklich aus. Du hast

- die zwei sichtbaren Komponenten Button und Image in die App eingebaut und
- eine unsichtbare Komponente Sound hinzugefügt.

Jetzt fehlt noch, dass dein Schaf »Mäh« macht, wenn du es willst. Teste auf deinem Smartphone oder im Emulator, ob deine App richtig aussieht.

Die Funktionalität für das Schaf

Wechsel nun in den Blocks-Editor, damit die App macht, was du willst.

Deine Aufgabe ist es, dass die App ein Geräusch, nämlich Mäh macht, wenn du auf den Button klickst.

1 **In den Blocks findest du deinen erstellten Screen1. Darunter sind alle Komponenten aufgelistet, die du im Designer hinzugefügt hast. Klicke auf Button1.**

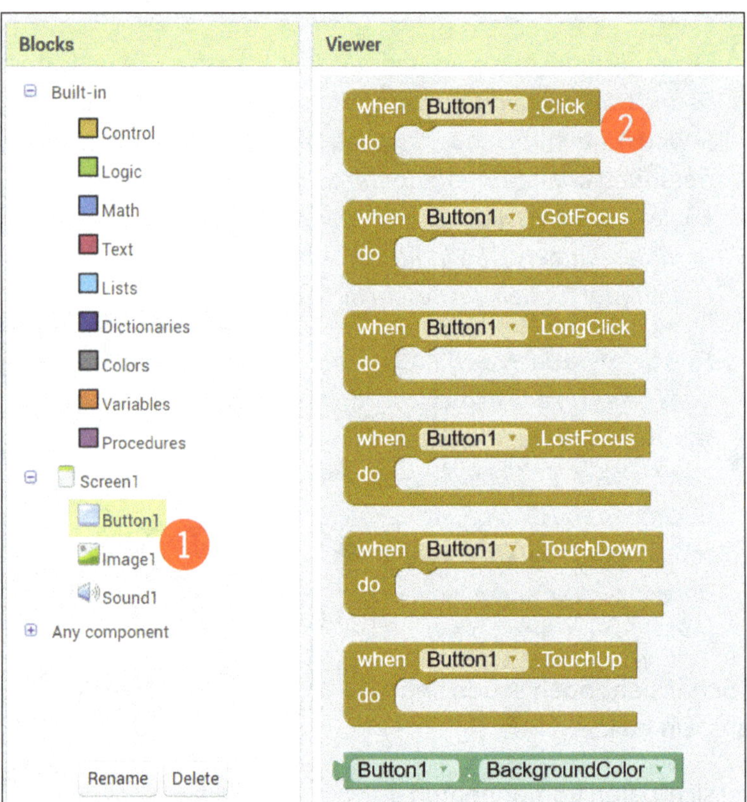

Es öffnet sich ein zweites Fenster, in dem du verschiedene Programmbausteine auswählen kannst, die alle mit dem Button1 zu tun haben.

2 **Klicke auf den Programmbaustein when Button1.Click do und ziehe diesen in den Viewer.**

Eine kleine Erinnerungshilfe:

- *when bedeutet »wenn«,*
- *Button1 ist dein eingefügter Button,*
- *.Click bedeutet »wird angeklickt« und*
- *do bedeutet »dann tue etwas«.*

Also bedeutet dieser Programmblock übersetzt »Wenn Button1 angeklickt wird, dann tue etwas«.

Was dann getan werden soll, kommt jetzt hinter das do.

3 **Klicke in den Blocks auf Sound1.**

Hier siehst du nun alle Programmbausteine, die du mit dem Sound benutzen kannst. Die orangenen Programmbausteine geben eine Bedingung vor, die lila Programmbausteine führen etwas aus (wie den Sound abspielen). Mit den dunkelgrünen Programmbausteinen kann etwas verändert werden und mit den hellgrünen Programmbausteinen können Werte ausgelesen, also entgegengenommen werden.

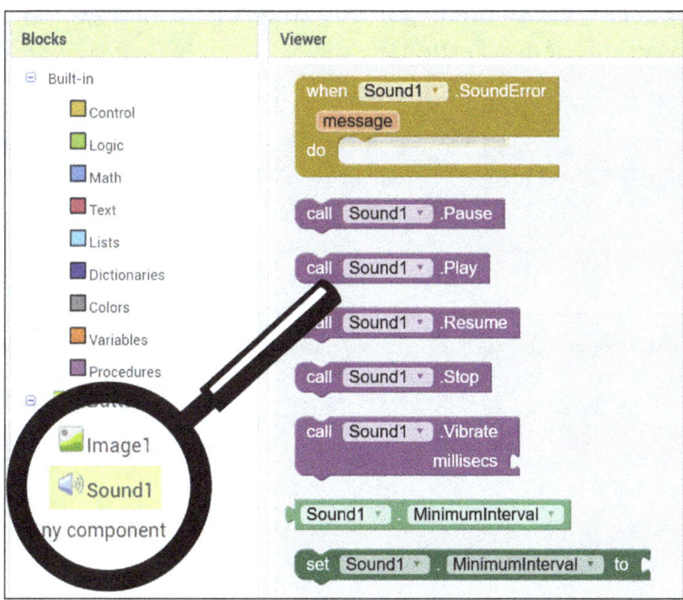

4 Klicke auf den Programmbaustein call Sound1.Play und ziehe diesen in den Viewer.

Hier die Übersetzungshilfe:

- call bedeutet »rufe auf«,
- Sound1 ist der Sound, den du hinzugefügt hast,
- .Play bedeutet »abspielen«.

Also bedeutet dieser Programmblock übersetzt »Rufe Sound1 auf und spiele ihn ab«.

5 Setze den Programmbaustein call Sound1.Play jetzt hinter das do des Programmbausteins when Button1.Click do.

Das ganze Programm lautet jetzt also »Wenn Button1 angeklickt wird, dann rufe Sound1 auf und spiele ihn ab«. Prima, das ist genau das, was du wolltest.

Die App *Das mähende Schaf* ist fertig. Viel Spaß beim Mähen! Vielleicht findest du ja noch andere Bilder und Geräusche?

Dein eigenes Malprogramm

Hier erstellst du dein eigenes Malprogramm, bei dem du mit dem Finger zeichnen kannst und das auch noch in verschiedenen Farben.

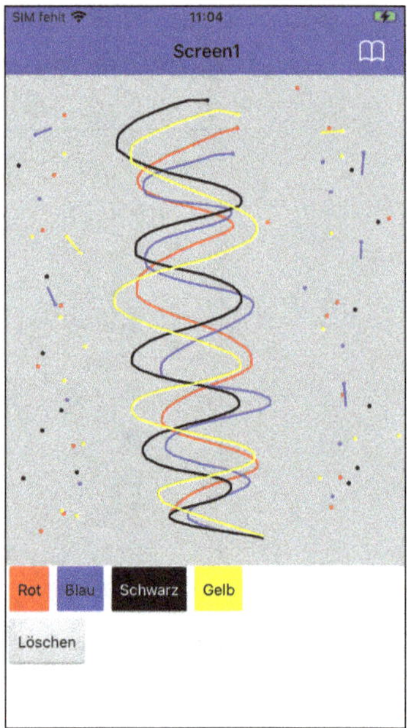

Deine Aufgaben sind:

- *ein* Canvas *(»Leinwand«) als Zeichenfläche einzufügen,*
- *einen* Button *einzufügen, um die Zeichenfläche wieder zu löschen, und*
- *vier* Buttons *für vier Farben hinzuzufügen.*

Bevor es losgeht, musst du ein neues Projekt erstellen, das *Malprogramm* heißen könnte. Um deine App während des Programmierens zu testen, verbindest du den App Inventor direkt mit deinem Smartphone oder Tablet.

Falls du dich nicht mehr daran erinnerst, wie du ein Projekt anlegst oder den App Inventor mit dem Smartphone verbindest, dann schaue doch noch einmal in Kapitel 2, »Deine erste App«, nach, da wurde das ganz genau erklärt.

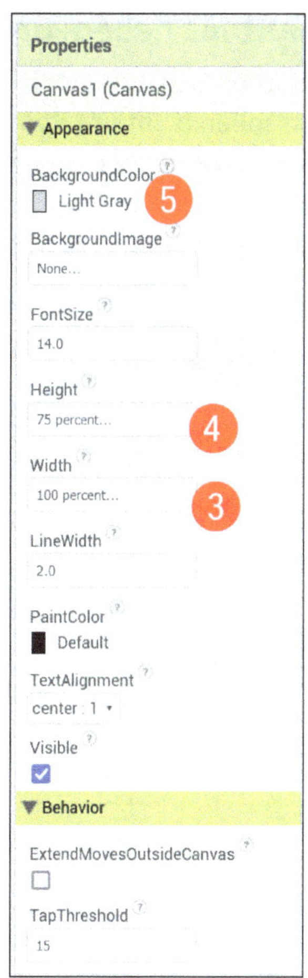

1. **Wähle im Designer unter Palette die Kategorie Drawing and Animation (»Zeichnung und Animation«) aus.**
2. **Ziehe ein Canvas von der Palette in den Viewer.**

   Dies ist deine Zeichenfläche.

   Unter Components ist der Canvas1 aufgetaucht und die Properties des Canvas1 sind verfügbar.

3 **Ändere in den Properties die Width (»Breite«) des Canvas1 auf `100` percent (100 Prozent der Breite deines Bildschirms).**

4 **Ändere die Height (»Höhe«) des Canvas1 auf `80` percent (das sind nur 80 % der Bildschirmhöhe, da du noch Platz für deine Buttons brauchst).**

Damit du deine Zeichenfläche vom weißen Hintergrund unterscheiden kannst, solltest du noch die Hintergrundfarbe ändern.

5 **Klicke unter BackgroundColor auf das kleine Farbfeld und wähle dann Light Gray aus.**

Buttons neben- und untereinander

Nun brauchst du noch vier Buttons für die vier verschiedenen Farben. Aber diese sollen nicht untereinander, sondern nebeneinander angeordnet werden. Dafür brauchst du eine neue Komponente: das HorizontalArrangement (horizontale Anordnung). Alle Komponenten, die du da hineinziehst, werden nebeneinander (also horizontal) angeordnet.

Normalerweise werden alle Komponenten, die du in den Screen ziehst, untereinander angeordnet. Möchtest du das ändern, findest du die Komponenten dazu in der Palette *unter* Layout*.*

1 **In der Palette unter Layout ziehst du die Komponente HorizontalArrangement unter das Canvas1 in den Screen1.**

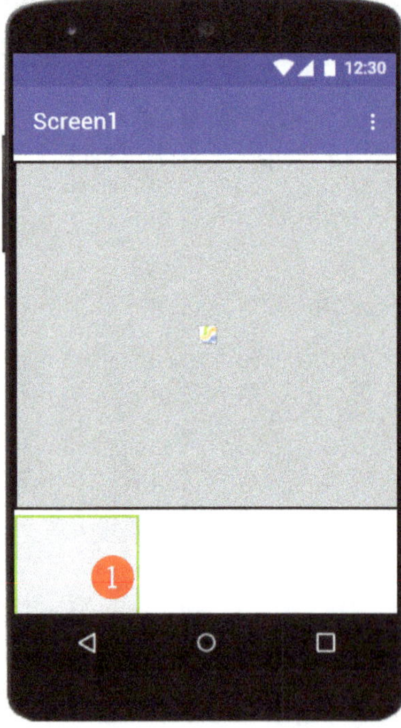

2 **Ziehe einen Button aus der Kategorie User Interface in das Horizontal-Arrangement1.**

Der Button1 taucht jetzt in den Components unter dem Horizontal-Arrangement1 auf.

3 **Ändere die Properties des Button1. Setze Text auf `Rot` und ändere die BackgroundColor ebenfalls auf `Red` (»Rot«).**

Wirf ab und zu einen Blick auf deine App. Sieht alles richtig aus? Dann geht es direkt weiter.

4 **Ziehe jetzt einen weiteren Button aus der Palette auf den Button1 im Viewer und füge so einen weiteren Button direkt neben dem Button1 ein.**

Dein neuer Button2 taucht nun rechts neben dem Button1 auf? Sehr gut! Jetzt passt du auch hier die Farbe und den Text an.

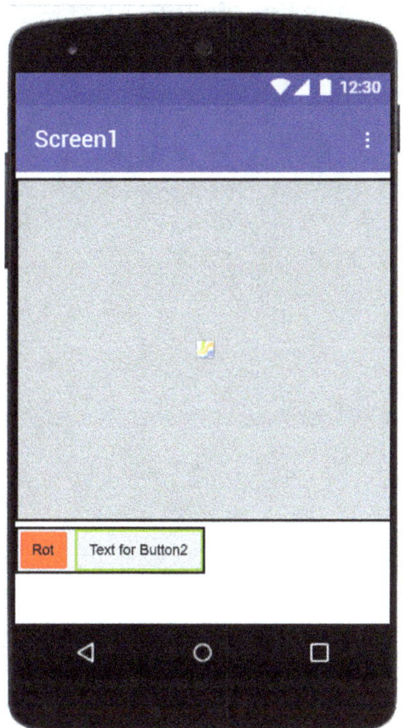

5 **Ändere die Properties des Button2. Verändere den Text des Button2 auf `Blau` und stelle `Blue` (Blau) als BackgroundColor ein.**

Toll! Jetzt weißt du, wie es geht.

6 **Mit den anderen beiden Buttons machst du es genauso. Du brauchst noch einen Button für Schwarz (Black) und einen für Gelb (Yellow).**

Wenn du einen schwarzen Hintergrund wählst und die Textfarbe auch schwarz ist, dann kannst du den Text nicht mehr sehen. Ändere deshalb bei dem schwarzen Button die Textcolor *(Textfarbe) in den* Properties *auf* `White` *(Weiß).*

Deine App sieht schon fast perfekt aus. Es fehlt jetzt nur noch ein Button, mit dem du die Zeichnungen wieder löschen kannst, wenn du ein neues Bild malen willst.

7 **Füge unter den anderen Buttons einen neuen Button in den Viewer ein und ändere den Text des neuen Buttons auf `Löschen`.**

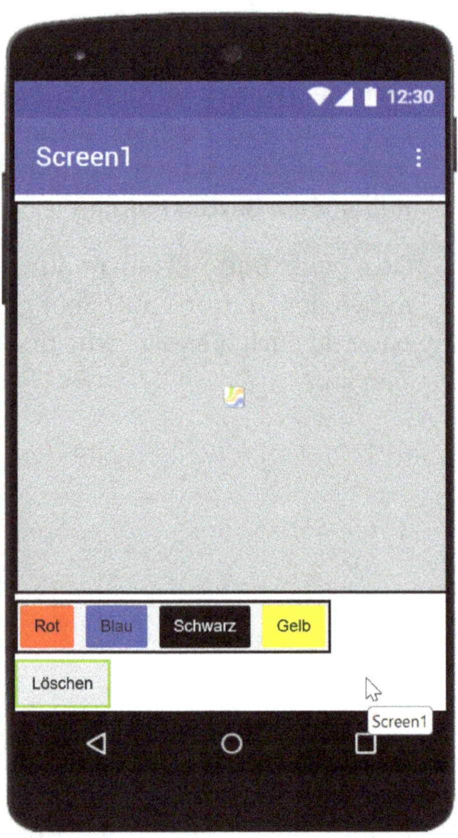

Super, dein Malprogramm sieht schon genauso aus, wie es sein soll. Du hast

» ein Canvas als Zeichenfläche vorgesehen und

» Buttons nebeneinander für die gewünschten Farben und einen für die Löschfunktion eingefügt.

Teste auf deinem Smartphone oder im Emulator, ob deine App richtig aussieht.

Die Funktionalität für das Malprogramm

Jetzt soll dein Malprogramm natürlich auch funktionieren. Wechsel dazu in den Blocks-Editor, damit du bald die ersten Dinge malen kannst.

Deine Aufgabe ist es, dafür zu sorgen, dass du mit dem Finger auf der Zeichenfläche malen kannst und das in verschiedenen Farben.

1 **In den Blocks findest du deinen Screen1. Darunter sind alle Komponenten aufgelistet, die du im Designer hinzugefügt hast. Klicke auf Canvas1.**

Es öffnet sich ein zweites Fenster, in dem du alle Programmbausteine findest, die etwas mit dem Canvas1 zu tun haben.

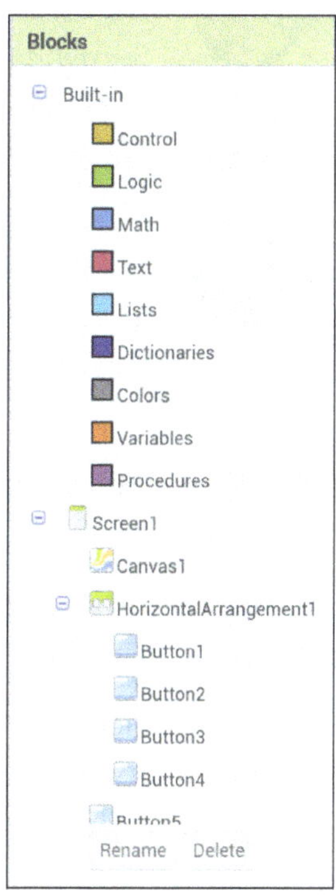

2 **Klicke auf den Programmbaustein when Canvas1.TouchDown do und ziehe diesen in den Viewer.**

Hast du schon eine Ahnung, was dieser neue Programmbaustein macht? Die meisten Wörter kennst du schon. Du willst auf dem Canvas1 malen können, also muss etwas passieren, wenn du das Canvas1 berührst. Genau dabei hilft dir dieser Baustein.

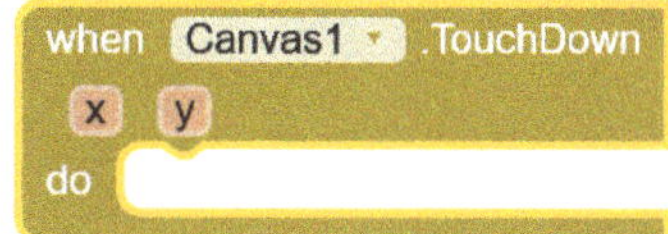

- when bedeutet »wenn«,
- Canvas1 ist deine eingefügte Zeichenfläche,

- .TouchDown bedeutet »wird berührt« und
- do bedeutet »dann tue etwas«.

Also bedeutet dieser Programmblock übersetzt »Wenn Canvas1 berührt wird, dann tue etwas«.

Dir sind bestimmt schon das x und das y aufgefallen. Diese beiden brauchst du, damit du weißt, wo das Canvas1 berührt wurde, damit wir genau da einen Punkt oder einen Strich malen können. Das x gibt dabei die Entfernung von der berührten Stelle zu der linken Seite des Canvas an. Das y gibt die Entfernung zum oberen Rand an.

Im Designer *bestimmt die Anordnung der Komponenten (zum Beispiel der Buttons) das Aussehen deiner App. Im* Blocks*-Editor dagegen kannst du die Befehle beliebig anordnen. Es kommt nur auf die richtige Zusammensetzung der Befehlsblöcke an, nicht darauf, wo du diese auf der Fläche ablegst.*

Was auf dem Canvas1 passieren soll, wenn es berührt wird, kommt jetzt hinter das do.

3 Klicke in den Blocks auf Canvas1.

Da jetzt etwas passieren soll – es soll nämlich auf dem Canvas1 gemalt werden –, schaust du dir die lila Programmbausteine an.

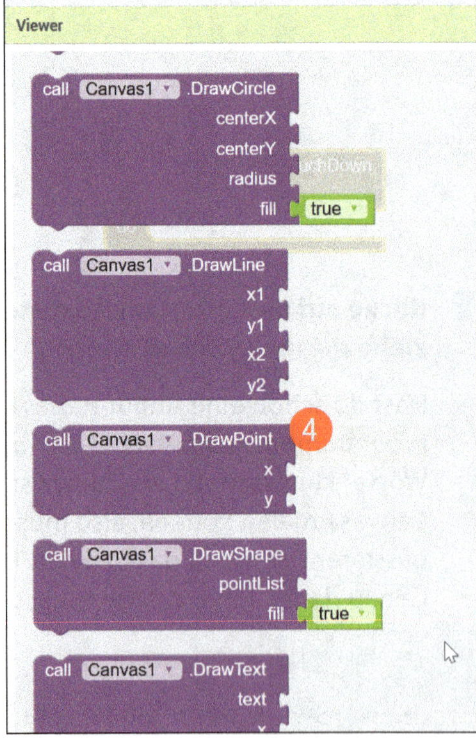

4 Klicke auf den Programmbaustein call Canvas1.DrawPoint und ziehe diesen in den Viewer.

Wie gewohnt die Übersetzungshilfe:

- call bedeutet »rufe auf«,
- Canvas1 ist die Zeichenfläche, die du hinzugefügt hast und
- .DrawPoint bedeutet »male einen Punkt«.
- x ist die Entfernung von der linken Seite des Canvas zu dem Punkt, an dem etwas gemalt werden soll.
- y ist die Entfernung von der oberen Seite des Canvas zu dem Punkt, an dem etwas gemalt werden soll.

Also bedeutet dieser Programmblock übersetzt »Rufe Canvas1 auf und male an der Stelle, die x vom linken Rand entfernt ist und y vom oberen Rand, einen Punkt«.

5 Setze den Programmbaustein call Canvas1.DrawPoint jetzt hinter das do des Programmbausteins when Canvas1.TouchDown do.

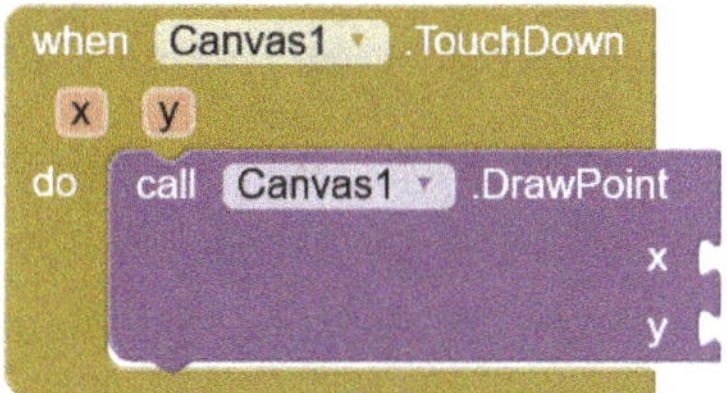

Das ganze Programm lautet jetzt also »Wenn Canvas1 berührt wird, dann male an die Stelle, die x vom linken Rand entfernt ist und y vom oberen Rand, einen Punkt«. Sehr gut! Aber wie du an den offenen Puzzlestellen bemerkt hast, fehlt noch etwas. Du musst dem Programmstück noch sagen, wo denn das x und das y genau sind.

6 Gehe mit der Maus über das *x* des Programmbausteins when Canvas1.TouchDown do, ohne zu klicken.

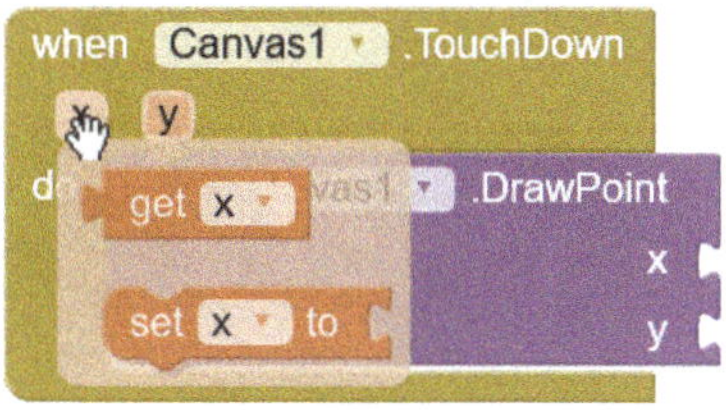

Es öffnet sich ein kleines Fenster an der Stelle.

7 **Klicke den Programmbaustein get x an und ziehe ihn an die freie Stelle des Programmbausteins call Canvas1.DrawPoint, an der ein *x* steht.**

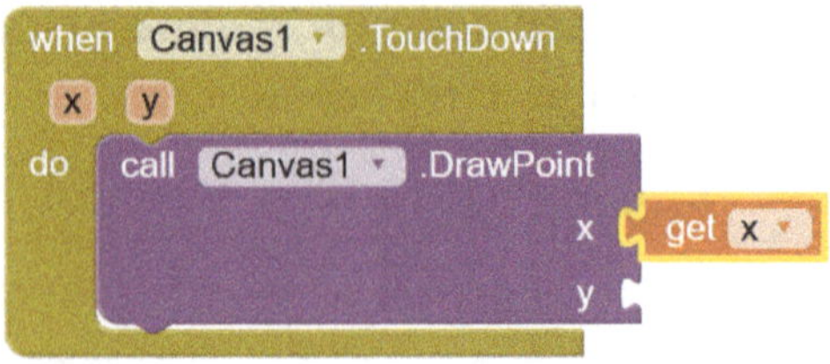

8 **Wiederhole die letzten zwei Schritte für das *y*.**

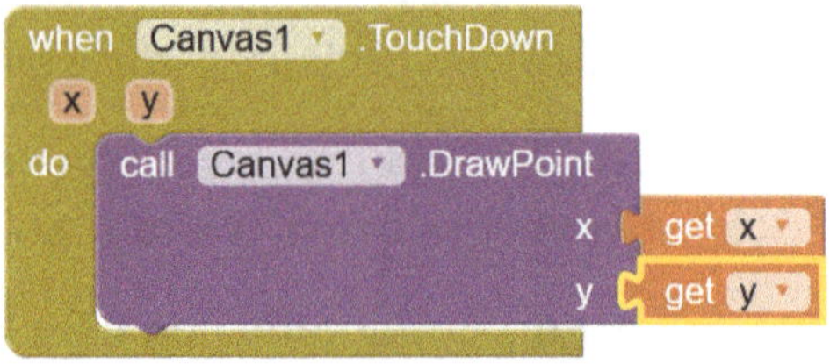

Klasse! Du kannst jetzt überall auf der Zeichenfläche kleine schwarze Punkte machen. Probiere es gleich mal aus, indem du dein Smartphone oder Tablet wieder verbindest. Falls es noch nicht klappt, schaue dir die letzten Schritte noch einmal genau an und vergleiche es mit deiner Lösung.

Aber nur schwarze Punkte reichen nicht. Du willst ja auch bunte Bilder malen können.

9 **Klicke in Blocks auf den Button1 und ziehe den Programmbaustein when Button1.Click do in den Viewer.**

Button1 ist der rote Button. Wenn dieser angeklickt wird, willst du, dass sich die Malfarbe auf Rot verändert. Die Farbe, mit der du auf das Canvas1 malst, gehört zum Canvas1 und deshalb findest du den richtigen Programmblock beim Canvas1.

10 **Klicke auf das Canvas1 in den Blocks, finde den grünen Programmbaustein set Canvas1.PaintColor to und ziehe es hinter das do des Programmbausteins when Button1.Click do.**

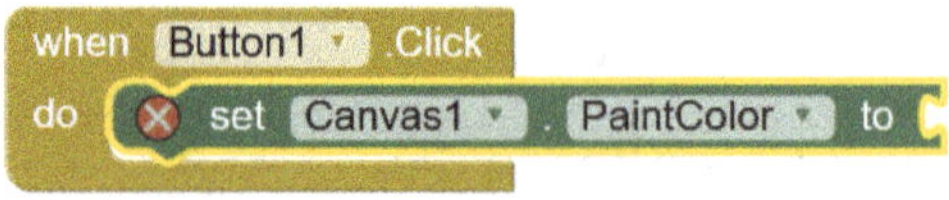

Der neue grüne Programmbaustein kann etwas verändern:

- Set bedeutet »Ändere«,
- Canvas1 ist die Zeichenfläche, die du hinzugefügt hast,

- .PaintColor bedeutet »Malfarbe« und
- to heißt »zu«.

Also bedeutet dieser Programmblock übersetzt »Ändere beim Canvas1 die Malfarbe auf«.

Jetzt fehlt dir noch die Farbe. Du willst ja die rote Malfarbe benutzen.

Wenn du ein Warndreieck oder ein rotes Kreuz im Viewer siehst, dann bedeutet das: Hier fehlt etwas oder es stimmt etwas nicht.

11 Klicke in den Blocks auf Colors. Dort findest du alle Farben. Ziehe die rote Farbe hinter das to.

```
when Button1 .Click
do set Canvas1 . PaintColor to
```

Ein Farbbutton ist fertig. Drei fehlen noch! Du kannst die rote Malfarbe auch direkt einmal ausprobieren, indem du auf den roten Button klickst. Auf der Zeichenfläche erscheint ein roter Punkt.

12 Klicke auf den Button2. Ziehe den Programmbaustein when Button2. Click do in den Viewer. Hinter das do fügst du wieder den Programmbaustein set Canvas1.PaintColor to ein und wählst die Farbe Blau.

13 Wiederhole das für den Button3, der Schwarz als Farbe bekommt, und den Button4, der Gelb bekommt.

```
when Button1 .Click
do set Canvas1 . PaintColor to

when Button2 .Click
do set Canvas1 . PaintColor to

when Button3 .Click
do set Canvas1 . PaintColor to

when Button4 .Click
do set Canvas1 . PaintColor to
```

Probiere es direkt einmal aus. Du kannst jetzt zwischen den Farben hin und her wechseln, indem du den Button mit der Farbe anklickst, die du haben möchtest. Jetzt kannst du schon viele bunte Punkte auf die Zeichenfläche zaubern.

Du merkst natürlich, dass deine Zeichenfläche immer voller wird. Wenn du ein neues Bild zeichnen willst, musst du von der Zeichenfläche wieder alles entfernen. Und genau das machst du jetzt.

14 **Klicke in den Blocks auf den Button5 und ziehe den Programmbaustein when Button2.Click do in den Viewer.**

Jetzt musst du den Programmbaustein finden, der die Zeichenfläche von allen gemalten Dingen bereinigt. Da du die Zeichenfläche bereinigen willst, muss der gesuchte Programmbaustein bei dem Canvas1 zu finden sein.

15 **In den Blocks suchst du beim Canvas1 den Programmbaustein call Canvas1.Clear. Füge diesen in den Programmbaustein des Button5 ein.**

Der neue Programmbaustein hat diese Funktion:

- call bedeutet »rufe auf«,
- Canvas1 ist deine Zeichenfläche,
- .Clear bedeutet »bereinigen«.

Also bedeutet dieser Programmblock übersetzt »Rufe Canvas1 auf und bereinige es«.

Das ganze Programm lautet jetzt »Wenn Button5 angeklickt wird, dann rufe Canvas1 auf und bereinige ihn«. Toll, du kannst gemalte Bilder wieder löschen! Probiere es gleich mal aus. Ist alles verschwunden? Dann füge noch ein paar Punkte hinzu und probiere es noch einmal.

So weit, so gut! Eine Sache fehlt dir aber noch. Nur Punkte malen reicht dir natürlich nicht. Du willst auch noch Linien malen können, damit du richtige Zeichnungen anfertigen kannst.

16 Klicke auf Canvas1 in den Blocks. Ziehe den Programmbaustein when Canvas1.Dragged do in den Viewer.

Dies ist wieder ein neuer Programmbaustein. Die Punkte auf deiner Zeichenfläche konnten wir malen, indem wir uns die Stelle gemerkt haben, an dem die Zeichenfläche berührt wird. Damit deine App eine Linie zeichnen kann, muss sich die Zeichenfläche Canvas1 merken, wo du mit deinem Finger auf der Zeichenfläche eine Linie ziehst. Und genau das heißt Dragged (»Ziehen«).

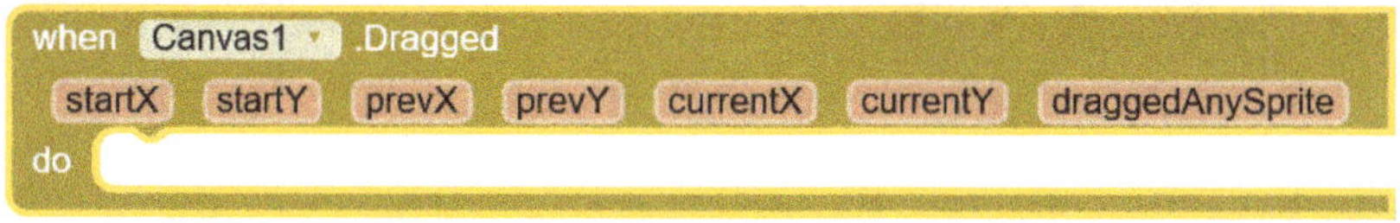

when Canvas1 .Dragged
startX startY prevX prevY currentX currentY draggedAnySprite
do

Du siehst jetzt schon die roten Buttons innerhalb des Programmbausteins mit den Namen *startX*, *startY* und noch ein paar andere. Diese brauchen wir erst gleich. Gut! Die Zeichenfläche weiß nun, dass etwas passieren soll, wenn du deinen Finger darüber ziehst. Du willst, dass genau dort eine Linie gezeichnet wird.

17 Ziehe call Canvas1.DrawLine in den Viewer in das neue when Canvas1. Dragged do. DrawLine bedeutet »male eine Linie«.

Dir fallen natürlich sofort die offenen Puzzlestellen auf. Diese musst du nun füllen. Und zwar soll die Linie immer von dem Punkt gezeichnet werden, an dem dein Finger vorher war, bis zu dem Punkt, an dem dein Finger momentan ist. Dazu brauchst du wieder *x* und *y*.

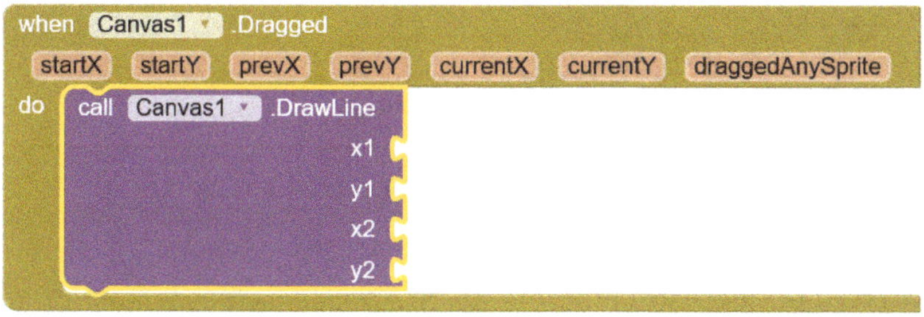

when Canvas1 .Dragged
startX startY prevX prevY currentX currentY draggedAnySprite
do call Canvas1 .DrawLine
x1
y1
x2
y2

»Vorher« heißt auf Englisch previously. Wenn du dir jetzt die roten Buttons noch einmal ansiehst, erkennst du prevX und prevY. Das ist genau die Stelle, an dem dein Finger vorher war. Also schnell die Puzzleteile anhängen!

18 Gehe mit der Maus über das prevX, ohne zu klicken, und warte, bis ein Fenster erscheint. Klicke den get prevX-Baustein an und ziehe ihn hinter das *x1*.

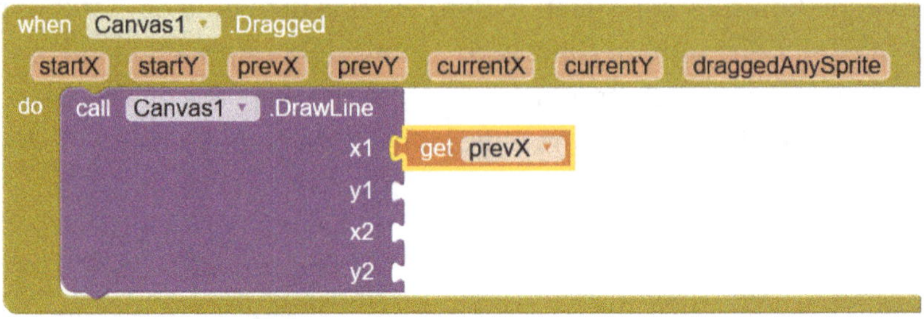

19 Wiederhole dies mit dem *y1*, indem du von dem prevY den get prevY-Baustein hinter das *y1* setzt.

Prima! Fast fertig. Jetzt fehlt noch die momentane Position deines Fingers, damit der Strich immer bis dahin gemalt wird. Und »momentan« heißt auf Englisch current. Und wenn du die roten Buttons ansiehst, findest du dort genau die Bausteine, die du brauchst.

20 Gehe mit der Maus über das currentX und ziehe den Baustein get currentX hinter das *x2*.

21 Wiederhole dies mit dem *y2*, indem du von dem currentY den get currentY-Baustein hinter das *y2* setzt.

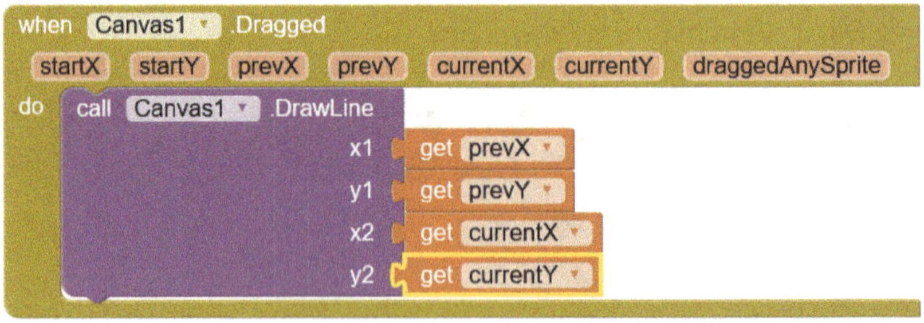

Jawohl, du hast es geschafft. Probiere deine App *Mein eigenes Malprogramm* direkt aus. Du kannst bunte Punkte und bunte Linien malen und alles auch wieder löschen, wenn du etwas Neues malen willst.

Wenn du Lust hast, kannst du deine App auch noch erweitern.

» Füge noch Buttons für andere Farben hinzu oder verändere deine Farben.

» Schau dir die lila Programmbausteine an, die beim Canvas1 in den Blocks zu finden sind und tausche diese gegen den DrawPoint-Baustein aus. Der Baustein DrawCircle kann zum Beispiel große Kreise zeichnen.

Oder probiere dich einmal an einer App für Fortgeschrittene im nächsten Kapitel.

Kapitel 4
Apps für Fortgeschrittene

Super, wenn du hier angekommen bist, hast du schon mindestens eine oder vielleicht sogar mehrere Apps erfolgreich entwickelt. Auch in diesem Kapitel hast du wieder zwei Apps zur Auswahl, die du auch gerne beide nacheinander programmieren kannst.

Die Auswahl lautet:

- *Maulwurf-Jagd*
- *Pinguin-Lagesteuerung*

Die *Maulwurf-Jagd* ist ein lustiges Spiel, bei dem es darum geht, einen Maulwurf (möglichst oft und schnell) zu fangen, der immer wieder an verschiedenen Positionen des Bildschirms erscheint. Um das Spiel zu einer echten Herausforderung zu machen, kannst du am Ende auch die Geschwindigkeit steigern, sodass es immer schwieriger wird, den Maulwurf zu fangen.

Bei der App *Pinguin-Steuerung* kannst du einen Pinguin mittels des Orientierungssensors deines Smartphones oder Tablets über den Bildschirm steuern. Passende Spielideen sind zum Beispiel das Einsammeln von Fischen oder auch die Flucht vor einem Hai. Da sind deiner Kreativität keine Grenzen gesetzt. Falls du kein Android-Gerät hast, kannst du stattdessen eine Steuerung über die Pfeiltasten auf der Tastatur deines Computers bauen.

Maulwurf-Jagd

Los geht es nun mit der *Maulwurf-Jagd*.

Ziel der Programmierung ist es, dass

- *ein Maulwurf immer wieder nach einer bestimmten Zeit (zum Beispiel jede Sekunde) an einer* zufälligen Position *auf dem Spielfeld erscheint,*
- *der Spieler den Maulwurf durch* Antippen *fangen kann (wenn er denn schnell genug ist) und*
- Punkte *hochgezählt werden, wenn der Spieler den Maulwurf erwischt.*

Bevor es losgeht, musst du (wie immer) ein neues Projekt erstellen, das Maulwurf-Jagd heißen könnte. Du kannst auch direkt den App Inventor mit deinem Smartphone oder Tablet verbinden, falls du eines hast, oder den Emulator starten.

Falls du dich nicht mehr daran erinnerst, wie das genau geht, schaue doch noch einmal in Kapitel 2 nach, da wurde das ganz genau erklärt.

Nur Buchstaben, Zahlen und Unterstriche sind im Projektnamen erlaubt. Außerdem muss der Projektname mit einem Buchstaben beginnen.

Jetzt geht es an die Programmierung! Da du ja bereits ein fortgeschrittener Programmierer bist, wirst du dir selbst das Design deiner App überlegen.

Suche die Komponenten zusammen

Im Designer geht es los:

1. **Die App soll im Querformat angezeigt werden. Stelle deshalb für den Screen im Bereich Properties den Eintrag ScreenOrientation auf Landscape.**

   Jetzt hat sich die Ausrichtung des Bildschirms gedreht, so als hättest du das Smartphone quer in der Hand. So kannst du später mit beiden Daumen gleichzeitig auf Maulwurf-Jagd gehen.

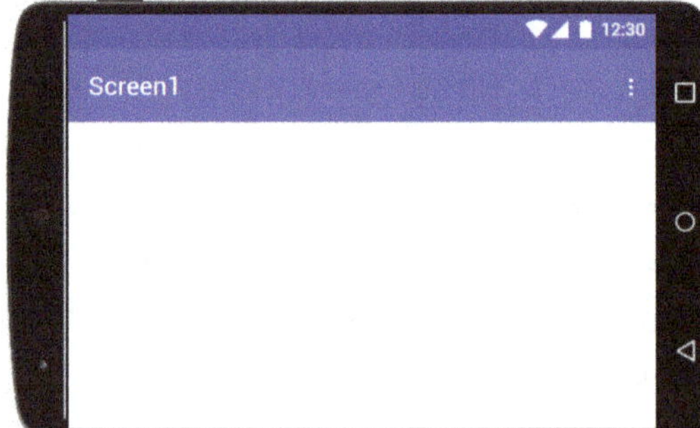

2. **Jetzt geht es an das Spielfeld. Dazu fügst du ein Canvas ein. Dieses findest du in der Palette unter Drawing and Animation.**

   Aktuell ist das Spielfeld noch recht klein.

3. **Passe die Höhe (Height) und Breite (Width) des Canvas so an, dass das Spielfeld fast den gesamten Bildschirm ausfüllt.**

Du kannst die Höhe und Breite entweder über eine bestimmte Anzahl Pixel (»pixels«) oder einen Prozentanteil (»percent«) angeben oder du probierst einmal die Einstellung Fill parent aus. Findest du heraus, was diese Einstellung tut? Die Größe des Spielfeldes kannst du auch später noch jederzeit anpassen.

4 **Weise dem Spielfeld eine Farbe (über BackgroundColor) oder ein richtiges Bild (über BackgroundImage) zu.**

Wie man ein Bild aus dem Internet speichert und in die App einfügt, kannst du in Kapitel 3 im Abschnitt »App mit Bild« nachlesen.

5 **Baue einen Button für den Neustart-Knopf und ein Label für die Punkteanzeige ein.**

Wie du einen Button einbaust, hast du schon in Kapitel 2 gelernt, und ein Label funktioniert ganz ähnlich wie eine Textbox. Bestimmt schaffst du es, beide Elemente zu finden und auf dem Screen zu platzieren.

6 **Jetzt bist du als fortgeschrittener App-Entwickler gefragt: Überlege dir, wie du die drei Elemente (Canvas, Button und Label) anordnen möchtest und wie sie aussehen (Größe, Farbe, Form etc.) sollen.**

7 **Zu einem guten Programmierstil gehört, dass alle Komponenten einer App sinnvoll benannt sind. Gib den drei Komponenten Canvas, Label und Button über Rename (in Components) sinnvolle Namen.**

Du kannst auch den Titel des Screens (unter Properties) noch anpassen.

8 **Passe die Texte der Punkteanzeige und des Buttons an.**

Den Text der Punkteanzeige musst du auf `0` setzen, da der Spieler zu Beginn ja noch keine Punkte hat. Den Text auf dem Neustart-Knopf könntest du zum Beispiel in `Neustart` ändern. Die Beschriftung änderst du, indem du das entsprechende Element anklickst und dann unter Properties den Text änderst.

Vergiss das Testen nicht. Sieht deine App so aus, wie du es gerne hättest? Falls du gerne noch mehr über die Anordnung der Elemente auf dem Bildschirm erfahren möchtest, schau im Abschnitt »Buttons neben- und untereinander« in Kapitel 3 nach.

Das Spielfeld ist bereit, es könnte so ähnlich aussehen wie in der Abbildung. Nun fehlt nur noch der Maulwurf.

9 **Für den Maulwurf brauchst du ein ImageSprite. Ein ImageSprite ist ein Bild, das sich bewegen kann. Dieses findest du unter Drawing and Animation.**

Wichtig ist, dass du das ImageSprite *direkt auf das Canvas (also das »Spielfeld«) ziehst, denn der Maulwurf soll ja auf der Spielfläche unterwegs sein.*

10 **Lade auch hier wieder ein Bild hoch und lege die Größe fest.**

Am besten passen würde natürlich ein Bild von einem Maulwurf. Wo du kostenfrei Bilder herunterladen kannst und wie du sie in deine App einbaust, kannst du in Abschnitt »App mit Bild« in Kapitel 3 nachlesen.

11 **Na, hast du daran gedacht, das ImageSprite umzubenennen? Nein? Nicht schlimm, dann tue das einfach jetzt noch, damit du später den Maulwurf immer schnell findest.**

12 **Als letzten Bestandteil deiner App brauchst du noch eine Clock (»Uhr«), damit du später einstellen kannst, nach welcher Zeit der Maulwurf an einer neuen Position erscheinen soll.**

Die Uhr findest du in der Kategorie Sensors.

13 **Benenne auch diese Komponente um.**

Wie wäre es mit dem Namen `Uhr`?

Eine Clock *ist eine besondere Komponente, sie ist nämlich sozusagen unsichtbar. Falls du die* Clock *bereits in den* Viewer *hineingezogen hast, hast du sicher bemerkt, dass unterhalb des Displays die Beschriftung* Non-visible components *erschienen ist.*

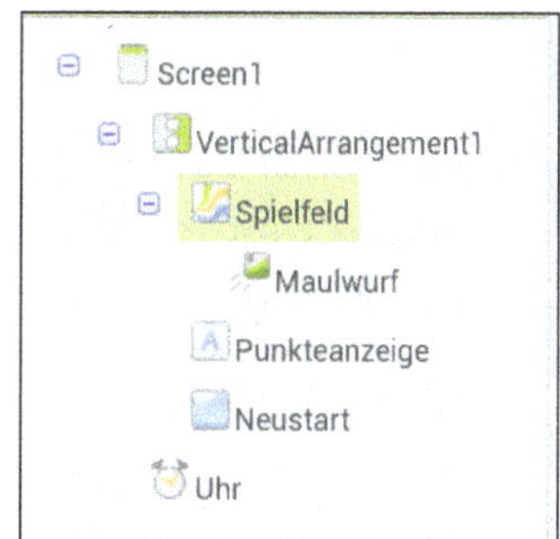

14 Für den Anfang kannst du in den Properties der Clock das TimerInterval, also die Zeit, nach der der Maulwurf an eine andere Position springen soll, auf 2000 festlegen.

Die Zeitspanne dauert damit 2000 Millisekunden (das entspricht zwei Sekunden).

Super, die Arbeit im Designer ist geschafft. Du hast

- alle sichtbaren Komponenten (Canvas, Label, Button und ImageSprite) in die App eingebaut,
- den Hintergrund, den Maulwurf, die Punkteanzeige und den Neustart-Knopf nach deinen Wünschen hübsch gestaltet und
- einen Timer (mittels Clock) hinzugefügt.

Jetzt fehlt nur noch die Funktionalität. Aber vorher solltest du das Aussehen deiner App noch einmal auf dem Smartphone oder im Emulator testen. Wenn der Hintergrund die richtige Farbe hat und dich der Maulwurf anlacht, kann es weitergehen.

Bring den Maulwurf in Bewegung

Wechsel nun in den Blocks-Editor.

Als Erstes soll sich der Maulwurf über das Spielfeld bewegen, also nach Ablauf des TimerIntervalls (welches du oben auf 2 Sekunden gesetzt hast) an einer neuen zufälligen Position erscheinen.

1 **Der Maulwurf soll sich bewegen (auf Englisch heißt das »move to«). Daher benötigst du den Baustein call Maulwurf.MoveTo, welchen du in der Kategorie Maulwurf findest.**

Wenn du zuvor im Designer den Maulwurf anders benannt hast, musst du in der entsprechenden Kategorie suchen.

2 **Das *x* und *y* beschreiben die Position, an die der Maulwurf springen soll. Für einen ersten Test kannst du beides einfach mal auf 50 setzen.**

Das *x* und das *y* nennt man Koordinaten. Ein Koordinatensystem mit x- und y-Achse kennst du vielleicht schon aus dem Mathematikunterricht.

Zahlen findest du in der Kategorie Math. *Dabei steht zuerst immer eine 0 in dem Block, die du aber in jede beliebige andere Zahl ändern kannst.*

Wenn du deine App nun testest, wirst du merken, dass auch nach längerem Warten noch gar nichts passiert. Das liegt daran, dass du ja auch noch gar nicht programmiert hast, wann der Maulwurf sich bewegen soll.

3 **Um dem Maulwurf mitzuteilen, wann er sich denn bewegen soll, brauchst du den Baustein when Uhr.Timer do aus der Kategorie Uhr. Diesen baust du um den bisherigen Block herum.**

Denke immer daran, dass sowohl die Bausteine als auch die Kategorien bei dir anders heißen können, je nachdem, wie du die Komponenten im Designer *benannt hast.*

So sollte der gesamte Block nun bei dir aussehen, wobei die Namen »Uhr« und »Maulwurf« auch anders lauten können, wenn du diese anders benannt hast.

```
when Uhr .Timer
do  call Maulwurf .MoveTo
                        x  50
                        y  50
```

Wenn du nun deine App testest, siehst du, wie der Maulwurf nach zwei Sekunden an die neue Position (x = 50 und y = 50) springt.

Falls du den Sprung verpasst hast, starte die App einfach noch einmal neu, indem du am Computer die Verbindung über Reset Connection zurücksetzt und dann noch einmal neu herstellst.

Nach dem ersten Sprung sieht es so aus, als würde sich der Maulwurf nicht mehr bewegen. In Wahrheit springt er tatsächlich auch weiterhin alle 2 Sekunden, nur eben immer an die gleiche Position.

Im nächsten Schritt geht es darum, den Maulwurf an eine zufällige Position (statt der festen Position bei x = 50 und y = 50) hüpfen zu lassen.

4 **Lösche die beiden Zahlenbausteine mit dem Wert 50 für die x- und die y-Position.**

Löschen kannst du Programmbausteine, indem du sie in den Mülleimer (rechts unten) verschiebst.

Wenn deine App noch läuft (auf einem Smartphone oder auch im Emulator), erhältst du beim Entfernen der beiden Zahlen eine Warnung mit dem Titel Runtime Error. *Das ist ein wichtiger Hinweis, da dein Programm nun nicht mehr lauffähig, also nicht mehr funktionstüchtig ist. Das liegt daran, dass die Anzahl der Argumente, also die Zahl der Puzzlesteine, die hinten angehängt werden, falsch ist, du also statt zwei nun nur noch eine oder auch keine Koordinate angibst. Du musst die App erst schließen, dann kannst du die Meldung auf* Dismiss *wegklicken (ansonsten erscheint die Meldung immer wieder). Anschließend musst du die fehlenden Argumente – diesmal mit Zufallszahlen – wieder füllen.*

5 **Wähle dazu aus der Kategorie Math den Baustein random integer from 1 to 100 (»Zufallszahl zwischen 1 und 100«) aus und stecke ihn an die x- und auch an die y-Position.**

Jetzt ist das Programm wieder lauffähig und du kannst deine App noch einmal testen. Aber was ist das? Der Maulwurf springt nur in der oberen linken Ecke des Spielfeldes herum! Das liegt daran, dass er nur auf Positionen im Bereich x = 1, y = 1 (das ist ganz oben in der Ecke) und x = 100, y = 100 springt. Damit der Maulwurf auf dem gesamten Spielfeld umherspringt, ist eine kleine Anpassung nötig.

6 **Statt der Zahl 100 kannst du bei der x-Position auch die Width (»Breite«) des Spielfeldes und bei der y-Position die Height (»Höhe«) eintragen. Dazu verwendest du die Bausteine Spielfeld.Width und Spielfeld. Height aus der Kategorie Spielfeld.**

Nun sollte dein Maulwurf wild über das gesamte Spielfeld hüpfen. Falls er dies nicht tut, vergleiche deinen Programmcode mit unserer Lösung.

Super, du hast es geschafft, den Maulwurf nach einem bestimmten Zeitintervall (bisher waren dies immer 2 Sekunden) an eine zufällige Position auf dem Spielfeld zu bewegen. Bisher passiert aber noch nichts, wenn der Spieler es schafft, den Maulwurf zu erwischen. Das wird sich nun ändern!

Fang den Maulwurf

1 **Zum Glück gibt es den Programmblock when Maulwurf.Touched (»wenn der Maulwurf berührt wird«), der dir bei dieser Herausforderung hilft. Ziehe diesen Baustein in den Viewer.**

Aber was soll eigentlich passieren, wenn der Maulwurf berührt wird? Klar, der Punktestand soll sich um einen Punkt erhöhen.

2 **Dazu brauchst du als Erstes den Block set Punkteanzeige.Text to aus der Kategorie Punkteanzeige (oder wie du das Label zu Beginn im Designer benannt hast). Diesen Programmblock ziehst du in die orangene Klammer rein, da das ja nur passieren soll, wenn der Maulwurf auch berührt wird.**

3 **Als Nächstes brauchst du den Addieren-Block aus der Math-Kategorie, da ja zum bisherigen Punktestand ein Punkt addiert werden soll.**

4 **In eine der Lücken gehört der bisherige Punktestand, den du mit dem Befehl Punkteanzeige.Text in der Kategorie Punkteanzeige findest.**

5 **In die andere Lücke musst du nun nur noch die Zahl 1 eintragen.**

Jetzt kannst du losspielen und deinen ersten Rekord aufstellen. Falls du Probleme hattest, findest du hier den zweiten Programmteil zum Vergleich:

```
when Maulwurf .Touched
 x  y
do  set Punkteanzeige . Text to  Punkteanzeige . Text + 1
```

Aber was ist, wenn jemand anderes dein Spiel ausprobieren möchte? Dazu brauchst du noch den Neustart-Knopf, aber keine Sorge, das geht ganz schnell.

Spiele, so oft du willst

1 **Um den Neustart-Knopf zu programmieren, brauchst du den Baustein when Neustart.Click (oder wie auch immer du den Button zu Beginn im Designer benannt hast).**

Das bedeutet »wenn der Neustart-Knopf angeklickt wird«.

2 **Darin muss lediglich die Punkteanzeige wieder auf 0 gesetzt werden.**

Den Baustein kennst du schon vom Hochzählen der Punkte, nur, dass der Text der Punkteanzeige diesmal einfach auf die Zahl 0 gesetzt wird.

Spitze, das Spiel Maulwurf-Jagd ist fertig. Viel Spaß beim Spielen! Wer fängt am schnellsten den Maulwurf?

Wenn euch der Maulwurf zu langsam ist, könnt ihr das Tempo jederzeit steigern, indem ihr im Designer die Clock anklickt und dort das TimerInterval von 2000 (was ja 2 Sekunden sind) auf 1000 oder, wenn ihr geübt seid, sogar auf einen noch kleineren Wert setzt.

Ihr möchtet eure App noch weiter entwickeln und damit noch interessanter machen? Dann findet ihr hier noch ein paar Ideen und Tipps dazu:

» Eine erste Erweiterungsmöglichkeit ist, dass der Maulwurf nach einer Berührung sofort die Position wechselt, damit der Spieler nicht an derselben Stelle mehrfach hintereinander Punkte sammeln kann. Dazu musst du den gesamten call Maulwurf.MoveTo-Block zusätzlich in den when Maulwurf.Touched-Block einbauen.

- Die Geschwindigkeit könnte sich erhöhen, je mehr Punkte der Spieler schon hat. Dazu musst du im Block when Maulwurf.Touched ergänzen, dass das TimerInterval beispielsweise auf »vorheriger Wert minus 100« gesetzt wird. Wichtig ist dann, dass du im Block zum Neustart das TimerInterval wieder auf den Ausgangswert (zum Beispiel 2000) zurücksetzt.
- In einer Profi-Version des Spiels könnte es ein zweites Tier (vielleicht einen Wurm) geben, der ebenfalls wild über das Spielfeld hüpft, den der Spieler aber nicht berühren darf. Wenn der Wurm dann doch versehentlich angeklickt wird, wird dem Spieler ein Punkt abgezogen. Um diese Spielerweiterung einzubauen, musst du einige der Schritte für den Maulwurf für das zweite Tier wiederholen und am Ende im when Wurm.Touched-Block einen Punkt subtrahieren statt addieren. Kriegst du auch diese Herausforderung gemeistert?

Aber das sind nur ein paar Ideen von uns, dir fallen sicher noch andere tolle Erweiterungen ein. Auf geht's! Dir und deinen Freunden viel Spaß bei der Maulwurf-Jagd!

Pinguin-Lagesteuerung

Wenn du schon alle Rekorde in der Maulwurf-Jagd gebrochen hast, findest du hier eine weitere Herausforderung: die *Pinguin-Lagesteuerung*.

Das Besondere an dieser App ist die Steuerung über den Orientierungssensor (auch Lagesensor genannt) deines Smartphones oder Tablets.

Da du gleich mit dem Orientierungssensor deines Geräts arbeiten willst, ist es am besten, wenn du als Erstes die Funktion Display automatisch drehen deines Smartphones oder Tablets ausschaltest.

Erstelle zuerst wieder ein neues Projekt, das du zum Beispiel Pinguin-Lagesteuerung nennen kannst.

Suche die Komponenten zusammen

Jetzt geht es los. Zuerst wirst du alle nötigen Komponenten im Designer zusammenstellen und nach deinen Wünschen gestalten. Anschließend programmierst du dann im Blocks-Editor die Lagesteuerung.

1 **Genau wie für die App *Maulwurf-Jagd* benötigst du ein Canvas und darauf ein ImageSprite.**

Beide Komponenten kannst du nach deinen Wünschen ausgestalten. Als Erstes solltest du die *Größen* (Höhe und Breite) festlegen. Danach kannst du dir passende *Bilder* aussuchen und hochladen. Eine Idee ist, als Hintergrund (Canvas) eine Eislandschaft zu verwenden und als Figur (ImageSprite) einen Pinguin.

Denk immer daran, die Elemente so umzubenennen, dass du sie später (im Blocks*-Editor) einfach wiederfindest. Wie das geht, wurde im Abschnitt »Maulwurf-Jagd« weiter vorne in diesem Kapitel erklärt.*

2 **Jetzt fehlt noch die wichtigste Komponente: der OrientationSensor aus der Kategorie Sensors.**

Elemente, die nicht direkt im Display sichtbar werden, wie zum Beispiel der Orientierungssensor, erscheinen unterhalb des Displays mit der Beschriftung »Non-visible components«.

3 **Für diese App verwendest du am besten den Portrait-Modus (also das Smartphone im Hochformat), da sonst die Steuerung verdreht ist.**

Wenn du noch mehr Übung mit der Programmierung für den Orientierungssensor hast, kannst du gerne versuchen, diesen auch im Querformat, also im Landscape-Modus zu verwenden.

Damit sind die Vorbereitungen im Designer bereits abgeschlossen. Du kannst später noch weitere Komponenten hinzufügen, um aus der Lagesteuerung ein richtiges Spiel zu machen. Dazu kannst du alles verwenden, was du in den vorherigen Apps schon gelernt hast.

Der Orientierungssensor steuert den Pinguin

Hier dreht sich alles um den neuen Sensor: den OrientationSensor (auf Deutsch »Orientierungssensor«).

In praktisch jedem Smartphone und Tablet ist ein Orientierungssensor eingebaut. Er misst, wie das Gerät gehalten wird. Eine Drehung nach rechts und links wird dabei im Wert roll *gespeichert. Wird das Gerät nach vorne oder hinten gekippt, verändert sich der Wert* pitch.

Falls du kein Smartphone oder Tablet mit Orientierungssensor hast, findest du weiter unten auch einen Abschnitt, in dem gezeigt wird, wie du den Pinguin auch mit Buttons steuern kannst.

Der Pinguin soll immer dann seine Position ändern, wenn das Smartphone (oder Tablet) bewegt wird. Das bedeutet, dass die Position des Pinguins immer dann geändert werden muss, wenn sich die Orientierung des Gerätes (und damit die Werte des eingebauten Orientierungssensors) ändert.

1. **Als Erstes brauchst du den Baustein when Orientierungssensor.OrientationChanged aus der Kategorie Orientierungssensor.**

   OrientationChanged heißt »Orientierung ändert sich«.

Falls du im Designer *den »OrientationSensor1« anders benannt hast, heißt dieser bei dir nicht »Orientierungssensor«.*

2. **Wenn sich nun die Orientierung verändert, soll der Pinguin seine Position ändern. Das geht mit dem Baustein call Pinguin.MoveTo.**

   Dabei kann bei dir statt des Wortes »Pinguin« auch ein anderer Name stehen, je nachdem wie du das ImageSprite im Designer benannt hast.

   Aber wie soll sich die Position ändern? Na, wie die Werte des Orientierungssensors!

3. **Die *x-Position* des Pinguins ergibt sich aus dem roll-Wert des Orientierungssensors und die *y-Position* aus dem pitch-Wert. Die nötigen Bausteine findest du bei pitch und roll im Block.**

   Nun sollte sich der Pinguin beim Kippen des Handys schon ein wenig bewegen. Falls dies bei dir noch nicht funktioniert, kannst du deinen Code mit unserem Code abgleichen.

```
when Orientierungssensor .OrientationChanged
  azimuth  pitch  roll
do  call Pinguin .MoveTo
                   x  get roll
                   y  get pitch
```

Der Pinguin läuft über das ganze Spielfeld

Aber irgendwie verhält sich der Pinguin noch nicht wie gewünscht … Schau dir noch einmal die Werte des Orientierungssensors an.

Um den Orientierungssensor besser zu verstehen, hilft es, die Sensorwerte (also »roll« und »pitch«) auf dem Display deines Smartphones (oder Tablets) anzuzeigen. Dazu kannst du (im Designer*) ein* Label *(zum Beispiel mit dem Namen* `Sensorwert`*) einbauen, das den aktuellen roll- oder pitch-Wert anzeigt. Dazu musst du an den Baustein* set Sensorwert.Text to *den Stein* Orientierungssensor.Roll *oder* Orientierungssensor.Pitch *anhängen.*

Kippst du das Handy ganz nach *links*, nimmt der roll-Wert den Wert »90« an. Daher wandert der Pinguin dann bis zur Position x = 90.

Kippst du das Handy ganz nach *rechts*, nimmt der roll-Wert den Wert »–90« an. Da der Pinguin aber schon bei x = 0 ganz am linken Rand steht, kannst du diese Bewegung gar nicht mehr auf dem Display sehen.

Kippst du das Handy ganz nach *vorne*, nimmt der pitch-Wert den Wert »90« an. Deshalb wandert der Pinguin nun nach unten bis zum Wert y = 90.

Kippst du das Handy ganz nach *hinten*, nimmt der pitch-Wert den Wert »–90« an. Da der Pinguin aber schon bei y = 0 ganz am oberen Rand steht, kannst du diese Bewegung ebenfalls nicht auf dem Display sehen.

Damit sich der Pinguin über die gesamte Fläche bewegt, musst du mit dem roll- und pitch-Wert noch ein wenig rechnen.

1. **Damit der Pinguin, wenn das Handy flach auf der Hand liegt, also nicht gekippt wird, sondern in der Mitte der Spielfläche steht, addierst du auf den roll- bzw. pitch-Wert die Größe des halben Canvas.**

   Das bedeutet, dass du an die x-Position des call Pinguin.MoveTo-Blocks nicht direkt Orientierungssensor.Roll anhängst, sondern zuerst mittels des Additionsblocks (+) zum roll-Wert den Wert Spielfeld.Width/2 addierst.

   Die Berechnung für die x-Position sieht am Ende so aus wie in der Abbildung.

Für die y-Position musst du nur »Roll« gegen »Pitch« und »Width« gegen »Height« (Höhe) austauschen.

Jetzt bewegt sich der Pinguin bereits im mittleren Bereich deines Canvas. Das ist super!

2 **Falls du die Steuerung gerne umkehren möchtest, wenn du also willst, dass der Pinguin nach oben läuft, wenn du das Handy nach vorne kippst, und nach rechts, wenn du das Handy nach rechts kippst, musst du den roll- und pitch-Wert negieren.**

Negieren *bedeutet, dass man das Vorzeichen (+ oder –) einer Zahl umdreht. Aus dem Wert »–15« wird durch Negieren der Wert »15« und entsprechend aus dem Wert »27« der Wert »–27«.*

Um also die Steuerung umzukehren, musst du vor die Bausteine Orientierungssensor.Roll und Orientierungssensor.Pitch den Baustein neg aus der Kategorie Math einfügen.

Vielleicht ist es dir schon aufgefallen … Egal wie stark du dein Handy auch kippst, der Pinguin erreicht einfach nicht die Ecken des Canvas. Das liegt daran, dass die Werte für roll oder pitch nur zwischen –90 und 90 variieren, dein Canvas aber sehr wahrscheinlich größer als 100 x 100 Pixel ist.

3 **Wenn du möchtest, kannst du den roll- und den pitch-Wert so umrechnen, dass der Pinguin über das gesamte Canvas laufen kann. Dafür brauchst du einige mathematische Befehle, die du hintereinander ausführen musst.**

- Der roll- und der pitch-Wert können Werte zwischen –90 und 90 annehmen.
- Zuerst muss der roll- und der pitch-Wert durch 90 geteilt werden. Dadurch nimmt er nun Werte zwischen –1 und 1 an.

- Der zweite Schritt ist nun, diesen Wert mit der halben Breite oder Höhe des Canvas zu multiplizieren. Somit können Werte von -Spielfeld.Width/2 bis Spielfeld.Width/2 in x-Richtung und -Spielfeld.Height/2 bis Spielfeld.Height/2 in y-Richtung erreicht werden.

- Am Ende wird (wie bereits in Schritt 1 erklärt) noch Spielfeld.Width/2 bzw. Spielfeld.Height/2 addiert.

Die Rechnung kannst du für die y-Position wieder mit »Pitch« statt »Roll« und »Height« statt »Width« anpassen.

Super, du hast deine erste eigene Lagesteuerung programmiert und kannst den Pinguin nun durch das Kippen deines Geräts über den Bildschirm steuern. Herzlichen Glückwunsch, nun bist du ein echter App-Profi!

Im nächsten Abschnitt wird dir gezeigt, wie du den Pinguin auch mittels Buttons steuern kannst, falls du kein Android-Gerät mit Orientierungssensor hast. Wenn du aber über ein Smartphone oder Tablet verfügst, kannst du den nächsten Abschnitt überspringen und direkt zu den Spielideen springen.

Den Pinguin mit Buttons steuern

Falls du kein Android-Gerät zur Verfügung hast, kannst du den Pinguin statt mit dem Orientierungssensor auch über vier Buttons steuern.

Los geht es dazu wieder im Designer:

1. **Als Erstes brauchst du (genau wie in der Variante fürs Smartphone) ein Canvas und ein ImageSprite. Passe diese nach deinem Geschmack an (Größe, Farbe, eventuell Bild hochladen).**

2 **Des Weiteren brauchst du vier Buttons, über die du den Pinguin (oder eine andere Figur) nach oben, unten, links und rechts steuern kannst.**

Deine App könnte dann zum Beispiel so aussehen wie in der Abbildung.

Wichtig ist, dass du nicht nur die Buttons beschriftest (zum Beispiel oben, unten, links, rechts), sondern auch ihre Namen anpasst, damit du die vier Buttons später im Blocks*-Editor unterscheiden kannst.*

Weiter geht es nun im Blocks-Editor. Dort musst du nun jeden der vier Buttons so programmieren, dass sich der Pinguin bei einem Klick auf den Button in die entsprechende Richtung bewegt.

Los geht es mit dem Button, der den Pinguin nach oben bewegt. Wir haben ihn in `rauf` umbenannt. (Bei dir kann er auch einen anderen Namen haben.)

1 **Damit der Pinguin auf einen Klick reagiert, brauchst du den Befehlsblock when oben.Click, den du in der Kategorie deines Buttons findest.**

2 **Wenn der Button angeklickt wird, soll der Pinguin seine Position ändern. Das geht mit dem Baustein call Pinguin.MoveTo.**

Dabei kann bei dir statt des Wortes »Pinguin« auch ein anderer Name stehen, je nachdem wie du das ImageSprite im Designer benannt hast.

3. **Da du gerade den Rauf-Button programmierst, soll die x-Position des Pinguins bei einem Klick beibehalten werden. An die x-Position kannst du den Baustein Pinguin.X ohne Veränderung anhängen.**

4. **Der Pinguin soll sich aber bei einem Klick ein Stück nach oben bewegen, das bedeutet, dass die y-Position kleiner werden muss. Die bisherige y-Position (Pinguin.Y) soll um die Zahl 5 verringert werden. Dafür brauchst du den Subtraktionsblock (-) aus der Kategorie Math.**

Wenn du ein Objekt (hier den Pinguin) auf einem Canvas platzieren oder verschieben willst, denk immer daran, dass der Nullpunkt *(x = 0, y = 0) oben links in der Ecke liegt.*

Jetzt kannst du deine App ausprobieren. Bei jedem Klick auf den Rauf-Button sollte dein Pinguin ein Stückchen nach oben wandern. Falls du Probleme hast, vergleiche deinen Programmblock mit unserer Lösung.

5. **Nun ist es an der Zeit, diese Idee auch auf die anderen drei Buttons zu übertragen.**

   Beim Runter-Button brauchst du lediglich aus der Subtraktion (–) eine Addition (+) zu machen. Beim Links- und Rechts-Button musst du statt der y-Position die x-Position verändern (die y-Position bleibt unverändert). Probiere einfach aus, wann du eine Addition und wann eine Subtraktion einbauen musst.

Es ist wieder Zeit zum Testen. Arbeiten alle vier Buttons so, wie du es dir vorstellst? Prima! Dann ist deine Pinguin-Lagesteuerung fertig.

Jetzt sind deine Spielideen gefragt

Wenn du nun die Lage- oder auch Button-Steuerung des Pinguins fertig programmiert hast, kannst du auch noch ein richtiges Spiel mit dem Pinguin entwickeln. Hier findest du ein paar Ideen, was du machen könntest. Aber vielleicht hast du ja auch eigene Ideen?

- Du könntest zusätzlich einen Schneemann (ein weiteres ImageSprite) auf dem Spielfeld platzieren und mit dem Pinguin diesen fangen. Um auf eine Kollision des Schneemanns mit dem Pinguin zu reagieren, brauchst du den Baustein when Schneemann.CollidedWith. Wenn also der Schneemann und der Pinguin sich berühren, soll der Schneemann an eine *zufällige Position* auf dem Spielfeld springen. Wie man ein ImageSprite an eine zufällige Position verschiebt, hast du schon in der App »Maulwurf-Jagd« gelernt.
- Um das Spiel noch ein wenig spannender zu gestalten, könntest du einen *Punktezähler* einbauen. Auch das kennst du schon aus der vorherigen App.
- Du könntest auch einen Feind des Pinguins, zum Beispiel einen Seelöwen, einbauen, den der Pinguin nicht berühren darf. Vielleicht gibt das dann Punktabzug.
- Du kannst bekannte App-Spiele nachbauen. Ein berühmtes Beispiel ist *Flappy Bird*. In diesem Spiel muss der Spieler einen Vogel rauf und runter steuern, um herannahenden Hindernissen (Röhren) auszuweichen. In der Originalversion wurde der Vogel mittels zweier Buttons gesteuert, aber es geht auch mit dem Orientierungssensor. Mit dieser kostenlosen App nahm der vietnamesische Programmierer Dong Nguyen 2013 allein durch Werbung bis zu 50.000 Dollar pro Tag ein, bevor er sie am 7. Februar 2014 wegen des »zu großen Erfolgs« selbst wieder aus dem App-Store entfernte.
- Mit ein bisschen Kreativität kannst du auch Spiele, die normalerweise nicht mit Smartphones gespielt werden, nachbauen. Wie wäre es zum Beispiel mit einer Partie *Minigolf* oder *Billard*?

Egal für welche Spielidee du dich entscheidest, wir wünschen dir viel Spaß beim Programmieren und anschließenden Spielen.

Und wir gratulieren dir ganz herzlich: Du bist nun ein *fortgeschrittener App-Entwickler*!

Im nächsten Kapitel erfährst du, welche Sensoren dein Smartphone noch hat und lernst komplexere Programmierbefehle, um deine Apps noch interessanter zu gestalten.

Kapitel 5
App-Ideen für Profis

In diesem Kapitel lernst du noch einige wichtige Programmierbefehle und weitere Sensoren kennen, die du in deinen Apps nutzen kannst. Ganz zum Schluss wirst du sogar in der Lage sein, deine App gegen den ungewollten Zugriff von neugierigen Nasen zu schützen.

Mit verschiedenen Levels arbeiten

Um deine (in den vorherigen Kapiteln programmierten) Apps noch spannender zu machen, kannst du verschiedene *Level* (zum Beispiel mit unterschiedlichen Geschwindigkeiten) einbauen. In welchem Level sich der Spieler befindet, kannst du in einer Variable speichern und jederzeit im Spiel anpassen.

Eine Variable ist ein Speicherplatz, an dem du einen Wert (zum Beispiel eine Zahl für das aktuelle Level) speichern und diesen im Spiel jederzeit überschreiben (also anpassen) kannst. Eine Variable ist ein Programmierkonstrukt, daher findest du die Kategorie Variables (»Variablen«) im Blocks-Editor unter Built-in.

Um eine Variable anzulegen, brauchst du den Block initialize global name to. Den Namen darfst du selbst auswählen (somit ist es auch möglich, mehrere Variablen zu nutzen) und rechts kannst du direkt den Startwert anhängen (zum Beispiel 0).

```
initialize global name to 0
```

Initialisieren einer Variable bedeutet, dass ein Speicherplatz reserviert wird. In diesen Speicherplatz (also in die Variable) kannst du dann beispielsweise eine Zahl speichern.

Wenn der Spieler nun das nächste Level erreicht, kannst du die Variable mittels set global name to um 1 erhöhen.

```
set global name to get global name + 1
```

Vielleicht möchtest du ja einen Ton ausgeben, wenn der Spieler das dritte Level erreicht? Dies kannst du mit einer if-Abfrage programmieren.

```
if get global name = 3
then call Sound1 .Play
```

Eine if-Abfrage ist ein sehr wichtiger Baustein für Programme. Damit steuert der Programmierer den Programmablauf im Falle eines bestimmten Ereignisses. Das englische Wort if heißt auf Deutsch »falls« oder »wenn« und then steht für »dann«.

Mit einer if-Abfrage kannst du Bedingungen programmieren, wie zum Beispiel »Wenn die Variable Name gleich 3 ist, dann spiele einen Ton ab«.

Eine if-Abfrage kannst du auch nutzen, um dem Spieler unter einer bestimmten Bedingung eine Meldung oder ein weiteres Objekt anzuzeigen.

Mehrere Screens kombinieren

Wenn du dich in den vorherigen Kapiteln ein wenig ausgetobt hast, wirst du sicher gemerkt haben, dass für umfangreichere Apps ein einziger Screen nicht immer ausreicht. Deshalb lernst du hier, wie du in einer App auch mehrere Screens kombinieren kannst.

Screens einbauen

Vielleicht ist es dir schon aufgefallen: Oben in der grünen Leiste im App Inventor kannst du zwischen den Screens wechseln, weitere Screens hinzufügen und Screens löschen.

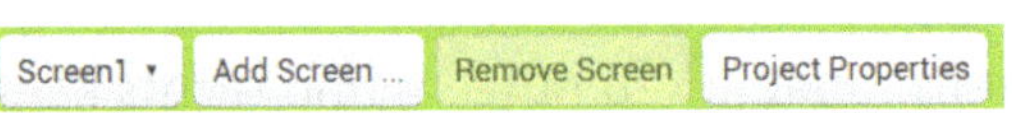

1. **Füge mit Add Screen ... zwei neue Screens hinzu, sodass insgesamt dann drei Screens in der App sind.**

   Der erste Screen soll die Übersichtsseite, also das Auswahlmenü, darstellen und heißt im Beispiel Uebersicht.

   Der zweite Screen dient der Ansicht von Fotos und trägt hier den Namen Fotoanzeige.

   Der dritte Screen ermöglicht es dem Nutzer, einen Internetbrowser zu benutzen und heißt daher Internet.

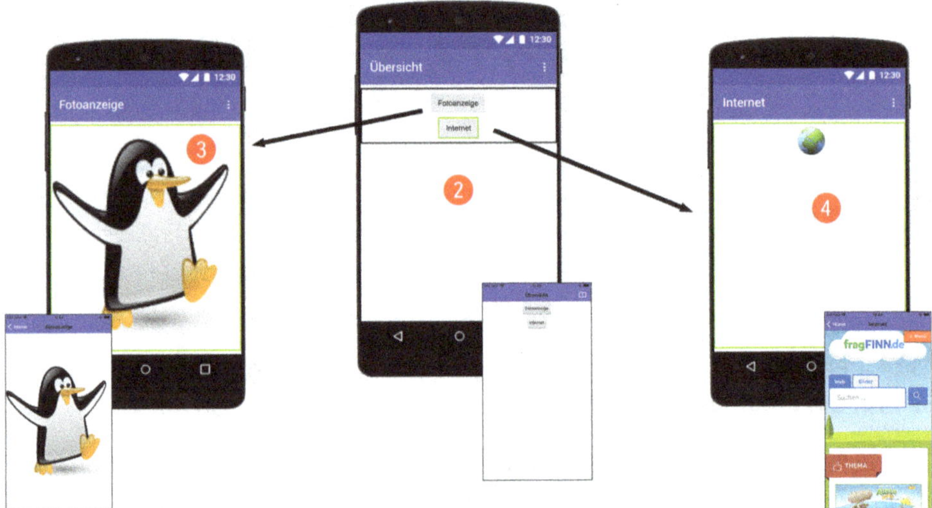

2. **Auf dem ersten Screen »Übersicht« sollen lediglich zwei Buttons sein, mit denen der Nutzer später zu den anderen beiden Screens weitergeleitet wird.**

   Ändere die Namen und Texte der Buttons so, dass du und der spätere Nutzer wissen, wozu sie da sind.

3 **Auf den Screen »Fotoanzeige« kannst du ein beliebiges Bild laden, damit du später in der App testen kannst, ob du nach einem Klick auf den Button Fotoanzeige auch auf dem richtigen Screen landest.**

4 **Der dritte Screen »Internet« besteht nur aus dem WebViewer. Diesen findest du in der Palette unter User Interface.**

Der WebViewer kann Internetseiten anzeigen. Am einfachsten zum Testen ist es, wenn du in den Properties unter HomeUrl eine beliebige Internetadresse einträgst.

Die eingegebene Internetadresse muss mit http://... *beginnen. Du könntest also zum Beispiel eine Suchseite wie »Frag-Finn« (*https://www.fragfinn.de*) eingeben.*

Wenn du nun deine App testest, wirst du einen der drei Screens sehen. Da die Weiterleitung über die beiden Buttons noch nicht programmiert ist, kannst du innerhalb der App noch nicht zwischen den Screens wechseln. Um dennoch alle drei Screens auszuprobieren, kannst du im App Inventor links neben dem Button Add Screen ... zwischen den Screens wechseln. Der Wechsel passiert dann auch sofort in deiner App (auf dem Smartphone oder im Emulator).

Verlinken

Da die App später auch ohne den App Inventor funktionieren soll, musst du nun noch die Verlinkung über die beiden Buttons einbauen.

1 **Nur der Screen Übersicht muss hier programmiert werden.**

Achte darauf, dass du den richtigen Screen (den mit den beiden Buttons) ausgewählt hast, bevor du loslegst.

2 **Als Erstes brauchst du die Steuerung für den Buttonklick, also den Befehl when FotoanzeigeButton.Click .**

Das kennst du ja schon.

3 **Dann brauchst du den Befehl open another screen screenName, den du unter Built-in und Control findest.**

Open another screen heißt so viel wie »öffne einen anderen Screen«.

4 Wie du sicher schon vermutest, musst du dahinter noch den Namen des Screens auswählen, den du öffnen möchtest.

In unserem Beispiel heißt der gewünschte Screen »Fotoanzeige«. Dazu klickst du auf das kleine Dreieck hinter Screen1 und wählst den Fotoanzeige-Screen aus.

Insgesamt besteht der Befehlsblock für den ersten Button aus drei Bausteinen:

```
when FotoanzeigeButton .Click
do   open another screen screenName Fotoanzeige
```

5 Wiederhole die Schritte 2 bis 4 auch für den zweiten Button, der den Nutzer auf den Screen mit dem WebViewer führen soll.

Es ist wieder Zeit zum Testen! Gehe im App Inventor auf den Übersichts-Screen, damit du von dort die beiden anderen Screens aufrufen kannst. Falls etwas nicht funktioniert, kontrolliere ganz genau die Schreibweisen. Sowohl in der HomeUrl als auch bei den Screen-Namen kommt es auf jeden Buchstaben und auch auf die Groß- und Kleinschreibung an.

Jetzt ist es geschafft! Du hast eine App aus mehreren Screens gebaut, die sogar untereinander verlinkt sind. Super!

Durchblick im Supermarkt – Barcodes scannen

Barcodes kennst du bestimmt, das sind diese schwarz-weißen Strichmuster auf vielen Waren im Supermarkt.

Diese kann aber nicht nur das Gerät an der Supermarktkasse einscannen, sondern auch dein Smartphone. Mit dieser Smartphone-Funktion kannst du dir ganz leicht einen Einkaufszettel erstellen, ohne alle Produktnamen mühsam einzutippen. Auch kannst du mit dem Smartphone selbst Barcodes erzeugen, ausdrucken und so eigene Informationen speichern.

Die Komponenten

1. **Als Erstes brauchst du natürlich aus der Palette den BarcodeScanner unter Sensors.**

   Der Barcodescanner ist eine unsichtbare Komponente und taucht daher unterhalb des Handydisplays auf.

Falls du auf deinem Smartphone keine andere App mit einem Barcodescanner installiert hast, musst du das Häkchen in den Properties *bei* UseExternalScanner *entfernen. Falls du dir unsicher bist, ob eine solche App auf deinem Gerät vorhanden ist, oder falls du diese nicht verwenden möchtest, kannst du das Häkchen ebenfalls entfernen.*

2. **Dann benötigt die App einen Button, mit dem du den Scan später startest.**

   Diesen solltest du auch wieder umbenennen und passend beschriften.

3. **Außerdem ist ein Label sinnvoll, um den eingelesenen Code direkt ausgeben zu können. Ziehe auch dieses in deine App.**

   Damit hast du auch schon alle nötigen Komponenten zusammen. Natürlich kannst du deine App später noch weiter ausgestalten, aber zum Kennenlernen des Barcodescanners reichen diese drei.

Die Funktionalität

1. **Wenn der Button Startknopf angeklickt wird, muss der Befehl call BarcodeScanner1.DoScan aufgerufen werden.**

   Beachte, dass du hier bereits zwei Befehle zusammenfügen musst.

2. **Um den eingescannten Code anzuzeigen, kannst du den Befehlsblock when BarcodeScanner1.AfterScan nutzen.**

   Das englische *AfterScan* bedeutet »nach dem Scannen«.

3 **In diesen Block setzt du dann jenen zum Überschreiben des Texts im Label ein, also set CodeAnzeige.text to.**

4 **Zum Schluss musst du diesen Text auf das Ergebnis (»Result«) des Barcodescanners setzen. Dafür klickst du im Befehlsblock when BarcodeScanner1.AfterScan auf `result` und nimmst dir den get result-Block.**

Um deine App nun zu testen, brauchst du ein Produkt mit Barcode, also zum Beispiel eine Wasserflasche oder eine Tafel Schokolade. So hast du auch gleich noch eine Stärkung, bevor du dich an die nächste Herausforderung begibst.

Wenn alles funktioniert hat, hat deine App nun eine lange Zahlenfolge ausgespuckt. Der Computer in der Supermarktkasse schlägt mithilfe dieser Zahlenkombination in einer Tabelle (»Datenbank«) den Preis für das Produkt nach.

Aber wir Menschen würden doch gerne einen kleinen Text speichern. Dafür gibt es neben den Strichcodes noch *QR-Codes*. Dies sind quadratische Anordnungen von schwarzen und weißen Vierecken. In diesen kann man auch eine umfangreichere Information, sogar einen kleinen Text, speichern.

Probiere es aus und scanne mit deiner selbst erstellten App den Code oben. Na, was liest du? Ja, genau richtig: »Super gemacht!«

QR-Codes kannst du im Internet ganz einfach selbst erstellen! Du brauchst nur einen beliebigen (nicht zu langen) Text einzutippen und die Webseite (zum Beispiel www.mal-den-code.de) erzeugt dir daraus einen QR-Code. Diesen kannst du dann ausdrucken und zum Beispiel als Erinnerung an die Zimmertür kleben. Beim Rausgehen brauchst du nur den Code zu scannen und schon fällt dir wieder ein, was du nicht vergessen darfst. Und gleichzeitig erfährt dein Bruder nicht, was er zum Geburtstag geschenkt bekommt. Du kannst den Code auch deinen Freunden weiterreichen, solange sie auch deine App auf einem Smartphone haben.

Mit dem Smartphone reden: Die Sprachsteuerung

Gerade für sehbehinderte oder gar blinde Menschen, die Nachrichten nicht einfach vom Display ablesen können, oder auch für alle, die zum Beispiel während der Autofahrt eine SMS vorgelesen bekommen möchten, ist *TextToSpeech* eine hilfreiche Erfindung. Auch in die umgekehrte Richtung ist dies sehr hilfreich, denn der blinde Smartphone-Nutzer möchte sicher auf die Nachricht antworten, kann aber seine Antwort nicht bzw. nur mühsam über die Bildschirmtastatur eingeben. Auch hierzu gibt es eine Lösung: *SpeechRecognizer*.

TextToSpeech *(auf Deutsch »Text zu Sprache«) bedeutet, dass Text, der normalerweise direkt auf dem Display angezeigt würde, von einer Computerstimme laut vorgelesen wird.*

Um auch über die Spracheingabe antworten zu können, gibt es einen SpeechRecognizer *(auf Deutsch »Sprach-Erkenner«).*

Sicher fallen dir schon viele Situationen ein, wo man eine solche *Sprachsteuerung* gut gebrauchen kann.

TextToSpeech

TextToSpeech dient dazu, eine Nachricht vorzulesen, für alle, die (aktuell) nicht auf das Display schauen können oder zum Beispiel noch nicht lesen gelernt haben.

Zum Kennenlernen dieser Komponente soll deine App auf Knopfdruck eine kurze Nachricht vorlesen.

1. **Füge als Erstes in dein neues Projekt einen Button ein, der später die Sprachausgabe starten soll.**
2. **Dann benötigst du die unsichtbare Komponente TextToSpeech, die du in der Palette unter Media findest.**

Damit hast du die beiden wichtigen Komponenten eingefügt und kannst dich an die Programmierung im Blocks-Editor begeben.

1. **Um die Sprachausgabe auf Knopfdruck zu starten, brauchst du den Baustein when SprachausgabeButton.Click.**
2. **Um einen Text auch wirklich sprachlich ausgeben zu lassen, musst du den Befehl call TextToSpeech1.Speak message einbauen.**

   Speak message bedeutet »sprich Nachricht«.

3 **Wie du dir sicher schon gedacht hast, wird an message noch die Nachricht angehängt, die vorgelesen werden soll. Dazu verwendest du einen einfachen Textbaustein, in den du dann selbst eine Nachricht eintippst.**

Um die Nachricht »Hallo, wie geht es dir?« vorzulesen, brauchst du das Programmstück aus der Abbildung.

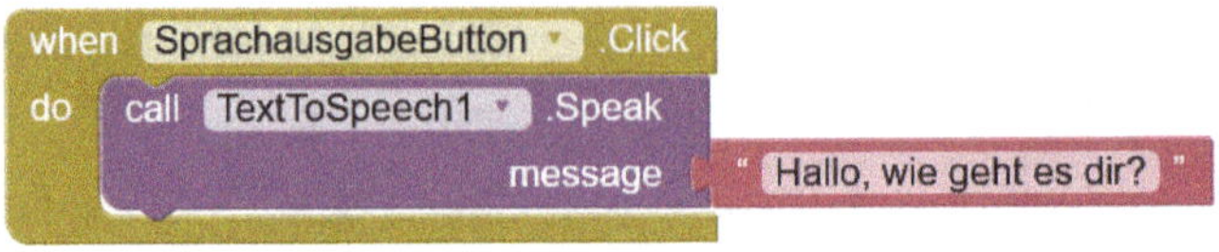

Hast du die freundliche Frauenstimme gehört? Na, das klingt doch schon ganz prima. Fordere sie gerne auch mit längeren Texten ein wenig heraus.

SpeechRecognizer

Um auf eine vorgelesene Nachricht auch antworten zu können, musst du noch einen Spracherkenner einbauen.

1 **Füge noch einen Button hinzu, der später die Spracherkennung starten soll.**

2 **Weiterhin brauchst du ein Label auf dem angezeigt wird, was du eingesprochen hast, bzw. das, was die Spracherkennung erfasst hat.**

3 **Dann benötigst du die unsichtbare Komponente SpeechRecognizer, die du ebenfalls in der Palette unter Media findest.**

Weiter geht es im Blocks-Editor.

1 **Ausgelöst werden soll die Spracherkennung über einen Klick auf den entsprechenden Button.**

2 **Der Befehl zum Starten der Spracherkennung lautet call SpeechRecognizer1.GetText und ist in der Kategorie SpeechRecognizer zu finden.**

GetText bedeutet so viel wie »Hol den Text«. Damit ist der Programmblock zum Starten der Spracherkennung bereits fertig.

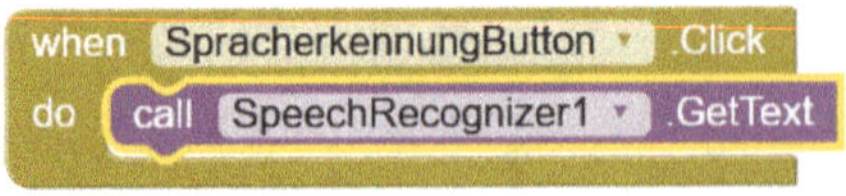

3 **Nun soll der eingesprochene Text auf dem Label angezeigt werden. Den Text des Labels kannst du mit set GesprochenerText.Text to ändern.**

4 **Dieser Text soll auf das Ergebnis der Spracherkennung, also SpeechRecognizer1.Result, gesetzt werden.**

Wenn du diese beiden Befehle kombinierst und in den bestehenden when SpracheingabeButton.Click-Befehl einfügst, wird der eingesprochene Text immer erst beim nächsten Klick auf den Button ausgegeben.

5 **Damit der Text auch direkt nach der Spracheingabe im Label erscheint, musst du den Block when SpeechRecognizer1.AfterGettingText benutzen.**

AfterGettingText bedeutet auf Deutsch »nach Erhalt des Textes«.

Insgesamt hast du nun einen zweiten Programmblock, der den Text im Label aktualisiert.

```
when SpeechRecognizer1 .AfterGettingText
  result  partial
do  set GesprochnerText . Text to  SpeechRecognizer1 . Result
```

Herzlichen Glückwunsch, dein Handy spricht mit dir!

Wenn du die Sprachsteuerung auf einem Apple-Gerät ausprobierst, kann es sein, dass die Spracherkennung nur Englisch versteht. Das liegt nicht an deiner Programmierung, sondern hier funktioniert leider etwas noch nicht beim App Inventor.

Apps mit Sprachsteuerung

Diese Funktionalität kannst du nun in vielen Apps verwenden, um die Steuerung zu vereinfachen oder ein Spiel witziger zu machen. Hier ein paar Ideen …

» Du kannst das Ergebnis der Spracheingabe mit bestimmten Begriffen abgleichen und so ein Ereignis per Sprache auslösen. Ein einfaches Beispiel wäre, die Textfarbe des Labels aufgrund der Spracheingabe anzupassen. Sagt der Nutzer zum Beispiel das Wort »Blau«, so soll der Text in der Farbe Blau erscheinen.

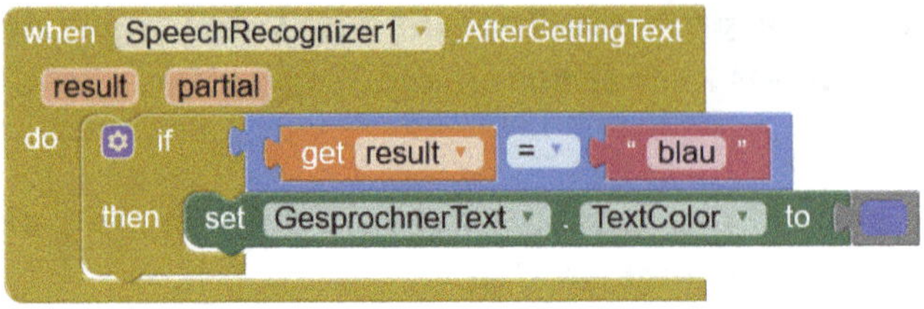

```
when SpeechRecognizer1 .AfterGettingText
  result  partial
do  if    get result = " blau "
    then  set GesprochnerText . TextColor to
```

Hier wurde ein wichtiges Programmierelement verwendet: die if-Abfrage. Die hast du am Anfang dieses Kapitels im Abschnitt »Mit verschiedenen Levels arbeiten« kennengelernt. Falls du dir nicht mehr sicher bist, wie diese Programmiertechnik funktioniert, blättere noch einmal ein paar Seiten zurück.

» Mit der gleichen Technik kannst du neben Textfarben auch die Richtung festlegen, in die sich ein Objekt bewegt. Somit könntest du den Pinguin aus der App »Pinguin-Laufsteuerung« in Kapitel 4 mit deiner Stimme steuern. Dazu baust du am besten die Steuerung per Buttons um und reagierst nicht auf den Klick, sondern auf das gesprochene Wort. Damit das Ganze auch funktioniert, musst du dem Benutzer in der App mitteilen, welche Begriffe (zum Beispiel »rechts«, »links«, »rauf« und »runter«) der Pinguin versteht.

» Auch kannst du eine App programmieren, die sich mit dem Nutzer unterhält oder ihm Fragen beantwortet. Das funktioniert zwar nicht für beliebige Sätze (weil du ja nicht ewig an dieser App programmieren willst), aber du bekommst einen Eindruck, wie die professionellen Systeme wie »Siri« von Apple, »Cortana« von Windows oder auch »OK Google« von Android funktionieren. Für ein erstes Beispiel kannst du auf die Frage »Wie geht es dir?« eines Nutzers mit »Mir geht es gut!« antworten.

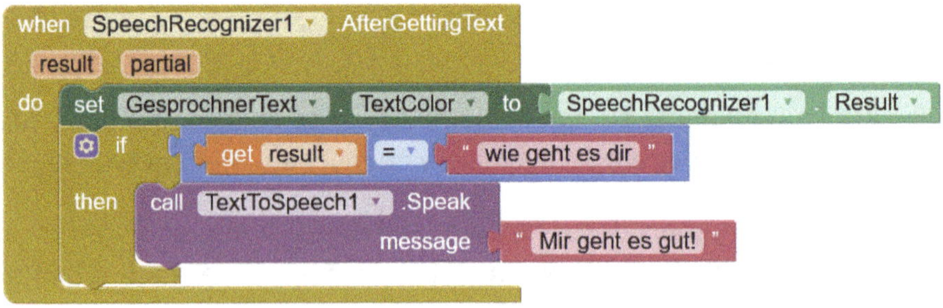

```
when SpeechRecognizer1 .AfterGettingText
  result  partial
do  set GesprochnerText . TextColor to SpeechRecognizer1 . Result
    if    get result = " wie geht es dir "
    then  call TextToSpeech1 .Speak
                       message " Mir geht es gut! "
```

Die Zeile zur Textausgabe im Label GesprochenerText *ist nicht zwingend nötig, aber sie erleichtert das Testen, da du so sehen kannst, was die Sprachsteuerung erkannt hat. An dieser Ausgabe wirst du auch sehen, dass der erkannte Text immer komplett klein geschrieben ist. Somit wäre ein Vergleich des Resultats mit dem Text »Wie geht es dir?« nicht sinnvoll. In der Sprache der Programmierer heißt die Ausgabe von Zwischenergebnissen zum Testen:* Debug-Ausgabe.

Je mehr solcher Regeln du in deine App einfügst, desto interessanter wird das Gespräch. Vielleicht hast du ja Lust, der App ein wenig Wissen über dein Lieblingshobby beizubringen?

Wo bin ich? – GPS-Ortung

Wenn du gerne draußen unterwegs bist, kennst du das sicher. Du bist im Wald oder auf Feldern unterwegs. Du findest eine ganz tolle Stelle und fragst dich: Wo bin ich eigentlich (schließlich gibt es keine Straßenschilder)? Und wie kann ich mir diesen tollen Ort merken?

Die Antwort lautet: über die *GPS-Koordinaten* des Ortes.

GPS *steht für* Global Positioning System *(auf Deutsch »Globales Positionsbestimmungssystem«). Mithilfe dieses Systems kann jeder Ort auf der Welt ganz genau durch zwei Koordinaten angegeben werden. Das Ganze funktioniert ähnlich wie ein Koordinatensystem. Statt x- und y-Koordinate gibt es einen* Längen- *(auf Englisch* longitude*) und einen* Breitengrad *(auf Englisch* latitude*).*

Damit dein Smartphone herausfinden kann, wo (also an welchem Längen- und Breitengrad) es sich befindet, kreisen eine ganze Menge Satelliten um unsere Erde. Diese senden durchgehend ihre Position und die aktuelle Zeit aus. Mithilfe der Signale mehrerer solcher Satelliten kann dein Smartphone berechnen, wo es sich auf der Erde befindet.

Wenn dich das Thema GPS-Ortung näher interessiert, findest du im Internet sehr viele (auch einfache) Erklärungen. Für uns ist wichtig, dass die exakten Koordinaten eines Punktes aus Längen- und Breitengrad (also longitude und latitude) bestehen.

Anzeige des Längen- und Breitengrades

Nun geht es ans Designen:

1 **Damit du die Koordinaten später nicht durcheinanderbringst, lässt du sie am besten mit Beschriftung auf dem Display anzeigen.**

Um die Werte neben den Beschriftungen anzuordnen, eignet sich ein ScreenArrangement aus der Kategorie Layout. Wie genau du ScreenArrangements verwendest, hast du im Abschnitt »Buttons neben- und untereinander« in Kapitel 3 gelernt.

2 **In das gewählte Layout kannst du nun vier Label ziehen. Zwei für die Beschriftungen `Längengrad` und `Breitengrad` und zwei für die Anzeige der Werte.**

Wenn du zu Beginn in die Labels zur Anzeige »???« schreibst, könnte deine App so aussehen wie in der Abbildung.

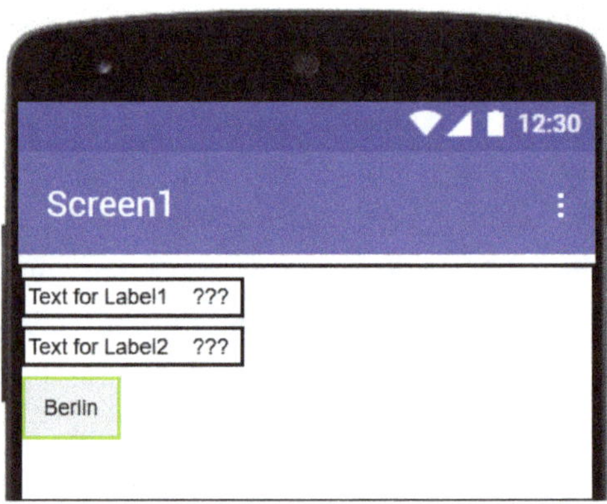

3 **Nun fehlt nur noch der LocationSensor aus der Palette unter Sensors.**

Auch wenn das Design hier noch nicht optimal ist, reicht es zum Kennenlernen des Sensors vollkommen aus. Wechsel nun also zum Programmieren in den Blocks-Editor.

1 **Zuerst musst du bestimmen, wann die GPS-Daten aktualisiert werden sollen. Eine Möglichkeit ist, dass dies immer passiert, wenn der Ort gewechselt wird. Das legst du mit dem Block when LocationSensor1.LocationChanged fest.**

2 **Damit sich auch die Anzeige ändert, musst du mit set LaengengradAnzeige.Text to bzw. mit set BreitengradAnzeige.Text to die bisherigen Werte überschreiben.**

3 **Überschrieben werden sollen die Labels mit dem longitude-Wert beim Längengrad und dem latitude-Wert beim Breitengrad.**

Insgesamt sieht die Anzeige des aktuellen Längen- und Breitengrades dann so wie in der Abbildung aus.

```
when LocationSensor1 .LocationChanged
  latitude  longitude  altitude  speed
do  set LängengradAnzeige . Text to  get longitude
    set BreitengradAnzeige . Text to  get latitude
```

Die Genauigkeit der Koordinaten und auch die Zeit bis zur Anzeige kann von Gerät zu Gerät variieren. Bitte habe ein wenig Geduld und teste deine App im Freien, damit dein Gerät auch die Signale der Satelliten gut empfangen kann.

Die Ortungs-App

Jetzt, wo die Anzeige der Koordinaten funktioniert, kannst du dir überlegen, wie du deine Ortungs-App gestalten möchtest.

» Eine einfache Anpassung wäre, dass die Anzeige der Koordinaten auf *Knopfdruck* (also über einen Button) gesteuert wird.

» Weiter könntest du den *schönsten Ort speichern*. Dazu solltest du weitere Labels einfügen und einen zweiten Button zum Speichern einer ganz besonderen Position.

» Du kannst dir auch in der App die *Koordinaten eines bestimmten Ortes* angeben lassen. Dafür brauchst du einen Button und drei Label. Mit folgendem Programmblock fragst du die Koordinaten von Berlin ab.

```
when StarteSucheButton .Click
do  set LängengradAnzeige . Text to
    set BreitengradAnzeige . Text to
```

An die beiden offenen Enden musst du noch die Programmblöcke zum Berechnen des Breiten- und Längengrades anbauen.

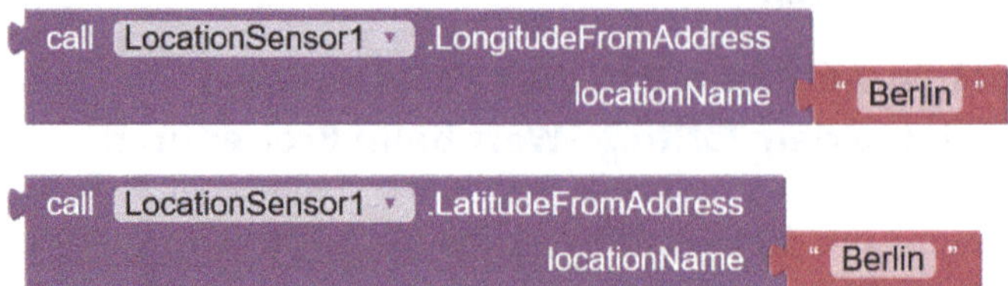

» Natürlich ist es nicht sehr spannend, immer wieder die Koordinaten von einem festen Ort abzufragen und anzuzeigen. Wenn du deine App zusätzlich mit der *Sprachsteuerung* aus dem vorherigen Abschnitt kombinierst, kann der Nutzer seinen Wunschort nennen und deine App gibt die zugehörigen Koordinaten aus.

Sicher ist sicher - Passwort-Sperre

Zum Abschluss dieses Kapitels steht noch ein wichtiges Thema an: die *Sicherheit*. Hier lernst du, wie du deine App (oder auch Teile davon) per *Passwort* schützen kannst.

Sicher bist du schon ganz oft sogenannten Login-Formularen begegnet. Meist gibt man dort einen Nutzernamen und ein Passwort ein und drückt anschließend auf Login. Genau dies wirst du hier nachbauen.

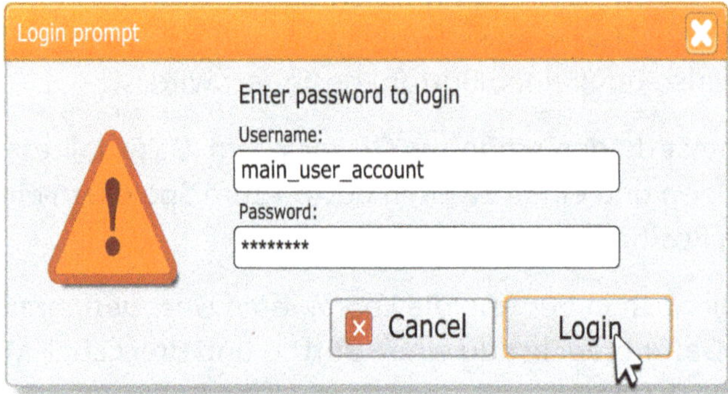

Wie du vielleicht schon weißt, sind Passwörter unterschiedlich sicher. *Das Passwort »Anna123« ist nicht so sicher wie »K73fh+9§hcq0«, da ein Fremder es viel schneller erraten kann. So ähnlich ist es auch mit* Authentifizierungsverfahren *im Allgemeinen. Wenn du dich authentifizieren musst, heißt das, dass du nachweisen musst, dass du wirklich du bist. Zum Beispiel haben Banken besonders starke Sicherheitsmechanismen, damit niemand unerlaubt an dein Konto rankommt. Passwörter zu vergleichen, wie wir das hier tun, gehört zu den eher unsicheren Authentifizierungsverfahren, daher solltest du mit dieser Methode keine allzu wichtigen Geheimnisse abspeichern. Aber es reicht auf jeden Fall, um neugierige Nasen, die dein Handy in die Finger bekommen, davon abzuhalten, dein Geheimnis zu sehen.*

Sicher ist sicher, also auf geht es zu deinem ersten eigenen Sicherheitsverfahren.

Login-Bildschirm gestalten

1. **Um ein Eingabefenster zu bauen, brauchst du eine Textbox, in die später der Nutzername eingetragen wird. Nenne ihn zum Beispiel »Name-Eingabe«.**
2. **Dann brauchst du natürlich das Passwortfeld.**
3. **Einen Button, auf dem `Login` stehen könnte.**
4. **Einen weiteren Button, auf dem `Logout` stehen könnte.**
5. **Damit du die Passwortsperre testen kannst, füge noch ein Bild (Image) hinzu.**

   Lade zwei Bilder hoch. Eines, das jeder sehen darf, und eines, das nur für dich sichtbar werden soll. In unserem Beispiel wird dies eine »geschlossene Schatztruhe« (darf jeder sehen) und eine »offene Truhe« (stellt das Geheimnis dar) sein.

Achte nach dem Hochladen beider Bilder darauf, dass in den Properties *des Images das öffentliche Bild ausgewählt ist, denn dieses wird ja direkt am Anfang angezeigt.*

Wenn deine App nun so ähnlich aussieht wie das Beispiel mit der geschlossenen Schatztruhe, dann kann es im Blocks-Editor weitergehen.

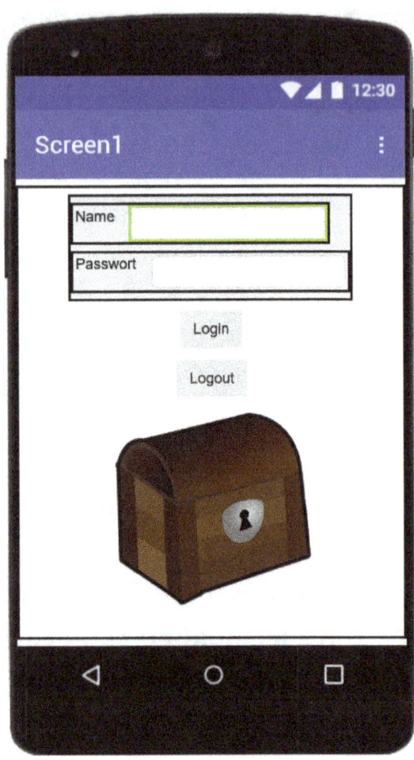

Geheimnis verstecken

Los geht es (wie so oft) beim Klick auf den Button. Fange am besten mit dem Login-Button an.

1. **Zunächst brauchst du eine if-Abfrage.**

   Du willst später gleichzeitig den richtigen Namen und auch das richtige Passwort abfragen. Beginne aber zuerst einmal damit, nur das Namensfeld zu prüfen.

2. **Da du den eingegebenen Namen ja mit einem festgelegten (vermutlich deinem eigenen) abgleichen willst, brauchst du den Baustein mit dem Gleichheitszeichen aus der Kategorie Math.**

   Auf die eine Seite des Gleichheitszeichens kommt nun der Text, der in das Namensfeld eingegeben wurde. Dieser Text ist in NameEingabe.Text gespeichert.

Auf die andere Seite kommt der festgelegte Name zum Abgleich. Diesen kannst du mittels des Textbausteins mit den Anführungszeichen einfügen.

```
NameEingabe . Text = " Nadine "
```

3 **Falls nun die Bedingung erfüllt ist, also der richtige Name eingegeben wurde, soll das geheime Bild (geöffnete Schatztruhe) sichtbar werden. Dazu musst du unter then den Befehl set Bild.Picture to mit dem Namen der Bilddatei kombinieren.**

Es ist Zeit zum Testen. Bisher wird nur das Namensfeld überprüft. Starte also die App und versuche, dich mit richtigem und auch falschem Namen einzuloggen. Kannst du dein geheimes Bild sehen, wenn du den richtigen Namen eingegeben hast?

Falls es noch nicht ganz klappt, vergleiche dein Programm mit unserer Lösung.

```
when LoginButton .Click
do  if    NameEingabe . Text = " Nadine "
    then  set Bild . Picture to Truhe_auf.png
```

4 **Nur der Name wäre aber ein sehr unsicherer Schutz! Daher kommt nun auch noch die Abfrage des Passwortes hinzu. Dazu musst du zwei Bedingungen mit einem and-Baustein verbinden.**

Einen solchen and*-Baustein nennen Informatiker* logischen Operator, *daher ist er in der Kategorie* Logic *zu finden. Der Baustein bewirkt, dass beide (also die erste* und *die zweite) Bedingungen erfüllt sein müssen. Ein weiterer Operator ist der* or*-Baustein, dieser überprüft, ob mindestens eine von beiden Bedingungen erfüllt ist, also die erste oder die zweite oder auch beide.*

5 **Die zweite Bedingung sieht ganz ähnlich aus wie die erste, nur geht es diesmal nicht um das Namensfeld, sondern um das Passwortfeld.**

Wenn du die Bedingungen korrekt kombiniert hast, wird das geheime Bild nun nur noch sichtbar, wenn der richtige Name und auch das richtige Passwort eingegeben wurden.

and PasswortEingabe . Text = " ghj&(/%%("

6 **Zum Schluss fehlt nur noch die Programmierung für den Logout-Button. Wenn dieser angeklickt wird, soll wieder das öffentliche Bild erscheinen.**

when LogoutButton .Click
do set Bild . Picture to Truhe_zu.png

Super, nun kannst du sogar selbst Passwort-Sperren in deine Apps einbauen. Du hast es zum Super-Profi-App-Entwickler geschafft. Herzlichen Glückwunsch!

Aber keine Sorge, deinen weiteren App-Ideen sind noch lange keine Grenzen gesetzt. Der App Inventor hat noch zahlreiche weitere Möglichkeiten. Du kannst zum Beispiel mit Apps

» *LEGO Mindstorms Roboter* ansteuern,
» auf die *Kamera* des Smartphones zugreifen,
» eine eigene *Datenbank* (Speicherplatz für viele Daten) anlegen und sogar
» *E-Mails* schreiben und *Twitter* lesen.

Im nächsten Kapitel erfährst du, wie du vorgehen kannst, um deine eigenen App-Ideen umzusetzen.

Kapitel 6
Apps entwickeln

Du bist vom Anfänger in der App-Entwicklung mit dem App Inventor zum Profi geworden und kennst dich hervorragend mit den Sensoren deines Smartphones aus. Jetzt hast du viele Ideen für weitere Apps.
In diesem Kapitel erfährst du, wie du von deiner App-Idee zu einem Design und dann zur fertigen App gelangst. Das nennt der *Developer* (»Entwickler«) einen *Entwicklungsprozess*.

Alles startet mit einer Idee

Wenn du anfängst, Apps zu entwickeln, werden dir sehr schnell viele Ideen für eigene Apps in den Kopf kommen. Leider vergisst man häufig viele tolle Ideen.

Besorge dir also am besten ein kleines Notizbuch, das du immer mitnimmst. Wenn dir dann eine Idee kommt oder du dich mit jemandem unterhältst, der eine App benötigt, kannst du das schnell notieren. Natürlich gibt es auch Apps, die du zum Notieren deiner App-Ideen nutzen kannst. Auch eine solche könntest du selbst entwickeln.

Über viele App-Ideen wirst du erst einmal länger nachdenken müssen, ob diese auch realisierbar sind. Apps auf Smartphones können schon richtig viel, aber natürlich auch nicht alles.

Planung ist die halbe App

Du bist von deiner Idee überzeugt? Super! Dann kommt jetzt die Planungsphase der App. Dazu schreibst du dir in wenigen Stichworten auf, was deine App können soll.

Bei der Planung solltest du dich zuerst auf das Wichtigste beschränken. Du kannst deine App ja jederzeit mit weiteren tollen Funktionen oder einem schicken Design ausbauen.

Nun überlege dir, wie deine App funktionieren soll:

- Was sieht der Nutzer zuerst, wenn er deine App startet?
- Was soll er als Erstes tun können?
- Was sind die nächsten Schritte, die er in deiner App tun kann?
- Wann soll deine App beendet werden?

Zu jedem Stichwort notierst du dir, welche Komponenten und insbesondere welche Sensoren des Smartphones du dafür benötigst. Beachte dabei auch das Tippen oder Ziehen auf dem Bildschirm.

Design macht den Unterschied

Damit deine App erfolgreich wird, solltest du genau über das Aussehen deiner App nachdenken. Wichtig sind nicht nur schöne Farben und Bilder, sondern auch eine verständliche Bedienung. Es ist ganz wichtig, dass jeder, der deine App bedient, immer ganz genau weiß, was er machen muss.

Wenn die Bedienung deiner App zu kompliziert oder umständlich ist, sind die Nutzer deiner App schnell frustriert und löschen deine App wieder von ihrem Smartphone. Dies willst du als App-Entwickler natürlich auf keinen Fall!

Hier kommt der *Prototyp* ins Spiel. Ein Prototyp zeigt, wie die fertige App aussieht und funktionieren könnte, ohne dass du bereits im App Inventor die App programmiert hast. Meist sprechen Informatiker von Paper-Prototypen, da diese häufig tatsächlich aus Papier sind. Durch einen Prototyp kannst du viele Fehler vermeiden.

Den Prototyp zeichnest du auf ein Blatt Papier. Du beginnst mit deinem Startbildschirm (»Screen«), von dort zeichnest du einen Pfeil zu einem neuen Screen, der nach deinem Startbildschirm kommen soll. Zeichne auch den zweiten Screen so, wie er in deiner Vorstellung ungefähr aussehen soll. Achte darauf, den Pfeil so einzuzeichnen, dass auch eine andere Person erkennt, wie man vom Startbildschirm zum zweiten Screen kommt. Zusätzlich solltest du an den Pfeil schreiben, was der Nutzer tun muss, um zum nächsten Screen zu kommen, beispielsweise auf den Bildschirm tippen oder auf einen Button klicken. Dies führst du fort, bis du den Ablauf deiner App vor dir siehst und zufrieden bist.

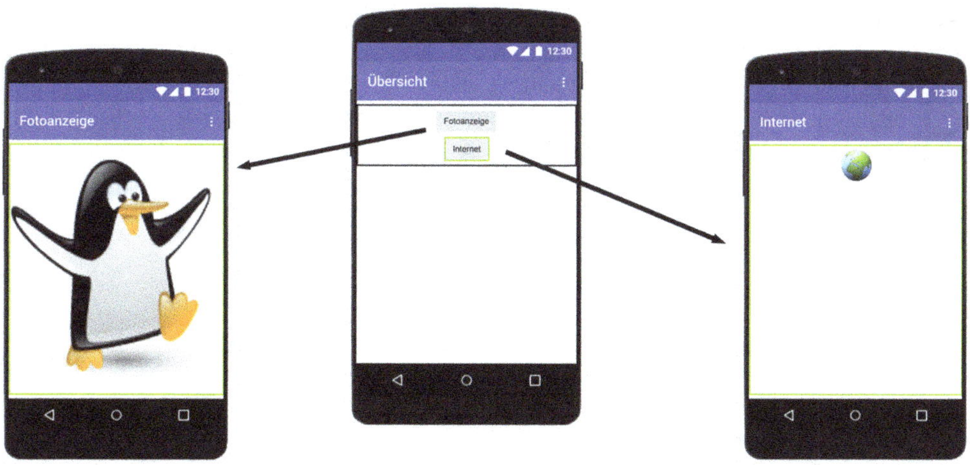

Umsetzen und Schritt für Schritt testen

Jetzt geht es an die Umsetzung. Folge deinem Prototyp und setze beginnend mit dem Startscreen Schritt für Schritt jeden Screen um. Teste dabei immer direkt, ob sich dein Screen so verhält, wie du es erwartest.

Die fertige App auf dem Smartphone installieren

Damit deine App dauerhaft auf deinem Smartphone vorhanden ist und auch deine Freunde sich diese installieren können, musst du noch ein paar kleine Schritte machen und eine Einstellung auf deinem Smartphone ändern.

Die Installation deiner App auf einem Apple-Gerät ist leider noch zu kompliziert. Aber es wird schon an einer Lösung gearbeitet. Du kannst den aktuellen Stand immer mal auf der Webseite https://appinventor.mit.edu/ios_tips/ nachschauen.

Normalerweise verbietet dein Smartphone, dass du Apps installierst, die nicht aus dem Google Play Store oder App Store kommen. Das ist normalerweise auch richtig und wichtig, da du dir sonst nicht sicher sein kannst, dass keine schädlichen Apps auf dein Smartphone gelangen. Da du aber selbst die App erstellt hast, weißt du ja, dass deine App nicht schädlich ist, deshalb kannst du diesen Schutz auf deinem Smartphone zur Installation deiner eigenen App kurzzeitig aufheben.

Wenn du deine App erst einmal auf deinem Smartphone installiert hast, wird sie sich nicht mehr verändern, egal was du später im App Inventor noch einmal anpasst. Falls du also deine App noch einmal verbessert hast, musst du die App danach wieder neu auf dem Smartphone installieren. Dabei wird die alte durch die neue Version ersetzt.

1. **Öffne das Projekt im App Inventor.**
2. **Klicke in der Menüleiste oben im App Inventor auf Build.**

3. **Wähle den Menüpunkt Android App (.apk) aus.**

   Es erscheint ein Ladebalken. Aus deinem App Inventor-Projekt wird jetzt eine Datei mit der Dateiendung .apk erstellt, die auf deinem Smartphone installiert werden kann. Und dies geht ganz einfach.

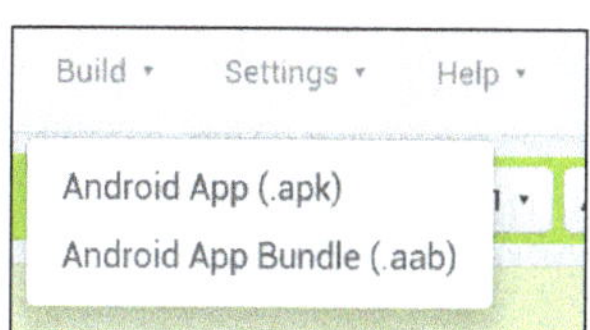

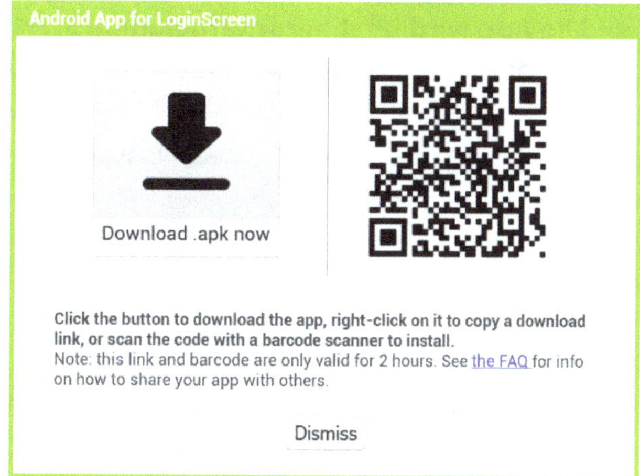

Wenn der Ladebalken verschwunden ist, siehst du einen QR-Code.

4 **Öffne jetzt auf deinem Smartphone die App MIT AI2 Companion, die du schon zum Testen deiner App benutzt hast.**

5 **Klicke auf scan QR code.**

6 **Scanne den QR-Code auf deinem Monitor.**

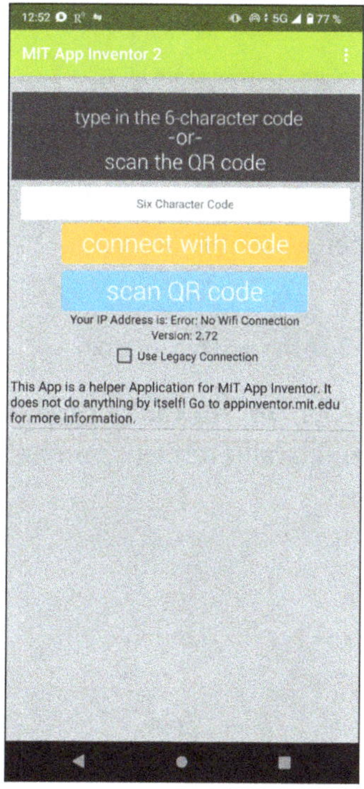

7 **Die App wird jetzt heruntergeladen. Starte das Installieren, indem du auf deinem Smartphone oder Tablet auf Öffnen klickst.**

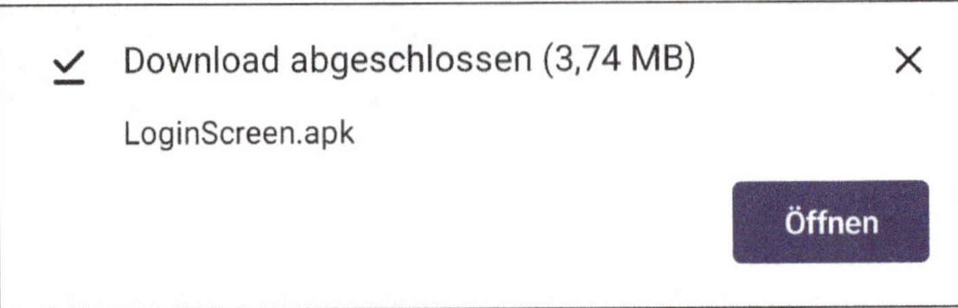

Du siehst jetzt einen Hinweis, dass es momentan nicht erlaubt ist unbekannte Apps zu installieren.

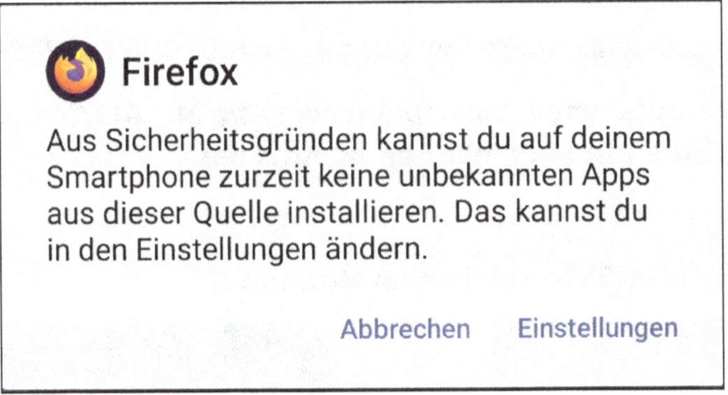

8 **Klicke auf EINSTELLUNGEN, um die Sicherheitseinstellungen zu ändern.**

Das Symbol oben links und auch der Programmname Firefox können sich je nach Smartphone-Modell und installierten Apps ein wenig unterscheiden.

9 **Klicke auf den Schieberegler hinter Dieser Quelle vertrauen.**

Dieser sollte sich dadurch nach rechts verschieben. Im Normalfall sollte die Möglichkeit, Apps aus unbekannten Quellen zu installieren, ausgeschaltet sein. Der Schieberegler sollte also links stehen.

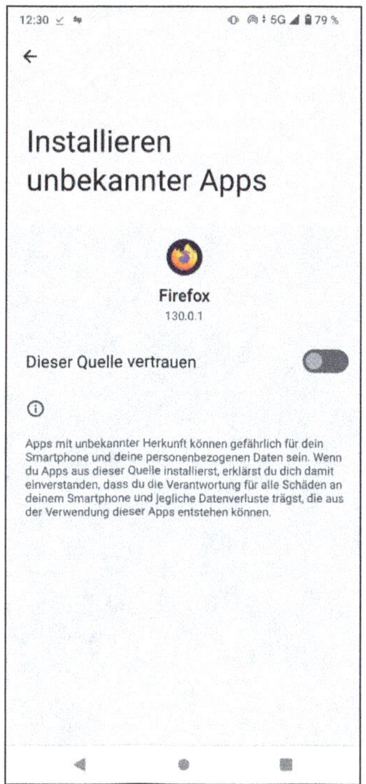

10 **Klicke auf Installieren, um die App auf deinem Smartphone zu installieren.**

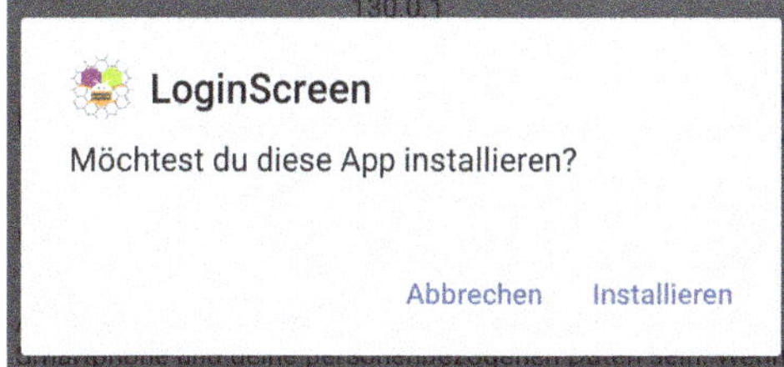

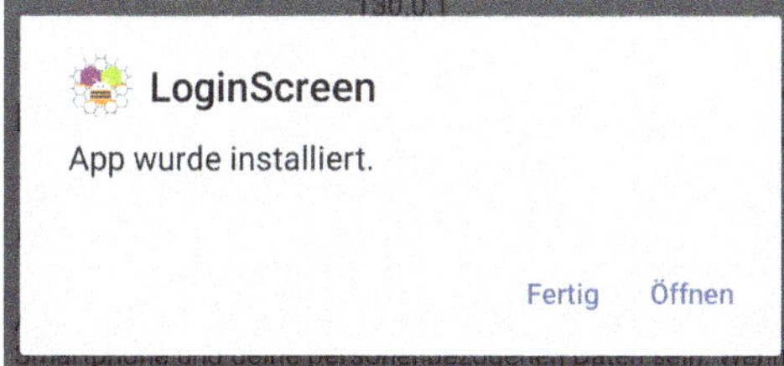

11 **Wenn die App installiert ist, klicke auf öffnen.**

Toll! Deine App ist jetzt auf deinem Smartphone installiert und du kannst die App bei deinen anderen Apps finden. Deine Freunde können die App auch genauso auf ihrem eigenen Smartphone installieren.

Vergiss nicht, die Sicherheitseinstellungen auf deinem Smartphone wieder hochzusetzen.

Kapitel 7
Und die Profis?

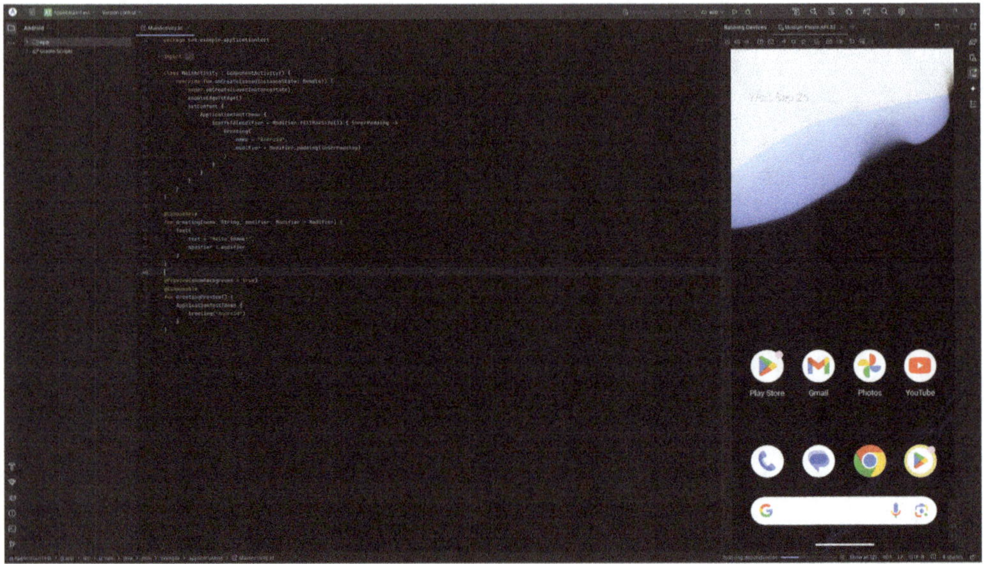

Du bist jetzt sogar schon in den Profibereich bei der Programmierung mit dem App Inventor vorgedrungen und hast viele tolle Apps programmiert und alle möglichen Sensoren ausprobiert. Vielleicht fragst du dich jetzt, was du danach noch lernen kannst. Ziemlich viel! Die Programmierung mit dem App Inventor ist gerade einmal der Anfang der Möglichkeiten, die du als Programmierer hast.

Der App Inventor ist so gemacht, dass du keine schlimmen Fehler machen kannst. Oft gibt dir der App Inventor Hinweise, zum Beispiel, wenn etwas falsch ist oder fehlt. Das Nutzen der vorhandenen Sensoren im App Inventor ist aber nur deshalb so einfach, weil Developer für diese Sensoren bereits Programme geschrieben haben, die du nutzt. Hinter jedem Programmbaustein, den du im Blocks-Editor in den Viewer ziehst, steht ein solches Programm.

Jedoch kannst du keine neuen Sensoren ansteuern, die nicht im App Inventor zur Verfügung stehen, und auch bei einigen anderen Dingen, wie der Kommunikation über das Internet bist du eingeschränkt. Willst du also wirklich alle Funktionen deines Smartphones nutzen, musst du den App Inventor verlassen.

Das Programmieren funktioniert dann noch ähnlich, sieht aber sehr viel komplizierter aus, da du nicht mehr mit Programmbausteinen programmierst, sondern alle Befehle tippen musst. Diese Form des Programmierens in *Textform* nennt man *textuell*. Es gibt aber auch hierfür Hilfen, die zum Beispiel Fehler im Programmcode finden.

Wenn du neue Herausforderungen suchst und schon alles verstanden hast, was man mit dem App Inventor machen kann, dann kannst du ja mal einen Blick zu den Profis riskieren.

Android-Apps werden in der Programmiersprache *Java* oder *Kotlin* geschrieben. Apple-Apps werden in der Programmiersprache *Swift* entwickelt. Die Sprachen ähneln sich aber sehr. Du weißt ja, wie man im App Inventor einen Button hinzufügt und die Buttonbeschriftung in den Properties auf Schwarz und die Hintergrundfarbe ebenfalls auf Schwarz (»Black«) ändert.

Die Java-Befehle für diese Einstellungen lauten so:

```
Button1.Text("Schwarz");
Button1.BackgroundColor(COLOR_BLACK);
```

Erkennst du die Ähnlichkeit zu den Programmbausteinen im App Inventor? Die Ähnlichkeit ist natürlich Absicht, damit dir das Einarbeiten in die Programmiersprachen leichter fällt.

Falls du also neue Herausforderungen suchst und einen Schritt in die Welt der textuellen App-Programmierung machen möchtest, empfehlen wir dir, als Nächstes eine der Programmiersprachen zu erlernen …

Kapitel 8
Auf Wiedersehen …

Du hast nun die letzte Seite dieses Buches erreicht und es wird Zeit, Abschied zu nehmen. Wir freuen uns, dass wir dich so begeistern konnten, dass du bis hier, bis ganz ans Ende des Buchs, gelesen hast. Wir hoffen, dass dir unser Buch gefallen hat und wir dich motivieren konnten, noch viele weitere Apps zu entwickeln. Vielleicht haben wir ja bald eine von dir entwickelte App auf unseren Smartphones?

So oder so wünschen wir dir superviel Spaß und Erfolg bei der Erstellung weiterer informativer, nützlicher oder auch einfach spaßiger Apps.

Zum Wiederfinden

Über die Autoren

Nadine Bergner liebt es, wenn Dinge (und ganz besonders Apps) genau so funktionieren, wie sie es sich vorstellt. Sie ist Professorin an einer Universität und gemeinsam mit ihrem Team arbeitet sie daran, mit spannenden Workshops im Schülerlabor »InfoSphere« in Aachen Jung und Alt für die Informatik zu begeistern.

Nadine benutzt ihr Smartphone am liebsten, um Fotos zu schießen, Spontankäufe zu erledigen und überall auf der Welt ihre Mails zu checken.

Thiemo Leonhardt liebt es, sich Apps und Spiele auszudenken, bei denen man etwas lernen kann. Er ist Softwareentwickler und setzt gerne Ideen in die Tat um. Er liebt alles, was blinkt, zusammengesteckt und programmiert werden kann.

Thiemo benutzt sein Smartphone am liebsten, um Staus zu entkommen, seine Fußballtipps abzugeben und Apps zu programmieren.

Widmung

Wir widmen dieses Buch allen kleinen und großen App-Entwicklern, die mit ihren kreativen Ideen dazu beitragen, unsere digitale Welt ein Stückchen interessanter, spannender, informativer oder einfach spaßiger zu machen.

Danke

Wir möchten uns bei allen bedanken, die mit uns gemeinsam oder woanders auf der Welt tolle Informatikprojekte (darunter auch ganz viele Apps) entwickeln und uns mit ihren kreativen Ideen, neugierigen Fragen und glänzenden Augen so oft begeistern.

Zu den Screenshots und Programmen in diesem Buch

Der MIT App Inventor (http://appinventor.mit.edu) wurde ursprünglich von einem Entwicklerteam um Mark Friedman und Hal Abelson bei Google entwickelt und 2012 an das MIT (Massachusetts Institute of Technology) übergeben. Der MIT App Inventor wird unter der Creative Commons Attribution-ShareAlike 4.0 Unported License veröffentlicht: https://creativecommons.org/licenses/by-sa/4.0/ Alle Screenshots und alle Programme zum App Inventor in diesem Buch stehen unter derselben Lizenz.

C. Ermel und O. Runge

Programmieren und zeichnen mit Python für Dummies Junior

2. Auflage 2022 **ISBN:** 978-3-527-71995-2

224 Seiten

Format: 176 mm x 240 mm

Ladenpreis: 18,- €*

Zaubere tolle Bilder mit dem Computer! Du brauchst dafür nur ein paar einfache Befehle aus der Programmiersprache Python.

W. Eagle et al.

TikTok-Videos selber machen für Dummies Junior

1. Auflage 2023 **ISBN:** 978-3-527-72133-7

160 Seiten

Format: 176 mm x 240 mm

Ladenpreis: 17,-€*

Werde Teil der TikTok Community und begeistere andere mit deinen Ideen. In diesem Buch erfährst du, wie du Videos mit dem Smartphone erstellst, bearbeitest und mit deinen Freunden teilst.

C. Ermel und N. Rosenfeld

Spaß mit Elektronik für Dummies Junior

1. Auflage 2020 **ISBN:** 978-3-527-71705-7

198 Seiten

Format: 176 mm x 240 mm

Ladenpreis: 15,- €*

In diesem Buch lernst du, Schaltungen für coole Gadgets aufzubauen: eine Glückwunschkarte, die leuchtet, eine blinkende Weihnachtsbaumkugel, einen klingenden Draht und anderes mehr.

* Der €-Preis gilt nur für Deutschland. Preisänderungen und Irrtümer vorbehalten.

N. Bergner und T. Leonhardt

Eigene Chatbots programmieren für Dummies Junior

1. Auflage 2020	**ISBN:** 978-3-527-71768-2
Reihe:	...für Dummies
168 Seiten	
Format:	176 mm x 240 mm
Ladenpreis:	15,– €*

Kurztext:
In diesem Buch lernst du, einen Chatbot zu entwickeln, der immer besser auf seinen Chatpartner reagiert. Du verstehst dadurch besser, wie Alexa, Siri und Co. funktionieren, und erkennst auch ihre Grenzen.

M. Ponce Kärgel

Hörspiel und Podcast selber machen für Dummies Junior

2., vollst. überarb. u. erw. Auflage 2024	**ISBN:** 978-3-527-72243-3
208 Seiten	
Format:	176 mm x 240 mm
Ladenpreis:	18,– €*

Steig ein in die Welt der Hörspiele und Podcasts. Egal ob du dein eigenes Hörspiel aufnehmen, dir eigene Storys ausdenken oder deine Meinungen in einem Podcast mit anderen teilen möchtest: Marco Ponce Kärgel zeigt dir, wie du Audiobeiträge produzieren und veröffentlichen kannst.

U. Schmid, K. Weitz und M. Siebers

Künstliche Intelligenz selber programmieren für Dummies Junior

2., vollst. überarb. u. erw. Auflage 2024	**ISBN:** 978-3-527-72188-7
160 Seiten	
Format:	176 mm x 240 mm
Ladenpreis:	15,– €*

Finde heraus, was Künstliche Intelligenz ist und wie sie funktioniert. Dieses Buch hilft dir dabei: Anhand von anschaulichen Beispielen schaust du unter die Haube und erhältst einen Einblick, wie KI-Systeme gebaut werden können.

* Der €-Preis gilt nur für Deutschland. Preisänderungen und Irrtümer vorbehalten.

www.ingramcontent.com/pod-product-compliance
Lightning Source LLC
LaVergne TN
LVHW061937220826
846092LV00004B/1025

* 9 7 8 3 5 2 7 7 2 2 8 5 3 *